G000074933

Germ Gambits

Germ Gambits

THE BIOWEAPONS DILEMMA, IRAQ AND BEYOND

Amy E. Smithson

Stanford Security Studies
An Imprint of Stanford University Press
Stanford, California

Stanford University Press
Stanford, California

©2011 by the Board of Trustees of the Leland Stanford Junior University.
All rights reserved.

No part of this book may be reproduced or transmitted in any form or by any means,
electronic or mechanical, including photocopying and recording, or in any information
storage or retrieval system without the prior written permission of Stanford University Press.

Special discounts for bulk quantities of Stanford Security Studies are available to
corporations, professional associations, and other organizations. For details and discount
information, contact the special sales department of Stanford University Press.
Tel: (650) 736-1782, Fax: (650) 736-1784

Printed in the United States of America on acid-free, archival-quality paper

Library of Congress Cataloging-in-Publication Data

Smithson, Amy E., author.
    Germ gambits : the bioweapons dilemma : Iraq and beyond / Amy E. Smithson.
        pages cm
    Includes bibliographical references and index.
    ISBN 978-0-8047-7552-6 (cloth : alk. paper)—ISBN 978-0-8047-7553-3 (alk. paper)
    1. United Nations. Special Commission on Iraq—History. 2. Biological arms control—
Verification—Iraq—History. I. Title.
    UG447.8.S585 2011
    327.1'74509567—dc22   2011015778

Typeset by Classic Typography in 10/14 Minion

To Gilford Eugene and Janine, NGL, for
nurturing a bookworm into a book author

CONTENTS

Foreword ix
Rolf Ekeus

Acknowledgments xiii

Introduction 1
1 UNSCOM's Inception and Infancy 9
2 UNSCOM's Initial Biological Inspections 35
3 From Hiatus to the Hunt 57
4 UNSCOM Shreds Iraq's Cover Stories 75
5 Defection and Artifice 94
6 Inspections in a Fact-Free Zone 119
7 Tentacles and Disintegration 146
8 Lessons Experienced I: Inspection Prerequisites 170
9 Lessons Experienced II: Sharpening the Tools of Inspection 203
10 Gambits Present and Future 228

Notes 253
Index 357

In addition, see the webpage at http://www.sup.org/book.cgi?id=20908, which contains extended annotations for many of the endnotes.

FOREWORD

Rolf Ekeus

THE DECISION IN April 1991 by the United Nations (UN) Security Council that Iraq's weapons of mass destruction should be eliminated is an event in history with only one precedent, the decision under the Treaty of Versailles in 1919 that Germany, defeated in the First World War, should be fully disarmed. In the end the mission to disarm Germany failed, due to Germany's systematic obstruction of the efforts by the Allied Control Commission, responsible for implementing the provisions of the Treaty.

The disarmament of Iraq was the major component of Security Council Resolution 687(1991), constituting the ceasefire in the 1991 war between Iraq and a coalition led by the United States in support of the liberation of Kuwait.

The Special Commission, UNSCOM, set up by the Security Council to oversee the disarmament of Iraq was, like the Control Commission, faced with systematic obstructions. However, as we now have learned, UNSCOM overcame a multitude of challenges. When it effectively ended its operations in Iraq in late 1998, UNSCOM had thoroughly cleansed Iraq of its prohibited biological and chemical weapons, equipment, and installations, as well as its means of delivery, including relevant missiles. Also, nuclear weapons capabilities had been eliminated in cooperation between UNSCOM and the International Atomic Energy Agency's Action Team, specially created for the purpose of taking care of Iraq's nuclear capability.

The by far most difficult task for UNSCOM, embodied in its mission, was to identify and eliminate Iraq's clandestine biological weapons (BW) program.

This is the story of how this was done. Amy Smithson has approached her task of telling that story in a way that penetrates the complexities; clarifies the many obscure points; describes the operations; and provides understanding of the science of biological weapons research, development, and production. In addition, she demonstrates an understanding of the formidable political, organizational, and methodological difficulties facing UNSCOM, its leadership, and its inspectors, something which only a few commentators and observers have been able to do.

Iraq's biological weapons program constituted the most secret elements of Iraq's total destructive capabilities. The existence of BW in Iraq was denied from the beginning of UNSCOM's operations. That explains why it took UNSCOM four years of intensive work until the inspections yielded results. Not until spring 1995 could the Special Commission make the first disclosures to the UN Security Council about the existence in Iraq of the top-secret BW program, although Iraq did not admit this until July 1995, when officials acknowledged an offensive biological weapons program. In early August they also recognized that Iraq in late 1990 had weaponized its warfare agents by filling them in bombs and in a number (twenty-five) of missiles. The political impact in Iraq of these disclosures rocked the stability of the regime, with the lasting effect of undermining the power structures around Saddam Hussein, the president of the country. Thus Saddam's son-in-law Hussein Kamal, who had been put in charge of all activities relevant to Iraq's weapons of mass destruction, in August 1995 defected to Jordan, though he later returned to Iraq and was killed by the regime.

It must be stated that one non-technical reason for UNSCOM's progress and final success in eliminating the prohibited items in the face of Iraq's obstructive policy was that, as a subsidiary organ of the Security Council, it normally could enjoy the support of a united Council in pressing Iraq to accommodate the inspectors in matters of access to facilities, aerial surveillance, and so on. It fell upon UNSCOM's leadership to cultivate Security Council unity in support and understanding of the Special Commission's operations. In 1998 the unity in support for UNSCOM fell apart. Even if UNSCOM as an institution finally broke, it must firmly be stated that its mission before that had succeeded.

It is generally recognized that verification and monitoring of the implementation of the prohibitions of the 1972 Biological and Toxin Weapons Convention is a challenging task. Some governments even maintain that a verification protocol to the BWC would not be workable. UNSCOM, admittedly armed with far-reaching rights and strong technical and political backup, could prove the opposite, namely that a verification and monitoring system could work even under the most difficult and challenging conditions. Thus the team of inspectors who succeeded in identifying and eliminating Iraq's secret BW program did what many thought would be impossible, namely to disclose a highly clandestine BW program. The work took its time. It was not until mid-1996 when the sprawling Al Hakam biological warfare agent production facility could be finally destroyed.

In this book Amy Smithson tells the fascinating story of how the BW inspectors, through brilliant individual and collective work, succeeded in breaking the Iraqi resistance. She describes in detail how UNSCOM's methodological approaches, based upon material balance analysis, fast laboratory analysis, and aerial surveillance from high and low altitude, backed up by photo analysis and systematic site inspections, including no-notice inspections and refined interviewing techniques, against all odds led to detection, disclosures, and, ultimately, success.

With a great sense of humor and in almost literary terms she describes the individual inspectors, their personality profiles, and their very different temperaments and intellectual approaches, all based on repeated interviews. She gives each one of them their due, such as the heroic, and ultimately tragic, personality of David Kelly.

Iraq's denials and falsified declarations, the intimidating attitude of the Iraqi counterparts, physical obstructions of the inspectors, and the political games played by the government constituted tremendous obstacles for the inspection regime. In this book Amy Smithson gives us a narrative on how UNSCOM succeeded in overcoming these obstacles. To quantify the extent of progress made by the BW inspection team, one should note that Iraq's original declaration in 1992 on its holdings of declarable material amounted to 17 pages and in 1997 to 639 pages.

In addition to its search-and-destroy mission, the BW team was tasked with building a system for monitoring Iraq's laboratories and other biological and medical institutions that had a potential for research, development, and production of biological agents that could theoretically become a part of a restored biological warfare agent program. As a matter of fact, this country-wide mapping of all of Iraq's capabilities in the biological field contributed to the quick progress from 1996 to 1998 and provided the inspection team with large quantities of data and inside information that could assure UNSCOM about the full accomplishment of its task of identifying and eliminating Iraq's

BW capability. The system the inspectors thus created for the monitoring of Iraq is a unique and successful example of how a monitoring structure could be shaped and operated under a future potential monitoring and verification protocol to the BWC of 1972.

Now, with most data on Iraq's WMD programs, including its BW activities, received as a consequence of the work of the Iraq Survey Group evaluating after the war the remnants of Iraq's WMD capabilities, it must be recognized that the UNSCOM inspections really have turned out to be something of a complete success. UNSCOM had been tasked with responsibility for eliminating all the prohibited items. And it did so in full. Rarely has any UN mission been accomplished to a hundred percent. UNSCOM did that against the odds based on the experiences of the Allied Commission in Germany in the 1920s and 1930s.

It is important to understand how UNSCOM succeeded. Amy Smithson provides us with a high-quality study that will be indispensable for understanding the drama contained in the work of breaking the ultimate secrets of Iraq's BW program, while at the same time it creates a foundation for designs of future arms control regimes and initiatives.

ACKNOWLEDGMENTS

EVERY BOOK HAS ITS GENESIS; the starting point for this one came in the spring of 2002, when Western government officials, independent security analysts, and scientists met to discuss what should be done about various weapons proliferation problems. On the topic of biological weapons, discussion soon focused on what had transpired with the United Nations Special Commission (UNSCOM). Plenty of individuals volunteered information about the inspections and what should be learned from that experience. On the basis of my prior interactions with UNSCOM inspectors, I knew that people considered nonproliferation "experts" were voicing several factually erroneous statements and opinions that mangled the policy, technical, and operational lessons that should be drawn from these inspections. The only person in the room who participated directly in UNSCOM's investigation of Iraq's bioweapons program was chief inspector David Kelly. He said not a word. Somewhat stunned, neither did I.

When the meeting broke for coffee, I asked David whether he thought the time had come for the people who actually performed UNSCOM's inspections to tell the tale of what really happened and impart their views on the future significance of that experience. He agreed that a report to that effect would be beneficial. Thereafter, the Carnegie Corporation of New York graciously provided grant assistance to enable the interviews that fueled this book. Pat Nicholas Moore of Carnegie was supportive when the richness of interview data morphed the report into a book-length manuscript.

As the book took shape Amanda Moodie, Jessica Varnum, and Kirk Bansak scrubbed it for clarity and grammar. I am grateful for their assistance.

Numerous UNSCOM inspectors and officials generously lent their time, insights, and technical acumen to this book. Some requested anonymity, but others agreed to go on the record, and therefore I can thank them publicly for their invaluable assistance to this project. In alphabetical order, these individuals are Rod Barton, Stephen Black, Pierce Corden, Charles Duelfer, Rolf Ekeus, Doug Englund, David Franz, Robert Gallucci, David Huxsoll, Robert Kadlec, Hamish Killip, Gabriele Kraatz-Wadsack, Debra Krikorian, William Lebherz, Ron Manley, Jeff Mohr, Ake Sellstrom, Richard Spertzel, Terence Taylor, and Raymond Zilinskas. Janice Kelly granted permission for David Kelly's recollections and insights to be attributed by name. Several inspectors, particularly Spertzel and Kraatz-Wadsack, also spent considerable additional time reviewing the manuscript for accuracy.

In addition, I thank these intrepid, savvy individuals for their service to the international community as UNSCOM inspectors. They did the improbable—the unmasking of Iraq's covert bioweapons program. I hope that the lessons from their experience will be heeded and translated into stronger nonproliferation tools.

Amy E. Smithson
Washington, DC
July 1, 2011

Germ Gambits

INTRODUCTION

JUST AS FORCES OF NATURE can create disastrous upheaval, so too can human-engineered activities indelibly shape destiny. Humans have courted inconceivable jeopardy by harnessing a natural force, disease, for pernicious reasons. One of several historical cases, Iraq's covert biological weapons program, imperiled the Middle East until international inspectors found and shut down the program in the 1990s. Contemporarily, the lack of governance of the life sciences could exacerbate the proliferation of biological weapons, a matter with direct implications for the security and well-being of present and future generations.

Iraq's notorious dictator of the late twentieth century, Saddam Hussein, triggered the events recounted in this book when he embarked on an ultra-secret program to acquire germ weapons. Alone, this initial decision was somewhat chancy, particularly when juxtaposed with Saddam's decision to try to obtain nuclear weapons. The pursuit of nuclear weapons draws international opprobrium, but some still view nuclear arms as the epitome of power and prestige.[1] While governments have even been known to parade nuclear arms through capital streets, such fanfare or tolerance for a biological arsenal is unimaginable. Biological weapons are perhaps the most insidious and feared of all weapons because deliberately released contagious diseases are the equivalent of a self-sustaining attack that could cause unlimited harm among human, animal, or plant populations. Even if non-communicable diseases are employed, the wind can sweep an aerosol of biowarfare agent off target, engulfing more victims. As if these attributes are not atrocious enough, some

1

diseases entail considerable suffering prior to death, and biowarfare agents can be stealthily dispersed.[2]

In an attempt to preserve peace and mankind, the international community banned biological weapons in 1972.[3] Neither the contemptible characteristics of biological weapons nor Iraq's signature of the Biological and Toxin Weapons Convention dissuaded Saddam's quest for these weapons.[4] Moreover, Iraq's leaders were probably confident that Western intelligence did not have a firm fix on Iraq's bioweapons program. In contrast to Israel's 1981 preemptive attack on the Osiraq reactor, which set back Saddam's nuclear weapons aspirations, Iraq's germ agent production facility, Al Hakam, remained untouched before and during the 1991 Gulf War.[5] Prior to that war, Iraq loaded enough biowarfare agents into weapons to devastate vast populations.

Swiftly defeated, Iraq accepted ceasefire conditions that required Baghdad to relinquish its unconventional weapons and pertinent capabilities to the United Nations Special Commission (UNSCOM), which the United Nations (UN) Security Council established to oversee Iraq's disarmament. A defiant Saddam wagered anew by launching an elaborate concealment and deception strategy to hide his bioweapons program and other unconventional weapons capabilities. In Baghdad, the risk must have seemed reasonable, for it pitted a government with enormous resources at the ready to conceal an unobtrusive weapons program against a small cadre of inspectors who lacked concrete data that Iraq even had biological weapons.

Surely the odds in this contest favored Iraq, not UNSCOM. The biological inspectors set about their work even before the international community truly began to examine the feasibility of verifying whether offensive military activity was being surreptitiously conducted at so-called dual-use biological facilities—sites that house equipment, materials, capabilities, and personnel that can perform peaceful activities just as readily as prohibited military work.[6] Though an influential school of thought proclaimed biological inspections to be a weak, even a losing, proposition, UNSCOM inspectors persevered in the face of Iraqi obfuscation, in 1995 exposing Saddam's coveted bioweapons program for the world to see. In mid-1996, they oversaw the demolition of the crown jewel of Iraq's biowarfare program, Al Hakam. Had the outcome been different, Saddam's continued germ gambits might have drastically altered geopolitical history in the Middle East and spiraled into global public health and security catastrophes.

OTHER FACETS OF THIS CHRONICLE

While on one level this book is about monumental security and public health risks, other prominent themes emerge in the text. History is susceptible to individuals, organizations, and governments that deliberately twist facts to burnish their image or to justify a preferred course of action. Posterity benefits, however, from a historical record of what really transpired, how, and why.[7] Like so many events, UNSCOM's bioweapons inspections have been prey to factual reinvention and subjective interpretation. To hear some tell it, all the inspectors did was follow a clear, plentiful trail of intelligence right to Iraq's bioweapons program. Other disputable contentions are that Saddam's powerful son-in-law Hussein Kamal and the Haidar farm cache of documents that Iraq turned over to UNSCOM after Kamal's August 1995 defection provided the inspectors with significant new insights into Iraq's bioweapons program. UNSCOM's biological inspectors experienced their fair share of success, mediocrity, and failure. In this book, the inspectors themselves debunk the myths, relating what actually happened amidst the sands of Iraq.

Saddam's showdown with UNSCOM is also cause for reflection in relation to contemporary matters of international security policy and process. UNSCOM appeared on the global stage at the dawn of a major transitional phase in modern world order. Amidst the flotsam of the Cold War, the world was simultaneously becoming increasingly fragmented yet bound by economic interdependence. The power of multinational corporations was on the rise, and governments had to reckon with multibillionaires and nongovernmental organizations with issue agendas and the growing ability to sway international policies, programs, and phenomena.[8] Many galling problems also commanded the attention of international leaders, such as failing states; criminal gangs, drug cartels, and terrorists maneuvering on a global scale; climate change; and human rights crises. No state alone, no matter how powerful, could manage what was spilling across borders to disturb the domestic security and well-being of so many nations in unprecedented ways, so leaders began searching for new formulas and mechanisms and cautiously reshaping the roles and missions of alliances and international law and organizations. For some, the post–Cold War environment underscored the need for more robust global governance, but many still firmly embraced the Westphalian principle of state sovereignty.[9]

On this level, UNSCOM's experience can be read as a cautionary tale about the innate tensions between governments and international organizations and the evolving roles of each in the international arena. UNSCOM's spur-of-the-moment creation, direct reporting chain to the Security Council, and narrow geographic and functional mandate set it apart from other UN organizations.[10] Once a ceasefire was in effect, many assumed that the worst of the "Iraq problem" was behind them, and nations contributed resources to enable UNSCOM's operations.[11] When Iraq did not readily forfeit its prohibited weapons capabilities, however, the *realpolitik* of economic and other national priorities encroached steadily on UNSCOM's international support. UNSCOM reported what its inspectors uncovered, but governments' tolerance for the facts shrank with successive headlines about Iraqi citizens suffering under economic sanctions.[12] The diplomatic solution for this political quagmire was to allow limited sales of Iraqi oil in 1996 to fund humanitarian aid to Iraq and in 1999 to shoot the messenger and replace UNSCOM with a less robust inspectorate. The interactions of states with UNSCOM on such matters as intelligence sharing and UNSCOM's eventual fate offer insight into nations' reluctance to cede important authorities to and vest significant capabilities in international organizations. Therefore, one salient point amongst these pages concerns the rocky road ahead for initiatives to strengthen international laws, organizations, and mechanisms.

On yet another level, the narrative underscores the travails of collecting information about activities of security interest and concern in an increasingly complex world. Even in an age when ludicrous amounts of information are at everyone's fingertips, vital data can still go undetected or can be collected but overlooked or misunderstood. Intelligence gatherers and analysts have long known the predicaments of "background noise" and misinterpreted data, having presented leaders with inaccurate or incomplete assessments only to encounter shattering unanticipated events.[13] Indeed, the intelligence preceding the 1991 and 2003 Gulf Wars underrated and overrated, respectively, Iraq's bioweapons capabilities, shortcomings that can be attributed to overreliance on remote monitoring and defectors.[14]

Even if remote sensors could deliver reams of pertinent data and defectors proffered nothing but accurate information, intelligence and security analysts would still have to contend with the infamous "grey area." This term refers to the zone in which it is very difficult to differentiate between the offensive military capabilities that treaties prohibit and permissible defense and legitimate private sector activities.[15] In the biological realm, this grey area can be particularly vexing because the Convention allows its members to retain and work with pathogens, even ones known to have been weaponized, to maintain defenses and pursue research to find cures and treatments for diseases.[16]

UNSCOM's inspectors worked in the thick of the biological grey area, so their experience is germane to the long-simmering debate about the verifiability of the bioweapons ban, namely whether inspections can make a meaningful contribution to deciphering activities at dual-use facilities. This debate centers on the tensions between the intrusiveness and effectiveness of inspections and the need to prevent the compromise of national security and trade secrets unrelated to the treaty's prohibitions. The political faultlines that have permeated arms control debates in general have also colored discussions of the Convention's verifiability. Briefly, conservatives have a propensity to eschew arms control as anathema to peace through strength, skeptical that inspections will catch treaty violators, while liberals are apt to laud arms control as more likely to avert war and less costly than arms races, depicting inspections as imperfect but capable of detecting cheating in time to respond to the threat.[17]

Treaties inked during the height of the Cold War relied on "national technical means," a euphemism for spy satellites and other sources of intelligence to monitor compliance.[18] Ushering on-site inspections into the architecture of modern treaties, U.S. President Ronald Reagan brandished the Russian proverb "trust but verify" to summarize the purpose of inspections in arms control.[19] Inspections proved their mettle in the implementation of the 1987 Intermediate-Range Nuclear Forces Treaty and matured with the 1991 Strategic Arms Reduction Treaty, the 1993 Chemical Weapons Convention, and the 1997 additional safeguards protocol to the Nuclear Nonproliferation Treaty. Routine inspections guard against the presence of prohibited capabilities or activities at declared military and commercial facilities, while challenge inspections are meant to investigate compliance concerns at any undeclared location in participating states.[20]

So much doubt remained about the utility of inspections in a biological setting that members of the Convention did not convene to evaluate methods to verify the treaty until 1992. Talks to draft a legally binding verification protocol for the Convention began in 1995 with negotiators using a slightly different lexicon for routine and challenge inspection concepts.[21] The protocol negotiations faltered in 2001, and then folded in 2002.[22] Bookending these talks and UNSCOM's field experience with biological inspections, the administrations of U.S. Presidents George H.W. Bush and George W. Bush pronounced the Convention "not effectively verifiable" and "inherently unverifiable," while Barack Obama's deemed the draft protocol incapable of achieving "meaningful verification or greater security."[23]

Against this backdrop, what is to be made of the experience of UNSCOM's biological inspectors? To some, UNSCOM's experience is so singular that it is not applicable to other arms control and nonproliferation accords, including the Convention. Iraq's disarmament was supposed to be cooperative, but UNSCOM at times relied on challenge-inspection-like tactics and the Security Council's authority and threat to punish Iraqi noncompliance with military strikes.[24] Treaties have their own governing bodies, but all grievous compliance problems get referred to the same court of last resort, the Security Council, which can mete out political, economic, and military penalties as it did with Iraq.[25] Though UNSCOM's inspectors pioneered inspection practices, they largely went about their jobs plying many of the basic tools used to police other arms control and nonproliferation regimes either before or after the UNSCOM years. Arguably, therefore, UNSCOM's lessons should translate into other contexts.[26]

Of note, the achievements of UNSCOM's bioweapons inspectors appear to undermine the claim that the Convention is unverifiable. After all, UNSCOM inspectors detected Iraq's bioweapons program using measures comparable to routine inspections. The inspections also generated copious data that shed light on Iraq's bioweapons program as well as the legitimate, peaceful activity conducted in Iraq's dual-use facilities.[27]

Since the UNSCOM years, the job of collecting data to inform a bioweapons compliance assessment has gotten thornier because of the astonishing rate of discovery in the life sciences and the globalization of dual-use biological know-how, technology, equipment, and capabilities. Separately or together, these factors could accelerate the attempts of governments and subnational actors to acquire germ weapons. Whereas the military exploitation of chemistry begat the hallmark weapons of World War I (explosives and poison gas) and of physics World War II's atomic bomb, the militarization of the fruits of modern biology may be the distinguishing feature of future conflict.[28] As proven repeatedly over the past century, intelligence alone has yielded imprecise data and assessments about dual-use biological activities.[29] With the prospect of militarized biology looming larger than ever, at the very time when intelligence agencies need to be right on top of matters biological, the background noise is rising to a deafening level. These circumstances raise the question of whether intelligence can and should serve as the only alert system for suspect bioweapons activities.

SCOPE, METHODOLOGY, AND ROADMAP

This book's primary purpose is to capture how UNSCOM inspectors managed to root out Iraq's bioweapons program against considerable odds—sketchy intelligence, scant direct precedents to inform their efforts, the challenges of discriminating offensive military work from legitimate biological activity, and Iraq's campaign to impede the inspections. Secondarily, the book aims to glean from this experience the lessons that should be applied to reduce the chances that the world will stand again at the precipice of manmade biological disaster.

Like every book, this one has its limitations. Without access to interview the Iraqis, this history of UNSCOM's biological inspections is from the inspectors' perspective. To a certain extent, this ground has already been tilled; some inspectors have written about their experiences with UNSCOM.[30] The book is based on interviews with those who played enduring roles or participated at key junctures in UNSCOM's bioweapons inspections. Over ten of these centerpiece inspectors reviewed the book's historical chapters for accuracy and completeness. The recollections of UNSCOM insiders who worked side-by-side with UNSCOM's biological specialists supplement these pivotal interviews and further cross-check and round out the history. Official documents, news reports, analyses, and technical resources also buttress the text. The resulting collective history is authoritative, vibrant, and absent the bias or limited experience that may hinder autobiographical accounts.

Next, while the book includes considerable information about Iraq's germ weapons program, it should not be considered a definitive history of that program, nor is it intended to be. More information about the evolution and specific capabilities of Iraq's bioweapons program can be found in the official reports of UNSCOM, which delineate the major landmarks and provide ample detail. The Iraq Survey Group also added some elements to the historical record.[31]

Chapters 1 thru 7 present the history of UNSCOM's biological inspections. Chapter 1 describes UNSCOM's establishment, Iraq's early biological declarations, the pre-1991 Gulf War intelligence assessments, the onset of UNSCOM's operations in Iraq, Baghdad's concealment and deception strategy and tricks, and the reasons why Iraqi leaders may have gone to such lengths to keep the bioweapons program. Chapter 2 details UNSCOM's first pair of biological inspections, which featured surprises for the inspectors and their Iraqi counterparts. Chapter 3 examines why UNSCOM suspended biological inspections for over two years, and then turns to the factors that helped to kick UNSCOM's biological inspections into a higher gear. The inspection activities that produced data sufficiently damning to compel Iraq's July 1, 1995, confession about the limited production of biowarfare agents are the subject of Chapter 4. Chapter 5 covers the events, revelations, and misperceptions surrounding UNSCOM's biological investigation and the defection of Kamal, a central figure in Iraq's unconventional weapons programs. Chapter 6 relates the inspectors' struggle to confirm important details associated with Iraq's testing, production, filling, deployment, and unilateral destruction of its biological arsenal. Chapter 7 spells out how UNSCOM navigated this bumpy terrain as other interests vied for political support in the Security Council.

In addition to the historical record, UNSCOM's biological inspectors divulged the lessons of their experience. In Chapter 8, the inspectors address factors that can be categorized as essential prerequisites for the successful conduct of inspections, namely recruiting personnel with the appropriate skills, augmenting those skills with specialized training, avoiding the handicap of a predetermined mind-set, capturing field experience during an inspection process to improve the efficiency of inspections, figuring out how to incorporate intelligence into inspections, recognizing the inevitability of mistakes during inspections, and bridging the communications gap between scientists, diplomats, and policymakers. Tool by inspection tool, in Chapter 9 the inspectors explain the inner workings of on-site observation, interviews, documentation review, and sampling. They also collectively articulate how to improve the tradecraft of inspections and evaluate the overall utility of inspecting dual-use biological facilities. Finally, Chapter 10 places the events in this book in a broader historical and scientific context, closing with a multifaceted strategy to curb biological risks.

1 UNSCOM'S INCEPTION AND INFANCY

WITH IRAQI ARMED FORCES at a significant disadvantage,[1] the outcome of the 1991 Gulf War was sufficiently foreseeable for some to turn to post-war planning before the onset of hostilities. Before 1990 ended, possible ceasefire conditions and mechanisms were discussed in the capitals of major Coalition partners, particularly with regard to the disposition of Iraq's weapons of mass destruction after the war. As policymakers mulled over whether to demand Iraq's complete unconditional surrender against less draconian options, the draft of what became United Nations (UN) Security Council Resolution 687 began to circulate in the Security Council's chambers.[2] The resolution stipulated that Iraq agree unconditionally to allow the UN to remove, render harmless, or destroy its weapons of mass destruction and ballistic missiles; established the UN Special Commission (UNSCOM) to effect the majority of that mandate; and directly linked the lifting of trade sanctions to Iraq's compliance with the disarmament mandate. The Security Council's approval of Resolution 687 on April 3, 1991, set UNSCOM on a course of forced disarmament of a sovereign nation defeated in war, a feat rarely attempted, much less successfully executed, in modern history.[3]

This chapter first recounts the circumstances surrounding the creation of UNSCOM. Iraq's initial null and elliptical declarations about its biological activities are then juxtaposed against the Western intelligence assessment of Iraq's bioweapons status prior to the 1991 war. The narrative then describes UNSCOM's early inspections, the strategy and tactics Iraq employed to try to dupe the inspectors, the reasons Saddam Hussein sought to retain a biological weapons capability, and the adjustments the inspectors began to make to contend with Iraq's uncooperative behavior.

From the outset, UNSCOM and Baghdad took calculated risks. As Iraq chanced that it could swiftly hide incriminating evidence and fool the inspectors, UNSCOM's meager corps of inspectors set out to disarm it unaware of Saddam's already activated concealment strategy and the true scope of Iraq's unconventional weapons programs. Just as UNSCOM's inspectors did not know how far and hard they could push Iraq to find the truth, Saddam could not predict the skill level and determination of the inspectors or the Security Council's resolve to enforce the ceasefire conditions. Amidst those early postwar months, the leaders of UNSCOM and Iraq received disquieting glimpses of the challenges ahead but neither knew just how demanding it would be for UNSCOM to certify Iraq's disarmament to the Security Council or for Iraq to persuade UNSCOM and the Security Council that its unconventional weapons ambitions and capabilities were a thing of the past.

OPTIMISTIC EXPECTATIONS

The U.S. and British governments prepared the first draft of Resolution 687, putting UNSCOM in charge of all disarmament efforts in Iraq.[4] Without expert technical advice on what would be needed to find and secure Iraq's chemical arsenal and ballistic missiles, to determine the extent of its suspected nuclear and biological weapons programs, and to disarm it of these capabilities, Resolution 687's architects based the disarmament framework largely on what U.S. and British intelligence services knew about Iraq's weapons of mass destruction programs and the idea that a step-by-step process would be needed. The group drafting process took a week or two at the most. "We were really under intense time pressure," said Robert Gallucci, who later became UNSCOM's first deputy executive chairman.[5] The French argued that the International Atomic Energy Agency (IAEA), which judged Iraq's nuclear pursuits before the 1991 Gulf War to be purely peaceful in nature, had to be in charge of destroying any nuclear weapons capabilities that might be uncovered. The final version of Resolution 687 thus directed the IAEA to carry out these duties with UNSCOM's cooperation and assistance but gave UNSCOM alone the authority to designate additional sites for inspection that Iraq did not voluntarily identify as being involved with prohibited weapons activities.[6]

One feature of the ceasefire resolution quick to draw derision was its "laughable" deadlines for reporting and activity, described in Table 1.1. Those with field experience in the safe destruction of weapons found fault even with the fifteen-day deadline for Iraq to submit a declaration, the simplest task to be accomplished. Deadpanned one such expert, "People who didn't have a great deal of expertise came up with those deadlines."[7] The group that penned Resolution 687 "just made those deadlines up," conceded Gallucci.[8] The resolution's terms reflected the political pressure to end hostilities, the unusual international political environment just after the Cold War, and the speed of Iraq's defeat.[9] An overall sense of optimism infused multilateral efforts to address global problems in the early 1990s, making for a "gold rush mood . . . that everything would be over in a few months. It wasn't apparent right away that the inspections would get tough."[10] Recalling this buoyant period, "We took on the Iraqis, they got whipped, everything of interest had been bombed to smithereens, and the Iraqis would want to get out from underneath the sanctions and would cooperate. In that sense, the deadlines weren't seen as unrealistic."[11]

Table 1.1. Resolution 687 deadlines

Activity	Number of Days to Complete	Responsible Party
File declarations on chemical, biological, and ballistic missile capabilities*	15 days following passage of Resolution 687	Iraq
Submit plan to Security Council outlining how UNSCOM would be created and Iraq would surrender the proscribed weapons capabilities	45 days following passage of Resolution 687	Secretary-General, in consultation with governments and international organizations
Establish UNSCOM, launch inspections to verify Iraq's declarations, and assume control of Iraq's proscribed weapons capabilities	45 days following Security Council approval of the plan	Secretary-General, in consultation with governments and international organizations, as appropriate
Submit plan to Security Council for ongoing monitoring and verification of Iraq	120 days following passage of Resolution 687	Secretary-General, in consultation with UNSCOM
Review the need for sanctions on Iraq's sale of oil in view of Iraqi compliance with all relevant UN resolutions	Every 60 days following passage of Resolution 687	Security Council

NOTE: * To cover the locations, amounts, and types of (1) all chemical and biological agent stockpiles, subsystems, components, and all research, development, support, and production facilities; and (2) all ballistic missiles with a range over 150 kilometers, related major missile parts, and missile production and repair facilities.

SOURCE: UN Security Council, Resolution 687 (1991), adopted on April 3, 1991, Doc. S/RES/687, April 8, 1991, paras. 8-10.

Before long, the U.S. State Department shifted Gallucci to New York to buttress U.S. Ambassador to the UN Thomas Pickering's drive to win Security Council approval of the resolution and to set up UNSCOM. Joking that he had not been to the UN since a fifth-grade field trip, Gallucci was thrown into meetings with Secretary-General Javier Peres de Cuellar and UN Undersecretary for Disarmament Yasushi Akashi, who advised following UN practice and staffing UNSCOM with diplomats representing an equitable geographic balance from around the world. Knowing that specific technical skill sets would be required to locate and eliminate Iraq's weapons and that "diplomats from Uruguay don't do that," Gallucci felt that he "was awkwardly positioned in these talks." Worse, he was firmly instructed not only to press for Swedish diplomat Rolf Ekeus as UNSCOM's executive chairman but to nominate himself as Ekeus's deputy. This "doubly ugly, perfectly awful" situation mortified Gallucci, who groped for the right words to convey U.S. preferences to the world's top diplomats.[12]

On April 3, the clock started ticking on Resolution 687's deadlines.[13] Ambassador Ekeus remembered being approached the very next day about the UNSCOM job. Regarding the text of Resolution 687, Ekeus was struck by how unmistakably paragraph 22 tied Iraq's disarmament to the lifting of trade sanctions. Ekeus believed that Baghdad had a strong motivation to cooperate fully with UNSCOM since oil sales were Iraq's primary source of income. Moreover, he anticipated sharp criticism from Iraq if he did not proceed summarily. As he swung into action to launch UNSCOM, the humanitarian costs of extended sanctions weighed heavily on him: "I felt I had to rush, that I couldn't even allow more than one day than is absolutely necessary before completing my task."[14] Convinced that Iraq could be swiftly disarmed, Ekeus accepted the UNSCOM chairmanship on the condition that the Swedish government did not replace him as ambassador to the Conference on Security and Cooperation in Europe, allowing him to return to Geneva within a year or so.[15] As with Ekeus, prevailing opinion among policymakers and UNSCOM insiders held that UNSCOM would only be in existence for a year or two at the most.[16]

Landing in New York, Ekeus provided UNSCOM dexterous leadership. A "hands-off" manager, Ekeus's "let-science-lead-the-way" philosophy about running UNSCOM put scientists in the field for the technical work of inspection and destruction while he stuck to the diplomacy, informing the Security Council of their progress and sustaining support for UNSCOM's operations.[17] UNSCOM inspectors lauded Ekeus for his discretion, attentive listening, reasonable command of the technical issues, readiness to innovate, and willing-ness and ability to navigate political pressures in search of the truth. Ekeus also got very high marks for seeking his inspectors' counsel, asking the right questions, giving them liberty to do their work, heeding their recommenda-tions, and backing his inspectors in public even if he privately disagreed with them.[18] Everyone wanted something from this Swedish diplomat with the shock of white hair, but Ekeus adroitly juggled it all until the timing was right for action.[19] One of his juggling tools was language. Fluent in English, Ekeus spoke it with an intonation and phrasing that alternately charmed, informed, or paralyzed his inspectors, the Iraqis, international envoys, policymakers, and the media. Plying this "Swinglish," "Ekeus could be very unclear if he chose to do so," said Gallucci, "but very precise when he wished."[20] By all ac-counts, Ekeus was the right steward for UNSCOM.

To illustrate, Gallucci credited Ekeus with a structural proposal for UNSCOM that found the acceptable middle ground between doing things the typical UN way and the need to send technically qualified inspectors quickly into Iraq.[21] A group of international diplomats would advise UNSCOM, while technical experts would do the heavy lifting, inspections. "Splitting the dif-ference, the UNSCOM commissioners were the geographically equitable bit and the small inspectorate was filled with specialists who did the pointy-end-of-the-stick work."[22] Thus the Secretary-General's plan for UNSCOM called for a headquarters staff of roughly twenty-five people, divided into nuclear, ballistic missile, chemical, biological, and future compliance sections to pro-vide planning and operational support for inspections. As needed, govern-ments would loan technical experts to UNSCOM for the inspections.[23] The inspectorate's tasks were basically to gather and assess information, dispose of weapons and relevant facilities, and monitor and verify compliance.[24] Otherwise, Washington's expectations for UNSCOM were modest, accord-ing to Charles Duelfer, who later followed Gallucci as Ekeus's deputy: "We assumed UNSCOM would resolve some war termination issues temporarily and that its activities would keep sanctions in place, sort of kicking the rock down the road, which was the traditional U.S. approach with Iraq."[25]

IRAQ'S INITIAL DECLARATIONS

Meanwhile, Saddam was also banking on UNSCOM to be short-lived. As elaborated further on, Saddam's inner circle concocted a scheme to dupe the UN's inspectors and the world into believing that Iraq was meeting the disarmament mandate. Accordingly, Iraq's April 18, 1991, declaration contained data about Iraq's chemical arsenal but was silent on Iraq's production and weaponization of the nerve agent VX, understated Iraq's holdings of long-range missiles, claimed its nuclear activities were civilian and peaceful, and asserted that Iraq did not hold "any biological weapons or related items."[26] These declarations and Iraq's revelations to the first bioweapons inspection team roughly paralleled the open source data about Iraq's unconventional weapons programs.[27]

Of Iraq's first declarations, one European diplomat said with a grin, "[W]e expected to be entertained by Iraq's dishonesty and indeed we were."[28] Inside UNSCOM, similar sarcasm greeted Iraq's complete denial of nuclear and biological weapons programs. "There was only one surprise about the initial Iraqi declaration—that they declared their chemical weapons," said Gallucci. "Our job was to find and destroy their weapons. We took that declaration to mean that they weren't going to help us do that."[29] For his part, Ekeus was certain Iraq had used chemical weapons during the 1980s war, but he "wasn't sure what Iraq may or may not have done" in the biological weapons area and "didn't like that they submitted a very few lines." He was "a bit skeptical, but I thought perhaps their declaration was sloppy" because they had just fifteen days to assemble it.[30]

Surmising that Iraq had moved many pertinent items during the war, Ekeus gave Iraq the opportunity to "get it straight."[31] He fired off a letter that inferred that Iraq surely had equipment and materials relevant to the manufacture of biological weapons because many such dual-use items are employed in legitimate activities. Ekeus requested that Iraq detail its biological production capacity and activities involving dangerous pathogens. He pointed Iraq specifically to the list of items that negotiators in Geneva had compiled as useful for possible monitoring of the Biological and Toxin Weapons Convention, the 1975 germ weapons ban that Iraq acceded to in mid-1991.[32] Thus Ekeus signaled his dissatisfaction with the lack of content in Iraq's biological declaration, his sense of fair play, and his savvy in high-stakes maneuvering in the international arena.

Iraq's initial declarations revealed just how tall an order it would be to meet the deadlines to render harmless or destroy Iraq's weaponry. First, the declaration had sufficient data to underscore that the destruction of Iraq's chemical arsenal alone was a mammoth task. Ekeus quickly assembled a special advisory panel in mid-May 1991 to plot UNSCOM's first chemical weapons inspections as UNSCOM's advisory commission convened for the first time. Among the commissioners, "nobody even raised an eyebrow at the absence of a biological weapons declaration," said Ron Manley, who oversaw the inventorying and destruction of Iraq's chemical weapons.[33] At this juncture, the concerns that policymakers, intelligence analysts, and weapons experts relayed to UNSCOM focused on the small number of long-range missiles that Iraq declared. "Everyone thought they were playing with one or two things at Salman Pak. Why would countries be more concerned at that time about a biological program in Iraq if they still weren't concerned about a Soviet biological program? Of course, there were rumors, and people might think the declaration was not the truth," said a senior UNSCOM official, "but they didn't think there was much to the Iraqi program anyhow."[34] Although the commissioners made no particular fuss about Iraq's skimpy biological declaration, there were nagging worries that Iraq's nuclear, biological, and ballistic missile declarations omitted more than they revealed.

In mid-May 1991, Iraq twice emphasized to UNSCOM that it did not have a biological weapons program. First, Baghdad sent UNSCOM a brief statement that Iraq did not have biological weapons.[35] Then, the Iraqis clarified their initial declaration, stating that they did not have a central military research laboratory and did not immunize their armed forces against diseases other than typhoid. Although the Al Daura Foot and Mouth Disease Vaccine Production Department, which made vaccine, had biosafety containment capacity of the highest level, namely "P4" containment for work with highly infectious pathogens, Iraq declared no other P3 or P4 containment facilities. Iraq also submitted a one-half page table that listed three vaccine production facilities, the Al Daura plant, the Al Kindi Company at Abu Ghraib, and the Serum and Vaccine Institute at Al Ameriyah, with the latter two equipped with basic laboratory capabilities. Al Ameriyah manufactured cholera and typhoid vaccines for humans while Al Kindi, which Iraq said was destroyed by bombing, had made ten livestock vaccines. Iraq identified a fourth facility, the "Al-Hukm plant," with basic laboratory capabilities and facilities to maintain and repair equipment to make vaccines, single-cell protein, and other products.[36]

On July 18, Iraq sent the UN a list of ten dual-use biological facilities.[37] This list described Al Hukm (or Al Hakam) as having mostly inoperable fermentation equipment moved from Al Kindi and Al Taji. Along with additional detail about the four sites named in mid-May, Iraq briefly mentioned the Al Taji plant, the Agricultural Research and Water Resources Center at

Al Fudhaliyah, and Salman Pak, stating the latter had a laboratory to test foods and liquids for contamination. Three bakeries with large production capacities capped Iraq's list.[38] With these clarifications, Iraq began shifting from complete denial of a bioweapons program to an attempt to hide it in the open, stepping up its public relations campaign to show that it was cooperating fully with UNSCOM and shedding its prohibited weapons to quicken the lifting of economic sanctions. Baghdad later boasted, for example, that Iraq had declared Salman Pak to UNSCOM before the inspectors arrived, though it failed to mention that it had characterized the site as a food-testing laboratory, not a center of bioweapons activities.[39]

THE INTELLIGENCE TAKE ON IRAQ'S BIOLOGICAL WEAPONS CAPABILITIES

Western intelligence reports on a possible Iraqi biological weapons program date into the 1980s.[40] In early 1989, an Israeli official stated that Iraq had completed bioweapons research and development but not yet produced germ arms. U.S. intelligence sources seconded Israel's assessment and identified Salman Pak as engaged in biowarfare research for over a year.[41] In April 1990, Saddam denied to a visiting U.S. congressional delegation that Iraq had biological weapons.[42] By August 1990, however, U.S. military officials had reportedly voiced concerns about intelligence indicating that Iraq had produced a biowarfare agent and Saddam had supposedly bragged to other Mid-East leaders that biological weapons would stop U.S. forces.[43] A month later, Central Intelligence Agency (CIA) Director William Webster told Congress that while Iraq's chemical weapons capability was much larger and more advanced, Iraq had also produced germ agents. Specifying that Iraq had made anthrax and botulinum toxin, U.S. intelligence projected that Iraq would have a "militarily significant number" of biological weapons by early 1991.[44]

The U.S. intelligence community also assessed Iraq to be developing and perhaps to have made other unspecified biowarfare agents and to be working on a long-range delivery capability, such as a biological warhead for SCUD-B missiles. The CIA stated that by the end of 1990, Iraq had "deployed a militarily significant number of bombs and artillery rockets filled with botulinum toxin and anthrax."[45] The CIA further observed, "Saddam probably has little fear of the political consequences of using biological weapons. He has the dubious distinction of being the first to use nerve agents on the battlefield and successfully weathered the limited international response to this use."[46]

Contrasting U.S. intelligence reports noted that "[s]ince Iraq's doctrine for BW [biological weapons] remains unknown, the potential use of BW by Iraq cannot be described with confidence. The type of weapons, their fills, employment techniques, and other critical factors are not known."[47] Another U.S. intelligence view depicted germs as Saddam's weapon of last resort, projecting that he was likely to retain personal command and control authority to use this weapon.[48] Chatting with top lieutenants just before Coalition bombing started, Saddam specified that he would delegate final command authority in the event of his death and spoke of the use of the kind of agent that lasts "many years," the method of delivery, and targets.[49]

Other Western intelligence assessments of Iraq's bioweapons status were described as guesswork or as quite indeterminate. The Australian intelligence service "had almost no information on it, and to make matters worse the U.S. knew little more than we did. We thought it possible that Iraq had some biological weapons, but this assessment was based more on probabilities than evidence." Australia's intelligence point man on chemical and biological assessments before the 1991 Gulf War, Rod Barton, said, "We argued that since Iraq had developed chemical weapons, it might also have gone down the biological route. The best we could advise the Australian Defence Force was that the usual ones, such as anthrax, should be anticipated."[50] British intelligence analysts could not rule out the possibility that the Soviets might have given Iraq help with bioweapons.[51] The British pre-war view was "much more hard-line" than the U.S. assessment. "The U.K. thought they had a full-scale bio-warfare program, but we didn't know whether they had weaponized agents."[52]

Risk avoidance, not hard intelligence, apparently drove some Coalition decisions regarding medical precautions for soldiers: "Nobody had any convincing evidence that there was any biological weapons threat from Iraq, but it was decided that we couldn't take the risk of not vaccinating our troops. In 1991, the U.K. inoculated its troops against anthrax, plague, botulinum toxin, and pertussis because it speeds up the effectiveness of the anthrax vaccine," said Manley. "This was done just as a precaution. Pre-war intelligence wasn't all that fabulous. They vaccinated for anthrax and botulinum toxin because they figured that everybody does anthrax. They were wrong about the plague."[53] The U.S. government also played it safe, vaccinating troops for anthrax, botulinum toxin, yellow fever, and typhoid and identifying medical treatments for biological weapons.[54] Australia issued respirators and offered its troops anthrax vaccinations.[55]

The meager signatures, or telltale signs, of a germ weapons program in comparison to those for chemical or nuclear weapons programs made it problematic for military planners to identify bombing targets to incapacitate Iraq's critical military biological capabilities rapidly. The Desert Storm bombing campaign hit Salman Pak, long suspected as the heart of the bioweapons program. Coalition attacks inflicted significant damage on the Al Muthanna State Establishment for Pesticide Production, targeted because it was a chemical weapons facility, not because of suspected bioweapons activity. Coalition bombers struck the single-cell protein plant at Al Taji, a suspected bioweapons production and storage facility.[56] Table 1.2 summarizes the pre-war intelligence about the involvement of several Iraqi facilities in the bioweapons program, the military action against each site, and the role of each facility in Iraq's bioweapons program, as uncovered by UNSCOM's inspections.[57]

Table 1.2. Pre-1991 Gulf War assessment of Iraqi facilities versus their apparent role in Iraq's bioweapons program

Name of Facility	Pre-1991 Gulf War Assessment	Action Taken in 1991 Gulf War	Role in Iraq's Bioweapons Program
Salman Pak	Suspected research and development, production, storage	Bombed	Research, development, testing, pilot-scale production; unconfirmed as storage site
Al Hakam	Not identified	None	Production, storage of bulk agent; storage site for six tons of growth media; planned also as research, development, testing, filling site
Al Taji Single-Cell Protein Plant	Possible production, storage	Bombed	Botulinum toxin production site; weapons development site; some equipment moved to Al Hakam
Al Kindi Veterinary Vaccine Production Plant	Production of botulinum toxin	Bombed	Some equipment moved to Al Hakam; storage site for about 1.5 tons of growth media
Al Fudhaliyah Agricultural and Water Research Center	European company purportedly shipped fermenters to site, possible production	Bombed	Aflatoxin production site; equipment confiscated for bioweapons program
Al Daura Foot and Mouth Disease Vaccine Plant	Known high-level containment production capacity	None	Bulk production of botulinum toxin; anthrax DNA also found in samples from equipment; research site for viral agents

Table 1.2. (continued)

Name of Facility	Pre-1991 Gulf War Assessment	Action Taken in 1991 Gulf War	Role in Iraq's Bioweapons Program
Al Latifayah Explosives and Ammunition Plant at Al Qa Qaa	Possible production and filling facility at eastern end of Al Qa Qaa complex	Bombed	Role as explosives plant accepted; storage site for fermenters
Al Ameriyah Serum and Vaccine Institute	No connection to bioweapons program identified	None	Storage site for a ton of growth media, biowarfare agent seed stocks
Mosul Sugar Factory	No connection to bioweapons program identified	None	Hide site for chemical and possible biological bomb-making machinery from Al Muthanna
Al Muthanna State Establishment for Pesticide Production	Chemical weapons research, development, testing, production, storage	Bombed	Bioweapons research, development, testing, filling
Infant Formula Plant at Abu Ghraib	Reserve production, filling facility	Bombed	Planned, equipped to manufacture growth media for Al Hakam
Bunkers	Nineteen twelve-frame bunkers identified as likely bioweapons storage	Bombed	Weapons stored on banks of Tigris Canal, at Airfield 37, Al Mansuriyah railway tunnel, Al Azziziyah firing range
Al Adile Medical Warehouse	No connection to bioweapons program identified	None	Storage site for 11 tons of growth media
Al Razi Research Institute (at Salman Pak)	No connection to program identified	None	Storage site for 2.5 tons of growth media

SOURCES: UN Security Council, *Twenty-Second Quarterly Report on the Activities of the United Nations Monitoring, Verification and Inspection Commission in Accordance with Paragraph 12 of Security Council Resolution 1284 (1999)*, Doc. S/2005/545, August 30, 2005, Appendix, paras. 4, 7-12; UN Security Council, *Letter Dated 25 January 1999 from the Executive Chairman of the Special Commission Established by the Secretary-General Pursuant to Paragraph 9 (b) (i) of Security Council Resolution 687 (1991) Addressed to the President of the Security Council*, Doc. S/1999/94, January 29, 1999, Appendix C, paras. 150–161; Armed Forces Medical Intelligence, "Information on Iraq's Biological Warfare Program," Memorandum to John Deutch, Under Secretary of Defense for Acquisitions (Washington, DC, November 12, 1993); "Identification of BW Related Facility at Latifiya," Memorandum to CENTCOM FWD/CCJ2-T (Washington, DC, February 26, 1991); Central Intelligence Agency, *Intelligence Related to Possible Sources of Biological Agent Exposure During the Gulf War* (August 2000), Appendix B, http://www.gulflink.osd.mil/library/43917.htm; Defense Intelligence Agency, "Collateral Risk Due to Allied Air Strikes on Iraqi Biological Warfare (BW) Facilities," Memorandum to U.S. Army Lt. Gen. Eichelberger (Washington, DC, n.d.); Directorate of Intelligence, Central Intelligence Agency, *Prewar Status of Iraq's Weapons of Mass Destruction*, Top Secret Report, DocID 934037 (Washington, DC, March 20, 1991), 4, 8–9, 27–28, http://www.gwu.edu/~nsarchiv/NSAEBB/NSAEBB80/; David Kelly, PhD (former UNSCOM chief biological weapons inspector), interview with author, Washington, DC, December 17, 2002; Hamish Killip (former UNSCOM chief biological weapons inspector), interview with author, Isle of Man, August 22, 2005; Richard Spertzel, PhD (former UNSCOM chief biological weapons inspector), interview with author, Washington, DC, July 1, 2005; Gabriele Kraatz-Wadsack, DVM (former UNSCOM chief biological weapons inspector), interview with author, Berlin, August 15, 2005.

The Coalition also bombed targets that were not, according to UNSCOM's investigation and Iraq's admissions, really part of the bioweapons program. The Al Kindi Veterinary Vaccine Production Plant at Abu Ghraib was bombed because intelligence identified it as a producer of botulinum toxin, but this site stored growth media and apparently supplied fermenters for the program. Significant air-handling and processing capability, ties to Salman Pak, possible handling of botulinum toxin, and the planned receipt of fermentation equipment earned the Al Latifayah Explosives and Ammunition Plant identification as a suspected biowarfare production facility. In addition, nineteen storage bunkers were on the Desert Storm target list.[58] On January 21–22, 1991, U.S. F-117 stealth fighters bombed the Infant Formula Plant near Abu Ghraib, also supposedly connected to the bioweapons program. Intelligence indicated that this site had never produced infant formula, yet had fermentation capabilities, ventilation systems, a camouflaged roof, and unusual security for a commercial factory. In April 1992, intelligence labeled this plant, known as Project 600, a reserve biowarfare production site. The factory was also suspected to be a biological weaponization and filling site.[59] When the Iraqis took CNN's Peter Arnett to the bombed facility on January 23 and Arnett described the plant as the only source of infant formula in Iraq, an international uproar ensued. UNSCOM determined that the factory never operated and that Iraq's bioweapons technicians were on loan there.[60]

Finally, Coalition fighter aircraft did not attack several facilities that were part of Iraq's bioweapons program, according to UNSCOM inspections and the admissions that the UNSCOM inspections compelled Iraq to make. The Coalition did not bomb the Al Daura Foot and Mouth Disease Vaccine Plant, the Al Ameriyah Serum and Vaccine Institute, or the program's centerpiece, Al Hakam.[61] Though Al Hakam had been captured on overhead imagery, Western analysts had not pegged it as a military biological facility. "Every aspect of the place reeked of it being a military production facility. The physical layout was a characteristic signature, as was the spacing between the buildings, along with its isolation. The laboratory was constructed in the telltale H shape, the place had bermed buildings, physical protection, bunkers, and dummy bunkers," said UNSCOM inspector Robert Kadlec. Calling UNSCOM's post-war discovery that Al Hakam was Iraq's main bioweapons production site "a big surprise" to Western intelligence, Kadlec wondered "what that says about our collection and assessment capabilities."[62]

In sum, pre-war intelligence about Iraq's bioweapons program was hardly conclusive. "In the Western intelligence community, it's fair to say that we did not have a firm idea about an Iraqi bioweapons program prior to the Gulf War. Remember, Salman Pak was bombed, but not Al Hakam."[63] An UNSCOM inspector who reviewed the data closely described the reports as "fantasy in some way. There was a tremendous vacuum of intelligence" on the bioweapons program.[64] More charitably, Gallucci said, "We thought we knew something about what Iraq had, which was no nuclear weapons, lots of chemical weapons, and maybe something in bio. That turned out to be roughly accurate."[65]

An individual's impression of the caliber of the intelligence on Iraq's bio-warfare capabilities depended on whether he or she had a clear understanding of how intelligence is collected and evaluated, had read all intelligence traffic and formal assessments, or had occasionally been briefed on the matter. In addition, a person's predispositions about the danger presented by biological weapons and the overall utility of intelligence influenced how that person processed the intelligence data. While policymakers may take steps to avoid risk on the basis of imprecise intelligence, in general they are not as likely to pursue a risky or difficult activity if they lack confidence in the intelligence. To the extent that pre-war intelligence did not convince policymakers and diplomats that Iraq possessed a bioweapons program, they were not inclined to push UNSCOM to investigate the matter.

THE ONSET OF UNSCOM INSPECTIONS

UNSCOM stood up with no budget and practically nothing in place save a handful of individuals borrowed from the UN Department of Disarmament Affairs and advanced by a few supportive governments.[66] Under considerable political pressure to field inspection teams right away, Ekeus scrambled to bring aboard enough staff and logistical capabilities to start inspections. "I didn't even allow the luxury of doing all of the necessary hiring, preparations, and logistics before beginning to send in teams."[67] From his tenure at the Conference on Disarmament, the Geneva-based international forum for disarmament negotiations that dates back to 1960, Ekeus knew many of the world's top technical experts on weapons of mass destruction and disarmament. He dipped into his rolodex to recruit headquarters staff, commissioners, and inspectors.[68]

One of the first experts that Ekeus brought to UNSCOM was Nikita Smidovich.[69] A lawyer by discipline with an aptitude for strategic thinking,

Smidovich joined the Soviet Foreign Ministry in 1975. Described as "[b]rilliant and hardworking . . . Nikita was never convinced that things sometimes just happened. For him, there was always a reason."[70] He had earned Ekeus's admiration for his handling of chemical and biological disarmament matters in Geneva. In January 1991, Smidovich helped to "host" a team of U.S. and British biological experts who visited four Soviet Biopreparat facilities at the invitation of President Mikhail Gorbachev. Smidovich fenced diplomatically with this scientific delegation to ensure that Moscow could maintain plausible deniability that anything untoward was taking place at these facilities, which Western intelligence said were part of the U.S.S.R.'s bioweapons program.[71] With such stonewalling credentials, Smidovich was tailor made to deal with Baghdad. He garnered a reputation as "the Duracell Man of UNSCOM's talks with the Iraqis," his patience "[f]uelled by a stream of black coffee and nicotine."[72] While at UNSCOM Smidovich concentrated on missile matters, but Ekeus at one point directed him to watch over the biological portfolio, and the biological team often relied on his long-term perspective and unflappable diplomatic skills.

Though Ekeus often succeeded in hand-picking talent, he also had to make do with the personnel that governments sent his way, sometimes stipulating that their experts lead inspections.[73] Offsetting such petty gamesmanship, UNSCOM received many resources.[74] Preparing to work with the IAEA, UNSCOM listed items that its inspectors should seek related to uranium enrichment activities and asked U.S., Russian, Chinese, British, and French nuclear laboratories to prepare a similar list related to the design and development of a nuclear implosion system or device. When weapons designers from these five countries met to exchange sensitive data, the discussion quickly crossed into classified material, one of several early UNSCOM experiences that participants found remarkable.[75]

The IAEA's standing inspector corps and logistical capability allowed it to send in an inspection team, led by David Kay, in mid-May. UNSCOM personnel joined the IAEA on the mission. At Iraq's lone declared nuclear site, Al Tuwaitha, the inspectors found what the IAEA had not on previous inspections at Al Tuwaitha, namely 2.26 grams of plutonium, strongly indicative of a nuclear weapons program since there are no peaceful uses for plutonium. The IAEA/UNSCOM team also exercised UNSCOM's right to inspect undeclared sites and went to Al Tarmiya, also suspected of involvement in nuclear weapons activities. The inspectors noted extensive physical changes to disguise the nature of the work performed at both sites.[76]

Despite pressure to get a team into Iraq quickly, Ekeus knew that he first had to secure sweeping rights for his inspectors. In addition to diplomatic immunity for the UNSCOM and IAEA personnel, in early May 1991 Iraq agreed to grant the inspectors

- Complete and un-delayed freedom of entry and exit and of movement throughout Iraq without advance notice, with necessary supplies and equipment
- Unobstructed, no-notice access to any site, above or below ground, and to multiple facilities simultaneously
- The prerogative to examine any document, photocopy, and retain it; to photograph and videotape, move, and retain any item UNSCOM deemed pertinent to the implementation of its mandate; to take and analyze any type of sample, including analysis at laboratories outside of Iraq; and to interview Iraqi personnel
- The power to designate items for storage, destruction, or rendering harmless and any facility for inspection or continued monitoring
- The right to install ongoing monitoring equipment and build facilities to enable various activities (such as storage, destruction of items, testing, observation)
- The use of aerial surveillance and unrestricted communications (such as radio and satellite)

Iraq further pledged to ensure the safety of the inspectors and cover some inspection costs (such as for office space). Though Iraq agreed to these terms while the first inspection was under way, Baghdad flouted them almost from the outset. In response, the Security Council passed other measures to reinforce the rights of the inspectors.[77]

UNSCOM's first solo inspection surveyed Iraq's main chemical weapons research, development, production, filling, and storage facility, called the State Establishment for Pesticide Production at Al Muthanna, from June 9 to 15, 1991. Australian Peter Dunn, a scientist who participated in the UN Secretary-General's March 1984 investigation of Iran's allegations of Iraqi chemical weapons use, led the mission.[78] Dunn and Australian intelligence analyst Barton, who later joined UNSCOM's nucleus of bioweapons inspectors, did their final planning as they flew into Bahrain to stage the mission. Since Al Muthanna had been bombed during the war, Barton and Dunn expected a dangerous mess, but they had only five days of training and mock inspections at an old military facility in Bahrain to prepare a team of chemical agent detection specialists, structural engineers, and decontamination and explosive ordnance technicians.[79] In addition to the years he spent poring over data on foreign unconventional weapons programs, Barton had an extensive background in the paper trail of transactions left by a weapons program from his work in support of the multilateral export control cooperative, the Australia Group.[80]

This initial team included Hamish Killip, a retired colonel of the British Royal Engineers. A chemical engineer by training, Killip had been an analyst and manager at Britain's chemical and biological defense facility at Porton Down. With an easygoing smile and an understated persuasive manner, Killip had a flair for taking the Iraqis and his fellow inspectors by surprise.[81] Killip used encyclopedic knowledge of weapons systems and testing, engineering skills, and eagle-eyed powers of observation to scrutinize Iraqi claims about their bioweapons tests and capabilities.[82] For his distinguished service as one of UNSCOM's core biological inspectors, Killip received the Order of the British Empire.[83]

Overloaded just arranging the initial inspection logistics, said Killip, UNSCOM's small headquarters staff made a fundamental opening gaffe: "No assessment was done of Iraq's initial declarations other than by individuals who drew their own conclusions as to their shortcomings. All that the inspectors in Iraq had was the raw Iraqi declarations, photocopied to the point of illegibility."[84] Recapping the inspectorate's beginning, a senior UNSCOM official said, "UNSCOM had no clue; it was just a bunch of people coming from all over the world, drawing as best they could from their own experience. The initial thought was that all there would be to this job was to run bulldozers over a few missiles and chemical rockets."[85] In the field with little instruction beyond "go verify the declaration," the inspectors, said Killip, had difficulty wrapping their minds around what UNSCOM was supposed to do in practice beyond counting weapons. Almost right away they saw that the numbers of Iraqi missiles, chemical bombs, and other materials did not correspond to Iraq's declarations, and they got various other indications that their job called for much more than just checklist counting.[86]

At Al Muthanna, the inspectors saw unexploded ordnance everywhere, and the chemical detectors alarmed frequently every day. The toxic mess aside, Killip, who was "looking for signs of cooperation or non-cooperation" from the beginning, noticed that the electricity was off in some buildings and documents were piled in stacks as if in readiness for burning. Killip recognized the signs of passive resistance, though the Iraqis seemed somewhat cooperative.[87] Having pored over satellite images of Al Muthanna for years,

Barton was surprised to find a large animal house, necessary for testing of agents, and other buildings that were not at all what he had anticipated. A sobering appraisal of the complexity and size of the chemical weapons destruction job ahead, of the mission Barton said, "Everything considered, it was quite a success, but, on reflection, we missed a lot."[88]

Barton's regret from that first mission was that he had seen but not necessarily understood the proverbial needle in the haystack. Among the many thousands of munitions at Al Muthanna, Barton had seen bombs with black stripes on them. With about twenty people and six days to cover this massive site, the inspectors split into smaller teams to survey different buildings. Killip recalled that Barton's "outfit did the filling station, where, in their original packing cases, there were a number of assembled bombs with black stripes."[89] With R-400 bombs literally "all over the place . . . we never stopped to do an inventory of how many with which type of markings were there," said Barton.[90] Killip and Barton spoke with team chief Dunn about the need to understand the meaning of the different markings on the munitions. Killip also advised that the inspectors determine who the senior managers of the chemical weapons program were and solicit their descriptions of the size and scope of Iraq's chemical arsenal, its supporting infrastructure, and the upcoming destruction job. Such recommendations ran counter to the UN's legal advice to the early UNSCOM teams to operate circumspectly, not asking the Iraqis their names. Some inspectors were told not to speak with Iraqis that UNSCOM believed to be important figures in the chemical weapons program. These conservative protocol guidelines and the political circumstances in which UNSCOM was operating made it tough for early UNSCOM team chiefs to contemplate pushing the Iraqis to clarify markings on munitions, grant access to the managers of Iraq's weapons programs, or pursue other anomalies that inspectors noticed.[91]

Moreover, the need to survey all of Al Muthanna left the inspectors scant time to investigate anything unusual that they observed. On another early mission to Al Muthanna, Barton remembered that he and Killip "kept going on and on about the dump site, wanting to exploit it for evidence," apparently annoying the team chief. "Early on, the Iraqis still didn't have everything cleaned up and stuff like that—biological bombs—were just sitting out in the open. The rubbish dumps contained more relevant things, drop tanks and spray tanks, that were important clues to the chemical and biological programs." Plus, Barton explained, "at that time, no one at a senior level was really interested in trying to dig out a covert biological weapons program."[92] Killip and Barton were not the type, however, to give up easily.

When Killip and Barton subsequently asked the Iraqis about the black markings on the R-400s, they came up with "all sorts of explanations and none made sense. 'Oh, that's the only paint we had available' was the type of thing they would say," recalled Killip. The Iraqis gave Killip similar noncommittal responses about another munition, the LD-250. Another factor that stood out for Killip was that "none of the cases that had the black-striped bombs had any shrapnel markings, so they had been put there since the war." Before they were destroyed along with Iraq's chemical weaponry, the inspectors checked the black-striped R-400s and found them empty, with a blue "epoxy coating on the inside to help keep contents stable. At the time, we did not suspect their true nature."[93] Of their circumstances, Barton said, "We were still working out the fundamental lines of questioning. We didn't know what facilities were involved, what agents they were working with, how far they had gotten. We didn't know whether we were missing something or whether they really didn't have anything." In hindsight, Barton noted that the plan for UNSCOM's first mission should have included leaving a team at Al Muthanna "to look more carefully at the bombs, to get the lot and serial numbers, to ask about the different colored stripes."[94] The black stripes, UNSCOM's bioweapons hunters later learned, distinguished the R-400 bombs that were to be filled with biological agent as opposed to chemical agents. Iraq apparently also planned to use the LD-250 bombs to deliver germ agents.

Soon after UNSCOM's first team departed on June 15, Kay returned at the helm of IAEA inspectors on June 22. Satellite imagery showed the Iraqis burying and moving large objects just before his first inspection at Al Tuwaitha, so Kay's team was to determine what the Iraqis were trying to hide. On June 28, Kay's inspectors photographed a convoy of over eighty trucks scurrying out the back gate of Al Fallujah carrying calutrons, equipment to enrich uranium. When Iraqis started firing weapons over the inspectors' heads, Ekeus, monitoring events via telephone, ordered them to stop chasing the convoy. Unbeknownst to UNSCOM, this incident pressed Iraq's leaders to elect to destroy unilaterally its remaining prohibited weapons, mostly biological agents and missiles.[95]

Throughout July, Iraq continued to hinder the inspectors in ways large and small, particularly trying to restrict UNSCOM's use of aircraft to ferry teams quickly to locations and also to detect the unauthorized Iraqi movement of weapons or other items of interest.[96] Having stymied Kay's nuclear team at Al Fallujah without suffering severe consequences, "Iraq early on learned a very important lesson in that they could blatantly block an UNSCOM inspection. Even while U.S. forces still surrounded Iraq, the Security Council gave Iraq the equivalent of a parking ticket—sending two Swedes to Baghdad to really let them have it," Duelfer said half in jest. "Then, they got 707," which was inspector-speak for the UN's rebuke of Iraq in mid-August 1991.[97] Security Council Resolution 707 demanded that Iraq give the inspectors "full, final and complete disclosure" about its weapons programs, provide "immediate, unconditional and unrestricted access to any and all areas, facilities, equipment, records, and means of transportation," and "cease immediately any attempt to conceal, or any movement or destruction of any material or equipment" related to its weapons programs.[98] Exceeding Resolution 687, Resolution 707 insisted that Iraq disclose "all aspects" of prohibited weapons programs. The notion that UNSCOM would investigate what happened in Iraq's weapons programs in the past was without precedent in the history of arms reduction or elimination, stated an UNSCOM veteran.[99] "That," said Duelfer, "set a lot of the tone for what unfolded subsequently."[100]

IRAQ'S CONCEALMENT STRATEGY AND TACTICS

While UNSCOM and the Security Council reacted to the early worrisome signs of Iraq's noncooperation, they had no idea that Saddam already had thousands of Iraqi foot soldiers at work implementing a concealment strategy designed to attrite the inspectorate. Iraq's leaders deduced that they did not have much to fear from UNSCOM inspections. After all, their points of reference were the pre-1991 Gulf War IAEA safeguards inspections that did not detect Iraq's nuclear weapons program and the UN Secretary-General's special investigations of charges of chemical weapons use during the 1980s Iran-Iraq War that concluded poison gas attacks occurred but did not specify Iraq as the perpetrator.[101] So Baghdad decided to employ the mixture of cooperation and concealment that kept IAEA inspectors at bay before the 1991 war.[102] "Iraq had expected the inspection process to be a typical UN operation: desk-jockey bureaucrats would come along, gratefully accept the obsolete and dangerous weapons handed over to them by the Iraqis and believe what they were told about the extent of the past weapons program."[103]

Much like those who were standing up the inspectorate, Iraq's leaders assumed that UNSCOM inspections would only last for a few months and the sanctions regime a few years. Iraq formed a high-level committee, which in April 1991 decided to file incomplete declarations and to submit only part of Iraq's weapons, associated components, materials, and production capabilities for inspection, rendering harmless, or destruction. Overall, Iraq would give up only its least modern weapons and keep, if possible, the documentation and production capability necessary to resurrect its weapons programs. In addition, Iraq resolved to hide its bioweapons program completely, to preserve the program's production capabilities, and to withhold from UNSCOM the number and type of missile warheads Iraq had for biological and chemical weapons.[104] Apparently, Saddam gave the order to hide the bioweapons program personally, reportedly saying, "We will confess, but not to the biological program."[105]

Responsibility for implementing these decisions fell to Iraq's massive security, intelligence, and military bureaucracies.[106] Iraq thus created and moved a central, comprehensive archive of critical documents from place to place, reportedly often stashing it in the basements of government buildings.[107] The directors of Iraqi facilities involved in prohibited military activities had standing orders to be able to evacuate evidence or destroy any important items that remained behind within fifteen minutes.[108] Inside facilities, the Iraqis set up obstacles to hinder or completely block the inspectors' access to certain areas and to frustrate and distort their ability to determine what occurred there. When UNSCOM pressed Iraq for documentation, the Iraqis frequently extracted critical records, redacted the originals, or substituted counterfeit ones.[109]

Iraq also created business and research veneers, or cover stories, for facilities involved in weapons development and production to try to preserve as much pertinent physical infrastructure, intellectual capital, and materials as possible to be able to restart its weapons programs.[110] In April 1991, Saddam also reportedly approved Hussein Kamal's decision not to declare Al Hakam as part of Iraq's military biological program. Not only was everyone to recite the agreed cover stories, chief germ weaponeer Rihab Taha also compelled all the scientists who worked on germ weapons at Salman Pak and Al Hakam to sign oaths not to reveal anything to UNSCOM about the development status of any agent or Iraq's ability to produce such agents. Anyone breaking this pledge, it specifically stated, would be executed.[111] Iraq's *modus operandi* was to admit something only when UNSCOM could prove it.[112]

In addition, before the first biological inspection the Iraqis sanitized several biological facilities—demolishing buildings, replastering and repainting walls, removing and rearranging key items, pouring new concrete floors, regrading and removing soil, and scrubbing facilities. The intent of these makeovers was to confound the inspectors' efforts to determine the original purpose of facilities and to impede UNSCOM from detecting biowarfare agents via sampling.[113] The Iraqis also practiced inspections at key facilities, trying to figure out what the inspectors would see and how to handle their inquiries.[114] After Iraqi leaders decided in June to destroy the biological arsenal, they blew up or melted weapons and components and planted misleading materials at destruction sites to muddle the evidence about the capabilities Iraq was trying to retain.[115]

To further complicate UNSCOM's efforts, when the inspectors were in Iraq, a complement of security officials, which the inspectors collectively called "minders," would watch them around the clock. Always in the inspectors' midst or hovering nearby when they were in the field, the minders were ready to intercede with theatrics or genuine hostility if the inspectors closed in on incriminating evidence.[116] Sometimes the minders engaged in relatively harmless or juvenile harassment, but they tried more intense forms of psychological intimidation with some inspectors.[117] Verbally, the Iraqis often tried to browbeat the inspectors, once even loudly berating Ekeus.[118]

In addition to garden variety harassment, the Iraqi minders, guards, and officials at inspection sites had an array of tactics designed to put UNSCOM inspectors in seeming risk of physical harm with death threats and mobs that formed a gauntlet for the inspectors.[119] Sometimes, the Iraqis placed the inspectors in actual physical jeopardy, causing vehicle crashes en route to inspection sites, brandishing guns, and even firing guns over the heads of the inspectors. The Iraqis also staged health- and even life-threatening booby traps at inspection sites to buy time to sweep evidence from a site or to sort out what to do.[120] On less harrowing days, the Iraqis stalled the inspectors by purportedly losing the keys to a building or room, which they did so frequently it became a joke.[121] Some inspectors took this pestering, challenging, and sometimes hostile environment in stride, but others buckled under the pressure.[122]

A final dimension of Iraq's deception policy was to gain advance notice of inspection plans and to understand what evidence UNSCOM had about Iraq's weapons programs.[123] From the outset, UNSCOM took precautions to protect sensitive data, but Iraq's efforts to infiltrate UNSCOM were nonetheless a magnet for controversy.[124] Arguably, Iraq's snooping on UNSCOM had no real influence on the outcome of events.[125] Moreover, UNSCOM's inspection track record disproved the standard criticism that the international nature of the UN renders the successful conduct of sensitive or assertive inspections impossible.

THE REASONS FOR IRAQ'S BIG BLUFF

Many factors appear to have motivated Iraq's grand and risky concealment and deception program, which exposed the prohibited items that Iraq did not forfeit to possible discovery by the inspectors and Iraq to potential punishment for noncompliance. For starters, Saddam and his inner circle may have thought it advisable not to cooperate with UNSCOM on principle, given U.S. leadership in the 1991 Gulf War. Standing up to the United States was certainly popular in the Arab world.[126]

The roots of Iraq's prolonged bioweapons standoff with UNSCOM, however, likely ran much deeper than attempting to embarrass a global superpower by proxy. Within months, UNSCOM articulated plans not just to eliminate Iraq's chemical arsenal but to disable the remaining production capability at Al Muthanna, and inspectors zeroed in on and started dismantling Iraq's nuclear weapons program as well. These events may have redoubled Baghdad's determination to preserve the bioweapons program. Small in comparison to Iraq's chemical and nuclear weapons programs, it may have been perceived by Iraq's leaders as the easiest to hide.[127]

For Iraq, giving up the country's bioweapons program was an unattractive and perhaps unthinkable option for three major reasons. First, if Iraq's enemies knew or suspected Iraq had any unconventional weapons, Iraqi leaders assumed they would temper any plans to provoke or attack Iraq. Baghdad's extension of the range of its SCUD missiles altered Middle Eastern security dynamics and contributed to the perception that even a defeated Iraq was still a regional power.[128] So long as UNSCOM was unable to account for some SCUDs, Iraq's unconventional weapons capability was more worrisome. According to one of Saddam's chief U.S. interlocutors after the 2003 Gulf War, Saddam thought it was "absolutely" necessary to perpetuate the perception that Iraq retained weapons of mass destruction.[129]

Second, to the extent that the legitimacy of Saddam's rule depended on the assertion that Iraq won the 1980s war with Iran, Saddam could ill afford for ordinary Iraqis to see Iraq stripped of its unconventional weaponry. After all, Iraqis viewed chemical weapons as the equalizer in a war that otherwise Iraq would have lost.[130] Moreover, some Iraqi officials could not imagine Saddam humiliating himself by admitting he had no weapons left. Even Iraqis who knew about the destruction of the biological munitions and bulk agent believed that Saddam had found a way to preserve some weapons.[131] Thus feeding the myth of a lingering viable unconventional weapons capability in Iraq was equally important to regime survival, internally and externally.

A final contributing factor was Saddam's view of his own legacy. Wanting to claim the mantle of Nebuchadnezzar, Saddam always thought in strategic political terms and had ambitions that Iraq would be *the* leading Arab nation.[132] With such lofty aims, Saddam had no choice but to hang on, at the very least, to some ability to resuscitate his nuclear, biological, and missile programs. To have a fighting chance to realize his goals, Saddam kept the teams of critical nuclear, biological, and missile scientists together to perform what research they could, given the sanctions and the presence of inspectors. Saddam met regularly with his weaponeers, and Iraq never handed over its archive of weapons cookbooks and manuals.[133] No matter what the costs, which eventually included his rule and his life, Saddam never relinquished his dream of regional domination or blinked in his bluff that Iraq still had unconventional weapons.

Regardless of the motives, the thoroughness and aggressiveness of Iraqi concealment practices placed a considerable burden on UNSCOM inspectors, noted Gallucci:

> These circumstances meant that inspectors had no choice other than to assume that nothing they were being told could be assumed to be true. They had to go and verify every single, little thing, to see manifest proof. If someone said, "I'm sorry, we've lost the keys," then the inspector had to assume they were buying time to clean what's behind that door or gate, and it was very important to get whatever they were hiding. That inspector had to bust down the door if they didn't produce the keys. If they told the inspector that so-and-so wasn't available, then the assumption had to be that they haven't had sufficient time to work that person over, to get them properly "prepared" for the interview. When the lies are so abundant and flagrant, the inspectors have to work under worst case assumptions.[134]

To implement its mandate, UNSCOM could not afford to leave an unturned stone.

UNSCOM INCUBATES INSPECTION STRATEGY, TACTICS, AND TOOLS

Within weeks, Iraq blatantly disregarded the Security Council's latest commands when it detained a Kay-led team on September 23, 1991, and confiscated the documents the inspectors had found about Iraq's nuclear weapons program. The next day, after the inspectors tried to remove documents from Iraq's Atomic Energy Commission, the Iraqis held Kay's forty-four inspectors at gunpoint in a nearby parking lot for four days before allowing them to depart with Iraq's nuclear bomb blueprints.[135] This incident highlighted just how high the stakes were in this disarmament showdown.

Individually and collectively, the UNSCOM inspectors recognized they were in something of a fix. The Security Council's resolutions were simultaneously clear, yet nonspecific. UNSCOM inspectors knew that intelligence would not always be that accurate and were generally aware of efforts to disarm Germany following World Wars I and II. However, as Killip put it, "there wasn't exactly a file we could pull up to tell us how it had been done previously."[136] Though the Allies recorded details of these large-scale disarmament efforts, time-pressed UNSCOM personnel hardly had the luxury to sift through dusty archives for practical guidance.[137] Other reference points for UNSCOM included the inspections of the IAEA, the mid-1980s confidence-building measures in the European theater, the 1987 Intermediate-Range Nuclear Forces Treaty, and the 1990 Conventional Forces in Europe Treaty, all of which carefully balanced inspection intrusiveness to enable a reasonably high confidence of compliance while protecting national security and business information not related to treaty obligations. Usually, when inspectors visited declared sites to view facilities and equipment their access was controlled to achieve that balance.[138] A significant advance beyond the sole reliance on national technical means (such as satellites) to assess compliance, these first-generation on-site inspection tools were virtually untried in the area of biological weaponry. Not until 1995 did negotiations to craft a verification protocol for the 1972 international bioweapons ban even begin.[139]

Iraq's behavior, stated UNSCOM historian Stephen Black, obliged the inspectors to create "verification tools and capabilities that were unimaginable in the spring of 1991."[140] For instance, Ekeus began authorizing no-notice inspections of nondeclared sites before Chemical Weapons Convention negotiators even agreed to the concept of a challenge inspection.[141] Geneva diplomats had codified some controlled access to documents and personnel, but they had not dared to license inspectors to examine every document and computer record at a site, to ask personnel affiliated with a weapons program to account repeatedly for pertinent activities, much less to interview individuals who had only tangential involvement with a weapons program (such as janitors and drivers). As noted, Kay's team left Iraq's Atomic Energy Commission with virtually every document in sight, and UNSCOM later dispatched many other missions to search for documents and other items Iraq was hiding. Of necessity, UNSCOM incubated inspection strategies and practices because Iraq's declarations were clearly lacking and the inspectors had to know the full scope of the Iraqi weapons programs to certify to the Security Council that all such weapons were destroyed, removed, or rendered harmless.

To pinpoint what the Iraqis were *not* telling UNSCOM, the inspectors first reviewed the declarations, making margin notes based on assigned percentages to the different phases of a weapons program (for example, research, testing, production). Next, the inspectors listed what they needed to know to be able to certify whether "x" was true and designated the level of confidence with which they were able to verify that part of the program at that time. This exercise allowed the inspectors to determine how significant Iraq's omissions were and then to specify how many important questions the Iraqis had answered, or not.[142]

The need for a straight accounting on the number and types of chemical rounds still in Iraq in the fall of 1991 prompted UNSCOM inspectors to blaze more trails. Killip and fellow inspector Igor Mitrokin struck on the idea of a mass balance of materials, a concept discussed in arms control circles but never applied in practice. The inspectors could match a full listing of materials coming into a weapons program to accounts of materials and weapons subsequently produced and expended for various reasons to give them a firmer idea of what remained. Next, the inspectors could contrast this mass balance with the Iraqi declarations to provide more confidence in how accurate the declarations were, identify what resources might have been diverted, and decide the timing and content of reports to the Security Council. Starting modestly, UNSCOM asked Iraq for data on the material streams leading into one type of weapon, the R-400 bombs. Iraq refused the request, probably concerned that such data might point to Iraq's use of the R-400 in its biowarfare program. Forced to resort to other novel methods to obtain evidence to corroborate the material inputs, production and consumption rates, and remaining materials in Iraq's weapons programs, UNSCOM acquired documents from suppliers, interviewed scientists and others ancillary to the weapons programs, and collected and analyzed samples.[143]

Though capable of innovating inspection strategies, tactics, and tools, the inspectors were at a loss to resolve the quandary that grew from the Security Council's failure to stipulate the standard of proof for UNSCOM's work. If the inspectors found all but a handful of weapons, was that sufficient to certify Iraq as disarmed? Were records that Iraq provided enough to verify Iraq's

declarations or was some other documentary or physical evidence (such as records from suppliers or sample analysis) required for verification?[144] Were Iraq
to keep even a few unconventional warheads and missiles from UNSCOM,
Baghdad could plunge the Middle East into another conflict, so the standard
of proof was hardly a trivial matter. The inspectors therefore were in the perpetually indefensible position of trying to prove a negative—that Iraq's declarations were not true.[145] Absent full declarations and unimpeded access,
the inspectors had to be at their wiliest to sift the factual from the fabricated
in Iraq's declarations, and UNSCOM's wisest course was to report the facts
unvarnished.

2 UNSCOM'S INITIAL BIOLOGICAL INSPECTIONS

IN AUGUST 1991, the biological weapons portfolio appeared to be the least problem facing the United Nations Special Commission (UNSCOM) because Iraq only declared several dual-use biological facilities and Western intelligence on Iraq's biowarfare program was hardly definitive. As for Executive Chairman Rolf Ekeus, many generals had told him the military had no interest in biological weapons, "so I thought it would be the same for Iraq. My mind-set was that Iraq probably had very little in the biological area."[1] Nonetheless, Ekeus knew a due diligence approach was necessary, so he dispatched the initial bioweapons teams with the same no-nonsense directions he gave all inspectors: "The starting point was to see if the declaration was correct, to meet the personnel involved on these sites, to see if what they said was coherent, and then to start getting the documentation, mainly the import documents." Due to the brevity of Iraq's biological declaration, Ekeus added, the inspectors also had to check "specifically of what was not really known."[2]

This chapter chronicles UNSCOM's inaugural biological inspections, attempting to convey what it was like to wear the shoes of UNSCOM biological inspectors. These teams did not have the benefit of the clarity that hindsight provides. Instead, they faced the related hazards of possibly overlooking critical evidence and of maybe not discerning a weapons program amidst the jumble of evidence around them. For their part, the Iraqis chanced how much of their biowarfare program assets they could "hide in the open" and still perhaps elude the inspectors' recognition of these assets as part of a military activity. For both UNSCOM and Iraq, the stakes of the early biological inspections were very high.

A FIRECRACKER START

David C. Kelly, a former chief of microbiology in the United Kingdom's chemical and biological weapons defense facility, led UNSCOM's first biological inspection. To the task he brought field experience from inspections of dual-use
facilities in the Soviet bioweapons program.[3] Kelly became a mainstay of the
inner circle that busted Iraq's bioweapons program, the chief of thirty-seven
UNSCOM teams. A Welsh biologist who sported wire-rimmed spectacles, Kelly
focused analytically on the research and development aspects of Iraq's program.
In recognition of his service and contributions to the unraveling of the Soviet
and Iraqi bioweapons programs, in 1996 Kelly was appointed to the British
Order of St. Michael and St. George. "[A] scientist to his core," Kelly "found it
difficult to make declarative statements beyond his view of the evidence."[4] Kelly
was "quiet, persistent, well informed, scientifically indomitable, and, in terms
of biological warfare knowledge, [unable to] be overtrumped."[5] On UNSCOM's
first biological inspection, this unassuming scientist began to demonstrate his
knack for getting interviewees to divulge more than they intended.[6]

Together with Nikita Smidovich, one of Ekeus's top lieutenants, Kelly fashioned a questionnaire to extract more detail from the Iraqis about the ten facilities they identified as having dual-purpose equipment and capabilities and
perhaps about other Iraqi biological sites.[7] Kelly intended to slip his twenty-
eight specialists in microbiology, medicine, biotechnology, safety, and communications into Iraq quietly, but the Iraqis expected the Kelly team because
UNSCOM followed its previous practice of announcing inbound inspections.[8]
At Habbaniyah Military Airfield on August 2, an Iraqi delegation greeted the
team, including Rihab Taha, soon to be shoved into the limelight.[9] Getting right
down to business, Kelly asked for an 8:00 P.M. meeting. After the exchange of
courtesies at the Palestine Hotel, Brig. Gen. Hossam Amin, who headed the na-
scent National Monitoring Directorate, dropped the first bombshell.

Amin said that Iraq was prepared to cooperate with UNSCOM, and then,
as David Huxsoll put it, Amin began to "lay it on the table." Huxsoll, a veterinarian who directed the U.S. Army Medical Research Institute for Infectious
Diseases and later the Plum Island Animal Research Disease Center, was in-
timately familiar with the fine line between defensive and offensive research.
He measured Amin's words closely. Calling Iraq's earlier declaration incor-
rect, Amin identified Salman Pak as a center for military biological research
and stated Iraq had engaged in a research program for "military purposes"
under the auspices of the Technical Research Center, where Ahmed Murtada
oversaw electronic, forensic, and biological research. Taha, he said, led a small

military biological research group of ten and reported to Murtada. Amin said that research was limited to work on three agents, volunteering a list of publications from Salman Pak and of the agents studied, including Iraq's sources for those pathogens. Amin concluded that Iraq had never produced agents or had biological weapons.[10]

Taha followed, explaining briefly why they chose to work with anthrax, botulinum toxin, and *Clostridium perfringens*. Their research, she claimed, consisted of academic studies about the properties of the agents, their sensitivity to antibiotics, their resistance to the environment, and issues related to immunization. Concerned that Salman Pak would be bombed, they halted the work in August 1990, autoclaved the agents, and evacuated the facility.[11] Taha's very nervous demeanor belied the pressure of the moment.[12]

Kelly instantly began trying to determine what the Iraqis meant by a program of military research. "The Biological and Toxin Weapons Convention does not ban research, and defensive work with known biowarfare agents is permissible, but at a certain point, a country that wants these weapons is going to do things to make decisions about the suitability of agents for offensive purposes, and that is when the thin line is crossed," explained Huxsoll. Kelly inquired "about various defensive research activities with several questions and various angles, and the answer always came back that they did not do that."[13] For example, Kelly asked whether Iraq vaccinated its soldiers against the agents they were working with and was told that the Ministry of Health vaccinated Iraqi citizens, including soldiers, against typhoid and cholera.[14] He asked for more detail about the tests conducted with the three agents, and Taha said they had tested these three agents to determine their LD_{50}, a technical abbreviation for a standard toxicity test to identify how much of a substance is needed to kill 50 percent of the test animals.[15] In other words, what the Iraqis described in various ways was not a defensive program. "For me," said Huxsoll, "that left only one option as to what they were doing. They never labeled their work as defensive and they certainly weren't describing defensive work, so at the very least it raised the questions of what they were doing and why."[16]

So Kelly finally asked point blank if their work was defensive, and Amin's reply was, "Oh no, not defensive." Amin then blurted that the research was offensive. Kelly asked again whether Amin was talking about a defensive program, and Amin tried to recover by saying that it could be for offensive purposes, defensive purposes, or both.[17] After this eyebrow-raising exchange, Kelly inquired why Iraq had started an offensive bioweapons program. Amin replied that Iraq began the program in the 1980s when it was worried that Iran and Israel might have such weapons. Amin repeatedly stressed that the program was limited to research and strenuously denied that Iraq had manufactured biowarfare agents or weapons. Kelly also asked why they were revealing this program at this point, and Amin said they were concerned that this work would be misinterpreted and used for propaganda purposes. Kelly requested a statement about their work at Salman Pak, and the Iraqis later produced a handwritten version for him bearing Amin's signature. That night, the Iraqis gave Kelly a list of ten facilities in response to UNSCOM's questionnaire.[18]

After this encounter, some inspectors thought the Iraqis had just confessed to an offensive research program, others that the Iraqis said or meant to say that their work was confined to permitted defensive activities. "So," recalled Huxsoll, "there was varying interpretation of this statement amongst the team, but all of the inspectors had sufficient information that there was undoubtedly some kind of a program there. What it was had to be settled."[19]

Kelly, who had intended to inspect the Foot and Mouth Disease Vaccine plant at Al Daura first, said Iraq's acknowledgment of Salman Pak "actually threw me" and that he knew he had to head there the next day.[20] Shortly after 10:00 P.M., Kelly notified the Iraqis that Salman Pak would be inspected.[21] Later that night, some inspectors reviewing Iraq's facilities list saw it included the "Al Hukm plant" (or Al Hakam) and the notation that some fermenters were stored there.[22]

At this stage, the inspectors were trying to gauge what the Iraqis were saying and had done, and the Iraqis were trying to determine what the inspectors already knew. With Amin's slip of the tongue and their pre-emptive declaration of Al Hakam, the inspectors appeared to have the upper hand. Retired British Army Col. Hamish Killip, a member of UNSCOM's first inspection team at the Al Muthanna chemical weapons compound and of Kelly's maiden biological team, mused that "they must have been kicking themselves" because Iraq revealed at the outset more than the inspectors could independently confirm.[23] That night, the inspectors pondered how, if at all, Al Hakam might be linked to Iraq's bioweapons program.[24]

INITIAL IMPRESSIONS OF SALMAN PAK: BOMBS, BULLDOZERS, AND BALONEY

The next day, right away the inspectors noticed that in addition to two exterior fences, which were standard for an Iraqi government or military facility, Salman Pak had an electrified third fence.[25] The Forensic Science Complex, including the bunker area across from it, the administrative building, and the chemical analysis laboratory all had additional security.[26] The team's second impression was of the unexploded ordnance everywhere.[27] Because Salman Pak was home to several military facilities, Coalition bombers had hit it on the basis of intelligence that a laboratory, a production facility, and bunkers there were associated with bioweapons activities.[28]

Assessing the biological capacity at facilities with significant bomb damage was already a challenge, but as Kelly's inspectors fanned out across Salman Pak they soon realized that the Iraqis had deliberately altered many structures. Nonetheless, capacities and pieces of equipment important to bioweapons activity might still be visible. Work with large primates, the closest substitute for the human physiology, points to offensive weapons testing, so the inspectors looked for signature pieces of equipment in the laboratory and testing facility, such as large animal cages and aerosol test chambers. They also kept an eye out for the level of biosafety containment (for example, air-handling capacity) and extra security to assist their evaluation.[29]

A Coalition bomb had dropped right down the elevator shaft of the main administrative office of the electronics department, causing the top floors of this green six-story reinforced concrete structure to pancake onto each other. Outfitted with a library, a canteen, electronics laboratories, and radio workshops, this building also had a large basement with photographic facilities and storage areas. The inspectors found about a dozen aircraft drones in the basement, which set off red flags in the minds of some of them because drones can be used to disperse a biological aerosol.[30] Unbeknownst to their Iraqi escorts, a quartet of inspectors slipped onto the building's fourth floor, which the Iraqis had not yet sanitized. Among other items, they found a computer printout with a logo of a bird with outstretched wings and tail marked "Al Hazen." Later, the inspectors learned this logo belonged to the Iraqi intelligence services, which was involved in bioweapons research aimed at what might be termed "dirty tricks" for use against Saddam Hussein's opponents. A subsidiary of the Al Hazen Institute located on the Salman Pak peninsula had conducted this type of research.[31]

The main biological forensics building, which had extensive bomb damage, contained three animal laboratories, a few offices, and an underground storage area where the inspectors found unassembled animal cages large enough for monkeys. The Iraqis initially maintained that this building's original purpose, particularly Taha's laboratories, was to test food for contamination.

A few inspectors had seen satellite images of the building under construction that clearly showed "clean" and "dirty" corridors indicative of a toxicology test facility, not a food-testing lab. Taha's research group worked in a trio of laboratories, one for each agent they studied. The inspectors saw that imported ceramic tiles covered the floors and walls of the laboratories to facilitate cleaning, and the animal room had separate, stepped-up air-handling equipment. A fifth room housed seven- and fourteen-liter fermenters, and a sixth was for service activities such as glassware washing and autoclaving.[32]

In the biological forensics complex, the Chemical Analytical Laboratory, which a German company had built as a turnkey facility, had fume hoods and air-scrubbing ventilation systems.[33] Inside the one-story administrative building, the inspectors found shelves in the basement emptied of documents and two large piles of ashes on the floor. Also in this complex was an underground cold storage facility with a large vaulted door that the inspectors deemed "admirably suited for the bulk storage of microorganisms."[34] The eight support buildings for the main forensics building, which would have been of considerable interest to the inspectors, were totally demolished. Gone were the buildings that held an incinerator to burn the carcasses of test animals and a 150-liter Chemap fermenter that Taha said was used to scale up the production of agent for tests. The Iraqis had covered this area with a fresh layer of topsoil, leaving two bulldozers in full view. The inspectors concluded, "there was no point in taking any samples."[35]

Elsewhere, the inspectors came across other buildings that had obviously undergone pre-inspection makeovers, as well as other peculiar things and people.[36] For instance, in several places expensive equipment and machine tools were sitting by the roadside, including near a research facility that the inspectors eventually identified as the Ibn-Sina Center, the biological branch of the aforementioned Al Hazen Institute. This facility included a health clinic, a small animal house, and a two-suite bacteriology laboratory. Later, a closer look at this laboratory revealed the telltale markings of an airlock to provide biosafety containment for research with highly infectious, lethal pathogens. At the time UNSCOM did not know that this laboratory had housed biowarfare research in 1974.[37] Another oddity involved an Iraqi physician providing medical assistance, who volunteered for no reason that he had no experience with exposures to dangerous pathogens. Pressing his luck, he said he was not familiar with the basic equipment in the UNSCOM team medic's toolkit, a statement the inspectors found difficult to swallow.[38]

IRAQI-SPEAK ABOUT THEIR "LIMITED" RESEARCH PROGRAM

Kelly agreed with Killip that it was important to let the program's managers describe Iraq's governmental and commercial biological research, development, production, and public health activities. So, while his team surveyed Salman Pak, Kelly interviewed Iraqi officials in the site's firehouse, leaving only to look at something of interest or concern. Following hierarchical order, Kelly questioned Murtada, Taha, and a few agricultural and public health officials to get a sense for the overall status of biological activities in Iraq.[39] Kelly nicknamed the first inspection the "Taha road show" because to the extent possible the Iraqis channeled all questions through her. Kelly appreciated that this tactic "constrained how information got to us. They made it tough to talk to other people, identify inconsistencies, leverage in and move forward. Of course, it also made it quite obvious to some of us that they were lying."[40]

Taha depicted a modest research program that graduated from small fermenters for laboratory-scale production of botulinum toxin and anthrax to a 150-liter Chemap fermenter. Her staff had also made *Clostridium perfringens* and two surrogate agents that could be used in testing activities without endangering the staff, *B. subtilis* and *B. thuringiensis*. They autoclaved the agents in August 1990, she said. The research was exploratory, never advancing to applied research.[41] Kelly had a hard time correlating what he was hearing with what he knew about how military programs in general and military bioweapons programs in particular operate. For example, he thought it was preposterous to claim that any military research program of the nature described would involve only ten people, a point that Huxsoll seconded.[42]

Kelly asked for documentation to substantiate their work. Taha claimed she had none—no research logs, no process flow diagrams for the production of the agents, no medical records or supply receipts or even personal diaries and bank account records. This complete paperwork vacuum made no sense: scientists are trained to document everything. Kelly said, "They may or may not have destroyed the actual specific documents associated with the program, both in terms of the production and in terms of research and reports, but there are documents that were never destroyed . . . which indicated to me that they had something substantial going on."[43] Responding to the inspectors' growing dissatisfaction, Taha finally gave Kelly ten research papers that she said captured her team's work over the program's four-year lifetime.[44] The inspectors expected professional papers with research data and results.

Instead, the documents were a stylistic, linguistic, and substantive hodge-podge, with some in English, some in Arabic, and some even handwritten. Taha claimed this material, stamped secret, went to Murtada and his boss, Amir Al Sa'adi, a senior official in the Ministry of Industry and Military Industrialization, when she was reviewed for promotion. Anyone who ever worked in a research institute or a bureaucracy could see these documents were entirely inappropriate for a performance evaluation, so Taha's explanation did not seem reasonable.[45]

The next day, Taha literally cornered Huxsoll for a talk. Paraphrasing Taha's words, Huxsoll said, "She was eager, pressing to see what I thought. She said, 'I'm wondering if our program was as good as the U.S. program? Are we doing the things that the U.S. did in its offensive program?' This wasn't just a passing comment. She stayed on that subject, wanting to talk about it."[46] Anyone starting a germ weapons program would logically go to school on what they could acquire about the U.S. bioweapons program to save time and effort, so Taha's queries were natural for someone wanting to see how they rated against the competition, or for someone cut off from their international and domestic peers.[47]

The inspectors considered ten documents a paltry output for a ten-person staff over several years. With the "publish or perish" rule of thumb, publications are the lifeblood of scientific careers. Scientists engaged in legitimate biological defense research still publish, which makes lack of publications a classic warning sign that personnel may be engaged in questionable work. Scientists at the State Company for Drug Industries at Samarra, the Nuclear Research Institute at Al Tuwaitha, university laboratories, and elsewhere published 10,100 papers from 1969 to 1991 on their research, including work with Crimean Congo hemorrhagic virus, *Brucella*, and mycotoxins. Interestingly, anthrax is endemic in Iraq and constitutes a public health concern, but Iraqi scientists published only one research paper on anthrax in over twenty years. Likewise, Iraqi scientists prepared only one article on *Clostridium botulinum* during that time frame. Salman Pak's scientists said they did not publish at all from 1969 to 1991.[48]

During interviews, Kelly and his colleagues focused on determining the research program's overall goals and management, such as who above Taha, other than Murtada, asked for this work and oversaw its conduct. At the time, Kelly reasoned that this type of a project could not be started "without any control, without any direction, without any objective."[49] Somebody had to be paying the bills and setting performance measures for the program. At first, the Iraqis would not name anyone outside of Salman Pak, saying the program was so small, exploratory, and isolated that it was not connected to other organizations and facilities. They firmly denied ever making any expansion plans and pledged never to restart the program.[50] Funds for Taha's group came from the Technical Research Center, and Taha reported directly to Murtada, the center's director since 1987. The Iraqis also said that the "Al Hakim [sic] project was funded centrally, not from [that] budget."[51] Al Hakam, they said, was a warehouse and they had moved some items there, specifying fermenters from the Al Kindi Veterinary Vaccine Production Plant.[52]

On August 4, Taha mentioned that the 150-liter Chemap fermenter came from the State Establishment for Pesticide Production at Al Muthanna, which had no use for it. Iraq's chemical weapons program was located at Al Muthanna. Taha said that the anthrax, botulinum toxin, and *Clostridium perfringens* research started in 1986, use of the 150-liter fermenter in 1988. Taha also spoke about a Karl Kolb inhalation chamber imported for food testing, claiming they used it just once a year. Under questioning for the chamber's whereabouts, Taha listed three different locations. Of the primate cages, Taha said they were unused.[53]

When interviewed, Sinan Abdul Hasen told of several activities associated with offensive objectives, listing not a single defensive work product from Taha's group. Absorbing Sinan's statement, Kelly reeled off a series of questions about the standard objectives for a defensive biological research program, such as, Does the Iraqi government produce vaccines for its troops? Did it have plans to vaccinate its troops? Does it produce protective equipment? Did they test protective equipment against the agents they worked with? To these and other questions, Sinan answered, "No, none of this."[54] Thus the Iraqis described offensive research, but they labeled it defensive and hoped the label would stick.

Though Taha intermittently restated that her team had autoclaved its stocks of biowarfare agents in 1990, on August 5 she handed Kelly a collection of seed cultures and asked him to sign for their receipt.[55] To clarify what he was being given, Kelly asked whether the collection was all of the pathogens that Iraq had imported or worked with in the program, but he found Taha's explanation unsatisfactory. Therefore, he signed for the vials but stipulated that their receipt "did not demonstrate the totality of their program."[56] The handover consisted of 103 reference strains that Iraq had purchased from seed culture suppliers overseas, such as the American Type Culture Collection and the Pasteur Institute. The Iraqis said they used thirteen of the vials, leaving the remainder unopened. In contrast to their earlier inability to produce any documentation of the program's transactions, the Iraqis provided import records for each strain, including date of import, source, and quantity.[57] UNSCOM sent this collection to Britain's Chemical and Biological Defence Establishment to confirm the contents of the vials.[58] The collection included brucellosis and tularemia strains that other nations had militarized and seed stocks of biowarfare agent simulants.[59]

Also that day, UNSCOM and Iraq issued dueling press statements. Hewing to Amin's remarks, UNSCOM stated that Iraq had withheld declaration of "biological research for military purposes" at Salman Pak out of concern that this activity would be "misconstrued by the world at large."[60] Iraq's Foreign Ministry said that Iraq had informed UNSCOM of "the existence of research work regarding the biological factors for military purposes."[61]

MORE FIREWORKS IN THE CLOSING DAYS

To piece together Salman Pak's production and testing capabilities, the inspectors tried to find carcasses of test animals. Wearing full protective gear to dig near the main forensics building, the inspectors were disturbed when Iraqis wandered unprotected throughout the dig site with no concern for its potential hazards. Failing to locate any carcasses fairly soon, the inspectors realized that they lacked sufficient personnel vaccinated against anthrax to sustain the dig and aborted the effort.[62]

The Iraqis also meandered about, picking up whatever caught their eye near a suite of five bunkers where all sorts of unexploded munitions and booby traps had clearly been set to slow or injure the inspectors. Western intelligence images showed that the Iraqis had reentered these bunkers shortly after Salman Pak was bombed, and the inspectors hoped the bunkers might contain clues about what they tried to salvage. With hot temperatures causing some ordnance to detonate spontaneously, the team's explosive ordnance disposal specialists needed over two days to clear this area. The team took dirt and small stone samples from two bunkers. On the afternoon of August 4, the inspectors encountered three sealed cobalt-60 radiation sources inside the partially open door of the smallest bunker. The Iraqis claimed that the bunker belonged to the anti-terrorist unit and produced a displeased colonel who gave an uncomfortable, unconvincing explanation for the presence of the cobalt-60.[63]

Livid that the Iraqis had intentionally jeopardized the health and safety of his inspectors, Kelly demanded to see Taha. Murtada appeared on the scene. Kelly characterized the ensuing exchange as a turning point in the inspection because "[t]hat was when we got additional acknowledgment of the offensive program."[64] Kelly pressed Murtada, charging that if Iraq was engaged in ordinary defensive research, it would have nothing to hide because the bioweapons ban permits such research. Murtada exclaimed that the research could be used for defensive or offensive purposes and that Saddam's son-in-law, Minister of Defense Hussein Kamal, personally blessed the program when he headed the Military Industrialization Commission. He also contradicted Taha's 1986 start date by saying that the program began in 1987.[65] The linkage of Saddam's inner circle to the program was an important insight. With Kelly the next day, both Amin and Murtada characterized the program as for offensive or defensive purposes, and Murtada went on the record about Kamal's role.[66]

Of course, the inspectors wanted to see the Karl Kolb inhalation chamber used for the LD_{50} tests. At first unable to recall what happened to it, eventually the Iraqis said it had sustained bomb damage.[67] On the inspection's last day, the inspectors asked to see the site and were taken to a cleared area with bulldozer tracks so fresh that the Iraqis had apparently knocked down their aerosol test facility while the team was on site. Two trees bumped by heavy equipment during the demolition bore fresh scars. Even though there were no signs of blast damage, Taha was adamant that bombing had pulverized the facility.[68] Then the Iraqis switched to say that the facility was partially damaged by bombing and that it was easier to tear it down than to repair it. The Iraqis said the building consisted primarily of an anteroom and a test chamber.[69] The inspectors knew from the transformer still attached to the power pole that the site's power supply was modest. Taha claimed that water had been brought in by tanker, but there were no signs of sewage piping. The inspectors deducted that the aerosol chamber was isolated from the other units of Salman Pak to minimize the possible hazard from its activities or to keep its operation secret.[70]

Persisting on the chamber's whereabouts, the Iraqis led the inspectors to and through a multi-acre trash heap on the main road to Baghdad, in an area known as Jurf Al-Nadaf, stopping precisely in front of the chamber. "Amid rubbish," said Kelly, "crushed by a Caterpillar" sat the chamber.[71] No bomb damage was visible. Heavy machinery had clearly mashed the chamber to roughly six inches in height in some places, but the inspectors could see that the chamber's interior was spacious enough to fit mid-sized primates.[72] The Iraqis claimed to have dumped the chamber there a month earlier, but there was no dust or trash on it. Sampling from the chamber, the inspectors concluded, would have been pointless, and they had no means to impound it.[73]

The perplexed inspectors wondered why the Iraqis would go to the trouble to crush such an expensive piece of equipment, haul it off site, and then take them to see it. "There was absolutely no necessity for them to provide it," stated Kelly.[74] "It was hard to figure," said Huxsoll, "whether this was just a goof on their part due to lack of instructions or a deliberate attempt to tip us to the program that they represented as having been terminated."[75] Killip inferred that the Iraqis deemed it important that the inspectors not see the chamber as part of a suite, with intact ventilation systems and the animal cages the inspectors had found, because that would have facilitated a much better idea of how the Iraqis had used it. Plus, the Iraqis might have hoped the inspectors would believe that the Salman Pak test facility was the only one involved in the program.[76] Then again, the inspectors also pondered whether the chamber had even been located at the bulldozed site at Salman Pak.[77]

Subsequent analysis of aerial images showed that Iraq had "sanitized" Salman Pak in the two weeks before the inspection.[78] Iraq chose the lesser of two evils by admitting the inspectors to a site so blatantly prepared rather than blocking the inspection altogether.[79] The absence of equipment, other than a few animal cages, made it "very difficult" to determine "with any degree of precision the type of work carried out in the buildings."[80] Huxsoll thought the Iraqis "anticipated certain questions, and they were prepared to try to pass the program off as having been ended. They assumed that maybe the inspectors would go home and be satisfied. It seemed as though they wanted us to conclude that the biological program had not reached the maturity of the chemical or nuclear programs."[81] Other inspectors also believed Iraq had a game plan from the outset to conceal the program, saying and showing just enough to persuade some inspectors that nothing was sufficiently wrong to demand additional inspections.[82] Put another way, the Iraqis were betting on human nature—that a group of inspectors with varied backgrounds, each of whom had seen and heard different things while at Salman Pak, would not reach a uniform conclusion that Iraq had engaged in offensive bioweapons work.

DERAILED BY OTHER PRIORITIES AND RESOURCE CONSTRAINTS

During the inspection, the Iraqis explained that they listed Al Hakam in their response to UNSCOM's questionnaire because the site was pressed into service during the post-war insurgency in Iraq. Buildings everywhere were being looted, the Iraqis said, so to protect important assets they transferred fermenters from Salman Pak to Al Hakam. The Iraqis explained that Al Hakam was the only other facility belonging to the Technical Research Center, which meant it might be more than just a warehouse.[83] "The Iraqi disclosure of Al Hakam when we knew nothing about it—that was the really crazy thing that happened in BW1."[84]

Kelly's instincts told him to get to Al Hakam right away, and he also planned to inspect at least Al Daura within the next five days. Then, fate intervened.[85]

David Kay's IAEA 4/UNSCOM 6 team was in Iraq trying to pin down Iraq's uranium enrichment capabilities and how much progress Iraq might have made toward a nuclear bomb. Back at the Palestine Hotel after their fifth day at Salman Pak, Kelly and a few of his inspectors "were sitting around the table, getting prepared for Al Hakam. We knew it was important." According to Killip, "David Kay came in and said he had permission to use all our resources," so half in jest, the biological inspectors pelted Kay with bread rolls.[86] With his interpreters, vehicles, and communications gear diverted to Kay's team, Kelly had no choice but to cut his inspection short.[87] In the eyes of Killip, this was a major opportunity missed:

> In retrospect, that turned out to be a disaster. If we had gotten to Hakam in August, maybe Hakam wouldn't have been as cleaned up as it was later. No telling what we would have found. The Iraqis were on the run, and the single-cell protein [one of Iraq's cover stories for Al Hakam] hare would never have been run. If we had managed to get there as early as we could have, we could have caused mayhem.[88]

Kelly harbored similar regrets, for UNSCOM's first biological team had many unanswered questions, including

- Why were the Iraqis so evasive (altering buildings, failing to produce records) if their research program was defensive?
- Given the Iraqis' vacillation on timelines, how far back did the program really date, and what was its real chain of command and objectives?
- Was Taha really the person running the program, and, if so, was her staff limited to just ten people?
- Were the microbial agents the Iraqis mentioned and handed over the only ones Iraq worked with?
- Since the Iraqis did toxicity tests and pilot-scale production, had they proceeded to the next logical step, namely full-scale production? Had the Iraqis gone even further, to fill weapons with agents?
- If Salman Pak had produced so many surprises, what else might be uncovered at the other sites, particularly this place called Al Hakam?

Kelly left thoroughly persuaded that Iraq was trying to mask a germ weapons program and determined to return as soon as possible to pursue the matter.[89]

When the team met at the Holiday Inn in Bahrain to debrief and prepare to file their report, inspectors gave Kelly photographs of areas at Salman Pak that he had not personally seen. One set of photographs was of a small, two-story building the Iraqis presented as a chemical storage facility, which had a completely open, air-conditioned storage room in the cellar capable of storage down to forty to forty-six degrees Fahrenheit. From photos, Kelly realized this location was ideal for biological weapons storage, and the Iraqis later admitted they had used it to fill munitions.[90] Still other photos showed the hallmarks of a facility built to facilitate decontamination. Amidst the bomb damage was a fully tiled area, with sealed floors that curved into the walls. A ventilation system was partially visible. This facility was an animal house. Days later, Kelly was still steaming that this inspector waited until Bahrain to tell him about it.[91]

As noted, not all of Kelly's inspectors were convinced that the Iraqis were up to anything nefarious.[92] More to the point, the inspectors had incriminating and contradictory statements and negative evidence but no absolute proof of biological malfeasance, so the mission report provided the known facts and a reasonable interpretation of them given Iraqi behavior. Thus Kelly tried to set the stage for future inspections of Iraqi biological facilities.[93] Among the report's major statements about Salman Pak: "[I]t was apparent that the emphasis was on offensive research," and "since key buildings (e.g., fermentation laboratory and aerosol testing chamber) have been physically removed, a weapon filling and storage facility could well have been removed."[94] The inspectors assessed the forensics department, where Taha's team worked, as providing "an excellent base for the BW [biological weapons] research programme and was ideally positioned for expansion of that programme should the decision have been made."[95] In short, the BW1 inspectors questioned Iraqi claims about the program's research-only scope as well as its operational time frame.[96]

Kelly's inspection report detailing Iraq's admission to a military biological research program hit diplomats' desks along with a report on the progress of the nuclear inspections. UNSCOM staff briefed the Security Council, which discussed the matter for about an hour before deciding that the circumstances weighed heavily against the removal of sanctions.[97] Since Iraq had also blocked UNSCOM's U-2 surveillance flights and use of helicopters and not cooperated with inspectors on the ground, in mid-August 1991 UN Security Council Resolution 707 declared Iraq to be in material breach of Resolution 687. Resolution

707 contained a nine-point list of demands for Iraq's full cooperation with in-spections, including with the investigation of Iraq's past weapons programs.[98]

MORE SUSPICIONS BLOSSOM WITH UNSCOM BW2

Though intelligence had not identified Al Hakam, the UNSCOM 15/BW2 mis-sion, which ran from September 20 to October 3, 1991, went there first be-cause during the BW1 inspection this site had popped up out of nowhere and the Iraqis had discussed it so casually. "I wouldn't have been surprised," said Huxsoll, the team's leader, "if they had just taken us to a warehouse."[99] The first day of the BW2 mission left an indelible impression on Kelly partly because the inspectors had no idea where or what Al Hakam was. Over the Euphrates and into the desert the Iraqis led the caravan, turning at a nondescript little sign that read "special projects."[100]

With no villages nearby, Al Hakam was literally in the middle of no-where.[101] Inside the main gate, the inspectors passed a domineering mural of Saddam Hussein and looked out at a facility that stretched practically as far as the eye could see. All of a sudden, the Iraqis began describing Al Hakam as a single-cell protein plant. Al Hakam had a few clusters of buildings. Get-ting from one group of buildings to another required a five to ten minute car ride, which many inspectors recognized was not in line with the commercial practice of situating buildings closely.[102] None of the inspectors had seen any announcement of this huge production complex, and it seemed strange that Al Hakam had begun operations with no public fanfare whatsoever.[103]

The Iraqis attributed Al Hakam's isolated location to the nearby petro-chemical refinery, which would facilitate efforts to develop new spin-off ani-mal feed products.[104] Al Hakam had triple-barbed-wire-topped fences and an eight-foot concrete wall running along the side of the facility that bordered the entrance road; guards manned the main gate and towers. Nearby, the inspectors could see surface-to-air missile and anti-aircraft batteries. The Iraqis explained that such security was necessary because Bedouins would rob an unprotected site, but many inspectors found the security remarkable for a supposed chicken feed plant.[105] Artillery and air defense missile batteries dotted the Iraqi countryside, so Al Hakam's security was not really all that extraordinary since the facility was also reasonably close to a major rocket filling station and one of Iraq's most important industrial sites, Al Qa Qaa.[106]

The building cluster nearest to the gate consisted of an administrative building, a small fermentation plant for three fermenters, an animal house, and a research building. The sole graduate student in the laboratory, surrounded by pristine books and brand new Pasteur flasks, could barely say anything in response to Kelly's questions about his work. Given the lack of equipment, the Iraqis' attempt to portray this laboratory as engaged in single-cell research floundered. Huxsoll was not buying the sales pitch: "I got the feeling that it was just for us to see that day."[107] One inspector noticed evidence of an airlock in the building, which seemed out of place for single-cell protein research.[108]

The inspectors quickly found other things askew at Al Hakam, for instance at the animal house, which the Iraqis kept saying was for chickens. The inspectors saw some chickens, but after they found animal cages large enough for goats and cows, the Iraqis revealed their plan to conduct nutritional studies on large animals using their feed product. The facility otherwise appeared outfitted for small animals, such as guinea pigs and dogs, right down to its outdoor dog run. Behind the animal house sat an incinerator, which the Iraqis stated was mandatory for poultry farms. This rule struck the inspectors as unusual because death due to a dangerous illness is the only reason to incinerate animal carcasses, and diseased animals should not be present at a single-cell protein research facility.[109]

The Iraqis presented Nassir Al-Hindawi, one of Iraq's most senior microbiologists, as Al Hakam's director. Hindawi's credibility as the facility's director began to erode when he could not even state basic facts about Al Hakam, such as the facility's number of employees and its budget.[110] In his office, inspectors found seed cultures not at all suited for a site making single-cell protein.[111] Accompanying Huxsoll around the site, Hindawi, who spoke polished English, alerted him that a long metal building had something "really interesting" in it, namely hundreds of thousands of dollars worth of equipment (for example, fermenters, dryers, control units) damaged when the Iraqi army tore the items out of Kuwaiti facilities. Addressing Huxsoll solicitously as "professor," Hindawi asserted "without hesitation" that Iraq had no biological weapons. A research program, he noted, was another matter.[112] For three days, the inspectors pored over Al Hakam, trying to figure out the place.

To begin with, not much single-cell protein production was taking place, despite the storage of keg-sized containers of growth media in one of the climate-controlled warehouses. "There was a fair amount of media there, but seeing this stuff for the first time and not comparing it with anything, it was hard to say what the significance of that media cache was," said Huxsoll. "The single-cell protein operation was strictly in a research stage at that point, but they were planning for a bigger production facility, which was what would be needed if they hoped to have an economic impact."[113] Had time permitted, a closer examination of the growth media would have revealed more links between Al Hakam and the Ministry of Defense.[114]

Located at the southern part of the site, the single-cell protein line consisted of 1,500- and 2,500-liter fermenters manufactured in Iraq.[115] This production line was in a warehouse-like building with an open interior and no specialized ventilation system or other physical barriers to limit the exposure of personnel to lethal or infectious agents. Inspectors familiar with more rudimentary ways of biowarfare manufacture came away convinced that the line was set up to make pathogens. Of the lack of biosafety containment, Kelly said, "I would have wrapped those fermenters in plastic bags and decontaminated afterwards. Effective, no big deal."[116]

In the room next to the fermenters were five black 5,000-liter tanks with pressure gauges and sterilization lines. The Iraqis explained that these vessels were used to hold water and acid to make steam to clean the single-cell protein line, which the inspectors accepted.[117] A sloppy coat of black paint camouflaged these high-grade stainless steel tanks. Use of such tanks to store water would be very costly and inappropriate for a commercial plant, but UNSCOM BW2 did not have an inspector with industrial or production credentials who would recognize that "these were the most expensive water storage tanks ever!"[118] In hindsight, Kelly said, "We really didn't look at them carefully because they actually were tanks to store pathogens."[119]

Otherwise, for all of its size, Al Hakam was devoid of industrial or research activity. Several empty buildings awaited equipment. At the northern end of the site, the Iraqis set up two 1,850-liter and seven 1,480-liter fermenters that were transferred from the Al Kindi Veterinary Vaccine Production Plant before the 1991 war. The building's staff spoke quite openly about their difficulties operating this equipment.[120] Al Hakam was also squeaky clean, literally acid-washed. "Everyone thought Al Hakam had just been put into place," said Kelly, who retrospectively understood that a scrub-down of the site accounted for its spotlessness. "At the time, I did not believe it had been used."[121]

Finally, Al Hakam's numerous bunkers seized the inspectors' attention. The ones underground were air-conditioned and, according to the Iraqis, used to store growth media. The largest bunker, close to the single-cell protein plant, was empty.[122] The site also had crude above-ground bunkers to store chemical solvents. For every functional bunker, there were two or three dummies with soil mounded behind a fake concrete entrance. The inspectors had the Iraqis open the dummies with earth-moving equipment. "What kind of commercial facility," wondered Huxsoll, "builds a capacity like that?"[123] Kelly reckoned that "they just couldn't provide a rational explanation for the bunkers. It was just suspicious."[124]

Analysis of several swab samples from the interior surfaces of Al Hakam's equipment, where steam sterilization can rid smooth surfaces of residues, came back negative for biowarfare agents. Had the inspectors sampled intrusively, taking apart equipment to sample its rings or seals, the chance of detecting trace amounts of biowarfare agents would have increased. In addition, the inspectors erred in sampling Al Hakam's human waste cesspool instead of the fermentation process waste cesspool.[125]

UNSCOM BW2's mission was largely to investigate facilities that might have produced bulk agents had Iraq scaled up its program from Salman Pak's apparently limited production capacity.[126] Huxsoll thought that of all the sites the inspectors saw on the first two inspections, Al Hakam was the best suited for bulk production.[127] Of Al Hakam, Kelly said "I immediately thought this was a very, very strange facility."[128] Huxsoll's team left Al Hakam with eight more facilities listed for inspection.[129]

OTHER STOPS ON THE UNSCOM BW2 ITINERARY

After Al Hakam, the UNSCOM BW2 team spent a day and a half at Samarra Drug Industries. Built by the Soviets, this multilevel plant was importing raw medications in bulk and reformulating them into 180 final products (for example, tablets and capsules) instead of making their own products from scratch.[130] Samarra had huge fermenters as well as large stainless steel tanks for such oral preparations as cherry cough syrup. The inspectors saw the plant's operations from start to finish, including the mixers and tablet formulation, and the pill coating and encapsulation.[131] At the heavily bombed Agricultural and Water Research Center at Al Fudhaliyah, there was only one laboratory in anything approximating working order. The institute, said Kelly, was "essentially derelict, with no obvious biological weapons signature," so the inspectors questioned why they were there and had similar thoughts about a defunct bakery they quickly inspected.[132]

Coalition bombers also struck the Al Kindi Veterinary Vaccine Production Plant, which made several vaccines for animal diseases. This plant's fermenters made anaerobes, organisms that grow without air. *Clostridium botu-linum* is an anaerobe and a known biowarfare agent that Iraq declared was part of its military research program. Though Iraq had transported some of the plant's fermenters to Al Hakam before the war, the remaining Italian-made fermenters had a 1,800-liter capacity. The Al Kindi staff said they were having contamination problems with the hoses connecting the tanks, but Huxsoll thought it took sheer ingenuity to have the plant operating at all given the severity of its bomb damage. With the mission's packed itinerary, the inspectors had little time to review documents to confirm the staff's assertions that the plant was shipping livestock vaccines to neighboring countries.[133] Before leaving, Huxsoll got Al Kindi's director to provide the location of Iraq's sole slaughterhouse by engaging him in a discussion of whether Iraq had any problems with the sale of contaminated meat. According to an intelligence tip, shortly after the 1991 Gulf War uniformed military officers removed stainless steel tanks from a slaughterhouse. So with no advance notice the BW2 team dropped by the slaughterhouse that afternoon. As with the mission's other three no-notice inspections, the team found nothing to indicate the facility's involvement in Iraq's bioweapons program.[134] UNSCOM BW2 also inspected the Serum and Vaccine Institute at Al Ameriyah, which made vaccines for humans, researched vaccines for diseases endemic to Iraq (such as cholera), evaluated the safety and efficacy of imported human vaccines, and distributed vaccines. As Al Ameriyah's operators spoke about possibly producing new vaccines for pertussis, tetanus toxoid, and diphtheria toxoid, Huxsoll concluded that they were not as technically savvy as the Al Kindi staff.[135]

UNSCOM BW2's next stop was the Al Daura Foot and Mouth Disease Vaccine Plant, the French-built turnkey facility with a process design to make cells on the clean side of the facility, then on the other side to inoculate the tanks, allow the foot and mouth virus to grow to the necessary titer, and finally to inactivate the virus for a killed vaccine. Sound containment is required because foot and mouth disease spreads swiftly among animals with hooves (such as cattle) and kills about 50 percent of the animals infected.[136] Virologist Hazem Ali was the plant's director. Touring the facility, Kelly could not help but notice there were no mid-level managers around but otherwise the plant was "full of very attractive young Iraqi ladies, absolutely full of them, all apparently busy, but busy doing absolutely nothing. Every single one of them knew Hazem Ali."[137] The inspectors examined Al Daura's equipment, but "nothing struck me as unusual about the fermenters," recalled Huxsoll. "I thought they were pretty much standard."[138] As was the case at Al Hakam, the

Iraqis had left small signs in plain view that the fermenters had been modi-fied. The inspectors picked up on alterations in the plant's original design, which the Iraqis chalked up to their efforts to meet the Food and Agriculture Organization's requirements for a diagnostic laboratory.[139]

Al Daura had not been bombed, and the inspectors had a difficult time attributing the plant's significant drop in post-war production to the generic aftereffects of the war, the staff's inability to get technical assistance from the French, or something else. Huxsoll reasoned that if the Iraqis did have a bio-weapons program, they would have wanted to protect the program's human assets. Al Daura was designed to safeguard the environment outside of the plant from an accident, not the people working there. To have an effective weapon, a high infectivity titer would have been required of any agents made there, which would have made it risky for the personnel involved. Therefore, Huxsoll rated Al Daura "a last resort place to make biological weapons."[140] Although "there was obviously something wrong about Al Daura," said Kelly, "we saw nothing about the plant that meant you could argue that it was not a foot and mouth disease vaccine facility."[141]

UNSCOM BW2's report separated the ten sites the team examined into three categories, the first being sites the inspectors could readily rule out as having no past or probable future connection to a bioweapons program. UNSCOM would not need to monitor facilities such as the out-of-business bakery, Samarra Drug Industries, the blood bank, the slaughterhouse, and a dairy.[142] Sites with no discernable association with a bioweapons activity but clear capabilities to make warfare agents illicitly went into a second category. Though Huxsoll's team viewed Al Ameriyah and the Al Kindi as legitimate commercial facilities, they recommended these two sites submit certain data on an annual basis (for example, statements on activities, imports, produc-tion) and that inspectors check Al Kindi in person each year. In addition to these measures, the BW2 team recommended that Al Daura be required to notify UNSCOM of equipment purchases, structural changes to the plant, and any change in use from the production of vaccine.[143]

The inspectors ranked Al Hakam alone in a third category as being a major compliance concern. Their roster of worries included Al Hakam's

- Isolated location, bunkers and other military features, and military layout
- Significant security
- Weak economic rationale for the site's product
- Quick, secret construction and operation

These inconsistencies with standard commercial practices fed suspicions that Al Hakam was a covert military facility.[144] The team agreed unanimously that the rational next step for a bioweapons program after research at Salman Pak was a plan for development and production, hence the inspectors recommended future monitoring of Al Hakam to clarify the use of the facility.[145] UNSCOM's press release from the BW2 inspection alluded to Al Hakam's association with a weapons program.[146]

TAKING STOCK AFTER UNSCOM'S FIRST INSPECTIONS

With its first two inspections, UNSCOM went on record with noteworthy concerns about two of the five facilities eventually confirmed to be part of Iraq's bioweapons program and recommended that Al Hakam and Al Daura be watched closely. Though the inspectors did not find evidence of weaponization, "there was never a question in my mind as to what they were up to," said Huxsoll, "especially after having seen Salman Pak and Al Hakam."[147]

Soon after Huxsoll's team exited Iraq the hunt for Iraq's nuclear program again took center stage. Working from intelligence that records pertaining to Iraq's nuclear weaponization efforts were stashed in downtown Baghdad, another Kay-led team found some of the sought-after documents at the Nuclear Design Center. The Iraqis confiscated the documents at gunpoint in front of CNN cameras but the very next day, the inspectors hit the document jackpot again at a nondescript building near their hotel. Iraq held the inspectors hostage for four days in the parking lot before releasing them and the documents on September 28.[148]

Whether blocking surveillance flights, playing shell games with documents, or menacing unarmed inspectors, Iraq was hardly a partner in disarmament. Reports from the chemical, missile, and nuclear inspection teams often had disturbing revelations. The Security Council was particularly taken aback by the unveiling of Iraq's nuclear program, after which Iraq became the first nation ever to be stripped of the right of civilian nuclear activity.[149]

In that context, the first biological weapons inspection report was "vague, and that started the impression that there wasn't much going on in the biological area. The report said that their bio program could be either offensive or defensive. Also, it said that the Iraqis were contradicting themselves. Well, you can't make very much out of that," said a senior UNSCOM official. "The same was true with the second inspection report." Noting that UNSCOM's 1995 biological inspection reports used much stronger language, this UNSCOM insider said that after the first two inspections "people were thinking the Iraqi biological weapons program probably hadn't gotten very far. Most decision makers could easily accept that. Bio just didn't get the attention."[150] Contributing to this ambivalent attitude, Iraq strenuously denied having a bioweapons program.[151] In mid-November 1991, Ekeus said, "Iraq had a very advanced military offensive program in biological research. So it is peculiar we have not found a real production plant yet."[152] As if to put any lingering misgivings to rest, Iraqi Deputy Prime Minister Tariq Aziz sent Ekeus a letter stating that Iraq's program was for defensive purposes.[153]

3 FROM HIATUS TO THE HUNT

NOT LONG AFTER United Nations Special Commission (UNSCOM) Executive Chairman Rolf Ekeus gave the United Nations (UN) Security Council his first major progress report detailing Iraq's obstructionism, the Council approved the UNSCOM and International Atomic Energy Agency plan for long-term monitoring and verification. Resolution 715 restated UNSCOM's authority to select undeclared sites for inspection and overflight and reiterated the Security Council's demand for full and immediate Iraqi compliance and cooperation.[1] The ongoing monitoring plan extended indefinitely the inspectors' rights to go anywhere in Iraq at any time, on short notice, and without impediments. This plan confined Iraq's activity with pathogens to research of indigenous diseases and work at civilian facilities and listed the types of materials, equipment, and facilities to be declared and monitored.[2] For over two years, Iraq shunned Resolution 715.[3]

Most inspectors on the first two biological teams came away understanding that Iraq had a covert bioweapons program and that resources were needed to pin them down on it.[4] For Ekeus, those inspections planted seeds of doubt, but he was fixated on biosafety containment as indispensable for a bioweapons program until an inspector he regarded highly, Johan Santesson, explained that biosafety was preferable but not essential for bioweapons work. Santesson also told Ekeus that the Iraqis lacked modern biosafety standards and were not answering the inspectors' questions straightforwardly.[5] In December 1991, UNSCOM's commissioners found serious gaps in Iraq's chemical and biological declarations. Not only did the first two biological inspections raise questions about the extent of Iraq's military biological program, it omitted huge quantities of munitions from its chemical declaration, and a joint chemical and biological inspection team caught Iraq hiding one hundred pieces of chemical-bomb-building machinery at a sugar factory in Mosul.[6] In January 1992, Ekeus sent a team to tell Amer Rasheed, a senior figure in Iraq's military industry, that Iraq needed to make full declarations and accept Resolution 715, but Rasheed gave no ground.[7]

With bravado, in March 1992 Iraq began asserting that UNSCOM had completed its disarmament work, a propaganda campaign that anchored Saddam Hussein's strategy to repeal sanctions and fueled global dissension over how to handle the situation in Iraq.[8] That same month, Iraq's new declaration revealed another flagrant falsehood that contradicted its earlier statements. Iraq's March 1992 declaration said that Iraq had previously destroyed eighty-nine SCUD missiles unilaterally.[9] With Iraq already a proven cheater on its nuclear program, Ekeus's tolerance was thinning. An air of resignation settled over UNSCOM; the inspectors knew they could accept nothing Iraq said at face value.[10]

This chapter first outlines the reasons why UNSCOM did not pursue immediately its in-house worries that Iraq's biological declarations were inaccurate and incomplete, thus increasing the risk that Iraq would bury further any evidence of its bioweapons program. Next, the chapter relates the transition of UNSCOM's biological inspection efforts to a more assertive stance with the addition of key personnel and a series of 1994 inspections that raised more indications of Iraq's likely production of germ agents. The narrative then describes how UNSCOM began to stalk Iraq's bioweapons programs in late 1994.

THE HIATUS IN UNSCOM'S BIOLOGICAL INSPECTIONS

Other than one biological inspection mission in 1993, the last three months of 1991, the entire year of 1992, and the remainder of 1993 passed without any dedicated biological inspections.[11] The Iraqis "caught a break because bio inspections didn't really resume in earnest again until 1994."[12] In the early 1990s UNSCOM averaged two inspections per month, each lasting about two weeks. From June 1991 until the end of 1993, nineteen missile and twelve chemical teams went to Iraq in comparison to three biological teams.[13] The hiatus conveys the impression that somewhere along the line—in UNSCOM's leadership, in the intelligence assessments and political direction from governments, or among UNSCOM's biological inspectors—someone was negligent, incompetent, or perhaps willfully blind to the possibility of an Iraqi bioweapons program. UNSCOM insiders pointed to several reasons for the lull in biological inspections.

One explanation was that in the early years biological inspections lost the competition for logistical resources to nuclear, chemical, and missile inspection teams. In the fall of 1991, UNSCOM began to relieve considerable political pressure to show disarmament results when bulldozers crushed empty chemical munitions, the first step in eliminating Iraq's huge chemical arsenal.[14] The missile group was destroying missiles and support equipment during that fall, trying to ascertain whether undeclared SCUDs remained in Iraq, and dismantling Iraq's super gun. Finally, nuclear inspectors had yanked the cover off of Iraq's weaponization program and were trying to curb Baghdad's quest for the bomb. With no weapons to destroy and no certainty that Iraq had germ weapons or a weapons program, biological inspections took a back seat to other priorities.[15] Cracked UNSCOM historian Steve Black, in 1991 "uncovering the massive biological weapons program just wasn't on the bullet points, maybe a mention of biological on the second briefing page."[16]

Next, as noted in Chapter 1, Western intelligence about Iraq's bioweapons program was neither voluminous nor strong. The September 1991 biological team went to most, if not all, of the sites that intelligence had linked to a possible bioweapons program. According to Ekeus, "very quickly, UNSCOM exhausted its possible biological inspection targets."[17] Data declarations can also identify inspection sites, but in April 1992 Iraq declared just half a dozen dual-use biological facilities,[18] a fraction of Iraq's biological sites. Without other data to prompt biological inspections, Ekeus did not receive proposals for more missions. "If there was a persistent or even a semi-persistent effort to get an inspection launched I think he would have approved of it. There wasn't."[19] While UNSCOM piggybacked a few biological experts and sites onto three chemical inspection teams, Ekeus stressed, "This break was because I was missing targets. Where should we go?"[20]

Another factor that helped sideline biological inspections was that UNSCOM was getting by with a joint chemical and biological desk. Plus, mostly chemical specialists rotated through this post. "Some people who worked the desk early on did not have the appropriate biological skill set or had a mind-set that Iraq didn't really have an offensive bio program. You can't have a true inquiry with that type of mind-set."[21] During this time, U.S. Army

Maj. Karen Jansen staffed the joint desk and went to Al Hakam, Salman Pak, and other Iraqi biological sites.[22] Jansen's co-workers said she did not believe Iraq would have made biowarfare agents without biosafety precautions. She told Ekeus "nothing more could be done" to pursue the matter and shared similar views with others.[23] Jansen's last mission generated a blaze of publicity when for over two weeks the Iraqis blocked her team, which was acting on an intelligence tip about the location of critical documents on Iraq's prohibited weapons programs, from entering the Ministry of Agriculture. Publicly, Jansen insinuated before she left UNSCOM in July 1992 that UNSCOM could not uncover a covert bioweapons program.[24] Next, the chemical and biological desk fell to Annick Paul-Henriot, a lawyer and UN civil servant who lacked the substantive expertise to drive an investigation of Iraq's bioweapons program but actively supported the more assertive approach that took shape in the spring of 1994.[25] So the absence of appropriately skilled and open-minded biological expertise contributed to the gap in UNSCOM's biological inspections between 1991 and 1994.[26]

After the Ministry of Agriculture standoff, UNSCOM redesigned the rules of inspection specifically to thwart Iraq's delay and concealment tactics, so that Iraq had "no space to maneuver," in the words of Ekeus. "If the Iraqis stopped the inspectors at the gate, the inspectors blocked all entrances and exits and stationed a helicopter above to see what was going on inside the site, if they were trying to take something away. To avoid getting totally blocked outside the gate even if Saddam were inside in bed," these rules, said Ekeus, required a senior Iraqi official to "go immediately to the site and allow a team of limited size to enter for an unlimited period of time."[27] New rules were in effect, but biological teams were still not back in the fray in Iraq.

Intermittently, Ekeus received intelligence or information from other sources about Iraqi bioweapons activities. A 1992 report held that Iraq had deployed germ weapons, another that it had progressed to animal and weapons testing.[28] In February 1995, Iraq's former military intelligence chief, Gen. Wafiq Al-Sammarra'i, alleged that Iraq had buried two hundred anthrax-filled bombs close to Saddam's hometown of Tikrit and claimed to have seen documentary evidence about bioweapons before he fled into hiding in northern Iraq.[29] Some nations, however, were always ready to downplay any suspicions about an Iraqi bioweapons program.[30]

Another factor complicating Ekeus's efforts to decide which way the scales tipped was that his first few chief biological inspectors, all esteemed individuals, disagreed about whether Iraq had a bioweapons program. In mid-March 1993, UNSCOM dispatched its sole biological inspection for the year, headed by David Franz, then the deputy director of the U.S. Army Medical Research Institute for Infectious Diseases. Like chief inspector David Kelly, Franz had inspected the commercial biological facilities that the USSR used to mask its bioweapons program.[31] For Franz, the defining characteristic of the UNSCOM 53/BW3 mission was that Iraqi biosafety precautions were inadequate for commercial or possible military activity. At the Al Kindi Veterinary Vaccine Production Plant, for example, vents above the workers inoculating eggs to grow the Newcastle virus for vaccine were exhausting live virus outside of the building, putting workers and the public at risk.[32] Al Hakam's pilot plant and the new building to make single-cell protein were crude metal buildings with big exhaust fans, large doors to move equipment, and no air-handling capacity whatsoever. "With zero containment" save the distance provided by the surrounding desert, Franz said, "I thought it was too dangerous to produce agent there."[33]

At Al Hakam, except for the drying of beer mash waste, nothing was happening. Franz noticed little plastic bags with an unknown powdery substance that he also saw in a green drier at the pilot-scale production plant. Though inspectors did not request a bag of this material for sampling purposes, it was probably bentonite. UNSCOM later learned Iraq was mixing bentonite with the biopesticide *B. thuringiensis*, which weapons programs used to simulate anthrax.[34] Outside of a very contentious plant manager at the Foot and Mouth Disease Vaccine Plant at Al Daura and a few other oddities, the inspection was uneventful.[35] The UNSCOM 53/BW3 report found no evidence of illicit activity at Al Daura, Al Kindi, or the other sites visited but cast Al Hakam as possibly involved in a bioweapons program and recommended continued monitoring of sites with dual-use capabilities.[36] Though not as damning as the first two inspection reports, Franz's assessment looked neutral in comparison to the rose-colored report of UNSCOM's next biological team.[37] From where he sat, Ekeus knew that Iraq claimed Al Hakam made single-cell protein and recalled that "none of our biologists came forward and said Al Hakam was not that. They said the amount of security was odd," which ignited Ekeus's suspicions but was insufficient to alter UNSCOM's priorities.[38] In sum, several interlocking factors, all conducive to stasis, contributed to the hiatus in UNSCOM's biological inspections.

In September 1993, Ekeus and his deputy, Pierce Corden, met in New York with an Iraqi delegation led by Rasheed about the chemical, biological, and missile portfolios. The biological discussions concentrated on Iraq's past biological activities and current capabilities.[39] Rihab Taha, named as the head of Iraq's military biological research program, gave a blackboard presentation showing that only a few grams of warfare agent could have been produced at Salman Pak. Ekeus felt that Taha's explanation was reasonable and prepared a statement to that effect. However, he issued a cautionary statement after twin warnings from Santesson and Corden that the Iraqis were not telling the truth. In an awkward position, UNSCOM could not just close the biological portfolio yet could not pin down the Iraqis: "At that time, we didn't have enough knowledge inside UNSCOM to really challenge them."[40]

In late November 1993, Iraq finally accepted Resolution 715. This act was a turning point in UNSCOM's bioweapons inspections, forcing an end to the hiatus. To perform ongoing monitoring and verification of Iraq's biological facilities, UNSCOM had to acquire in-house biological expertise to construct and operate a monitoring system.[41]

UNSCOM BEEFS UP ITS BIOLOGICAL STAFF

Resolution 715 required Iraq to hand over basic data about its biological sites to enable remote and on-site monitoring to guard against the use of civilian facilities for military purposes. Iraq gave UNSCOM data in dribs and drabs, in January 1994 tendering files on thirty sites.[42] That spring UNSCOM initiated what were known as "baseline" inspections at Iraqi biological sites. Any deviations from the detailed data gathered during this baseline process would alert the inspectors to a possible shift in facility operations from legitimate purposes.[43]

To aid the inspectors, UNSCOM needed to create a database on Iraq's so-called dual-use equipment, which could readily be diverted from civilian to military uses. Resolution 715 required Iraq to declare its dual-use equipment, but the inspectors often found undeclared items that Iraq then had to declare. Short-handed, UNSCOM requested two people to analyze this new data and UNSCOM's other biological files. In the spring of 1994, Richard Spertzel and Raymond Zilinskas joined the biological desk, with Zilinskas bearing the brunt of creating the equipment database.[44] Spertzel, a veterinarian and retired colonel whose career spanned production and testing of biowarfare agents in the U.S. weapons program to research improving U.S. biological defenses, was a heavy lifter on UNSCOM's biological team for the next four years. A hard-charging workaholic, Spertzel dazzled others with his memory: "Spertzel has massive background data, most of which he kept in his head," said Charles Duelfer, former UNSCOM deputy executive chairman. "He seemed to know every detail from every conversation he ever had with Iraqis."[45] Spertzel also had the "big picture" of how everything fit together across Iraq's facilities to constitute a bioweapons program.[46]

At this juncture, two veterans of UNSCOM's first inspection of Al Muthanna, Rod Barton and Hamish Killip, became more intensely involved in biological inspections, though Barton did not join the headquarters staff until September 1994. The first biological inspection chief, Kelly, also began spending more time at headquarters and leading teams into Iraq. Two other essential members of the team that spearheaded UNSCOM's breakthrough on Iraq's covert bioweapons program were Gabriele Kraatz-Wadsack, who landed in Baghdad in January 1995 to direct the final preparations for ongoing monitoring, and Nikita Smidovich, known for his diplomatic skills and strategic thinking. Not wishing to offend Paul-Henriot but wanting a more seasoned hand in the mix, Ekeus quietly asked Smidovich to keep an eye on biological matters late in 1994. When Paul-Henriot died in January 1995, Ekeus appointed Smidovich to supervise the biologists, but he was still primarily responsible for the missile portfolio.[47]

On arrival, Spertzel's first order of business was to assess Iraq's biological activities. Periodically, UNSCOM assembled different expert panels that sent Iraq new questionnaires about its biological activities when Iraq did not really answer the previous question set. Since UNSCOM asked the Iraqis many of the same questions several times using different wording, Spertzel performed the inspectorate's first comparative analysis of Iraq's responses. He discovered that Iraq often answered the same question in mutually exclusive ways.[48] Spertzel then absorbed every piece of relevant intelligence in UNSCOM's files and every scrap of paper that the inspectors collected, including equipment lists and employee records. Among the more interesting documents in the UNSCOM files were those related to Iraq's attempts in 1987 and 1988 to purchase an air-handling system for high-level biosafety containment for buildings E and H at a site called Project 324. These intelligence data, which predated the 1991 war, indicated Iraq was shopping for blowers, ductworks, seals, high efficiency particulate air filters, the whole works. The location of Project 324 was unknown, but the ventilation system ordered would aid work with highly infectious or lethal microorganisms.[49]

The more puzzle pieces that Spertzel put on the table, the more logical relationships between Iraq's biological facilities came into view. Spertzel emerged from his dive into the files convinced that UNSCOM needed to investigate Iraq's covert bioweapons program. Paul-Henriot tenaciously promoted this plan, and Spertzel briefed his findings to the May 1994 meeting of UNSCOM's commissioners.[50] Kelly and Killip had advocated such an inquiry after the August 1991 inspection at Salman Pak, suggesting that Iraq's illicit program could be cracked by concentrating first on the people and organizations likely to be involved.[51]

The central figures in UNSCOM's biological brain trust—Kelly, Spertzel, Killip, Barton, Kraatz-Wadsack, and Smidovich—each brought complementary expertise to the endeavor.[52] Smidovich regularly unleashed his diplomatic skills to help the bioweapons inspectors outfox the Iraqis. Along with their knowledge, "the biologists each had their own kingdoms that they could tap into on a particular issue," and they used those networks as force multipliers during the investigation of Iraq's bioweapons program.[53] "These scientists would argue endlessly over the facts, their importance, and what they meant," said Duelfer. "It was a relief when they all agreed on something."[54] The issues at hand easily lent themselves to multiple interpretations, and none of the biologists was reticent about arguing a point. "We ran the gamut from bunny huggers who would give the Iraqis the benefit of the doubt to those who always thought they were lying," said Killip. With their different technical specialties, he continued, "Each person was free to question the other's point of view. On missions, we'd each work according to our area of expertise, which meant the lead rotated. We operated independently, interactively, and very collegially. We made decisions by consensus."[55] In this manner and sometimes working from the faintest traces of evidence, UNSCOM's biological inspectors pieced together an impressively complete picture of Iraq's bioweapons program, though these same inspectors would readily point out what remains unclear. On the critical issues, however, one or the other of these bioweapons hunters was right almost all the time.[56]

THE NON-INSPECTION

In April 1994, the first biological baseline team went to Iraq. Two military officers, Volker Beck of Germany and Patrice Binder of France, led UNSCOM 72/BW4 to university and medical laboratories, food control facilities, breweries, Al Hakam, Al Kindi, Al Daura, and producers of fertilizer, pesticide, and castor oil to assess whether UNSCOM should monitor these sites.[57] The situation reports filed from the field indicate the team dwelled on minor declaration errors.[58]

Word seeped back to UNSCOM headquarters that Beck and Binder were thwarting any initiative on the part of their inspectors. Team member Jeff Mohr quipped that the team could hardly be effective when its leaders were treating the inspection like it "was a vacation in Iraq." Beck and Binder had the team spend more time drinking tea than investigating. Some inspectors were so fed up that they joked about mutiny.[59] Beck, however, told the press of a "highly successful mission" in which his team had been to forty-one sites and concluded that "there are no more gaps left to be filled" in the data that UNSCOM needed about Iraq's biological activities to start monitoring them; that Iraq's military defensive research was "basic, at the laboratory level;" and that "there is no suspicion that they are hiding any biological warfare programme."[60]

According to the May 1994 BW4 inspection report, Iraqi biological facilities did not need to be monitored unless they had high-level biosafety containment. This report glossed over considerable indications that Iraq had engaged in offensive biological activities and left unstated that modern containment infrastructure, while desirable, was hardly a prerequisite for research, development, testing, production, and filling of biowarfare agents. UNSCOM's in-house biological experts and some other inspectors were appalled. Paul-Henriot somehow managed to bury the BW4 report for roughly a year, by which time other inspectors had collected evidence that strongly pointed to an Iraqi bioweapons program.[61]

THE BIOLOGICAL BASELINE INSPECTIONS

Back-to-back-to-back inspections from May to September 1994 created an incredibly detailed database on Iraq's biological facilities. From an evolving list of all sites in Iraq that could conceivably have dual-use equipment (for example, milling machines and fermenters) or pertinent biological research, development, testing, and production activities, UNSCOM determined the sites to be surveyed. Facilities made the list because Iraq declared them, intelligence data indicated a reason for inspection, UNSCOM staff dug up information that merited their inclusion, or UNSCOM inspections generated more data about other sites to be included. The list ran the gamut from dairy and detergent factories to pharmaceutical companies and military sites such as Salman Pak. To tailor monitoring to each site, the inspectors checked each facility's activities, inventoried and tagged dual-use equipment, prepared site diagrams, and gathered information on the pertinent capabilities of facility personnel.[62]

From May 29 to June 6, 1994, Franz led an inventory and tag team, UNSCOM 78/BW5, to thirty-one sites. Franz told one inspector, an expert in the production of biowarfare agents, to wander Al Hakam with a critical eye and chat up the technical staff.[63] From the way the technicians laid out the fermenters, tanks, centrifuges, and other equipment, everything looked like, felt like, and even smelled like a weapons shop to this inspector. For example, the Iraqis fed their biopesticide materials from a spray drier into a cyclone collector and then into a bag filter, an arrangement appropriate for making particles in the one- to ten-micron-size range, which is ideal for biowarfare agents. The spray head in the drier was identical to the one chosen for the long defunct U.S. biowarfare program.[64] On the list of agents the Iraqis worked with, this inspector saw the Vollum strain of anthrax, which the Americans and British had weaponized.[65] All around Al Hakam, this inspector saw a carbon copy of the old U.S. bioweapons program, which is why the inspector strongly recommended that the spray drier be sampled to assay the particle size of the *B. thuringiensis* it made.[66]

This inspector also probed the operational knowledge of Al Hakam's plant foreman and staff on such topics as putting valves on fermenters to avoid contamination of the organisms before fermentation. With gentle steering, a discussion on the logistical challenges of trucking in water for their early production operations segued into a dialogue about the necessity of pure water for the production of agents such as tularemia and plague. "I spoke about agents and they came back at me with statements that indicated production knowledge associated with agents. We had a specific conversation about sight glass placement in the fermentation line for making biological warfare agents," as well as other technical aspects of biowarfare agent production.[67]

At Al Kindi, the UNSCOM BW5 inspectors described the vaccine plant as capable of producing human pathogens. While at Al Daura, the UNSCOM BW5 inspectors took note of the facility's odd air-handling capacity, negative air flow in certain areas and positive air flow in others. The inspectors also tagged items that could be used to deliver biological agents at the Plant Protection Divisions at Abu Ghraib and at Khan Bani Sa'ad Airport. The team recommended careful monitoring of Al Hakam, Al Kindi, and Al Daura, including the possible placement of video cameras for remote monitoring. Franz's team proposed less intense monitoring of the Agricultural and Biological Research Center at Al Tuwaitha and Khalis Alcohol, a site with significant fermentation capacity. The team consensus was that "Iraq possesses the necessary infrastructure to develop and support an effective—although modest by world standards—biological warfare program."[68]

From June 25 to July 5, Mohr led UNSCOM 84/BW6 in an assessment of thirty-five sites, determining that twelve, including eight that Iraq had not declared, required ongoing monitoring.[69] At Al Hakam, the inspectors interviewed Taha and one of her assistants, Abdul Rahman Thamer. Both attributed Al Hakam's high security to the standing requirement to include passive protection in all facilities built at the end of the Iran-Iraq War. Taha became Al Hakam's director, they said, after Nassir Al-Hindawi retired. The duo tried to explain away Thamer's attempt to buy four spray dryers made to their specifications from Niro Atomiser by saying the dryers were to be used to make biopesticide and had nothing to do with Iraq's former military biological research. They insisted that anthrax production never exceeded the flask scale at Salman Pak. Such work, Taha and Thamer contended, was no longer of interest.[70]

The spray dryer configurations on Al Hakam's single-cell protein and biopesticide production lines drew the BW6 team's attention. Some thought that no one in their right mind would make particles under ten microns without any containment; others knew that the Iraqis could moderate the risk of drying biowarfare agents with personal protective equipment. Some inspectors appreciated that a particle size of fifty to eighty microns, which does not float away, was much more appropriate for biopesticide production.[71] The inspectors were also struck by "large quantities of growth media," approximately 125 drums of Oxoid media and other media in styrofoam boxes, marked with Ministry of Defense and Technical Scientific Materials Import Division labels.[72] Though the Iraqis said they had been making single-cell protein for months, they had only a few bags of product. Mohr's team reported that Al Hakam was not well suited for commercial operations and had the capability to make biowarfare agents.[73]

During a no-notice inspection at Al Daura, the displeased Iraqis accused Mohr's inspectors of wasting their time.[74] When this team pulled another no-notice inspection at Salman Pak, the Iraqis began to stall once they understood the team was going to excavate an area on the southern part of the peninsula to determine what was hidden in twenty-six trenches the Iraqis dug after the 1991 war. First, the Iraqis stated the area was farmland.[75] Next, they directed gunfire at the inspectors who remained there overnight, then failed to provide a full water tanker to enable operations in the heat of day. Just before the dig started, the Iraqis claimed the site might contain the remains of Iranian soldiers from the Iran-Iraq War and later produced religious officials to berate the inspectors about desecrating burial sites, including one who threatened to incite a media scandal.[76] At one point, National Monitoring Directorate chief Hossam Amin hauled in an oddly dressed "farmer" who said the very deep trenches were for irrigation.[77] With guidance from New York the inspectors moved ahead cautiously, using ground penetrating radar and an ultrasonic range device to try to detect munitions, containers of agent, or underground spaces that might indicate buried items. They dug eight trenches but found nothing of note. Laboratory analysis of the soil samples taken at various levels and locations in these trenches all returned negative for classic biowarfare toxins and pathogens.[78] To discourage further UNSCOM exploration of the area, Iraq installed a large fish pond in August 1996.[79]

In mid-summer 1994, Ekeus informed the Security Council that since all known weapons had been destroyed, barring verification problems with Iraq's past weapons programs, UNSCOM only needed time to get the ongoing monitoring system up and running.[80] Shortly thereafter, Ekeus deployed an extended biological baseline inspection, UNSCOM 87/BW8, which ran from July 25 to September 7, 1994. This team developed monitoring protocols for fifty-five biological sites. Kelly and Killip were the mainstays of this mission, which averaged two sites a day and imported fresh inspectors every couple of weeks. Killip called the UNSCOM 87/BW8 mission one of their "best pieces of work, a hands-on assessment of Iraq's ability to engage in biological warfare activities." Though packed with expertise, even the UNSCOM BW8 team did not pick up on some inchoate things. The inspectors made no record of the unusually large quantities of complex growth media at several sites, nor did they see the welding indicating the modification of fermenters to enable anaerobic production at Al Daura or the black paint slapped on stainless steel tanks at Al Hakam.[81] After the mission, Kelly described UNSCOM as "deeply suspicious" because the Iraqis were "less than candid in discussing" some pertinent biological activities, there were "unusual weapons, bombs for which there was no rational explanation," and at some sites "buildings, equipment have been removed."[82]

Cumulatively, the baseline missions covered some two hundred biological facilities.[83] Along the way, the inspectors found numerous pieces of equipment that merited declaration and also standardized how inspectors classified different types of equipment.[84] UNSCOM rated seventy-nine sites according to their need for monitoring, with "A" denoting facilities requiring the clos-est monitoring and "D" those meriting occasional declarations or check-ups, such as dairy processors and small college laboratories.[85]

While the baseline inspection reports did not specify anything particu-larly alarming about Iraq's possible biowarfare program,[86] some teams in-cluded true experts in the fermentation of warfare agents and commercial products. These individuals discerned and could substantiate why something that looked or sounded right to other inspectors really was off kilter with Iraq's declarations. As UNSCOM pursued investigative leads, Iraq's responses to questions became more outlandish. "Iraq had all of these denials and crazy explanations that didn't hold together," said Ekeus, "and the inspectors saw right through it."[87]

INTERVIEWS BEGIN TO REVEAL, CONNECT THE DOTS

UNSCOM barely received a drip of biological intelligence in its early years, but in late May or early June 1994, Israel contacted UNSCOM to convey the likelihood that Iraq had purchased significant quantities of growth media. In September 1994, Russian officials spoke of chemical equipment that Iraq could have adapted for a bioweapons program and stated that Moscow believed Iraq had a bioweapons program. Germany coughed up some pertinent intelli-gence, and toward the end of their regular briefings U.S. intelligence officials added that Iraq had weaponized biological agents, though they provided little data to support their assessment.[88] These activities signaled political support for UNSCOM to initiate a biological investigation.

In the fall of 1994, Ekeus told the Security Council UNSCOM could start ongoing monitoring and verification tests but that troubling gaps in Iraq's declarations remained, particularly in the biological area.[89] The press reported that UNSCOM might never make headway on Iraq's germ weapons program, while Ekeus publicly reiterated that such weapons were "the most difficult for us to verify, and the easiest to hide."[90] Meanwhile, two UNSCOM biological staffers were so discouraged at Ekeus's reluctance to pursue Iraq's bioweap-ons program aggressively that they asked to meet him outside the office and subsequently tutored him on the technical requirements for a bioweapons program, how Iraq could veil one, and the evidence pointing to a program in Iraq.[91] At an October 26, 1994, meeting, Ekeus found the case about Iraq's bioweapons program substantial enough to authorize an investigation.[92]

In mid-November, the UNSCOM 104/BW15 interview mission delved into the links between Salman Pak, Iraq's only admitted military biological facility, and other organizations; revisited Iraq's logic and rationale for its "defensive" biological activities; and tried to establish a material balance for equipment, media, and cell cultures at Salman Pak and other facilities possibly associated with the program.[93] While in Bahrain, the team, which included Kelly, Spertzel, Killip, and Barton, prepared a list of possible interviewees. The inspectors believed Taha reported to Lt. Gen. Hussein Kamal, Saddam's powerful son-in-law, but Duelfer declined their wish to interview him, so the inspectors homed in on Taha's research group.[94]

Iraq produced twenty-eight individuals for interviews, including nine of the ten people that Iraq identified as Taha's researchers. The inspectors learned that Taha's workers had transferred as a unit from Salman Pak to Al Hakam in 1988, so this group did not move because their laboratories were destroyed in the Gulf War. However, Taha's staffers were tight-lipped about their work at Al Hakam. A fermenter technician, for instance, doggedly claimed the Al Hakam fermenters were never used and his only daily activity was to read. The inspectors first interviewed the junior scientists separately, asking about their experiments, their interaction with other researchers, dates and locations of activities, the outcomes of the research, the equipment involved and its origin, and all manner of other details. All Taha's staffers said they kept not a scrap of paper and knew nothing about work in neighboring laboratories, implausible assertions in the world of science, in which peer review and painstaking records are core practices. "Even after that initial pass," said Barton, "it all seemed completely fabricated."[95]

Killip queried Amin about the relevance of the Al Hazen Institute to Iraq's biological work, and though this facility had once conducted research to develop biological "dirty tricks," Amin demurred that UNSCOM should not be concerned with an organization that existed long ago.[96] While straight answers were rare, the inspectors hit pay dirt with employees of the Technical Scientific Materials Import Division (TSMID), an acronym the Iraqis used but the inspectors did not really understand. A chief purchasing clerk explained that TSMID was situated organizationally in the Ministry of Trade but was the only import office for the Technical Research Center. Both the clerk and a co-worker said that TSMID actually reported to the military.[97] The TSMID clerk also mentioned a 1992 order to destroy all purchasing records, but Amin casually interrupted him to say the accurate date for that order was 1991.[98] TSMID's linkage to the military bolstered the case that the Technical Research Center and Al Hakam were military operations under civilian cover. Slowly, the inspectors were getting a better idea that the results of the biological work at Salman Pak and Al Hakam ended up in military hands.

Taha, saved for last, related her progression from part-time work on bacterial pesticides at Al Muthanna to a full-time post testing food for contamination at Salman Pak after she completed a doctorate in microbiology in the United Kingdom. She depicted the branching of her research into a biodefense program as altruistic: her work would protect not only Iraq's hierarchy from food poisoning but all Iraqis from the harm of germs. The scientific gulf between food and water contamination and biodefense research left Kelly plenty of room to work. In various ways Kelly asked Taha who had authorized the change in the direction of her research, its increased manpower and funding, and what the research intended to achieve. Gradually cornered, Taha gave evasions that became shriller until Kelly gently insisted that she please stop. Taha disintegrated into tears and stomped from the room. Next, Amin appeared to accuse Kelly of insulting all Iraqi women and threatened to halt the interview unless Spertzel booted Kelly from the team. Spertzel did not retreat, so Amin dictated that Kelly use notes to pass his questions to Taha from another room. Nonplussed, Spertzel called a lunch break. When they reconvened, Taha insisted that Kelly write his questions for other inspectors to ask, but Spertzel countered that he would tell Ekeus of the mission's collapse. Minutes later, Amin proposed the *status quo ante*, that Kelly pose questions through an interpreter.[99]

Despite Taha's meltdown and her staff's dissembling, the inspectors gained some definition on Iraq's bioweapons efforts. They learned that the same cluster of researchers migrated from facility to facility and that the Technical Research Center was the only client of TSMID, a military organization. From that, the inspectors soon pieced together the trail of completed and attempted purchases for key equipment and materials into the program, namely fermenters, ventilation equipment, and growth media. Amidst the interviewees' crazy answers they dropped "hard" facts (such as dates and locations) that contradicted Iraq's verbal accounts and written replies to UNSCOM's questionnaires. These tidbits provided investigatory leads, and the disparity in the interviewees' responses indicated to the inspectors that they had been coached about what not to say, not what to say. Concentrating on how much could be scraped together from what the Iraqis did not say,[100] the inspectors began to reverse engineer significant aspects of the activities in Iraq's bioweapons program.

AL HAKAM GOES UNDER THE INSPECTION MICROSCOPE

UNSCOM had overlapping biological teams in Iraq in December 1994. UNSCOM 99/BW13 concentrated on equipment inventory activities while UNSCOM 106/BW17 collected data at several sites and UNSCOM 105/BW16 continued preparations for interim monitoring at Al Hakam.[101] Kelly led the latter team, which included an expert in fermentation processing, Bill Lebherz, who identified several instances in which Al Hakam's setup, equipment and process flow, logistics, and expansion plans did not correlate with rational business operations. For starters, Al Hakam's research buildings, normally the engine driving product discovery and improvement, were sparsely and sometimes inappropriately equipped and practically empty save a couple of staff and a few bony chickens in the animal house. After inspectors found media for isolating and growing cholera and *Y. pestis* in a laboratory, the next day the Iraqis made a big production of tossing the boxes of the media onto a bonfire, claiming no need for it.[102]

In a bermed building in the northern production area, the Iraqis were making single-cell protein from beer mash. Across the road, they were arranging fairly sophisticated scale-up experiments to take their single-cell protein production into continuous flow fermentation with a line that included a 50,000-liter fermenter. The southern production building contained operational lines to produce a biopesticide and a biofertilizer. The 500-liter fermenter on their *B. thuringiensis* biopesticide line yielded a very modest output, so the Iraqis were setting up a new line with four 5,000-liter Iraqi-made-fermenters, and a clean-in-place facility next door that would enable overnight cleaning of this new line. Even with expanded capacity, these lines would yield a small percentage of Iraq's stated needs for biopesticide and single-cell protein. "The Iraqis said they needed to start somewhere, but if I were looking for a place to put money," said Lebherz, "this would be about the stupidest investment I could make."[103] Tellingly, the process flow diagrams of the biopesticide line showed it was the same process used for anthrax, and the same equipment on the single-cell protein line could be used to make concentrated botulinum toxin.[104]

Lebherz also noticed but the mission report did not specifically mention that Iraq had purchased far more growth media than could be consumed prior to its expiration using Al Hakam's fermentation capacity. Large containers were stored in one of the southern bunkers and a nearby warehouse. The Iraqis had also begun operating before having the necessary logistics in place for water and electrical power. Finally, the wide separation of the production buildings would make business sense only if the manufacturing process were hazardous or if product "A" had to be kept separate from product "B," as is the case for pharmaceuticals. A final oddity was the document stipulating that Al Hakam's roads be covered quickly with sand to make the facility less visible from the air, which the Iraqis attributed to concern about an Iranian attack, though Al Hakam was built after the Iran-Iraq War. The BW16 team sampled the waste tanks at Al Hakam's single-cell protein plant, but the results were inconclusive.[105] In December, another biological team sampled the spray dryer on the biopesticide line and sent these samples to two U.S. laboratories.[106] As a priority, UNSCOM planned an in-depth analysis of the inconsistencies of what Iraq had declared about Al Hakam.[107]

The BW16 team conducted a snap inspection of Salman Pak on its last day in Iraq. Kelly evidently caught the Iraqis off-guard because a heated exchange occurred before they opened the main gate. Recent images showed new excavation activity at Salman Pak, and the team was to determine whether Iraq was laying a new building foundation or burying something. Though the team split in two, the inspectors did not locate the excavation site in their limited time there.[108]

In mid-December, Ekeus appraised the Security Council of UNSCOM's budding biological investigation, reporting that "Iraq's account is minimal and has no inherent logic. . . . the indications all point to an offensive programme."[109] Ekeus also spoke to the press about UNSCOM's growing concerns that Iraq was concealing a bioweapons program much larger than the limited, practically directionless research they had admitted. UNSCOM planned stepped-up biological inspections in early 1995 because, Ekeus said, "They have a capability which we have not as yet put our hands on fully; a capability to mass-produce microbiologic items—viruses and bacteria—for warfare purposes."[110]

During final preparations for ongoing monitoring, the inspectors began installing temperature sensors on fermenters and video cameras aimed at different parts of select facilities (such as entry and exit gates, or production areas) to be continuously and remotely monitored. Eventually UNSCOM set up fourteen such cameras at Al Hakam alone.[111] In December 1994, UNSCOM put in the first two cameras, one for the single-cell protein line and another for the biopesticide line.[112] Briefly on one of the last days of 1994, the biopesticide line camera captured an employee wearing gloves and respiratory protective gear from the shoulders up, evidently taking samples from a fermenter. If biopesticide were being made, such safety precautions were overboard.[113] Some UNSCOM inspectors saw the video clip as possible confirmation that when the facility was "hot" the Iraqis suited up staff to safeguard them. If so, the camera may well have caught the Iraqis making biowarfare agent.[114] An anthrax production run, however, would have required roughly five more days, and the worker was only seen in protective gear once.[115] Another explanation was that the Iraqis, who understood the purposes of the cameras and were aware that they became operational on December 19, might have been trying to provoke an UNSCOM response. No such reaction occurred, however, because the transmission tower linked to UNSCOM's Baghdad monitoring center was not yet functional.[116] Instead, once again, the biological inspectors mused over what the Iraqis were really up to at Al Hakam.

4 UNSCOM SHREDS IRAQ'S COVER STORIES

WHEN THE United Nations Special Commission's (UNSCOM's) inspectors finally put the hammer down to investigate Iraq's biological activities, the momentum quickly swung in UNSCOM's favor. This chapter first describes how the inspectors converted a few intelligence tips into documentary confirmation and on-the-ground evidence pointing to Iraq's covert bioweapons program. Chapter highlights include UNSCOM's tracking of Iraq's huge cache of growth media and rebuttal of Iraq's increasingly preposterous stories about this media and why Iraq had assembled so many capabilities consistent with offensive bioweapons activity. Trying to bluff their way past UNSCOM's evidence, Iraqi leaders faced the unmasking of their long-denied covert bioweapons program.

Evidence in hand, UNSCOM put the facts about Iraq's probable bioweapons program before an international group of technical experts and then the Security Council. As the narrative next relates, Iraqi officials made a last-ditch effort to get some benefit out of this sticky situation. On the short end of their own deal, Iraq confessed to the limited production of germ warfare agents. This decision reflected a calculation by senior Iraqi officials that admission of some production would satisfy the inspectors and the international community, giving Iraq a chance to conceal the remainder of the program, retain dual-use biological items important to a rejuvenated weapons program, and avert significant punishment. The inspectors, however, recognized Iraq's confession as half-baked and pressed Iraq right away to disclose its bioweapons activities fully.

TURNING INTELLIGENCE TIPS INTO DAMNING EVIDENCE

The pace with which UNSCOM accumulated evidence about an Iraqi bio-weapons program accelerated in early 1995. First, an Israeli intelligence officer gave two detailed briefings to UNSCOM's core biological staff—David Kelly, Richard Spertzel, and Rod Barton. Intelligence indicated that Iraq had ordered high efficiency particulate air (HEPA) filters for buildings E and H at Project 324, which along with Project 85 had some affiliation with Iraq's bioweapons program. The location and function of these sites was unknown. The Israeli briefing also covered possible suppliers to the program and items and dates of purchase. For example, Iraq's Technical Scientific Materials Import Division (TSMID) had purchased thirty-nine metric tons of growth media, including "several" tons of growth media from the British company Oxoid in 1988.[1] Intelligence reports of the mysterious Project 324 were already in UNSCOM's possession in the spring of 1994. After the Israeli briefing, UNSCOM staffers scoured maps for this facility's possible location, focusing on Iraq's western desert.[2]

As is often the case with raw intelligence data, the Israeli briefing gave the biological team an idea of what they might be dealing with but did not provide a clear picture of what Iraq had done or might be doing. At this point, the inspectors could identify many details to chase down, rule out, or confirm. "The information had some detail" said Barton, "but it really wasn't terribly specific so we had to do the legwork ourselves."[3] The same day that Israeli intelligence began to brief UNSCOM, the biological inspectors met with Hossam Amin, the head of Iraq's National Monitoring Directorate, and told him that Iraq needed to explain its large growth media imports. UNSCOM Executive Chairman Rolf Ekeus also met with Gen. Amer Rasheed, who deflected suggestions that Iraq had a bioweapons program and said that UNSCOM should go straight to Iraq's overseas suppliers for more information on these matters.[4] UNSCOM had already secured information from other types of suppliers and would have done this anyway. Barton, who was well versed in just how much data corporate files contained given his tenure with the Australia Group, gave the biological team a jumpstart on this process. In the end, Rasheed's bravado backfired because UNSCOM's consultations with suppliers cornered Iraq.

In mid-January 1995, Ekeus sent letters asking several countries for information about the possible sale of growth media to Iraq.[5] Some countries responded in writing and provided some information; others gave the biological team a briefing or encouraged UNSCOM to speak directly with the companies or individuals involved.[6] In late January, Oxoid wrote to UNSCOM, opening the door for Barton to call the company's manager to arrange a visit. Given the unusually large quantity that Iraq had purchased in 1988—twenty-two tons—the manager quoted the sales figure to Barton from memory then sent documentation via facsimile. When Barton visited Oxoid later, the company turned over more records.[7]

So UNSCOM personnel visited the various companies, explaining why they wanted to know about Iraq's purchases and what Iraq expressed interest in buying. The corporate officials usually relaxed once they realized Iraq was the focus of the investigation. Barton and Spertzel received significant cooperation from Fluka AG, Niro Atomizer Inc., Chemap AG, and Olsa S.P.A.[8] These companies supplied pro forma invoices, letters of credit, sales records, shipping documents, and miscellaneous correspondence with the Iraqis related to the products of interest to the inspectors. This process turned up several hundred documents that allowed considerable insight into Iraq's attempted and sometimes successful procurement of dual-purpose equipment and material that it diverted to its bioweapons program. Niro staff also said that in 1988 the company shipped two spray driers to Iraq capable of generating very small particle sizes.[9] Olsa representatives stated that Iraq wanted two fermenters and six storage tanks but that the company sold Iraq six fermenters, which could be rapidly disconnected and put on skids.[10]

Working with the suppliers, UNSCOM gathered about twenty truly key documents. When combined with records the inspectors obtained from Iraqi banks on these transactions, this paper trail elucidated Iraq's biological procurement activities.[11] UNSCOM could use this data to squeeze the truth out of the Iraqis and to make a noncompliance case to the Security Council and the global public, showing independent confirmation of what had really transpired. Therefore, the inspectors considered information from suppliers to be "indispensable."[12]

Using classic tradecraft, the inspectors labored to break the codes on Iraqi letters of credit and orders related to TSMID's purchases for the bioweapons program. After a few months of effort in early 1995, Barton, Spertzel, and Nikita Smidovich figured out which numbers in the numerical strings on the paperwork referred to the year of the transaction, the transaction's involvement in the bioweapons program, the identifying number for the specific item, and the sequence of TSMID's annual communications about each transaction. As UNSCOM amassed more documents from sources outside of Iraq and from document search missions, the ability to decipher these numbers was essential to its understanding of the program and efforts to impel Iraq to be more forthcoming.[13]

In January 1995, UNSCOM also received the analytical report from the samples taken from a dryer at Al Hakam, which confirmed what UNSCOM's inspectors had suspected since June 1994. A dryer on the biopesticide line was making ultra-fine particle sizes of ten microns or less, which meant the biopesticide would not adhere to plants. The analysis also found that the *B. thuringiensis* lacked the crystal to make the material virulent for plant pests, further making the Al Hakam product useless.[14] UNSCOM became even more persuaded that Al Hakam's biopesticide production effort was just for show after Iraqi farmers later said the biopesticide, called Al Nasir, was worthless for pest control. The tiny particle size from the spray dryer on Al Hakam's biopesticide line was, however, ideal for dried biowarfare agents. Other aspects of the initial analysis performed on this sample indicated that Iraq might have been headed in that direction.[15]

AWASH IN GROWTH MEDIA

Soon after the Israeli intelligence briefing, UNSCOM headquarters directed the Baghdad office to take a closer look at the air-handling system for Al Hakam's animal building. Gabriele Kraatz-Wadsack, a military veterinarian and microbiologist who landed in Baghdad on January 12, 1995, as the new chief inspector for ongoing monitoring and verification of biological facilities, took on this request on her first day on the job. A researcher in the German Army's Medical Service, Kraatz-Wadsack was a petite blonde with a fondness for wearing Escada when not in combat boots scouring the crannies of Iraq's biological facilities. Little escaped her notice. She earned the nickname "gentle hammer" by remaining nonplussed and respectfully refusing to back down when the Iraqis went into bully mode.[16] After her tenure at UNSCOM Kraatz-Wadsack, now a senior official in the United Nations (UN) Office for Disarmament Affairs, was promoted to full colonel, one of a handful of women to achieve that rank in the German Armed Forces.

At Al Hakam, Kraatz-Wadsack eschewed a handshake and conversational pleasantries with Rihab Taha. Stating her name, Kraatz-Wadsack simply asked how to get to the roof of the research and toxicology buildings. The air-handling system had very large, bifurcated plenums, but Kraatz-Wadsack was not concerned because there were no HEPA filters or other indicators of controlled air handling. Kraatz-Wadsack photographed all of the air-handling pipes on the roof and relayed her findings to UNSCOM headquarters.[17] Among those familiar with the former U.S. and British bioweapons programs, the bifurcated plenums signaled that the building's air-handling system was designed to perform at a more capable, high-containment level. UNSCOM now had reason to believe that TSMID may have ordered the HEPA filters for these buildings at Al Hakam.[18]

Kraatz-Wadsack's next task was to find whatever growth media she could in Iraq, but she received no reason or other guidance for the growth media hunt. With only Iraq's declaration to give her clues, she started at the Al Adile Medical Warehouse, identified as storing a modest amount of growth media for distribution to Iraqi hospitals. Kraatz-Wadsack noticed that Iraqi secret police joined her escort, which she found strange for a trip to a warehouse. At Al Adile, she and two other UNSCOM staffers examined the 1- to 5-kilogram-sized containers of growth media and found everything consistent with the site's declaration. Touring the rest of the site, Kraatz-Wadsack was adamant that the one locked door at Al Adile be opened. The Iraqis said that room just had some expired media, so she was taken aback to find it stacked floor to ceiling with 25-, 50-, and 100-kilogram-sized barrels of growth media. When Kraatz-Wadsack stated that this obviously made their declaration false, the Iraqis shrugged that it was only a matter of a mistakenly placed decimal point, and besides, the media was expired. With the secret police listening attentively, Kraatz-Wadsack held her ground. The Iraqis corrected their declaration before she departed for UNSCOM's Baghdad Monitoring and Verification Center at the Al Kanat Hotel, which the inspectors called the Canal Hotel. Kraatz-Wadsack knew that the amount of growth media at Al Adile was totally out of proportion with hospital consumption or normal scientific activities.[19]

Media must be sterile for seed cultures to grow. Once a container of media is opened, the contents need to be used in fairly short order or the media will deteriorate. Experiments and hospital diagnostic tests require small amounts of media, so it was utterly ridiculous to buy a 50-kilogram barrel of media for either purpose. The containers at Al Adile had to be special orders because suppliers offer much smaller quantities for normal scientific and hospital use. Media should be viable well beyond the suppliers' conservative five-year expiration date. The import date for the eleven tons of media at Al Adile was 1988, which meant this media was likely still usable. The Iraqis gave her no documentation or explanation for this huge media stash, so Kraatz-Wadsack logically deduced Iraq meant to produce something with it. Her report contained a brief analysis that the quantity of media at Al Adile was far in excess of what Iraq would need for hospital diagnostics.[20]

Continuing her media hunt, over the next five days Kraatz-Wadsack went to other facilities she thought would reasonably have media. She turned up 2.5 tons at the Al Razi Institute, roughly 1.5 tons at Al Kindi, 1 ton at Al Ameriyah, and 6 tons beneath Al Hakam's research and development buildings, where some of the barrels bore double labels. All together, Kraatz-Wadsack found 22 tons of media.[21] Already aware of roughly 39 tons of growth media sold to Iraq, the inspectors in New York presumed Iraq had 17 tons hidden elsewhere or had consumed that amount for some purpose. The results of Kraatz-Wadsack's media hunt prompted a flurry of inspections and consultative meetings to explore why Iraq had ordered such huge media supplies to begin with, what really happened with the media, and why Iraq had purchased and attempted to acquire other specialized equipment. From January to the end of March 1995, UNSCOM sent six biological teams into Iraq. With so much data pointing to Iraq's production of biowarfare agents, UNSCOM began to press harder.[22] To have sanctions lifted, Iraq needed UNSCOM to close the biological portfolio, but the inspectors wasted no time in conveying their concerns to Iraq.

INSPECTIONS CLARIFY FUZZY INTELLIGENCE DATA

As UNSCOM cranked up this investigation, at moments of the inspectors' choosing they confronted the Iraqis with evidence that contradicted their current version of events. This tactic kept Iraq in a state of perpetual uncertainty about exactly how much the inspectors knew or could prove. Therefore, at times the Iraqis admitted more than UNSCOM had evidence of or said something that they had no idea would help the inspectors piece things together. The UNSCOM 113/BW22 mission, which took place from January 23 to February 3, had several such moments.

The team of Spertzel, Kelly, Killip, and Barton pushed the Iraqis on their questionable purchases, including the air-filtration equipment. A single-cell protein plant, they told Taha, would benefit from filtered input air but certainly not negative air pressure and filtered output air. Scrambling, Taha said that the HEPA filters were for the chicken house so that any animals outside would not catch diseases from Al Hakam's chickens. This argument did not wash with the inspectors because no commercial outfit would squander money on that level of precaution for a building described as a feeding house for chickens. In a pinch, the Iraqis mistakenly decided to try to prove Al Hakam's civilian purpose by giving UNSCOM the architectural drawings for Al Hakam.[23]

In addition, Spertzel's team interviewed twenty-seven other Iraqis, including the engineers at the Baghdad University of Technology and the Al Faw Construction Establishment, regarding their design work for Al Hakam. Al Faw was part of the Military Industrialization Commission. Asked where high-containment air-handling equipment would be needed at Al Hakam, one engineer said that this equipment was for Project 900. Another Al Faw engineer who worked on Al Hakam's water, electrical, and waste systems, however, called the Al Hakam work Project 324. Spertzel instantly connected these numbers to the intelligence reports.[24]

Back at the Canal Hotel that evening, on the unfurled architectural drawings the inspectors saw that letters identified the buildings. According to the Al Faw plans, building E was an animal toxicity test facility, not a glorified chicken house. Building H was designed as a high-containment laboratory. All of a sudden, clear as day, this data fit with the mysterious Project 324 that intelligence linked to Iraq's bioweapons program.[25]

The next day brought another important development to nail down Al Hakam as a purposefully built bioweapons facility. First, Spertzel nonchalantly mentioned to Taha that he had heard two different numbers, Project 900 and Project 324, used to refer to Al Hakam. Taha replied that Project 324 was the designation for all of Al Hakam and Project 900 was the number that Baghdad University of Technology engineers used for the buildings they designed, the animal house and research laboratory. For Spertzel, this was the "irrefutable defining moment" of the effort to unmask Iraq's bioweapons program.[26] Following Kraatz-Wadsack's footsteps, the inspectors also went to Al Hakam to scrutinize the ventilation systems atop buildings E and H to reconfirm they were set up for high-containment operations.[27] Al Hakam's true purpose was becoming increasingly unmistakable.

The inspectors also began to query the Iraqis generally about why TSMID purchased tons of growth media for Salman Pak. At this juncture, the inspectors had evidence that Iraq had imported large amounts of growth media on three separate occasions. Taha and two other officials explained that TSMID had acquired the media for the Ministry of Health, which had depleted its foreign currency account, for diagnostic tests at Iraq's hospitals. The director of TSMID opined that it was not unusual for one branch of the Iraqi government to get foreign currency from another to buy supplies. Collectively, this trio attributed the oversized orders to a practice leftover from the Iran-Iraq War, when large orders of all sorts of things seemed wise given Iraq's import woes.[28] Already this explanation had little credibility, giving Charles Duelfer, then UNSCOM's deputy executive chairman, good reason to label Iraq's growth media tales the "progressive idiocy theory."[29]

In a subsequent interview session, the inspectors tossed out a few figures about Iraq's import of different types of media (such as casein), to which the Iraqis said they would try to ascertain how much they had imported.[30] To stimulate their cooperation, Barton laid down photocopies of two letters of credit related to their purchase of ten tons of growth media and watched the color drain from the faces of the Iraqi scientists and a quartet of generals across the table. He asked for all of their credit records related to media imports. "That was all I had," said Barton. "Not a full house, just two deuces. So I played them both."[31] This maneuver flushed the Iraqis into producing more documents, which showed their purchase of an additional four tons of media that UNSCOM had not known about and aired the Swiss company Fluka as one of Iraq's media suppliers.[32] At one point during the mission, Iraq's Minister of Health even appeared to reiterate that TSMID bought the media on behalf of his normal procurement organization, the State Company for Marketing Drugs and Medical Appliances.[33]

When the inspectors asked to see the media remaining from the TSMID purchases, the Iraqis began weaving a fantastic tale about the 1989 distribution of the missing seventeen tons of media to the pathology laboratories in some, but not all, of the hospitals in seven of Iraq's provinces. Still wondering why a comparatively small subset of Iraqi hospitals received this huge amount of media, the dumbfounded inspectors heard Amin assert that people had stolen the media from the hospitals during the post-war riots. Among the counterpoints the inspectors raised, Iraq ordered only a few types of media (such as thioglycolate broth, casein, yeast extract, peptone, tryptone, and glucose) in overwhelming quantities, yet hospital diagnostics called for a wide variety of media.[34] Due to information from the company Oxoid, UNSCOM also knew that in 1988 Iraq's Health Ministry had placed smaller orders for diagnostic media.[35] Since the missing media was unavailable for examination, the inspectors asked for documentation of its purchase, receipt, and transport. Later in the mission, Iraq handed over twenty-three documents about the Ministry of Health's receipt of the media and its partial distribution to regional hospitals.[36] The documents were in pristine condition, and the inspectors joked that the ink on them was practically still drying. UNSCOM sent the documents to the U.S. Federal Bureau of Investigation for forensic analysis to verify the obvious.[37]

Several days later, UNSCOM was back in Iraq to lay the foundation for a visit by Ekeus. A one-man biological advance team, Spertzel leaned on Taha for a more plausible explanation about the missing media, only to hear the same absurd story about sending the hospitals tons of media, which was all lost, stolen, or destroyed after the war. Under the circumstances, Al Hakam could no longer be considered a biowarfare agent production facility in waiting. After two days of eliptical discussion, Spertzel told Taha that UNSCOM believed that Iraq's bioweapons program involved more sites than Iraq had declared and that Iraq had produced and weaponized agents. Stone-faced, Taha offered to relay this assessment to higher authorities.[38]

IRAQ'S SCHEHERAZADE CHARADE OVER THE GROWTH MEDIA

Not only was Iraq clinging tenaciously to its cover stories in interviews, it officially gave UNSCOM a new full, final, and complete declaration that budged not an inch from the original one submitted in May 1992.[39] Inside UNSCOM, by this time wags called Iraq's biological declarations "full, final, and complete fairy tales."[40]

Publicly, Ekeus stepped up the pressure, comparing the Iraqis' cascade of stories to those of Scheherazade in *The Book of One Thousand and One Nights*. "We say, 'Do you have cages for monkeys?' They say, 'No, never any experiments on primates.' We say, 'What about these cages, with animal hair?' They say, 'Oh, *those* cages—we planned to use them for medical research.' Their story changes every night," said Ekeus. "They admit only what we can prove."[41] Returning from a meeting in Baghdad in late February, Ekeus told the Security Council that UNSCOM was making progress in all areas except those related to Iraq's biological activities, past and present. While Iraq was no longer disavowing the large growth media purchases, Ekeus stated that it still had no credible explanations for the disposition of twenty to thirty tons of it. Iraq, he added, had all of the elements necessary to make biological weapons and had perhaps taken that step.[42] In another public comment, Ekeus said that the missing media "can only coincide with the production of biological weapons."[43]

As part of UNSCOM's full-court press, Ekeus asked CBW commissioner Terry Taylor to try to get to the bottom of Iraq's stories about imports of dual-use biological items. Before leading UNSCOM 114/BW23 in mid-March 1995, Taylor viewed videos of UNSCOM's early inspections, including one that chemical inspectors had shot at Al Adile at least three years earlier with the media containers clearly visible. Taylor could only shake his head at the miss, at what might have happened had the chemical inspectors realized what they saw or UNSCOM required its teams to share data across the inspection disciplines.[44]

The BW23 team spoke with various Iraqis likely to know about the media imports, but they just repeated the song and dance about its distribution to hospitals and its theft and demise in riots. Taylor showed them some of the suppliers' records on the shipment of the media to Iraq and explained that preliminary analysis showed the twenty-three documents Iraq had provided in January were counterfeits. The Iraqis seemed nonplussed.[45]

Next, at the Ministry of Health, the finance manager there told the inspectors he had never heard of TSMID and that it was against Iraqi regulations for one branch of government to borrow money from another. In the ministry's document repository, the inspectors found no records related to TSMID, to any supply orders placed through another ministry, or to any orders of growth media valued at over half a million dollars. In the glowering presence of Taha and Amin, the inspectors later questioned a stock clerk from the State Company for Drugs and Medical Appliances, Abdul Razzack Jasem, who looked thoroughly intimidated before he uttered a word. Intermittently over the next two days, the inspectors queried Razzack about receipts for the incoming media, the sales vouchers, and the store inventory records that Iraq gave the inspectors in January to document the media imports. Razzack told the inspectors that he had handwritten those documents from detailed notes in his notebook, which he had since lost. He called these re-created documents "originals" and claimed the copies were needed because the receipts went up in flames and the sales vouchers were in a box that fell off the back of a truck. As these asinine tales spilled from Razzack, the inspectors stifled their laughter with difficulty.[46]

To confirm Razzack's account, the inspectors trekked to the warehouse. The metal file cabinet that purportedly stored Razzack's records was in good shape, with all of the other drawers filled with files. Apparently, the growth media documents were the only ones to catch fire. Razzack said that the electrical cable of a broken x-ray machine next to the cabinet ignited the fire. The Iraqis had no explanation for how a broken machine, even if it had been connected to an electrical socket, could start a fire. "It was complete and utter nonsense," said Taylor. The inspectors requested the records of the fire station's response to this blaze, but Razzack said those records were also destroyed.[47] The final Iraqi explanation about this "selective" fire was that the records were actually destroyed as part of a standing order to eliminate documents five years after their creation.[48] The team had heard enough.

To close the mission formally, the inspectors met the Iraqis. Passing off the inspectors' concerns about forged documents, Amin looked at Taylor, a retired colonel, and said that as a military man Taylor could surely understand how documents got destroyed in wartime and how important it was to restore good records and order. Amin nonchalantly described the documents as "not forged, but reconstructed."[49] The inspectors told the Iraqis that the Security Council would have to be told that Iraq had given UNSCOM false documents and that their story about the media was neither true nor plausible.[50] As Taylor's team departed the National Monitoring Directorate building, Razzack chased after them to say that he had misspoken because the inspectors never asked for the "original, original documents." He explained that he was ordered to re-create the documents from memory after the war and he considered those the "originals." He stuck with the claim that the Ministry of Health imported the media but admitted that the whole hospital distribution scheme was a ploy. The so-called original, originals were the real import records, which Iraq later sent to UNSCOM.[51] Iraq publicly announced it would give UNSCOM the "missing biological weapons information."[52]

In the first quarter of 1995, the inspectors also peppered the Iraqis with questions about why TSMID bought four filling machines, which could be used to transfer agents into munitions, and tried to buy a contained spray drier capable of making ultra-fine particles in 1989. After some not-so-artful dodging, the Iraqis consolidated on the following explanations. The equipment was to be used in a biopesticide project at Salman Pak, although Iraq previously had made no mention of such work there. The Iraqis said they removed all equipment from Salman Pak before the war to avoid losing it to bombing, but they stated the filling machines were destroyed during the war. Hemming and hawing about the attempted aerosolization chamber purchase, the Iraqis claimed they needed a new one to provide spare parts for Salman Pak's chamber. Iraq completely refused to acknowledge that TSMID tried to acquire various anthrax strains used in other countries' bioweapons programs even though UNSCOM had corroborated TSMID's attempts with the culture collections abroad. The Iraqis also found little relevance in UNSCOM's point that the Al Hakam spray drier could make particle sizes far better suited to disperse biowarfare agents than biopesticides.[53]

THE DEMOLITION OF IRAQ'S COVER STORIES

In early April 1995, Oxoid and Fluka gave UNSCOM documents showing Iraq's copious growth media purchases. To make a plausible argument that the missing growth media was consumed at Al Hakam in the production of biowarfare agents, UNSCOM had to determine when Al Hakam as a facility became operational and whether from that point the facility had fermenters with sufficient capacity working to process tons of growth media. In March 1995 Smidovich asked Bill Lebherz, who had extensive experience setting up fermentation processing lines, to evaluate about a hundred pages of documents that UNSCOM had about Al Hakam. Lebherz concluded that the earliest date that Al Hakam could have been fully operational was March 1989, when its steam generator was in place.[54]

In a late March 1995 meeting, the Iraqi delegation included Riyad Al Qaysi, the deputy foreign minister; Gen. Amer Rasheed, the deputy for research and development at the Ministry of Industry and Military Industrialization and soon to be appointed Iraq's Minister of Oil; and Rasheed's bride, Taha. Ekeus had said enough publicly about Iraq's suspected bioweapons program that UNSCOM's credibility was on the line, and the Iraqis all knew the consequences of having their cover stories crumble.[55] Ekeus first reminded the Iraqis that a lifting of sanctions would not be in order until biological matters were resolved and then contended that Iraq had made a large amount of biowarfare agent.[56] Next, Smidovich gave an overview of the probable fate of the unaccounted-for media, crowned with the assertion that Al Hakam produced bulk biological warfare agents. Still trying to cover Iraq's tracks, Rasheed replied that in a fluke the growth media order just kept escalating in size as it passed up the bureaucratic chain for approval.[57] Despite the minister of health's vouching for hospital usage, neither that story or the enlargement of the media order to tens of tons fit for Ekeus, who noted there was no way that Iraq needed such a huge quantity of media for hospitals. "You're not telling the truth," he said to Rasheed.[58] Deputy Prime Minister Tariq Aziz retorted that Iraq had a choice of appointing politicians or scientists to ministerial posts, and in this case they chose a politician. He then dismissed the health minister as an idiot and said sheer stupidity caused this lie about the media. For Ekeus, "this moment was decisive. Even if we couldn't do the final accounting for all of the media, clearly any thought of giving them a clean bill of health on the biological program was off."[59]

The next morning, Taha tried to salvage the hospital diagnostics segment of the cover story by attributing the conservative order of growth media to the recommendations of the World Health Organization, noting that in 1989 Iraq ran 1.8 million hospital diagnostic tests. Quoting Iraqi Ministry of Health statistics, Spertzel briefly rejoined that Iraqi hospitals barely used kilogram quantities for diagnostics, not tons. Consistent with that usage and the need to avoid compromise of the media, he asserted that hospitals routinely ordered in much smaller containers. At a white easel, Taha wrote calculations showing that UNSCOM's assertions were not feasible because one 450-liter fermenter was working at Al Hakam during the time in question. She said contamination had rendered the two 1,850-liter fermenters transferred from Al Kindi inoperable and that the 1,450-liter vessels at Al Hakam were mixing or inactivation tanks, not fermenters. Describing how much agent could be made in two hours, Taha calculated that over twenty-six years would be needed to process all seventeen tons of media in Al Hakam's mixing tanks, as she called them. The inspectors remained silent.[60] Taha noted that Al Hakam was devoid of the necessary biosafety containment features to allow production of hazardous agents. Al Hakam, she said, never installed HEPA filters in any buildings, and Iraq ordered the other equipment of concern to UNSCOM for use with the biopesticide and single-cell protein production lines.[61] Ekeus, who felt he had extended himself with the assertion that Iraq had made a lot of biowarfare agent, was very upset that his inspectors did not instantly rebut Taha's account.[62]

Meanwhile that day, Kraatz-Wadsack again took the direct approach to obtain the data necessary to pinpoint Al Hakam's capacity. Kraatz-Wadsack prepared an itemized table listing the fermenters by UNSCOM's tag number and creating columns for the dates of their acquisition in country; their transfer to Al Hakam, installation, and establishment of operational capability; and their downtimes for maintenance or problems. At Al Hakam, Abdul Rahman Thamer, Taha's deputy, filled the table in from memory in fifteen minutes. According to Thamer, the fermenters all worked from the start and had no significant operational problems, which meant that Al Hakam's fermenters could have processed all of the missing media to make biowarfare agents.[63] Later that night, Kraatz-Wadsack briefed Ekeus and his biological brain trust on the Al Hakam fermenter data, after which Spertzel and Barton burned midnight oil preparing UNSCOM's reply.[64]

The next day, UNSCOM showed how Al Hakam could have used the missing media to make biowarfare agents over a seven-month period from March 1989. At the same white easel, Barton unfolded a calculation that integrated the growth media with the fermenter availability and capacity for the sum of Al Hakam's anthrax and botulinim toxin production output. Taha immediately raised objections about downtime and unavailable spare parts for the vessels, which she again insisted were mixing tanks.[65] Barton explained that UNSCOM's experts had examined the vessels, which could be used as fermenters. More important, he reminded Taha that she and her staff called them fermenters. Barton laid on the table Iraq's declarations, which described the vessels as fermenters and bore Taha's signature. In a tearful fit, Taha blurted that UNSCOM forced her to sign the declarations. Rasheed injected that no one needed a fourth-grade mathematics lesson and began yelling at Barton, accusing him of lying. Ekeus interceded to close the meeting, stating that UNSCOM needed to know what really happened and asking if Iraq had anything else to declare.[66] Ekeus, who was "not impressed for a second" by Taha's tears, recalled feeling very pleased.[67]

UNSCOM TAKES ITS CASE TO THE SECURITY COUNCIL

Through public statements and consultations with governments, UNSCOM telegraphed the contents of its upcoming report.[68] In line with UNSCOM practice before taking a major issue to the Security Council, in early April UNSCOM convened an international panel of experts to review the evidence.[69] While Kraatz-Wadsack presented the methodology for the media inventory, Smidovich and Spertzel gave the big-picture analysis, including a comparison of the inventory data with the import documentation for the media. They also reviewed such matters as the Al Hakam spray drier calibrated to make particle sizes of less than ten microns and the procurement pattern that was inconsistent with commercial production. Purchases of concern included the ventilation system apparently destined for Al Hakam, the filling machines ordered in 1989, the attempted order of an inhalation chamber during that time frame, the large fermenters ordered for Al Taji but intended for Al Hakam, and the virulent anthrax strains. Al Hakam's layout was also more like a military facility than a commercial plant.[70] Indeed, Al Hakam was almost a smaller cookie cutter duplicate of Iraq's main chemical weapons production facility, Al Muthanna.[71]

The experts asked about Iraq's false stories, the forged documents, the purported use of the equipment, and even the amount of mice feces on the top of some media barrels.[72] Their discussion, however, boiled down to the missing growth media, which the experts unanimously and informally agreed was used for covert production of biowarfare agents.[73] The experts' official report stated that Iraq's declaration was incomplete and its biological program was broader and more advanced than declared. The panel also identified the need for further UNSCOM investigation of Iraq's inadequate explanations for its large media purchases and Al Hakam's capabilities and activities; the possibility that Al Muthanna was involved in the biological program; and the prospect that weaponization had occurred.[74] With that, the stage was set for UNSCOM to present its findings to the Security Council.

UNSCOM's report to the Security Council had to be carefully worded because absent Iraq's admission of a bioweapons program, some would view the evidence as circumstantial. At that point, France and Russia were ready to endorse sanctions relief over U.S. and British objections. Ekeus drew on his legal training to get the right balance: "I was not the prosecutor, I was the investigator. In this report, I presented very carefully what Iraq was saying. To put it another way, I was very honestly presenting their lies and arguments."[75] Thus the report gave Iraq's account that its large order of growth media in 1988 was a singular error, then countered that UNSCOM had data indicating that Iraq also made significant media purchases in 1989 and 1990.[76] Juxtaposing Iraq's statements with the factual evidence, the report catalogued what did not add up regarding growth media, equipment, lethal pathogens, and Al Hakam's incongruous infrastructure. The report's summation of Iraq's attempted or successful acquisition of items of concern was "the only conclusion that can be drawn is that there is a high risk that they had been purchased and in part used for proscribed purposes—the production of agents for biological weapons."[77] The report was so damning that France and Russia had no choice but to join the chorus calling for Iraq to come clean.[78] Ekeus made UNSCOM's position clear, telling the *New York Times*: "Confession is not enough. We need to get our hands on it and destroy it."[79]

Not ready to give up yet, Iraq put on a last-ditch propaganda campaign, opening the doors of Al Hakam to a couple of TV reporters in early April. Taha then entertained a pack of foreign reporters, saying that Al Hakam was producing about five tons of biopesticide per month and pointing to Iraq's inability to import stirrers for fermenters as the obstacle to expanding output to two million tons of animal feed annually.[80] Taha was surrounded by some six hundred fat hens, a sharp contrast to the few scrawny chickens that inspectors saw at Al Hakam earlier. Asked if Al Hakam could be converted to make bio-warfare agent, Taha explained that "[t]his is a problem for all biological facilities. Their purposes can be changed, but, believe me, this project is for purely civilian use." She assured the journalists that for the time being Iraq only needed "fat chickens and lots of eggs."[81] Taha added that the seventeen tons of media imported by the Ministry of Health was used "for medical purposes. There is nothing special in this site," she claimed. "Nothing serious."[82] As a final touch, Taha's staff not only showed how they were tracking the flock's daily egg production, they offered the reporters a tray of eggs as they left.[83]

THE "DEAL" WITH AZIZ

From May 29 to June 1, Ekeus was in Iraq with a full team to address outstanding issues. Miffed about the aftershocks from UNSCOM's Security Council report, the Iraqis refused to meet with UNSCOM's biological experts and even balked at their attending talks on the chemical portfolio. Unbeknownst to the biological team, in May the Iraqis floated the idea of private discussions between Aziz and Ekeus to break the biological logjam, foreshadowing to Duelfer that Iraq would have a biological deal for the inspectorate if UNSCOM reported positively on the status of chemical and missile disarmament activities.[84]

Ekeus approached this meeting carefully. UNSCOM had a gun, so to speak, but it was not smoking, meaning UNSCOM did not have a biological weapon or a positive sample for any biowarfare agent. Ekeus's challenge was to convince Aziz that Iraq's least detrimental course would be to acknowledge the bioweapons program. So Ekeus rattled off the list of questionable matters regarding Iraq's biological activities and told Aziz that while both UNSCOM and Iraq could appeal to the Security Council, it would be best if Iraq conceded the program because he was pretty confident that the Security Council would agree with UNSCOM's assessment. Aziz tried to get something positive if anything was to be relinquished, so he bartered for a clean bill of health on the missile, chemical, and nuclear portfolios for a promise to address the biological issues to UNSCOM's "satisfaction" in late June.[85] In short, Aziz implied that further discussion of Iraq's biological activities would require halting the investigations of Iraq's past weapons programs and lifting the sanctions. UNSCOM's ongoing monitoring and verification activities, Aziz said, could continue. Ekeus rejoined that UNSCOM's next report could be more positively worded where appropriate, but Iraq had to make a biological mea culpa. A deal of sorts was thus cut, but to Iraq's detriment Ekeus more or less printed the terms in UNSCOM's June report.[86] Before leaving Baghdad, Ekeus described the state of affairs as "focusing upon how to solve the problems rather than solving them."[87]

With the next report to the Security Council due in days, the UNSCOM staff spent hours combing the text "so that every word could be interpreted as half-full or half-empty."[88] UNSCOM's mid-June 1995 report said that the number of uncertainties in the chemical and missile areas had decreased and the remaining issues were of a technical nature, which could be read positively if one were so inclined.[89] However, the June report was hardly a picnic for Iraq. UNSCOM repeated almost verbatim the "high-risk" statement about what Iraq had probably done with the biological materials and equipment it had acquired.[90] What pleased Iraq was UNSCOM's assessment that Iraq was not capable at that time of attacking other countries in the region.[91] When Ekeus briefed this report to the Security Council, he also emphasized "the fantastic work that had been done by UNSCOM's biologists."[92]

Ekeus told the press that the Security Council had disparaged Iraq's behavior with the biological inspectors and widely criticized and rejected Aziz's proposed exchange of biological cooperation for positive chemical and missile reports.[93] Though Ekeus appeared puzzled that Iraq would continue to stonewall UNSCOM on its biological program and foment a crisis in the Security Council, he forecast that Iraq would soon call a meeting "to declare its biological weapons programme."[94] Ekeus knew UNSCOM had Iraq cornered.

THE MOTHER OF ALL MEA CULPAS: PART I

Out of options, Iraq invited Ekeus to return to Baghdad with his biological experts to receive a presentation. On arrival, Aziz told Ekeus that UNSCOM's June 20 report to the Security Council had had sufficient positive aspects for them to move ahead with a biological disclosure.[95] On the evening of July 1 at the Military Industrialization Commission building, the UNSCOM delegation met with Al Qaysi, Rasheed, and Taha. Rasheed opened the meeting and then deferred to Taha. Referring to notes and avoiding eye contact, in less than thirty minutes Taha reviewed Iraq's mid-1988 decision to build Al Hakam to make anthrax and botulinum toxin and to store both agents there in concentrated form. Agent production began in 1989 and continued until 1990. The production of the 9,000 liters of liquid botulinum toxin consumed seventeen tons of media. Iraq also made some 600 liters of liquid anthrax. The program involved no other agents, and Taha held that Iraq never put any anthrax or botulinum toxin into munitions. Instead, upcoming hostilities drove orders to destroy the agent, a task her staff completed in October 1990 using chemical deactivation and heat.[96]

Indicating the difference between a scientific and political sense of achievement in these circumstances, Ekeus recalled being "very satisfied by Iraq's admission of the biological weapons program in July 1995," but remembered that his biological team, with questions unanswered about weaponization, the missing growth media, and other details, "did not have the same feeling of triumph."[97] Discussing the matter after the meeting broke, the inspectors found it absurd that Iraq would go to all the trouble to produce bulk quantities of biowarfare agents if not to put it in weapons.[98] Also, Taha claimed that Iraq had ordered the destruction of the bulk agent in August 1990, on the eve of Iraq's invasion of Kuwait. Getting rid of a secret weapon, the inspectors joked, was just what a nation would do right before it went to war.[99] The inspectors recognized that this confession was carefully attuned to what Iraq thought UNSCOM knew or had proof of, hence the disclosure of a limited program consisting of bulk production of just two biowarfare agents, only at Al Hakam.[100] The inspectors, however, were hardly the type to be hoodwinked.

The next day, Smidovich, Barton, and Spertzel met with Rasheed and Taha to clarify Iraq's disclosure. Asked directly if Iraq weaponized the agent, Taha and Rasheed flatly denied it. Rasheed said they did not even "think" about doing that, a claim that begged the inspectors' credulity. The husband-and-wife duo repeated the phrase "step by step" to describe the program. Iraq had not moved from the production step to the weaponization step because they ran out of time. Iraq attempted to save equipment only to use it for peaceful purposes, they lectured, not to resume making bioweapons. Not impressed, the inspectors queried Iraq's starting date for the program, the participation of other organizations (for example, the military), and the material balance of the amount of agent supposedly produced in comparison with the growth media supply. Then the inspectors tried to persuade Rasheed and Taha to reconsider their account and to submit a new declaration.[101]

Of course, Rasheed's claim that Iraq never even contemplated the weaponization of biological agents was disingenuous. As early as 1987 and 1988 the Iraqi Army had issued training manuals that specifically described different types of agents, their routes of transmission, how to store and deliver them, and factors influencing the effective dispersal of biological agents.[102] UNSCOM did not know how far back the bioweapons program dated, but the inspectors logically assumed that no country embarks on making a weapon without first reflecting on its possible uses in war. For the time being, Ekeus told the Iraqis their disclosures were welcome but that they needed to expand their account on weaponization and to revise their declaration.[103]

The Ekeus delegation departed Baghdad with news that Iraq had admitted production of biowarfare agents at Al Hakam.[104] Iraq immediately tried to put the best possible face on the revelation. Iraq's Foreign Minister Muhammad Sa'id al-Sahhaf practically boasted that there had been no weapons and that the bulk agent was destroyed before the war because it was too dangerous to keep. Iraq had lost interest in biological weapons, he said, and would provide a new declaration in mid-July.[105]

The United States pounced on Iraq's statement as a half-truth, at best. Pointing out that Iraq claimed the program existed for such a brief time, U.S. Ambassador to the UN Madeleine Albright said, "After admitting that it had lied for four years about production of biological agents, Iraq now wishes us to believe that it never even thought about weaponizing and storing these agents." She concluded that "Iraq has a credibility problem not only because of its uninterrupted record of lying for four years, but because it has not yet produced a story that is internally consistent."[106]

As it had done with its 1991 disclosure of research, Baghdad calculated that some governments, not understanding or perhaps not even caring that the whole truth had yet to emerge, would contentedly accept that only production occurred. Perhaps even more important, Iraq's quasi-confession gambit would tilt the international political environment toward the lifting of sanctions.[107] Iraq, in other words, again deftly and distinctly shifted the burden of proof back to UNSCOM.

5 DEFECTION AND ARTIFICE

IRAQ PROVIDED THE United Nations Special Commission (UNSCOM) with a new full, final, and complete data declaration on its bioweapons program not long after Iraq's July 1 admission of agent manufacturing at Al Hakam. This chapter delineates events in the late summer of 1995 that were bizarre even by Iraqi standards of theatricality, initiated by the defection of a central figure in Iraq's weapons programs, Saddam Hussein's son-in-law Hussein Kamal. As described, Kamal's defection compelled Baghdad's rush to make a second bioweapons confession, confirming the inspectors' beliefs that Iraq had weaponized germ agents. Swiftly afterward, the Iraqis detoured UNSCOM Executive Chairman Rolf Ekeus to the mock discovery of a large collection of documents on Iraq's weapons programs, coincidentally located at Kamal's farm and thus the exclamation point to Iraq's shallow attempt to blame Kamal for Iraq's concealment program.

The chapter next expounds on Ekeus's debriefing of Kamal and UNSCOM's inspections on the heels of Iraq's avowal of weaponization. The Iraqis were wagering that UNSCOM would accept their recent statements of weaponization at face value and conclude that Iraq had relinquished the entirety of its bioweapons program. Given Iraq's history of evasiveness, the inspectors were wary of another Iraqi stratagem. These inspections raised ambiguities about Iraq's accounts. The chapter wraps with a critical examination of whether the farm documents and Kamal's remarks about Iraq's bioweapons activities advanced UNSCOM's factual knowledge and overall understanding of Iraq's bioweapons program.

IRAQ REVERTS TO FORM

Richard Spertzel headed a mission, UNSCOM 121/BW26, in mid-July 1995 to review and discuss the draft declaration with the Iraqis. The Iraqis had fluffed the number of pages but not added much substance. They held to the lines that research at Salman Pak involved mainly three agents and that they made anthrax and botulinum toxin on limited and large scales, respectively, at Al Hakam.[1] In addition to accounts of the production and destruction of bulk anthrax and botulinum toxin, the declaration stated that only the State Organization for Technical Industries and the Military Industrialization Commission had been involved in decisions pertaining to the program. No committees had been created to direct or coordinate the bioweapons program, and no link or relationship existed between the bioweapons program and the Ministry of Defense. The declaration barely conceded any activity at Al Muthanna, and it did not mention production of biowarfare agents at Al Daura, Al Taji, or Al Fudhaliyah. Moreover, the declaration contained data that the Iraqis underscored as reported from "memory," not records.[2]

As UNSCOM had long suspected, Iraq took extensive steps to rid Al Hakam of incriminating evidence before the first biological inspection in August 1991. The declaration described decontamination efforts, the removal and destruction of equipment, and the painting of items to camouflage their true purpose. For example, they painted all five 5,000-liter holding tanks black so they appeared made of carbon rather than stainless steel.[3]

Such titillating details aside, the draft declaration had so many shortcomings that Spertzel advised the Iraqis not to submit it formally. For one thing, Spertzel knew that Iraq's statement that Al Hakam was closed in August and September of 1990 was untrue because UNSCOM had imagery from that time showing activity at the site. The Iraqis then changed the date of Al Hakam's closure to the summer of 1991, when they claimed to have dumped deactivated bulk agent in the desert off the northern end of the facility. Spertzel also told Rihab Taha that he believed that they had loaded weapons with biowarfare agents, describing to her Al Muthanna's likely role in the testing and filling of biological weapons.[4]

Spertzel made the weaponization assertion forcefully to Taha because on the way to Baghdad, he and fellow inspector Rod Barton had stopped in Germany to visit a small company that sold perforated cylinders to the Iraqis. UNSCOM had a telex about Iraq's order of these cylinders, which required precision tool work to make 8- to 30-micron-sized particles spin out as the cylinders rotated. Unlike the companies that sold the Iraqis growth media and other equipment, this company's officials refused to say anything about their interactions with the Iraqis, who had paid this company with a suitcase full of cash, perhaps trying to hide a purchase useful for dispersing biowarfare agents. Combined, these factors made the inspectors more confident that Taha's July 1 claim that Iraq had not even thought about weaponization was false. Eventually, UNSCOM's bioweapons inspectors came to call this cylindrical system the "parallel Zubaidy device" because of its similarities to one that the inspectors would soon learn an Iraqi scientist by that name tried to develop.[5] Taha brushed off Spertzel's contentions of more extensive offensive bioweapons activities.[6] In doing so, Taha signaled that Iraq's "cooperation" about its bioweapons program would be fleeting and drew the line for Iraq's next biological confrontation with UNSCOM.

Iraq complicated matters with a July 17 ultimatum that UNSCOM must wrap its work up by the end of August, enabling the lifting of sanctions, or Iraq would cease to cooperate with UNSCOM. The lift-or-leave threat reportedly originated with Iraq's Revolutionary Command Council. Saddam issued the warning initially, leaving other senior officials to repeat it.[7] For example, when Ekeus went to Baghdad to try to sort things out, Deputy Prime Minister Tariq Aziz accentuated this threat on August 5 and again on August 7 after Ekeus returned to New York.[8] To add punch to their threat, the Iraqis handed Ekeus a formal biological declaration that was less informative than the draft.[9] Knowing that Iraq had submitted another deficient biological declaration and that outstanding issues remained in UNSCOM's other investigations, Ekeus could hardly acquiesce to Iraq's blackmail. Instead, he prepared to withdraw UNSCOM's inspectors from Iraq.

Ekeus's muted public reaction to Iraq's biological declaration was that it was "not thoroughly complete."[10] Among the areas in which UNSCOM inspectors found the declaration wanting was Iraq's description of the program's management. Iraq portrayed the bioweapons program as launched without any planning or connection to, any coordination with, or any assistance from any government entity other than the Technical Research Center. For example, the Iraqis stated that the program had no relationship "whatsoever" with the Ministry of Defense,[11] an assertion the inspectors viewed as preposterous. Weapons programs do not materialize unbidden. An unexpected turn of events intervened as UNSCOM's biological inspectors were bracing for stonewalling from the Iraqis.

KAMAL FLIES THE COOP

A high-level defection from a totalitarian society can cause an uproar. The shunned nation's leaders will worry about how the defection of a prominent artist or sports figure reflects on their country, and if the defector held a position of responsibility, concerns will center on the likelihood of him or her divulging state secrets. On the opposite side of the equation, intelligence agencies and the media will clamor to interview the defector. Such was the case when Lt. Gen. Hussein Kamal fled on August 7, 1995, to Amman, Jordan.[12]

A first cousin of Saddam and husband of Saddam's daughter Raghad, Kamal held significant interest for intelligence agencies and the media. Described as perhaps the most powerful man in Iraq other than Saddam, Kamal was first fired from being Iraq's minister of defense then resurrected about six months later to head the Special Security Organization, which was in charge of Saddam's personal security and played a significant role in Iraq's unconventional weapons programs. Until 1990, Kamal was minister of industry and military industrialization. Although he never sat on Iraq's powerful Revolutionary Command Council, at the time of his defection Kamal ran the Military Industrialization Commission, which also had a key role in Iraq's weapons of mass destruction programs.[13] According to Spertzel, under Kamal's stewardship "[t]he development of biological weapons took on the highest priority, 'so that anything they wanted for the program they got.'"[14]

Pivotal to Iraq's unconventional weapons programs for over a decade, Kamal left Baghdad in something of a fix after his defection. Trying to turn the situation to their advantage, the Iraqis used the defection as the artifice to lay the entire blame for the hiding of Iraq's weapons programs on Kamal. Iraq wasted no time launching a campaign to that effect.[15] In a televised speech, Saddam called Kamal a traitor whose purpose in defecting was to keep sanctions in place.[16] Aziz told the media how shocked the Iraqi government was. Insinuating that he would have acted earlier to clear everything up, Aziz said that Kamal alone knew the technical details of the weapons programs. Only when Aziz discovered that Kamal had requested a pair of confidential reports on Iraq's biological and nuclear programs just before he defected did Aziz realize "that Mr. Ekeus was not getting all the information," at which point Aziz knew that he had to set the record straight with UNSCOM.[17]

Ekeus seized the opportunity to ratchet up the pressure on Iraq. He told the press that largely because of UNSCOM's inability to verify Iraq's biological declaration the prospect of lifting the sanctions on Iraq soon was miniscule.

As U.S. intelligence officials descended on Jordan to debrief Kamal, Iraq reversed course on its ultimatum to stop cooperating with UNSCOM and branded its just-submitted final biological declaration "null and void."[18] Iraq knew that Britain's MI-6 and UNSCOM were angling to debrief Kamal as well.[19] Kamal's defection triggered something of "a contest between Baghdad and the defectors to be the first to bare sensitive secrets and reap the public relations reward."[20] Inside UNSCOM, the inspectors thought the Iraqi hierarchy was worried that Kamal would talk not only of weaponized biological agents but of Iraqi biological tests on human subjects.[21] In Baghdad, Saddam's advisers calculated Iraq's next steps partly from a list of what Kamal knew about Iraq's weapons programs that Iraq had yet to tell UNSCOM.[22]

In a 3:00 A.M. telephone call a few days after the defection, Gen. Amer Rasheed, Iraq's oil minister, told Ekeus that Aziz requested a meeting. The timing of the call alone conveyed the Iraqis' urgency to scapegoat Kamal and preempt his revelations. Aware that Ekeus had already scheduled a trip to Amman to meet Kamal, Rasheed noted that Iraq would regard it as "an unfriendly act" if Ekeus saw Kamal before he visited Baghdad.[23] Rasheed then sent a written invitation that impugned Kamal for concealing information about the weapons programs, for giving orders to subordinates to do the same, and for commanding his subordinates not to disclose their actions to him or Aziz.[24] Back in Iraq on August 17, Ekeus knew that his position was "fantastically good."[25]

THE MOTHER OF ALL MEA CULPAS: PART II

Ekeus's trip to Baghdad had more than the standard Iraqi quotient of drama. Several senior Iraqi officials headlined the opening meeting on August 17 wherein the Iraqis serially pledged cooperation and blamed Kamal solely for the prolonged deception of UNSCOM and the International Atomic Energy Agency. Afterward, the Iraqis held a special meeting to show willingness to be forthcoming in the biological area.[26]

Iraq's second biological mea culpa began with Aziz and Rasheed telling Ekeus that UNSCOM had repeatedly inspected a biological facility but had not understood its involvement in the weapons program. They were referring to Al Daura, which they said Iraq had converted at the end of 1990 to make botulinum toxin rather than foot and mouth disease vaccine. They informed Ekeus that the day after the Security Council's November 29, 1990, vote to use force, if necessary, to evict Iraq from Kuwait, Iraqi leaders decided to fill weapons with biological agents. In her briefing, Taha spoke of the filling of 191 bombs and SCUD missile warheads with 8,500 liters of concentrated anthrax and at least 19,000 liters of concentrated botulinum toxin at Al Muthanna from December 1 to 23, 1990. Iraq hid the SCUD warheads by a canal at the Tigris River, while the bombs went to Airfield 37 and Al Azziziyah during the Gulf War.[27] Saddam later claimed to have ordered the elimination of Iraq's biological arsenal in 1991.[28] Taha said her staff destroyed the bulk agent and munitions in the summer of 1991, not in October 1990 as previously declared.[29] Field trials with R-400 bombs were part of Iraq's weaponization efforts, which Taha dated to September 1989.[30] Iraq also stated that it had developed the anti-crop agent wheat smut.[31]

As the account emerged over the course of a couple of days, Ekeus was not convinced that he was getting the whole story. At one point he appealed personally to Aziz for the truth. "I told him that he had misled me for such a long time, that he had lied about Iraq having no biological weapons. I asked him how I could trust him. Again, Aziz blamed everything on Hussein Kamal." Aziz's reply was no surprise to Ekeus, who observed, "People have forgotten the systematic and fantastic lying by the top Iraqi leaders."[32] Kamal, Aziz contended, kept everyone in the dark, hiding the truth about the bioweapons program even from his closest aid, Rasheed, whose wife, Taha, ran the bioweapons program. The preposterousness of that assertion did not faze Aziz.[33] Just after accusing Kamal and telling Ekeus he had no responsibility for the biological portfolio, Aziz claimed personal credit for withholding information on biological weapons.[34]

During the next two days, the Iraqis paraded people in front of Ekeus to relate what they had done in the nuclear, chemical, biological, or missile programs.[35] Aziz or Rasheed repeatedly encouraged Ekeus's staff to "ask anything" and then shouted at each hapless individual to tell the UNSCOM delegation whatever they wanted to know. "I'm sure these poor people didn't tell us everything because they were scared," said Ekeus. "The whole episode had an atmosphere almost of panic."[36] On August 19 Tariq Al-Zubaidy spoke about the development and purportedly unsuccessful testing of an aerosol generator to disperse biowarfare agents. As noted earlier, UNSCOM had already begun to investigate Iraq's development of a similar dispersal device.[37] UNSCOM had also suspected that some of the warheads that Iraq had declared as chemical delivery systems might have instead been designated for biological agent delivery.[38] Other details to emerge on August 19 included the filling of R-400 bombs with 2,200 liters of concentrated aflatoxin, which was produced at Al Fudhaliyah; the performance of studies involving *Clostridium perfringens*; the conduct of research on viruses for military utility; work on an unmanned drone to deliver biological agents; the existence of a modest ricin research effort for medical purposes; and the involvement of a total of twenty facilities in the bioweapons program.[39]

Ekeus later likened Iraq's second biological weapons mea culpa to a scene out of the film *Casablanca*. Amidst the revelations, Aziz and Rasheed acted stunned that Kamal had kept the bioweapons program secret from them.[40] Aziz and Rasheed claimed they had been under Kamal's orders not to speak about Iraq's weapons programs.[41]

THE HAIDAR FARM CACHE

While in Baghdad, Ekeus complained angrily to Rasheed that Iraq had provided some very interesting new documentation on the nuclear program but nothing to clarify the chemical, missile, and biological programs. With that, the Iraqis could add the capstone to their campaign to blame Kamal for withholding critical data on Iraq's weapons programs. While Ekeus was en route to Habbaniyah Military Airfield on August 20, Hossam Amin, chief of the National Monitoring Directorate, told Ekeus that he had something interesting to show him. "Initially, I said I wasn't interested because I thought he would take us on another detour," said Ekeus.[42] Amin persisted, and Ekeus's entourage wound its way to a farm near Haidar that the Iraqis said belonged to Kamal. The Iraqis played for dramatic effect; the entire delegation milled around until Amin beckoned him to the windows of one of the sheds, where inside he saw metal containers. Ekeus asked to open the doors but the Iraqis claimed not to have a key. "This was just more theater on their part," recalled Ekeus. "So, we broke the locks on the doors, and there sat this enormous group of boxes."[43]

Shiny steel trunks, 147 of them, containing documents, microfiches, computer disks, photographs, and videotapes about Iraq's weapons programs were stacked haphazardly in these chicken coops. Amidst the trunks was a small wooden box with a red photograph album perched atop of it. Nary a speck of dust was on the album, and the cleanliness of the trunks indicated that they had not been there long.[44] By packaging it differently, the Iraqi officials wanted to draw the inspectors to the box of biological documents.

While the inspectors began opening the trunks, the Iraqis quickly produced a local farmer to describe how Kamal had had the documents hauled to the farmhouse two days before he defected.[45] Conferring with his staff, Ekeus reassigned an UNSCOM inspection team already in Iraq to secure the documents, remove them to UNSCOM's Baghdad office, and conduct a preliminary assessment of the cache.[46] He then departed for Jordan.

The Iraqis began trumpeting how the material that Ekeus "discovered" at Kamal's farm proved that Kamal was guilty of withholding the truth from UNSCOM all these years. They depicted this cache as Kamal's personal collection of critical data to be used to reconstitute Iraq's weapons of mass destruction programs. Rasheed said the documents "strip[ped] Hussein Kamal from the information he might give to Ekeus during their meeting in Amman," accused Kamal of being a CIA agent, and predicted that Kamal would misinform Ekeus as part of his plan to prolong the sanctions.[47]

Ekeus, for one, did not swallow the Iraqi spin. A couple of days later, he stated, "I find it hard to believe that such documents relating to secret nuclear, biological and missile programs would be left in such a place."[48] Attributing the systemic hiding of these documents to the Iraqi special forces, Ekeus said that Kamal laughed about the incident and denied putting any documents at the farm. The Iraqis, meanwhile, came up with other interesting yet ridiculous stories for how the documents ended up in a chicken coop.[49]

In actuality, the Special Security Organization took over the farm ten days before Ekeus's detour. Once inspectors went carefully through the documents, they recognized the glaring absence of any records related to the Military Industrialization Commission, the Ministry of Defense, or any armed forces involvement in the weapons programs and a shortage of documents related to production, procurement, and suppliers. Apparently, Iraqi security personnel had hastily culled the documents to remove items inconsistent with Iraq's contemporary version of the total truth.[50] However, the volume of documents was so large that "they missed a number of things they probably should have withheld" from UNSCOM.[51] Not long after UNSCOM took possession of the Haidar farm collection the Iraqis claimed that the cache resulted from a high-level order issued in the summer of 1991 to collect and protect important documents for all weapons of mass destruction programs. The Special Security Organization was the guardian of the cache, but the Iraqis said that there was no paper trail (such as the order itself or receipts) for the implementation of this order.[52] One of the Haidar farm documents contradicted this statement, namely an edict of that nature signed by Kamal, dating to December 1990.[53]

Thus, in dramatic fashion, Iraq managed to spill the biological weapons beans first, an act that generated headlines as Ekeus briefed the press and the Security Council. While he commended Iraq's openness, Ekeus cautioned that UNSCOM had to verify what Iraq said. UNSCOM had significant experience with the inaccuracy of Iraq's declarations. To wit, after this latest confession, Iraq declared invalid an entirely false biological declaration given to UNSCOM just two weeks earlier.[54] Ekeus articulated two biological verification concerns rising from his meetings with Aziz and Rasheed. First, UNSCOM needed to account for Iraq's biological weapons. Second, questions about the missing growth media and the possibilities that Iraq may have made and retained additional bulk agent with it still demanded answers. He also indicated that UNSCOM already possessed documentation to refute Iraq's verbal statements about the extent of the bioweapons program.[55]

EKEUS'S DEBRIEFING OF KAMAL

When Kamal met Ekeus on the evening of August 22, he dwelled on how he would come to power in Iraq. Kamal seemed uncomfortable with the details about the weapons programs, perhaps because he lacked technical expertise or felt it was beneath him to speak of such matters.[56] Subtracting the time consumed by Kamal's political musings and interpretation delays, Ekeus spoke with Kamal for fifteen to twenty minutes apiece on the chemical, biological, nuclear, and missile portfolios. The UNSCOM team posed general questions, assuming they would be able to ask Kamal for more detail later.[57]

The transcript of this meeting contradicts the impression that Kamal revealed copious information to UNSCOM about Iraq's biological weapons program. In some instances, Kamal simply confirmed data that Ekeus or senior UNSCOM official Nikita Smidovich provided. For example, Kamal corroborated that

- Nassir Al-Hindawi was a leading figure in the bioweapons program.
- Al Fudhaliyah was a production site for biowarfare agents.
- The program included a plant pathogen to cripple wheat crops.
- Al Daura was involved in the bioweapons program, includving the conduct of research into more exotic biological agents.
- In December 1990 Iraq filled bombs and twenty-five warheads with biological agents at Al Muthanna.

Kamal briefly described anthrax as the centerpiece of the Iraqi program and indicated that Iraq had researched other biological agents, though he was unable to recall what he said were the "medical terms" for those other agents. According to Kamal, Iraq also pursued an agent to poison water supplies because Iran had a fresh water lake. Kamal attributed the general motivation for Iraq's biological weapons program to the Iranian military threat.[58]

On weaponization matters, Kamal added that an epoxy resin coated Iraq's biological bombs and in 1986 Iraq's development of a missile to disperse biological agents progressed past a parachute delivery system to the employment of a proximity fuse to enable above-ground detonation. Iraq, he said, did not flight test a biological missile warhead. Kamal stated that he ordered the destruction of all of Iraq's unconventional weapons, including the stocks of biological agents and weapons, a process that began before the first biological inspection in August 1991. He reported that UNSCOM inspectors had located the site where Iraq had buried biological munitions, a possible reference to Al Nibai. Complimenting Ekeus, Kamal said UNSCOM's inspections compelled Iraq to destroy its weapons: "You have important role in Iraq with this. You should not underestimate yourself. You are very effective in Iraq."[59]

Looking at organizational charts and diagrams of the Iraqi bioweapons program prepared by UNSCOM, Kamal said that the program's chain of command ran down from Lt. Gen. Amir Al Sa'adi, one of his top deputies, to Rasheed to Murtada to Hindawi to Taha. The bioweapons program moved from Al Muthanna to Salman Pak and finally to Al Hakam, where they made bulk agents. Some personnel were dispatched from Salman Pak back to Al Muthanna or to Al Daura, which, according to Kamal, made mostly anthrax. Kamal ended the interview with wry remarks about the Iraqi leadership's vacillating claims on the culpability for Iraq's weapons programs and relationship with UNSCOM.[60]

Ekeus attempted another debriefing on October 3, 1995, but Kamal kept postponing. When the pair finally met, Kamal seemed listless. Not inclined to entertain questions, Kamal said little except to complain about his health and Iraqi politics.[61] In mid-February 1996 Kamal returned to Iraq, where he was promptly arrested and shot.[62]

In contrast to several public statements about his meeting in Baghdad with Aziz and Rasheed, practically all that Ekeus would say about his August 22 meeting with Kamal was that it was "positive."[63] UNSCOM had reason to remain tightlipped about the Kamal debriefing. The more the Iraqis thought that Kamal had told the inspectors, the more they would feel pressed to reveal themselves.[64]

INSPECTIONS ON THE HEELS OF KAMAL'S DEFECTION

As long as it was possible that Kamal would speak with UNSCOM and Western intelligence officials, UNSCOM's biological team made every effort to exploit Baghdad's uncertainty about how much Kamal divulged. As Ekeus debriefed Kamal in Amman, Spertzel's UNSCOM 125/BW27 team was bound for Iraq, where over the course of nine days the team attempted to get the Iraqis to flesh out their statements to Ekeus's delegation. The BW27 team interviewed about seventy-five scientists, technicians, policymakers, and others who took part in the bioweapons program. A few weeks later, David Kelly headed UNSCOM 126/BW28, which conducted more interviews and inspected all the sites that Iraq named as part of their weapons program. During the BW27 mission, for the first time the inspectors interviewed at length Al Sa'adi, Kamal's senior deputy and a special adviser to Saddam.[65]

Like Aziz, Ahmed Murtada, the Technical Research Center director who presided over Iraq's interactions with the BW27 and BW28 teams, proclaimed Iraq's August declaration a dead letter and touted his order that all Iraqis be completely forthright in their interviews.[66] Well-versed at that point in the fluid boundaries of the word *truth* regarding Iraqi accounts of the bioweapons program, the inspectors pressed methodically for the Iraqis to explain the purpose, scale, methodologies, materials requirements, personnel involved, and outcomes of all facets of Iraq's biological research, development, testing, production, and weaponization activities. Other than playing the dupe to Kamal as mastermind of Iraq's concealment machinations, Iraq's ploy at this point was to appear to relinquish its bioweapons program entirely in hopes of retaining capabilities relevant to reviving it.

The Iraqis brought before these two teams appeared ill at ease. An Iraqi scientist who had told Ekeus days earlier that his research with ricin was only for medical purposes gave four different accounts of his activities before finally telling the inspectors that Iraq was interested in ricin as a weapon and had conducted artillery field tests with that agent.[67] UNSCOM personnel sensed that the fluctuation of the rules for how Iraqis were to comport themselves with the inspectors created a chancy situation for the Iraqis. With their livelihoods and their physical well-being on the line, some Iraqis may have doubted that Murtada's order to tell the truth was genuine.[68] All the inspectors knew for certain was that the Iraqis were vacillating on details that were important to getting a straight account of Iraq's agent production and filling of weapons. For instance, the Iraqis said that instead of putting botulinum toxin into fifteen warheads, the actual number was only thirteen and that two warheads contained aflatoxin. In contrast to the previous statement that they had buried all of the biological SCUD warheads in pits by the Tigris River Canal, the Iraqis told Kelly's team that they hid ten anthrax-filled warheads in a railroad tunnel at Al Mansuriyah during the Gulf War. Kelly's team saw twenty-five pits on the banks of the canal, but the Iraqis explained that some were too shallow so they buried only fifteen warheads there.[69]

For a while after Kamal's defection, some inspectors felt the Iraqis were quite cooperative.[70] The Iraqis stood for hours in bunkers and gave fairly extensive explanations of how they had stored mobile tanks of bulk agent there. When the BW28 team went to Al Daura, the Iraqis showed the inspectors how they had altered the commandeered facility and its equipment to enable production of botulinum toxin. In 1990 Hazem Ali and some Al Hakam workers substituted for the regular vaccine production staff, breeching Al Daura's original containment structure and erecting a new partition under the misguided belief that they could run both vaccine and biowarfare agent processes in parallel. They removed the partition before UNSCOM's BW2 inspection team went there in September 1991, leaving only odd little holes here and there in the wall where the partition had been attached, noticeable only with up-close examination.[71] To enable the anaerobic production of *Clostridium botulinum* in seven fermenters designed for cell cultures, the Iraqis added a mounting flange so that a probe could be inserted on top. Prior to the BW2 team's visit, the Iraqis removed these additions and repaired these fermenters, leaving a welding mark about the size of a coin. Previous UNSCOM inspectors had not seen the minor visual signs denoting the modification of the fermenters and the temporary containment partition.[72]

At Al Taji, the inspectors questioned Al-Hindawi at length about the manufacture of botulinum toxin at this site, but he also extensively explained the site's single-cell protein work and methanol plant. Kelly and veteran inspector Hamish Killip had the Iraqis lead them to the exact locations of weapons field tests with animals, asking the Iraqis to describe these events in as much detail as possible, which provided very instructive points of comparison with the Haidar farm videos even though no markings from the tests remained.[73]

The Spertzel and Kelly teams sifted through the Iraqis' recently revised verbal accounts of their bioweapons program at a deliberately detailed level. As the inspectors spotlighted different activities, the Iraqis adjusted some accounts and provided new information. For example, the Iraqis stated that they went into crash bioweapons agent production mode right after Iraq's invasion of Kuwait in August 1990 and began filling weapons in December 1990. That same month, Iraq also mounted a rush effort to improve its biological delivery systems, field testing a modified aircraft drop tank and a remotely piloted vehicle in January 1991.[74] In interview, the Iraqis explained that Kamal had pushed for a better delivery system after reading a November 1990 Israeli newspaper article that said 98 percent of all Israelis would perish in an anthrax attack.[75]

The inspections following Iraq's second biological mea culpa largely centered on verifying the basic facts of the new Iraqi statements about quantities of agent produced and weaponization activities. As of mid-August 1995, UNSCOM could only account for the disposition of 28 of the 182 munitions that Iraq said it had filled with germ agents and was already questioning Iraq's claim to have made only 182 biological munitions. At this juncture, Iraq's biowarfare program was regarded "as the most alarming and elusive of all of the weapons of mass destruction endeavors undertaken by Iraq."[76]

In addition, this pair of missions raised a new crop of issues for the UNSCOM biological team to investigate. In contrast to the concentrated effort to develop the spray tank delivery system and the manufacture of other military items through mid-January 1991, the Iraqis said that they had stopped making biowarfare agents on December 31, 1990. In light of eyewitness reports of activity at Iraq's biological production facilities in early January 1991 and the growth media that Iraq could not account for, the UNSCOM inspectors had to consider that Iraq could have made significant quantities of agent during this two-week period of time.[77] The Iraqis were also describing different rationales for their bioweapons program. Initially, they attributed their program to a need to offset numerically superior Iranian forces or to counterbalance Israel's possible unconventional arsenal, but then they stated their germs were a last-resort weapon in the context of a nuclear attack, implying an equalizer for a U.S. nuclear attack.[78] Divulging their research with agents such as hemorrhagic conjunctivitis, the Iraqis implied that Western armies were potential targets since the underlying assumption of using incapacitating agents would be to force Western countries to sap their war effort by expending significant resources to care for ill soldiers.[79]

The inspectors needed to examine the timeline and progression of the bioweapons program closely to check against the possibility that Iraq could have made considerably more progress than it had admitted. The Iraqis dated the onset of their bioweapons work to 1974, describing a meagerly staffed program that was dormant for an extended period of time and wherein proposals to develop new capabilities or produce biological agents got sidetracked. Some questions arose out of the Iraqis' description of their weapons tests and their work with viral agents, mycotoxins, and *Clostridium perfringens*. However, the Iraqi research on and their production of aflatoxin was what really stumped the inspectors. Aflatoxin, which causes liver cancer, was not a classic biowarfare agent. A mycologist, Mohammed Emad Al-Diyat, claimed to have made 1,850 liters of aflatoxin in glass flasks at Al Fudhaliyah over several months. Because the glass flasks were stacked atop each other and had to be shaken daily, the inspectors could not grasp how this approach could have succeeded.[80]

Iraqis' accounts of their disposal of biological munitions and bulk agent also bore careful investigation. The Iraqis stated that they had deactivated the bulk anthrax, botulinum toxin, *Clostridium perfringens*, and aflatoxin with chemicals, thereafter dumping the deactivated anthrax near Al Hakam. UNSCOM interviewed drivers who recalled trucking the material to a site in the desert. The Iraqis claimed that they blew up, burned, and buried biological warheads and bombs. In late August 1995, the inspectors visited a site where the Iraqis claimed they had buried the biological warhead remnants, but then the Iraqis said they were unable to identify the burial location. The Iraqis also said that they threw empty bomb casings into the Euphrates River.[81] UNSCOM later went to extensive lengths to verify Iraq's statements and found some physical evidence of disposed weapons. More often than not, however, both documentation and physical evidence were lacking.

DEFICIENCIES IN IRAQ'S BIOLOGICAL ACCOUNT PERSIST

Though Iraq finally admitted it had weaponized biological agents, the inspectors believed they were still getting the runaround from the Iraqis. Thus, in mid-October 1995, UNSCOM reported that the biological documents Iraq had provided to date, including those from the Haidar farm, probably were "a fraction of all of the documents" that a weapons program of that size would have generated and that Iraq had yet to give "a full and correct account of its biological weapons programme."[82] UNSCOM's view of the status of its other disarmament efforts was also quite grim. To show Baghdad's displeasure, Iraqi Vice President Taha Muhieddine Maarouf accused Ekeus of being a liar.[83]

Iraq's revised draft full, final, and complete biological declaration of November 5, 1995, did little to improve the circumstances.[84] In its mid-December
report, UNSCOM contended that the Iraqis apparently were trying to minimize their research results and how far they had gone with production and
weaponization activities. The declaration's figures about the number of biological munitions made, filled, and destroyed were especially worrisome and contradicted findings from inspections and evidence in UNSCOM's possession
that proved Iraq's bioweapons program was more advanced. Not surprisingly,
the inspectorate requested that Iraq re-submit a new biological declaration.[85]

UNSCOM's concerns that the Iraqis were attempting to evade sanctions
to import equipment to maintain its missiles were borne out in early December 1995, when the Jordanians intercepted a shipment of gyroscopes,
a key component for missile guidance systems, from Russia to Iraq.[86] The
absence of physical evidence or documentation for the disposition of the
biowarfare agent that Iraq admitted producing and Iraq's continuing lack
of a credible explanation for the missing growth media, as Ekeus explained,
"creates obvious concern when you marry that together (with the fact) that
we no longer have full accounting of Iraq's missiles."[87] Thus, within a few
months of Iraq's second major biological mea culpa, Baghdad was actively
fostering the appearance that it still had or was trying to sustain an operational bioweapons capability.

THE VALUE OF KAMAL'S DEFECTION TO UNSCOM'S
BIOLOGICAL INVESTIGATION

Analysts, public officials, government agencies, and the media have remarked
on the tremendous value of two sources of information to UNSCOM's investigation of Iraq's bioweapons program, namely Ekeus's debriefing of Kamal
and the Haidar farm documents. Among the statements about the biological
investigation's profit from Kamal are the following:

- "The 1995 defection of Iraqi General Hussein Kemal led to the
  discovery of Iraq's biological-weapons program, which Iraq had not
  declared."[88]
- Kamal was "a gold mine of information. He had a good memory and,
  piece by piece, he laid out the main personnel, sites and progress of
  each WMD program."[89]
- "When a son-in-law of Saddam Hussein defected in 1995, the UN
  learned the truth about what was going on at al-Hakem."[90]

- "No concrete information on the scope of Iraq's biological warfare program was available until August 1995, when Iraq disclosed, after Husayn Kamil's defection, the existence of an offensive biological warfare (BW) capability . . . after years of claiming that they had conducted only defensive research."[91]
- "Rumors of an Iraqi biological weapons programme had continued to reach the inspectors. However, it was not until August 1995 that hard evidence became available."[92]
- "Absolute proof that Iraq still had an active biological-weapons program came in August 1995, when Kamal surprised the world and fled to Jordan."[93]

Even major political figures warped reality. In 2002, U.S. President George W. Bush said, "In 1995, after several years of deceit by the Iraqi regime, the head of Iraq's military industries defected. It was then that the regime was forced to admit that it had produced more than 30,000 liters of anthrax and other deadly biological agents."[94] British Prime Minister Tony Blair similarly misspoke: "It was only four years later, after the defection of Saddam's son-in-law to Jordan, that the offensive biological weapons and the full extent of the nuclear programme were discovered."[95]

Such assertions are considerably off the mark of what actually transpired. UNSCOM inspectors leveraged the documentation they obtained of various incriminating Iraqi purchases, sample analysis from an Al Hakam spray drier, calculations about production capacity at Al Hakam that strongly contrasted Iraq's cover stories for that facility, and other incriminating evidence to compel Iraq's July 1 admission of production of biological agents over a month prior to Kamal's defection. From the moment the words spilled from Taha's and Rasheed's lips, UNSCOM's inspectors did not buy the absurd claim that Iraq had abstained from filling weapons with anthrax and botulinum toxin. Instead, they advised the Iraqis more than once before Kamal defected that they believed Iraq had weaponized biological agents, and Ekeus informed the Security Council in early July 1995 that Iraq had likely filled munitions with biological agents.[96] Thus UNSCOM's unmasking of Iraq's offensive biological weapons program was already well under way before Kamal and his entourage trekked overnight to Jordan.

In all fairness, UNSCOM to a certain extent fed the impression of the make-or-break role of the Kamal defection in its investigation of all of Iraq's weapons programs. Ekeus, for example, described Kamal's information to a reporter as "almost embarrassing, it was so extensive."[97] UNSCOM's final substantive report also separated the organization's history into pre- and post-Kamal defection categories. The text implies that UNSCOM did not really appreciate the depth and scope of Iraq's weapons programs prior to Kamal's defection and that only afterward did it move into an assertive investigative mode.[98] If the inspectors were the blind man feeling the elephant, they may not have measured the exact length of the tusks, but they were tugging at the beast's tail with every investigative means at their disposal, resulting in Iraq's July 1, 1995, admission.

As it turned out, for several reasons Kamal was not exactly the windfall of biological information for UNSCOM that many subsequently portrayed him to be. Table 5.1 summarizes the main data points pertinent to Iraq's biological weapons program discussed during Ekeus's debriefing of Kamal, stipulates UNSCOM's level of understanding about each data point prior to July 1, 1995, and why, and recaps Iraq's statements in the July-to-September-1995 time period. This comparison puts into perspective Kamal's relative contribution to advancing UNSCOM's state of knowledge regarding Iraq's biological weapons program. Moreover, this table accentuates what UNSCOM knew or suspected before Iraq began confessing its deeds with germ weapons.

Table 5.1. Synopsis of the value of Kamal's debriefing to UNSCOM's investigation of Iraq's biological weapons activities

Data Point from Ekeus's Meeting with Kamal	UNSCOM's Knowledge Prior to Kamal's Defection and Iraq's July 1, 1995 Admission of a Limited Offensive Program	Kamal's Comments*	Iraqi Government Statements, July–September 1995**
Management of Iraq's bioweapons program	Suspected that Taha reported to Murtada, Al-Hindawi was involved, and Kamal had a major role; did not believe Rasheed was a line manager or know of Al Sa'adi's role	Described Al Sa'adi as involved, indicated Rasheed reported to Al Sa'adi and was Murtada's boss, and noted Al-Hindawi was engaged while anthrax research was being done	Beginning with Al Sa'adi's engagement with inspectors on UNSCOM BW27 mission, his involvement was evident to inspectors
Movement of Taha's core bioweapons group from Al Muthanna to Salman Pak to Al Hakam, also worked at Al Daura	Knew Taha's group worked at first three sites; did not know they had also worked at Al Daura	Stated Taha's group also went to Al Daura	On August 17, 1995, admitted 1990 conversion of Al Daura for military purposes

Table 5.1. (continued)

Data Point from Ekeus's Meeting with Kamal	UNSCOM's Knowledge Prior to Kamal's Defection and Iraq's July 1, 1995 Admission of a Limited Offensive Program	Kamal's Comments*	Iraqi Government Statements, July–September 1995**
Involvement of Salman Pak in bioweapons program	Knew because (1) identified by intelligence prior to 1991 Gulf War; (2) Iraq admitted militarily applicable research at Salman Pak during first inspection	Stated Taha's core group worked at Salman Pak after Al Muthanna, before Al Hakam	No noteworthy elaboration of previous declarations
Involvement of Al Muthanna in bioweapons program	Suspected because (1) Iraqis said during UNSCOM BW1 Taha's group initially worked at Al Muthanna, which had expertise and equipment to test, produce, and fill chemical weapons; (2) suspected some Iraqis worked in both chemical and biological programs	Agreed that Iraq filled weapons with agent; stated filling was done at Al Muthanna	On August 17, 1995, admitted filling SCUDs and bombs with biowarfare agents in December 1990
Involvement of Al Fudhaliyah in bioweapons program	Not suspected	Identified Al Fudhaliyah as location where biological weapons were produced	On August 19, 1995, admitted aflatoxin was produced at Al Fudhaliyah
Involvement of Al Hakam in bioweapons program	Knew because of (1) various incongruities between site capabilities and stated commercial purposes (such as drier generating small particles); (2) incriminating data that UNSCOM obtained from Iraq's suppliers	Stated bulk agent was manufactured at Al Hakam, a site chosen because of its isolation	On July 1, 1995, Iraq admitted production of bulk anthrax and botulinum toxin at Al Hakam
Research and production of biowarfare agents at Al Daura	Suspected because of (1) facility capabilities, including high-level containment; (2) site's failure to resume vaccine production; and (3) lack of cooperation during inspections, which led UNSCOM to monitor Al Daura closely	Stated Al Daura produced anthrax; agreed that research was conducted there on other agents, but none specified	On August 17, 1995, admitted 1990 conversion of Al Daura to produce botulinum toxin, but thereafter steadfastly denied making anthrax at Al Daura
Anthrax as primary biological weapon	Knew because (1) Iraq admitted considerable research on anthrax; (2) Iraq procured the Vollum strain of anthrax deliberately; (3) Al Hakam's process layout and capabilities were consistent with anthrax production; and (4) Iraq ordered large amounts of growth media appropriate to anthrax production (such as yeast extract)	Stated the main focus was on anthrax, though also mentioned botulinum toxin and research on other agents	On July 1, 1995, admitted bulk production of anthrax at Al Hakam

Table 5.1. (continued)

Data Point from Ekeus's Meeting with Kamal	UNSCOM's Knowledge Prior to Kamal's Defection and Iraq's July 1, 1995 Admission of a Limited Offensive Program	Kamal's Comments*	Iraqi Government Statements, July–September 1995**
Work with wheat smut	Suspected work with other agents, not wheat smut specifically	Stated Iraq began work on agent to contaminate Iran's wheat crops during 1980s war, possibly weaponized before 1991 Gulf War	On August 17, 1995, admitted development of wheat smut
Work with agent to poison water supply	Suspected work with other agents, perhaps cholera, a water-borne disease included in other nations' past bioweapons programs (such as Japan and United States)	Stated Iraq attempted, but did not succeed in developing agent to poison Iran's water supply	No specific mention of an agent aimed at water supplies
Work on other agents	Knew because (1) UNSCOM confirmed that Iraq procured other pathogen strains from culture collections abroad; (2) Taha gave 103 reference strains to UNSCOM BW1, but inspectors were not confident that represented the entirety of Iraq's efforts	Stated research was conducted on other unspecified agents	On August 19, 1995, admitted research on viruses and mycotoxins, modest ricin research program; during UNSCOM BW27 admitted development of ricin
Weaponization of biological agents	Strongly suspected, which led Ekeus to brief the Security Council in early July 1995 that it made no sense for Iraq to produce bulk agents but not weaponize them; UNSCOM also had evidence of Iraqi efforts to develop biological delivery systems (for example, parallel Zubaidy device, biological missile warheads)	Stated that filling was accomplished at Al Muthanna and that biological bombs had an epoxy coating; agreed that twenty-five missile warheads were filled with agent	On August 17, 1995, admitted Iraq filled R-400A bombs and missile warheads with biological agents and then deployed and hid the weapons; during UNSCOM BW27 admitted testing ricin in artillery shells
Sophistication of biological delivery systems	Suspected and briefed Security Council in early July 1995 of Iraq's likely weaponization of biological agents; knew Iraq had loaded SCUD warheads with chemical agents, so biological warheads were a possibility	Stated Iraq tested proximity fuses used in artillery rounds to enable above-ground detonation; capability demonstrated with warhead separation during Iraq's attacks on Israel	On August 17 and 19, 1995, admitted filling missile warheads and R-400 bombs, development of unmanned drone and spray tank delivery systems
Flight tests of missiles with biological payload	Suspected because (1) weaponization suspected; (2) work with anthrax simulant *B. thuringiensis* at Al Hakam opened possibility of tests	Stated no flight tests of biological missiles	Denied flight testing biological warheads

Table 5.1. (continued)

Data Point from Ekeus's Meeting with Kamal	UNSCOM's Knowledge Prior to Kamal's Defection and Iraq's July 1, 1995 Admission of a Limited Offensive Program	Kamal's Comments*	Iraqi Government Statements, July–September 1995**
Deployment, hiding of Iraq's biological weapons	Suspected because (1) an intelligence tip led UNSCOM to inspect Airfield 37 in November 1991, but Iraq had already removed bombs from the site; (2) weaponization suspected	Stated that weapons were buried at site north of Baghdad that UNSCOM had inspected	On August 17, 1995, admitted biological bombs were deployed to Airfield 37 and Al Azzizziyah and SCUDs to Tigris River canal; during UNSCOM BW28 added a tunnel at Al Mansuriyah as a biological warhead hide site
Destruction of Iraq's biological weapons	Suspected because production and weaponization suspected, but UNSCOM unable to confirm due to lack of physical evidence, documentation	Stated he ordered destruction of all chemical and biological agents and weapons; stated biological weapons and agent were destroyed during the month UNSCOM began biological inspections	On August 17, 1995, revised July 1, 1995 statement to include destruction of weapons and moved destruction date from October 1990 to June–July 1991
Target(s) of Iraq's biological weapons program	Knew because of (1) previous statements of Iraqis about Iran and Israel; (2) the history of the 1980s and Iraq's enmity for Israel	Identified Iran as a target, discussed Iraq's bombing of Israel	Acknowledged verbally and in declarations prior to July 1, 1995

NOTES: * UNSCOM officials consider the entire transcript of this meeting somewhat suspect because Ekeus's regular interpreter was not present. Jordan's King Hussein provided an interpreter.

** On numerous occasions after September 1995, Iraq altered key data (including dates of activities, numbers of items and materials, and people involved) in its verbal and written accounts of events.

Any number of reasons could explain why Kamal was not more informative, including the possibility that he did not know as much as many assumed he did. Kamal had managerial skills but apparently lacked the scientific or engineering training that would facilitate a grasp of technically complicated weapons programs.[99] An Iraqi defector from Saddam's nuclear weapons program, Khidhir Hamza, even described Kamal as "semiliterate."[100] Another possibility is that he may not have been accurately informed of the real status of weapons development; scientists running these programs, fearing for their lives, could have exaggerated test results and weapons capabilities.[101]

Ekeus said he did not necessarily expect Kamal to know all of the technical details but rather to function like the CEO of a big corporation. Therefore, on most matters of crucial interest to UNSCOM's biological investigation, "Kamal knew very little. Plus, he was not an especially bright person."[102] Moreover, according to Hamza, Kamal had had surgery to remove a brain tumor in 1992 and afterward experienced significant memory lapses. "Two years after," said Hamza, "he didn't even recognize the new chairman of Atomic Energy, a man he knew quite well."[103] The possibility that Kamal had diminished mental capacity provides another explanation for the technical errors in his accounts of weapons programs. Some UNSCOM inspectors were aware that Kamal had undergone brain surgery, others were not. One UNSCOM staffer found Kamal to be coherent during one of UNSCOM's two interviews with him; Ekeus did not.[104]

In sum, the value of Kamal's defection to the bioweapons investigation was not in what Kamal said to Ekeus but rather in what Iraq's leadership feared he would tell UNSCOM. "As far as biology was concerned, H. K. told the chairman nothing that was of any value to us in the biology section," said Spertzel. "Everything he said about bio was in generalities, nothing specific."[105] From the date of Kamal's defection until his ill-considered return to Iraq, UNSCOM's inspectors describe the Iraqis as being more cooperative than at any other time. "A lot has been made about what Kamal told us about the biological weapons program, but he didn't get things right," said UNSCOM bioweapons inspector Rod Barton. "After the defection, the Iraqis told us most of the rest, but they only did that because they thought that Kamal Hussein might have told us things."[106] As the next chapters describe, Iraq's cooperation evaporated not long after Kamal returned to Baghdad.

THE VALUE OF THE HAIDAR FARM DOCUMENTS TO UNSCOM'S BIOLOGICAL INVESTIGATION

Similar to the depictions of the value of Kamal's debriefing, there have been misperceptions about how much UNSCOM's biological inspectors learned from the Haidar farm documents. Once again, media hyperbole came into play: "In desperation, Saddam began turning over reams of documents detailing the size and scope of his biological-weapons program."[107] Another report held that the "discovery" of the Haidar farm documents "meant that Iraq could no longer deny the program's existence."[108] Even inside UNSCOM, some inspectors working other portfolios thought the Haidar documents were a bonanza for the biological inspectors that considerably advanced their knowledge of Iraq's germ weapons program.[109] These views were, however, off target.

The entire Haidar farm stash consisted of roughly seven hundred thousand documents, but the overwhelming majority pertained to the nuclear, missile, and chemical programs.[110] In contrast, "We were pretty disappointed because we only got this small box. Christmas hasn't visited us," quipped Barton.[111] UNSCOM biological inspectors catalogued the approximately two hundred biological documents at the Canal Hotel, and Barton used a small suitcase to carry them back to New York for further analysis. Spertzel described the biological weapons documents as "the equivalent of Taha's bottom desk drawer."[112] Taha later said she had assembled the biological segment of the document cache. Most were of an administrative nature, such as requests for published scientific journal articles to be photocopied or reprints of published articles about pathogens research and production methods. Amidst these mundane items were multiple drafts of the 1988 and 1990 annual reports for the bioweapons program, but the annual report for the key year of 1989 was missing. Operating manuals and operating logs for the fermenters, which the inspectors would have found very useful, were also omitted.[113]

The farm cache included the full, unedited texts of some of the biological documents that Iraq had previously given to UNSCOM, allowing the biological inspectors to analyze how the Iraqis redacted and altered documents to attempt to mislead UNSCOM.[114] Some of the Haidar farm biological documents contained data that appeared to be exaggerated, perhaps because the weapons scientists padded their accomplishments to impress their bosses. For example, some documents stated that 5,000 liters of botulinum toxin was made at Al Daura and 2,200 liters of aflatoxin at Al Fudhaliyah, quantities UNSCOM could never confirm.[115] By far, the most valuable Haidar farm documents were the two annual reports and a few draft reports on animal tests and field tests of weapons. The inspectors asked for the 1989 annual report and other key documents but the Iraqis said they had destroyed such items.[116]

UNSCOM's biological team also found some utility in the photograph album and videos from the farm. The album was a red, three-ring binder with numbered pages and pictures dating through 1989. Some pages had been removed.[117] This album listed the biological agent tests that the Iraqis conducted and contained photographs of inhalation tests with rabbits, dogs, sheep, and donkeys. Other photographs showed fermenters and rocket warheads.[118] One worrisome photograph was of a human arm covered with lesions.[119]

Also, six or seven videos from the Haidar farm constituted important historical documentation of Iraq's laboratory inhalation tests and munitions tests. The Iraqis performed most of their biological laboratory tests at Al Muthanna, which had staff experienced in using the facility's inhalation chamber with chemical agents. Al Muthanna's chamber was better than Salman Pak's because it was completely sealed, situated inside a second physical containment barrier to prevent the accidental release of agent. The testing control room at Al Muthanna was also well protected. The Iraqis tested biological agents on rodents, dogs, donkeys, and primates. Videos showed several inhalation tests.[120] Most of the videos, however, were of the trials with munitions and spray tanks at Al Muthanna's test range, Al Hammadiyat.[121] The images of these trials were irrefutable proof that UNSCOM was justified in asserting that Iraq had weaponized biological agents.[122]

The effective dispersal of biological agents is a technically demanding endeavor, and staff expertise to run competent weapons field tests can take considerable time to develop. Studying the testing videos gave the UNSCOM biological team insight into the type of tests the Iraqis performed, the quality of their weapons testing methodology, the scientific and operational skills of those involved in the bioweapons program, and the overall caliber and scope of the bioweapons program as a whole. In general, the videos showed the Iraqis gradually improving their skills as they conducted standard weapons tests. The Iraqis employed tests that were reasonably similar to how other countries had tested munitions, but they did not do anything that was cutting edge technically. The videos also brought home another important point for the inspectors as they saw Iraqi technicians trying to chase down wounded animals in several of the tests. Iraq's bioweaponeers were under significant pressure to produce certain results; the tests had to kill a certain number of animals. So long as "x" number of animals died, the scientists could avoid punishment. Sometimes the animals were staked closer to the munition to get the desired result. The test result forms lacked a box to indicate whether the animals perished from the munition's blast effects or exposure to a biowarfare agent, so the exact cause of death was immaterial. Some of Iraq's bioweapons tests were therefore not true trials. In light of this evidence, UNSCOM's biological inspectors had to consider carefully whether the Iraqis' verbal and written claims about the capabilities of their agents and weapons systems were realistic.[123]

The UNSCOM biological team gleaned more from the videos than the Iraqis realized they were revealing. Part of what the inspectors learned was who exactly was involved in what activities. Taha and two of her principal assistants, Sinan Abdul Hasen and Brig. Gen. Mohammed Mahmoud Bilal, appeared frequently. Bilal's presence initially caused some uncertainty because he was in charge of weaponizing chemical agents and that meant he performed similar duties in the bioweapons program.[124] The inspectors pored over the videos for other minute forensic details about the equipment present in different tests and such factors as the number, type, color, and positioning of test items so they could meticulously plan their lines of questioning. They interviewed each and every Iraqi scientist and technician seen on tape, asking very specific questions that were based on what the videos factually established. Through repeated interviews with a variety of individuals, the biological team learned more about Iraq's biological weapons testing and its biowarfare program.[125]

In sum, the collection of biological documents was "barely enough to lead to more discussion with the Iraqis," said Barton. "The Haidar farm documents really weren't the jackpot for us that they were for the other teams."[126] UNSCOM's official description of the value of the biological documents was much the same: "Most of these documents related to research and did not add a great deal to the Commission's overall understanding of the programme."[127] UNSCOM's biological team, however, made the most of the modest material they had, particularly the videos, to further their investigation.[128]

THEORIES ABOUT KAMAL'S DEFECTION

Inside UNSCOM, theories abounded regarding the real motives behind Kamal's defection and return to Iraq because those motives could abet UNSCOM's understanding of both former and contemporary control over Iraq's weapons programs.[129] At times, however, UNSCOM personnel were reduced to the same connect-the-dots theorizing that Sovietologists used after a Red Square parade to project Soviet power shifts on the basis of the proximity of officials in the Kremlin's viewing stands to the Communist Party secretary.

Two schools of thought about Kamal's defection predominated. First, Iraq's July 1 admission of limited offensive biowarfare activities so infuriated Russia, France, and other countries that were pushing to have sanctions lifted that Kamal fled because internally he was blamed for these terribly embarrassing circumstances.[130] Another possibility was that Kamal's defection was an elaborate Iraqi plot to allow the Iraqis to escape the corner they had painted themselves into over the previous five years. Accordingly, Kamal agreed to be the scapegoat to give Iraq the excuse to cough up a fuller, though not complete version of the truth. The voluntary scapegoat theory might explain why Kamal thought he could return safely to Iraq.[131] If indeed that was the plan, Saddam had a change of heart while Kamal courted the Western media and intelligence agencies. Kamal was murdered on his return to Iraq in February 1996, perhaps because "Iraqi leaders blamed him for the collapse of the big lie."[132] Kamal's violent death diminished the credibility of the scapegoat theory.

Dismissing speculation that Iraq had anything to gain from Kamal's defection, an UNSCOM veteran argued that Kamal chose to abandon Iraq. "Think about it, Kamal actually spoiled a lot for them. Before his defection they had started the same tactics that they used in 1998 to try to force UNSCOM out, telling UNSCOM that if we did not report Iraq was compliant with the resolution they would cease to cooperate," said this official. "This defection was a great embarrassment in front of the whole world and cost the Iraqis at least three years. There were definitely better ways to come clean about the program."[133]

Building on the notion that Kamal left of his own volition, Ekeus thought Kamal was convinced that if he told the truth his fellow Iraqis would overthrow Saddam and he could return to lead Iraq.[134] Ekeus felt that much of what was said about the defection, particularly that UNSCOM caught Iraq's bioweapons program because of Kamal, was wrong. Rather, Ekeus said that Kamal "was forced to defect because we detected the hidden biological weapons program. . . . We did not discover it as a result of his defection."[135]

6 INSPECTIONS IN A FACT-FREE ZONE

AFTER IRAQ'S ADMISSION, the United Nations Special Commission (UNSCOM) had the responsibility to disarm the Iraqi bioweapons program. This chapter first illuminates how UNSCOM eliminated the program's critical infrastructure, then describes UNSCOM's monitoring program for Iraq's remaining dual-use biological capabilities, notably the interaction of the monitors with the teams investigating Iraq's past bioweapons activities. The chapter next chronicles the UNSCOM missions that hunted documents and took samples to find evidence to close the gaps and untangle the inconsistencies in Iraq's accounts about its production of biowarfare agents and its testing, filling, and unilateral disposal of weapons and bulk agent.

In early 1996, Iraq resumed its familiar mix of superficial cooperation and substantial evasiveness. Baghdad was venturing anew that it would win the war of attrition that began with UNSCOM's creation in 1991 because the stresses of the links between UNSCOM's disarmament mandate and sanctions on Iraqi oil sales were beginning to show more prominently. The more international discomfort about the suffering of Iraqi citizens, the weaker the political support for UNSCOM to resolve each and every ambiguity in Iraq's declarations. Sooner or later, Saddam Hussein assumed, the political scales would tip in Baghdad's favor. In the meantime, Saddam was willing to brave further reprisal for his defiance of the terms of Resolution 687.

DESTRUCTION OF THE INFRASTRUCTURE OF IRAQ'S BIOWARFARE PROGRAM

Given UNSCOM's mandate to oversee the destruction or rendering harmless of weapons, production facilities, materials, and equipment directly relevant to prohibited weapons activities, one of its first priorities at this juncture was to scope out the biological materials, equipment, and infrastructure that had to be eliminated. This undertaking was complicated and potentially controversial, since Iraq had commandeered civilian facilities for military purposes and built some structures at Al Hakam after 1991 purportedly to house commercial activity. Iraq's degraded economy following years of war and economic sanctions also made it difficult for some to contemplate destruction of items that could be used to improve the standard of living in Iraq.

From December 5 to 17, 1995, Gabriele Kraatz-Wadsack led UNSCOM 127/BW29 to the facilities involved in Iraq's bioweapons program to assess the requirements for and feasibility of destroying Iraq's bioweapons infrastructure and materials. An accurate inventory of all equipment at these sites was a prerequisite for destruction. At Al Hakam alone, among numerous production and warehouse buildings and bunkers, UNSCOM inventoried and tagged over one thousand pieces of laboratory, processing, and control equipment and a large filling line.[1]

The Iraqis were quite cooperative and genial throughout the period of time until Hussein Kamal returned to Iraq in early 1996. The inspectors queried Al Hakam's staff about their use(s) of various pieces of equipment to check their accounts against what the Iraqis had told UNSCOM in the fall of 1995. Inspector Debra Krikorian, for one, felt that the Iraqis' accounts about equipment use for agent production correlated fairly well. At Al Daura, for instance, the Iraqis went to great lengths to explain what they did to try to make vaccine and botulinum toxin simultaneously, even pointing out where guards were stationed when biowarfare agent was being made.[2]

Kraatz-Wadsack's team sealed the entire Al Hakam and Al Daura sites, placing tamperproof tape on building doors to safeguard against removal of the equipment. At other sites, the inspectors also sealed the rooms containing large quantities of growth media. Pending a decision on the disposition of Al Hakam and Al Daura, in mid-December 1995 UNSCOM Executive Chairman Rolf Ekeus asked Iraq to cease all activities at these sites. Iraq cooperated.[3]

Prior to the BW29 mission, some of UNSCOM's in-house biological experts preferred to see Al Hakam leveled and, at the least, the equipment directly engaged in biowarfare agent production from Al Daura destroyed. Others did not want to demolish all of Al Hakam or Al Daura. Ekeus sought a legal opinion, and UNSCOM lawyers stated that Al Hakam was to be razed since Iraq did not disclose it as a bioweapons facility under United Nations

(UN) Resolution 687. A more moderate, render-harmless stance was taken with Al Daura, a civilian facility that Iraq had co-opted for biowarfare agent production. The site's air-handling system would be destroyed, and any pertinent items from Al Daura and other civilian facilities (such as Al Fudhaliyah) that Iraq used in the biowarfare program would be demolished.[4]

UNSCOM 134/BW31 eradicated the most identifiable vestiges of Iraq's bioweapons program during a six-week mission in May and June 1996 that UNSCOM attempted to conduct in a low-profile manner to increase the prospects of Iraqi cooperation. Iraq was obligated to provide the principal workforce and the materials for the demolition, so team chief Terence Taylor first needed Iraq's agreement on the specifics of the destruction plan. Roughly two weeks passed as the Iraqis made a last-ditch pitch for UNSCOM to spare everything and then anything from the ax to use the items for civilian purposes. From Deputy Prime Minister Tariq Aziz on down, the Iraqis lobbied Taylor, knowing that chief inspectors had leeway in their execution of missions.[5]

On the day that destruction was to begin, Iraq started trying other delay tactics. Hossam Amin, the head of the National Monitoring Directorate, sent a handful of teenagers, a couple of small tractors, and a sputtering truck to Al Hakam to do the task. Protesting that demolition work was inappropriate for teens, Taylor threatened to have Ekeus brief the Security Council, so the next day Amin sent an adult work crew and better equipment. Then the Iraqis said that they did not have sufficient RDX explosive for the demolition. Taylor shifted to a two-birds-with-one-stone destruction strategy: Al Hakam was blown to bits with the powerful, high-quality HMX explosive that Iraq had acquired for the precise detonations needed in nuclear devices. To drive home the point that UNSCOM was really going to level the entire facility, the first building brought down was Rihab Taha's animal house, which had not been used for agent production.[6]

Other than the Iraqis' continuing pleas to save even toilet bowls from obliteration, the oddest incident during this mission was when the Iraqis drove up with a truckload of equipment they claimed to be returning for destruction after thieves supposedly looted an equipment-filled bunker at Al Hakam in January 1996. The truck contained a 400-liter pilot plant, complete with a water purification unit. UNSCOM had audited this bunker in 1994 and inventoried and sealed its contents in December 1995. Inspectors on UNSCOM's April and May 1996 pre-destruction missions twice checked and resealed this bunker, so this extreme story bewildered the inspectors. Their prevailing

theory was that once the Iraqis saw that the inspectors were carefully comparing the equipment to be destroyed with previous inventory records they knew
they had to return this equipment, which they had hoped to salvage.[7]

Otherwise, the destruction proceeded in a business-like manner. One by
one, the buildings collapsed into rubble under the supervision of Australian
structural engineer Owen Hammond, who led the last weeks of the mission.
After mixing water into the large containers of growth media collected from
Al Adile, Al Hakam, Al Razi, Al Kindi, and Al Ameriyah, the remains were
dumped into pits at Al Hakam. The demolition team dismantled the air-
handling system at Al Daura and gathered at Al Hakam all of the equipment
used to produce biowarfare agents from Salman Pak, Al Fudhaliyah, and Al
Daura. After being blown up, cut up, or crushed with a bulldozer, the equipment remnants were sealed in cement and buried. Once Al Hakam's power
lines and fences were felled, Al Hakam was again a vast expanse of sand.[8]

MONITORING 'ROUND THE CLOCK

Interspersed with inspection missions focused primarily on interviews, sampling, and document sweeps, UNSCOM's biological monitors in Baghdad
kept tabs on dual-use biological sites in Iraq to guard against contemporary
and future proliferation. UNSCOM declared its biological monitoring program operational in April 1995 after an extensive series of baseline inspections
to identify sites that warranted monitoring and to collect detailed data about
their equipment, infrastructure capabilities, the operational requirements
and patterns for their declared civil activities, and their personnel.[9] Kraatz-
Wadsack, who supervised the establishment and operation of this monitoring
program, noted that the Iraqis were irritated and resigned to such close oversight. The monitors dropped in on very high-risk sites twice each month to increase deterrence of misbehavior and chances of catching foul play. Checking
on over eighty-five facilities, the monitors continued to encounter contradictions with Iraq's declaration and other problems, such as the removal of tags
from equipment and hundreds of items of undeclared dual-use equipment.[10]

Like the monitoring teams in other disciplines, Kraatz-Wadsack's did
their fair share of comparing what they saw on the ground to their lists of
dual-use equipment. For this reason, some inspectors regarded the monitors
as second-class citizens within UNSCOM.[11] Some espousing this caste-sys-
tem attitude believed that lowly monitors were not to be involved in the more
glamorous tasks of uncovering and eliminating past weapons activities.

While this in-house division of labor may have held true in the chemical and missile portfolios, the biological monitors did more than ordinary
check-box work and were frequently called on to flesh out the manpower of
incoming inspection teams.[12] Using a formula that Kraatz-Wadsack devised,
the biological monitors surveilled the rate at which Iraq's dual-use facilities
consumed key materials and utilities (for example, power and water), the
frequency of production runs, equipment maintenance activities, whether
production parameters were within the expected operational range for the
facility's product(s), and other data points so they could assess site status
on the basis of factors far more informative than just the size of fermenters.
An important part of this equation involved manpower, namely the whereabouts and activities of known or suspected bioweaponeers. The monitors
interviewed such individuals, as well as other scientists and managers, on
their site visits to help account for and evaluate activities. Tailored to each
site, questionnaires guided these interviews so that the Iraqis had to explain
every deviation from the baseline data regarding research activity, production output, management or staffing, funding levels or sources, consultants
or collaborating organizations, numbers and types of raw materials used for
site activity, utility and raw materials consumption, and equipment status and
maintenance. The monitors also went over any alteration to buildings or capabilities with a fine-toothed comb and incessantly poked their noses into anything and everything that had to do with Iraq's biological capabilities, from its
crop-dusting activities to its stocks of microorganisms.[13]

Iraq also had to file a steady stream of reports with the biological monitors, including advance notice of key equipment transfers or modifications
and timely notification of usual but pertinent activities, such as disease outbreaks.[14] The monitors placed critical pieces of equipment under twenty-
four-hour video surveillance and sometimes used other remote sensors. If
something looked amiss, the monitors could quickly follow up on site with
questions, an inventory check, and other activities. The biological monitors'
reports on worrisome activities or anomalies sometimes triggered investigation missions. For example, the Sterne strain of anthrax was in legitimate use
at Al Kindi Veterinary Vaccine Plant to make vaccine, but when monitors
found a document there about another strain of anthrax, Richard Spertzel led
an interview mission to delve into the matter.[15]

The line separating legitimate commercial activity from warfare agent
production was so fine that the monitors had to stay right on top of every facet

of Iraqi biological activity. If a facility used castor beans to make brake fluid, then the monitors knew they also had to track what happened to the leftover pulp because it contained ricin residue. Similarly, because Iraq had weaponized aflatoxin, the monitors called on Iraqi scientists to explain any work they did with *Aspergillus* spp., so they could evaluate if it remained within the realm of peaceful activity. In addition, the biological monitors occasionally turned up new sites that warranted routine monitoring. For instance, the monitors identified a site with fermenters, centrifuges, a spray drier, and other downstream processing equipment—three total process lines that Iraq had failed to declare. Elsewhere, they discovered undeclared filter presses, biological safety cabinets, fermenter control units, and other undeclared dual-use equipment.[16]

From the front lines in Iraq Kraatz-Wadsack paid no heed to the roiling debate in Geneva negotiations about whether monitoring the ban on biological weapons was even feasible.[17] Instead, she created tools that enabled the monitors to gather and feed as much relevant data as possible into the inspection process. These monitoring barometers helped UNSCOM continually reassess the risk that dual-use facilities posed regarding the covert manufacture of biowarfare agent and also informed UNSCOM's understanding of the breadth and depth of Iraq's past bioweapons activities.

CHASING THE PAPER TRAIL

When the Iraqis reverted to obfuscation in the spring of 1996, UNSCOM had little choice but to ply increasingly creative and aggressive inspection tactics to till for hard facts about Iraq's past germ weapons program and guard against continuing covert military activities at dozens of Iraqi biological facilities. In the wake of Lt. Gen. Amir Al Sa'adi's statement to Ekeus in April 1996 that Iraq had furnished UNSCOM with all of its documents related to its weapons of mass destruction programs, UNSCOM mounted document search missions.[18] In early May 1996, Hamish Killip led the first of several dedicated biological paper chases. The inspectors first blitzed through buildings for a quick appraisal of their contents and then swept them more systematically room by room, looking in all drawers, containers, and spaces for relevant documents. They identified the location of computers during the initial reconnaissance of buildings and subsequently exploited their electronic records.[19] "Every little pencil they purchased has three requisition copies. We've found documents in other programs going back to the late 1950s," said Kraatz-Wadsack, one of many inspectors who believed Iraq still had bioweapons program documents stashed somewhere.[20]

Indeed, Killip's UNSCOM 142/BW34 team found fifteen documents pertaining to growth media alone, others on fermentation processes (for example, flow diagrams and equipment drawings with details about fermenters and spray driers), and printouts from a database search for information on botulinum toxin, with the latest dated 1985. The Iraqis spun a variety of entertaining reasons for this database search.[21] The inspectors deduced, however, that Iraqi scientists did what anyone else would do when given an assignment outside their prior experience and knowledge; they conducted "a literature survey," said Killip. "Interestingly, they very quickly found that one of the best sources . . . was that series of volumes produced by SIPRI, the Stockholm International Peace Research Institute" in the early 1970s that leapfrogged them to pertinent articles and "fairly obscure patents that had details of specific types of dissemination equipment rather than having to make very detailed searches."[22]

Surprisingly, the team recovered some of its most interesting documents at Al Hakam and Al Daura Foot and Mouth Disease Vaccine Plant.[23] Two documents found on the BW34 mission shed light on Al Hakam's professed effort to develop single-cell protein to feed Iraq's chickens. Taha's deputy, Abdul Rahman Thamer explained that one document was a bill for 120 hatching chickens that were to be test subjects for Al Hakam's chicken feed, but the team also found a bill for 1,200 kilograms of special chicken fodder.[24] The second document made it hard for anyone to keep swallowing the notion that Al Hakam was ever a chicken feed plant. The BW34 report from Al Daura also conveyed the absurd circumstances that sometimes arose during inspections. Tongue in cheek, the inspectors reported that it was "remarkable" that the large slaughterhouse adjacent to Al Daura had not a single document and that although the Al Daura staff "worked hard to produce the correct keys to open locked doors. They frequently failed" and therefore "gratefully accepted" the team's offer of bolt cutters.[25]

During the UNSCOM 145/BW35 mission, David Kelly's team chased the paper trail from May 11 to May 20 at Samarra State Company for Drug Industries, the Al Ameriyah Serum and Vaccine Institute, and the Al Kindi Veterinary Vaccine Production Plant at Abu Ghraib. Among the 186 documents of interest found were classified records about Samarra Drug Industries' links to Al Muthanna, the Ministry of Defense, the Iraqi Intelligence Services, and the Ibn Al-Baetar Center at Al Taji.[26] Interviews with Brig. Gen. Mohammed

Mahmoud Bilal and the Al Ameriyah institute's former director, Faisal Ghazi, confirmed the inspectors' impression that the Iraqis had made a studious attempt to remove incriminating documents from the Serum and Vaccine Institute before the team arrived.[27] Oddly, a folder placed neatly atop the desk of the facility's director, where the inspectors were sure to spot it, held documents that the inspectors surmised had been stashed elsewhere, perhaps in Ghazi's home.[28] Seven of these records related to the transfer of the Al Ameriyah institute from the Ministry of Health to Al Muthanna from 1990 to 1991 and linked the institute to the Military Industrialization Commission. Ghazi explained that he had initiated the institute's takeover because the Military Industrialization Commission offered a better pay scale and higher funding for research and operations. He then ruminated about the days when Taha and Thamer had done graduate studies with him; both later became principal players in Iraq's bioweapons program.[29]

Three other documents from that same folder discussed the possible establishment of a genetic engineering program to develop vaccines at the Serum and Vaccine Institute. Ali Al Za'ag, who headed that research unit, denied any military purpose for his genetic engineering work. Bilal said he simultaneously directed both Al Muthanna and Al Ameriyah during the 1990–1991 time period, but that Al Za'ag's work was not part of the bioweapons program. Bilal flatly denied that Al Muthanna had any consequential involvement in the bioweapons program.[30] Trying to pin down Al Muthanna's role in the bioweapons program, UNSCOM later excavated beneath Taha's laboratory there, but the results of the dig did not advance their understanding of the work done by Taha's biological research group at Al Muthanna from 1985 to 1987.[31]

The UNSCOM BW35 team found documents that helped to elucidate the relationships between various organizations and activities in Iraq's bioweapons program.[32] For example, documents about the collaboration between the Technical Research Center and Al Muthanna on ricin research in the 1989–1990 time frame helped clarify how Al Muthanna fit into the picture.[33] Still, many unanswered questions remained about who really formulated the overall strategy and policy decisions for Iraq's bioweapons program and who made specific operational decisions about the research, production, testing, and deployment of weapons.

In addition to document sweeps and interviews, the UNSCOM BW35 team undertook intensive and intrusive sampling activities in mid-May 1996. This team collected 270 samples at Al Hakam, 31 at Al Daura, 6 at the Agriculture and Water Research Center at Al Fudhaliyah, and 28 at Salman Pak.[34] At Al Hakam and Al Daura, UNSCOM sampled structures and equipment, including all of the equipment used in preparation of seed cultures, batch cultivation, harvesting, subsequent processing of the agent, and transport or storage of the agent (including fermenters, drying equipment, and holding tanks). The inspectors also sampled laboratory equipment such as incubators, aerosol sampling equipment, centrifuges, anaerobic jars, and isolation hoods. To take dry swabs from multiple sites from the interior surfaces and fittings of the equipment, the inspectors opened large items such as fermenters and tanks. In storage, the inspectors found two pH probes that they sampled. The inspectors swabbed the remains of R-400 bombs that were salvaged from a river and materials from Al Hakam's waste pit, both of which were in a maintenance shed there. At a vehicle repair shop at Salman Pak, they collected samples from aerosol generation equipment and air samplers.[35] In Mosul, they sampled a Niro spray drier at a metallurgical repair shop.[36] The inspectors split all samples with the Iraqis. When UNSCOM sent the samples for analysis, the package included 6 samples that another inspection team had taken late in the summer of 1995 from castor bean mash present at Al Fallujah III and from a purported dump site for bulk agent located six kilometers from Al Hakam.[37]

IRAQ'S PREPOSTEROUS CLAIMS CONTINUE

As much as UNSCOM had gotten Iraq to disclose about its germ warfare activities, in 1996 Iraq was still making claims about the program's conduct that were outlandish to some inspectors. The draft full, final, and complete disclosure that Iraq gave the UNSCOM BW35 team on May 18, 1996, stated that the Ministry of Defense had "no role in the programme right up to the time of its demise" except for briefly when the weapons were deployed.[38] Iraq identified only two areas of limited military participation in the bioweapons program. First, the military provided logistical support for bioweapons tests and for the dispersal, guarding, and disposal of the weapons. Second, the Air Force Command was involved in the selection of weapons storage sites, modification of spray tanks as a dispersal system, and destruction of biological munitions. Iraq declared that no biological defensive program existed, stating that its troops relied only on chemical protective clothes and masks and received no specialized training. Nor, Iraq stated, was an operational concept for the use of biological weapons even developed. The declaration, however, described the initial purpose of biological weapons as an offshoot of a strategy to use chemical weapons to deter Iran's use of human wave offensives in the 1980s and secondarily to serve as a "viable" deterrent to Israel's weapons of mass destruction. Finally, Iraq stated that none of the military personnel who participated in the bioweapons program could provide "any assurance" that any of Iraq's biological weapons were able to "function reliably."[39]

According to Al Sa'adi, the military contribution to the bioweapons program was slight because the program was Kamal's pet project. Kamal made all of the major policy decisions, considered the program the ace up his sleeve, and planned to surprise the military with a new weapons capability at a time of his choosing. Al Sa'adi maintained that an April 1990 Arab intelligence report about the potential for an Israeli pre-emptive strike against Iraq had goaded Kamal into ordering a re-intensified bioweapons development effort.[40] In many countries, a single individual, no matter how influential, could not conceivably launch and run such a significant military program without extensive military involvement. A military concept of use, at least a rudimentary strategic plan, was a predicate to weaponization. The inspectors thought this pet project tale was possible in the scheme of Iraqi politics, but the Iraqi program progressed all the way to weaponization and deployment of munitions. Without coordination with and input from the military, many inspectors believed it unlikely that a bioweapons program would go that far.[41]

Furthermore, UNSCOM's inspectors knew full well by that time that several individuals with significant, integral roles in Iraq's germ weapons program were military officers. Al Sa'adi, who was Kamal's senior deputy at the Military Industrialization Commission, and Bilal, who oversaw the filling of munitions with biological agents, were both generals. Majid Ismael, Taha's deputy who supervised the production of botulinum toxin at Al Taji, Al Daura, and Al Hakam, held the rank of colonel.[42] Verbal statements from Murtada and other Iraqis to Ekeus in August 1995 and also to biological inspectors in September and October 1995 did not correspond at all to Iraq's subsequent stance of no military involvement before the deployment of weapons.[43]

Despite such contradictions, Iraq clung to this and other equally nonsensical statements (such as the fate of the unaccounted-for growth media). The Iraqis could or would not substantiate their declaration, but inspections occasionally turned up evidence to refute Iraq's version of events. UNSCOM deemed this 622-page declaration incomplete, a conclusion seconded by a panel of outside experts that UNSCOM convened.[44]

DIGGING FOR DONKEYS AND OTHER HARD EVIDENCE

In mid-1996, the Iraqis continued see-sawing back and forth in their cooperation with UNSCOM. One week they refused to provide people for interviews
and barred inspectors from places controlled by the Revolutionary Guards,
the next they handed Ekeus folders of information on Iraq's prohibited chemical, biological, and missile programs. A short time later, the Iraqis flipped
again, declining to amend their account of events even when UNSCOM bioweapons inspectors put contradictory factual evidence before them.[45]

At the beginning of July 1996, Ekeus sent inspectors to Iraq to interview
personnel involved in the production of agent, filling of munitions, and the
destruction of Iraq's biological arsenal, the beginning of a process that would
try to confirm Iraq's latest declaration. UNSCOM aborted one interview mission after just a day and scrubbed another entirely because of Iraq's lack of
cooperation, but the inspectors finally got some discussion going with the
Iraqis in mid-September 1996.[46] UNSCOM was casting its net for interviews
as widely and inventively as possible, trying to pick up information from
people at the heart of the bioweapons program as well as those in peripheral
roles (for example, facility janitors and truck drivers). All together, UNSCOM
inspectors interviewed roughly four hundred bureaucrats, scientists, security
and military personnel, and civilians who in some way took part in the bioweapons program.[47]

UNSCOM's October 11, 1996, report to the Security Council characterized
Iraq's most recent biological declaration as lengthy but stated that Baghdad
was still under-reporting imports of materials procured for the bioweapons
program. Furthermore, Iraq had not given UNSCOM substantiating evidence for the quantities of warfare agents it claimed to have made in 1987,
1988, and 1989; accurate data for its weapons field tests; or any documentation on its destruction of bulk agents and biological weapons. In view of this,
UNSCOM concluded that Iraq might have retained biowarfare agents and related materials.[48]

In mid-November 1996, Ekeus dispatched more biological samplers into
Iraq. With Kelly again at the helm, the UNSCOM 163/BW43 team was after
hard evidence on matters that Iraq refused to document. First, the inspectors
returned to Al Hakam to sample for residues of the biological agents that the
Iraqis said they made, tested, deactivated, and disposed of there. They dug
down to a lined waste pit in the southern production area, which had no liquid or hard waste. Near what had been buildings 31 and 33 in the northern

area, the inspectors unearthed and sampled from two septic tanks. The Iraqis said they had treated the bulk anthrax with formaldehyde and potassium permanganate and lastly with steam sterilization then poured the deactivated agent into the dump tank by building 31. Later, the Iraqis said they drained the deactivated agent into mobile tanks and took it into the desert beyond Al Hakam's northern production area to a dump site that Taha's assistant Thamer identified. The inspectors set up a ten-by-ten-meter grid at this location and collected samples at three depths—on the surface, at eight inches, and at sixteen inches deep. The inspectors sent the samples to one French and two U.S. laboratories for analysis.[49]

Next to the former utility building for the large production building that used to be in the northern part of Al Hakam the BW43 team also dug for R-400 munitions to see if the Iraqis had filled or buried there any of the R-400s that they said they had assembled at Al Hakam.[50] The Iraqis also led the inspectors to two places outside of the Al Hakam fence where in August 1990 they supposedly tested the size of the booster charge needed to disseminate botulinum toxin with a couple of R-400s filled with that agent. When the Iraqis kept pointing to different spots as the location of the tests, the inspectors knew it was a goose chase. Killip, a munitions expert, also saw that these areas had none of the markings or damage characteristic of test sites, no matter how long ago the tests occurred, so the inspectors decided not to collect samples.[51]

The UNSCOM BW43 team also got the runaround when they attempted to confirm Iraq's declaration about animal tests with anthrax and botulinum toxin. At Salman Pak, the Iraqis pointed to a location where they said they had buried dead sheep and donkeys. Each time the inspectors established a trench and found no animal carcasses, the Iraqis suddenly recalled the right place was just next to the previously identified burial site. After digging three large trenches, Kelly, clearly irritated by the Iraqi shenanigans, called off this dig.[52]

WRESTLING WITH THE AMBIGUITIES OF IRAQ'S BIOWARFARE AGENT PRODUCTION

As 1996 began, Iraq was still being moderately open with UNSCOM, providing some documents. The Iraqis told the inspectors that in addition to bioweapons trials at Al Muthanna's test sites, they conducted weapons tests at Al Hakam, where they originally planned to fill weapons too. Instead, they had just assembled the R-400 bombs there and sent them to Al Muthanna for filling. Hoping to profit from this atmosphere of cooperation, in early 1996 Spertzel led a pair of teams looking into Iraq's past weapons program. The second of these missions, UNSCOM 139/BW33, ran from February 24 to March 1 and attempted to clarify on an agent-by-agent and site-by-site basis what Iraq's capacity and capability were for biowarfare agent production. Although production occurred mainly at Al Hakam and Al Daura, Iraq also made agent at Salman Pak, Al Taji, and Al Fudhaliyah. Trying to assess how much of each kind of agent Iraq produced, the inspectors considered such factors as

- The size and number of the fermenters involved
- The transfer of equipment from site to site
- The installation dates of equipment at various sites
- The operability of various pieces of equipment given their availability and condition, such as downtime required for clean-up between production runs and maintenance, the presence of key workers
- The amount of available growth media suitable for each type of agent
- The time required for fermentation of each agent
- How much agent Iraq stated was consumed in weapons tests and in filling munitions[53]

With this number of variables, the calculations were complex; the complications rose as the Iraqis moved fluidly from one explanation to another about their production of biowarfare agents.

They claimed, for example, that their production of botulinum toxin at Al Hakam in 1989 was 40 percent of what they could have made under ideal conditions and by continuously operating the equipment on site at the time. Lacking the 1989 annual report for the bioweapons program, the inspectors had only what the Iraqis said and evidence obtained from other sources for points of reference. UNSCOM concluded that Iraq's general story about making a total of 19,000 liters of botulinum toxin was "credible" but that a confident assessment was not possible because it had evidence that contradicted Iraq's production figures for 1987–1988, which in turn called into question exactly when Iraq began producing botulinum toxin and conducted its weapons field trials with it.[54] For anthrax, the Iraqis verbally described running two lines of fermenters at Al Hakam in a manner that would have yielded much more agent in 1990 than the production figures given in Iraq's 1990 annual program report and November 1995 draft declaration. As was the case for botulinum toxin, inconsistency in the 1990 anthrax production quantities opened concerns about the amount of anthrax Iraq claimed to produce in 1989.[55] Perhaps the only bright spot of the BW33 mission, the inspectors' interview of Ali Shehab Ahmed, did not generate any major concerns about how much *Clostridium perfringens* Iraq said it made, only the continuing curiosity that Iraq made this agent but never loaded it into weapons.[56]

The inspectors also needed to determine how much biological agent simulant Iraq made because their production of these simulants involved the same fermentation lines, growth media, and personnel used to manufacture actual biowarfare agents. In late August 1995 and during the UNSCOM BW33 inspection, the Iraqis gave divergent accounts of how much *Bacillus subtilis* they produced to use in weapons tests. In the interim, under the pressure of UNSCOM's investigation, the Iraqis conceded that they had conducted more field trials than they first admitted, and UNSCOM suspected that Iraq had undertaken even more tests. Trapped by their own statements, the Iraqis produced either too much or too little simulant for the number of trials they said they conducted for the Zubaidy helicopter spray device in March–April 1988, for static 122mm rocket tests in November 1989, for dynamic tests of 122mm rockets in May 1990, and for tests with R-400 bombs in August 1990 and the drop tank in January 1991. Two Iraqi written sources indicated that the production line at Al Hakam with fermenters originally from Al Taji made 150 liters of *B. subtilis*, while the Olsa fermenters from Al Kindi made 8,275 liters. From the verbal accounts of fermenter operations at Al Hakam the inspectors calculated that 2,401 liters and 12,600 liters of *B. subtilis*, respectively, could easily have been made in the Al Taji and Al Kindi lines.[57] Likewise, Iraq's statements about the amount of *B. thuringiensis* produced had some worrisome variances, and it was not clear what Iraq did with this simulant. The Iraqis claimed they did not contemplate drying it in their spray driers.[58] This statement had negligible credibility since the inspectors already had sample analysis showing that the Al Nasir biopesticide made at Al Hakam, although useless for killing plant pests, was a dried *B. thuringiensis* product.[59]

The upshot of UNSCOM's assessment after UNSCOM BW33 was that Iraq could have made considerably larger quantities of bacterial agents than claimed, especially for the year 1989. Moreover, Iraq could not have made as much *B. subtilis* in March 1988 as stated given the available fermentation capacity.[60] Lacking authoritative documentation, UNSCOM habitually qualified its confidence in its assessments of how much biowarfare agent Iraq made. UNSCOM's calculations became even more uncertain when the Iraqis told the UNSCOM BW33 team that beyond their claimed usage of the growth media that the Technical Scientific Materials Import Division purchased, they diverted media from other sources to make biowarfare agent.[61]

If the bacterial agent production figures were wobbly, the account for the manufacture of aflatoxin was dumbfounding. Setting aside questions of why Iraq would work with this agent in the first place, Iraq said aflatoxin was made in flasks of up to 5 liters stacked inside of modified ovens, incubators, and environmental chambers. The stated production amount did not match how much aflatoxin Iraq said was consumed in its static and dynamic trials of 122mm rockets in November 1989 and in May 1990, respectively, and in their static trials of R-400 bombs in August 1990. Iraq's stated production method required the rotation of the stacked glass flasks in very close quarters on a daily basis. Iraqi workers had literally zero margin for error in this turning process lest they break significant numbers of flasks. Aware that the media consumption and agent production numbers did not correlate, the Iraqis discussed in front of the inspectors how much agent really had to be filled into each munition and whether the May 1990 trials involved thirty or forty rockets. Al Sa'adi was so appalled by Mohammed Emad Al-Diyat's version of the production process and results that he ordered him to present new figures. The following day the account swung significantly. For instance, the Iraqis changed the amount of solvent used to extract the agent, which gave them a higher yield, and said that instead of cramming 3,750 flasks in an environmental chamber, the actual figure was more like 2,000.[62] Moreover, Iraq also stated in a mid-1990 document that aflatoxin retained its stability in long-term storage, an assertion supposedly proven by the activity of aflatoxin stored for a year and then used in a field test. Given the November 1989 and May 1990 field tests, this claim either meant that Iraq made aflatoxin in 1988, which countermanded Iraqi statements, or that it made far more aflatoxin before May 1989 than its stated capacity would allow.[63] With so many inconsistencies in the aflatoxin account, UNSCOM BW33 concluded that Iraq's story was "patently contrived."[64]

As for Iraq's other biowarfare agents, it apparently did not make large quantities of trichothecene. Also, since the Iraqis considered their November 1989 field trial with ricin to be a failure, Technical Research Center Director Ahmed Murtada reportedly called off additional ricin production. Al Sa'adi said that a November 1989 wheat smut field trial with one 122mm rocket was viewed as unsuccessful, but a document from the Haidar farm stated that

the wheat smut field trial involved three rockets and led to a recommendation to weaponize this agent.[65] With no documents forthcoming from Iraq
to corroborate its production accounts, so little lined up with known facts or
standard operational practices for the production of biological materials that
UNSCOM's April 1996 report averred that Iraqi officials adjusted their data
on bulk agent production according to whatever information the inspectors
put in front of them.[66]

SAMPLE RESULTS CONTRADICT THE IRAQIS

In mid-January 1997 the biologists on UNSCOM 169/BW45 expected and received little help from the Iraqis.[67] Armed with the results of analyses performed on samples that UNSCOM BW35 took in May 1996, the inspectors
were prepared for a difficult meeting with the Iraqis. Tests using three methods, culture for bacteria, immunoassay, and polymerase chain reaction (PCR)
screened the samples for the presence of eight biowarfare agents. From the
first two methods, all results were negative save one immunoassay, which returned a positive for *C. botulinum* Types A and B. The more advanced PCR
analyses returned several positive anthrax and botulinum toxin results from
the 270 and 31 samples taken, respectively, at Al Hakam and Al Daura, as
Table 6.1 shows.[68] These results reflected the advances in analytical techniques
made in the 1990s that allowed UNSCOM to detect the molecular signatures
of biowarfare agents despite Iraq's repeated efforts to cleanse its facilities of
evidence of illicit activity.[69]

   The results most likely to have taken the Iraqis off guard were those showing traces of anthrax DNA in samples taken from a fermenter, a storage vessel,
and a transfer tank. In rebuttal, the Iraqis claimed they had never even used
that particular fermenter or transfer tank in the weapons program.[70] None
of the Al Daura samples returned any evidence of botulinum toxin, the only
agent Iraq said was produced at that site. Moreover, the inspectors informed
the Iraqis that results showed *Clostridium botulinum* type B on a pH probe
found at Al Hakam, when Iraq had previously stated that it produced and
weaponized only *Clostridium botulinum* type A.[71]

   In addition, the BW45 inspectors told the Iraqis that analysis of the samples from the purported dump site for deactivated bulk agent just outside of
Al Hakam's northern boundary returned fourteen positive hits for the Vollum
strain of *Bacillus anthracis*. Oddly, the positives for live agent came from all
three depths in the area sampled, except from the samples taken in the exact
middle of the grid. On some samples, the results were as high as one hundred

Table 6.1. Results of polymerase chain reaction analysis from
Al Hakam and Al Daura samples

Facility	Sample Location	Agent Identified	Number of Positive Results
Al Hakam	Vials from dump site	B. anthracis	2
	Centrifuge rotor	B. anthracis, C. botulinum, Type A	1
	pH probes	C. botulinum, Types A, B	2
	Vials	C. botulinum, Type A	3
	Preparative fermenter	B. anthracis	1
	Preparative fermenter	C. botulinum	1
	Fermenter	B. anthracis	1 (not confirmed as virulent)
	Transfer vessel	B. anthracis	1 (not confirmed as virulent)
Al Daura	Storage vessel	B. anthracis	1
	Fermenter	B. anthracis	1 (not confirmed as virulent)
	Transfer vessel	B. anthracis	1 (not confirmed as virulent)

SOURCES: Cdr. James Burans, "Update on Sampling and Analysis of Samples Collected at Al Hakam and the Hoof and Mouth Vaccine Facility: 'Saddam, Are You Sure You Cleaned That Equipment?'" briefing slides (Washington, DC, Naval Medical Research Institute, n.d.); United Nations Special Commission, *Draft Inspection Report: UNSCOM 145/BW35*, Chief Inspector David C. Kelly (New York, n.d.), 20.

spores per gram, a high concentration over five years after the supposed disposal of the deactivated anthrax. Meanwhile, the samples taken from the building 33 waste tank at Al Hakam, where the Iraqis said they temporarily stored the deactivated agent before dumping it, tested negative for anthrax.[72] Faced with these results, which told the inspectors that something was out of kilter, Bilal appeared uncomfortable. Several explanations were possible, including that the Iraqis had not followed the stipulated deactivation procedures or had used an ineffective method. Alternatively, since the temporary storage tank samples were negative but the dump site had live anthrax, the results could indicate that Iraq seeded the purported dump site with anthrax in a clumsy attempt to give the inspectors something to corroborate destruction of the agent or to mislead them about what really happened with the bulk anthrax.[73] Since the finding of live agent did not jibe with inactivation of the anthrax, the Iraqis claimed first that the Vollum strain was endemic, which was untrue, and then that the live spores must have come from discarded material from previous production runs at Al Hakam.[74] At one point, the Iraqis also produced gate receipts denoting who entered and exited facilities, promoting the receipts as proof of the agent destruction.[75]

With Iraq's story about the disposition of the bulk agent in disarray, the BW45 inspectors resumed their efforts to straighten out and authenticate Iraq's data about the bulk production of agents and to identify relevant individuals in the program's chain of command. One set of the inspectors' questions focused on the production engineering. With personnel that Iraq declared had worked in the program, the inspectors explored such issues as their equipment operations and limitations; their production volume, rate, and output for anthrax and botulinum toxin; the possibilities of production runs resulting in different quantities of agent; and their agent-storage capacity. The inspectors also requested interviews with others who helped procure equipment and materials and with technicians who serviced the equipment at Al Hakam because they might have been able to provide some insight into operational capabilities and downtimes for the production lines there.[76]

The mission encountered lots of delay from the Iraqis. For example, Taha and Bilal, dressed up from attending the Military Industrial Commission's Science Day, strolled late into a session delving into the Arabian Trading Company's facilitation of imports for the bioweapons program. Much later, it came to light that Saddam had given this pair awards that day for developing anthrax and botulinum toxin weapons, the principal achievements of their scientific careers.[77] Taha appeared that day only, otherwise snubbing the inspectors. The statements of the Iraqis who showed up tied neatly into Iraq's contemporary written declaration. Spertzel added an interview session on Saturday to try to cull more useful data, but Iraq refused to produce most of the requested interviewees. Overall, the mission made little progress.[78] Similarly, during Spertzel's UNSCOM 174/BW47 mission the Iraqis were uncooperative, other than statements from Bilal, Murtada, and Nassir Al-Hindawi that Iraq's single-cell protein activity at Al Taji and Al Hakam was a smokescreen for bioweapons work.[79]

What Iraq did with the growth media figured centrally in UNSCOM's efforts to clear up how much of which biowarfare agents Iraq made. Iraq still could not account for 2.5 tons of growth media that UNSCOM documented with records from Iraq's suppliers. The inspectors had to pursue this matter because 2.5 tons of media can produce very large amounts of warfare agents.[80]

In addition, considerable uncertainty surrounded Iraq's use of peptone, yeast extract, and tryptone that the Technical Scientific Materials Import

Division imported. Before the growth media was destroyed in mid-1996, the inspectors found barrels with broken seals, and sometimes the plastic liner bags inside held less media than the quantity on the label. Moreover, the labels on some of the interior bags sometimes did not match the production lot and container numbers of the labels on the exterior of the drums. The Iraqis claimed they never inventoried the media and even if they had, the records of exactly what happened with it had long since been destroyed.[81] Thus the irregularities with the contents of many barrels caused suspicions that Iraq might have imported or made more media and placed it in the original bags and containers. Either possibility would indicate that Iraq could have produced considerably more bulk agent than declared.

These concerns elevated when the inspectors learned that Iraq specifically assessed the performance of domestically produced growth media versus imported media and also had an indigenous capability to make growth media. For example, comparative studies at Salman Pak demonstrated that *Clostridium botulinum* yielded comparable quantities of toxin and a lethality of toxin whether grown in thioglycollate medium or casein-yeast extract-glucose broth, the latter being the imported medium used at Al Hakam.[82] Iraq could make several types of growth media (such as thioglycollate) from materials readily available inside the country. After inspectors found a document about a comparative study of *Clostridium perfringens* grown from peptone at Al Tuwaitha, the staff there showed Kraatz-Wadsack a hall, at that point empty, where they had produced large quantities of peptone.[83] Moreover, UNSCOM validated in mid-1997 that Iraq had sufficient domestic industrial capacity and skills to manufacture dual-use equipment (for example, double-jacketed fermenters, separating centrifuges, and spray dryers).[84] In short, Iraq could sustain a bioweapons program wholly without external supplies because Iraq had the seed cultures of warfare agents, the ability to make the necessary equipment and growth media, and the domestic technical know-how to research, develop, produce, and weaponize biological agents.

TWISTED TALES: IRAQ'S ACCOUNTS OF BIOWEAPONS TESTS, NUMBERS, MARKINGS, AND DISPOSAL

After August 1995, Iraq's accounts were all over the map about the number of weapons tests, the quantity of weapons made and filled with which agents, the markings on munitions, and the disposal of bulk agent and munitions.[85] UNSCOM 133/BW30, which ran from January 12 to 18, 1996, tried to get a handle on the agents employed in different weapons tests, the sequence in which Iraq filled biological bombs and SCUD warheads, and when Iraq marked its biological munitions to distinguish them from conventional or chemical rounds. The inspectors interviewed numerous Iraqis about what occurred with biological agents and SCUD warheads, R-400 bombs, LD-250 bombs, 122mm rockets, and other dispersal devices. Then, after Al Sa'adi summoned several generals to give UNSCOM presentations on Iraq's various munitions in mid-May 1996, he served notice that Iraq's next biological declaration would be its last.[86]

Though markings on munitions might help UNSCOM settle discrepancies in Iraq's account about the number of weapons filled with the different agents, the inspectors knew they needed other evidence because the markings were just paint. Iraq's stories about markings and the agent fills, however, changed with disturbing frequency. Not long after August 1995, the Iraqis first claimed that the biological rounds had no special markings because only those immediately involved in the biowarfare program handled them. That tale quickly disintegrated because Iraq also said the munitions were dispersed before the Gulf War and the inspectors pointed out that the security and military personnel moving, storing, and perhaps firing them would probably depend on unique markings to know they were handling the correct weapons. Moreover, the inspectors reminded the Iraqis that early UNSCOM inspectors took ample photographs of munitions with different markings. Iraq then claimed that munitions with two longitudinal black stripes were the ones filled with biological agents or made for that purpose.[87] Iraq's assertion that all biological weapons were thus marked was suspect because the inspectors knew that Iraq did not usually employ markings to differentiate various types of rounds.[88]

Spertzel headed an October 14–23, 1996, inspection that drilled the Iraqis on the discrepancies between Iraq's declaration about its field tests of biological weapons and what UNSCOM knew about those tests, largely from forensic examination of the Haidar farm videos. The inspectors derived copious factual details from these videos that they juxtaposed to Iraq's declaration and the Iraqis' verbal statements. Sometimes the inspectors showed the Iraqis clips of the tests to spur their recollections of the trials conducted from 1988 to 1990 with experimental devices, LD-250 bombs, and 122mm rockets. UNSCOM concluded that Iraq had failed to declare some field trials because the Iraqis interviewed who helped to prepare the June 1996 declaration gave accounts that stuck closely to that report, whereas other interviewees' memories fit with the Haidar farm documentation about the field trials for the LD-250 bombs and 122mm rockets.[89] Moreover, Iraq repudiated field tests with six R-400 bombs at Al Muhammadiyat that Iraq described in its June 1996 declaration, in the Haidar farm documents, and in the verbal accounts of staff who conducted these trials.[90] The Iraqis offered the inspectors so little other documentation (for example, receipts of transfer of items or orders for activities) that UNSCOM judged Iraq's accounts of its field trials to be askew on both minor and significant details.

Killip directed missions with the goal of cracking what had really happened with the Iraqi field tests and the disposal of the bulk agent and munitions.[91] For instance, he went to Al Muthanna's facility at Al Muhammadiyat and to Abu Abaida Air Base, where, Iraq claimed, bioweapons tests had been performed.[92] When he had so little to go on, Killip preferred to get a baseline account from a key participant in an event and then take other Iraqis who were also involved to the "scene of the crime," as he called it, to get them to reconstruct weapons tests or demolition.[93] Site by site, UNSCOM inspectors went to locations where the Iraqis stored or filled weapons before, during, and immediately after the Gulf War. For example, more than once inspectors scoured an abandoned railway tunnel at Al Mansuriyah and the banks of the Tigris Canal near Baghdad, which Iraq said were temporary hiding places for ten and fifteen biological-filled SCUD warheads, respectively. Iraq said that in roughly mid-July 1991 it took the biological SCUD warheads to specific areas at Al Nibai, a desert site about one hundred miles northwest of Baghdad, for destruction.[94] In 1992, when missile and chemical inspectors first saw fragments of Al Hussein warheads at Al Nibai, the Iraqis said they were chemical warheads. Unaware that some of these remnants might have been from biological warheads, the inspectors took no samples in 1992.[95]

During UNSCOM 167/BW44 in mid-December 1996, Spertzel's team interviewed seventeen Iraqis about the filling, deployment, interim storage, and destruction of Iraq's biological weapons. Iraq did not even initially mention aflatoxin as a SCUD warhead fill, and after August 1995 the Iraqis switched the number of warheads filled with different agents whenever it suited them.[96] The Iraqis also told inconsistent stories about the transport of the SCUD warheads from the Tigris Canal and the Al Mansuriyah tunnel to Al Nibai. The Iraqis said they took the missile warheads to Al Nibai and blew them up in one or two explosions on July 9, 10, or both, 1991.[97] The BW44 team drove a Land Rover into a pit the Iraqis identified as a destruction site at Al Nibai and dug around for a bit before returning to Baghdad. As planned, a U.S. satellite took images of the team's vehicles, which the inspectors parked in a north-south direction to permit a reliable geographic orientation in this flat desert area. As the inspectors expected, when they compared shots of this pseudo-excavation to historical images of Al Nibai from July 9–10, 1991, there was no sign of activity at Al Nibai on those two days in July 1991. Once again, UNSCOM caught Iraq in a lie.[98] By that time, UNSCOM had exposed so many Iraqi falsehoods that a senior UN official said, "Saddam's only recourse was to try to shut down UNSCOM."[99]

Killip's teams also went to Al Nibai more than once, in mid-1997 excavating various locations where Iraq had destroyed twenty-five biological SCUD warheads, the Iraqis said. Examination of the physical evidence from these debris fields pointed toward the destruction of fifteen of the biological warheads at different times, which ran counter to Iraq's account of how it destroyed the biological missile warheads.[100] Killip's team also went to two sites where Iraq said it had stored biological bombs before they were taken for destruction in early July 1991, namely Airfield 37, where according to Iraq's declaration 78 R-400 biological bombs were buried for about five months, and the Al Azziziyah firing range, which the Iraqis said was the transient storage site for 79 biological R-400s.[101] In April 1992 Iraq told UNSCOM inspectors that 40 chemical R-400s were destroyed at Al Azziziyah. After August 1995, the Iraqi line was that they filled 166 R-400 bombs with biowarfare agents. However, the diary of a junior army officer who supposedly witnessed the disposal operations noted that 157 items were blown up at Al Azziziyah. Once Iraq turned a portion of this officer's diary over to UNSCOM, the Iraqis asserted they had filled only 157 R-400s with germ agents and destroyed that very quantity of R-400s at the firing range. Furthermore, the Iraqis then recalled that they never destroyed any chemical R-400s at Al Azziziyah. Killip headed mid-February and mid-May 1997 missions to Al Azziziyah to investigate.[102]

Using a map that Bilal and another of Taha's key aides, Sinan Abdul Hasen, provided, the inspectors dug for parts and pieces of the R-400s, which they catalogued and photographed. At a disposal pit not on this map, the inspectors unearthed pieces of twenty bombs and three intact R-400s. Black stripes marked two of the intact R-400s, which according to the Iraqis indicated an anthrax or botulinum toxin fill; one had no stripe, which Iraq claimed meant an aflatoxin fill. Bilal and Sinan said that the agent fill was inactivated prior to the placement of explosives on either side of the bombs for demolition. For this intact trio of R-400s, they assumed the explosives had misfired. To make the burial site look like an ordnance dump, the Iraqis scattered ammunition on top of it. An already dangerous dig became even more so because the Iraqis ambled through the area with lit cigarettes, increasing the risk to the inspectors. Largely for safety reasons, Killip halted the dig after recovering remnants of 25 R-400s, far short of the Iraqi figure of 157 R-400s.[103]

Samples from the intact R-400s showed residues of potassium permanganate, which Iraq said was used along with formaldehyde to deactivate anthrax and botulinum toxin. Sample results showed the DNA of impure botulinum in all three bombs. If the Iraqi explanation of their munition markings was true, the R-400 with no black stripes should have contained the residues of bleach, which the Iraqis claimed they used to deactivate aflatoxin. This sampling result certainly undercut Iraq's verbal explanation of their munitions markings and also raised problems with Iraq's declaration about how many weapons were filled with different agents.[104]

On the first UNSCOM inspection at Al Muthanna in 1991, Killip and fellow inspector Rod Barton had wondered about the significance of green, yellow, and black markings on the R-400s.[105] In September 1991, the Iraqis told UNSCOM that fifty-eight empty R-400s at Al Muthanna were designated for chemical agents and were never filled. After August 1995, the Iraqis claimed that thirty-seven of the R-400s destroyed at Al Muthanna were actually designated for biological agents. Of those thirty-seven R-400s, twenty-six had black stripes and eleven did not. Barton and Killip spent roughly two weeks trying to reconcile Iraq's declaration with the videos and photographs of munitions destroyed at Al Muthanna but were not entirely successful partly because some weapons were not clearly visible.[106] Adding to the ever erratic Iraqi story about munition markings and other codes used in the bioweapons program, a number of the R-400s destroyed at Al Muthanna were also marked with a circle and the Iraqi letter for "A."[107] One such R-400, brought from the Al Waleed Airbase in far western Iraq, had no black stripe but did have a circled A.[108] The inspectors questioned any Iraqis who had handled the biological munitions about markings on the weapons because they already knew Iraq employed a letter code to designate their biological agents.[109]

At that juncture, Iraq declared that the biological R-400s had a white circle and the letters A, B, or C on them, and the missile warheads were marked with the numbers 3 through 5.[110] According to the key written in the red photograph album from the Haidar farm, "A" was code for *Clostridium botulinum*

Type A, "B" for *Bacillus anthracis*, and "C" for *Clostridium perfringens*.[111] This code, however, did not synchronize with the agent code letters in other documents the inspectors found or that Iraq used in its declarations, where agent "C" stood for aflatoxin. For example, the 1990 annual report for the bioweapons program used the letter "G" to refer to *Clostridium perfringens*, noting that Iraq had performed a pathogenicity test with this agent in 1990. Moreover, this report also described agent "C" as a cancer-causing agent and stated that 2,200 liters of that agent was made in 1990, the exact amount of aflatoxin Iraq declared it had produced.[112] Said Kelly, the Iraqis "just could not get a consistent story" between their documents, the actual munitions, and their verbal accounts about their agent coding system.[113]

With the R-400 remnants from Al Azziziyah, the inspectors turned to yet another distinguishing physical characteristic that might help determine which bombs were supposed to be for chemical versus biological agents. Iraq declared making 100 R-400 bombs for agent "A" (botulinum toxin), 75 for agent "B" (anthrax), and 25 for agent "C" (aflatoxin).[114] They explained that they ordered 200 R-400-A's, which were specifically for biological agents and had an internal blue epoxy coating. The Iraqis stated, however, that they made only 175 of the planned allotment of R-400-A's when they determined that aflatoxin reacted negatively to the epoxy coating.[115] For that reason, the Iraqis said that they put aflatoxin in 25 standard R-400s. The Iraqis also declared that in the waning days of December 1990 they were unable to fill all of the R-400s because they required the remaining bulk agent at Al Muthanna to fill the SCUD warheads.[116]

To complicate matters, after August 1995 the Iraqis initially said they filled ten SCUD warheads with anthrax and fifteen with botulinum toxin. In September 1995, Iraq first changed its story to loading half of the SCUD warheads with anthrax and half with botulinum toxin, then settled on the line of ten anthrax-filled, thirteen botulinum-toxin-filled, and two aflatoxin-filled warheads.[117] Next, in its May 1996 declaration, Iraq stated that sixteen SCUD warheads were filled with botulinum toxin, five with anthrax, and four with aflatoxin.[118] These zig-zagging accounts were part of what threw off UNSCOM's efforts to square the quantity of different agents produced with the amounts needed for weapons tests and filling of 157 R-400 bombs.

The tale of the R-400s was as contorted as that of the biological SCUDs. Iraq reportedly made 1,550 R-400s. UNSCOM inspectors witnessed the destruction of 395 of them after the Gulf War and found sufficient evidence to back up Iraq's statement that 160 R-400s were destroyed during the Gulf War. Much of the accounting problem pertained to over 1,000 R-400s that Iraq claimed to have destroyed unilaterally. Of that number, Iraq declared making 200 R-400-A's for biological agents and filling 157 of them, which left 43 empty biological bombs.[119] UNSCOM could not reliably account for all of the filled biological R-400s perhaps blown up at Al Azziziyah or determine how many of the 58 empty R-400s disposed of at Al Muthanna under UNSCOM supervision were destined for chemical or biological fills.[120] Iraq unilaterally destroyed another 308 R-400s that it said were never filled with anything deadly, creating another accounting headache for the inspectors. Iraq provided a receipt that the Nasr State Establishment, which manufactured the bombs, sent to Al Muthanna. This receipt did not say "melt the R-400s," it just said "melt." Not surprisingly, the inspectors did not consider this receipt convincing evidence that Iraq had destroyed 308 R-400s.[121] In verbal and written accounts, Iraq gave different numbers for how many R-400s were manufactured, filled, and destroyed in one way or another,[122] rendering UNSCOM unable to confirm much of anything about the R-400s.

The aflatoxin conundrum lent further uncertainty to what agents Iraq loaded into R-400s and SCUD warheads. The scientist responsible for making the aflatoxin, Al-Diyat, reportedly left Iraq in 1997, never to be heard from again. As noted, Al-Diyat's production method for aflatoxin—the daily rolling of glassware inside incubators—was questionable. This approach might have yielded enough aflatoxin for weapons tests, but the inspectors thought that the output was unlikely to be sufficient to fill the number of weapons Iraq said it loaded with aflatoxin.[123] Iraq first told UNSCOM that 16 of the 25 regular R-400s were filled with aflatoxin but later lowered that number to 7 to fit with the 157 biological R-400s recorded in the Army officer's diary about destruction operations at Al Azziziyah. Iraq claimed that four SCUDs contained aflatoxin.[124] The riddle became even more perplexing when samples taken from the stainless steel remnants of at least seven warheads revealed only the DNA of *B. anthracis*. Analysis did not detect any residues of aflatoxin or botulinum toxin, which the Iraqis also said they put into SCUD warheads.[125] Thus forensic evidence once again cast serious doubt on Iraq's nomadic bioweapons accounts, shown in Tables 6.2 and 6.3. The inspectors dug, sampled, searched for corroborating documentation, conducted numerous interviews, and consulted satellite imagery in their efforts to get at the truth.

Attempting to make the missile warhead numbers fit, in early August 1998 Amer Rasheed told an UNSCOM team led by Nikita Smidovich that Iraq did not dispute the laboratory analysis detecting anthrax in at least seven destroyed SCUD warheads. Rasheed then announced that Iraq must have filled sixteen SCUD warheads with anthrax instead of botulinum toxin. Flipping Iraq's previous account, he claimed that five SCUDs contained botulinum toxin. Perhaps trying to keep a rough balance in how much agent was put into munitions, Rasheed added that Iraq modified more R-400s for a botulinum toxin fill than declared and that fewer R-400s were filled with anthrax than previously claimed. He dismissed Iraq's prior statements about the allocation of agent into SCUD warheads, asserting that biologists were not so smart with math. For Rasheed's statement to be true, Iraq needed to have made more anthrax and less botulinum toxin, which would mean Iraq consumed more yeast extract for anthrax production instead of thioglycolate to make botulinum toxin. Rasheed's statement did not match Iraq's declaration about the consumption of growth media. Nor did it correspond to Iraq's account about the temporary

Table 6.2. Iraq's meandering account of SCUD warheads filled with biowarfare agents

Date of Statement	Anthrax	Botulinum Toxin	Aflatoxin
August 17, 1995*	10	15	0
Late September 1995 (statement to BW28 team) **	10	13	2
June 1996 declaration, December 1996 interviews	5	16	4
August 1998 (Amer Rasheed statement)	16	5	4
August 1998 (Amir Al Sa'adi reversion to *status quo ante*)	5	16	4

NOTES: * On August 17, 1995, the Iraqis initially stated that there were seventy-five SCUD warheads filled with chemical agents and twenty-five SCUD warheads filled with biological agents, a total of one hundred warheads filled with unconventional payloads.

** During UNSCOM 126/BW28, the Iraqis stated that there were fifty SCUD warheads filled with chemical agents and twenty-five SCUD warheads filled with biological agents, a total of seventy-five warheads filled with unconventional payloads.

SOURCES: National Monitoring Directorate, Republic of Iraq, *Full, Final and Complete Disclosure of Iraq's Past Biological Programme,* May 1996, paras. 2.5, 6.6, 6.7, pages 41, 179–181, 183–184; United Nations Security Council, *Letter Dated 25 January 1999 from the Executive Chairman of the Special Commission Established by the Secretary-General Pursuant to Paragraph 9 (b) (i) of Security Council Resolution 687 (1991) Addressed to the President of the Security Council,* Doc. S/1999/94, January 29, 1999, Appendix I, para. 25; Appendix III, paras. 32, 35, 38; Richard Spertzel, PhD (former UNSCOM chief biological weapons inspector), interview with author, Washington, DC, July 1, 2005; David Kelly, PhD (former UNSCOM chief biological weapons inspector), interview with author, Washington, DC, December 17, 2002; Hamish Killip (former UNSCOM chief biological weapons inspector), interview with author, Isle of Man, August 22, 2005.

Table 6.3. Iraq's various accounts of R-400 bombs filled with biowarfare agents

Date of Statement	Anthrax	Botulinum Toxin	Aflatoxin
August 17, 1995	200	200	0
Late September 1995 (statement to BW28 team)	50	100	11
September 1996	50	100	7
July 1998 (Amer Rasheed statement)	Fewer than 50	Over 100	Did Not Mention
August 1998 (Amir Al Sa'adi reversion to *status quo ante*)	50	100	7

SOURCES: United Nations Security Council, *Letter Dated 25 January 1999 from the Executive Chairman of the Special Commission established by the Secretary-General Pursuant to Paragraph 9 (b) (i) of Security Council Resolution 687 (1991) Addressed to the President of the Security Council*, Doc. S/1999/94, January 29, 1999, Appendix III, para. 39, 41–42; 45, 47; National Monitoring Directorate, Republic of Iraq, *Full, Final and Complete Disclosure of Iraq's Past Biological Programme*, May 1996, Chapter VI, para. 6.2.5, page 172, para. 6.4.2.1, pages 172, 177; Richard Spertzel, PhD (former UNSCOM chief biological weapons inspector), interview with author, Washington, DC, July 1, 2005; David Kelly, PhD (former UNSCOM chief biological weapons inspector), interview with author, Washington, DC, December 17, 2002; Hamish Killip (former UNSCOM chief biological weapons inspector), interview with author, Isle of Man, August 22, 2005.

storage in early 1991 of SCUD warheads filled with anthrax and botulinum toxin in the Al Mansuriyah railway tunnel and by the Tigris Canal. Once the inspectors put Rasheed's version of events in writing, Al Sa'adi sent UNSCOM a letter in mid-August 1998 disavowing Rasheed's numbers and confirming the account in Iraq's full, final, and complete declaration.[126] With such escapades, the Iraqis seemed flippant about the inspection process, recanting data almost as quickly as they presented it to the inspectors for "clarification."[127]

UNSCOM recognized the high stakes resting on a premature certification that the essential elements of Iraq's bioweapons program had been demolished or rendered harmless. "There was no bunker with barrels full of anthrax that we could show to the world. This was a slow process of assembling a jigsaw puzzle. With chemicals and missiles, we went in knowing the outlines of the puzzle and whether it had five hundred or five thousand pieces," said an UNSCOM staffer. "With the biologicals, we never had a good feeling for how big the puzzle was, whether we had found the corner pieces, or whether we had two or two hundred missing pieces."[128] With new, dramatic evidence of biological foul play hard to come by, retaining Security Council support for UNSCOM's inspections against competing political priorities became ever more challenging.

7 TENTACLES AND DISINTEGRATION

MANY KEY RECORDS about Iraq's bioweapons program (for example, the "cook-books" and annual program reports) were not among the document-filled trunks that the Iraqis guided United Nations Special Commission (UNSCOM) Executive Chairman Rolf Ekeus to at the Haidar farm in August 1995. Despite going to great lengths to verify the accuracy and completeness of Iraq's decla-rations, in early 1997 UNSCOM's biological inspectors knew that important gaps in information persisted, which fostered suspicions about Iraq's past bio-weapons program. Moreover, Iraq was improving its domestic capabilities to make dual-use biological equipment and materials and had kept its core bio-weaponeers together at Al Hakam until its mid-1996 destruction. Thereafter, Rihab Taha's group of weaponeers worked at the National Monitoring Direc-torate.[1] UNSCOM could not ignore indications that Iraq might be creating and conserving capacities to restart the program.

The security stakes were considerable if UNSCOM were to certify prema-turely to the Security Council that Iraq was out of the bioweapons business, only to have it resurrect its germ weapons program. This chapter describes the tailored investigatory missions that UNSCOM fielded and the interna-tional panels of experts that concurred with the belief of UNSCOM's in-house biological team that Iraq was withholding significant evidence. Maintaining concealment and obstruction activities, Saddam Hussein was speculating that he could outlast the international community's support for UNSCOM. Although Iraq suffered additional targeted military strikes before UNSCOM's demise, Saddam turned out to be correct. This chapter conveys what trans-

pired during UNSCOM's final biological inspections and the festering political circumstances that led to the collapse of the inspectorate.

SCOURING IRAQ FOR ADDITIONAL BIOWEAPONEERS
AND EVIDENCE

Early in 1997, UNSCOM's biological inspectors considered new angles they
could leverage to learn more about Iraq's weapons program. Knowing that
anyone who ever earned a PhD has an uncanny ability to lay hands on the
raw documentation for their dissertation even twenty-five years after defend-
ing it, the inspectors decided to cull for any additional scientists with links to
the program. If these scientists were true to their training, they probably kept
pertinent records despite orders to destroy them. The inspectors opted to cast
the net widely, screening the professional histories of Iraqi scientists for those
with certain academic degrees and research interests such as genetic engineering. Rather than rely on intelligence leads, they pulled the publications of
Iraqi scientists and narrowed the possibilities to a list of roughly fifteen scientists that UNSCOM had yet to interview in-depth who had a skill set suited to
weapons work.[2]

Team chief Terence Taylor maintained tight secrecy about the objectives
and tactics for UNSCOM 180/BW48, informing only two senior inspectors
about the inspection targets in advance. The real objectives of this mid-April
1997 mission were to locate listed individuals at nine different academic sites,
but the Iraqis were confused about the inspectors' purpose. Professor Moona
Al Jaboori, who did research with mushrooms at Al Tuwaitha, was a scientist
of interest. When previously interviewed, Al Jaboori showed inspectors photographs of her work. Though the UNSCOM biological team believed that
she was somehow involved in Iraq's research on fungal agents, the inspectors
came up empty-handed from their search of Al Jaboori's office and the files of
scientists of interest at the rest of the universities, save one.[3]

At the Pharmaceutical College of Baghdad University, UNSCOM looked
for Professor Shakir al-Akidy, a British-educated pharmacologist who sat on
Iraq's Scientific Research Council. Al-Akidy was not in his office, and the
inspectors, who lacked a photograph of him, did not tell the Iraqi minders
who they were seeking lest al-Akidy be warned and leave campus. So the inspectors wandered the campus all morning looking for al-Akidy and positioned themselves in building stairwells and exits to check the bags of Iraqis

to prevent the removal of items of interest to UNSCOM. An inspector at the top of a stairwell summoned Taylor when he found a bunch of Arabic documents in a professor's possession.[4] Taylor, whose Iraqi minder was off smoking a cigarette, suspected the man was al-Akidy because he was wearing a natty, perhaps even British suit. When Taylor greeted him by name, al-Akidy acknowledged his identity. Asking about the professor's papers, Taylor examined the clear plastic folder in his hands that had a driver's license application showing on both sides. Al-Akidy said it was his wife's license application, but as Taylor thumbed through the papers, Taylor's interpreter urgently nudged him in the back, their prearranged sign that he had seen something of interest. The interpreter had seen an Arabic report about animal trials conducted with ricin.[5]

Taylor invited al-Akidy to return to his office for a talk, where the professor gave Taylor an English version of the animal testing report, notes from his meetings with military officers, and other documents about the testing and production of ricin. As Taylor quickly but thoroughly questioned the man, two seasoned inspectors rapidly appeared to search the professor's office from top to bottom—checking the garbage can, beneath the carpet, every drawer or possible space for documents. In a stack of research papers, the inspectors found more reports about the production of ricin. By the time Taylor's minder returned from his break, Taylor had elicited from al-Akidy the gist of his ricin work, and UNSCOM had documentation of it. Taylor described al-Akidy as a nice, well-published scientist, but "by the time this was over, his lovely suit was drenched with sweat."[6]

Before the BW48 team cornered al-Akidy, Iraq had stated that it made roughly 10 liters of ricin from 100 kilograms of castor beans for a November 1990 field test with 155mm artillery shells. Al-Akidy's documents showed that in the fall of 1990 Iraq harvested a far larger castor bean crop to support the manufacture of ricin.[7] Despite extensive efforts, UNSCOM was unable to compile a complete account of Iraq's work with ricin.[8]

At the Chemical Engineering Design Center, the BW48 team uncovered old plans to make large fermenters for Al Hakam and Al Tuwaitha, showing Iraq's intent to expand production capacity at Al Hakam for biowarfare agents and at Al Tuwaitha perhaps for growth media to supply Al Hakam. During the mission, the Iraqis delayed the inspectors' entrance to a site and the team watched as smoke rose from the roof of a building inside the gates. The inspectors knew that documents related to their investigation were probably going up in flames, though they joked that the smoke signaled the selection of a new pope. Dismissing the inspectors' complaints, the Iraqis stated that a janitor just happened to be burning tar on the roof.[9]

Though UNSCOM made headway elaborating Iraq's activities with ricin, Iraq's work with viral agents remained unclear. The BW2 team first encountered the virologist Hazem Ali at Al Daura Foot and Mouth Disease Vaccine Plant, where the high-level containment features kept the inspectors preoccupied with the site's production capacity, not its research activities. Early inspectors had, however, quickly picked up on the considerable capacity at the Al Kindi Veterinary Vaccine Plant to produce viral agents via egg inoculation. When the inspectors later found a document indicating Iraq had tried to order egg incubators, suspicions heightened that Iraq might have engaged in the development and production of viral agents.[10] The virologist Ali later oversaw the development and manufacture of rapid detection kits for microbiological agents at the Al Razi Research Institute, a shop that Hussein Kamal set up in 1992 to house Ali's civilian work. There, a photograph of Ali clasping Saddam's hand attested to his political connections. As chief biological inspector Gabriele Kraatz-Wadsack put it, "he knew his science, and he must have done something to earn that handshake."[11] UNSCOM learned that Kamal was somewhat fixated on viruses. He appointed Ali to initiate a viral weapons research and development program at Al Daura using the same methodology Iraq employed with bacterial weapons, namely to focus on non-pathogenic surrogates to develop the ability to produce the agent at a laboratory and pilot scale and then to introduce virulent strains.[12] UNSCOM, however, did not know of Ali's viral research at Al Daura until after Iraq's mid-August 1995 confessions.

In the 1970s, Iraqi scientists published research papers on camel pox, but UNSCOM had nothing to indicate contemporary Iraqi interest in this virus until Ali volunteered to chief biological inspector David Kelly after Iraq's August 1995 admissions that he was working on it. To punctuate his revelation, Ali brought out a research notebook, supposedly his own, which documented work with two other viruses but did not mention camel pox. If not for Ali's words, Kelly admitted that "we would not have had an inkling of their camel pox work."[13] Chief biological inspector Richard Spertzel saw Ali's voluntary statement about his camel pox research as calculated to provide a plausible alibi for Iraq in case UNSCOM independently found evidence indicating Iraqi interest in or activity with smallpox, which UNSCOM did.[14] Ali's disclosure did little to calm the inspectors' concerns that Iraq's goal might have been the development of smallpox. According to a May 1994 U.S. Defense Intelligence Agency report, Russia shared smallpox with North Korea and Iraq in the late 1980s or early 1990s.[15] The Iraqis also insinuated to some inspectors that Iraq possessed variola, the virus that causes smallpox.[16]

On top of that, though the World Health Organization declared smallpox eradicated in 1979, the inspectors knew that Iraq continued to make smallpox vaccine at least until 1989 and perhaps into the 1990s. Iraq also tested the efficacy of its vaccine in rabbits into the 1990s and immunized its troops against both anthrax and smallpox at least until 1990 and apparently on into the decade. A research reprint on smallpox that bore Rihab Taha's signature was in the Haidar farm documents, so smallpox was of interest within Iraq's biowarfare program. Also, a Kelly-led team found an industrial freeze drier with "smallpox machine" written on it in Arabic at the repair shop of the State Company for Marketing Drugs and Medical Appliances, known as Kimadia. Kelly noted that this smallpox reference could have been to vaccinia virus, the live virus in the smallpox vaccine, or to the variola virus.[17]

In this context, the inspectors considered Ali's activity with camel pox a tune-up for work with smallpox itself.[18] Still, definitive evidence about Iraq's possession of smallpox and conclusive answers about Iraq's viral research activities never materialized.[19] Though the inspectors frequently dropped in with no notice on various biological facilities in Iraq over the next couple of years, their efforts to uncover the tentacles of various Iraqi bioweapons activities rarely brought anything of major significance to light.

SHIFTING POLITICAL WINDS BUFFET UNSCOM

Since UNSCOM's disarmament mission ran counter to the principle of state sovereignty at the heart of the United Nations (UN) Charter, the inspectorate, observed Ekeus, was virtually guaranteed an uneasy status within UN diplomatic circles. Ekeus toiled to maintain sufficient political support for robust inspections.[20] His task became more difficult as time passed. Some states wanted to lift the sanctions for humanitarian reasons, others to resume trade. By 1998, Moscow's strong interests in reestablishing trade with Baghdad had earned Russia the nickname the "Iraqi Interest Section of the Security Council."[21] Still other nations had different agendas. The United States, for example, sought an end to Saddam Hussein's regime. On March 26, 1997, U.S. Secretary of State Madeleine Albright stated Washington would not support the lifting of sanctions even if UNSCOM certified that Iraq met the disarmament requirements of Resolution 687.[22] Not only were Albright's remarks "questionable from the standpoint of international law," noted Ekeus, the practical effect was that the position "gave the Iraqis little incentive to cooperate with inspections."[23]

Pitted against a nation determined to hang onto the vestiges of its weapons programs and developments demanding priority from global leaders, UNSCOM faced mounting odds against it. "If the inspectors are capable and the inspected party has depth of resistance, then continuing Security Council support and enforcement is required. Failing such support the inspected state will always be able to outlast and overcome the inspectors," reasoned UNSCOM historian Stephen Black. "It is after all a contest between hundreds of inspectors and tens of thousands of cheaters."[24] In mid-1997, UNSCOM had documentary evidence that Iraqi leaders had ordered Iraq's strategic unconventional weapons capability to be maintained. Referring to Iraq's neverending supply of explanations to dismiss any evidence contradicting Iraq's declarations, Ekeus said, "They are very, very innovative. This is frustrating and irritating sometimes, but also amusing, highly amusing."[25] Though he retained his sense of humor, after years of wrangling with the Iraqis Ekeus resigned as chief of UNSCOM on May 1, 1997, noting shortly thereafter that UNSCOM had no choice but to stop in its tracks when Iraqis pulled weapons on inspectors.[26] When Australian diplomat Richard Butler took the reins of the inspectorate on July 1, he described Iraq's bioweapons activities as a "big concern," adding that "[i]n the hideous world of weapons of mass destruction, the biological stuff is just awful."[27]

From May to September 1997, UNSCOM pressed intensely, sending nine biological teams to Iraq.[28] In late July 1997, the UNSCOM 192/BW52 mission inspected several locations, including the headquarters of the Iraqi Air Force, which Baghdad labeled a sensitive site. Kraatz-Wadsack, the chief inspector, ran into objections from the Iraqis, who tried to limit their access first by reducing the number of inspectors who entered the building and then by denying entry to certain floors. Kraatz-Wadsack agreed that only the team's deputy and an interpreter would accompany her into the building's nerve center, the operations room. In a safe there, she found a document marked with the Arabic word for "special;" in Iraqi lingo, special weapons meant chemical and biological weapons. While the Iraqi minders stalled over Kraatz-Wadsack's request to copy this seven-page document, the interpreter helped her read and take notes on the document. Titled "I-I War Special Munitions," this report explained Iraq's expenditure of weapons during the Iran-Iraq War and included numbers that showed that Iraq had fired significantly fewer chemical rounds from 1983 to 1988 than declared to UNSCOM. In other words, this document was proof of a major problem with Iraq's chemical weapons declaration. Realizing this, the chief minder ripped the paper from Kraatz-Wadsack's hands. The ensuing verbal fracas culminated in the minders pulling Kalashnikovs on the inspectors, Kraatz-Wadsack's telephone call to Butler, and a compromise whereby the document was sealed and left in Iraqi custody, to be given to Butler during a scheduled visit to Iraq.[29]

For this maiden trip at the end of July 1997, Butler asked his biological, chemical, and missile teams to carve a path for progress, which they did at the working level only to have Butler accept terms more favorable to Iraq that Deputy Prime Minister Tariq Aziz dictated a few hours later. Stunned and offended at being undercut, the inspectors planned to depart Iraq the next morning. When Butler heard of this mutiny, he apologized to his inspectors, only to stray again from the text his staff carefully prepared for his closing meeting with Aziz. Speaking off the cuff, Butler got closer to the original agreement but also insinuated that he did not trust UNSCOM's senior experts. Afterward, the inspectors fumed.[30] Butler was off to a rocky start.

During his second trip to Baghdad in early August 1997, Aziz played hardball with Butler, telling him Iraq would never relinquish the report on the consumption of special munitions in the Iran-Iraq War and branding further discussions "useless."[31] On his third try in September, Butler firmly requested that Iraq provide a new declaration addressing the many remaining uncertainties about its bioweapons activities as well as those in the chemical and missile portfolios. Iraq had to substantiate its statements, Butler said.[32] Instead, Baghdad dealt Butler several rapid lessons in just how grueling it would be to pry loose the truth.

In July 1997, UNSCOM began to unravel a connection between a food testing laboratory at Baghdad University and Saddam's Special Security Organization, or SSO. This laboratory had declared thirty-eight items of equipment, but a biological monitoring team identified fifty-seven pieces of equipment that should have been declared on the laboratory's first floor alone. Before long, team chief Kraatz-Wadsack also found two well-fed, caged rats placed with food and water inside a desk drawer in an otherwise empty office that the Iraqis delayed opening for over an hour. The office also contained handwritten notes on animal experiments, but this laboratory had not declared it was conducting any animal tests. The Iraqis shoved forward a graduate student from Baghdad University's biology department to explain the circumstances, and her hysteria only escalated when Kraatz-Wadsack found that other desk drawers contained unidentified frozen material in vials and growth media that she said she planned to destroy, along with the rats, in the laboratory's autoclaves because only one was functioning over at the university. Kraatz-Wadsack and her monitors dropped by the university, where ten of the biology department's eleven autoclaves were in working order. The monitors remained suspicious about what was really happening at the food testing laboratory. A Spertzel-led interview mission, UNSCOM 193/BW56, raised the matter with the dean of the biology department at Baghdad University, Alice Melkonian, but did not decipher the situation.[33]

Chief biological inspector Diane Seaman returned to the food testing laboratory on September 25, 1997, entering via the back door to avoid losing time to the exchange of pleasantries over tea with its director. She literally ran into two men, one toting a briefcase. They ran back inside with Seaman in hot pursuit. She seized and searched the briefcase. The documents inside on SSO letterhead pertained to the SSO's program to test Saddam's food and clothing to prevent his assassination, including a list of hospitals in the testing program. While Iraq should have declared this activity, which involved pathogens and animal testing, Saddam's personal testing program was not of major consequence to the bioweapons program.[34]

Another intriguing item surfaced during a September 1997 inspection at Al Faw, the engineering design center that drew the plans for Al Hakam. While reviewing designs for fermentation plants, Kraatz-Wadsack plucked an incriminating and controversial record from the center's files. Dated April 1995, this document detailed an Iraqi trip to Moscow that month to tour a single-cell protein plant and discuss the purchase of a new fifty-cubic-meter production line. Iraq also asked Russia for high-caliber ventilation equipment, which was clearly not required for single-cell protein production. Sanctions prohibited these sales.[35] Butler wrote Russia's UN Ambassador Sergei Lavrov two letters, the first asking for an explanation of why Iraq was exploring such an import with Russia and the second requesting that Russia allow an UNSCOM team access to investigate the matter. Lavrov's reply to both letters was, more or less, "get lost."[36] Like some other countries, Russia's more pressing interests had long since veered toward doing business with Baghdad, regardless of sanctions. Iraq owed Moscow from $7 to $9 billion for military equipment purchased prior to the 1991 Gulf War.[37]

According to a veteran UNSCOM staffer, as the "finds" of UNSCOM became less spectacular, Security Council support for the hunt for the remains of Iraq's prohibited weapons capabilities wavered. In short, "sanctions fatigue" arrived in the mid- to late-1990s:

> As time went on, the Iraqis played their hand with more skill. This wasn't just politics between the UN and Iraq it was also the Security Council and the Secretary-General's office and whoever else Iraq could interest in its views. The overall sentiment was that this was dragging on much longer than it should. Security Council members would ask, what is UNSCOM still looking for?[38]

To those impatient for the removal of sanctions, progress was barely perceptible. Some also saw the remaining issues as small, technical details and posited that in trying circumstances sometimes victory is best declared once most of the problem has been addressed.[39]

Even the inspectorate's staunchest supporters, such as the United States and the United Kingdom, had to give other matters priority. For example, the war in Bosnia and its horrific ethnic cleansing campaign began dominating headlines in 1992 and drew peacekeeping intervention from the United Nations Protection Force and eventually the active involvement of North Atlantic Treaty Organization forces.[40] When another gruesome genocide campaign erupted in Rwanda in 1994, first the French government and then the UN intervened to restore peace and order.[41] At times, the troubles in Iraq looked modest by comparison to events elsewhere, which contributed to the increasingly tepid political support for UNSCOM.

Iraq handed Spertzel, who took a team into Iraq to stalk the origins of Iraq's bioweapons program, yet another full, final, and complete biological declaration on September 11, 1997. After the mission, Spertzel's team took two days in Bahrain to review the 639-page document and expeditiously pronounced it somewhat more coherent but still wanting.[42] The evaluations of Spertzel's team and that of an outside group of experts, discussed further on, featured prominently in Butler's October 6 report to the Security Council. This report underlined Iraq's failure to provide any new documentation on its past bioweapons activities and listed eleven areas of noncompliance concern, including the understated production of bulk agent and mismatched data on biological munitions made and destroyed. UNSCOM concluded that the new

Iraqi declaration did not "give a remotely credible account of Iraq's biological warfare programme" and was "unredeemed by progress or any approximation of the known facts about Iraq's programme."[43] Rising to UNSCOM's recommendation that the Security Council demand that Iraq submit a full declaration once and for all, the U.S. government prepared a resolution that the British backed but that drew abstaining votes from China, Egypt, France, Kenya, and Russia. With such evidence of the fissuring of the Security Council's support for UNSCOM, Iraq became more obstinate.[44]

IRAQ UPS THE ANTE

On October 29, Iraq announced that it would not tolerate U.S. inspectors on UNSCOM teams and barred two incoming U.S. inspectors. Next, Iraq booted six UNSCOM inspectors with U.S. citizenship from Iraq on November 13.[45] Since the authority to set policy on inspection team composition and the conduct of inspections rested with UNSCOM, Butler pulled his personnel from the country. UNSCOM could monitor some activities remotely via the video cameras at numerous facilities, but the Iraqis blocked some cameras and moved equipment. For example, Iraq removed two 22-liter fermenters from the view of a camera at Al Tuwaitha, prompting UNSCOM to raise concerns with Iraq about their location. The Iraqis then fed the media information about the UNSCOM tag numbers on this equipment before leading camera crews to the storage area at Al Tuwaitha where they conveniently saw the tagged fermenters. The press, which Iraq converted into pseudo-inspectors in its public relations campaign, reported that Baghdad was doing nothing wrong. In short, the Iraqis cooked up this situation to emphasize their frequent argument that UNSCOM was making a big deal out of nothing.[46]

Terming Iraq's attempts to dictate the makeup of inspection teams a "material breach" of the 1991 ceasefire conditions worthy of military reprisal, the United States and Great Britain sent aircraft carriers to the region. On November 21, 1997, UNSCOM commissioners met in emergency session to advise the Security Council how to improve the effectiveness of UNSCOM operations. That very day, Iraq readmitted UNSCOM inspectors, including four Americans.[47] The inspectors scrambled to track down various items of equipment and resume normal operations.[48] Right away, however, they faced another problem. On November 23, Iraq declared Saddam's palaces, ministries, and other so-called sensitive sites exempt from UNSCOM inspections.[49] The presidential facilities were known to be under the control of Iraq's special security forces, which UNSCOM believed to be responsible for executing Iraq's programs to cloak prohibited weapons and related materials and records. Some said that Iraq raised barriers against U.S. inspectors and on access to these sites because UNSCOM's biological inspectors were getting too close for Baghdad's comfort.[50] Once again, Iraq was ignoring the terms of Resolution 687 to provide UNSCOM full and unconditional access to all locations in Iraq.[51] Both Butler and UN Secretary-General Kofi Annan tried to arbitrate the crisis.

During these talks UNSCOM went about its business as best it could, continuing a series of inspections to re-inventory the dual-use equipment at Iraq's biological sites and check against prohibited activity. UNSCOM also investigated the possibility that Iraq had tested biological agents on humans, an issue long raised in intelligence reports. Some of the aerosolization chambers Iraq imported were large enough to hold big animals or humans.[52] A photograph from the Haidar farm album showed lesions on a human arm, without explanation. The lesions could have resulted from a worker's accidental exposure to an agent, and Taha eventually stated that a staffer working with a fermenter at Salman Pak experienced a cutaneous exposure to anthrax.[53] Or, the photograph might have been from a human test.[54] A high-level defector claimed that on July 1 and August 15, 1995, Iraqi General Service agents took political prisoners from Abu Ghraib prison to a military facility at Al Haditha to be test subjects for chemical and biological agents. At Butler's request, Kraatz-Wadsack led a subset of the UNSCOM 227 team to the prison in mid-January 1998. Abu Ghraib had reasonably comprehensive records on its prisoners for other years but none for the 1994–1995 time frame. The team also came up empty-handed at another prison and at five other sites where they searched for documentation of human testing. Thereafter, Iraq again broke off cooperation with UNSCOM.[55]

With Baghdad standing its ground, the United States threatened military force to compel Iraqi compliance. The United States confined the goal of punitive attacks to "seriously diminishing" Iraq's weapons of mass destruction capabilities, but a U.S. push to establish an automatic trigger of Iraqi misbehavior that would initiate military strikes floundered in the Security Council.[56] Annan went to Baghdad, striking a bargain with Aziz on February 23, 1998, that the secretary general stated Saddam would keep. "I think I can do business with him," Annan said of Saddam.[57] The deal stipulated that inspectors would go to the presidential sites with senior diplomats in tow, ostensibly to be witness to anything found and ensure that UNSCOM was not treading too heavily on Iraq's sovereign right to protect its national security.[58]

Though the terms of the Annan agreement applied only to eight presidential sites, this deal unmistakably undercut the authority of the inspectorate by implying that UNSCOM inspectors could not be trusted to do their work without diplomatic babysitters.[59] Moreover, Annan's terms of access, observed Ekeus, were "a parody" of those Ekeus obtained in the summer of 1992.[60] When the inspectors finally went to the presidential sites in April 1998 nothing was there save the spectacle of Saddam's ultra-luxurious abodes.[61] Butler's April 16, 1998, report to the Security Council concluded that Iraq manufactured the four-month crisis, failed to heed Security Council demands to allow access to sites, and in general so gummed up UNSCOM inspections that "virtually no progress in verifying disarmament [could] be reported."[62] The report also chided Iraq for attempting "disarmament by declaration," short-hand for Baghdad's incantations that Iraq simply no longer had any prohibited weapons.[63]

OUTSIDE TECHNICAL EXPERTS REINFORCE UNSCOM'S VIEW

From its earliest days, UNSCOM routinely called in panels of outside experts to review the status of its activities or Iraqi declarations in all areas, continuing the practice into the mid- and late-1990s. A group of outside experts determined in March 1997 that Iraq had

- Not properly declared its imports for the bioweapons program
- Under-reported production of bulk biowarfare agent
- Not made the agent aflatoxin as it described
- Not produced enough evidence on the destruction of bulk agent and filled munitions
- Not given UNSCOM a comprehensive account of the bioweapons program[64]

The panel's conclusions virtually mirrored those of UNSCOM's biological staff.

Six months later, UNSCOM invited fifteen experts from thirteen nations to New York to review Iraq's biological full, final, and complete declaration of September 1997. Unanimously, the outside experts pronounced the lengthy declaration to be "incomplete," with "significant inaccuracies" and "outstanding problems [that] are numerous and grave" concerning the full scope of Iraq's bioweapons program, from planning and definition through production and weapons testing to the ultimate destruction of the agent and munitions. The experts proposed a review of all evidence associated with the program—UNSCOM reports, videos, photographs, records of physical evidence, documents from Iraq and other sources, and testimony from Iraqi personnel.[65] Iraq usually glossed over the negative assessments of these panels, but Baghdad seized this recommendation in an effort to boost the stature of outside technical reviews.

After the fall of 1995, Iraq repeatedly blamed the lack of progress in resolving outstanding issues about Iraq's bioweapons activities on the bias of UNSCOM's inspectors. Expecting outside experts to be more sympathetic and conclude that Iraq had given a reasonably full and accurate account of its biowarfare activities, Baghdad really escalated the pressure for independent and neutral experts to assess the situation following the destruction of Al Hakam in mid-1996. Iraq's proposals found a receptive audience among those who did not understand the significance of the outstanding issues, who had other reasons for wanting the repeal of sanctions, and who questioned why UNSCOM did not just close the biological file.[66] In a December 1997 meeting in Baghdad Butler and Aziz revived the concept of high-level outside reviews, which Butler christened technical evaluation meetings (TEMs). Butler initially accepted disadvantageous terms for the TEMs, but after coaching from his staff secured agreement that UNSCOM would recruit experts and prepare a background dossier for them about the unresolved matters. Iraq was free to present additional data during TEMs.[67]

Two TEMs convened simultaneously in February 1998, one on the special missile warheads for chemical and biological agents and another on Iraq's activities with the nerve agent VX. This latter TEM examined a controversy that clouded UNSCOM's waning years, the apparently contradictory test results from U.S., Swiss, and French laboratories of samples taken from the remnants of missile warheads dug out of a pit at Al Taji. Iraq and those who backed lifting of sanctions intimated that UNSCOM had planted incriminating evidence, that its sampling procedures were untrustworthy, or that the U.S. analysis was rigged.[68] The VX TEM concluded that all three laboratories found VX degradation products, which was at odds with Iraq's declaration that the warheads it destroyed unilaterally were never filled with poison gas.[69]

Butler put the biological TEM in the hands of a Swedish chemical defense expert who was on the VX TEM and had a flair for diplomacy and experience as an inspector, Ake Sellstrom. The panel seated a broad spectrum of technical experts from around the world. First, the UNSCOM biological staff briefed the experts in New York City for six days, working from thick books of background materials and carefully stating the source of each piece of data. Sellstrom then assigned various experts the lead on subtopics.[70]

Though Iraq wanted the biological TEM held in Baghdad, to lessen the potential for publicity the panel went to Vienna from March 20 to 27, 1998. Lt. Gen. Amir Al Sa'adi headed the Iraqi delegation of fewer than ten. Several senior staff in the Iraqi biowarfare program, such as Taha, Technical Research Center Director Ahmed Murtada, and Nassir Al-Hindawi, were absent. Though other Iraqi technical staffers were present, Al Sa'adi assumed center stage, saying that he would answer all questions, no matter how technical.[71] On the first day, Al Sa'adi tried to bully the Chinese expert, Guo Anfeng.[72] Also, one of the experts queried Al Sa'adi for about two hours about Iraq's weaponization of biowarfare agents, expending all of his prepared questions. Later realizing that Al Sa'adi's long-winded replies contained few, if any, definitive answers, that evening this expert asked Hamish Killip to question Al Sa'adi. The next day, Killip probed Al Sa'adi for hours on just one issue related to weaponization to demonstrate to the outside experts how the Iraqis had mastered the art of empty verbosity.[73]

One by one over the five days, the other experts led the questioning on their assigned topics. Among Al Sa'adi's more arresting statements was that Iraq really planned to fill the drop tanks that it tested for use with Mirage F-1 aircraft with botulinum toxin rather than with anthrax. This statement implied that Iraq would have needed to make larger amounts of botulinum toxin because Iraq planned to make a dozen drop tanks that could hold 2,000 liters of agent apiece. The Iraqis also upset another applecart when they announced that they considered the Zubaidy device to be ineffective. Iraqi documents stated that Iraq had successfully tested the Zubaidy with an anthrax simulant.[74] The Zubaidy used German precision-crafted perforated cylinders, so the inspectors considered this device quite capable of disseminating biowarfare agents.[75]

Occasionally, Al Sa'adi turned to his technical experts for information or they openly disputed him about an answer. Sellstrom viewed these mini-disputes as a deliberate tactic to convey the sense that the truth was being told.[76] However, little clarity emerged. Presented with the panel's calculations about the quantity and types of agents produced, the Iraqis fumbled for technically coherent answers, sometimes even getting confused consulting their own documents. The Iraqis persisted with the tale that they rolled glass flasks daily to make aflatoxin though this method rendered it almost impossible to have made the quantity of agent they declared.[77] Al Sa'adi fielded the panel's questions while simultaneously complaining that Iraq could not afford to send its leading experts to Vienna to provide thorough answers. Unwittingly, Al Sa'adi fed the impression that Iraq was trying to skate through the evaluation on rhetoric.[78] As this farce unfolded before the outside experts, Kelly observed, "They were probably more horrified than any of the UNSCOM inspectors. It really was an amazing performance."[79] With so many questions unanswered, the panel requested that Iraq supply more information, and Iraq provided additional documents about two months later.[80]

The April 1, 1998, TEM report charged that Iraq's biological declaration was "incomplete and inadequate" with "major mistakes, inconsistencies and gaps." The experts said that the Iraqis had provided "no additional confidence in the veracity and expanse" of their declaration and did not supply "any new technical information of substance."[81] The panel characterized the Iraqi accounts as not "technically coherent," and complained that Al Sa'adi gave most responses at the "general and political level" or said that Iraq would respond later.[82] Practically nothing about Iraq's account made sense to the TEM experts—not the rationale for the bioweapons program and its expansion; the purported management of it; the reasons the Iraqis selected agents for research, development, and production; the discrepancies surrounding growth media, production capacity, and the quality and quantity of agents supposedly produced; the agents that Iraq said it put in certain weapons systems; or the contradictions in the number of special missile warheads reportedly produced and destroyed. The report also scoffed at Iraq's claim that its bioweapons scientists were not very skilled, noting that they managed to make considerable progress in a relatively short period of time.[83] Furthermore, the TEM experts stated that it was "absurd" for Iraq to continue to deny that many individuals working from a coordinated plan were necessary to execute its concealment strategy to hide the bioweapons program, as evidenced by forged documents, altered materials, and shifting verbal accounts.[84]

Finally, the experts concluded that Iraq's material balance gave "no confidence" that Iraq had destroyed its weapons, bulk agent, media, and seed stocks. The panel determined that Iraq's declaration did "not provide a clear understanding of the current status of the BW programme or *whether, or when*, it was terminated."[85] When composing the report, experts from the countries expected to be friendliest to Iraq actually became Baghdad's harshest critics. One such expert insisted on the "whether, or when" phrasing.[86] Some viewed the consensus TEM assessment as tougher than UNSCOM's evaluation.[87] While it was important for scientific reasons, Ekeus noted that the TEM's unanimity was of even greater political consequence because it stymied countries, such as Russia, that were pressing to remove sanctions.[88] Butler highlighted the panel's conclusions to the Security Council in his April 1998 report. However, he also voiced concern that "[t]he technical evaluation meetings have become an extremely time-consuming process for the Commission and have slowed down and, in some cases, led to the postponement of important field work."[89]

UNSCOM'S POLITICAL SUPPORT SPIRALS DOWNWARD

Undaunted, in late April 1998 Iraq's Aziz wrote the Security Council a letter stating that sanctions must be lifted "without any restrictions or conditions" and renewing Iraq's threat to stop cooperating with UNSCOM.[90] Trying to regain some political momentum, in early June UNSCOM gave an unprecedented two-day briefing to the Security Council on the outstanding issues in each area of proscribed weaponry, including a litany of verification problems with every aspect of Iraq's bioweapons program.[91] "We made a serious attempt to tell them in practical and technical terms what this was about, what we did and didn't know, using all sorts of data and satellite photos to illustrate certain issues," recalled an UNSCOM staffer. Nothing changed in the Security Council, where "gradually the burden had shifted from Iraq having to prove that it had disarmed to UNSCOM having to prove that there was still something to find."[92]

With Security Council support flagging, Butler traveled to Baghdad in June to lay out his "road map" for progress, which essentially consisted of having the most senior UNSCOM and Iraqi personnel work out the biggest unresolved issues. Aziz insisted that Butler explain his "top down" concept, which apparently flustered Butler.[93] Though he had just complained to the Security Council that the meetings of outside experts detracted from UNSCOM's inspections, Butler agreed to convene another such group to examine the outstanding issues in biology, starting with the material balance problems in biological weapons.[94]

Reprising his role, Sellstrom took a second group of experts to Baghdad in mid-July 1998 to address Iraq's response to the April 1 TEM report. The panel was designated UNSCOM 250/BW69. Sellstrom adopted a more assertive approach to this TEM, sequentially raising each of the eighteen outstanding issues, noting what the Iraqi declaration said, and then asking the Iraqis for official information to support their statement. Each time, the Iraqis came forward with what little they had to back up their account and Sellstrom recessed the experts to consider the evidence, intoning before their departure that the Security Council, indeed the world, would hear this panel's judgment.[95] Al Sa'adi generally argued that Iraq had no additional documents but that need not matter either because Iraq had destroyed all biological weapons, bulk agent, and materials or because whatever might be left, growth media or warfare agent, would no longer be effective. In the face of UNSCOM's sample analysis showing anthrax residues in at least seven SCUD warheads, though Iraq declared filling only five warheads with that agent, Al Sa'adi posited that the fragments might have come from one warhead, not multiple warheads. Taha also tried to justify the finding of anthrax in samples taken from Al Daura, where Iraq declared producing only botulinum toxin, by explaining that cross contamination could have occurred from a 2,550-liter tank used to transfer agent from Al Hakam to Al Daura.[96]

Moreover, Aziz took the unusual step of asking to see Sellstrom on the third day of the TEM. Aziz indicated that it would be better if Sellstrom changed his approach, but Sellstrom persisted.[97] This expert panel was just as unfavorable as its predecessors about the caliber of Iraq's biological declaration and Iraq's lack of forthrightness with UNSCOM. They concluded that it was not possible to confirm a material balance for growth media or for Iraq's production of bulk biowarfare agent. Nor could the Iraqi accounts about R-400 bombs and biological SCUD warheads be verified. The report also questioned Iraq's statements about other biological delivery systems such as drop tanks and commercial insecticide generators.[98]

Not long after this TEM report, UNSCOM's fortunes began to spiral downward precipitously. Arguing that Iraq had eliminated its nuclear weapons program, at the end of July Russia introduced a resolution in the Security Council to curtail UNSCOM's activities to ongoing monitoring and verification alone. Though the measure did not pass, it signaled Russia's determination to rescind the sanctions.[99] In Baghdad, Aziz told Butler on August 3 that Iraq would allow UNSCOM to continue monitoring dual-use facilities but would cease assistance with the investigation of past weapons activities. Aziz also stated that Iraq would stop cooperating altogether if the Security Council did not lift sanctions in October.[100] UNSCOM objected to the rationale behind Iraq's threats, namely that if UNSCOM could not prove that Iraq did not retain prohibited weapons, then Iraq must be in compliance with Resolution 687. Iraq quit working with UNSCOM on August 5. While deploring Iraq's decision, Annan attempted to resurrect Iraqi cooperation by suggesting a "comprehensive review" that would "more closely" involve the Iraqis.[101] Annan's trial balloon fell flat in London and Washington.[102]

On the heels of these developments, UNSCOM inspector Scott Ritter unexpectedly resigned. Ritter headed UNSCOM's efforts to decipher, explain, expose, and frustrate if not countermand Iraq's concealment and deception activities for prohibited weapons systems. He claimed that UNSCOM was on the verge of getting its hands on Iraq's illicit weapons but could not do that since the Security Council and the United States would not give the inspectors sufficient backing. Ritter first asserted that the U.S. government repeatedly delayed or blocked inspection plans between November 1997 and August 1998, then later charged that UNSCOM was a pawn of U.S. intelligence agencies.[103] Then an Israeli newspaper reported that Ritter shared intelligence with Israel about Iraq, making Ritter a gift to Iraqi propagandists, who converted his comment "into proof that [Iraq's] charges of Israeli and American espionage were true."[104] Iraq quickly accused Ritter of being an American spy. Meanwhile, UNSCOM inspectors believed that Ritter's activities and manner of resignation hastened UNSCOM's disintegration.[105]

From that point, the fall of 1998 mimicked the previous autumn, with a negative UNSCOM report to the Security Council, more Iraqi stonewalling of UNSCOM, threatened U.S. and British military reprisals, and Annan's intercession to break the impasse. Of this political firestorm, Charles Duelfer, then UNSCOM's executive deputy director said, "There were powerful forces at work, and UNSCOM was in the middle."[106] On October 6, UNSCOM reported that while disarmament work with Iraq's chemical and missile programs might be nearing its conclusion, the same could not be said for Iraq's biological weapons program. Dropping a reminder that Iraq for years completely denied having a bioweapons program until UNSCOM's investigation established that it did, the report advised against falling for Iraq's ploy to shift the burden of proof to UNSCOM to demonstrate that Iraq was still withholding weapons, pertinent capabilities, and evidence.[107] To illustrate, UNSCOM's biological monitoring teams identified and tagged some 150 undeclared pieces of dual-use equipment from April to October 1998.[108] On September 9, the Security Council rebuffed Iraq's extortion attempt by deciding to withhold any further status review that could lead to the removal of sanctions until Iraq resumed full cooperation with UNSCOM. The Security Council also announced "its willingness to consider" Annan's proposed comprehensive review and invited his counsel on the matter.[109]

While mediating with Iraq, Annan publicly forecast a grim future for UNSCOM. "I personally believe, as I think a lot of Security Council members believe with 100 percent certainty," said Annan, "that Iraq being fully disarmed is never going to be possible."[110] At the end of October 1998, just as the Security Council approved Annan's proposed comprehensive review, Iraq suspended all cooperation with UNSCOM and ordered U.S. inspectors to depart Iraq.[111] The Security Council denounced Iraq on November 5, and six days later UNSCOM withdrew all of its personnel from Baghdad.[112] With inbound U.S. aircraft carriers accentuating the threat of military strikes, Iraq blinked on November 14. Aziz sent Annan a letter agreeing to allow the inspectors to return, appending Iraq's terms for a comprehensive review.[113]

The July biological TEM recommended that no new assessment of Iraq's biological declaration should be attempted unless and until Iraq provided new data, so on November 18, 1998, Butler wrote Aziz requesting new documentation, materials, declarations, or explanations.[114] Inside UNSCOM, the inspectors sensed that this political storm was unlikely to blow over, with one noting that the French, Russian, and Chinese diplomats had their "knives . . . out for UNSCOM."[115] As inspections resumed, Russia unsuccessfully bid again for a Security Council resolution to halt UNSCOM's investigation of past weapons programs and change how UNSCOM conducted inspections.[116]

THE LAST HURRAH

In the fall of 1998, Spertzel left UNSCOM and Butler appointed Kraatz-Wadsack to head UNSCOM's biological desk. That December, UNSCOM sent three final biological teams into Iraq. UNSCOM 253/BW70 obtained no new information about Iraq's biowarfare activities and concluded that many worrisome uncertainties remained about Iraq's biological research and development work, management and expansion of the program, rationale for the bioweapons program, and doctrine for the use of germ weapons. Over two tons of growth media was still unaccounted for, and two missions, UNSCOM 256/BW71 and UNSCOM 260/BW72, addressed this matter.[117]

One unsettled growth media issue was the fate of 2.5 tons of yeast extract that Iraq imported from H.E. Daniel Ltd. in 1989 and 1990. This company's labels were found on the plastic liner bags inside some 25-kilogram containers of growth media located at facilities possibly linked to Iraq's production of biowarfare agents. After exploring the matter at Samarra State Company for Drug Industries, the BW71 inspectors concluded that the lion's share of the yeast extract was consumed making a commercial product. Though Samarra Drug Industries also sent small amounts of the media to facilities involved in Iraq's bioweapons program (for example, Al Razi Institute), the remaining yeast extract did not make a significant contribution to Iraq's bioweapons activities. The inspectors were unable to determine why the H.E. Daniel Ltd. labels were on the bags inside the growth media containers.[118]

During the BW70 mission, which Kraatz-Wadsack led, bioweapons inspector Rod Barton spent over two days posing questions and allowing Taha, her deputy Abdul Rahman Thamer, a security official, and Murtada to talk all day and late into the night about evacuating critical facilities during the war and taking the growth media to a school at Al Asmara, which was subsequently looted. In vivid detail, they spoke of finding the place knee-deep in growth media and other debris and of cleaning up the mess. The Iraqis said that the chaos after the war made an investigation of the theft impractical, so there was no police report on the crime even though roughly a half ton to a ton of growth media was supposedly stolen from the school. At that point, Barton established that growth media was never stored at Al Asmara, via three documents from the Haidar farm cache about the police investigation of the ransacking of the school. These reports listed the items stored there and exactly what was stolen, but did not mention growth media. The next morning, Taha countered that the growth media was not on the list because it was considered such a sensitive matter. Barton rejoined that one top-secret report was circulated only to Murtada, whose handwritten notes were in the margins, and surely Taha would have conveyed the actual circumstances to her boss. "Then they changed their story to something else that was utter nonsense," said Barton. "They were caught in another lie and they knew it."[119]

In large part, the last UNSCOM biological weapons inspections greatly resembled the first. The inspectors assiduously searched for the truth about Iraq's bioweapons program, and Taha and her cohorts spun tall tales to hide it. UNSCOM's report to the Security Council, filed December 15, stated that Iraq did not keep its mid-November pledge to provide documents and access to resolve outstanding issues in the missile, chemical, and biological areas. The report indicated that many troubling gaps remained in Iraq's accounts. UNSCOM, therefore, did not have sufficient new information to enable a comprehensive review.[120]

On December 16, UNSCOM's staff and UN humanitarian workers flew to Bahrain.[121] That day, U.S. President Bill Clinton and British Prime Minister Tony Blair decided to proceed with the air strikes against Baghdad.[122] Over roughly seventy hours, U.S. and British forces struck one hundred targets in Iraq's political and military infrastructure. UNSCOM had identified many of the sites hit as possibly being involved in Iraq's weapons of mass destruction programs, including Al Tikrit, Samarra, Al Kindi, and Baghdad University's Biological Research Center.[123] Operation Desert Fox, as this campaign was called, ended on December 19.

UNSCOM GETS THE GUILLOTINE

When charges emerged that the U.S. government, with the help of UNSCOM, had installed an eavesdropping device in UNSCOM's Baghdad office, the propaganda scales tipped radically in Iraq's favor.[124] For some, this revelation added believability to claims that the underlying purpose of UNSCOM's investigation of Iraq's concealment and deception activities was to spy on Iraq's military forces and security services on behalf of the United States, aiding U.S. plans to unseat Saddam. From the onset, according to media reports, CIA agents were on UNSCOM's teams.[125] The U.S. government first professed innocence then asserted that UNSCOM had no knowledge of the secret operation to plant U.S. intelligence agents and equipment in it.[126]

On the counteroffensive, UNSCOM denied awareness of any U.S. intelligence infiltration. Explaining that it assessed inspectors on the basis of their skills, UNSCOM allowed that some intelligence officers might have been on its teams, but not because of their organizational affiliation. Moreover, UNSCOM certainly did not plan its missions in conjunction with any intelligence agency.[127] Reportedly persuaded that UNSCOM was complicit in the U.S. abuse of the inspectorate, Annan pushed Butler to resign. One of Annan's advisers anonymously stated, "The United Nations cannot be party to an operation to overthrow one of its member states. In the most fundamental way, that is what is wrong with the UNSCOM operation."[128]

Butler tried to salvage the situation by hurriedly releasing what became known as the "Final Compendium Report" even as Security Council votes swung to support a Canadian proposal to bypass the planned comprehensive review and instead create three panels to consider humanitarian issues in Iraq, the disposition of prisoners of war and Kuwaiti property, and the disarmament charter and future monitoring and verification arrangements. The

262-page compendium report catalogued countless Iraqi actions that looked yet were anything but innocuous. The biological section of the report reprised many of UNSCOM's familiar statements about the incompleteness of the Iraqi declaration and how many facets of Iraq's pertinent and proscribed activities (including weapons manufacture, testing, and disposal) UNSCOM could not confirm because Iraq failed to facilitate verification. The report stated that "except in some limited areas, documentation provided by Iraq is grossly inadequate for verification" of Iraq's biological declaration and that "[t]he Commission has little or no confidence in Iraq's accounting for proscribed items for which physical evidence is lacking or inconclusive."[129]

In addition to the uncertainty of whether the Iraqis used the unaccounted for growth media to make biowarfare agents, UNSCOM asserted that Iraq "considerably understated" its production of bulk agent. For example, the Iraqis reported obtaining reasonable levels of botulinum toxin when they used thioglycollate broth at half of the manufacturer's recommended strength. Therefore, had the Iraqis produced botulinum toxin according to their own formula, they could have manufactured far more than they declared. Iraq's explanation for making just a small amount of *Clostridium perfringens* was that they did not have enough of the right growth media or available personnel to make more. However, the company that supplied Iraq with significant quantities of peptone gave UNSCOM inspectors sales documents showing that Iraq had plenty of peptone to have made much more *Clostridium perfringens*.[130]

The report detailed many instances in which the Iraqis very deliberately deceived the inspectors and attempted to hide and preserve capabilities pertinent to a germ warfare program.[131] Referring several times to Iraq's claims to have "obliterated" its bioweapons program in 1991, the report baldly stated, "[t]here is little confidence that [Iraq's biological weapons] programme has been ended."[132] Iraq certainly handcuffed the inspectors with its efforts to keep weapons-relevant capabilities in the nuclear, chemical, and missile areas, but the compendium report implied that Iraq's biological malfeasance was the most grievous.[133]

UNSCOM's report made little difference in the overall trajectory of the unfolding political events; the Security Council rippled with negatively tinged talk about UNSCOM.[134] Moscow's diplomats were particularly vocal. Russian political counselor Vladimir Dedouchkine quipped, "UNSCOM is history. It's a plain fact that UNSCOM cannot even think of trying to come back."[135] The Security Council adopted Canada's tri-panel approach to chart a course out of the stalemate. Brazil's Celso Amorim, the Security Council president, headed the panels. The disarmament panel was to find a way "to re-establish an effective disarmament/ongoing monitoring and verification regime in Iraq."[136] Butler announced in early February 1999 that he would step down in June, but with his inspectors unable to watch Iraq's dual-use facilities closely, Butler warned in March that Iraq could mount a "crash" resumption of its biowarfare program. Using a chemical agent to make his point, Butler cautioned, "They can make aspirin before lunch, and they can be making mustard gas after lunch."[137]

Echoing Butler's view, at the end of March the Amorin disarmament panel acknowledged that "Iraq possesses the capability and knowledge base through which biological warfare agents could be produced quickly and in volume."[138] Noting the outstanding issues in all prohibited weapons areas, the Amorim panel urged that monitoring and verification continue because Iraq was not providing any information, exculpatory or otherwise, to the inspectors. The panel recommended preserving the inspectors' full rights by having them retain a complete array of inspection tools and full access to all Iraqi sites, while at the same time altering the "intensity, frequency, intrusiveness, and methods" of inspections to accomplish them "with due regard to Iraqi sovereignty, dignity and sensitivities."[139] The inspectorate would continue to derive its authority directly from the Security Council, but its advisory commission would be reformulated, and the Security Council would have a say in its membership. More inspectors would be brought aboard, but the Security Council might also review who was hired. The Amorim panel stated that these new "reinforced" arrangements "would be, if anything, more intensive than the one so far practiced."[140] However, to UNSCOM insiders and watchers, the Amorim report effectively ended the level of independence seen in UNSCOM's operations. This restructuring paved the way for the increased politicization of the inspectorate and the gradual substitution of an equitable geographic distribution of personnel as the defining characteristic of the inspector corps rather than the premium UNSCOM had placed on inspectors having the necessary technical skills for the job.

The Security Council quickly approved the Amorim plan for a new United Nations Monitoring, Verification, and Inspection Commission, or UNMOVIC, but Aziz announced in mid-April 1999 that Iraq would not go along with the new process.[141] Eight months went by before the UN passed Resolution 1284 on December 17, 1999, replacing UNSCOM with UNMOVIC.[142] Russia rejected

Annan's nomination of Ekeus to lead UNMOVIC, and France and China argued that a new organization needed new blood.[143] In March 2000, Hans Blix, the former director-general of the International Atomic Energy Agency, became UNMOVIC's chief. Iraq, however, did not allow the return of inspectors until the United States and the United Kingdom threatened hostilities, so UNMOVIC did not set foot in Iraq until November 27, 2002, almost four years after UNSCOM departed Iraq.[144]

Ever outspoken, Butler blamed the demise of UNSCOM directly on Russia, China, and France, which fussed about small quantities of VX in the testing samples left behind in UNSCOM's Baghdad laboratory during the hasty departure in mid-December 1998. By insisting on analysis of these test standards, this trio of nations hinted that UNSCOM's technicians spiked their analytical results. Butler was particularly critical of Russia's role and also observed that Annan had it out for UNSCOM because it was "too independent."[145]

Other factors surely contributed to UNSCOM's downfall, including the assertions that UNSCOM was a pawn of the U.S. policy advocating regime change in Iraq, the unabashed push of Russia and France to end sanctions on Iraq, the technical complexity of the issues that UNSCOM inspectors were trying to parse, and the desire to alleviate the humanitarian plight of Iraqi civilians. Given the artfully chosen words and the ready assurances of a continued, vigorous pursuit of Iraqi compliance with Resolution 687, some nations may not have even perceived a significant difference between the structure and authority of UNSCOM and its successor, UNMOVIC. Whatever the reasons for the UN's switch to UNMOVIC, nothing can diminish the remarkable feat that UNSCOM's inspectors pulled off under the most trying of circumstances, the exposure of Iraq's covert bioweapons program to the world.

8 LESSONS EXPERIENCED I: INSPECTION PREREQUISITES

"LESSONS LEARNED" is the customary phrase to denote the knowledge gained from an event or process; it implies careful, critical examination of the activities to distill the lessons that should yield changes to policies, programs, or practices. Lessons can be positive or negative, and the notion of making a deliberate effort to learn from experience is certainly laudable. After all, absent the study of history and improvement of the mechanisms that guide human behavior, past mistakes are likely to be repeated.

In practice, however, often the same lessons are experienced repeatedly, meaning that either learning did not occur or the follow-through process to amend policy, programs, or operational practices was faulty. In the hope that the wisdom gained will be applied in the future, two chapters of this book look analytically at the experiences of those who participated extensively or at key junctures in biological inspections for the United Nations Special Commission (UNSCOM). This chapter focuses on the factors that are integral to the success of field inspections yet at the same time auxiliary to their actual practice, while the next takes on inspection tools, tactics, and strategies. These lessons are relevant to inspections of biological activities and other types of weaponry. Only to the extent that these lessons are harnessed to improve future inspections will they make the transition into lessons learned; hence, the expectant "lessons experienced" title of these chapters.[1]

The stakes of international inspections to determine compliance with prohibitions on offensive bioweapons activities are very high, whether the inspections are associated with the 1925 Geneva Protocol, which bans the use of these weapons; with the 1975 Biological and Toxin Weapons Convention, which outlaws their development, production, and stockpiling yet presently lacks verification provisions; or with other mandates, such as United Nations (UN) Security Council Resolution 687, that might be imposed on specific nations. A hidden bioweapons program poses a major threat to countries in the same region as the proliferator and to global security and public health. Had UNSCOM's bioweapons inspectors been less conscientious and persistent, then Iraq would likely have sustained a covert germ weapons capability that could have significantly altered Middle Eastern and even global history. One could argue, therefore, that the welfare of future generations will depend to a certain extent on whether international leaders, security analysts, scientists, and the public study, learn from, and actually implement the lessons of UNSCOM's biological inspections.

THE PROVERBIAL "RIGHT STUFF"

The U.S. National Aeronautics and Space Agency searched exhaustively to secure the most qualified individuals to land the first man on the moon.[2] Though UNSCOM often had to assemble inspection teams on the spur of the moment, the right personnel were no less essential to successful inspections.[3] Time permitting, team chiefs defined the expertise needed for a mission, and UNSCOM petitioned countries that routinely seconded personnel to the inspectorate, requesting specialists by name if possible. For the most part, "the UN could pretty well get any expert in the world."[4] Sometimes, however, UNSCOM sent teams into Iraq on less than a day's notice, which meant the chiefs had little idea of their mission and had to make due with assigned personnel. Even team chiefs who deployed after reasonable mission preparation often did not know who would be on their teams because nations made specialists available at the last minute. Countries sometimes sent military officers or government officials who did not understand the science or technology involved, or academics who had no practical experience.[5]

Inside UNSCOM, those who had no real or applicable technical expertise earned the unflattering nickname of "oxygen thieves."[6] Baffled that those calling the shots did not dispatch the appropriate specialists to hunt Iraq's bioweapons program, one inspector said, "I don't know how the countries involved or UNSCOM chose people to go over. I guess it was a political thing. A lot of the people who could have made significant contributions to identifying and deciphering that program never even went to Iraq."[7] Some nations also handicapped these sparsely staffed teams with inspectors who defaulted on assignments or behaved inappropriately.[8]

Defining the appropriate qualities for a bioweapons inspector turns out to be an exercise in common sense. The task calls for practical experience in applicable disciplines, an understanding of past bioweapons programs, the ability to think creatively and objectively about the potential to employ dual-use equipment and settings for legitimate and prohibited military activities, and acute powers of observation.[9] Teams not predominated by those who have worked in laboratories or production facilities will hardly be suited to differentiate between a lawful facility and one covering up weapons-related activities. A stunned inspector recalled how no one else on one team "had any in-depth knowledge that would allow them to see the equipment layout and process design and evaluate it." One apparently hapless inspector "showed me a picture of a centrifuge and asked what it was."[10] Similarly shocked at how many of his predecessors had categorized equipment improperly, inspector William Lebherz said, "They seemed to bring in people who were management level/PhD types, not folks accustomed to putting their hands on steam generators and fermenters. UNSCOM really needed more of the latter kind of expertise, sooner."[11]

In hindsight, loading the early UNSCOM biological teams with military personnel who did not have the appropriate skills was an error, said UNSCOM chief bioweapons inspector David Franz.[12] Along this line of thought, David Kelly, who led over thirty-five UNSCOM biological teams, argued that "having the right expertise on the team was *the* crucial thing. Teams need to be tailored to the mission; otherwise, the inspectors will not pick up on things in real time."[13]

Inspectors with extensive relevant work experience will comprehend what is fitting for the facilities they examine. For instance, whereas commercial plants have quality assurance or quality control procedures to reduce human and other errors, mistakes are more common in research laboratories where graduate students may be loosely supervised. Table 8.1 describes the appropriate backgrounds for inspectors according to the facility to be inspected. Qualified inspectors will know such things as how to evaluate research activity and culture collections; how the pipes should connect on process lines; whether supplies, fermentation, containment, waste handling, and storage capacity are in line with a site's production history and objectives; and where to look in a facility's records and infrastructure to confirm legitimate activity or signs of foul play. Appropriately experienced inspectors will have a better feel for whether the anomalies found are more consistent with human error

Table 8.1. Expertise critical to inspections of biological sites

Type of Expertise	Inspection Target	Knowledge Critical to Inspections
Experienced researchers, tailored to the organism(s) the target facility is working with	Research laboratories; cell-culture production facilities	Laboratory standard operating procedures (SOPs), biosafety, management of culture collections, record keeping
Chemical, electrical, and design engineers; microbiologists with a background in large-scale fermentation; physicists; all with extensive experience in commercial plants	Production facilities	Ability to assess whether equipment, materials, process layout, waste handling, biosafety containment, and staff skills match product(s) site professes to make; process SOPs; production supplies; business and regulatory practices
Background in past bioweapons production, program management, and doctrine; biodefense; munitions and aerosol dispersal experts	Production facilities	Ability to identify equipment and infrastructure suitable for making warfare agents, weapons development, testing, filling, and storage; to calculate bulk production capacity; to identify newest and vintage equipment and technical approaches
Interpreters, preferably with some knowledge of life sciences	All facilities	Nuances of local communications (such as language, facial expressions, body language) and customs

SOURCES: Hamish Killip (former UNSCOM chief biological weapons inspector), interview with author, Isle of Man, August 22, 2005; Richard Spertzel, PhD (former UNSCOM chief biological weapons inspector), interview with author, Washington, DC, July 1, 2005; David Franz, DVM, PhD (former UNSCOM chief biological weapons inspector), interview with author, Washington, DC, June 29, 2005; William Lebherz (former UNSCOM industrial biotechnology expert), interview with author, Washington, DC, February 13, 2006; Gabriele Kraatz-Wadsack, DVM (former UNSCOM chief biological weapons inspector), interview with author, Berlin, August 15, 2005; Stephen Black (UNSCOM historian), interview with author, Washington, DC, November 16, 2007; David Huxsoll, DVM (former UNSCOM chief biological weapons inspector), interview with author, Washington, DC, June 21, 2005; Terence Taylor (former UNSCOM CBW commissioner and chief inspector), interview with author, Washington, DC, May 12, 2005; former UNSCOM inspector and chief of product development in an offensive biological weapons program, interview with author, Washington, DC, February 21, 2006; former UNSCOM chief inspector, interview with author, London, August 18, 2005.

or nefarious purposes. Mixing commercial and bioweapons experts on teams sent to production facilities would abet a holistic, well-informed evaluation.

Finally, garden variety or diplomatic circuit interpreters may not be familiar with scientific jargon, have regional experience, or be prepared for the stress of field missions.[14] The right interpreters can boost inspection efficiency by quickly reading documents on site, indicating whether certain matters should be pursued, and even alerting inspectors when interviewees might not be telling the truth.[15] Interpreters should be recruited with full cognizance of their role in determining the success of inspections.

The political expectation that any international inspection effort have an equitable geographic balance of inspectors can be handled deftly through external supervisory and review groups, as UNSCOM did with its commissioners and technical evaluation meetings.[16] As Chapter 7 accentuates, outside experts serving in a review or oversight capacity can make a valuable contribution to the overall process. The rigor and effectiveness of any future inspections will hinge on whether primacy is given to composing teams with individuals who have backgrounds befitting inspection tasks, regardless of nationality.

THE ENCUMBRANCES OF THE "WESTERN" FRAME OF REFERENCE

In three different respects, a "Western mind-set" hindered some inspectors' evaluations of whether and how Iraq made biological weapons. The suppositions in questions were that Iraq would (1) opt for the standard biowarfare agents and formulate a top-of-the-line end product; (2) operate at a level of efficiency similar to that found in the West; and, (3) use modern biosafety precautions for offensive weapons work. *Biosafety* consists of the physical barriers and operational practices necessary to prevent accidents with dangerous pathogens and to minimize the harm to workers and the public in the event of mishaps.[17] Not all inspectors held these assumptions but they were prevalent enough to cause many serious disagreements about Iraq's past bioweapons activities and possible continuation of such work amidst UNSCOM inspections.

Iraqi Departures from the "Classic" Bioweapons Program

In some ways, Iraq saved time and resources by patterning its efforts on previous weapons programs, so many inspectors thought it would aim for agents that had been previously weaponized (for example, tularemia or plague). While the Iraqis consulted the literature about classic bioweapons agents and pursued some, even using the same strains of anthrax and botulinum toxin as other countries,[18] they also departed notably from these expectations by weaponizing *Clostridium perfringens* and aflatoxin, which, respectively, cause the skin-eating disease gas gangrene and liver cancer.[19] Not only did Iraq's pick of *Clostridium perfringens* seem odd, "Western inspectors didn't think that aflatoxin made sense as a weapon, but it did for the Iraqis, and *that*," said UNSCOM commissioner and chief inspector Terence Taylor, "is what was important."[20] Caught off guard, some inspectors had difficulty wrapping their minds around Iraq's bioweapons choices.[21]

A slurry of biowarfare agent is generally less stable for long-term storage, more vulnerable to damaging environmental effects, and more difficult to disperse than a dried agent.[22] With the availability of equipment to dry agents, create ultra-small particle sizes, and coat the particles with materials to enhance their dispersability and to harden agents against environmental effects, some inspectors also projected that Iraq would dry and micro-encapsulate its germ agents.[23] The Iraqis, however, expediently copied the operational approach of their chemical weapons program, which was to produce new poison gas at intervals and flush and refill munitions. Iraq's "bioweapons program was just a higher offshoot of their chemical program," said Taylor.[24] By following this pattern with its initial production runs of bulk biological agent, Iraq relieved the pressure to master the ability to freeze dry its agents.[25]

Iraq's less-than-optimal end product and weapons refilling practices seemed strange, even backward to some inspectors, given the state of technology and know-how when Iraq's bioweapons program matured. The Iraqis, however, may have viewed the situation differently. An Iraqi general reportedly considered the biowarfare program to be a success if Iraq managed to put one anthrax spore over Tel Aviv,[26] an achievement barometer that clearly differed from Western weapons programs. UNSCOM found convincing evidence that Iraq was moving toward drying of biowarfare agents, but the question of whether Iraq successfully dried biowarfare agents remained open.

Efficiency Culture Clash

"Insha'Allah," if Allah wills, is a constant refrain in Iraq that denotes a cultural clash with the notion of effectively marshalling resources (such as money and manpower) to achieve an end result. The manner in which Iraq ran research and production operations contradicted Western expectations about how to structure, plan, staff, and manage a weapons program. Calling the bioweapons program a pet project of Lt. Gen. Hussein Kamal, head of the Military Industrialization Commission, the Iraqis said the program unfolded with practically no military involvement. This claim rang false to inspectors fixated on how a weapon could possibly be integrated into military doctrine and operations without significant military input into its plans and specifications.[27] According to Huda Amash, a senior scientist and the only woman on Iraq's Revolutionary Command Council, in the 1980s Iraq's bioweapons program was well-conceived and highly organized until Kamal took control of it. From that point, "the program became very decentralized," said inspector Robert Kadlec, "and the influential factors were who you knew and if you could sell a bag of camels to Saddam or Kamal."[28]

A few inspectors could envisage that in Saddam Hussein's Iraq a variety of things were done without the controls, managerial cross-checks, and oversight employed in other societies, but these circumstances became much clearer in hindsight and with information that Iraqis provided after the 2003 Gulf War.[29] At the time, however, many inspectors did not appreciate that "whether someone had great technical skills or was incompetent was irrelevant compared to their loyalty to the Ba'ath Party and to Saddam and his inner circle," noted Kadlec.[30] Once someone passed the loyalty litmus test, seconded Taylor, "they were just making the best use they could of available technical expertise and resources."[31]

Rihab Taha and her role in Iraq's bioweapons program embodied the Iraqi efficiency conundrum that bewildered many UNSCOM biological inspectors. Taha, presented during the UNSCOM's BW1 mission as the head of Iraq's military biological research group, earned a PhD in 1984 at the University of East Anglia.[32] When UNSCOM personnel pressed her during interviews, Taha sometimes cried and threw screaming, foot-stomping tantrums. Her UNSCOM interlocutors speculated that she was ashamed about her comparative lack of scientific prowess, afraid of imparting information that she should not, or stressed about getting caught in a lie.[33] UNSCOM personnel split on whether Taha was playing dumb or was dumb. Said chief inspector Jeff Mohr, "that's the kind of person I'd put up front because if she was as slow as she appeared to be, the inspectors weren't going to get too far with her."[34] Some inspectors concluded that Taha may not have ever run Al Hakam and could not possibly have been the real brains behind the whole bioweapons program. At most, they viewed Taha as a capable laboratory scientist who could follow a weapons cookbook.[35] Nassir Al-Hindawi, who wrote the paper that persuaded Saddam to pursue bioweapons and was initially presented as Al Hakam's director, led a list of candidates believed to have truly managed the line operations of the bioweapons program.[36] As it turned out, though the Iraqis might have segmented some military aspects of the program,[37] Taha was not just a stand-in manager. "No question about it, she led the program," said UNSCOM bioweapons inspector Rod Barton. "Not pegging her as the lead was characteristic of a misjudgment of inspectors appraising other efforts by Western standards. We were all guilty of this at times, myself included."[38]

Worlds Apart in Safety

Practically every inspector had tales about the Iraqi attitude about safety that left many inspectors agog. The Iraqis routinely transited excavation operations and areas with live ammunition without protective gear and with lit cigarettes, seemingly oblivious to the potential harm their actions could cause.[39] The inspectors repeatedly noticed major departures from modern safety practices at Iraq's biological facilities. The biosafety rules at the U.S. Army Medical Research Institute for Infectious Diseases, which David Huxsoll once managed, barred pregnant workers from handling high-risk pathogens. When Huxsoll saw a "clearly pregnant" technician at Al Ameriyah Vaccine and Serum Institute working with *Brucella*, "I just couldn't believe that."[40] Another inspector related how an inspection team withdrew from an area to don masks after encountering a senior scientist performing inoculations with *B. subtilis* on the bench "without any protection—no mask, no gloves, no cap."[41] Hence, prominent Western specialists on UNSCOM missions, including team chiefs, and also experts on the panels UNSCOM convened to review Iraq's program were of the opinion that nobody in their right mind would make biowarfare agents under such lax biosafety conditions.[42] This point of view was frequently heard in UNSCOM circles until the summer of 1995, when Iraq admitted production and weaponization of biowarfare agents.

Fortunately, the Western way of thinking about biosafety did not ensnare all UNSCOM inspectors. Not seeing familiar safety practices and equipment, "the Canadians, Brits, Aussies, and Swedes, we'd sit and talk about this," said Mohr. "We all pretty much said 'no way' at first and then we thought about it and said 'well, why not?' After that, we looked at things differently."[43] Inspectors who knew the history of biowarfare programs kept reminding skeptical colleagues that states suited up their production technicians and wrapped their fermenters to make biowarfare agent slurries.[44] Or, they harkened back to the not-so-long-ago days before stricter biosafety practices. "One of my professors, a cigarette smoker, instructed me how to use a pipette and suction from my mouth to withdraw microorganisms, like vaccinia virus, from one receptacle and deposit them in another," said a chief inspector who observed many colleagues unable to shake the Western biosafety mind-set.[45]

Iraq may have foregone biosafety for several reasons. First, after the 1991 Gulf War Iraqi scientists were isolated just as tougher biosafety standards came of age elsewhere, possibly contributing to Iraq's biosafety deficiencies.[46] Second, the Iraqis thought differently about safety and did not necessarily see anything wrong in their approach. "Safety was within tolerable levels as far as they were concerned," stated chief inspector Hamish Killip, who explained that although safety standards often looked suspect at Iraqi industrial plants, it would be naïve to conclude that the Iraqis operated at an actual lower level of safety.[47] So long as they were working with warfare agents in wet slurry form, the Iraqis may have viewed the safety risks as quite acceptable. The dangers of working without full biosafety precautions escalate considerably when a program advances to drying of biowarfare agents.[48] UNSCOM amassed evidence that Iraq intended to upgrade biosafety at Al Hakam, one of several harbingers of Iraq's possible plans to produce dried agents. Third, export controls and then sanctions complicated the acquisition of equipment and might have also compelled Iraq to cut biosafety corners or take other unusual steps to make weapons.[49] Finally, Iraq might have foregone some biosafety precautions to cut costs and to move its program ahead easier and faster.[50]

Numerous UNSCOM personnel concurred that assessing Iraqi facilities, personnel, and activities according to Western standards was a significant factor impeding the unmasking of Iraq's bioweapons program.[51] This mindset caused some UNSCOM teams to file watered-down reports, including one stipulating that absent certain biosafety conditions, a past, current, or future bioweapons program in Iraq was not a concern.[52] Moreover, this mind-set affected how the inspectors interacted with the Iraqis, often to the detriment of inspection goals. While the influences of one's societal upbringing and professional training can be difficult to blunt, training can assist inspectors in recognizing when their thought patterns and interpersonal skills can degrade their performance and how to adjust their behavior to be more effective inspectors.

TRAINING EXPERTS IN THE PRACTICALITIES OF INSPECTIONS

Even if individuals already possess the technical know-how and pertinent work experience to evaluate facilities and activities, odds are they have little awareness of inspection tradecraft. Lebherz, a biological production expert, fretted that he entered UNSCOM service figuratively blind of the expectations of him as an inspector.[53] Prior to a mission, UNSCOM personnel had a couple of days in Bahrain for some safety instruction; a generic background intelligence briefing; and overviews of logistical matters, the rules of inspection, and mission objectives. Sometimes teams rehearsed key tasks for the upcoming mission. New inspectors were not, however, instructed in fundamentals such as interview techniques, the operational aspects of inspection, tip-offs of bioweapons activities, and the most effective usage of their time on site.[54] Likewise, team chiefs received "practically zero training. The reality was that there was nobody to train them or, for that matter," said Taylor, "to tell the team chiefs what to do."[55]

UNSCOM Executive Chairman Rolf Ekeus held scientists in such high regard that he apparently equated their technical knowledge to an instant ability to perform inspections.[56] Though appreciative of Ekeus's confidence, the inspectors identified a lack of training as an UNSCOM weakness.[57] As the next chapter explains, savvy inspectors need certain skills and thought patterns that may differ from those used in their everyday jobs. Therefore, inspectors agreed that specialized training would significantly enhance the ability of future inspectors to do their jobs.[58]

UNSCOM's bioweapons inspectors counseled that training should focus partly on how to adjust basic skills so as to utilize them most effectively for inspections. Interviews need to be conducted in an unprejudiced manner. To illustrate, rather than the unbiased query, "How did you do it?," some UNSCOM inspectors, captive to their experience or preferred methodology, asked "Did you do it this way?" or "Why did you not do it with 'X' procedure or 'Y' piece of equipment?" The latter two phrasings of the question potentially interfere with forthright answers. Cumulatively, such leading questions could have also inappropriately imparted information about how to develop, test, manufacture, and weaponize agents more effectively. According to UNSCOM chief inspector Gabriele Kraatz-Wadsack, questioning in ways that ran counter to the true purpose of inspections "was a big problem. Having an academic discussion or open debate is different from how one should work on an inspection. Training inspectors not to prejudge or to preempt is very difficult."[59] An inspector's job is to collect evidence that conveys an impartial, full, and accurate accounting of events, to find out what happened rather than pass value judgments. Thus inspector training should help instill purely investigatory interviewing skills in scientists accustomed to arguing the supremacy of one technique or theory over another.

Training should address directly the likelihood that many called to serve as inspectors have no direct background in offensive bioweapons. Though all teams should have someone steeped in that expertise, all inspectors need some background in the practices of past weapons programs so that they can understand the approaches that proliferators might try to emulate in whole or in part. Instruction should cover military biowarfare doctrine, weapons research and development, laboratory and field testing, bulk agent production, post-production processing of the agent, and weapons filling and storage. At the same time, inspectors should be alerted that proliferators might customize weapons programs to their priorities and capabilities, perhaps not using the most advanced equipment or techniques. Examples should detail how the Japanese, U.S., and Iraqi weapons programs churned out agent without modern biosafety containment barriers. In addition to descriptions and diagrams, the training should include side-by-side photographs of the equipment, facilities, and operational practices (for example, toxicology and weapons field tests) from bioweapons programs to facilitate comparative observation and discussion.[60] UNSCOM's experience should be used to illustrate the pitfalls of going into the field with biases about how to plan, equip, and operate a bioweapons program.

Put another way, to evaluate individual facilities and a country's collective dual-use biological capabilities, inspectors need to be trained to "think about what the inspected site's personnel might have done there, not how the inspector would have done it," stated UNSCOM chief inspector Ron Manley.[61] When the first defector from the Soviet biological weapons program, Vladimir Pasechnik, told his British debriefers of the U.S.S.R.'s colossal program, Taylor recollected that "we didn't believe Pasechnik to start with because what he was saying was so alien to us." Noting similar disbelief among some inspectors in Iraq, Taylor recommended that "to offset the tendency to think Western, inspectors need to really understand the resources that a country has available—facilities, equipment, and, in particular, their scientific expertise."[62]

The Importance of Culture Sensitivity

Training should also immerse inspectors in the culture of the country being inspected so that how that society operates and its people behave can overlay everything the inspectors do, informing how they assess what they see on-site, interact with the locals, and evaluate data. To the extent possible, inspectors need to be able to get inside the minds of the locals to understand what motivates and influences them, to tune into the politics of their country and their immediate working environment, and to know what commands their respect or offends them. Ideally, expatriate scientists from academic, industrial, and government facilities—the most authentic source of such information—would instruct and regularly assist the inspectors. Otherwise, historians, sociologists, and political scientists who specialize in the country being inspected should brief the inspectors and be integrated periodically throughout an ongoing inspection effort to help inspectors read the actions of the locals and tweak tactics to suit cultural sensitivities. This approach will promote optimal results from individual and cumulative inspections.[63]

To underscore the importance of equipping inspectors with local cultural awareness, a societal difference that occurred often during UNSCOM's years pertained to lying. Lies are clearly wrong in some cultures; children are admonished to tell the truth and liars shamed and shunned. The Iraqis lied to the inspectors so frequently, nonchalantly, and flagrantly that some inspectors took umbrage, which had an impact on their ability to assess circumstances objectively. UNSCOM inspectors might have handled themselves differently had they been taught that in Iraqi society lying is considered a means to an end, not a cultural taboo. "The Iraqis didn't care if they told a hundred lies to reach the goal; to them it was insignificant to lie."[64]

Moreover, tutoring in the contemporary realities of life in Saddam's Iraq would have helped the inspectors appreciate that truth was also a life-or-death matter to the Iraqis. An Iraqi could no more blurt to inspectors how far work had progressed on "weapon x" than he or she could tell a superior that "weapon x" really did not function effectively.[65] The dangers were such that Iraqis schooled themselves not to satisfy idle curiosity about their colleagues' work. "The Iraqis knew full well to mind their own business," said Kadlec. "They used to say that just because you danced with the devil didn't mean that you slept with the devil."[66] Thus the onus was on the inspectors to transform these circumstances from a roadblock to an opportunity, a skill discussed in Chapter 9.

Inspectors and the Inspected: Matters of Comportment

Opinions diverged about how inspectors should interact with those they were inspecting. Some inspectors believed the Iraqis would not respond to them unless they were tough, even confrontational; others opted for a more personal, friendlier approach. At issue, in other words, was whether inspectors should be good cops, bad cops, or a bit of both.

Roughly 90 percent of the information that the inspectors had to verify about Iraq's biological activities was statements of fact, as in how many fermenters were involved in a specific production run, or how much growth media.[67] Chief bioweapons inspector Richard Spertzel believed that to make any progress judging the reliability of Iraq's "factual" statements, in extensive discussions a tough approach automatically had to be taken with high-ranking Iraqis, those with a certain attitude, and Iraqis who signaled they were not going to be cooperative.[68] Practitioners of the bad cop approach peppered the

UNSCOM inspector corps. "Some people treated the Iraqis with no respect, and the Iraqis fought them every inch of the way."[69] This approach included very harsh talk, even shouting that the Iraqis were lying or had committed war crimes. Some inspectors acted as though they disdained all Iraqis.[70] To their contemporaries, such behavior was not constructive because not all Iraqis had done bad things, and the Iraqis could not be scared into cooperation. An inspector's abrasive behavior could also justify Iraqi decisions to end an interview or restrict access at a facility.

Espousing a different philosophy on comportment, Huxsoll said, "We didn't know how they got into weapons work, what their motive was. The only way to try to understand their perspective is to try to walk in their shoes."[71] For Franz, "talking science is a good way to learn things. The carrot is better; you get more by trying to work with them than by beating them down."[72] Thus some inspectors engaged the Iraqis on subjects of mutual interest, noting that friendly listening yielded useful data.[73] Others scoffed at a kinder, gentler inspection philosophy: "Some inspectors thought that if they talked a lot of science to the Iraqis and were very nice that the Iraqis would just melt and tell the truth, but that will never happen," said a senior UNSCOM official. "It is a myth that someone will spill the beans in a spasm of truth because no one will tell you what their government does not allow them to say. Everyone knows that you never know who is listening, plus they don't have anything to gain from doing that."[74]

Still other inspectors advocated middle-of-the-road flexibility, mindful that it is human nature to respond to authority. The most productive approach, therefore, is to be firm, civil, straightforward, respectful, persistent, and professional.[75] Certain occasions might cause an inspector to divert momentarily from a courteous, authoritative approach: "If I saw a lack of cooperation or an advantage to taking a harder line, I went 'bad cop,' like when they blatantly stalled the Al Hakam destruction mission. Also, an inspector should probably go straight to 'bad cop' if he is really confident about what is behind a door," said Taylor. "An inspector onto something has to be hard, direct, and relentless, but even then should maintain a professional rapport, if possible."[76]

Occasionally, Iraqis tried to present information to inspectors unofficially in a whispered conversation or by slipping them a note or a document.[77] Surprisingly, the need for UNSCOM to be a totally above-board operation was not universally appreciated. Government officials and even some within UNSCOM advocated sneaking out documents and using force to collect evidence.[78] Some inspectors, Killip said, "sometimes fancied themselves as minor spooks."[79] First, inspectors should consider that the *sub rosa* information might be fabricated to bait the inspector and get them dismissed. Second, collaboration on the sly might jeopardize the informant's safety because Iraqi minders were always watching. Third, UNSCOM's mandate was to disarm Iraq openly and cooperatively, and the essence of UNSCOM's legitimacy was the legal and cooperative collection of all data. UNSCOM could not submit improperly obtained data to the Security Council lest Iraq or other countries deny the data's legitimacy or claim the inspectors had falsified it. Therefore, inspectors should discourage and decline such offers. Moreover, inspectors have no business soliciting anyone to slide them information on the side or to defect.[80] Due to the possible risks that inappropriate behavior poses to the inspectors, informants, and the entire inspection endeavor, training of future inspectors should clarify the boundaries and procedures to be observed.

INSTITUTIONAL LEARNING IN THE HEAT OF BATTLE

UNSCOM operated with scarce resources and at a feverish tempo that diluted the inspectorate's effectiveness. UNSCOM inspectors often began work before dawn and labored well into the night. During missions, inspectors were told to channel information about anomalies or other important findings to the team chief or another designated individual so that someone had the complete picture of what was unfolding. Operational security requirements and a team chief's preferences sometimes meant that a fraction of the team was fully briefed and included in key on-site meetings. Right after a mission, the inspectors spent roughly a day in Bahrain writing the part(s) of the inspection report related to their mission responsibilities, which team chiefs polished into final reports.[81]

The upshot of these circumstances was that many inspectors never saw the bigger picture or final reports. Conversely, many inspectors were not debriefed in a systematic fashion or asked for their analytical insights pertaining to their duties or other aspects of the mission. In other words, UNSCOM deployed tremendous and varied brainpower but did not reap its full benefits.[82] Inspection missions were always so time pressed that, as Kelly recalled, there never seemed to be time for "sharing of other interesting observations, so a lot of things didn't emerge."[83] For this reason, UNSCOM's bioweapons inspectors recommended that teams have a mandatory "hot wash" at the end of each mission.[84] A hot wash is a methodical and impartial debriefing of the participants in an event to facilitate a full exchange of information, improve analysis of the event, and thereby enhance the performance at similar events in the future.[85]

Post-mission hot washes would have required only a couple more hours from the inspectors in Bahrain. Arguably, rank-and-file inspectors would have then left the mission perhaps more satisfied that their time and talents had been put to good use. More important, UNSCOM as an institution would have benefited fully from their acumen to strengthen its analysis and to build an institutional memory to inform future inspections. Hot washes could have also fattened UNSCOM's factual database, fed into mission planning, and helped improve operational tactics and procedures.

Next, UNSCOM team chiefs worked mostly in isolation from their contemporaries because the inspections were ad hoc and also because, for security purposes, only individuals with a "need to know" had access to certain data. According to Kadlec, "the level of compartmentalization within UNSCOM was actually self-defeating; the only people that we fooled besides the Iraqis were ourselves."[86] Furthermore, UNSCOM was so time and budget strapped that the inspectorate did not gather its biological team chiefs so they could brief each other on their missions. Had the chiefs jointly combed their experiences to determine what Iraq was doing to hinder inspections and what response tactics worked best, team leadership and overall performance might have improved. UNSCOM's analysis and inspection planning could also have profited from pooling the chiefs' views, allowing them to connect the significance of data gathered at one facility to what was noted at different sites. Collectively, the chiefs might have dissected anomalies and trends to inform inspection priorities. In the event of another sustained international biological inspection effort, UNSCOM inspectors suggested biannual all-chiefs debriefings and brainstorming meetings.[87]

In addition, the UNSCOM inspectors recommended occasionally gathering the team chiefs across the inspection portfolios. UNSCOM's biological, chemical, and missile teams and the nuclear teams of the International Atomic Energy Agency (IAEA) were often conducting overlapping inspections of the same sites. However, these groups maintained separate databases and except for incidental or exceptional circumstances had no formal system to share data or insights of concern or common interest. A prime example of the consequences of such "stovepipes" was the linchpin physical evidence at the Al Adile warehouse that sat unexploited because data was not shared across disciplines. A chemical team went to Al Adile three years before Kraatz-Wadsack entered it in January 1995 and found growth media barrels stacked floor-to-ceiling there. Right away, Kraatz-Wadsack seized this discovery's relevance to UNSCOM's biological investigation. Video of the barrels sat in UNSCOM's chemical inspection files until Taylor came across it in preparation for a March 1995 inspection. Frustrated, Taylor surmised that the chemical inspectors had not understood the significance of this media cache. Had they promptly informed the biologists of this find, UNSCOM would have had cause much earlier to push Iraq to explain the need for this enormous amount of media, arguably leading to a much faster exposure of Iraq's bioweapons program.[88] Routine cross-fertilization among the team chiefs in all disciplines and the deployment of more cross-disciplinary teams are the underpinnings of more effective inspections.[89]

Most UNSCOM inspectors went to Iraq one or a few times, and even more seasoned ones had extended breaks between deployments. By default, files became UNSCOM's main reservoir of institutional memory, and the disarray of the archives "made it tough for a chief who wanted to look at previous reports, images, or videos from a certain site prior to taking a mission there. Often, these just couldn't be found," said Taylor.[90] In 1993–1994, UNSCOM began to establish a genuine data management system.[91] Accessible archives are critical to recognizing trends and anomalies that might alter inspection plans and outcomes. Not until Spertzel scoured every pertinent paper in UNSCOM's cabinets in the spring of 1994 did anyone recognize that UNSCOM already had an appreciable and damning paper trail on Iraq's bioweapons program. Only after Iraq ousted UNSCOM inspectors for an extended period of time in 1998 did the headquarters staff examine fully and critically the data collected in the various inspection disciplines.[92] An inspectorate can blunt the negative side-effects from a lack of personnel continuity and a feverish operational pace with team hot washes, periodic team chief meetings, and a proper and swift archiving of all data.[93]

THE ROLE OF INTELLIGENCE IN UNSCOM'S BIOLOGICAL INSPECTIONS

When it comes to the function of intelligence[94] in the midst of international agencies, one school of thought holds that intelligence may be a necessity for nations but this unseemly business has no place in international organizations that serve the global good, while the other posits that intelligence can be responsibly and usefully woven into international organizations when necessary. The tension between these two camps complicates efforts to introduce and work with intelligence in international settings. Moreover, intelligence officials worry that providing data to international organizations will compromise their sources and methods of collection and that loosely controlled access to their data will strip intelligence of its value. However, intelligence agencies exist to collect information, which is a very expensive task, so intelligence officials are almost always open to opportunities to barter information.[95]

Starting from Scratch

UNSCOM stood up in 1991 with only Iraq's more fictional than factual declarations on hand, as demonstrated by Baghdad's initial null biological weapons declaration. Thus UNSCOM had to scrape together whatever information it could to help direct its first missions.[96] Seeking information to compare to Iraq's declarations, Ekeus asked governments for pertinent intelligence.[97] Some countries lent a hand early and throughout UNSCOM's existence, others helped only on specific issues, and still others provided intelligence only after evaluating UNSCOM's operations for a while. Early on, only the United States and the United Kingdom worked with the inspectorate.[98]

The intelligence arrangements between the United States and UNSCOM had a rocky start and came to an ugly end. As UNSCOM was standing up, Robert Gallucci, soon to be UNSCOM's first deputy executive chairman, floated a trial balloon about the United States sharing intelligence with UNSCOM. A senior U.S. intelligence official told him, "Not a chance. None of these UN folks are cleared. You've got to be kidding."[99] The United States nonetheless answered Ekeus's call quickly, but the watered-down quality of the early U.S. intelligence belied the stereotypical concern that an international organization would not handle sensitive data responsibly.[100] Once UNSCOM began turning up copious amounts of fresh data because inspectors were inside so many Iraqi facilities, the U.S. intelligence community realized the possible benefits of helping UNSCOM.[101] U.S. officials upgraded what they provided, but they still "never went all the way with data."[102]

The U.S. government also put a U-2 aircraft at UNSCOM's disposal to snap images of sites and activities relevant to Iraq's compliance with Resolution 687. UNSCOM determined the targets for U-2 flights, and when the inspectors obtained information about an event, item, or facility, they could also ask U.S. analysts to search retroactively for relevant images.[103] When U.S. analysts first briefed Olive Branch imagery to Ekeus, he saw at a glance that the U-2 photos were all fuzzy, not the promised high-resolution images, and threw them in the trash to punctuate his request that henceforth they give actual images to UNSCOM.[104] The United States bowed to Ekeus's demand, but the photo interpreters' briefings were perfunctory because they had never been to Iraq and were not necessarily scientists. Gradually the photo interpreters accepted more interaction with UNSCOM's scientists, who had the technical know-how and on-site experience to enable more information to be derived from the images.[105]

The U.S. intelligence community created another capability called GATEWAY to aid and, quite frankly, benefit from UNSCOM inspections. Located in an annex of the U.S. Embassy in Bahrain, GATEWAY's purpose was to brief and debrief UNSCOM teams. The Central Intelligence Agency ran the place, with supplemental staff from Australia, Canada, and the United Kingdom.[106] GATEWAY provided a downgraded, generic brief for entire teams and a more detailed one for Westerners only. Even then, Manley quipped that the higher-grade briefing told "only half of the story."[107] Similarly, the GATEWAY debrief was a two-level affair. Teams exiting Iraq were debriefed as a group, although some team chiefs instructed their inspectors not to say anything. GATEWAY staff also corralled Western inspectors for separate debriefings and data collection (for example, copies of documents and photographs).[108] Although GATEWAY was clearly the largest operation of its kind, other countries (such as France and Russia) also had personnel in Bahrain to debrief the inspectors.[109] Though GATEWAY was somewhat awkward, several inspectors thought the UN did not recognize GATEWAY's constructive contribution to UNSCOM operations, such as helping to pinpoint compliance problems and inspection targets in Iraq.[110]

Navigating the Minefields of Intelligence Collaboration

As the summer of 1991 progressed, the scope and complexity of the mission assigned to UNSCOM became more evident and the volume of sensitive data derived from UNSCOM's inspections and sometimes from cooperative intelligence agencies was on the rise. Ekeus formed the Information Assessment Unit to manage intelligence data; create and maintain the databases for imagery, equipment, and sites; assess the data; prepare site briefings; recommend inspection missions; help inspection chiefs with report preparation; and serve as a liaison with cooperating intelligence agencies.[111] UNSCOM generally restricted access to the smallest possible number of people. Mainly the chairman and a few additional staffers, depending on the country providing data or the type of inspection conducted, received intelligence.[112] Taylor argued that including the designated chief inspector in pertinent intelligence briefings would cancel any tendency of the designated entry point(s) to serve as the sole judge and jury about what intelligence merits action.[113]

One long-held pretense surrounding international organizations and intelligence is that civil servant status in international agencies creates a genuine wall precluding personnel from relaying information to their home governments. Seconded from their governments, inspectors signed a pledge not to disclose to their government any UNSCOM information. Neither a pledge nor a full-time civil service employment contract can guarantee that staff will keep secrets.[114]

Another of UNSCOM's intelligence predicaments was that most cooperative intelligence services expected something in return, namely debriefs from inspections. The practical result of debriefs is that the intelligence agencies learn what data they provided to help target an inspection was accurate and what was not, which helps improve their collection and analysis. Debriefs incentivize intelligence services to keep cooperating with more or even better data to improve the success of inspections. Thus the inspectors support a two-way street: "For real inspections, the information has to flow both ways. This shouldn't be so political. It needs to be done matter-of-factly instead of making it some big hush-hush thing."[115] UNSCOM policy left the decision to share the results of an inspection with a collaborating intelligence service to the discretion of the individual(s) serving as that nation's point of contact. Some intelligence agencies discontinued their cooperation because their designated UNSCOM contact balked at sharing. To avert this problem, said UNSCOM inspectors, two-way street pragmatism should be a standing policy so that an international inspection agency can operate effectively.[116]

Another essential reason for an international organization to share select data is to augment its own internal analysis with access to advanced national technical and analytical capabilities, which are broader and deeper than what resides in international organizations. For example, in the summer of 1991 nuclear inspectors could tell that an Iraqi facility was making batteries but could not figure out what else the Iraqis were doing. UNSCOM shared a description of this site with a couple of nations, and their technical experts recognized the site's test stand as a hallmark of electromagnetic isotope separation activity. Also, UNSCOM sent samples to the laboratories of supportive governments, which identified VX in the nosecones of Iraqi missiles and characterized Iraq's binary chemical agents. In sum, national technical and analytical capabilities empowered UNSCOM to bear down on Iraq to uncover the truth.[117]

Any good or reasonable thing, however, can get carried too far, and UNSCOM's intelligence collaboration with the United States included the nightmare scenario of excess. The "Scott Ritter factor," as Gallucci called it, is "the idea that an international organization can be compromised if it crosses the boundary from collecting data needed to achieve the organization's mission to collecting intelligence to benefit individual countries."[118] Ritter had a central role in UNSCOM's activities to break Iraq's concealment and deception programs, which heightened concern that UNSCOM had gathered intelligence for U.S. purposes. UNSCOM inspectors agreed that inspectors must not engage in any collection activity that diverges from the direct inspection mandate. Ritter's handiwork, UNSCOM veterans concurred, contributed directly to UNSCOM's downfall.[119]

Other Intelligence Sore Spots

Some viewed the participation of individuals connected to the world of intelligence on UNSCOM's teams as controversial, if not by definition detrimental. Understanding the scope, complexity, and difficulty of their mandate, the UNSCOM staff took a pragmatic stance on these matters. "If someone had asked on that first mission for everyone who had no connections with intelligence to please step forward, only one or two would have done so. Otherwise, how would the UN have known anything?" said Killip. UNSCOM, he continued, recognized the sensitivity of having intelligence officers in its midst and tapdanced publicly around the issue with a neither-confirm-nor-deny policy.[120]

Another prickly aspect of intelligence concerned whether inspectors had access to the intelligence in UNSCOM's files and got an intelligence briefing prior to their service with UNSCOM. A number of UNSCOM's bioweapons inspectors received intelligence briefings from their governments, but many did not.[121] For some, the mixture of briefed and un-briefed personnel was problematic because some inspectors knew what to look for and others did not.[122] The intelligence-sharing dilemma thus created some friction within UNSCOM, which UNSCOM might have alleviated by placing such disparities in a positive light. To begin with, not everyone had a genuine need to know sensitive information, so it was unrealistic to expect everyone to be equally informed. Briefing intelligence to an expert on fermenters, for instance, makes little sense.[123] Kraatz-Wadsack further explained the upside of not being briefed:

> I didn't care if I had the intelligence data. With my eyes, I could see things. Having some inspectors with no preconditions and others with an intelligence background made for a stronger analysis with different perspectives. Both

types will sometimes miss something. Intelligence says building 18 has underground storage and the briefed person goes directly to building 18. I'm looking around wider and seeing what strikes me as out of place. That's the right combination, and team chiefs should give all inspectors the right to follow up the leads they find.[124]

Likewise, Taylor argued that inspectors without guidance of what they are supposed to find, a "fresh eyes" capacity, should be built into teams so they can freely bring their expertise to bear and challenge prevailing logic within the team and the inspectorate.[125]

Ground Truth Versus Satellites and Defectors

UNSCOM's biological inspectors had mostly realistic expectations of how often intelligence would be on the mark with regard to a covert germ weapons program. Unlike the large "footprints" that typify chemical and nuclear weapons programs (for example, nuclear reactor cooling towers), the signs of a bioweapons program are modest. Prior to the 1991 Gulf War, as noted in Chapter 1, Western intelligence missed facilities critical to Iraq's bioweapons program and mistakenly tagged several sites that were not part of it.[126]

First, the inspectors recognized that some intelligence leads can be very temporal, especially tips about the possible location of weapons and relevant equipment, materials, and documents. Iraq's standing system to move equipment and documents quickly to new hiding places exacerbated UNSCOM's need to investigate actionable intelligence rapidly. UNSCOM did not uniformly handle time-critical intelligence well, partly because in the early days the inspectorate did not consistently have sufficient resources available to act on leads and also because some staffers disregarded intelligence briefings.[127] For example, prior to July 1991 UNSCOM received intelligence that biological bombs were buried at Airfield 37, but UNSCOM did not send a team to the site until November 1991, when the inspectors found pits in the ground but did not push the Iraqis too hard for an explanation. In the fall of 1995, Iraq admitted storing biological bombs at Airfield 37 until their removal for destruction in July 1991.[128] Ekeus was known for authorizing time-sensitive missions to investigate solid intelligence leads, so once it had sufficient resources UNSCOM often got a team to a target within a week of receiving a credible tip, which is remarkable for an international entity.[129] Nonetheless, UNSCOM bioweapons inspectors listed the 1991 Airfield 37 mission as one of several that should have been launched faster and lasted longer to reap full benefit from the intelligence.[130]

Intelligence tips rarely led to pay dirt, but the inspectors accepted that misses came with the territory.[131] "Intelligence never guarantees that if inspectors go here or there they'll find this or that. The choice is to ignore intelligence or follow it up. Even if inspectors get only one hit in a hundred, that could be a cache of bioweapons. In my view," said Barton, "that's worth going to ninety-nine other places that are a dead end."[132] Convinced that rooftop equipment denoted a high-level containment ventilation system and a covert biological facility, intelligence analysts pushed for a no-notice inspection of a site. The equipment turned out to be a standard cooling system, the building a beef storage warehouse.[133] "The inspectors' job is to just investigate the lead and report the facts," said Kraatz-Wadsack. "Intelligence is never an assurance that something is there, so inspectors should not complain if it isn't; nor should the analysts call inspectors stupid because we don't find what their lead says was there. The blame game is useless."[134]

Antagonism arose, however, when the intelligence analysts acted as though their assessments were foolproof. When the inspectors went to locations but did not turn up what the analysts predicted, some analysts told the inspectors they were in error, sometimes insinuating they were incompetent or lazy. The inspectors found this incomprehensible because they literally had "ground truth" from being on site.[135] The caliber of overhead imagery in the 1990s was informative but hardly definitive. On the basis of imagery, in 1994 the inspectors dug trenches at the very spot on the Salman peninsula where intelligence analysts specified that critical items (for example, containers of bulk agent and animal carcasses from weapons tests) were buried. Rather than redirecting the effort while the team was on site, analysts told Kadlec after the mission that the dig was "somehow off a meter or two. This was unbelievable stonewalling in the face of facts witnessed on the ground by multiple reliable, technically trained individuals."[136] By withholding information from UNSCOM, intelligence officials may have somewhat preserved the façade that their analysis was accurate, but they did not facilitate a maximally assertive, open-minded investigation of Iraq's weapons programs. The uncomfortable thought that intelligence officials "are more inclined to prove their hypotheses than they are to test them" frequently crossed Franz's mind during his work with UNSCOM.[137]

In the field, inspectors witnessed some intelligence officials who could clearly see that what they projected was not in fact at a location, yet they *still* reported back to their agencies that the inspectors were at fault. The inspectors were floored that the truth took a back seat to protecting the original intelligence analysis and analysts' reputations. "There are limitations to what can be seen and understood from ninety miles above the earth," said chief inspector Doug Englund. "Surely we can all agree on that."[138] Moreover, the UNSCOM inspectors sometimes saw assessments built on information from Iraqi defectors that could have been significantly improved had the intelligence community consulted with UNSCOM personnel or other technical experts. For instance, the 2003 U.S. intelligence projection about a mobile biological weapons capability in Iraq, derived from an Iraqi defector code-named "Curveball" who admitted in February 2011 that he fed intelligence officials false information to try to topple Saddam, was notoriously wrong. Of such misfires, Kraatz-Wadsack said that sometimes intelligence analysts fall "in love with sexy information from a source and do not think clearly."[139] Were intelligence analysts held accountable for the failure to vet sources thoroughly, for not seeking data to contradict a prevailing theory, for not basing analysis on the most current data, or for noteworthy mistakes in judgment in the face of strong countervailing data, they might contribute more constructively to inspections.

THE UTILITY OF INTELLIGENCE TO UNSCOM'S BIOWEAPONS INSPECTIONS

Not long after UNSCOM stood up, the data advantage shifted radically from the intelligence agencies to UNSCOM's favor. "UNSCOM's activities began generating new information and new sites," said Ekeus, who held authority to designate nondeclared sites for inspection.[140] Intelligence services might update a briefing with a couple of new data points from a recent defector that sometimes lack technical or scientific detail and need to be verified by other means. In contrast, on a single inspection day UNSCOM collected hundreds of new facts by virtue of what its inspectors saw, documents they collected, and their discussions with Iraqis. The inspectors leveraged what they already knew to draw more information from the Iraqis and continued to turn up useful data despite Iraq's campaign to cleanse facilities of incriminating evidence. "All of this generates facts that can be confirmed or refuted and that can contribute to an assessment." Continuing, an UNSCOM official explained that the inspectorate updated its analysis on the basis of the most convincing facts from its newest batch of facts, not just a couple of data points. Plus, "[u]nlike intelligence officers who thought their photograph was of an underground facility, we could definitively say that no, it was a dry riverbed because we were there. A person never in Iraq does not really compare to someone who was. By 1993–1994, there was not a single expert in the world who knew our subjects better than us."[141] In short, UNSCOM was producing more and often far superior data about Iraq's weapons programs than the intelligence agencies, on the outside looking in, could derive from defectors or national technical means.[142]

These circumstances also help put into proper perspective the value of intelligence to UNSCOM's search for Iraq's bioweapons program. Barton said that intelligence leads on biological sites in Iraq were "not plentiful," but that the tips "on imports of media and a range of equipment were very useful, although we had to follow those up. UNSCOM probably could have generated that data anyway," continued Barton, "but the job would not have been as easy" because without some specifics (such as company names) governments might have rebuffed UNSCOM's request to cooperate.[143] In another take, Franz viewed "the early intelligence as more helpful than the later," specifically mentioning the overhead imagery as useful in orienting teams. However, Franz said that "there wasn't enough additional data to help UNSCOM with the people and the agents and who was responsible for what in the program."[144] Others were less charitable about the importance of intelligence to UNSCOM's investigation of Iraq's bioweapons program. According to Ekeus, "the role of intelligence was very little." UNSCOM, he explained, learned very quickly to base its actions about biological sites not on intelligence but on the data inspectors discovered in documents, through observation, and in interviews. "All of this information created its own dynamic. We generated our own data," stated Ekeus. "I very, very much believe that UNSCOM's most important information came from its own inspections."[145]

While crediting UNSCOM with creating the overwhelming majority of information that made it possible to uncover Iraq's biological weapons program, a senior UNSCOM official acknowledged that some contend it was UNSCOM's fault that it took the inspectors too long to do it while others make the inspectors unadulterated heroes by implying that they independently unearthed Iraq's bioweapons program without any support from governments. "Actually, somewhere in the middle is the truth."[146] As explained in Chapter 3, several reasons account for UNSCOM's delay in aggressive stalking of Iraq's bioweapons activities, and a few tips truly gave the inspectors a boost. However, the inspectors turned up far more information, both in quality and quantity, by running down those leads to flesh out what Iraq had done, not to mention by generating their own leads. Thus chief inspector Ake Sellstrom concluded that while "intelligence sometimes had the hottest information, it is wrong and very much oversimplified to characterize UNSCOM as not knowing anything that intelligence didn't already tell it."[147]

ERRORS IN A CONTEST OF SEEKERS AND CONCEALERS

According to UNSCOM inspectors, both the Iraqis and the inspectors made mistakes in judgment that aided the other side in this contest between seekers and concealers of the truth. As noted earlier, the inspectors viewed the Western mind-set as a causal factor in some individual and collective misjudgments about Iraq's biological activities. The inspectors chaffed about the sidelining of biological inspections for over two years, discussed in Chapter 3, as a major error with several contributing factors that kept UNSCOM from pushing Iraq much earlier and harder.[148]

The inspectors were the first to admit they did not recognize a few key clues that the Iraqis left in plain view. All the inspectors at Al Hakam walked right past the tanks in the southern production area that the Iraqis said they used to store water, having slapped black paint on them to mask their stainless steel composition. Use of such expensive equipment for water storage was wildly inconsistent with standard business practice. Bifurcated plenums sat openly atop the animal house and research buildings at Al Hakam and would have been indicative of a high-containment ventilation system, had UNSCOM examined the rooftops before mid-January 1995. At Al Daura, the technicians who altered the fermenters so they could function in an anaerobic capacity left coin-sized welding markings when they restored them. A high-containment capacity to produce single-cell protein was just as seriously out of place at Al Hakam as anaerobic fermenters were at Al Daura, originally designed to make foot and mouth disease vaccine. Questioning these irregularities would have made it more difficult for Iraq to hide the bioweapons program.[149] "Seeing things but not really understanding them, not spotting things at all, or seeing things and not following up on them—there were lots of missed opportunities early on," said Barton.[150] The remedies for such oversights include dispatching inspectors with the appropriate skill sets, a well-conceived inspection plan, and allotting teams sufficient time on site to review infrastructure and equipment thoroughly. Other fixes are discussed in the next chapter.

Nations build military research and production programs from their scientific communities, making human expertise another hide-in-the-open component of Iraq's bioweapons program. Not until 1996 did UNSCOM survey

Iraq's wider community of life scientists, results that guided inspections in 1997 that yielded new data about Iraq's work with ricin. UNSCOM should have asked cooperating intelligence agencies earlier for data to fuel such a survey.[151]

The inspectors also castigated themselves for sometimes not exploiting or asking timely questions about the clues they found, including the black-striped munitions seen on UNSCOM's first inspection at Al Muthanna, the large quantities of growth media the BW2 team observed at Al Hakam and subsequent teams saw in 1994, or the huge stash of growth media that an early chemical inspection team filmed at the Al Adile warehouse.[152] "We should have explored every little shred of evidence," said bioweapons inspector Debra Krikorian, "but we didn't take advantage of every opportunity."[153] Though the inspectors recognized that these anomalies would help clarify Iraq's biological activities, they attributed the failure to follow leads promptly to the early policy to heed diplomatic protocol, overscheduling of missions, some team chiefs who would not listen to inspectors' feedback, and UNSCOM's lack of resources. These causal factors could all be corrected.

On the other side, Iraq's leaders goofed before UNSCOM first stepped on Iraqi soil when they assumed that UNSCOM inspectors would be no more meticulous or consequential than those during previous international weapons inspections in Iraq. Having suffered no significant ill consequences from these inspections, Iraq's leaders evidently perceived no particular reason to dread UNSCOM and assumed it would be short-lived. After initiating the concealment-and-deception strategy, Iraqi leaders apparently saw little need to police its implementation closely.[154]

UNSCOM's first biological team found that the Iraqis did a slapdash job with clean-up and cover stories, whether it was leaving bulldozers parked beside freshly razed buildings at Salman Pak or describing offensive, not defensive, research activities. The lackadaisical execution of the cover stories was evident throughout UNSCOM's years. At Al Hakam in mid-January 1995, Kraatz-Wadsack spotted a trio of emaciated and badly pecked chickens in the atrium of the animal house that lent zero credibility to Iraq's assertion that Al Hakam was making single-cell protein feed.[155] Similarly, for years the inspectors turned up enlightening and inculpating documents and identified, tagged, and monitored equipment that could have been secreted elsewhere. These rank-and-file blunders benefited the inspectors.[156]

Iraq's strategic objectives over time drove Baghdad's calculations about how to manage the biological inspections. At first, Iraq intended to hide its bioweapons capability fully. With inspectors hot on the trail of Iraq's nuclear program in mid-1991, Iraqi leaders ordered the biological weapons and bulk agent destroyed to skirt getting caught red-handed and from 1992 to 1995 focused on retaining their industrial infrastructure and scientific know-how to make and weaponize agents. Then, after its mid-1995 admissions of production and weaponization, Iraq concentrated on sustaining the skills of its weaponeers.[157]

A second major factor influencing how Iraq handled the biological inspections was Baghdad's calculus of how much to reveal based on its guesstimate of what UNSCOM knew at that particular time. Using a partial-truth tactic that alternately served and harmed Iraq's interests, the Iraqis tossed the inspectors a bit of the truth, as necessary, hoping not to have to reveal larger truths about the program.[158] Iraq toiled to achieve the right balance of partial truths. Initially claiming no biological capability whatsoever, Iraq soon aligned its declaration with news coverage cued largely on intelligence reports of bioweapons activity at Salman Pak. Iraq next depicted its biological research program as trivial, which it was compared to Iraq's much larger chemical and nuclear weapons programs, and the inspectors could not immediately cry foul when Iraq generically labeled its work as for "military purposes" with defensive or offensive applications because the Biological and Toxin Weapons Convention expressly permits research with high-risk pathogens for prophylactic, protective, and other peaceful purposes. This permitted research is very difficult to distinguish from similar work for offensive military applications.[159] Iraq's scheme might have paid off more handsomely had the Iraqis executed it well. Instead, one Iraqi after another delineated work that correlated disturbingly with offensive bioweapons studies, as described in Chapter 2.

"I wonder why the Iraqis ever admitted a military biological research program in the first place. They could have said that they were looking into defensive measures at Salman Pak and just had a rudimentary defense program," stated Huxsoll.[160] Plus, the Iraqis perplexingly took the inspectors to a demolished aerosolization chamber indicating more substantial and offensive work after having crushed Salman Pak's chamber and hauled it to a roadside junk heap. Such missteps handed the inspectors threads that they could pull to unravel Iraq's bioweapons program.

By far, the biggest thread that Iraq disclosed was Al Hakam, which Iraq brought to light as an equipment storage and repair facility. According to Kelly, the Iraqis spoke of Al Hakam because "they thought we knew about it, but they did it in a minimalist way."[161] While Iraq's measured revelation of Al Hakam could be viewed as an inoculation against later accusations of trying to conceal a major dual-use plant, some saw Baghdad's exposure of Al Hakam, which had emerged unscathed from the 1991 Gulf War, as a squandering of Iraq's successful building and operation of a covert bioweapons facility.[162] The important lesson that Iraq took from this false move was not to concede anything that UNSCOM could not demonstrate. Thereafter, Iraq rarely volunteered anything, sometimes holding its ground despite evidence of Iraqi wrongdoing.[163]

After UNSCOM repeatedly stated concerns that Al Hakam was not a single-cell protein facility, Iraq pressed its luck to conserve and develop the skills of its weapons scientists to dry biowarfare agents by adding a second product line purportedly for a biopesticide. This venture backfired, as Chapter 3 describes, because an inspector identified a tell-tale equipment setup and samples showed the ultra-fine particle sizes of *B. thuringiensis*, an anthrax simulant, to be unusable for a biopesticide but ideal for biowarfare agents. Once UNSCOM really devoted resources to the task, the inspectors made quick work of Iraq's cover stories. "We started working this in earnest in November 1994," recapped Barton. "Iraq confessed on July 1 the following year."[164]

Iraq's shabby cover story problems, however, were minor compared to the predicament raised by its lack of documentation about the unilateral destruction of its biological arsenal. Iraq gave UNSCOM's chemical and missile inspectors accounts of what happened with bombs, rockets, and missiles long before Baghdad admitted weaponizing germs, and this came back to haunt them. Iraq's zig-zagging verbal and written accounts about the number of weapons and how and where the Iraqis hid and destroyed the weapons and bulk agent combined with the dearth of confirming documentation and physical evidence to create an asymptotic impasse between Baghdad and the inspectorate. Exacerbating the deadlock, the quantity of truth was so small compared to Iraq's fabrications over the years that some inspectors and policymakers became conditioned to believe Iraq incapable of telling the truth about anything on its biological or other weapons programs.[165] UNSCOM historian Stephen Black summed up the situation simply: "They shot themselves in the foot."[166] Perhaps a colossal lapse in judgment that prolonged sanctions, this situation might have stemmed from conflicting Iraqi policy objectives. Saddam wanted UNSCOM out of Iraq quickly, but he also intended for Iraq's enemies to worry that Iraq retained unconventional weapons and the ability to deliver them. Iraq's documentation drought was part of what led UNSCOM to broadcast repeatedly that it could not certify that Iraq no longer had hidden weapons or unaccounted-for ingredients to make them, and that served Saddam's bluff.[167]

OF PROOF AND PRISMS

One man's foolproof evidence is another's invitation to start debating exactly what that evidence means.[168] UNSCOM's mandate required the inspectorate to convey its findings—good, bad, or indifferent—about Iraq's declarations, dual-use facilities, and forfeiture of required items for destruction or rendering them harmless. Excepting examples of blatant Iraqi misbehavior, some countries routinely viewed UNSCOM's reports as justification to sustain sanctions while others did not. The same reports could be seen so differently in part because the Security Council never stipulated the standard of proof for UNSCOM's certification that Iraq had met the disarmament requirements.[169] Thus everyone could freely question what exactly constituted proof of compliance.

Iraq fabricated so much of its declarations and unilaterally destroyed or withheld so much evidence that UNSCOM was stuck in the untenable position of trying to prove a negative—that what Iraq was saying was not true. The inspectors cataloged Iraq's incongruous statements about facilities, equipment, and activities and then compared Iraq's explanations of how these items were being used for peaceful purposes against how they could be employed to make weapons. "That information convinces scientists, technologists, and industrial people," said Kelly, "but it does not convince diplomats, and that is the real problem."[170] As UNSCOM's finds of evidence of Iraqi noncompliance became less frequent or audacious, it was tougher for UNSCOM to retain political support. "Politicians assume that the whole arrangement isn't working, that the inspectors aren't effective, or that because nothing is being found, that proves nothing is there. Neither argument is right," said Gallucci. "Inspections that do not turn up illicit goods or activity may confirm compliance and serve to deter noncompliance, but it will always be impossible to prove a negative."[171]

A logic gap automatically grabs the attention of scientists, who innately see matters through the prism of logic. Kraatz-Wadsack noted right away the peculiarity of how reticent Taha was to discuss basic scientific aspects of Al Hakam's single-cell protein and biopesticide operations. At Al Daura, which

Iraq declared was producing six hundred thousand doses of foot and mouth disease vaccine annually, Kraatz-Wadsack saw no staff, functioning lights, or growth media prepared for production. Something must have happened to transform Iraq's most advanced biological plant, which was not bombed during the war, into a ghost town. "Things at Al Hakam were out of place, but Al Daura really gave me alarm because this place had so much more capability and was not at all as it should be. These were scientific operations, yet there was no scientific logic to what I was seeing or hearing," said Kraatz-Wadsack.[172] For anyone with industrial experience the notion that Al Hakam was a commercial outfit was implausible: "Their cover stories were very clearly cover stories. The whole time I was at Al Hakam, the Iraqis were telling me a mule was a horse."[173] Some inspectors described logic almost as a sixth sense that told them about Iraqi noncompliance. During the first biological inspection, "I knew in thirty minutes that they were hiding and concealing, and therefore by definition, I thought they were hiding something about a program," said Kelly. "The dilemma the inspectors had was actually translating that into evidence."[174]

Scientists, Krikorian cautioned, are not always paragons of objectivity. "Data can be politicized; people can choose to rely on selective information. Pictures and human intelligence can be deceiving. Having scientists who are really taught—and this is seldom done—to review information without bias is critical. A real compliance assessment," she insisted, "demands a balance of several types of data and also that both scientists and diplomats know the technical capabilities and limitations of the collection systems."[175]

With their natural gravitation to logic, however, some inspectors thought it was easier to make a compliance case to scientists.[176] When UNSCOM presented evidence of Iraq's hidden bioweapons program to international scientists in April 1995, the panel quickly concluded that Iraq had a larger, more sophisticated bioweapons program than Baghdad had declared.[177] Indeed, as discussed in Chapter 7, the inspectorate's independent review panels consistently found Iraq short of meeting its obligations under Resolution 687.

In contrast, sometimes the Security Council rebuffed data that UNSCOM's scientists considered hard proof of Iraq's noncompliance and mendacity. For example, Iraq declared that it had no uranium enrichment program, remembered Gallucci, only to have inspectors uncover first their electromagnetic isotope separation activities, then their work with gas centrifuges, chemical enrichment, and gaseous-diffusion enrichment. The Iraqis countered that they were only interested in power production and hid these enrichment efforts because Israel bombed the Osiraq reactor in 1981. UNSCOM pointed out that Iraq did not have a single nuclear power plant and that uranium enrichment was a neon indicator of a covert weapons program, but the diplomats demurred. "UNSCOM had to prove that Iraq had a nuclear weapons program by turning up an even hotter smoking gun. We had to get the blueprint for their weapons. That's a very difficult standard to meet, almost impossible, but that was what was needed to make the case to the Security Council," said Gallucci. "For scientists, the case that Iraq was proliferating was made with the first data about their uranium enrichment activities. The joke inside UNSCOM was whether a bomb design would be sufficient to convince the Security Council or if they actually needed to stand in the bomb crater."[178] Commented an UNSCOM commissioner, "If someone doesn't want to be convinced, it will be very difficult to prove compliance either way."[179]

Accordingly, UNSCOM's bioweapons inspectors were prone to think that some politicians based their decisions on factors unrelated to the data pertinent to compliance, others were not capable of understanding the science, and still others did not care or want to know the facts.[180] Kelly recalled that when UNSCOM reported that a handful of missiles were not accounted for in Iraq, the Russians argued that Iraq's remaining missiles "were of no significance" because no matter what they were loaded with they would not affect the military balance in the Middle East.[181] The inspectors concluded that diplomats and politicians were after the best evidence that supported their position or did not pin them down to one.[182] Thus a divide can fester between the worlds of science and politics, particularly when neither side necessarily appreciates fully what the other brings to the policymaking process.

In the fluid world of politics, diplomats and policymakers routinely trade one issue off of others.[183] The reasons for political compromises can be manifold, difficult to pinpoint, often at odds with scientific logic, and an encumbrance to definitive problem solving. As UNSCOM Deputy Executive Chairman Charles Duelfer put it, "The reality UNSCOM described was not the reality the UN Security Council wanted. The council wanted a less contentious version."[184] Scientists often struggled to understand diplomats and politicians. After hearing Manley's initial recommendations to destroy Iraq's chemical arsenal, Ekeus replied that he was not questioning Manley's science and asked whether the chemist had considered alternative "x." "He was looking at and incorporating the political angles. I never would have thought of that alternative," admitted Manley. "Scientists never do that; they look at it as how to solve a problem. Politicians have to take other things into account."[185] Ekeus understood that UNSCOM's scientists often overlooked the larger geo-political context in which the organization operated.[186] Unlike the immutable laws of science, the rules that do exist in politics appear made to be broken, which means anything can and does happen.

Political agendas that place personal, organizational, or national interests ahead of the global good can be highly objectionable, and some diplomats clearly wore political agendas on their sleeves. Others, however, asked Ekeus to help them comprehend UNSCOM's data.[187] In short, some policymakers attempted to scale the technical learning curves associated with the verification of unconventional arms capabilities. However, the frequency of UNSCOM's reporting could be seen as a gauge of policymakers' desire to grasp the facts. UNSCOM initially reported formally to the Security Council several times a year, then normalized to four annual reports, and finally slid to two annual reports. At first UNSCOM also gave the Security Council its field inspection reports, but around April 1992 the inspectorate began submitting executive summaries of these reports instead. "After a while they didn't seem to want even the executive summaries."[188] By this yardstick, as time wore on, the data that UNSCOM gathered appeared to play a less prominent role in Security Council deliberations.

While UNSCOM's bioweapons scientists regaled their contemporaries with lots of data, they maintained there was "an enormous difference, a huge gulf, in what one tells diplomats and what one says to scientists."[189] The infinite details that fascinate scientists are not necessarily suited to policymakers, and for the most part, the inspectors knew that what they presented verbally or sent in writing to the Security Council had to be short and snappy, with plain but not over-simplified language.[190] In addition to issues of technical substance and terminology, the international setting contributed to communications difficulties between scientists and diplomats because a large number of participants in any discussion or decision were not native speakers of English.[191]

If the IAEA's nuclear inspectors, who literally had calutron-sized physical evidence, felt they had a tough time convincing the Security Council that Iraq was hiding a nuclear program, UNSCOM's biological team had it worse. In-house, the biological inspectors thought that evidence of Iraq's attempt to obtain a negative pressure air-handling system for Al Hakam was the more significant indicator of a weapons program. No commercial enterprise would spend an exorbitant sum on a capability not essential for the plant's products, and high-level containment was totally unnecessary to make single-cell protein and biopesticide but very handy for bioweapons research and development. UNSCOM headlined its case to the Security Council in April 1995 with the missing growth media because non-technical audiences could most readily digest that issue.[192]

Ideally, said Englund, scientists and diplomats should be working with roughly the same information because the technical data feeds into the policy context and vice versa. "If the information is clear, then one ought to be able to make a compliance judgment."[193] Kraatz-Wadsack thought that more interaction between the inspectors and those receiving inspection reports would improve the overall process: "Inspectors see and learn first-hand, so they are best able to assess the validity of something. Considerable interaction between the field and intelligence analysts, diplomats, and policymakers about factual findings will reduce the chances that they will assume too much that may not be true."[194] One way to foster such interchange would be to include sporadically and from the outset a few diplomats or policymakers on missions as observers to heighten their understanding about the technical and operational aspects of inspections and promote confidence in the inspection results.[195] Intermediaries well-versed in both policy and technology might also help to bridge the communications gap so that scientists and policymakers can work together effectively.[196]

Taylor described UNSCOM as "a scientific exercise that unfolded in a political context."[197] Making decisions at the intersection of policy and science is always a challenge, but Franz asserted that decisions about "biological noncompliance are especially hard. In a nuclear context, the issues are crisper and cleaner, and the lines are brighter. We're still trying to figure out how to deal with this squishy field called biology. In the future," he predicted, "really hard decisions about compliance with bioweapons prohibitions will have to be made with a lot less information than we really need."[198] For the sake of global public health and security, policymakers and scientists alike should spare no effort now to ensure that every possible scrap of relevant factual data can be presented to policymakers to inform such decisions.

9 LESSONS EXPERIENCED II:
SHARPENING THE TOOLS OF INSPECTION

THE UNITED NATIONS Special Commission's (UNSCOM's) biological inspection missions had different basic objectives, including to clarify Iraq's declarations and conduct initial site visits; to establish baseline data for ongoing monitoring; to inventory, tag, and document dual-use equipment; to perform ongoing monitoring and verification; to destroy equipment and facilities used in Iraq's weapons program; to locate and review documents pertinent to dual-use activities; to interview relevant Iraqis; and to expound Iraq's past bioweapons activities. The bioweapons inspectors conducted some missions jointly with inspectors in UNSCOM's Baghdad monitoring and verification office or other inspection teams. The inspectors hunted and evaluated data related to the weapons, facilities, sites, equipment, technologies, documents, materials, human resources, finances, procurement, events, and activities of Iraq's germ weapons program. By examining data across these areas, the inspectors isolated patterns and factors that helped to expose more about the bioweapons program that Iraq was hiding.[1]

Time and distance from an event or process give participants opportunities to ruminate on the effectiveness of policies, practices, and actions, allowing them to project how things could be done better in similar circumstances in the future. All too often, lessons are identified and characterized but never utilized for constructive changes in policy and practice. As noted in Chapter 8, unapplied knowledge rests as a lesson experienced but not yet learned.[2]

This "lessons experienced" chapter addresses lessons about the actual conduct of field inspections. Drawn primarily from those with extensive experience inspecting dual-use biological facilities in Iraq, these observations pertain first to biological arms inspections, in which the lines between peaceful research, commercial production, and permitted defense activity and illegal offensive weapons work are notoriously thin. "This is not like finding a bomb in a building some place," said UNSCOM chief biological inspector David Huxsoll. "The challenge in biological inspections is to find information that can be easily disguised and doesn't leave much of a signature."[3] The lessons in this chapter, however, are easily translated to chemical, nuclear, missile, and conventional arms inspections.

Several lessons derive from the trails that UNSCOM blazed in inspection strategy and practices. True, since 1957 the International Atomic Energy Agency (IAEA) has been inspecting nuclear power plants and research reactors around the globe to see that they are safely operated and not serving as a cover to develop fissile materials for weapons. When UNSCOM was created, however, not that many countries had experience with IAEA inspections because of the relatively sparse number of nuclear reactors worldwide. The inspectorate for the Chemical Weapons Convention, which has sent teams to industrial and military chemical facilities in some eighty countries since 1997, was half a dozen years away from starting operations when UNSCOM inspectors set foot on Iraqi soil.[4] The conduct of biological inspections was still uncharted territory because the treaty banning this category of arms, the Biological and Toxin Weapons Convention, has no verification provisions whatsoever. So, to begin with, "there was a lot of hesitation to really utilize this funny thing called UNSCOM," said UNSCOM bioweapons inspector Debra Krikorian. Chapter 3 related other reasons that delayed assertive biological inspections, but Krikorian argued that "if all of the information and resources had been brought to bear, we could have exposed Iraq's bioweapons program a lot more effectively and efficiently."[5]

The urgency to inaugurate an inspection process and the novelty of it all can propel inspections before much actual thinking is done. Neither looking only where the inspected state opens doors or the "ready, fire, aim" approach will get the job done. Instead, inspectors should work from a model of a weapons program, including the military requirements for it and how that program might be set up in the country concerned. Factors to be considered would include whether the country imported or made key equipment and materials, custom built or converted industrial facilities for its weapons programs, and has appreciable scientific and technical sophistication. From that tailored model, inspectors can estimate what the weapons program might look like and derive key investigatory questions to guide initial inspection plans and objectives.[6] UNSCOM inspectors approximated this thought process on the fly, as Chapter 1 describes, working with declarations in hand to identify what the Iraqis had not told them about the phases typical to a weapons program. However, the early UNSCOM inspectors did not work up full, country-specific models of Iraq's various weapons programs. As needed, they tested new inspection concepts and adjusted and improved existing strategies and practices.

The following pages describe how UNSCOM's biological inspectors employed and fine-tuned the basic inspection tools of on-site observation, interviews, document reviews, and sampling. The chapter also includes a discussion of the advisability of a more aggressive inspection strategy. To close the chapter, the inspectors evaluate the overall effectiveness of inspections to determine whether a covert germ warfare program is nestled amidst a country's dual-use biological facilities.

The opinions of UNSCOM's bioweapons inspectors about the effectiveness of different inspection tools varied based on their personal experiences. Whereas chief UNSCOM biological weapons inspector Terence Taylor said formal interviews had little value, UNSCOM inspector Rod Barton rated interviews as "the key" inspection tool.[7] Though each inspector had their preferred tool(s), as a group they agreed that every tool served its purpose during UNSCOM's investigation of Iraq's bioweapons program, with the productivity of tools differing from one stage of the investigation to another. As a senior UNSCOM official explained, "The beauty is that we had all of these tools and could apply them as required. Inspectors should use the right tool at the right time. Saying that one tool is better than another isn't possible because at some time they are all good."[8]

ON-SITE OBSERVATION: BEYOND SEEING TO ACTIVE COMPREHENSION

Any data that inspectors have in advance from open sources or intelligence about a dual-use facility will help them anticipate a site's infrastructure, capabilities, equipment, unique features, and regulatory framework, as well as the likely number, disciplines, and skill levels of personnel. Advance information is important because many buildings can be relatively nondescript—a laboratory can be situated inside what otherwise looks like an administrative building. A pre-existing site dossier can inform the plan about how inspectors move through a facility in the manner most beneficial to inspection objectives. Even if a team arrives on site with nothing other than information from the inspected country, each inspector should be acutely aware that absent vigilant observation, they are likely to bypass obvious clues about what is really taking place at a facility.

UNSCOM provided chief inspectors with line diagrams of Iraqi facilities to help orient and organize their inspectors to work effectively as a team. On the basis of the team's mission, the site's characteristics, and the skills of inspectors, team chiefs assigned subteams and individuals specific tasks in advance, which is why all team members had to understand the site layout and the building and floor numbering systems so that they could exploit their assigned areas.[9] Huxsoll also employed site diagrams to ignite a collaborative tour of a facility. Unfolding the line diagram after introductions, the Iraqis clustered around it and, unprompted, sometimes began pointing to where they conducted various activities. Huxsoll continued to let the Iraqis talk about the facility as they walked through it, asking seemingly casual questions, such as, "Oh, why do you do that? Maybe they would just tell you," he said, "or maybe not."[10] Sometimes, it was reasonable to allow the Iraqis to guide a site tour, but when UNSCOM believed Iraq was hiding something or the inspectors were acting on an intelligence tip, the team went directly to certain parts of a site or fanned out quickly to limit the Iraqis' opportunities to destroy or stash evidence.[11]

Expertise in a certain technology or scientific discipline can cut both ways for an inspector. Someone who specializes in "x" might focus exclusively on that area, practically oblivious to other observable data important to the inspection.[12] In contrast, an inspector who is not a technical specialist but who has sharp eyes and a sizable curiosity can be unyielding, open, and comprehensive in examining a facility, as Krikorian explained. Tasked to learn about the welding equipment, capabilities, and activities at an Iraqi facility, Krikorian had never used a blowtorch and took nothing for granted. She looked "under every little piece of cloth, just kept prodding and poking" and thus found a drop tank to disperse biowarfare agent.[13] Said UNSCOM historian Steve Black, "Observation is better than comprehension at times, which often isn't acknowledged but is very important. Non-technical inspection tasks, like simple observation, generate essential knowledge."[14]

Most people do not exercise their full powers of observation, screening out the vast amount of data within eyesight and other senses to concentrate only on what they need to finish their current task. Entering an office, a person might be cognizant of photographs on the wall but not look closely at who was in them or the activity the photo captured. To be effective, inspectors have to be much more deliberate: they have to see such details, process the information, evaluate what it might mean, and, if appropriate, act on it.

UNSCOM chief bioweapons inspector Hamish Killip sharpened his observation skills, roundly recognized by his peers as remarkable, while on infantry patrol in Northern Ireland. Inspectors need the same hyper alertness that Killip and his fellow soldiers relied on to protect their lives as they passed through neighborhoods from one hour to the next, detecting small details such as whether cars had moved or a window was open or shut. Killip coached rookie inspectors to accumulate a mental inventory of a site, looking at things systematically, and, when they saw something odd, to discipline themselves to pursue why something would be that way instead of letting that information go past their eyes. For example, seeing an elevator, inspectors would need to investigate why it does not stop at the fifth floor and also to examine the machine room, taking in details such as the voltage powering the machines and the data plates, which could tell them whether equipment was made domestically or imported.[15] Krikorian watched for a satellite dish outside of Iraqi offices to help identify which Iraqis were trusted enough to have access to the outside world, a gauge of a person's importance in Iraq's hierarchy.[16] Inspectors who fully employed their powers of observation took in reams of data that informed and influenced their assessments.[17]

UNSCOM inspectors stretched their observational and analytical skills inventively, figuring out how to glean knowledge even from buildings completely stripped of equipment. When a novice inspector reported that a Salman Pak building contained nothing, Barton reeled off questions that might be answered when the inspector made the effort to observe the building intensely, thoughtfully, and systematically: "How long had it been empty? What could it have been equipped for? There were always clues: the amount of dust, the type of electrical fittings, the plumbing, the size of the entrance doors, overhead gantry cranes." The inspectors, Barton recounted, even read the patterns of pigeon droppings to learn something about past activities at a site.[18]

Search techniques have been developed for going through buildings, rooms, tunnels, and all manner of spaces, often relying on the same meticulous process to increase the chances that important details are not overlooked. UNSCOM taught inspectors to work always from top to bottom and left to right, looking deliberately at each object, and sometimes drilled newcomers to polish their observation skills. Items of interest could be found in predictable places, such as documents that slip behind a file cabinet drawer. To emphasize that point, in drills in Bahrain Black routinely placed a note promising its finder free beer in the bottom of a trash can. The overwhelming majority of new inspectors freshly instructed on how to search a room systematically overlooked the trash can, the obvious place to ditch something quickly.[19] Thus observation, an unheralded skill at everyone's disposal, often requires refinement and prompting so that inspectors are aware of how to apply this skill assiduously to discern the true nature of a facility's activities.

INTERVIEWS: ELICITING AND DISTINGUISHING TIDBITS OF THE TRUTH

Cumulatively, UNSCOM interviewed over two hundred people associated with Iraq's biowarfare program, and via this route it gained "the vast majority of the information that we had on the biological program."[20] The inspectors requested interviews with people named in documents (such as purchase records obtained from suppliers) or encountered during missions. Iraq frequently tendered them, which was quite remarkable.[21] The inspectors quizzed scientists and government officials from procurement officers to ministers, but they also knew that interviews with secretaries, janitors, farmers, and forklift drivers could be tremendously productive. Chief inspector David Kelly called the glasswasher a facility's "barometer of activity," so when Salman Pak's glasswasher claimed he hardly did any work, that meant that Rihab Taha's bioweapons research team was idle, which did not jibe with the amount and type of research the Iraqis described to the inspectors.[22]

Because they knew that definitive physical evidence would be hard to come by, the biological inspectors relied on interviews more heavily than did UNSCOM's other inspectors. Chief inspector Richard Spertzel called interviews the easiest way to try to get to the truth,[23] but finding the truth via interviews was anything but simple. Kelly's peers admired his polite but purposeful way of pinning an interviewee down on a question the person was trying to dodge by summarizing the interviewee's last statement, pausing to get the interviewee's confirmation that Kelly had understood them correctly before diverting to an observation about some pertinent scientific detail, and circling back to the original question, rephrased. With this technique, Kelly often numbed interviewees into giving up more detail than they intended as

they tried to find new ways to answer the same question.[24] With such interview styles, the inspectors pried more of the truth from the Iraqis.

The Iraqis though, were under considerable pressure not to divulge the
truth. They were instructed to maintain cover stories. Taha had bioweapons
scientists at Salman Pak and Al Hakam sign a death penalty oath not to say
anything about Iraq's ability to develop or produce any warfare agent, and all
of them were acutely aware that Iraq's internal security apparatus was monitoring their every word and move.[25] Some Iraqis "sweated like hell and shook
without being asked a question."[26] During an interview in mid-December
1996, Taha baldly stated the awful position the Iraqis were in when she exclaimed to Spertzel, "Dr. Spertzel, it is not a lie when you are ordered to lie."[27]

Iraq's cover stories generally changed as little as possible (for example, a
date) so that the Iraqis did not have to remember much new information. The
inspectors concluded that almost all interviewees had been coached on what
not to say, though not necessarily on what to say. When the Iraqis had to im-
provise about points their scripts did not address, the inspectors got an ear-
ful.[28] Over the years the tall tales stacked up, giving Iraqis, who had "to keep
the collective book on what was told to UNSCOM" a challenge, said former
UNSCOM Deputy Executive Chairman Duelfer.[29] To wiggle out of contradictions, the Iraqis usually blamed them on a person's drunkenness or stupidity.
At times, however, their contorted tales would get them into such impossible
positions that everyone would laugh.[30]

The lies Iraqis told came in all forms, from fibs about small details to whoppers that made significant differences in the amount of materials consumed or
the number of weapons made.[31] UNSCOM's purpose, noted Killip, was not to
catch the Iraqis in their lies but to get an accurate account of what happened.
In that context, a lie was "inconvenient and annoying, but sometimes it was
also quite useful," Killip explained. "When they were lying it meant they were
covering up, and the lie might provide a little bit of the shadow to tell you
where the truth was in the first place."[32]

A lie has more than one dimension, including when the lie is first told, the
temporal scope of the activity being lied about, how widespread the activity was, and the responsibilities of various people involved in the activity. A
lie about Iraq's biological program, for instance, might involve warfare agent
production just in 1990 and at Al Hakam, or it could cover a few years and
facilities. Unraveling a multifaceted lie is a thorny undertaking. To illustrate,
the tendency is to assume that the statements made later in an inspection

process may be closer to the truth, but the original statements could be more truthful because subordinates had not yet received orders to conceal the truth or closed ranks on how to do so. Just assessing how far back a lie went was difficult, but the inspectors also had to ascertain a lie's other facets, including the reason(s) the Iraqis told it.[33]

In interviews, the Iraqis did whatever they thought would satisfy, fool, or hinder the inspectors.[34] With an inexperienced inspector or one the Iraqis felt was not knowledgeable, almost by default they upped their antics. From the outset, the Iraqis watched for inspectors who nodded or smiled even when the Iraqis said something ridiculous or exhibited other behaviors that made them appear inducible. In September 1991, each evening Amer Rasheed, a senior Iraqi official, scanned film of the day's activities at Al Hakam to assess which inspectors were swallowing their cover story about single-cell protein production. Thus, in addition to gathering information on the inspectors' backgrounds, the Iraqis gauged their tenacity, willingness to negotiate, and level of sympathy to Iraq.[35] To make headway, the inspectors had to impress the Iraqis with how well they knew the subject matter so the Iraqis understood they could not just say anything. In addition to substantive expertise (such as in biological production or weaponry), the inspectors had to master the "golden nuggets," UNSCOM slang for what the Iraqis said when and where and the trajectory of what transpired throughout the inspections. This knowledge created a minefield for interviewees and allowed inspectors to manage or somewhat contain the lying. The golden nuggets also enabled inspectors to highlight contradictions in the Iraqis' accounts, which sometimes caused them to reveal more than intended as they scrambled to reconcile discrepancies.[36]

Some inspectors found the lies so distracting or irritating, however, that they interrupted an interviewee at the first remark they knew to be false. Others, understanding that a lie usually can contain a kernel of the truth, took full advantage of the lies. "I rarely pointed out the inconsistencies in their stories as they were talking, no matter how ludicrous. If you cut them off, you might not hear what it was they were trying to deceive you about or what they were trying to tell you. In some ways," said Killip, "the lie may be as valuable as the truth because it is the bodyguard of what they are trying to protect. After hearing the whole lot of it, then go back and pick it apart or try to decipher it."[37] The trick was to find the constructive element in what was said, to tell where the truth left off and the lie began.

In November 1994, the biological inspectors who conducted UNSCOM's first interview mission established the inspectorate's protocol for formal interviews. UNSCOM allowed only four Iraqis other than the interviewee in the room—an interpreter, a video camera operator, and two observers—all seated behind the interviewee so they could not cue that individual. Normally five or six inspectors faced the interviewee, with only one leading the questioning at a time while the others remained silent, passing a note to bring a pressing issue to the attention of the primary questioner. The team chief usually covered all of the subjects and then delegated additional questioning to others according to their expertise. The inspectors carefully planned an interview series, charting what they wanted to ask each interviewee. Inspectors posed roughly the same questions to individuals supposedly involved in the same activity so they could contrast their answers. At the end of every formal interview session, the inspectors usually compared notes, discussed whether they had heard one or more kernels of truth, devised follow-up questions, and decided whom to interview next to obtain more facts and insights.[38]

To establish a toehold to start to pin down a timeline and important data points, the inspectors tried to get the Iraqis to state a specific fact, usually a date.[39] The inspectors phrased some questions in "yes" or "no" form and made others more open-ended. Agile inspectors maneuvered with critical questions across the span of the interview, phrasing them differently so that the Iraqis could not avoid answering. Inspectors repeated important answers on the spot to ensure that they understood the answer properly and there were no interpretation problems. To make progress, patience and persistence were essential.[40]

By rote scientists describing an experiment mention research techniques, modifications to a process or equipment, and problems encountered along the way, so when the Iraqis did not speak of these customary factors it could also be instructive.[41] Physical signs of discomfort also conveyed useful information. For instance, the left side of Iraq's Deputy Prime Minister Tariq Aziz's face often twitched when he was nervous or perhaps not being honest.[42] The law enforcement maxim that a person looking up and to the left could be lying may not apply in Arab culture, which has a different perspective about lying. "To them it is no big deal to use any lie or a truckload of lies to reach their objective, and their eyes don't go up or left. They told plenty of lies where they didn't lose composure."[43] The inspectors realized that twitches and other "tells" did not guarantee mendacity, but they were always on the lookout for any Iraqi behavior, individually or collectively, that could assist the investigation.[44]

At signs of anxiety, vulnerability, or pliability, the inspectors pressed an interviewee harder.[45] "Inspectors have to know what buttons to push," stated Krikorian, who added that knowing an interviewee's background provided a significant advantage. "Agreeing with this in concept and knowing how to apply it are two totally different things; inspectors have to be taught this technique."[46] Knowledge of an interviewee's personal history can help inspectors figure out how to leverage their doubts about how much the inspectors know, who told the inspectors what, or who said something different from their account. When such uncertainties caused an interviewee to lose composure, inspectors could profit by asking the right questions.[47] Another way to throw the Iraqis off stride was "to make them angry, quite frankly." When angry, the Iraqis lost patience with their interpreters and broke into English, so inspectors could just speak English with them. "Sometimes," Taylor continued, "their English wasn't that good and by asking repeatedly for clarifications you could explore different aspects of what they said to learn more, always pushing them" to keep that edge of anger.[48]

Iraqi missteps could also be elicited by taking questions to a precise level of detail. The inspectors crafted manifold interlinked detailed questions—whether a tracked vehicle or a regular truck delivered certain items, the rank of the vehicle's driver, or the color of the rope that tied test donkeys to stakes.[49] Such questions shocked, irritated, and frustrated the Iraqis, which is why the inspectors found them so useful. Detailed questions could

- Extract a tremendous number of facts to be confirmed
- Identify individuals more likely to have really been involved in the activity of interest because they knew the answers
- Feed a tendency to make things up, which helped inspectors determine which Iraqis were telling the truth because the inspectors could usually dissect their accounts
- Cause the stories various Iraqis told to disintegrate and not match, which gave the inspectors justification to insist that the Iraqis straighten out their stories
- Cue the inspectors to which Iraqis had an eye for detail and good memories, identifying expedient routes to resolve matters in future interviews
- Expose the internal lies the Iraqis told each other[50]

Of this final point, Killip explained that detailed questions confirmed that the inspectors "were in the midst of a piece of theater. To create the right impression and protect themselves, they often said things for the camera to be reported up the chain."[51] Thus when the inspectors delved into the details the Iraqis detested it.

Every incongruity opened up a new line of questioning for the inspectors. Just because several people agreed that a weapon arrived at a site on a truck, however, does not mean that a weapon was ever there, much less brought by a truck. The Iraqis might have been instructed to give that detail as part of the cover story. Conversely, when people differed on a facet of a story—one saying the delivery vehicle was a flatbed truck, another a covered army truck—that could be the point at which the interviewees ran out of their shared cover story, *if* they were telling a lie. Or, they could have been trying to tell the truth but had foggy memories or just nervously or fearfully bobbled a detail.[52]

Although useful, small details can be the enemy of the larger truth. When differences on details could not be settled, the inspectors weighed their confidence that they had obtained the larger truth, that the Iraqis destroyed weapons at site "x," against the failure of interviewees to concur on the finer details.[53] The embodiment of the aphorism about the devil living in the details, inevitably the inspectors' opinions varied as to which details qualified as critical to the veracity of an account.

The inspectors also questioned the Iraqis on site, where they were supposed to be familiar with equipment, procedures, their job responsibilities, and events. For Taylor, impromptu interviews during no-notice inspections were the most useful inspection tool: "You're going to get the crown jewels at the instant that they are confronted," he said. "Once they had time to recover from the shock of your being there or to talk to colleagues, the odds of something productive coming out of it decreased. All my finds were from people who weren't expecting to see me, or vice versa."[54] Even when the Iraqis knew UNSCOM would visit a site, Iraqis who fumbled with equipment or for answers stood out as substitutes for the real scientists and technicians or as someone overly edgy about having inspectors in their midst. When the inspectors sometimes injected comments about procedures specific to performing an activity with biowarfare agents, the Iraqis occasionally joined in with opinions or details indicative of having actually worked with biowarfare agents.[55] Killip often took Iraqis who supposedly participated in an event of interest to a declared demolition or test site to reconstruct prior events. Going question by question, person by person down the line but just out of earshot of the others, Killip usually started his questioning from a solid data point like a date and then posed detailed questions about the objects involved, the sequence of activities, and how many workers and how much time specific tasks required. When the Iraqis gave different answers Killip huddled them together, listed their variances, told them somebody had clearly gotten something wrong, and then watched and listened as the Iraqis sorted matters out, sometimes arguing loudly and flinging their hands. The combination of being on site and interviewed collectively disarmed the Iraqis of their regular options to dissemble.[56]

In addition, the biological inspectors could break open an interview by introducing data from outside sources. The Iraqis knew that UNSCOM had U-2 aerial imagery and also probably historical U.S. satellite imagery prior to 1991. Simply mentioning that an Iraqi statement could be confirmed by outside means or offering to show them documents that contradicted their statements was sometimes enough to get the Iraqis to begin amending their accounts.[57] The inspectors contemplated carefully whether and when to introduce independently obtained data, such as documents from suppliers, sample results, and other items, holding such data in reserve for the proper moment to use them as leverage to squeeze essential or final elements of a story from the Iraqis. The inspectors threatened and actually introduced independent data sparingly but to great effect.[58] Often, only when UNSCOM could prove something would the Iraqis admit it. As Ekeus observed, "The Iraqi strategy was to admit only as much as they thought UNSCOM knew at the time. In 1991, the Iraqis admitted a research program, but no more; in July 1995 they said they produced agents, but not more."[59]

As much as the inspectors were able to wring from interviews about Iraq's germ warfare program, the ultimate truth remained elusive. Killip said, "You'll be left with something that is possible and something that is probable but you will probably not be able to swear it's the truth."[60] Normally, UNSCOM reported significant Iraqi noncompliance to the Security Council when they could buttress a probable account of events with hard evidence.

EXPLOITING THE PAPER TRAIL

When UNSCOM began operations, the inspectors routinely asked Iraq for documentation to support its declarations but were not overly concerned when the Iraqis slighted them, largely because of early held assumptions that

Iraq would forfeit its weapons in exchange for permission to resume oil sales. After inspections began to show galling inaccuracies in the Iraqi nuclear, chemical, and missile declarations, UNSCOM clamped down by driving Iraq at every opportunity to provide documentation and by designing ongoing monitoring procedures specifically to propel Iraq toward evidentiary support of declarations and statements. UNSCOM required the Iraqis, for instance, to submit ancillary records about monitored facilities, such as records for water and power consumption or the status any material produced from cradle to grave.[61]

The inspectors acquired documents in four basic ways: (1) the Iraqis purposefully gave them items; (2) the inspectors discovered relevant papers at facilities despite Iraq's cleanup and concealment program; (3) private companies outside of Iraq and cooperative intelligence services provided documents; and (4) the Iraqis turned over seven hundred thousand items in mid-August 1995 at the Haidar farm, a distinct subset of Iraqi-provided records because of the size of the cache. As discussed in Chapter 5, the Haidar farm papers contained much data useful to the nuclear, chemical, and missile inspectors, but the one "dinky little box containing mostly reprints of journal articles and document requests" was not a windfall for the bioweapons inspectors.[62]

When inspectors asked Iraq to open the books at facilities, the process was called a document audit. At Iraq's legitimate biological research or production facilities site managers could bring out reams of documentation dating back to the 1980s for the inspectors to review. Punctiliously, the Iraqis kept several copies of every type of record, color-coded for the different ministries overseeing a facility. Therefore, the inspectors were automatically on alert when Iraqi facility managers asserted they had no records on a piece of equipment, a material, or an activity. The Iraqis came up with incredulous excuses for having no paperwork, such as that the relevant documents fell off a truck, were burned in a fire, or never existed at all.[63] Otherwise, they often selected or manipulated the documents they gave the inspectors to try to convey Iraq's desired image about its biological activities. Accordingly, Taha gave UNSCOM's first biological inspectors ten documents in August 1991 redacted to make the work of her research group appear more innocuous. Sometimes the Iraqis tried to pass off forged records, as noted in Chapter 4, for the records they faked about the disposition of tons of imported growth media. Otherwise, they turned over a piece of paper with a few words on it or a receipt slip for a person's entry to a facility and claimed these scraps were documentation of an activity. The Iraqis kept up this parade of documentary chicanery until UNSCOM's final days.[64]

To circumvent documentary dead ends, the inspectors turned up the heat on the Iraqis with much more systematic pursuit of Iraq's records. The first document search mission in Iraq recovered Saddam's nuclear bomb blueprints in September 1991.[65] The bioweapons inspectors executed their first document search mission in the spring of 1996. After arrival on site, the inspectors split into subteams to scope a facility building by building, room by room for a quick sweep of all file cabinets, drawers, and other areas before returning to the more promising locations to examine paper and computer records more closely. Interpreters worked side by side with the inspectors to peg documents of interest. They found documents that pertained to bioweapons activities despite Iraq's assertion that it had given UNSCOM all documentation about its weapons of mass destruction programs and years after the Iraqis had issued orders for facility directors to hide such records. The inspectors photocopied any documents of interest.[66] Even seemingly bland paperwork could contain significant data. At the Baghdad Veterinary College in early 1997, a pamphlet about postgraduate studies at the Al Hazen Institute, which UNSCOM believed conducted Iraq's initial biowarfare research and development, pointed inspectors to new scientists who were possibly involved in the bioweapons program.[67] The inspectors also pulled the materials for all Iraqi scientists who published or spoke publicly about research interests pertinent to weapons work, instigating an inspection series in the spring of 1997 that bared a few bioweapons scientists, for example, ricin weaponeer Shakir al-Akidy.[68]

As the use of computers increased in Iraq in the 1990s, UNSCOM teams began incorporating computer experts and toting Arabic word processing programs to screen electronic data efficiently on site. UNSCOM occasionally confiscated computer hard drives containing data pertinent to bioweapons activities. With the advent of portable computer memory storage devices, the inspectors worried that agent cookbooks, test data, weapons blueprints, and other essential reference data could be stashed within minutes on a couple of zip drives and tossed over a fence while someone deleted the same files from a facility's computers.[69] However, computers wiped free of data would be a dead giveaway of impropriety. Computer forensics specialists can sometimes detect the timing of file deletions, which would be informative, and restore some or all of the contents. Moreover, even decades into the computer era organizations and individuals are still uncertain about to how to save records, so many facilities still maintain both electronic and hardcopy archives. When people collaborate on a project, practice shows that several are likely to download key documents regularly for review or to provide their input to jointly written documents, leaving an electronic trail and opening the possibility that key documents may remain available electronically after a hasty attempt to clear computers. Some personnel might send files to home computers, which inspectors could retrieve. Inspectors may also find backup hardcopies of important documents in individual offices because scientists tend to be slightly paranoid that a single erroneous keystroke could wipe out months of research. Finally, current operational documents, such as worksheets and protocols, are also likely to be printed for the easy access of laboratory and production line workers.[70] So, while the omnipresence of computers will undoubtedly challenge future efforts to recover documents, inspectors will still have several things working in their favor.

Documentation from sources outside of Iraq, such as suppliers, financiers, and shipping companies, shed considerable light on biological activities in Iraq. Most companies cooperated with the inspectors, a few sharing all written records of their contacts with the Iraqis. No one had tampered with these documents, so these data were very reliable. Outside documents gave the inspectors a better feel for the size and sophistication of Iraq's hidden program and what types of biowarfare capabilities they were pursuing. Records from equipment and material suppliers revealed what Iraq purchased and attempted to order, including performance specifications and quantities of items. Outside documents also provided new leads to investigate, including for capabilities Iraq did not declare. Bank records that listed the Iraqis who secured credit lines became an avenue to pry open Iraqi purchases, not to mention what was done with these items.[71] Finally, as noted earlier, in interviews documents from outside sources served as a fulcrum to get at the truth.

Opinions can differ and memories can fade, so an authentic and complete paper trail is probably the surest way for inspectors to assemble the history of a weapons program.[72] For many, documentary evidence is more persuasive than information that emerges from interviews. In hindsight, UNSCOM's bioweapons inspectors stated, they should have pushed hard, very hard to acquire documents in their very first inspections, not waiting until 1996 to begin sweeping Iraq's biological sites for documents, when arguably there was less to find.[73] Even still, one UNSCOM veteran rated the 1996–1997 document search missions as the single greatest source of useful information for the bioweapons inspectors.[74]

SAMPLING COMES OF AGE

Sampling is an inspection tool that gained considerable potency in the 1990s. The complexity of sampling is inherent in the types of samples that can be taken (for example, soil, liquid, and surface swipe), the variety of analytical techniques that can be employed (such as a DNA polymorphism, scanning electron microscope), and the endless number of locations that can be sampled (including fermenters, pipes, and building surfaces).[75] Sampling everything is cost prohibitive, so inspectors must decide when and where sampling is advisable.

Sampling technicalities aside, UNSCOM wrestled with other touchy issues, including the chance that some people could jump to erroneous conclusions because neither positive nor negative sampling results are necessarily definitive. As Huxsoll reminded, "sampling can be very useful, but the findings have to be put in context."[76] To wit, a positive result for anthrax from an environmental sample taken off the floor of a building could indicate anthrax was made there or that a technician who visited a farm with diseased cows subsequently tracked in the anthrax spores. A positive anthrax result from the gaskets on a fermenter constitutes a much more significant, convincing indicator of deliberate anthrax production because other logical explanations for the presence of anthrax on a fermenter's gaskets are not likely.[77] Technically savvy individuals know that negative results could be due to mistakes made in the taking and preservation of the samples, the injudicious selection of sampling locations, or the use of extraction techniques and analytical capabilities that were not strong or specific enough to obtain categorical results.[78] However, as the inspectors anticipated, Iraq pounced on any negative sampling results to proclaim innocence, which influenced UNSCOM's decision to sample circumspectly.[79]

Despite the potential downsides of sampling, the inspectors understood that physical evidence was the best, most persuasive data they could acquire. The inspectors were aware that the Iraqis never had a firm fix on the quality of the sample analysis capabilities available to UNSCOM.[80] When UNSCOM began inspections, however, field analysis of samples was not that workable of an option, and the laboratories analyzing the early samples could take over a month and a half to return results to UNSCOM.[81] Beginning in mid-1994 UNSCOM mounted several missions that focused on sampling and sometimes included excavation to find evidence of Iraqi biowarfare agent production, testing, weaponization, and destruction, but UNSCOM did not adopt standardized protocols for sampling and analysis until May 1995.[82] Some of the sampling locations more likely to provide definitive evidence were intrusive because they could interrupt facility operations and sometimes require equipment disassembly. The inspectors did not dismantle equipment for sampling until after Iraq's admission of weaponization, at which point they sampled the interior surfaces and fittings of equipment at Al Daura and Al Hakam. These sampling results, given in more detail in Chapter 6, significantly contradicted Iraq's declarations after mid-1995 that *Clostridium botulinum* Type B was never made at Al Hakam or anthrax at Al Daura.[83] This outcome underscored the point that the knack of sampling was whether the sample was collected at the right place and whether the right sample was taken.[84]

Another factor critical to the success of sampling is the sensitivity and power of the analytical technique(s) employed. Scientific advances, particularly the ability of polymerase chain reaction analysis to identify microorganisms swiftly from dead DNA, significantly improved the utility of sampling and forensic analysis during the 1990s. Huxsoll and Jeff Mohr, who led missions in 1991 and 1994 that involved sampling, observed that polymerase chain reaction analysis was so new that they were learning what would work.[85] From the early to the mid-1990s, however, "sampling technology changed by orders of magnitude. Those sampling advances were one of the principal contributory factors to making some progress on the biological program because what had been a successful way of covering things up in 1991 became less and less so," said Killip. "Analytical technique improvement meant some of the deception that they executed in 1991, like bombing a facility with formalin, was no longer adequate in 1996."[86] As more timely, sensitive, and specific analysis techniques became available, UNSCOM had a more powerful tool at its disposal.[87]

Following the 2001 anthrax letter attacks in America, considerable research brought more improvements in microbial forensics.[88] Several scientific disciplines, such as atomic force microscopy, bioinformatics, proteomics, ultra-high throughput DNA sequencing, genomics, nano-secondary ion mass spectrometry, and metabolomics have begun to alter significantly what can be expected from future investigation at dual-use biological facilities.[89] The ability to detect a covert bioweapons program through forensic investigation has shifted in favor of the inspectors. "With the current, extremely sensitive forensic techniques, if anyone used a warfare agent on a piece of equipment, it would be almost impossible to completely sanitize that equipment. A couple of copies of DNA would be found that would identify what they made in that equipment," said chief inspector Mohr. "Now there is absolutely no doubt that inspectors could go into a facility and tell what they've been doing for the last twenty years. The stuff would all be dead, but that doesn't matter."[90] Therefore, for any future effort to sort out bioweapons compliance, UNSCOM inspectors advised that the sooner and more intrusively sampling is done, the better.[91]

CASCADING INSPECTIONS

UNSCOM Executive Chairman Rolf Ekeus prudently secured Iraq's agreement that the inspectors had rights of full, unimpeded access to facilities and unfettered use of a variety of inspection tools before he sent in his first teams. The Iraqis flouted the inspectors' rights from the outset with ploys to create delays; with the movement of weapons, materials, and documents pertinent to Iraq's weapons programs; and with verbal and physical intimidation. Since Iraq's misbehaviors worked against effective inspections in multiple ways, UNSCOM's biological inspectors argued in retrospect that initiative should have been taken to overhaul some of the inspection terms solely under UNSCOM's control.

UNSCOM's internal inspection guidelines, influenced significantly by the inspectorate's reliance on seconded personnel, called for missions of relatively short duration with fixed entry and exit dates. UNSCOM initially sent separate chemical, missile, and biological teams into Iraq. Assigned to inspect so many pre-picked sites in a mission, inspection chiefs were always pushed "to get out of one place and on to the next, making it difficult to do justice to any of them. I was never on any inspection that was allowed to go where I thought I needed to go. Mostly this was because UNSCOM headquarters had certain information, called you to do a certain job, and gave you what they thought you needed to do that job," said Mohr. The early ground rules for inspections, he continued, also called for the team chief to tell the Iraqis the night before what site(s) the team would inspect the next day. In Mohr's words, "That made it absolutely futile. If there was anything for them to be worried about, they sanitized the area."[92]

Equally as frustrating for the inspectors, the tight scheduling of missions meant that "if the team found something wrong, there was no leeway to dig in other places, to keep pursuing the matter. Scientists follow leads, and that was not really possible under the circumstances."[93] When a team found something unusual, the Iraqis, aware of each team's schedule, knew just how long they needed to stall further activity at that site or over the remainder of the inspection mission to obfuscate any part of the trail to the bioweapons program that the inspectors managed to expose.[94] Another factor that played into Iraqi hands is that "the inspections had to start and restart," explained Killip. "If we'd been able to plow on and finish any one subject it would have been a lot better and quicker."[95]

To curtail Iraq's ability to evade them, UNSCOM inspectors devised inspection measures that outstripped those that the IAEA routinely employed and even those envisioned in the draft chemical weapons ban. For example, instead of inspecting as one unit, UNSCOM began splitting into subgroups that deployed simultaneously to different facilities. Ekeus also quickly began authorizing no-notice inspections so the Iraqis could not be certain of the inspection target until a team halted at a facility's front gate. Such adjustments aided inspection effectiveness, but if they had to do it again UNSCOM's biological inspectors would have instituted additional assertive tactics from the outset.

First, they suggested cascading inspections off of the first team sent into a country, rotating teams in one after another. The first team would quickly survey the sites of highest inspection priority, working from a list of inspection targets probably derived from intelligence, open source data, and declarations. The initial team would educate its relief team on the issues of concern, clues, anomalies, and any other information it developed about what was taking place at a nation's dual-use biological facilities. Thus outbound teams would recommend the inspection focal points for inbound ones, which would in turn develop their own new data. This cascade strategy would still incorporate inspection targets from fresh intelligence or open source data, but it would largely free successive teams to follow in a timely fashion the leads the inspectors found and to spend more time at facilities deserving in-depth examination. "At the outset is when inspectors can catch them with their pants down, if they think it through, keep a constant presence, and press really hard," said Barton.[96] To deprive the inspected state opportunities to mask evidence, the missions must be deployed without time gaps. The Iraqis, for example, were visibly upset when Kelly informed them he was going to inspect on Fridays, the Moslem holy day. Kelly and other chief inspectors ignored Iraqi rancor about this issue and proceeded with the job.[97]

This cascading strategy would arguably have broken open Iraq's bioweapons program much earlier because it would have robbed the Iraqis of time to regroup and cover their tracks. To illustrate the utility of cascading inspections, Barton and Killip point to the bombs with black stripes that they noticed on UNSCOM's maiden inspection in June 1991 at the Al Muthanna State Establishment for Pesticide Production. Common sense told them that it was important to determine the meaning of the markings on the munitions, but the inspectors, struggling just to get a rough estimate on the chemical arsenal, had no leeway to attend to details like munition markings. Similarly, UNSCOM's first several biological teams did not have sufficient time and resources to follow up on the black striped bombs, or why Al Hakam had a large amount of growth media sitting in a climate-controlled warehouse near a single-cell protein plant so clean it appeared unused, or other telltale leads. The sporadic presence of biological inspectors, combined with the lack of thorough debriefings of all team members so that their collective insights could be shared routinely with other team chiefs, gave the Iraqis ample opportunity to try to outfox the inspectors.[98]

UNSCOM's bioweapons inspectors argued that for additional punch, sampling and analysis be actively integrated into a cascading strategy. Franz, for one, "would rank all of the facilities by level of suspicion. In the Iraqi case, Al Hakam would have come out pretty high. Then, I would put together a comprehensive plan to sample early on and systematically, identifying what items should be sampled and how—like sampling the dryers and the crud around the O-rings and using PCR [polymerase chain reaction]." Franz emphasized that the idea was not "to sample eighty facilities, but rank them and sample the top four or five systematically. The point is to have a sampling plan."[99] Mohr, who led sampling teams for UNSCOM, observed that a hard-hitting sampling plan is important if there are concerns that the inspected state might attempt to purge facilities of incriminating evidence, as Iraq did even with UNSCOM inspectors in their midst. Such circumstances would warrant deployment of a field laboratory to perform preliminary sample analysis to inform the inspectors' efforts to evaluate leads and point them in the direction of new ones.

A major lesson of UNSCOM and a benefit of subsequent scientific advances is that any future inspectors should sample early, sample smart, and sample aggressively.[100]

Finally, the bioweapons inspectors recommended further strengthening a cascade strategy by purposefully identifying and interviewing all of the human assets possibly connected to a bioweapons program as soon as possible. UNSCOM did not initiate a more comprehensive search for scientists with skills and interests applicable to weapons work until early in 1997. To jumpstart inspections in the future, biological inspectors could request applicable information from intelligence agencies that regularly mine open sources to help ascertain who might be doing weapons-related work. "Intelligence agencies are collecting that type of information all the time, looking at all sorts of odd journals, documents, and specializations to get a handle on who might be involved in a program. In libraries, we'd look at MA and PhD theses and look at the examiners and who was setting up the research," said Killip.[101] In addition to what might be learned through interviews, as was the case with UNSCOM inspections, these scientists might be in possession of documentation important to understanding the scope and sophistication of a bioweapons program.

THE UTILITY OF INSPECTIONS OF DUAL-USE BIOLOGICAL FACILITIES

As noted in Chapter 1, prior to the 1991 Gulf War Western intelligence estimates about a bioweapons program in Iraq were sufficiently sketchy that few anticipated that UNSCOM's biological inspectors would be heavily tasked or tested. This supposition was not the only erroneous one circulating in early 1991. If asked at that time, many experts and policymakers would have thought it to be something of a losing proposition to dispatch inspectors to determine whether a nation was deliberately hiding germ warfare activities at dual-use biological facilities. International experts met in 1992 to evaluate the ability of twenty-one procedures to monitor compliance with the Biological and Toxin Weapons Convention,[102] but formal negotiations that began in 1995 to create a legally binding inspection protocol for the germ weapons ban lacked political momentum. Negotiators produced a draft text after six years, but the talks fell apart after the U.S. government pronounced the draft procedures inadequate to detect cheaters yet likely to compromise trade secrets and national security.[103]

Decision makers, analysts, and observers of UNSCOM's activities have opined about the role that UNSCOM's biological inspections had in containing the security threats in Saddam Hussein's Iraq and sometimes on whether that experience could be extrapolated to the monitoring of the international bioweapons ban. For instance, in mid-November 1997 U.S. Secretary of State Madeleine Albright called UNSCOM inspectors the "eyes and ears of the world" and lauded their ability to inhibit Iraq's bioweapons ambitions, whereas U.S. Under Secretary of State John Bolton indicated in mid-November 2001 that UNSCOM only partially fulfilled the United Nations' mandate to disarm Iraq of its bioweapons program.[104] Many factors impinge on the views of those who assess a process from the outside looking in, such as their ideological perspective, level of technical and operational expertise, and attachment to competing policy interests.

Arguably, the views of UNSCOM's biological inspectors, shaped predominantly from their firsthand field experience and technical expertise, deserve to be highlighted and weighted differently. A few UNSCOM inspectors have written about technical aspects of biological inspections, occasionally drawing broader conclusions about the effectiveness of a particular inspection tool or inspections in general.[105] As for the utility of biological inspections, UNSCOM veterans divide into camps. One school of thought considers inspections that detect and illuminate a covert bioweapons program to be a failure if after being informed about the cheating the international community does not impose penalties that compel compliance. Other inspectors separate inspections from the political decisions made in the name of inspection findings, accepting that the former can entail considerable accomplishments even while the latter, for any number of reasons, falls short of holding a cheater fully liable. Proponents in both camps agreed that the encroachment of politics into the technicalities of actual inspections can negatively affect the inspection process, in part because the inspected state may be emboldened to engage in obstructive or illicit behavior if it perceives that decision makers are reigning in the inspectors. UNSCOM inspectors flatly stated that when politics intruded into field operations, it encumbered their ability to out the truth.[106]

The camp that sees full punishment as integral to an inspection process resonates with themes from the long-standing debate about the utility of arms control, encapsulated by the quintessential phrase "after detection, then what?"[107] Spertzel stated that UNSCOM did not shut down Iraq's bioweapons program and inspections of biological facilities were unlikely to work absent the full cooperation of the inspected state. Into 1998 Iraq downplayed the sophistication and scope of its past bioweapons program and exaggerated its cooperation with UNSCOM, and Iraq's attitude led Spertzel to conclude that "it is extremely doubtful that any inspection regime will or can be successful."[108] On a different tack, two other bioweapons inspectors advised against translating UNSCOM's biological inspection experience into other settings because of the singular rigor of UNSCOM's mandate to conduct unimpeded inspections.[109]

In contrast, other UNSCOM staff proclaimed the bioweapons inspections a commendable success applicable to other settings, including to the Convention. For starters, Ekeus deemed the efforts of his bioweapons inspectors worthy of the Nobel Peace Prize. He described the principal lesson of UNSCOM as to allow "science to lead the way," in which case it is "possible with peaceful verification means to disarm a complex country even under the most challenging circumstances. When UNSCOM closed shop because of the political infighting and other issues," said Ekeus, "some outsiders thought that UNSCOM had not done the job. History shows, however, that UNSCOM really did disarm Iraq; very little was left there."[110] Ekeus's last remark refers to the work of the Iraq Survey Group, which scoured Iraq following the 2003 Gulf War but did not locate stocks of unconventional arms or significant evidence that Iraq had rebuilt its biological, chemical, or nuclear weapons programs.[111]

UNSCOM bioweapons inspectors were acutely aware that the credibility and effectiveness of an inspection process relied on its ability to enable distinctions to be made: "Inspectors have to evaluate sites not just for their possible bioweapons purposes but for their legitimate purposes as well."[112] UNSCOM personnel concluded that their experience demonstrated that inspections could sort peaceful biological research and production activities from offensive weapons work.[113] A half step further, several inspectors asserted that UNSCOM proved that what many presumed was improbable, if not impossible, could be done: "As far as arms control is concerned," said Killip, "what happened in Iraq shows that investigations can dig out a covert bioweapons program."[114]

Moving past the proposition that inspections can identify nations that violate the Convention, however, UNSCOM personnel warned against overloading an inspection process with sky-high expectations that inspections will yield every detail about a covert bioweapons program. "Clearly, it is easier to establish that prohibited activities are taking place than it is to learn their full scope," stated Black.[115] "Whether or not every small detail about the program is ultimately known," averred a senior UNSCOM official, "the political result can be achieved."[116] In the case of Iraq, the initial political result was that Baghdad acknowledged illicit bioweapons activity to the world.[117] Without inspections Iraq would have maintained and perhaps advanced and used this ghastly weapons capability.

UNSCOM personnel point to inspection benefits beyond a program's detection, though with caveats. They contend that inspections have deterrent effects but cannot state with certainty how deep into the chain of bioweapons acquisition activity a deterrent effect applies. While UNSCOM was operational, the biological staff believed that inspections dissuaded Iraq from producing and stockpiling biowarfare agents in bulk at declared facilities and from loading agents into delivery systems. However, the inspectors were unsure at the time if their work also deterred Iraq from additional bioweapons research and development activities or from perpetuating a bioweapons program at sites they did not monitor or investigate. To illustrate, the inspectors suspected but could not prove definitively that personnel at Al Hakam were drying *B. thuringiensis*, an anthrax simulant, to enhance their skills and knowledge to weaponize anthrax, not to support Al Hakam's purported biopesticide business. If inspections did not deter weapons activities fully, the UNSCOM inspectors counted the increased costs of any additional evasive measures that Iraq had to take to preserve a bioweapons program as another plus of inspections. Finally, so long as Iraq engaged in any bioweapons activities, Baghdad risked that UNSCOM inspectors would catch them again.[118]

Having bared Iraq's covert weapons program to the world and arguably made other positive contributions to reduce the possibility that Iraq was sustaining a bioweapons program, a number of UNSCOM biological inspectors considered the UNSCOM experience a roadmap that "should teach the international community the procedures for how to inspect biological facilities. A future inspection regime might adjust UNSCOM's basic procedures so that the inspections unfold in a collaborative manner with the inspected state."[119] Added inspector Robert Kadlec:

> If we fail as a nation to learn the lessons that we should from this experience—to categorize what went right, identify what went wrong, and to fix it for the next go-around—it will be our own fault. For some reason, there's always

a rush to do other things and we don't follow through and improve. I can't think of anything more important to do in the scheme of efforts to stop the proliferation of weapons of mass destruction.[120]

The urgency in Kadlec's remarks is due to a concern common to many UNSCOM bioweapons inspectors and security analysts, namely that advances in the life sciences are making biological weapons ever more accessible and attractive to state and non-state actors. Meanwhile, the international community lacks a standing bioweapons inspection capability. Given the complexities of inspecting dual-use biological facilities, several veteran UNSCOM inspectors recommended creating an on-call international biological inspection corps built from the lessons of UNSCOM's experience.[121]

10 GAMBITS PRESENT AND FUTURE

AFTER DRAWING SPECIFIC lessons from an experience, the final brick in the foundation to act on those lessons is to place the experience in a larger context. Peculiarities aside, all events have characteristics that allow linkage to a behavioral pattern, which improves understanding of the event, enables analysis to help forecast future occurrences, and informs prescriptive recommendations. Iraq was not the first nation to stockpile germ weapons, so it is reasonable to infer that it will not be the last. Although a behavioral pattern of proliferation is identifiable, the gravity of the biological threat that confronts present and future generations is more challenging to articulate.

This chapter provides an overview of the international security dynamics and scientific developments that will bear on whether nations and subnational actors aspire to obtain germ weapons and might successfully do so. From that broader context, U.S. and international leaders will be better positioned to determine what priority to give this matter compared to other security and public health risks. This context will also help policymakers to assess the tools at their disposal to constrain the bioweapons threat.

For decades, global concerns about weapons of mass destruction centered on nuclear arms, a preoccupation understandable in view of their potential to alter human history radically and to devastate the earth. For that reason, statesmen, security analysts, and technical specialists have devoted considerable effort since the end of World War II to establish, upgrade, and responsibly implement and verify the Nuclear Nonproliferation Treaty, nuclear testing, and nuclear arms reduction treaties.[1] The contemporaneous efforts of leaders and technical experts to restrict and eliminate biological weapons are meager by comparison. The 1925 Geneva Protocol prohibits the use of biological, toxin, and chemical weapons, while the 1972 Biological and Toxin Weapons Convention outlaws the development, production, and stockpiling of these arms. Since the international talks to fashion a verification protocol for the Convention buckled in 2001,[2] efforts to bolster compliance with the accord's prohibitions have faltered. Oddly enough, contemporaneously the realization that germ weapons could wreak a global holocaust among animal, plant, and human populations has become a staple of public discourse on security threats. Leaders from Canada, Germany, Japan, Poland, the United States, and other nations have called for action to constrain the biological weapons threat.[3]

HIJACKING NATURE FOR MILITARY PURPOSES

Since the beginning of time man has fashioned weapons for self-protection, hunting, and conquest, sometimes co-opting nature's sources of poison and disease for weaponry. Ancient warriors dipped the tips of arrows in poison; fouled water supplies with feces and the carcasses of dead animals; bombarded enemies with containers filled with snakes, disease-bearing rodents, and scorpions; and hurled human plague cadavers over the walls of besieged cities. Other early ventures into biological warfare include British attempts to transmit smallpox to American Indians in 1763 and to infect American soldiers and civilians with this virus during the Revolutionary War.[4] Man's early stabs at hijacking nature for biowarfare can be characterized as small-scale, opportunistic, and rudimentary; tactics often boiled down to capturing poisonous creatures and exploiting disease outbreaks already under way.

The character of biowarfare started to change in World War I, when governments began directing scientists to wage it more effectively. Advocates of bioweapons lauded their cheapness in comparison to other weapons; the difficulty of pinpointing a biological attacker; and, if contagious weapons were used, the self-perpetuating nature of the strike. Proponents also proclaimed the ability of bioweapons to offset an opponent's conventional military advantage and the surprise and psychological impact that would accompany their use. Furthermore, biological weapons leave infrastructure standing so that the victor can make full use of the industrial and other capacities of defeated nation(s). Historically, nations that deduce a threat from one or more adversaries, that appreciate and decide to act on their vulnerability to biological attack, and that consider germ warfare feasible and in some way advantageous have veered into the bioweapons business.[5] From the outside looking in, germ weapons work can be opaque, challenging intelligence agencies to assess the bioweapons capabilities of opponents. Hence, historically leaders have found it difficult to decide whether the biological threat facing them necessitates the establishment or acceleration of a bioweapons program or other military capability for deterrent, pre-emptive, or retaliatory purposes.

The first modern bioweapons campaign occurred during World War I. To undermine the Allied war effort, Germany targeted Allied military horses and mules, mostly with glanders and anthrax. From 1915 to 1918, saboteurs attacked military livestock in the United States, Argentina, Romania, Norway, and perhaps Spain, slipping the animals disease-laden sugar cubes, painting their nostrils with contaminated material, and sticking them with infected needles.[6]

Before and during World War II, several nations expanded or started bioweapons programs on the basis of fragmentary intelligence that potential opponents were seeking bioweapons. German researchers sporadically explored further offensive capabilities, covertly testing a biowarfare simulant in the Paris metro in 1933, experimenting with foot and mouth disease, spraying bacteria as anti-livestock and anti-crop agents, and working to weaponize anthrax. Unbeknownst to the Allies, in 1945 Adolf Hitler halted all German offensive bioweapons preparations in favor of biological defenses.[7]

Unsure of Germany's intentions and capabilities, from 1923 to 1940 France conducted animal toxicology experiments and field tested various munitions to study how to overcome the fragility of biowarfare agents during storage and dissemination, focusing on the generation of fine liquid aerosols. In a 1938 study of dispersal dynamics, French researchers released a biowarfare simulant along two lines of the Paris metro. French scientists developed defensive strategies and techniques, and they worked with many viral, bacterial, and toxin agents. After 1948, France investigated the dispersion of dried biowarfare agents, the interaction of biological and chemical agents, and incapacitating biological agents before stopping its program altogether in 1972.[8]

Like Hitler, Britain's Winston Churchill looked askance at biological warfare, but the United Kingdom nonetheless hedged its bets against possible German biological weapons. In 1936, the British initiated a research and development program that concentrated largely on anthrax and the development of an Allied anthrax cluster bomb codenamed the "N" bomb. The British also worked with plague and botulinum toxin, which they assessed to be viable weapons after aerosol toxicity tests. The British situated a biological research team at Porton Down, already home to their chemical weapons research. British experts concluded that anthrax field tests in the early 1940s at Gruinard Island provided irrefutable evidence that biological warfare could be waged effectively. The N bomb was slated for field tests in Canada and agent production in the United States when Allied victory over Germany arrived, undercutting the urgency to complete the N bomb. Cattle feed cakes spiked with anthrax—for retaliatory use—were the only biological weapon that the United Kingdom manufactured.[9]

As the Cold War took hold, the British military command issued orders to develop strategic biological arms for use against workers at major industrial sites. From 1948 to the mid-1950s, the British conducted multiple open-air trials at sea with towed arrays of test animals using simulants as well as the pathogens that cause anthrax, tularemia, plague, and Venezuelan equine encephalitis. The outcome of these trials, which studied the survivability of agents exposed to the elements and the effectiveness of various dispersal methods, contributed to Britain's determination that biological weapons had little strategic utility at that time. In the late 1950s, the program at Porton Down made the transition to defensive research only. Concerns remained, however, about Britain's vulnerability to a line source biological attack, in which the pathogen is dispersed in an extended line miles upwind of the intended target to achieve regional coverage. Until 1973 occasional British sea trials using biological simulants continued to look at the line source attack scenario, to develop detection systems, and to evaluate the feasibility of biological attacks against naval forces. In July 1963, the British also conducted a simulant trial in the London Underground system.[10] Vladimir Pasechnik, the director of the U.S.S.R.'s Institute of Ultra Pure Biopreparations before he defected to the United Kingdom in 1989, spurred the British to recalibrate the feasibility and strategic utility of biological weapons. Pasechnik provided stunning details of what Western intelligence had long suspected, a monumental covert Soviet bioweapons program.[11]

Across the Atlantic Ocean, Canada, which began investigating the potential of biowarfare before World War II, teamed with the United Kingdom and the United States to develop the anthrax N bomb. In 1950, Canada completed the development of a rinderpest vaccine to blunt an attack on Canada's cattle industry. Otherwise, Canada's biowarfare studies focused on insect vectors (such as fleas, mosquitoes, and flies) to deliver diseases; botulinum toxin, including production of Type A and B strains and development of toxoids for immunizations; the decay rate of pathogen aerosols; and the adaptation of viruses from one species to another to cultivate new diseases. Canadian bioweaponeers also worked extensively with brucellosis, tularemia, and anti-animal pathogens. At Suffield Experimental Station, Canada performed laboratory and field tests on a variety of weapons with lethal and nonlethal agents. Canada accomplished much of its bioweapons work in close collaboration with U.S. researchers, abandoning offensive research in 1969 as momentum gathered for a bioweapons ban.[12]

In its use of biological weapons, Japan's biowarfare program was unique among others of World War II vintage. Unit 731 and Unit 100 were the centerpieces of the Imperial Army's biowarfare program, the latter focusing principally on anti-crop and anti-livestock agents. Japan's bioweaponeers tested spray and artillery dispersal methods, nine types of biological bombs, and the use of insects as delivery vectors. Casualty estimates vary, but perhaps as many as ten thousand prisoners died in laboratory experiments and two hundred thousand Chinese soldiers and civilians died from May 1939 to the summer of 1942 in "field tests" of agents, including cholera, anthrax, plague, glanders, and typhoid fever. Japan's biowarriors dropped grain on at least eleven Chinese cities, anticipating that hungry citizens would consume the disease-laced granules. In addition, Unit 731 contaminated water supplies and released infected rodents and fleas. Unit 731 received special commendations for its contributions to Japan's war effort.[13]

After World War II, the United States granted amnesty to twenty-two Japanese bioweapons scientists for insight about Japan's biowarfare experimental results and delivery systems. The United States mobilized scientists toward the end of the war to design and generate a U.S. capability to detect, defend against, and conduct biowarfare attacks, if studies proved the latter feasible. Though the War Department uncloaked the program in 1947, early U.S. bioweapons scientists labored in secret at Edgewood Arsenal, Maryland, which also housed U.S. chemical weapons research, and at Ft. Detrick, Maryland, established as the hub of the U.S. bioweapons program in 1943. Now the U.S. Army Military Research Institute for Infectious Diseases (USAMRIID), Ft. Detrick conducted laboratory research and pilot-scale production. Ft. Detrick's Eight Ball facility housed explosive and inhalational tests of biowarfare agents, mostly with animals. Several biowarfare agents were also tested on human volunteers, followed by intensive health monitoring and medical treatment to preclude serious health problems.[14]

The U.S. outdoor testing program was substantial and varied. In 1949, Dugway Proving Ground, an arid unpopulated site near Salt Lake City, Utah, became the main U.S. location for outdoor biowarfare testing. However, from 1949 to 1953 the United States held outdoor trials in many other places, including unannounced trials with simulants over the San Francisco Bay area, Minneapolis, St. Louis, and the Pentagon and Norfolk areas of Virginia. To assess the suitability of mosquitoes to deliver the yellow fever virus, which had been approved for the U.S. arsenal, U.S. bioweaponeers released uninfected mosquitoes over Florida and Georgia in 1959. Operation Shipboard Hazard and Defense spread biological simulants and lethal agents from ships, from land, and from aerial platforms over several oceanic and coastland areas. Smaller-scale simulant tests in May 1965 involved National Airport and the Greyhound bus terminal in Washington, D.C., and, in June 1966, the New York City subway system.[15]

After screening numerous diseases for lethality, stability, infectivity, dispersal characteristics, and persistence, U.S. biological researchers settled on anthrax, tularemia, botulinum toxin, Staphylococcus aureaus enterotoxin, Q fever, and Venezuelan equine encephalomyelitis as the mainstays of the U.S. anti-personnel bioweapons program. The United States manufactured thousands of pounds of dry anti-personnel agents and thousands of gallons of liquid anti-personnel pathogens. For instance, it produced 20,178 gallons of liquid bulk biowarfare anti-personnel agents and 804 pounds of dry bulk tularemia, and filled munitions with 167.5 pounds of dry anthrax. The United States also manufactured 160,549 pounds of bulk wheat rust and rice blast, two anti-crop agents that were field tested. Pine Bluff, Arkansas, built in the early 1950s as the principal U.S. facility to produce anti-personnel and anti-crop agents, could initiate bomb-filling operations four days after receiving an order to do so.[16] At Ft. Terry on Plum Island, New York, in 1952 the United States activated an anti-animal research program that until 1954 worked with fifteen pathogens, including foot and mouth disease virus, African swine fever virus, rinderpest virus, and Newcastle disease virus.[17]

The United States developed several delivery systems for anti-crop, anti-livestock, and anti-personnel agents. For example, the M114 was a four-pound pipe-bomb-like device that held 320 milliliters of an anti-personnel agent, and the M33 cluster bomb consisted of 108 M114 mini-bombs. For anti-crop and anti-animal agents, the United States refined balloon bombs, spray tanks, and feather bombs, so nicknamed because they were to be stuffed with feathers inoculated with an agent. U.S. researchers also planned to use particulate bombs to deliver anti-animal agents, though U.S. work with anti-livestock agents did not progress to the point of stockpiling these agents. Among other delivery methods for anti-personnel agents, the United States designed and tested marine mines, drones, rockets, aerosol generators, and missiles. The United States filled 97,554 munitions of five types with anti-personnel agents and simulants.[18] Stating that "mankind already carries in its own hands too many of the seeds of its own destruction," on November 25, 1969, President Richard M. Nixon repudiated biowarfare and closed the U.S. offensive biological program, leaving in place a defensive program.[19]

With its first military biological research facility, the U.S.S.R. situated offensive biowarfare research under the same institutional roof with other legitimate biological research, a tactic that later facilitated Moscow's hidden bioweapons program. Some scientists at the Vaccine-Serum Laboratory, set up in 1926, concentrated on vaccines and medical treatments for the diseases that exacted a high toll on the soldiers in the early twentieth century, while others secretly explored how to wield disease as a weapon. Before long, the Soviets began to co-locate secret laboratories dedicated to bioweapons research in many civilian universities and technical institutes. Similar to U.S. and British researchers, early Soviet biowarriors considered several pathogens before zeroing in on anthrax, botulinum toxin, and typhus as having particular promise for warfare. The U.S.S.R. also worked with brucellosis, encephalitis, tuberculosis, tularemia, glanders, plague, cholera, Q fever, melioidosis, and tetanus, exploring ways to enhance the stability and lethality of these pathogens. After 1935, the U.S.S.R. began field testing several agents at Gorodomlya Island, in Seliger Lake, north of Moscow.[20]

The more recent decades of the Soviet bioweapons program must be discussed with some caution because public documentation of the immediate post–World War II years is scarce and the Soviets took the program underground in the 1970s to promote the appearance of adherence to the Biological and Toxin Weapons Convention. The U.S.S.R., which as a depository nation was a steward of this accord, steadfastly denied harboring an offensive bioweapons program after 1972.[21] Despite terse Russian government statements about the Soviet bioweapons program, the insider accounts of former Soviet bioweaponeers, on-site observation of the distinct features of many weapons institutes, and discussions with Russian scientists participating in collaborative research allow a reasonable composite of this program, unparalleled in its scale and sophistication.[22]

Rivaling the U.S.S.R.'s investment in nuclear weaponry, Moscow escalated its bioweapons program in the 1970s with a workforce of over sixty thousand scientists and technicians. Biopreparat, the collective name for a group of ostensibly civilian biopharmaceutical facilities, consisted of roughly forty sites that functioned primarily as weapons development and production facilities.[23] Biopreparat's flagship sites for work on bacterial and viral pathogens, respectively, were the All-Union Scientific Institute of Applied Microbiology at Obolensk and the State Research Center of Virology and Biotechnology in Novosibirsk, known as Vector. Other noteworthy Biopreparat sites were the Institute of Highly Pure Biopreparations in St. Petersburg, the Institute of Immunological Studies at Lyubuchany, and the Scientific Experimental Production Base in Stepnogorsk, Kazakhstan. At Stepnogorsk, the anthrax plant was adjacent to Progress, a commercial plant that made antibiotics and feed additives. With other plants at Sverdlovsk, Kurgan, and Penza, the U.S.S.R. could produce five hundred tons of anthrax annually.[24]

Another key component of the U.S.S.R.'s bioweapons complex was Vozrozhdeniye Island in the Aral Sea, where field tests were first held in the mid-1930s. In the early 1950s, the Soviets improved facilities on the island to support an expanded field test program that included anthrax, plague, Q fever, botulinum toxin, and smallpox. A smallpox aerosol that drifted off Vozrozhdeniye Island in late July 1971 infected a crew member aboard a research ship that later docked in Aralsk, Kazakhstan. Smallpox had not been seen in the U.S.S.R. for a decade, and Moscow did not report the outbreak to the World Health Organization, but epidemiological reports show that ten people contracted smallpox and three perished.[25]

Codenamed "Ekologiya," the U.S.S.R.'s anti-agricultural work involved about a dozen institutes and four test sites reporting to the Agriculture Ministry. Some ten thousand scientists and technicians developed and tested agents to decimate crops (for example, rye and wheat) and honed diseases such as rinderpest, foot and mouth disease, and African swine fever to use against animals.[26] The Health Ministry ran a series of anti-plague institutes in Irkutsk, Volgograd, Rostov, Saratov, and elsewhere that were linked to the weapons program, but largely conducted defensive research.[27]

After weaponizing classic agents such as anthrax, the Soviets turned to more exotic deeds, for example, pioneering the militarization of hemorrhagic fever viruses by successfully weaponizing Marburg.[28] In a program codenamed "Bonfire," the U.S.S.R. also exploited genetic engineering to make bacteria impervious to known antibiotics and develop two different strains of plague to resist five known antibiotics apiece. The Soviets spliced anthrax, plague, tularemia, and glanders strains to make these diseases resistant to known antibiotics and vaccines. They also converted *Legionella*, a bacterium that can cause pneumonia, into a virtual death sentence. In the mid-1980s, in a large program called "Factor," Soviet scientists tried to use genetic engineering to create entirely novel virulent strains, including ones that produced toxins. Other Soviet weaponeers conducted research with bioregulators and neuro-modulating peptides, incapacitating agents that would affect individual behavior, for instance by stimulating insomnia but not exhaustion and by increasing aggressiveness.[29]

The Soviets tested and accumulated several delivery systems for their biological arsenal, including sprayers, cluster bombs, intercontinental ballistic missiles, and cruise missiles. In addition to establishing a large standby production capacity to expedite the ability to fill munitions, the U.S.S.R. stockpiled hundreds of tons of anthrax and dozens of tons of plague and smallpox, mainly for use against U.S. and other Western non-battlefield targets. The Soviets periodically refreshed this bulk agent supply to maintain a fully virulent stockpile of liquid and freeze-dried anti-personnel agents.[30]

Contradicting insider accounts, Russia's 1992 voluntary declaration skirted outright admission of a prior offensive bioweapons program, stating that the U.S.S.R. did not amass biological weapons and attributing the failure of Soviet scientists to achieve "practical significant results in the military field" to inadequate methodology, equipment, and materials.[31] Moreover, governments and former Soviet bioweaponeers have publicly voiced suspicions that offensive research and development continues in Russia. Referring to Russian President Boris Yeltsin's spring 1992 statement that Russia was closing the bioweapons program, Ken Alibek, formerly the first deputy director of Biopreparat, observed, "When Yeltsin said, 'We stopped this activity,' he didn't mean that they stopped completely. In Russia, it doesn't work this way."[32] Key Russian military biological facilities, including the Center for Military-Technical Problems of Anti-Bacteriological Defense at Ekaterinburg, formerly Sverdlovsk; the Scientific Research Institute of Military Medicine in St. Petersburg; the Scientific Research Institute of Microbiology at Vyatka; and the Virology Center of the Scientific Research Institute of Microbiology at Sergeev-Posad, remain closed to outsiders.

Still other countries became involved in bioweaponry. In 1981, South Africa's defense minister authorized a covert program called Project Coast principally to develop weapons to eliminate enemies of the Apartheid-era regime. Project Coast scientists researched, tested, and produced small-scale quantities of several biological and chemical warfare agents until the program wound down in the early 1990s.[33] Libya, long depicted as having a bioweapons research and development program, denied any such activity after forfeiting its nuclear, chemical, and ballistic missile programs in mid-December 2003.[34] According to U.S., South Korean, and Russian intelligence estimates, North Korea got into the offensive bioweapons business in the 1960s. The continuing program reportedly involves several facilities and focuses on classic agents such as botulinum toxin, anthrax, plague, and perhaps smallpox. Some assessments allege that North Korea has stockpiled biowarfare agents, while others note that scientists in this isolated dictatorship are unlikely to have the state-of-the-art skills and equipment necessary for advanced biological weaponry.[35] Allegations of bioweapons programs have also swirled around China and a trio of Middle Eastern countries: Syria, Israel, and Iran.[36] Sites allegedly engaged in misconduct have not been inspected, and the public record contains scant credible evidence of contemporary bioweapons malfeasance in these nations.

Terrorism is a phenomenon as ancient as biological weapons, and subnational actors, too, have occasionally turned to germ warfare. Aum Shinrikyo, the Japanese cult that killed a dozen Tokyo subway commuters with the nerve agent sarin in mid-March 1995, also strove to obtain biological weapons. However, the cult's scientists failed utterly at two essential steps: (1) acquisition of virulent strains of the disease-causing agents they tried several times to disseminate from 1990 to 1995, and (2) development and testing of effective dispersal systems.[37] U.S. intelligence agencies, it is worth noting, were unaware of the cult's unconventional weapons programs until after the subway attack.[38]

Another cult, the Rajneesh, tested a plot to keep voters away from the polls in a Wasco County, Oregon, election by sprinkling a *Salmonella typhimurium* brew on salad bars and elsewhere, sickening 751. Two followers of the Bhagwan Shri Rajneesh received multiple lengthy prison sentences, though considerable time elapsed before public health authorities connected this surge in gastrointestinal illness to deliberate acts.[39] A more dramatic, quickly recognized string of bioterrorist attacks occurred in the fall of 2001, when five letters with dried anthrax were sent to U.S. media outlets and U.S. senators' offices. Five people died, and thousands took preventative antibiotics.[40] Far-reaching social disruption accompanied the 2001 anthrax attacks, which inspired a crescendo of bioterrorism hoaxes and plots and a handful of genuine incidents. For example, trying to compel the U.S. government not to implement new trucking regulations, in 2003 blackmailer(s) sent a chain of letters containing low-grade powdered ricin and threatened to make the U.S. capital "a ghost town."[41]

Despite the increase in activities indicating an interest in and intent to commit acts of bioterrorism, terrorist attacks with traditional tools (such as bombs and guns) dwarf bioterrorist events.[42] Nonetheless, the recent biowarfare exploits of subnational actors and the shift of some terrorist groups from moderately violent acts to mass casualty attacks have spurred security analysts and policymakers to rethink contemporary security threats.[43] Experts and policymakers consider a major bioterrorist attack to be a when-not-if matter, predicting such an attack in the not-too-distant future.[44] Economist Martin Shubik asserts that a paradigmatic shift has occurred as terrorists graduated from clubs to guns and bombs and now to unconventional weapons. Since the year 2000, terrorists, like nation-states, have been capable of waging war. Shubik argues the "high probability" that a few people could "wipe out a city" of millions, noting "there will be enough socially alienated, mad, and fanatical individuals to break taboos and overcome inhibitions" that may have kept past terrorists from using germs. Shubik characterizes mass casualty biological attacks as "inevitable" because "[b]iological weapons, with their easy accessibility, lack of effective international controls, and disproportionately large effectiveness, offer a singularly attractive mix to radical groups."[45]

Obvious generalizations emerge from this overview of mankind's forays into the biowarfare arena: some actors conclude that biological weapons are a desirable, suitable means to achieve their objectives, and those who do shroud their acquisition of bioweapons in utmost secrecy.[46] Beyond that, biowarfare programs come in all sizes and types, from grandiose, resource-rich, high-tech ones to small, almost primitive efforts funded on a shoestring. Some proliferators aimed for incapacitating diseases, others weaponized only anti-personnel diseases for which vaccinations and medical treatments existed, and yet others turned untreatable and even entirely novel diseases into weapons. Some bioweapons possessors used their arms against humans and animals, others stopped short of use but devoted extensive resources to develop, test, and stockpile these weapons. Whereas some nations invested seriously in anti-agricultural agents, terrorists to date have shunned those diseases in favor of anti-personnel agents. These variances complicate the efforts of security and intelligence analysts to identify or anticipate bioweapons programs and of policymakers to formulate steps to prevent and punish proliferation. As the next section of this chapter describes, changes are afoot that could propel governments and terrorists to recalculate whether to pursue biological weaponry, adding even more layers of complexity to the bioweapons quandary.

OTHER FACETS OF THE BIOLOGICAL RISK SPECTRUM

Terence Taylor, a United Nations Special Commission (UNSCOM) commissioner and chief bioweapons inspector, articulated a spectrum of biological risks that begins with natural outbreaks of infectious disease and re-emerging infectious diseases, moves on to the unintended consequences of dual-use biological research and laboratory accidents, spans the risks due to lack of awareness and negligence, and concludes with deliberate misuse of biology.[47] The first section of this chapter addressed that final category of risks, state-run bioweapons programs and bioterrorism. This section sets aside natural disease outbreaks, historically the largest type of biological risk,[48] to discuss the biological risks that man plays some part in causing and the status of options to reduce those risks.

Since 2003, nations that belong to the Convention have met occasionally to share information about national measures on bioweapons acquisition, disease surveillance, response to and mitigation of epidemics, codes of conduct for life scientists, and biosafety and biosecurity practices in biological facilities.[49] Briefly, the term *biosafety* refers to procedures to avert accidents with high-risk pathogens and physical containment barriers to reduce the scope of public health and environmental harm from any accidents that occur, while *biosecurity* measures are intended to foil the theft or diversion of high-risk pathogens.[50] The administration of U.S. President George W. Bush stifled attempts even to consolidate the information shared into global best practices or common guidelines.[51] Though this dialogue has been useful, talk alone falls far short of what is needed.

Research with pathogens is essential to decode their inner workings and to develop diagnostics, therapeutics, and vaccines to combat infectious disease. This research needs to thrive because it safeguards the public from natural eruptions of disease and also from repeats of history, given that both nations and terrorists have produced and used biological weapons. However, this pivotal biodefense and peaceful biological research brings with it three principal concomitant risks to public well-being.

The first such risk is that of human error, namely laboratory mishaps wherein scientists inadvertently infect themselves and perhaps others with disease(s). The United States, among other countries, has guidelines for institutions to evaluate biosafety risks and to furnish and manage the appropriate laboratory practices and physical containment barriers. The World Health Organization has also issued biosafety guidelines.[52] Still, examples abound of diseases acquired through mistakes at military and civilian facilities. With an errant needle prick, Nikolai Ustinov, chief of the Virus Culture Division at Vector, infected himself with the Marburg virus and succumbed to this gruesome hemorrhagic fever on April 30, 1988.[53] Early in 2004, two scientists working with SARS at the Institute for Virology in Beijing acquired the disease and spread it to others, leading to one death and the quarantining of over two hundred people. Also at Vector, a scientist working with the Ebola virus contracted the disease, dying in May 2004. The next month, the Southern Research Institute inadvertently mailed live anthrax samples to Children's Hospital and Research Center in Oakland, California, exposing seven scientists who assumed they were handling a dead pathogen.[54] In the United Kingdom, a faulty drainage system at vaccine and animal health facilities that worked with the foot and mouth disease virus in Surrey was the probable source of twin 2007 outbreaks of this disease, which is highly contagious to cloven-hoofed animals (for example, sheep).[55] Notably, all of these incidents took place at facilities supposedly operating under strict biosafety rules.

The significant number of laboratory-acquired diseases involving less notorious pathogens is indicative of widespread, lax biosafety practices.[56] Some biosafety shortcomings are downright elementary. According to a 2007 survey, 44 percent of 154 Middle Eastern scientists, 31 percent of 146 Eastern European scientists, and 21 percent of 300 Asian scientists polled were unable to stipulate their facility's biosafety level. Moreover, almost 50 percent of the Asian scientists and roughly 45 percent and 30 percent, respectively, of those in the Middle East and Eastern Europe would perform an experiment even if they did not have appropriate biosafety equipment.[57] In the same vein, UNSCOM inspectors observed outdated biosafety practices and a lack of containment in Iraqi facilities.

No country appears immune to eyebrow-raising biosafety mistakes, in part because facilities are not required to adopt biosafety rules. The World Health Organization's guidelines are voluntary, and for U.S. laboratories not receiving grants from the National Institutes of Health, the U.S. guidelines are optional. Without mandatory rules, workers may be inadequately trained and supervised in implementing biosafety practices. Moreover, laboratory staff can become cavalier about biosafety when there are no institutional or individual penalties for breaking the rules.

As if the frequency of biosafety gaffes is not worrisome enough, new techniques, equipment, and knowledge are propelling life sciences developments at a breakneck pace. Undoubtedly the life sciences revolution will yield quality-of-life-changing benefits in such areas as medicine, environmental remediation, energy generation, and agriculture.[58] Downsides, however, accompany any revolution: the second risk that attends the cutting-edge life sciences is that today's techniques, knowledge, materials, and equipment will be deliberately or inadvertently misapplied. According to biologist Malcolm Dando, "What would require the skills of a Nobel Prize winner in one decade will become commonplace laboratory practice in the next. All or almost all countries have the ability to produce deadly biotoxins cheaply."[59] As noted, Soviet bioweaponeers commandeered gene splicing know-how to harden diseases against known medications and to increase the lethality of diseases.[60] In addition to the intentional creation of more treacherous pathogens, genetic engineers have inadvertently made diseases more harmful.[61]

Once a skill set that relatively few could execute, genetic engineering has become commonplace; the same will soon be said about synthetic biology, the ability to generate microorganisms *de novo* from base pairs of nucleic acids. Already, scientists have artificially created the polio and 1918 influenza viruses, which killed and crippled tens of millions worldwide in the twentieth century.[62] The aforementioned Marburg was recovered from a full-length cDNA clone in 2006, bat SARS-like coronavirus recreated in 2008, and the *Mycomplasma mycoides* genome synthesized in 2010. Looking at the relative complexity of the pathogens synthesized, polio virus involved 7,741-base pairs, the Mycoplasma genome 1,080,000 base pairs.[63] Thus, not only are scientists able to reassemble pathogens faster, they are able to put together increasingly complex, large genomes. Variola major, the virus that causes the more lethal version of smallpox, has a comparatively modest number of base pairs, 186,102.[64] Synthetic biology therefore opens the door to the assembly from scratch of rare and tightly controlled pathogens as well as of eradicated diseases. Base pairs for synthetic assembly cost only a few dollars.[65]

Other important new technologies at the forefront of the life sciences revolution, such as RNA interference and nanobiotechnology, are also vulnerable to abuse. Malicious actors could combine sophisticated targeted-delivery technologies with bioregulators, which can be directed to manipulate the human immune, nervous, and endocrine systems.[66] Observed geneticist and molecular biologist Matthew Meselson, "A world in which these capabilities are widely employed for hostile purposes would be a world in which the very nature of conflict has radically changed. Therein could lie unprecedented opportunities for violence, coercion, repression, or subjugation."[67]

Scientists intent on discovery tend to work with single-minded purpose, perhaps not thinking through all of the safety angles or the unintended consequences of their work. Conscientious behavior can be promoted with policies and programs that carry mandatory noncompliance penalties, as demonstrated in the area of highway safety with drivers' education, speed limits, and seat belt and drunk driving laws. Comparable safeguards can govern the work of scientists. In 1975, amidst fears that recombinant DNA technology would harm laboratory workers, the public, and the environment, early genetic engineers to their credit assembled in Asilomar, California, having voluntarily agreed to cease recombinant DNA experiments until governing mechanisms could be instituted. The scientists fashioned what became the U.S. guidelines for oversight of genetic engineering research and biosafety, both of which revolve around institutional review processes for pertinent research.[68]

Conceptually, institutional peer review boards are the watchdogs to help ensure that research is performed responsibly and safely. However, the field of life sciences is so exciting that do-it-yourselfers, known as biohackers, are flocking to participate, taking advantage of advanced automated equipment that "de-skills" complex techniques and processes. These amateur scientists often work without oversight or any training in proper safety and security.[69] Lack of governance for self-taught biologists is troublesome, but it is far from the only issue confronting the life sciences community.

Even the traditional institutional review committee approach has its shortcomings. Only in a small number of nations (for example, Germany and the United Kingdom) are oversight panels mandatory for all facilities conducting recombinant DNA research. In the United States and many other countries, peer governance of scientific research is not exercised comprehensively or evenly.[70] Evidence also indicates that where such committees exist they do not always function effectively. Moreover, the self-regulatory approach is innately handicapped because "scientists hesitate to place any restrictions on each other's work and regard oversight mechanisms largely as a bureaucratic burden."[71] The flood of advances in the life sciences has underscored the need to update oversight mechanisms, and esteemed scientific advisory panels have proposed upgrades. The U.S. government has yet to act on recommendations, for example, to provide extra scrutiny for seven types of genetic engineering experiments.[72]

The third attendant risk to research with contagious, lethal diseases concerns the possibility that laboratory workers might misbehave or that the morally bankrupt could obtain high-risk pathogens. U.S. awareness of this problem intensified in 1995 when a lieutenant in the Aryan Nations, Larry Wayne Harris, used false pretenses to buy *Y. pestis* from a U.S. pathogen repository, which sent Harris three vials of the bubonic plague.[73] This incident sparked the maiden U.S. biosecurity regulations to control the transfer of and access to select pathogens. Known euphemistically as the "guns, guards, and gates" approach because physical security is one of its core components, biosecurity can also encompass licensing of facilities to work with pathogens; procedures to ensure the accountability of pathogens and to ascertain personnel reliability; pre-transport approval of transfers of pathogens and appropriate security during transport; oversight of scientific, commercial, and defense work with pathogens; and appropriate security for information related to processes and techniques useful in weaponizing an agent.[74]

Lapses occurred despite the tightening of security regulations in America and elsewhere. In August 2008, the Federal Bureau of Investigation fingered USAMRIID researcher Bruce Ivins as the perpetrator of the 2001 anthrax letter attacks. Beyond the unsettling contention that a twenty-six-year USAMRIID employee may have been the attacker, bioforensic and other evidence indicated that Ivins may have prepared the anthrax in question inside his Ft. Detrick laboratory.[75] Details about Ivins's behavior also fomented concerns about the "insider threat" scenario wherein a trusted employee engages in sabotage.[76] Less than a year later, an inventory of USAMRIID's culture collection turned up 9,220 vials not listed in the facility's computerized inventory, including vials of botulinum neurotoxins and the Ebola, Junin, Rift valley fever, and Venezuelan and Western equine encephalitis viruses. USAMRIID officials chalked this jumble up to errors made when the facility computerized its pathogen inventory in 2005 and samples that departing workers left behind in the facility's 335 freezers and refrigerators. Unable to rule out foul play, including the possibility that someone smuggled out vials, USAMRIID officials pointed to the facility's firm measures to deter misbehavior such as video cameras in the laboratories, exit checks of personnel, stepped-up personnel screening and pathogen cataloging and auditing procedures, and random internal inspections.[77]

Events at USAMRIID underline the difficulties of ensuring a secure environment for research with high-risk pathogens. The first obstacles are human imperfections. Employees hired through a personnel screening process that concentrates on criminal, financial, and professional background checks but superficially addresses mental health, substance abuse, and lifestyle issues means that laboratory workers could be high or inebriated on the job, emotionally disturbed, or extorted to protect revelation of private matters (for example, nudist club membership). U.S. biosecurity procedures do not require substance abuse screening and address mental health matters tangentially, but the U.S. National Advisory Board for Biosecurity did not advocate full-scope screening for researchers working with high-risk pathogens, citing apprehensions that more intrusive initial and ongoing personnel screening could cause scientists to abandon this specialized area of research.[78]

Another biosecurity predicament lies in the premise that laboratories can account definitively for their culture collections. A pathogen inventory is fundamentally different from a tally of nuclear warheads because fissile material can be counted, weighed, and confirmed. In contrast, scientists consider a precise inventory of culture collections to be somewhat futile because the very items to be cataloged, microorganisms, can be isolated from nature. Pathogens kept in-house can also be replicated and stored in deliberately mislabeled containers without drawing undue attention.[79] Moreover, as synthetic biologists worldwide sharpen the techniques to create pathogens artificially, the concepts of restricting access to pathogens and taking precise inventories will become less relevant to preventing villainy.[80] For these reasons, life scientists regard "locking up" pathogens as a costly hindrance with dubious security gains.

On top of these complications, the number of facilities and individuals working with high-risk pathogens is rising commensurate with the globalization of the research, pharmaceutical, and biotechnology industries. Knowledge and state-of-the-art equipment that automates previously labor-intensive processes are diffusing worldwide. So biodefense and public health research formerly consigned to a handful of government laboratories, universities, and contractors is now being outsourced to companies around the globe, partly because of less stringent regulatory burdens and lower labor costs.[81] Nations with already flourishing biotechnology industries or that are laying the foundation to become biological powerhouses include Brazil, Cuba, Egypt, India, Mexico, Russia, Singapore, South Korea, and Taiwan.[82]

In addition, concerns about emerging infectious diseases and bioterrorism are propelling an augmentation of high-containment laboratory capacity to enhance disease surveillance and conduct biodefense research. Since 2001, the United States raised from five to fifteen its number of Biosafety Level 4 laboratories. Level 4 is the highest level of biosafety for work with ultra lethal and contagious diseases at minimal risk to scientists and the public. Elsewhere, India has sixteen Level 3 facilities, is building six more, and is adding two Level 4 laboratories. Bangladesh, which already has one Level 3 laboratory, has another on the drawing board. Bhutan and Nepal each have a Level 3 laboratory planned.[83]

Just as with its biosafety guidelines, biological facilities are under no compunction to heed the World Health Organization's biosecurity guidelines.[84] Biorisk management practices around the world are of varied quality and effectiveness.[85] Although the World Health Organization has biorisk management training programs, this international public health watchdog's work is perpetually underfunded. With rare exceptions, biorisk management issues do not make it onto the agendas of global leaders. These circumstances combine to make it a challenge to chart an avenue to raise standards for biosecurity, biosafety, and genetic engineering research oversight worldwide.

In a nutshell, as wondrous life sciences discoveries materialized over the past few decades, Iraq and the former Soviet Union orchestrated programs to develop, produce, and weaponize diseases; noteworthy biosafety accidents and biosecurity lapses occurred, including at military biological facilities; and scientists performed trail-blazing and sometimes ill-advised experiments that, if duplicated by pernicious individuals, could cause considerable damage. The implications for bioweapons proliferation are worrisome. Other headline-dominating events—the 2001 U.S. anthrax letter attacks, the 2003 SARS outbreak, and projections of an influenza pandemic[86]—have heightened public awareness of how fast communicable diseases can hop national borders and bring mega-cities to a standstill, no matter whether the epidemic originates from nature, a laboratory mishap, or a deliberate human act. In the twenty-first century and beyond, the extent to which bioerrors, natural disease outbreaks, and acts of bioterror disrupt societal well-being worldwide will depend significantly on the individual and collective actions of leaders in government and the life sciences.

A consortium of nongovernmental entities can design and activate non-proliferation and biorisk management tools much more quickly than the cumbersome processes that generate standards, which normally involve national review boards, professional societies, government bureaucracies, and international negotiations. Indeed, the private sector has launched some tools to prevent the abuse of life sciences capabilities. Gene synthesis companies have begun implementing a graduated program to screen orders for genes to guard against the rogue assembly of dangerous pathogens.[87] Though a small percentage of life sciences experiments are of the type that would warrant concern, individual scientists and institutional review panels can now also obtain an impartial expert sanity check on possibly questionable research proposals by submitting the requisite information to an independent review panel accessible via the web.[88] Constructive, ground-breaking endeavors such as these are to be applauded and can serve as stopgaps to temper potentially wayward life sciences activities. Given the stakes to national and international security and public health, however, governments can hardly afford to sit on the sidelines hoping private sector mechanisms will fill the gaps in biorisk management. Biosafety, oversight of genetic engineering, and biosecurity practices are weak or altogether missing in far too many countries, and in many nations where biorisk management standards are in place, they need to be revamped to keep pace with science.

Moreover, biological facilities, including those possibly engaged in illicit activities, will continue to operate uninspected absent a verification protocol for the international bioweapons ban. Without the supplemental information that inspections could provide, the world's leaders are left indefinitely to make important national security, defense, and foreign policy decisions only on the basis of intelligence. Partly because the telltale signs of bioweapons programs are sparse and equivocal and biowarfare agents can be made with easily accessible items, intelligence agencies have repeatedly found it difficult to pinpoint these programs.[89] A high-level review commission stated in 2005 that the U.S. intelligence community "substantially underestimated the scale and maturity of Iraq's" bioweapons program prior to the 1991 Gulf War and that the U.S. intelligence assessment about the threat of Iraq's rejuvenated biological and chemical weapons programs, notably its alleged mobile bioweapons production trailers, prior to the 2003 Gulf War was "simply wrong."[90] The Iraq Survey Group, which had significant resources and unimpeded access in Iraq, located no cache of germ or poison weapons.[91] The United States restructured its intelligence community in 2004, but bureaucratic reorganization may not translate into improved bioweapons assessments.[92]

Even if the difficulty of bioweapons intelligence assessments were not at issue, the tendency of policymakers to view matters through a political prism, as discussed in Chapter 9, can stymie international action. Policy paralysis is far from ideal when bioweapons activities could jeopardize global health and peace. To illustrate, the U.S. intelligence community rightly ascribed the death of over sixty Soviet citizens to a leak of anthrax from a Sverdlovsk military base in early April 1979. Moscow attributed the deaths to consumption of contaminated meat, an explanation sufficiently plausible for many nations to reject the U.S. allegation.[93] The international community never censured Moscow, partly because U.S. noncompliance charges rested on intelligence alone.

More recent U.S. intelligence estimates about bioweapons programs, specifically about Iraq, may give international leaders room to question or dismiss outright future U.S. proliferation assessments. In short, the international community will likely require some other source of impartial, reliable data before agreeing to political, economic, or military punishments against a bioweapons proliferator. Therefore, an information gap related to the ability to patrol the prohibitions on development, production, and stockpiling of germ weapons constitutes another missing element in biorisk management, along with the holes in oversight of genetic engineering research, biosafety, and biosecurity practices.

A PATH TO CURB BIOLOGICAL PERILS

History reserves its harshest judgment for aggressors, oppressors, despots, and others who act with absolute depravity—the likes of Pol Pot, Hitler, and Shiro Ishii. Ishii, the Japanese contemporary of the notorious Joseph Mengele in World War II, tested biological agents on live humans and directed the battlefield use of germ weapons.[94] Any nation, terrorist group, or individual that acquires and callously unleashes bioweapons will be assured of a similarly ignominious legacy.

History can be almost as unsympathetic to leaders who are told of dangers threatening their citizens but shun reasonable steps to reduce and avert those dangers. Threats do not dissipate without purposeful effort, which is why since the mid-nineteenth century states have regularly agreed to build national capabilities to detect, report, and respond to disease outbreaks. Departing from the custom that public health capacities were largely a domestic concern, the 2005 iteration of the International Health Regulations stipulated closer international public health coordination.[95] In disquieting contrast, no proactive or coordinated global plan exists to address other potentially ruinous biological risks. One of history's greatest utilities is that it can chart the future; every component on the spectrum of biological risks has already transpired repeatedly.

The absence of an international biorisk management plan is partly due to the many moving pieces of the biohazards puzzle. Each of these pieces must be parsed to grasp how the potential causes of biological dangers intersect, and, in turn, how they relate to the various risk management tools.[96] The life sciences revolution encompasses metabolomics, genetic engineering, bioinformatics, synthetic biology, nanobiotechnology, and proteomics, to name a few disciplines, so basic familiarity with the constituent parts of this activity is an ambitious task. Comprehending the entire biohazards picture, which includes the globalization of biotechnology, a myriad of public health dilemmas, and the bioweapons proliferation angles is a downright intimidating undertaking. Nonetheless, the risk-causing factors and biorisk management tools have to be dealt with in an integrated fashion because the handling of each component has implications for all the others. To illustrate, building new high-containment laboratories to improve disease surveillance, a worthy objective, could have the unintended consequence of increasing the rate of biological accidents if these laboratories do not adhere to sound biosafety principles. The search for new medical treatments, whether for familiar public health menaces such as HIV/AIDS or previously weaponized diseases, could inadvertently result in more dangerous or novel pathogens absent conscientious peer oversight of research. Therefore an elevated problem-solving process that fuses the realms of life sciences, international security, commerce, and public health is required to confront and diminish present and future biological risks.

Such a holistic approach could be jumpstarted with a global summit on biorisk management.[97] Summits are fulcrums to chart a responsible global course to address multifaceted problems (for example, climate change) that affect all nations regardless of their level of development, cultural norms, or form of government. To that end, President Barack Obama convened a summit in April 2010 to create a strategy to confront the nuclear terrorist threat.[98] The mere scheduling of a summit initiates domestic and international meetings in which technical experts and mid-level officials evaluate decision options. Once leaders commit their political capital to a summit, everyone has incentive to avoid the embarrassment of or blame for the failure to hammer out a strategy.

The first objective of a summit would be to carve out global biorisk management standards. Industries accept standards because they establish a level competitive playing field, and countries that raise their practices to agreed standards will be more attractive to foreign investors. Standards can be configured in increasingly strict steps to permit nations with varying capabilities and resources to come into compliance in phases.[99] The workload leading into a biorisk management summit should be fairly modest because experts can pull proven models for biosafety and oversight of genetic engineering research off the shelf and update them to maximize their utility amidst a scientific revolution. Biosecurity, the latest biorisk management tool, has several components for which the security benefit remains unproven, making this tool ripe for evaluation and refinement.[100] A cost-benefit assessment could streamline and increase the effectiveness of biosecurity by emphasizing the measures most likely to prevent, deter, and detect misbehavior and devaluing or eliminating those for which the administrative burden and restriction on scientific freedom seriously outweigh the security gains.

To wit, the emphasis in biosecurity should be placed on personnel reliability rather than guns, guards, and gates. The time has come for life scientists to accept that working with certain materials, equipment, and technology is a responsibility, not a right, because their mistakes could have severe consequences for the public at large. Several professions with a significant bearing on public safety (for example, law enforcement and nuclear facility workers) have mandatory full-scope personnel screening to help short-circuit accidents and other employee misdeeds. Similarly, nations should consider requiring scientists working in high-biosafety containment laboratories to be screened initially and periodically after hiring for problems (such as depression, substance abuse, or susceptibility to coercion) that could negatively influence their reliability, trustworthiness, and reasoning.[101] Populating high-containment laboratories with scientists who exercise sound judgment reliably is a far more achievable route to reducing accidents and deliberate misbehavior than trying to inventory and padlock all high-risk pathogens.

To prepare scientists to exercise good judgment, a comprehensive, uniform educational requirement for good laboratory practices is warranted because budding scientists are often taught little about the safe and responsible practice of science. A 2009 survey of 765 scientists from eighty-one countries revealed widely varying perceptions of risk and frequent negligence in bio-safety and biosecurity.[102] Therefore, nations should contemplate requiring all colleges and universities granting undergraduate and graduate life sciences degrees to instruct future generations of scientists on the ethical consider-ations of life sciences research, the Convention's prohibitions, and the fun-damentals of biosafety, biosecurity, and research oversight. Nations might further agree that institutions working with high-risk pathogens should be obligated to provide their workers regular refresher training.[103]

Next, a three-tiered superstructure for biorisk management standards could be constructed with responsibilities assigned primarily at the institu-tional level, in significant cases bumped to a national level, and in select cir-cumstances also referred to the international level.[104] As this tiered structure is established, the linchpin role of the institutional biosafety officer in the day-to-day policing of agreed standards should be reinforced with the creation of institutional biosafety committees in all entities engaged in advanced life sciences research and the revitalization of existing committees so that they actively exercise the peer oversight intended. This peer governance approach departs from the state-centric model codified in arms control and nonprolif-eration treaties by literally designating a vast army of scientists to be sentinels in biological facilities worldwide, guarding against accidents and intentional misbehavior.[105] Scientists renowned for focusing on their petri dishes to the exclusion of everything else might implement standards lackadaisically un-less mandatory personal and institutional noncompliance penalties are at-tached to failure to observe standards. Fines, stripping individuals of access to high-risk pathogens, and the loss of facility certification typically motivate scientists to make a good faith effort in implementation. Initial and regular recertification of facilities using processes similar to those of the Interna-tional Organization for Standardization could also be agreed to confirm facil-ity compliance with biorisk management standards and to look for signs that a laboratory might have been usurped for malevolent purposes.[106]

Finally, to achieve a fully blended biorisk management strategy, a fresh and thorough look should be taken at the ability to detect germ warfare ac-tivities. The Convention has been described as "inherently unverifiable," an assertion still repeated.[107] The achievements of UNSCOM's biological inspec-tors directly challenge this platitude. UNSCOM detected Iraq's development, production, and weaponization of biowarfare agents with the rough equivalent of routine inspections at declared sites, reporting these matters to the Security Council before Iraq admitted culpability. Iraq declared the sites involved in its bioweapons program as civilian biological facilities, then during UNSCOM's initial biological inspection admitted conducting military biological research at Salman Pak. Thereafter, using ordinary inspection tools (such as observation, document tracking, interviews) and old-fashioned gumshoe detective work, the inspectors collected evidence that Iraq was hiding a bioweapons program behind a façade of civilian activity. Though UNSCOM's inspectors had limited success after 1995 using challenge tactics (for example, no-notice document searches) to ferret out the finer details about Iraq's bioweapons program, UNSCOM had already notified the international community about this weapons program. The many operational and technical lessons from UNSCOM's inspections are a valuable resource to plumb during a reevaluation of data-collection strategies, tactics, and tools that can be used to monitor biological facilities.[108]

Straightforward questions are in order to evaluate the limitations and prospective contributions of intelligence and inspections to the standing need to deter and detect bioweapons proliferation. A study of these tools should consider their utility in isolation of each other as well as the potential synergy between intelligence, increasingly powerful sampling and analysis capabilities, analysis of import and export data, and other on-site inspection tools. The global institutionalization of cross-cutting biosafety, biosecurity, and research oversight standards would generate a voluminous regulatory paper trail, so a thorough study should also contemplate how inspectors' perusal of such data could aid efforts to separate legitimate peaceful biological work from illicit biowarfare activities.[109] This appraisal could find that inspections can be expected to detect certain biowarfare activities reliably (for example, weapons filling, stockpiling, bulk agent production, and testing) but not necessarily others (such as offensive research or development). Whatever the study's conclusions, the analytical process entailed would identify alternatives to give global leaders more data of a higher quality about suspected bioweapons activities. The costs of war justified even partly by faulty intelligence are far too great for leaders not to be seriously motivated to promote tools to deter proliferation and provide the most comprehensive data possible to inform their decisions.[110]

Accordingly, leaders at a biological summit should consider a range of options to deter proliferation and to detect clandestine bioweapons activities, including transforming the currently voluntary annual data declarations by Convention members on pertinent biological activities and capacities into mandatory declarations, possibly adding useful data categories to the declarations, and augmenting international staff to evaluate the data.[111] The resumption of negotiations to add verification provisions to the Convention is another option, particularly if new talks aim for legally binding on-site inspection procedures only for activities deemed to be verifiable (such as stockpiling of weapons). Leaders could identify and frame other means to help monitor activities when on-site inspections are presumed incapable of providing data to help clarify compliance. While a more robust monitoring capability is being constructed, summit leaders could also weigh the temporary extension of the United Nations Secretary-General's authority to investigate alleged use of chemical and biological weapons to include the authority to investigate facilities suspected of bioweapons development, testing, production, and stockpiling.[112] In short, a rich, practical array of options can be placed on the agenda of a biorisk management summit, and existing international entities could implement most agreed-upon tasks.[113]

Absent a global biorisk management summit, the life sciences and the diffusion of dual-use biotechnology will race ahead largely unbound, courting biological accidents and bioweapons proliferation. International leaders have voiced concerns about all manner of biological threats (such as bioterrorism, covert national biowarfare programs, and laboratory mishaps), but they have otherwise left a leadership vacuum in their wake. A potential confluence of international interests to confront biological risks lies dormant. Once it is awakened, the building of an interlocking structure of global biorisk management standards and strengthened nonproliferation mechanisms becomes an achievable objective, because virtually all of the constituent tools already exist in some form. All that is missing is the leadership commitment to put the international community on a sustainable, forward-looking, and flexible path to curb biological perils.

NOTES

In addition, see the webpage at http://www.sup.org/book.cgi?id=20908, which contains extended annotations for many of the following endnotes. Note numbers on the webpage correspond to the note numbers that follow here.

Introduction

1. Michael I. Handel, *Weak States in the International System* (Abingdon: Routledge, 1990), 195–208.

2. According to Colin Powell, "Of all the various weapons of mass destruction, biological weapons are of the greatest concern to me." *Hearing Before the House Armed Services Committee*, 103rd Congress (March 30, 1993) (statement of Gen. Colin Powell, chairman of the U.S. Joint Chiefs of Staff). Also, Dr. Brock Chisholm: "Some seven ounces of a certain biological agent, if it could be effectively distributed, would be sufficient to kill all the people of the world.... Large armies, navies and air forces, including the Atomic bomb, which have been regarded as the symbol and fact of power, are now obsolete," quoted in Donald Avery, "The Canadian Biological Weapons Program and the Tripartite Alliance," in *Deadly Cultures: Biological Weapons Since 1945*, ed. Mark Wheelis, Lajos Rozsa, and Malcolm Dando (Cambridge, MA: Harvard University Press, 2004), 91; *The Biological Weapons Threat and Nonproliferation Options: A Survey of Senior U.S. Decision Makers and Policy Shapers* (Washington, DC: Center for Strategic and International Studies and the Carnegie Endowment for International Peace, November 2006); Frederick R. Sidell, Ernest T. Takafuji, and David R. Franz, eds., *Medical Aspects of Chemical and Biological Warfare* (Washington, DC: Office of The Surgeon General at Textbook of Military Medicine Publications, 1997).

3. For more, go to <http://www.opbw.org>. Also, Marie Isabelle Chevrier, "The Politics of Biological Disarmament," in Wheelis, Rozsa, and Dando, *Deadly Cultures*, 304–328.

4. United Nations (UN) Security Council, Resolution 687 (1991), adopted April 3, 1991, Doc. S/RES/687, April 8, 1991, http://www.un.org/Depts/unmovic/documents/687.pdf, para. C (7).

5. Rodger Claire, *Raid on the Sun: Inside Israel's Secret Campaign That Denied Saddam the Bomb* (New York: Broadway Publishing, 2004); Uri Bar-Joseph, *Two Minutes Over Baghdad* (Oxford: Routledge, 2003).

6. UN, *Special Conference of the States Parties to the Convention on the Prohibition of the Development, Production, and Stockpiling of Bacteriological (Biological) and Toxin Weapons and on Their Destruction, Final Report*, Doc. BWC/SPCONF/1, Geneva, September 19–30, 1994.

7. Martin Shubik, "Terrorism, Technology, and Socioeconomics of Death," *Comparative Strategy* 16, no.4 (October 1997): 406. Several scholars have noted the susceptibility of history to manipulation, including Margaret MacMillan, *Dangerous Games: The Uses and Abuses of History* (New York: Modern Library, 2009).

8. Examples include the International Campaign to Ban Landmines, which received the 1997 Nobel Peace Prize, and the public health, education, and development initiatives of the Bill and Melinda Gates Foundation. More information can be found, respectively, at <http://www.icbl.org/intro.php> and <http://www.gatesfoundation.org/Pages/home.aspx>.

9. Donald C. Daniel, Bradd C. Hayes, and Chantal de Jonge Oudraat, *Coercive Inducement and the Containment of International Crises* (Washington, DC: U.S. Institute of Peace, March 1999); P. J. Simmons and Chantal de Jonge Oudraat, *Managing Global Issues: Lessons Learned* (Washington, DC: Carnegie Endowment for International Peace, 2001); Ashraf Ghani and Clare Lockhart, *Fixing Failed States: A Framework for Rebuilding a Fractured World* (New York: Oxford University Press, 2008); Michael Barnett and Martha Finnemore, *Rules for the World: International Organizations in Global Politics* (Ithaca, NY: Cornell University Press, 2004); Chester A. Crocker, Fen Osler Hampson, and Pamela R. Aall, eds., *Turbulent Peace: The Challenges of Managing International Conflict* (Washington, DC: U.S. Institute of Peace, 2001); Thomas G. Weiss, David P. Forsythe, Roger A. Coate, and Kelly-Kate Pease, *The United Nations and Changing World Politics*, 5th ed. (Boulder, CO: Westview Press, 2006); James P. Muldoon Jr., *The Architecture of Global Governance: An Introduction to the Study of Global Governance* (Boulder, CO: Westview Press, 2008); Margaret P. Karns and Karen A. Mingst, *International Organizations: The Politics and Processes of Global Governance* (Boulder, CO: Lynne Rienner, 2004).

10. Dozens of organizations with global charters are affiliated with the UN, including the International Civil Aviation Organization, the World Trade Organization, and the UN Education, Scientific, and Cultural Organization. For more, go to <http://www.unsystem.org>.

11. Richard Lowry, *The Gulf War Chronicles: A Military History of the First War with Iraq* (New York: Universe, 2008); Michael R. Gordon, *The Generals' War: The Inside Story of the Conflict in the Gulf* (Boston: Back Bay Books, 1995); Graham S. Pearson, *The UNSCOM Saga: Chemical and Biological Weapons Non-Proliferation* (New York: St. Martin's Press, 1999), 176–187.

12. For the history and investigation of the Oil for Food program, go to <http://www.oilforfoodfacts.org/default.aspx>. Also, United States General Accounting Office, *United Nations: Observations on the Management and Oversight of the Oil for Food Program*, GAO-04-730T (Washington, DC, April 28, 2004).

13. Roberta Wohlstetter, *Pearl Harbor: Warning and Decision* (Stanford, CA: Stanford University Press, 1962); Abraham Rabinovich, *The Yom Kippur War: The Epic Encounter That Transformed the Middle East* (New York: Schocken, 2005); James J. Wirtz, *The Tet Offensive: Intelligence Failure in War* (Ithaca, NY: Cornell University Press, 1994). Also, Nassim Nicholas Taleb, *The Black Swan: The Impact of the Highly Improbable* (New York: Random House, 2007).

14. *Commission on the Intelligence Capabilities of the United States Regarding Weapons of Mass Destruction: Report to the President of the United States* (Washington, DC: U.S. Government Printing Office, March 31, 2005), 1, 82, 88–111. Also, Charles Duelfer, *Hide and Seek: The Search for Truth in Iraq* (New York: Public Affairs, 2009), 456, 470; Bob Drogin, *Curveball: Spies, Lies, and the Con Man Who Caused a War* (New York: Random House, 2007); The Royal Society, *New Approaches to Biological Risk Assessment* (London: Science Policy Centre, July 2009).

15. David Webb, "On the Definition of a Space Weapon (When Is a Space Weapon Not a Space Weapon?)," Praxis Center Metropolitan University, http://praxis.leeds met.ac.uk/praxis/documents/space_weapons.pdf. Also, Lynn R. Sykes, "False and Misleading Claims About Verification During the Debate on the Nuclear Comprehensive Test Ban Treaty," *F.A.S. Public Interest Report* 53, no. 3 (May–June 2000); Walter Krutzsch, "Law Enforcement Including Domestic Riot Control: The Intent of the CWC Negotiators" (paper presented at the 52nd CBW Pugwash Meeting, Noordwijk, The Netherlands, March 17–18, 2007); Jonathan B. Tucker, "The Body's Own Bioweapons," *Bulletin of the Atomic Scientists* 64, no. 1 (March-April 2008): 16–22.

16. Marie Isabelle Chevrier, "From Verification to Strengthening Compliance: Prospects and Challenges of the Biological Weapons Convention," *Politics and the Life Sciences* 14, no. 2 (August 1995): 212. Also, Douglas J. MacEachin, "Routine and Challenge: Two Pillars of Verification," *The CBW Conventions Bulletin* 39 (March 1998): 1.

17. Mark M. Lowenthal, "The Politics of Verification: What's New, What's Not," and Maria R. Alongi, "Verification and Congress: What Role for Politics," in *Verification: The Key to Arms Control in the 1990s*, ed. John G. Tower, James Brown, and William K. Cheek (New York: Brassey's, 1992), 13–34; Michael Krepon and Dan Caldwell, eds., *The Politics of Arms Control Treaty Ratification* (New York: St. Martin's Press, 1991); Michael Krepon, "The Politics of Treaty Verification and Compliance," in *Arms Control Verification: The Technologies That Make It Possible*, ed. Kosta Tsipis, David W. Hafemeister, and Penny Janeway (New York: Pergamon-Brassey's, 1986), 20–32; Rudolf Avenhaus, Nikolas Kyriakopoulos, Michael Richard, Gotthard Stern, eds., *Verifying Treaty Compliance: Limiting Weapons of Mass Destruction and Monitoring Kyoto Protocol Provisions* (New York: Springer, 2006).

18. Gerard Smith, *Doubletalk* (Lanham, MD: University Press of America, 1985); Hans Grumm, "IAEA Safeguards: Milestones in Development and Implementation," *IAEA Bulletin*, no. 3 (Vienna: International Atomic Energy Agency, 1987), 29–34; Bhupendra Jasani and Toshibomi Sakata, *Satellites for Arms Control and Crisis Monitoring* (Stockholm: Stockholm International Peace Research Institute, 1987); Tsipis, Hafemeister, and Janeway, *Arms Control Verification*, Chapters 7 to 20.

19. Ronald Reagan, remarks on signing the Intermediate-Range Nuclear Forces Treaty, Washington, DC, The White House, December 8, 1987.

20. Article XI of the 1991 Treaty Between the United States of America and the Union of Soviet Socialist Republics on the Reduction and Limitation of Offensive Strategic Arms. Also, Model Protocol Additional to the Agreement(s) Between State(s) and the International Atomic Energy Agency for the Application of Safeguards, Doc. INFCIRC/540, International Atomic Energy Agency, Vienna, September 1997; 1993 Convention on the Prohibition of the Development, Production, Stockpiling and Use of Chemical Weapons and on Their Destruction, Annex on Implementation and Verification.

21. Graham Pearson and Malcolm Dando, "On-Site Inspections in the Emerging BTWC Protocol," in "On-Site Inspections: Common Problems, Different Solutions," ed. Kerstin Hoffman, *Disarmament Forum*, no. 3 (1999): 78–82; Jez Littlewood, *The Biological Weapons Convention: A Revolution Failed* (Aldershot, U.K.: Ashgate Publishing, 2005), 89–138. Also, Protocol to the Convention on the Prohibition of the Development, Production and Stockpiling of Bacteriological (Biological) and Toxin Weapons and on Their Destruction, BWC/ADHOCGROUP/CRP.8, Ad Hoc Group, Geneva, April 3, 2001. For analysis, Graham S. Pearson, Malcolm R. Dando, and Nicholas A. Sims, "The Composite Protocol Text: An Effective Strengthening of the Biological and Toxin Weapons Convention," paper no. 20 (Bradford, U.K.: University of Bradford, Department of Peace Studies, April 2001); Marie Chevrier, "The Biological Weapons Convention: The Protocol That Almost Was," in *Verification Yearbook 2001*, ed. Trevor Findlay and Oliver Meier (London: Verification, Inspection, and Training Centre, 2001), 79–97; Model Protocol Additional to the Agreement(s), Doc. INFCIRC/540.

22. U.S. Ambassador Donald Mahley, Statement by the United States to the Ad Hoc Group of Biological Weapons Convention States Parties, Geneva, July 25, 2001. Also, Mike Allen, "US Seeks to Stiffen Pact on Germ War; Pact's Enforcement Mechanism Faulted," *Washington Post*, October 17, 2001, A21; Mike Allen and Steve Mufson, "U.S. Scuttles Germ War Conference; Move Stuns European Allies," *Washington Post*, December 8, 2001, A1; Littlewood, *The Biological Weapons Convention*.

23. Ronald Lehman, "Conference Can Strengthen Biological Weapons Regime," Geneva, September 10, 1991 (U.S. Information Agency); Wendy Lubetkin, "U.S. Welcomes Biological Weapons Convention Work Plan," Office of International Information Programs, U.S. Department of State, November 15, 2002, http://www.america.gov/

st/washfile-english/2002/November/20021115141419mkellerh@pd.state.gov0.4453089. html; "Under Secretary of State Ellen Tauscher: Address to States Parties of the BWC" (Geneva, Permanent Mission of the United States of America, December 9, 2009).

24. David Huxsoll, DVM (former UNSCOM chief biological weapons inspector), interview with author, Washington, DC, June 21, 2005; Ake Sellstrom, PhD (former UNSCOM chief inspector), interview with author, Stockholm, August 24, 2005. Also, Jessica Tuchman Mathews, *Iraq: A New Approach* (Washington, DC: Carnegie Endowment of International Peace, September 2002).

25. The referral of grave compliance problems to the Security Council is explicit in Article XII of the Chemical Weapons Convention and Article VI of the Biological Weapons Convention. The Security Council has also frequently been the forum for discussion and promulgation of punishments related to proven or suspected nuclear weapons proliferation problems. For sanctions related to Iran, see UN Security Council, Resolutions 1803 (2008), 1737 (2007), 1747 (2007), and 1696 (2006). For sanctions related to the Democratic People's Republic of Korea, see Resolutions 1874 (2009), 1695 (2006), 1718 (2006), and 825 (1993).

26. Similar to treaties reducing intermediate- and strategic-range nuclear arms, UNSCOM inspectors conducted baseline inspections to create a database of dual-use items at Iraqi facilities, tagging them with unique, tamperproof identifiers so that subsequent inspectors could check their location and status. UNSCOM deployed teams that focused on document searches and interviews and called its version of challenge inspections "no-notice inspections." UNSCOM inspectors used principles of managed access like those in the Chemical Weapons Convention to negotiate access (for example, number of inspectors permitted to enter, specific areas accessed) to sensitive parts of facilities. See the Chemical Weapons Convention, Verification Annex, Part X, paras. 46–52.

27. With a comparative analysis of Iraq's early declarations and a couple of intelligence tips as a springboard, UNSCOM's bioweapons inspectors employed routine inspection tools to nail Iraq as a cheater, which drove Iraq to admit it made germ warfare agents. Even with more intrusive no-notice inspections, they were unable to pin down all of the finer details of Iraq's bioweapons program.

28. Alan Beyerchen, "Clausewitz, Nonlinearity, and the Unpredictability of War," *International Security* 17, no. 3 (Winter 1992): 55–90. For this extrapolation of Beyerchen, punctuated with "World War III easily could be the biologist's war," see Shubik, "Terrorism, Technology, and Socioeconomics of Death," 404.

29. In addition to assessments prior to the 1991 and 2003 Gulf Wars, intelligence on suspected bioweapons programs before and during World I and II and throughout the Cold War fell short of the mark, as discussed in Chapter 10.

30. Allen A. St-Onge, "United Nations Biological Warfare Inspectors in Iraq: Implications for Biological Arms Control—One Canadian's Perspective," *Politics and the*

Life Sciences 14, no. 2 (August 1995): 259–261; Raymond A. Zilinskas, "Iraq's Biological Weapons: The Past as Future?" *Journal of American Medical Association* 278, no. 5 (August 6, 1997): 418–424. Also, Tim Trevan, *Saddam's Secrets: The Hunt for Iraq's Hidden Weapons* (London: HarperCollins, 1999); Rod Barton, *The Weapons Detective: The Inside Story of Australia's Top Weapons Inspector* (Melbourne: Black Inc. Agenda, 2006); Duelfer, *Hide and Seek*.

31. A library of UNSCOM reports can be found online at <http://www.un.org/Depts/unscom/unscmdoc.htm>. Also, Central Intelligence Agency, *Comprehensive Report of the Special Advisor to the DCI on Iraq's WMD* (Washington, DC, September 30, 2004); Milton Leitenberg, *Biological Weapons Arms Control*, PRAC Paper no. 16 (College Park, MD: Center for International and Security Studies at Maryland, May 1996), 22–38; Graham S. Pearson, "The Iraqi Biological Weapons Program," in Wheelis, Rozsa, and Dando, *Deadly Cultures*, 169–190.

Chapter 1

1. Juan J. Walte, "Next Comes Ground War: An Allied Blitzkrieg Is Likely," *USA Today*, January 18, 1991; "The Operation Desert Shield/Desert Storm Timeline," *DefenseLink*, August 8, 2000, http://www.defenselink.mil/news/newsarticle.aspx?id=45404; William M. Arkin, Gen. Charles Horner, and Rick Atkinson, "Fog of War," Special Project, The Washington Post Company, 1998, http://www.washington post.com/wp-srv/inatl/longterm/fogofwar/fogofwar.htm; "The Unfinished War: The Legacy of Desert Storm," *CNN Presents*, CNN, January 5, 2001, http://transcripts.cnn.com/TRANSCRIPTS/0101/05/cp.00.html; Guy Gugliotta and Caryle Murphy, "Jets Roar Off in Darkness at Start of 'Desert Storm,'" *Washington Post*, January 17, 1991, A1; "War in the Gulf: War Summary," *New York Times Late Edition*, February 24, 1991, section 1, part 1, p. 17; Rick Atkinson and Steve Coll, "Bush Orders Cease-Fire," *Washington Post*, February 28, 1991, A1.

2. Philip Towle, *Enforced Disarmament: From the Napoleonic Campaigns to the Gulf* (Oxford: New Oxford University Press, 1997), 186–187. Also, foreign ministry official, interview with author, London, August 17, 2005.

3. Towle, *Enforced Disarmament*. Also, Charles Duelfer, *Hide and Seek: The Search for Truth in Iraq* (New York: Public Affairs, 2009), 170.

4. Tim Trevan, *Saddam's Secrets: The Hunt for Iraq's Hidden Weapons* (London: HarperCollins, 1999), 46; Rod Barton, *The Weapons Detective: The Inside Story of Australia's Top Weapons Inspector* (Melbourne: Black Inc. Agenda, 2006), 60; Jean E. Krasno and James S. Sutterlin, *The United Nations and Iraq: Defanging the Viper* (Westport, CT: Praeger, 2003), 4–9.

5. Ambassador Robert Gallucci, PhD (former UNSCOM deputy executive chairman), interview with author, Washington, DC, March 13, 2006.

6. United Nations (UN) Security Council, Resolution 687 (1991), adopted April 3, 1991, Doc. S/RES/687, http://www.un.org/Depts/unmovic/documents/687.pdf paras. 9(b)

(i) and (ii); Trevan, *Saddam's Secrets*, 46–49; William M. Arkin, "Origins of the Iraq Mistake," *Early Warning* (blog), *Washington Post*, October 19, 2005, http://blog.washington post.com/earlywarning/2005/10/origins_of_the_iraq_mistake.html (site discontinued).

7. Former UNSCOM CBW commissioner, interview with author via telephone, January 23, 2006. Also, Ronald Manley, PhD (former UNSCOM chief chemical weapons inspector), interview with author, London, August 19, 2005; foreign ministry official, interview with author, August 17, 2005; Richard Butler, *The Greatest Threat: Iraq, Weapons of Mass Destruction, and the Crisis of Global Security* (New York: Public Affairs, 2000), 41–42.

8. Gallucci, interview.

9. Ibid.

10. Former UNSCOM chief inspector, interview with author, New York City, January 31, 2006.

11. Former UNSCOM CBW commissioner, interview with author, January 23, 2006. Also, Douglas Englund (former UNSCOM chief inspector), interview with author, Washington, DC, December 5, 2005; Robert Kadlec, MD (former UNSCOM inspector), interview with author, Washington, DC, February 23, 2006.

12. Gallucci, interview. Also, Terence Taylor (former UNSCOM commissioner and chief inspector), interview with author, Washington, DC, May 12, 2005.

13. United Nations Security Council, Resolution 687 (1991); United Nations Security Council, Resolution 661 (1990), adopted August 6, 1990, Doc. S/RES/661, http://www.unhcr.org/refworld/docid/3b00f16b24.html.

14. Ambassador Rolf Ekeus (former UNSCOM executive chairman), interview with author, Stockholm, August 24, 2005. Also, Trevan, *Saddam's Secrets*, 52.

15. Ake Sellstrom, PhD (former UNSCOM chief inspector), interview with author, Stockholm, August 24, 2005; Gabriele Kraatz-Wadsack, DVM (former UNSCOM chief biological weapons inspector), interview with author, Berlin, August 15, 2005; Gallucci, interview.

16. Taylor, interview; Manley, interview; Englund, interview; former senior UNSCOM official, interview with author, New York City, August 30, 2005; Pierce Corden, former UNSCOM deputy executive chairman, interview with author, Washington, DC, August 4, 2008.

17. Ekeus, interview. Lauding Ekeus's management style, Hamish Killip (former UNSCOM chief biological weapons inspector), interview with author, Isle of Man, August 22, 2005; Kraatz-Wadsack, interview; Englund, interview; Taylor, interview; former senior UNSCOM official, interview with author, August 30, 2005.

18. Richard Spertzel, PhD (former UNSCOM chief biological weapons inspector), interview with author, Washington, DC, July 1, 2005; David Kelly, PhD (former UNSCOM chief biological weapons inspector), interview with author, Washington, DC, December 17, 2002; Killip, interview; former UNSCOM chief inspector, interview with author, January 31, 2006; Englund, interview; former UNSCOM chief inspector,

interview with author, London, August 18, 2005; former senior UNSCOM official, interview with author, New York City, September 1, 2005; Sellstrom, interview; Debra Krikorian, PhD (former UNSCOM biological weapons inspector), interview with author, Washington, DC, June 21, 2005; former senior UNSCOM official, interview with author, August 30, 2005; Taylor, interview.

19. Kraatz-Wadsack, interview; Englund, interview; Rod Barton (former UNSCOM biological inspector), interview with author via telephone, May 20, 2005; former UNSCOM chief inspector, interview with author, January 31, 2006; Taylor, interview.

20. Gallucci, interview. Also, Trevan, *Saddam's Secrets*, 52.

21. Gallucci, interview.

22. Former UNSCOM CBW commissioner, interview with author, January 23, 2006.

23. UN Security Council, *Report of the Secretary-General on Setting up a Special Commission (UNSCOM) to Carry Out On-Site Inspection of Iraq's Biological, Chemical and Missile Capabilities*, Report of the Secretary-General on Implementation of Para. 9(b)(i) of Resolution 687 (1991), Doc. S/22508, April 18, 1991, paras. 5, 7, and 9.

24. UN Security Council, *Plan for the Implementation of Relevant Parts of Section C of Security Council Resolution 687 (1991)*, Report of the Secretary-General Pursuant to Paragraph 9(b) of Resolution 687, Doc. S/22614, May 17, 1991.

25. Charles Duelfer (former UNSCOM deputy executive chairman), interview with author, Washington, DC, November 15, 2007.

26. Letter from Ahmed Hussein, Iraqi Minister of Foreign Affairs, to Secretary-General Javier Perez de Cuellar, conveyed by Permanent Mission of Iraq to the UN, Ambassador Abdul Amir A. Al-Anbari, Permanent Representative to the UN (dated April 18, 1991), paras. 1–3. Also, UN Doc. S/22614, para. 7.

27. Stephen Black (former UNSCOM historian), interview with author, November 16, 2007, Washington, DC.

28. Foreign ministry official, interview with author, August 17, 2005.

29. Gallucci, interview.

30. Ekeus, interview.

31. Former senior UNSCOM official, interview with author, August 30, 2005.

32. Former senior UNSCOM official, interview with author, September 1, 2005; former UNSCOM CBW commissioner, interview with author, January 23, 2006.

33. Manley, interview.

34. Former senior UNSCOM official, interview with author, August 30, 2005. Also, *Deadly Enemies*, directed by Susan Lambert (New York: First Run Icarus Films, 2004), DVD; Ken Alibek with Stephen Handelman, *Biohazard* (New York: Random House, 1999).

35. Letter from Abdul Amir A. Al-Anbari, Permanent Representative of Iraq to the UN, to Rolf Ekeus, Executive Chairman of the Security Council Special Commission (New York, Permanent Mission of Iraq to the UN, dated May 16, 1991).

36. Letter from Abdul Amir A. Al-Anbari to Rolf Ekeus, letter no. 117 (New York, Permanent Mission of Iraq to the UN, dated May 22, 1991, stamped received, UN Office of the Special Commission, May 24, 1991).

37. Ekeus, interview; former senior UNSCOM official, interview with author, August 30, 2005; former senior UNSCOM official, interview with author, September 1, 2005; former UNSCOM CBW commissioner, interview with author, January 23, 2006; former UNSCOM chief inspector, interview with author, January 31, 2006.

38. Letter from Abdul Amir A. Al-Anbari to Rolf Ekeus, letter no. 1/7/230 (New York, Permanent Mission of Iraq to the UN, dated July 18, 1991), Annex B, pages 9–11, and transmittal letter.

39. Letter from the Charge d'Affaires A.I. of the Permanent Mission of Iraq to the UN addressed to the President of the Security Council (New York, Permanent Mission of Iraq to the UN, dated January 23, 1992), UN Doc. S/23472, 28.

40. *Joint Hearing on Biological Warfare Testing Before the U.S. House of Representatives Committee on Armed Services and the Subcommittee on Arms Control, International Security and Science, Committee on Foreign Affairs* (May 3, 1988) (statement of Thomas B. Welch, Deputy Assistant Secretary of Defense); CIA, "Iraqi Acquisition of Technical Expertise in Development of Biological and Chemical Agents," CIA Document 719580, marked "Not Finally Evaluated Intelligence" (Washington, DC, October 1987); Defense Intelligence Agency (DIA), "Biological Warfare Production and Use," DIA Document IR-2-201-0883-88, marked "Not Finally Evaluated Intelligence" (Washington, DC, June 1988).

41. "Israel Vows Action Against Iraqi Germ Research," *Washington Times*, January 19, 1989, A8; Stephen Engelberg, "Iraq Said to Study Biological Arms," *New York Times*, January 18, 1989, A7; Michael Binyon, "Iraq 'Developing Typhoid, Cholera and Anthrax Weapons,'" *The London Times*, January 19, 1989, 6.

42. Michael Gordon, "Confrontation in the Gulf; C.I.A. Fears Iraq Could Deploy Biological Arms by Early 1991," *New York Times*, September 29, 1990, A4.

43. "Fears of Bio-Warfare," *Newsweek*, August 26, 1990, 4.

44. Gordon, "Confrontation in the Gulf;" Molly Moore, "Iraq Said to Have Supply of Biological Weapons: Arsenal Adds to Peril of Forces in Gulf Region," *Washington Post*, September 29, 1990, A1. Also, James Gerstenzang, "Iraqi Pillaging Prompts U.S. War Warning," *Los Angeles Times*, September 29, 1990, A1; CIA, *Iraq's Biological Warfare Program: Saddam's Ace in the Hole*, Doc. SW-90-1152CX (Washington, DC, August 1990); Eric Nadler and Robert Windrem, "Deadly Contagion: How We Helped Iraq Get Germ Weapons," *New Republic*, February 4, 1991, 18–20.

45. CIA, Directorate of Intelligence, *Prewar Status of Iraq's Weapons of Mass Destruction*, Top Secret Report, DocID 934037 (Washington, DC, March 20, 1991), quote from page 27. See also pages 4, 8–9, and 28. Available at <http://www.gwu.edu/~nsarchiv/NSAEBB/NSAEBB80/>. Also, Armed Forces Medical Intelligence Center, *Iraq Biological Warfare Threat* (Washington, DC, October 22, 1990); DIA,

Interim Report on Iraq Biological Warfare (BW) (Washington, DC, December 17, 1990); CIA, *Bugs and Things* (Washington, DC, December 3, 1990).

46. CIA, *Prewar Status of Iraq's Weapons of Mass Destruction*, 27.

47. DIA, *Iraqi Biological Weapons (BW) Capabilities*, Background Paper for the Director, J-5 (Washington, DC, September 14, 1990). Also, *Commission on the Intelligence Capabilities of the United States Regarding Weapons of Mass Destruction: Report to the President of the United States* (Washington, DC: U.S. Government Printing Office, March 31, 2005), 81.

48. CIA, *Iraq's Potential for Chemical and Biological Warfare*, Document 62758, marked "Not Finally Evaluated Intelligence" (Washington, DC, September 1990), http://www.fas.org/irp/gulf/cia/960618/62758_01.htm; CIA, *Iraq's BW Mission Planning*, marked "Not Finally Evaluated Intelligence" (Washington, DC, 1992), http://www.gwu.edu/~nsarchiv/NSAEBB/NSAEBB80/.

49. CIA, "Regime Strategic Intent," in *Comprehensive Report of the Special Advisor to the DCI on Iraq's WMD*, vol. 1 (Washington, DC, September 30, 2004), 1–2, 8–11, 20–41, 45–48.

50. Barton, *The Weapons Detective*, 53–54.

51. Manley, interview; former UNSCOM biological weapons inspector, interview with author, Washington, DC, February 21, 2006.

52. Killip, interview.

53. Manley, interview. Also, Killip, interview; foreign ministry official, interview with author, August 17, 2005; Ministry of Defence, *Implementation of the Immunisation Programme Against Biological Warfare Agents for UK Forces During the Gulf Conflict 1990/1* (London: House of Lords, 1998), 13–69.

54. Kadlec, interview; former UNSCOM biological weapons inspector, interview with author, February 21, 2006. Also, Office of the Special Assistant to the Deputy Secretary of Defense for Gulf War Illnesses, "Vaccine Use During the Gulf War," Interim Report (Washington, DC: U.S. Department of Defense, December 7, 2000), Chapter IV, B, http://www.gulflink.osd.mil/va/.

55. Senate Foreign Affairs, Defence, and Trade Legislation Committee, Official Committee Hansard, Consideration of Budget Estimates (Canberra, Commonwealth of Australia, July 4, 2003), 27–29; Barton, *The Weapons Detective*, 54.

56. Kadlec, interview. Also, Armed Forces Medical Intelligence, *Information on Iraq's Biological Warfare Program*, Memorandum to John Deutch, Under Secretary of Defense for Acquisitions (Washington, DC, November 12, 1993).

57. UN Doc. S/1999/94, Appendix III, para. 161.

58. Armed Forces Medical Intelligence, *Information on Iraq's Biological Warfare Program*; DIA, *Collateral Risk Due to Allied Air Strikes on Iraqi Biological Warfare (BW) Facilities*, Memorandum to U.S. Army Lt. Gen. Eichelberger (Washington, DC, n.d.). Also, *Identification of BW Related Facility at Latifiya*, Memorandum to CENTCOM FWD/CCJ2-T (Washington, DC, February 26, 1991); Spertzel, interview with author, July 1, 2005.

59. Kadlec, interview; Spertzel, interview. Also, CIA, *Biological Weapons Production Capabilities of a Nutritional Plant Located Three Miles from the Abu-Ghraib Military Complex*, marked "Not Finally Evaluated Intelligence" (Washington, DC, November 1990); CIA, *Iraq Backup BW Production Plant*, Iraq-Kuwait: Situation Report, marked "Not Finally Evaluated Intelligence" (Washington, DC, January 1991); CIA, *Report on the Iraqi Biological Warfare Facilities at the Aqaba Establishment, and Projects 600 and 400*, marked "Not Finally Evaluated Intelligence" (Washington, DC, April 1992); Al Kamen, "Iraqi Factory's Product: Germ Warfare or Milk?" *Washington Post*, February 8, 1991, A1; Gregory Koblenz, "Countering Dual-Use Facilities: Lessons from Iraq and Sudan," *Jane's Intelligence Review* 11, no. 3 (March 1999): 50–52.

60. Koblenz, "Countering Dual-Use Facilities," 50–52. Also, Kadlec, interview; Spertzel, interview.

61. Armed Forces Medical Intelligence, *Information on Iraq's Biological Warfare Program*, November 12, 1993. Also, UN Security Council, *Twenty-Second Quarterly Report on the Activities of the United Nations Monitoring, Verification and Inspection Commission in Accordance with Paragraph 12 of Security Council Resolution 1284 (1999)*, Doc. S/2005/545, August 30, 2005, para. 12.

62. Kadlec, interview. Similarly, Barton, interview.

63. Barton, interview. Also, Englund, interview; former UNSCOM CBW commissioner, interview with author, January 23, 2006; former senior UNSCOM official, interview with author, September 1, 2005.

64. Raymond Zilinskas, PhD (former UNSCOM biological weapons inspector), interview with author, Washington, DC, October 4, 2005.

65. Gallucci, interview. Also, Duelfer, interview; Kadlec, interview.

66. Manley, interview; Killip, interview; Kelly, interview; Taylor, interview; Spertzel, interview; Krikorian, interview; former UNSCOM staff member, interview with author, New York City, September 1, 2005; former UNSCOM staff member, interview with author, New York City, September 2, 2005; former UNSCOM CBW commissioner, interview with author, January 23, 2006; former senior UNSCOM official, interview with author, August 30, 2005.

67. Ekeus, interview. Also, Manley, interview; Barton, *The Weapons Detective*, 61–62; Trevan, *Saddam's Secrets*, 53; Elaine Sciolino, "The Dauntingly Expensive Task of Imposing Arms Control," *New York Times*, April 28, 1991, sec. 4, p. 3; Jonathan C. Randal, "U.N. Experts Set to Inspect Iraq's A-Sites," *Washington Post*, May 16, 1991, A34.

68. Ekeus, interview. Also, Kadlec, interview; Kraatz-Wadsack, interview.

69. Trevan, *Saddam's Secrets*, 25.

70. Duelfer, *Hide and Seek*, 40–41.

71. David C. Kelly, "The Trilateral Agreement: Lessons for Biological Weapons Verification," in *Verification Yearbook 2002*, ed. Trevor Findlay and Oliver Meier (London: Verification, Inspection, and Training Centre, 2002), 93–109. Also, Tom Mangold and Jeff Goldberg, *Plague Wars* (New York: St. Martin's Press, 1999), 305; David E.

Hoffman, *The Dead Hand: The Untold Story of the Cold War Arms Race and Its Dangerous Legacy* (New York: Doubleday, 2009), 353–357.

72. Mangold and Goldberg, *Plague Wars*, 306.

73. Taylor, interview; former UNSCOM CBW commissioner, interview with author, January 23, 2006; Manley, interview.

74. UN Security Council, *First Report of the Executive Chairman of UNSCOM Under Resolution 687*, Doc. S/23165, October 25, 1991, Appendix VI.

75. Gallucci, interview; Trevan, *Saddam's Secrets*, 8.

76. Krasno and Sutterlin, *The United Nations and Iraq*, 49–52; Randal, "U.N. Experts Set to Inspect Iraq's A-Sites."

77. For the original terms, go to <http://www.un.org/Depts/unscom/General/basicfacts.html#ESTABLISH>. Also, Trevan, *Saddam's Secrets*, 60–62. For more on reinforcing Security Council statements, go to <http://www.un.org/Depts/unscom/unscmdoc.htm>.

78. Eliot Marshall, "Iraq's Chemical Warfare: Case Proved: A U.N. Team Found Mustard and Nerve Gas Bombs on the Battlefield; Now the Challenge Is to Prevent the War from Spreading," *Science* 224, no. 4645 (April 13, 1984): 130–132.

79. Barton, *The Weapons Detective*, 64.

80. Killip, interview; Barton, interview; Krikorian, interview; Kraatz-Wadsack, interview; William Lebherz (former UNSCOM industrial biotechnology expert), interview with author, Washington, DC, February 13, 2006. For more on the Australia Group, go to <http://www.australiagroup.net>.

81. Lebherz, interview.

82. Krikorian, interview; Kraatz-Wadsack, interview; former UNSCOM staff member, interview with author, New York City, September 2, 2005; Barton, *The Weapons Detective*, 64, 162–163.

83. Mangold and Goldberg, *Plague Wars*, 310.

84. Killip, interview.

85. Former senior UNSCOM official, interview with author, August 30, 2005.

86. Killip, interview. Also, Black, interview.

87. Killip, interview.

88. Barton, interview. Also, Barton, *The Weapons Detective*, 62–70.

89. Killip, interview; Barton, interview. Also, Ekeus, interview.

90. Barton, interview. Also, Killip, interview; Ekeus, interview.

91. Killip, interview.

92. Barton, interview.

93. Killip, interview.

94. Barton, interview.

95. CIA, "Biological Warfare," in *Comprehensive Report of the Special Advisor to the DCI on Iraq's WMD*, 50–51. Also, Paul Lewis, "Iraqis Fire to Bar U.N. Inspectors;

'We Can't Allow This,' Bush Says," *New York Times*, June 29, 1991, A1; Krasno and Sutterlin, *The United Nations and Iraq*, 52–56.

96. Raymond A. Zilinskas, "Detecting and Deterring Biological Weapons in Iraq: The Role of Aerial Surveillance," *Politics and the Life Sciences* 14, no. 2 (1995): 255–258; Krasno and Sutterlin, *The United Nations and Iraq*, 85–90.

97. Duelfer, interview.

98. UN Security Council, Resolution 707 (1991), Doc. S/RES/707, August 15, 1991, http://daccess-dds-ny.un.org/doc/RESOLUTION/GEN/NR0/596/43/IMG/NR059643.pdf?OpenElement, para. 3 (ii)(iii).

99. Former senior UNSCOM official, interview with author, August 20, 2005.

100. Duelfer, interview.

101. Lawrence Scheinman, *Cooperative Oversight of Dangerous Technologies: Lessons from the International Atomic Energy Safeguards System* (College Park, MD: Center for International and Security Studies at Maryland, January 2005); Joseph F. Pilat, "Iraq and the Future of Nonproliferation: The Roles of Inspections and Treaties," *Science* 255, no. 5049 (March 6, 1992): 1224–1229; *Report of the Mission Dispatched by the Secretary-General to Investigate Allegations of the Use of Chemical Weapons in the Conflict Between the Islamic Republic of Iran and Iraq*, UN Docs. S/19823 (April 25, 1988), S/20060 (July 20, 1988), S/20063 (July 25, 1988), and S/20134 (August 19, 1988); Trevan, *Saddam's Secrets*, 121.

102. Black, interview; Khidhir Hamza with Jeff Stein, *Saddam's Bombmaker: The Terrifying Inside Story of the Iraqi Nuclear and Biological Weapons Agenda* (New York: Scribner, 2000), 261; Mark Phythian, "UNSCOM in the Time of Cholera: The Continuing Lessons and Arms Control Implications of the UNSCOM Experience," *World Affairs* 163, no. 2 (Fall 2000): 56.

103. Trevan, *Saddam's Secrets*, 121. Also, 36–37.

104. UN Security Council, *Fourth Report of the Executive Chairman of the Special Commission Following the Adoption of Security Council Resolution 1051 (1996)*, Doc. S/1997/774, October 6, 1997, Annex, para. 107; UN Doc. S/1999/94, Annex D, paras. 2 and 32; CIA, "Biological Warfare," 1, 49–59; CIA, "Regime Strategy and WMD Timeline Events," in *Comprehensive Report of the Special Advisor to the DCI on Iraq's WMD*, vol. 1, pp. 4, 50; Duelfer, *Hide and Seek*, 377–381, 406–408; Ibrahim al-Marashi, "How Iraq Conceals and Obtains Its Weapons of Mass Destruction," *Middle East Review of International Affairs* 7, no. 1 (March 2003): 52.

105. Lisa Myers, "Saddam Talked of WMD Attack in U.S.: Tapes Show Him 'Almost Obsessed' with Weapons, Don't Prove He Had Them," NBC News, February 15, 2006, http://www.msnbc.msn.com/id/11373537/.

106. Al-Marashi, "How Iraq Conceals and Obtains Its Weapons of Mass Destruction," 52–53, 55–58, 60; UN Doc. S/1999/94, Annex D, paras. 13, 18, 19; Sean Boyne, "Inside Iraq's Security Network: Part I," *Jane's Intelligence Review* 9, no. 1 (July 1, 1997):

312–317; Sean Boyne, "Inside Iraq's Security Network: Part II," *Jane's Intelligence Review* 9, no. 8 (August 1997): 365–367; Sean Boyne, "Saddam's Shield: The Role of the Special Republican Guard," *Jane's Intelligence Review* 11, no. 1 (January 1999): 29–32; CIA, "Regime Strategic Intent," vol. 1, pp. 57–58, Annexes B, C, and D; Barton Gellman, "A Futile Game of Hide and Seek," *Washington Post*, October 11, 1998, A1.

107. Al-Marashi, "How Iraq Conceals and Obtains Its Weapons of Mass Destruction," 56–57; "Notes of Nikita Smidovich on a Meeting Between Hussein Kamal and UNSCOM and IAEA," Note for the File, UNSCOM/IAEA Sensitive (Amman, Jordan, August 22, 1995), 12, http://www.unmovic.org; Peter Grier, "Iraq-UN Standoff: A Miscalculation?" *Christian Science Monitor*, August 3, 1992, 7.

108. Krikorian, interview; *Iraq's Weapons of Mass Destruction: The Assessment of the British Government* (London, September 2002), 36; Gellman, "A Futile Game of Hide and Seek."

109. Barton, interview; Taylor, interview; Kraatz-Wadsack, interview; Spertzel, interview; Krikorian, interview; Hamza with Stein, *Saddam's Bombmaker*, 260–261.

110. Kelly, interview; Killip, interview; Kraatz-Wadsack, interview; former senior UNSCOM official, interview with author, August 30, 2005.

111. Spertzel, interview. Also, CIA, "Biological Warfare," 11–12.

112. Ekeus, interview; Kadlec, interview; former UNSCOM chief inspector, interview with author, January 31, 2006; former UNSCOM staff member, interview with author, September 2, 2005; Kraatz-Wadsack, interview; Taylor, interview. See also Jonathan B. Tucker, "Monitoring and Verification in a Non-Cooperative Environment: Lessons from the UN Experience in Iraq," *Nonproliferation Review* 3, no. 3 (Spring-Summer 1996): 1–14.

113. UN Doc. S/1999/94, Appendix III, paras. 196–202; Republic of Iraq, *Draft Full, Final and Complete Disclosure of Iraq's Past Biological Programme*, July 1995, 156–159; Government of the United Kingdom, "UN Special Commission BW Inspections in Iraq: Lessons for the Ad Hoc Experts' Group on Verification," BWC/CONF-III/VEREX-WP5 (White Paper presented during Third Review Conference of the Parties to the BWC, Geneva, UN, March 30–April 10, 1992), 2; UN Doc. S/2005/545, Annex, paras. 14, 44.

114. Barton, interview; Phythian, "UNSCOM in the Time of Cholera," 51–64; UN Doc. S/1999/94, Annex D, para. 15.

115. UN Doc. S/1999/94, Annex D, para. 4. Also, paras. 5–6; CIA, "Biological Warfare," 53.

116. Kelly, interview; Manley, interview; Krikorian, interview; Kraatz-Wadsack, interview; Spertzel, interview; Killip, interview. Also, Duelfer, *Hide and Seek*, 92–94; Barton, *The Weapons Detective*, 72, 81; Al-Marashi, "How Iraq Conceals and Obtains Its Weapons of Mass Destruction," 58; UN Doc. S/1999/94, Annex D, para. 32.

117. David Franz (former UNSCOM chief biological weapons inspector), interview with author, Washington, DC, June 29, 2005; Spertzel, interview; Killip, interview;

Manley, interview; former UNSCOM chief inspector, interview with author, August 18, 2005; Kraatz-Wadsack, interview; Krikorian, interview; former UNSCOM inspector and chief of product development in an offensive biological weapons program, interview with author, Washington, DC, February 21, 2006; former UNSCOM chief inspector, interview with author, January 31, 2006; former UNSCOM staff member, interview with author, New York City, September 2, 2005; former UNSCOM biological weapons inspector, interview with author, Washington, DC, September 17, 2005. Also, Barton, *The Weapons Detective*, 72, 81; Towle, *Enforced Disarmament*, 190. See also 75–77, 191.

118. Gallucci, interview.

119. Former UNSCOM chief inspector, interview with author, January 31, 2006; Gallucci, interview; Ekeus, interview; Sellstrom, interview; Spertzel, interview; Manley, interview; Barton, *The Weapons Detective*, 72, 81; UN Security Council, *Fourth Report of the Executive Chairman of Special Commission Established by the Secretary-General Pursuant to Paragraph 9 (b)(i) of Security Council Resolution 687 (1991)*, Doc. S/24984, December 17, 1992, Appendix II.

120. Duelfer, interview; Kadlec, interview; Jeffrey Mohr, PhD (former UNSCOM chief biological weapons inspector), interview with author via telephone, June 27, 2005; Spertzel, interview; Kraatz-Wadsack, interview; Kelly, interview; Krikorian, interview; Franz, interview; Killip, interview. Also, Barton, *The Weapons Detective*, 72, 81; Trevan, *Saddam's Secrets*, 15; Lewis, "Iraqis Fire to Bar U.N. Inspectors"; Gellman, "A Futile Game of Hide and Seek"; "We're Prepared to Stay Here," *Washington Post*, September 25, 1991, A21; Paul Lewis, "Baghdad Retains 40 U.N. Inspectors Who Find A-Plans," *New York Times*, September 24, 1991, A1.

121. Krikorian, interview; Kraatz-Wadsack, interview.

122. Gallucci, interview; Sellstrom, interview; Killip, interview; Kraatz-Wadsack, interview.

123. Spertzel, interview; former UNSCOM staff member, interview with author, September 2, 2005; former UNSCOM chief biological weapons inspector, interview with author, August 28, 2005; former senior UNSCOM official, interview with author, August 30, 2005. Also, Krasno and Sutterlin, *The United Nations and Iraq*, 46; Gellman, "A Futile Game of Hide and Seek"; Duelfer, *Hide and Seek*, 92–3, 113, 119; Al-Marashi, "How Iraq Conceals and Obtains Its Weapons of Mass Destruction," 58, 60; UN Doc. S/1999/94, Annex D, para. 32.

124. Ekeus, interview; Kelly, interview; Spertzel, interview; Taylor, interview; Mohr, interview; David Huxsoll, DVM (former UNSCOM chief biological weapons inspector), interview with author, Washington, DC, June 21, 2005; Barton, interview; former senior UNSCOM official, interview with author, August 30, 2005. Also, Duelfer, *Hide and Seek*, 94; Gellman, "A Futile Game of Hide and Seek."

125. Former senior UNSCOM official, interview with author, August 30, 2005.

126. R. Jeffrey Smith, "Secretive Iraq Parries U.N. Arms Inspectors: Technology, Patience Pry Open Weapons Data," *Washington Post*, November 4, 1994, A1; Richard J. Newman, "The Games Iraq Plays: Saddam Stands to Win a Lot More Than He Might Lose," *US News & World Report*, November 17, 1997, 48–51; Daniel Byman, Kenneth Pollack, and Mathew Waxman, "Coercing Saddam Hussein: Lessons from the Past," *Survival* 40, no. 3 (Autumn 1998): 127–151.

127. Former senior UNSCOM official, interview with author, August 30, 2005.

128. Killip, interview; Spertzel, interview; Huxsoll, interview; Kraatz-Wadsack, interview; CIA, "Regime Strategic Intent," 24–34, Annex D, 11–12, 40–44, 52–62; CIA, *Addendum to the Comprehensive Report of the Special Advisor to the DCI on Iraq's WMD* (Washington, DC, March 2005), Annex C, 27–42; "The Whore of Babylon and the Horseman of Plague," *The Economist*, April 12, 1997, 80; Duelfer, *Hide and Seek*, 408; Trevan, *Saddam's Secrets*, 36–37.

129. George Piro, interviewed by Scott Pelley, "Iraq War: Saddam's View," *60 Minutes*, CBS News Division, March 18, 2008. Also, Duelfer, *Hide and Seek*, 392–412.

130. CIA, "Regime Strategic Intent," 24–28. Also, Ekeus, interview; Phythian, "UNSCOM in the Time of Cholera," 62–64.

131. Duelfer, *Hide and Seek*, 405. Also, pages 167, 400–401. In addition, Kraatz-Wadsack, interview; former senior UNSCOM official, interview with author, August 30, 2005.

132. CIA, "Regime Strategic Intent," 22. Also, Ekeus, interview; Duelfer, *Hide and Seek*, 22, 386, 394, 400–408.

133. Ekeus, interview. Also, Gellman, "A Futile Game of Hide and Seek;" UN Doc. S/1999/94, Annex D, para. 2; CIA, "Regime Strategic Intent," 34.

134. Gallucci, interview. Similarly, Kraatz-Wadsack, interview.

135. John M. Goshko and Ann Devroy, "Iraq Holds U.N. Inspectors for 13 Hours, Seizes Data; Bush Makes Call For Firm Stance; Showdown Near," *Washington Post*, September 24, 1991, A1; John Lancaster and John M. Goshko, "Iraq Said to Yield on Nuclear Inspection; Baghdad Continues to Detain 44 Members of U.N. Team; Pentagon Orders Patriot Missiles Moved to Saudi Arabia," *Washington Post*, September 25, 1991, A1; Paul Lewis, "44 U.N. Inspectors Freed by Iraq with Secret Nuclear Documents," *New York Times*, September 28, 1991, A1; R. Jeffrey Smith and Michael Z. Wise, "Report Shows Extensive Iraqi Nuclear Effort; Records Seized by U.N. Team Indicate Testing of Missile Capable of Carrying A-Bomb," *Washington Post*, October 5, 1991, A1; David Albright and Mark Hibbs, "Iraq's Bomb: Blueprints and Artifacts," *Bulletin of the Atomic Scientists* 48, no. 1 (January-February 1992): 31–40.

136. Stephen Black, "Verification Under Duress: The Case of UNSCOM," in *Verification Yearbook*, ed. Trevor Findlay (London: Verification, Inspection, and Training Centre, 2000), 115–129. Killip, interview. Also, Ekeus, interview; Huxsoll, interview; Duelfer, interview.

137. Towle, *Enforced Disarmament*, 66–93, 152–168.

138. Wolfgang Fischer and Gotthard Stein, "On-Site Inspections: Experiences from Nuclear Safeguarding," in "On-Site Inspections: Common Problems, Different Solutions," ed. Kerstin Hoffman, *Disarmament Forum* no. 3 (1999): 45–54; Laura Rockwood, "Safeguards and Nonproliferation: The First Half Century from a Legal Perspective," paper presented at the 48th Annual Meeting of the Institute of Nuclear Materials Management, Tucson, AZ, July 8–12, 2007; John Carlson and Russell Leslie, "Special Inspections Revisited," paper presented at the 46th Annual Meeting of the Institute of Nuclear Materials Management, Phoenix, AZ, July 10–14, 2005. Also, U.S. Arms Control and Disarmament Agency, *Arms Control and Disarmament Agreements: Texts and Histories of the Negotiations* (Washington, DC, 1996), 234–247; Don O. Stovall, "The Stockholm Accord: On-Site Inspections in Eastern and Western Europe," in *Arms Control Verification and the New Role of On-Site Inspection*, ed. Lewis A. Dunn and Amy E. Gordon (Lexington, MA: Lexington Books, 1990), 15–38. In addition, Joseph P. Harahan, *On-Site Inspections Under the INF Treaty, A History of the On-Site Inspection Agency and Treaty Implementation, 1988–1991* (Washington, DC: U.S. Government Printing Office, 1993); Joseph P. Harahan and John C. Kuhn, III, *On-Site Inspections Under the CFE Treaty, A History of the On-Site Inspection Agency and CFE Treaty Implementation, 1990–1996* (Washington, DC: U.S. Department of Defense, 1996).

139. Kelly, "The Trilateral Agreement: Lessons for Biological Weapons Verification," 93–109; Hoffman, *The Dead Hand*, 345–357, 431–437, 460; Jonathan B. Tucker, "Verification of the Chemical Weapons Convention and Their Relevance to the Biological Weapons Convention," in *Biological Weapons Proliferation: Reasons for Concern, Courses of Action*, ed. Amy E. Smithson, report no. 24 (Washington, DC: Stimson Center, January 1998), 77–105; Jez Littlewood, *The Biological Weapons Convention: A Revolution Failed* (Aldershot, U.K.: Ashgate Publishing, 2005). Also, guest articles and news summaries in *The CBW Conventions Bulletin* at <http://www.sussex.ac.uk/Units/spru/hsp/pdfbulletin.html>.

140. Black, "UNSCOM and the Iraqi Biological Weapons Program: Technical Success, Political Failure," 304. Also, Gabriele Kraatz-Wadsack, "The Role of Scientists in Verification," in *Assessing the Threat of Weapons of Mass Destruction: The Role of Independent Scientists*, vol. 61, ed. John L. Finney and Ivo Slaus, NATO Science for Peace and Security Series E: Human and Societal Dynamics (Amsterdam: IOS Press, 2010), 43–54.

141. Amy E. Smithson, "Chemical Inspectors: On the Outside Looking In?" *Bulletin of the Atomic Scientists* 47, no. 8 (October 1991): 22–25.

142. Killip, interview.

143. Ibid. Also, Black, interview; former senior UNSCOM official, interview with author, August 30, 2005.

144. Kraatz-Wadsack, "The Role of Scientists in Verification," 43–44.

145. Killip, interview; Black, interview.

Chapter 2

1. Ambassador Rolf Ekeus (former UNSCOM executive chairman), interview with author, Stockholm, August 24, 2005.

2. Ibid. Also, Doug Englund (former UNSCOM chief inspector), interview with author, Washington, DC, December 5, 2005; Ron Manley, PhD (former UNSCOM chief chemical weapons inspector), interview with author, London, August 19, 2005.

3. David C. Kelly, "The Trilateral Agreement: Lessons for Biological Weapons Verification," in *Verification Yearbook 2002*, ed. Trevor Findlay and Oliver Meier (London: Verification, Inspection, and Training Centre, 2002), 93–109; David E. Hoffman, *The Dead Hand: The Untold Story of the Cold War Arms Race and Its Dangerous Legacy* (New York: Doubleday, 2009), 431–438.

4. Charles Duelfer, *Hide and Seek: The Search for Truth in Iraq* (New York: Public Affairs, 2009), p. 495, footnote 13.

5. Tom Mangold and Jeff Goldberg, *Plague Wars* (New York: St. Martin's Press, 1999), 307.

6. Debra Krikorian, PhD (former UNSCOM inspector), interview with author, Washington, DC, June 21, 2005; Hamish Killip (former UNSCOM chief biological weapons inspector), interview with author, Isle of Man, August 22, 2005; David Franz, DVM, PhD (former UNSCOM chief biological weapons inspector), interview with author, Washington, DC, June 29, 2005; Rod Barton (former UNSCOM biological weapons inspector), interview with author via telephone, May 20, 2005; former UNSCOM staff member, interview with author, New York City, September 2, 2005. Also, Mangold and Goldberg, *Plague Wars*, 309–310.

7. David Kelly, PhD (former UNSCOM chief biological weapons inspector), interview with author, Washington, DC, December 17, 2002. Also, Tim Trevan, *Saddam's Secrets: The Hunt for Saddam's Hidden Weapons* (London: HarperCollins, 1999), 27, 29.

8. Trevan, *Saddam's Secrets*, 24–25. Also, Walter Putnam, "Biological Weapons Inspection Team Begins Work in Iraq," Associated Press, August 3, 1991; United Nations, "UN Inspection Team on Iraq's Biological Weapons Capacity, Finds No Evidence of Current Stocks," Press Release, Doc. IK/46, August 14, 1991; R. Jeffrey Smith, "Iraq Admits to Germ Warfare Research," *Washington Post*, August 6, 1991, A11.

9. UNSCOM, *Draft Report on the First Biological Warfare Inspection in Iraq* (New York, n.d.), 12.

10. David Huxsoll, DVM (former UNSCOM chief biological weapons inspector), interview with author, Washington, DC, June 21, 2005; Kelly, interview; former UNSCOM biological weapons inspector, interview with author, Washington, DC, September 17, 2005; UNSCOM, *Draft Report on the First Biological Warfare Inspection in Iraq. 14.*

11. UNSCOM, Chief Inspector D. C. Kelly, *Report on the First Biological Warfare Inspection in Iraq: UNSCOM 7*, New York, August 16, 1991, para. 2; UNSCOM, *Draft Report on the First Biological Warfare Inspection in Iraq*, 14–15; Republic of Iraq, *A Full, Final and Comprehensive Report on {Biological Activity}*, May 1992, section 4, pp. 2–4; Smith, "Iraq Admits to Germ Warfare Research;" UN Security Council, *First Report of the Executive Chairman of UNSCOM Under Resolution 687*, Doc. S/23165, October 25, 1991, Appendix IV, para. 26.

12. Killip, interview; former UNSCOM biological weapons inspector, interview with author, September 17, 2005.

13. Huxsoll, interview.

14. UNSCOM, *Report on the First Biological Warfare Inspection in Iraq: UNSCOM 7*, para. 4(c); UNSCOM, *Draft Report on the First Biological Warfare Inspection in Iraq*, 15.

15. UNSCOM, *Report on the First Biological Warfare Inspection in Iraq: UNSCOM 7*, paras. 15–16. Also, Huxsoll, interview.

16. Huxsoll, interview.

17. Kelly, interview; former UNSCOM biological weapons inspector, interview with author, September 17, 2005; former senior UNSCOM official, interview with author, New York City, August 30, 2005.

18. Huxsoll, interview; Killip, interview; former UNSCOM biological weapons inspector, interview with author, September 17, 2005; UNSCOM, *Draft Report on the First Biological Warfare Inspection in Iraq*, 12, 14–15, 47. Also, Rod Barton, *The Weapons Detective: The Inside Story of Australia's Top Weapons Inspector* (Melbourne: Black Inc. Agenda, 2006), 165; Richard Spertzel, PhD (former UNSCOM chief bioweapons inspector), interview with author, Washington, DC, July 1, 2005.

19. Huxsoll, interview.Likewise, Kelly, interview; former UNSCOM biological weapons inspector, interview with author, September 17, 2005.

20. Kelly, interview.

21. UNSCOM, *Draft Report on the First Biological Warfare Inspection in Iraq*, 47.

22. Huxsoll, interview. See Letter from Abdul Amir A. Al-Anbari, Permanent Representative of Iraq to the UN, to Rolf Ekeus, Executive Chairman of the Security Council Special Commission, letter no. 117 (New York, Permanent Mission of Iraq to the UN, dated May 22, 1991, stamped received, UN Office of the Special Commission, May 24, 1991); Letter from Abdul Amir A. Al-Anbari to Rolf Ekeus, letter no. 1/7/230 (New York, Permanent Mission of Iraq to the UN, dated July 18, 1991).

23. Killip, interview.

24. Kelly, interview; Huxsoll, interview.

25. Kelly, interview; Killip, interview; former UNSCOM biological weapons inspector, interview with author, September 17, 2005; UNSCOM, *Draft Report on the First Biological Warfare Inspection in Iraq*, 15.

26. Kelly, interview; Huxsoll, interview. Also, Government of the United Kingdom, "UN Special Commission BW Inspections in Iraq: Lessons for the Ad Hoc

Experts' Group on Verification," BWC/CONF-III/VEREX-WP5 (White Paper presented during Third Review Conference of the Parties to the BWC, Geneva, UN, March 30–April 10, 1992), 6; Trevan, *Saddam's Secrets*, 32–34.

27. Kelly, interview; Killip, interview; former UNSCOM biological weapons inspector, interview with author, September 17, 2005.

28. Robert Kadlec, MD (former UNSCOM biological weapons inspector), interview with author, Washington, DC, February 23, 2006. Also, Huxsoll, interview; Killip, interview; Kelly, interview; UNSCOM, *Draft Report on the First Biological Warfare Inspection in Iraq*, 17.

29. Jeff Mohr, PhD (former UNSCOM chief biological weapons inspector), telephone interview with author, June 27, 2005; Killip, interview.

30. Former UNSCOM biological weapons inspector, interview with author, September 17, 2005. UNSCOM, *Draft Report on the First Biological Warfare Inspection in Iraq*, 18–19.

31. Killip, interview; Charles Duelfer (former UNSCOM deputy executive chairman), interview with author, Washington, DC, November 15, 2007; UNSCOM, *Draft Report on the First Biological Warfare Inspection in Iraq*, 18. Also, Central Intelligence Agency (CIA), *Comprehensive Report of the Special Advisor to the DCI on Iraq's WMD* (Washington, DC, September 30, 2004): "Regime Strategic Intent," vol. 1, Annex B, 6, 9 and "Biological Warfare," vol. 3, pp. 5–8, 16–17, 57.

32. UNSCOM, *Draft Report on the First Biological Warfare Inspection in Iraq*, 22–23, 31; Huxsoll, interview.

33. Huxsoll, interview; UNSCOM, *Draft Report on the First Biological Warfare Inspection in Iraq*, 24. Also, Rudolf Lambrecht and Gudrun Pott, "'Diyala' Secret Project," *Stern* (Hamburg), February 7, 1991 (translated in Doc. FBIS-WEU-91-032-A, Washington, DC, Federal Broadcast Information Service, February 15, 1991), 8–9.

34. UNSCOM, *Report on the First Biological Warfare Inspection in Iraq: UNSCOM 7*, para. 18. Also, UNSCOM, *Draft Report on the First Biological Warfare Inspection in Iraq*, 22–26.

35. UNSCOM, *Draft Report on the First Biological Warfare Inspection in Iraq*, 22–26, quote about not sampling from page 24. Also, former UNSCOM biological weapons inspector, interview with author, September 17, 2005.

36. Kelly, interview; Huxsoll, interview; Killip, interview.

37. Kelly, interview; Spertzel, interview; Kadlec, interview. For more on Al Hazen's bioweapons work, CIA, *Comprehensive Report of the Special Advisor to the DCI on Iraq's WMD*, vol. 3, 6 and Annex C of the March 2005 *Addendum to the Comprehensive Report*, 28; Graham S. Pearson, "The Iraqi Biological Weapons Program," in *Deadly Cultures: Biological Weapons Since 1945*, ed. Mark Wheelis, Lajos Rozsa, and Malcolm Dando (Cambridge, MA: Harvard University Press, 2004), 171–172.

38. Former UNSCOM biological weapons inspector, interview with author, September 17, 2005.

39. Kelly, interview; Killip, interview; Iraqi Foreign Ministry spokesman remarks (translated in Doc. FBIS-NES-1991, Washington, DC, Federal Broadcast Information Service, August 4, 1991), 35–36; UN Doc. IK/46.

40. Kelly, interview.

41. Trevan, *Saddam's Secrets*, 31–32. Also, UN Doc. S/23165, Appendix IV, para. 26.

42. Kelly, interview; Huxsoll, interview.

43. Kelly, interview.

44. "List of Biological Research and Reports Handed Over to the First Biological Lnspechon (sic) Team," in Republic of Iraq, *A Full, Final and Comprehensive Report on {Biological Activity}*, 15.

45. Kelly, interview. Also, Killip, interview; former UNSCOM biological weapons inspector, interview with author, September 17, 2005; Huxsoll, interview; foreign ministry official, interview with author, August 17, 2005; UNSCOM, *Report on the First Biological Warfare Inspection in Iraq: UNSCOM 7*, para. 6.

46. Huxsoll, interview.

47. Ibid.; UNSCOM, *Draft Report on the First Biological Warfare Inspection in Iraq*, 29.

48. *Collateral Analysis and Verification of Biological and Toxin Research in Iraq* (Toronto: External Affairs and International Trade, October 1991), 12, 34–35.

49. Kelly, interview.

50. UNSCOM, *Report on the First Biological Warfare Inspection in Iraq: UNSCOM 7*, para. 11. Also, UNSCOM, *Draft Report on the First Biological Warfare Inspection in Iraq*, 28–29.

51. UNSCOM, *Draft Report on the First Biological Warfare Inspection in Iraq*, 18.

52. Killip, interview; Huxsoll, interview.

53. UNSCOM, *Report on the First Biological Warfare Inspection in Iraq: UNSCOM 7*, para. 16; UNSCOM, *Draft Report on the First Biological Warfare Inspection in Iraq*, 32, 35; Barton, *The Weapons Detective*, 155.

54. Kelly, interview. Also, National Monitoring Directorate, Republic of Iraq, *Draft Full, Final and Complete Declaration of the Iraq National Biological Program*, May 1996, 202–203; Spertzel, interview.

55. "List of Bacteriological Isolates Handed Over to the First Biological Lnspechon (sic) Team," in Republic of Iraq, *A Full, Final and Comprehensive Report on {Biological Activity}*, 12–14. Also, UNSCOM, *Draft Report on the First Biological Warfare Inspection in Iraq*, 29–31; Kelly, interview; Killip, interview; Barton, interview; former senior UNSCOM official, interview with author, New York City, September 1, 2005; former UNSCOM biological weapons inspector, interview with author, September 17, 2005; UN Doc. IK/46.

56. Kelly, interview. Also, Walter Putnam, "Germ Warfare Team Ends Work; Nuclear Inspector Critical of Iraqis," Associated Press, August 7, 1991.

57. UN Security Council, *Twenty-Second Quarterly Report on the Activities of the United Nations Monitoring, Verification and Inspection Commission in Accordance with Paragraph 12 of Security Council Resolution 1284 (1999)*, Doc. S/2005/545, August 30, 2005,

Annex, para. 15. Also, "Supplier: American Type Culture Collection," Supplier Database (Washington, DC: Wisconsin Project), http://www.iraqwatch.org/suppliers/index.html; Eric Nadler and Robert Windrem, "Deadly Contagion: How We Helped Iraq Get Germ Weapons," *New Republic*, February 4, 1991, 18–20.

58. Spertzel, interview.

59. UN Doc. IK/46. Also, UN Doc. S/23165, Appendix IV, para. 26.

60. UN, "Aim of Biological Research Defensive, Iraq Tells UN Inspection Team," Press Release, Doc. IK/43, August 5, 1991.

61. Remarks of Iraqi Foreign Ministry spokesman on August 4, 1991, translated from Arabic in Foreign Broadcast Information Service, Doc. FBIS-NES-1991 (Washington, DC: Federal Broadcast Information Service, August 5, 1991), 35–36; Smith, "Iraq Admits to Germ Warfare Research."

62. Killip, interview. UNSCOM, *Draft Report on the First Biological Warfare Inspection in Iraq*, 4, 40.

63. Kelly, interview; Killip, interview; Krikorian, interview; former UNSCOM biological weapons inspector, interview with author, September 17, 2005. Also, UNSCOM, *Draft Report on the First Biological Warfare Inspection in Iraq*, 36–39; UNSCOM, *Report on the First Biological Warfare Inspection in Iraq: UNSCOM 7*, para. 19.

64. Kelly, interview.

65. UNSCOM, *Report on the First Biological Warfare Inspection in Iraq: UNSCOM 7*, paras. 2, 6, 7; Government of the United Kingdom, "UN Special Commission BW Inspections in Iraq," 5; UNSCOM, *Draft Report on the First Biological Warfare Inspection in Iraq*, 28–29. On this discussion between Murtada and Kelly, Kelly, interview; Killip, interview. Also, Spertzel, interview; Gabriele Kraatz-Wadsack, DVM (former UNSCOM chief biological weapons inspector), interview with author, August 15, 2005. See as well Trevan, *Saddam's Secrets*, 34–35.

66. "Annex Q: Transcript of Iraqi Admission of Both Offensive and Defensive Research Excerpt in Verbatim from Proceedings of the Meeting with Iraqi Officials on August 5, 1991," in *Report on the First Biological Warfare Inspection in Iraq: UNSCOM 7*.

67. Kelly, interview; Huxsoll, interview; former UNSCOM biological weapons inspector, interview with author, September 17, 2005; Killip, interview; Government of the United Kingdom, "UN Special Commission BW Inspection in Iraq," 6, 32.

68. Killip, interview. Also, UNSCOM, *Draft Report on the First Biological Warfare Inspection in Iraq*, 32; Republic of Iraq, *A Full, Final and Comprehensive Report on {Biological Activity}*, 4.

69. Huxsoll, interview.

70. UNSCOM, *Draft Report on the First Biological Warfare Inspection in Iraq*, 33–34. Also, Killip, interview.

71. Kelly, interview. Also, Huxsoll, interview; UN Security Council, *Letter Dated 25 January 1999 from the Executive Chairman of the Special Commission Established by the Secretary-General Pursuant to Paragraph 9 (b) (i) of Security Council Resolution*

687 (1991) Addressed to the President of the Security Council, Doc. S/1999/94, January 29, 1999, Appendix III, para. 161.

72. UNSCOM, *Report on the First Biological Warfare Inspection in Iraq: UNSCOM 7*, para. 17. Also, Huxsoll, interview; Killip, interview; former UNSCOM biological weapons inspector, interview with author, September 17, 2005.

73. Killip, interview. UNSCOM, *Draft Report on the First Biological Warfare Inspection in Iraq*, 33–34.

74. Kelly, interview.

75. Huxsoll, interview.

76. Killip, interview; Spertzel, interview.

77. UNSCOM, *Draft Report on the First Biological Warfare Inspection in Iraq*, 33–35.

78. Trevan, *Saddam's Secrets*, 33; William J. Broad and Judith Miller, "The Deal on Iraq: Secret Arsenal: The Hunt for the Germs of War," *New York Times*, February 26, 1998, A1.

79. Government of the United Kingdom, "UN Special Commission BW Inspections in Iraq," 7.

80. UNSCOM, *Draft Report on the First Biological Warfare Inspection in Iraq*, 35. Also, Kelly, interview.

81. Huxsoll, interview.

82. Kelly, interview; Killip, interview; Barton, interview; Spertzel, interview.

83. UNSCOM, *Draft Report on the First Biological Warfare Inspection in Iraq*, 16; Republic of Iraq, *A Full, Final and Comprehensive Report on {Biological Activity}*, 6, 9; Huxsoll, interview; Killip, interview.

84. Kraatz-Wadsack, interview.

85. Kelly, interview; Killip, interview.

86. Killip, interview. Also, Manley, interview.

87. Government of the United Kingdom, "UN Special Commission BW Inspections in Iraq," 6; Trevan, *Saddam's Secrets*, 36.

88. Killip, interview.

89. Kelly, interview. Also, Spertzel, interview; former UNSCOM CBW commissioner, telephone interview with author, January 23, 2006; Kraatz-Wadsack, interview. Also, Barton, *The Weapons Detective*, 78; Trevan, *Saddam's Secrets*, 37.

90. Kelly, interview.

91. Manley, interview; former UNSCOM CBW commissioner, interview with author, January 23, 2006.

92. Manley, interview. Also, Trevan, *Saddam's Secrets*, 37.

93. Kraatz-Wadsack, interview; Government of the United Kingdom, "UN Special Commission BW Inspections in Iraq," 7.

94. UNSCOM, *Report on the First Biological Warfare Inspection in Iraq: UNSCOM 7*, paras. 2, 5. Also, Government of the United Kingdom, "UN Special Commission BW Inspections in Iraq," 6.

95. UNSCOM, *Draft Report on the First Biological Warfare Inspection in Iraq*, 27.

96. UNSCOM, *Report on the First Biological Warfare Inspection in Iraq: UNSCOM 7*, para. 10; UNSCOM, *Draft Report on the First Biological Warfare Inspection in Iraq*, 47–48.

97. Former UNSCOM CBW commissioner, interview with author, January 23, 2006.

98. UN Security Council, Resolution 707 (1991), Doc. S/RES/707, August 15, 1991.

99. Huxsoll, interview.

100. Kelly, interview.

101. Barton, interview; Kelly, interview; Huxsoll, interview; former senior UNSCOM official, interview with author, September 1, 2005; William Lebherz (former UNSCOM industrial biotechnology expert), interview with author, Washington, DC, February 13, 2006.

102. Huxsoll, interview; Kelly, interview; Killip, interview; Lebherz, interview; former UNSCOM inspector and chief of product development in an offensive biological weapons program, interview with author, Washington, DC, February 21, 2006; Kelly, interview; Krikorian, interview; Trevan, *Saddam's Secrets*, 116–117.

103. Kelly, interview; Spertzel, interview. Also, UN Security Council, *Report of the Secretary-General on the Status of the Implementation of the Special Commission's Plan for the Ongoing Monitoring and Verification of Iraq's Compliance with Relevant Parts of Section C of Security Council Resolution 687 (1991)*, Doc. S/1995/284, April 10, 1995, Annex, para. 76.

104. Huxsoll, interview. Lebherz, interview.

105. Lebherz, interview; Killip, interview; Kelly, interview; Ray Zilinskas, PhD (former UNSCOM biological weapons inspector), interview with author, Washington, DC, October 4, 2005; Krikorian, interview; former senior UNSCOM official, interview with author, September 1, 2005; Barton, interview.

106. Killip, interview. Also, Barton, interview.

107. Huxsoll, interview. Also, Kelly, interview.

108. Recalling a BW2 inspector's description of signs of an airlock, Spertzel, interview.

109. Huxsoll, interview; Kelly, interview.

110. Former senior UNSCOM official, interview with author, September 1, 2005; Huxsoll, interview; Barton, *The Weapons Detective*, 117. Also, R. Jeffrey Smith, "Iraq's Drive for a Biological Arsenal; U.N. Pursing 25 Germ Warheads It Believes Are Still Loaded with Deadly Toxin," *Washington Post*, November 21, 1997, A1.

111. Spertzel, interview.

112. Huxsoll, interview. Also, Kadlec, interview.

113. Huxsoll, interview.

114. UNSCOM, *UNSCOM 84/BW6: Final Report*, June 20–July 12, 1994 (New York, n.d.), A19-1 to A19-3. Also, Spertzel, interview; Kraatz-Wadsack, interview.

115. Spertzel, interview. Also, Government of the United Kingdom, "UN Special Commission BW Inspections in Iraq," 10.

116. Kelly, interview. Concurring, Spertzel, interview; former UNSCOM inspector and chief of product development in an offensive biological weapons program, interview with author, February 21, 2006.

117. Kelly, interview; Huxsoll, interview; Spertzel, interview; Barton, interview.

118. Barton, interview.

119. Kelly, interview. Agreeing, Barton, interview; Killip, interview; Spertzel, interview.

120. Huxsoll, interview; Killip, interview.

121. Kelly, interview. Also, Kadlec, interview.

122. Kelly, interview; Huxsoll, interview.

123. Huxsoll, interview. Also, Government of the United Kingdom, "UN Special Commission BW Inspections in Iraq," 10.

124. Kelly, interview. Similarly, former UNSCOM chief biological weapons inspector, interview with author, August 28, 2005; Lebherz, interview.

125. Spertzel, interview; Huxsoll, interview; Killip, interview; UN Doc. S/2005/545, Annex, para. 17, p. 9.

126. Trevan, *Saddam's Secrets*, 114–115.

127. Huxsoll, interview.

128. Kelly, interview.

129. Huxsoll, interview; UN Doc. S/23165, Appendix IV, para. 27.

130. Huxsoll, interview with author; Government of the United Kingdom, "UN Special Commission BW Inspections in Iraq," 9. Giving a description of Samarra from his later inspection of the facility, Franz, interview.

131. Huxsoll, interview. Also, Krikorian, interview; former UNSCOM inspector and chief of product development in an offensive biological weapons program, interview with author, February 21, 2006.

132. Kelly, interview. Also, Government of the United Kingdom, "UN Special Commission BW Inspections in Iraq," 16; Trevan, *Saddam's Secrets*, 118.

133. Huxsoll, interview; Kelly, interview; Government of the United Kingdom, "UN Special Commission BW Inspections in Iraq," 16.

134. Huxsoll, interview. Also, UN Doc. S/23165, Appendix IV, para. 27.

135. Huxsoll, interview; Government of the United Kingdom, "UN Special Commission BW Inspections in Iraq," 9.

136. Ibid.; Kelly, interview.

137. Kelly, interview.

138. Huxsoll, interview.

139. Government of the United Kingdom, "UN Special Commission BW Inspections in Iraq," 8.

140. Huxsoll, interview.

141. Kelly, interview.

142. UN, "Several Iraqi Sites Recommended for Future Monitoring by Second UN Biological Weapons Inspection Team," Press Release, Doc. IK/69, October 31, 1991; Government of the United Kingdom, "UN Special Commission BW Inspections in Iraq," 8.

143. "Several Iraqi Sites Recommended for Future Monitoring by Second UN Biological Weapons Inspection Team," UN Doc. IK/69; Government of the United Kingdom, "UN Special Commission BW Inspections in Iraq," 8–9. Also, Trevan, *Saddam's Secrets*, 118; Letter from the Charge d'Affaires A.I. of the Permanent Mission of Iraq to the UN addressed to the President of the Security Council, (New York, Permanent Mission of Iraq to the UN, dated January 23, 1992), UN Doc. S/23472, 29.

144. Stephen Black, "The UN Special Commission and CBW Verification," *Chemical Weapons Convention Bulletin*, no. 32 (June 1996): 8; Government of the United Kingdom, "UN Special Commission BW Inspections in Iraq," 10, 16.

145. Huxsoll, interview; Kelly, interview; Englund, interview; former senior UNSCOM official, interview with author, September 1, 2005; UN Doc. S/23165, Appendix IV, para. 28.

146. "Several Iraqi Sites Recommended for Future Monitoring by Second UN Biological Weapons Inspection Team," UN Doc. IK/69.

147. Huxsoll, interview. Also, Kelly, interview.

148. John M. Goshko and Ann Devroy, "Iraq Holds U.N. Inspectors for 13 Hours, Seizes Data," *Washington Post*, September 24, 1991, A1; John Lancaster and John M. Goshko, "Iraq Said to Yield on Nuclear Inspection," *Washington Post*, September 25, 1991, A1; John Lancaster and John M. Goshko, "Iraq Seeks Deal to End U.N. Team Standoff," *Washington Post*, September 26, 1991, A1; Michael Z. Wise, "U.N. Team Finds New Evidence of Iraqi Coverup," *Washington Post*, October 1, 1991, A1; Jean E. Krasno and James S. Sutterlin, *The United Nations and Iraq: Defanging the Viper* (Westport, CT: Praeger, 2003), 57–59.

149. "British Expert on Iraq's Secret Arms Program," *Sunday Times* (London), February 14, 1999.

150. Former senior UNSCOM official, interview with author, August 30, 2005.

151. Republic of Iraq, "The Biological Aspects," Report to the Ad Hoc Group of Governmental Experts to Identify and Examine Potential Verification Measures from a Scientific and Technical Standpoint, BWC/CONF.III/VEREX/WP.19, Geneva, UN, April 6, 1992.

152. Paul Lewis, "UN Weapons Inspectors Renew Hunt in Iraq," *New York Times*, November 17, 1991, A12.

153. Spertzel, interview.

Chapter 3

1. United Nations (UN) Security Council, Resolution 715 (1991), Doc. S/RES/715, October 11, 1991.

2. UN Security Council, *Plan for Future Ongoing Monitoring and Verification of Iraq's Compliance with Relevant Parts of Section C of Security Council Resolution 687 (1991) Report of the Secretary-General*, Doc. S/22871/Rev.1 and S/22872/Rev.1, August 1, 1991. Also, Revised Annex III, UN Security Council, *Plan for Future Ongoing Monitoring and Verification of Iraq's Compliance with Relevant Parts of Section C of Security Council Resolution 687 (1991) Report of the Secretary-General*, Doc. S/1995/208, March 17, 1995.

3. Tim Trevan, *Saddam's Secrets: The Hunt for Saddam's Hidden Weapons* (London: HarperCollins, 1999), 7.

4. Ambassador Robert Gallucci, PhD (former UNSCOM deputy executive chairman), interview with author, Washington, DC, March 13, 2006; David Kelly, PhD (former UNSCOM chief biological weapons inspector), interview with author, Washington, DC, December 17, 2002; David Huxsoll, DVM (former UNSCOM chief biological weapons inspector), interview with author, Washington, DC, June 21, 2005; former UNSCOM CBW commissioner, interview with author via telephone, January 23, 2006; former UNSCOM chief inspector, interview with author, January 31, 2006.

5. Ambassador Rolf Ekeus (former UNSCOM executive chairman), interview with author, Stockholm, August 24, 2005. Concurring, Gallucci, interview; former UNSCOM CBW commissioner, interview with author, January 23, 2006. Also, Jez Littlewood, "Investigating Allegations of CBW Use: Reviving the UN Secretary-General's Mechanism," *Compliance Chronicles*, no. 3 (Ottawa, Canadian Centre for Treaty Compliance, December 2006): 1–36; UN Security Council, *Report of the Mission Dispatched by the Secretary-General to Investigate Reports of the Use of Chemical Weapons in Azerbaijan*, Doc. S/24344, July 24, 1992.

6. Former UNSCOM CBW commissioner, interview with author, January 23, 2006. Also, Frank J. Prial, "U.N. Team Finds Chemical Arms 4 Times Greater Than Iraq Claims," *New York Times*, July 31, 1991, A1; UN Security Council, *Third Report of the Executive Chairman of Special Commission Established by the Secretary-General Pursuant to Paragraph 9 (b)(i) of Security Council Resolution 687 (1991)*, Doc. S/24108, June 16, 1992, Appendix II, paras. 1–2.

7. Former UNSCOM CBW commissioner, interview with author, January 23, 2006.

8. Stephen Black, "The Death of UNSCOM: The CBW Colloquium," *ASA Newsletter*, no. 76 (January 2000); Charles Duelfer, *Hide and Seek: The Search for Truth in Iraq* (New York: Public Affairs, 2009), 82, 90, 105, 178–179, 449.

9. Letter from Muhammad Said Al-Sahhaf, Minister of Foreign Affairs, to Rolf Ekeus, Executive Chairman of the Special Commission (dated March 19, 1992, transmitted by Ambassador Abdul Amir A. Al-Anbari, Permanent Representative to the

UN, March 20, 1992), Annex A. Also, Appendix III, para. 2; Annex, para. 23. Also, UN Doc. S/24108, Annex, para. 14.

10. Ron Manley, PhD (former UNSCOM chief chemical weapons inspector), interview with author, London, August 19, 2005; former senior UNSCOM official, interview with author, New York City, August 30, 2005.

11. Graham S. Pearson, *The UNSCOM Saga: Chemical and Biological Weapons Non-Proliferation* (New York: St. Martin's Press, 1999), 130.

12. Rod Barton (former UNSCOM biological weapons inspector), interview with author via telephone, May 20, 2005. Similarly, former senior UNSCOM official, interview with author, August 30, 2005; Rod Barton, *The Weapons Detective: The Inside Story of Australia's Top Weapons Inspector* (Melbourne: Black Inc. Agenda, 2006), 117.

13. Former senior UNSCOM official, interview with author, August 30, 2005. Also, UN Security Council, *Fourth Report of the Executive Chairman of Special Commission Established by the Secretary-General Pursuant to Paragraph 9 (b)(i) of Security Council Resolution 687 (1991)*, Doc. S/24984, December 17, 1992, Appendix III, para. 4; UN Security Council, *Fifth Report of the Executive Chairman of Special Commission Established by the Secretary-General Pursuant to Paragraph 9 (b)(i) of Security Council Resolution 687 (1991)*, Doc. S/25977, June 21, 1993, Appendix II, para. 7.

14. Manley, interview; UN Security Council, *First Report of the Executive Chairman UNSCOM Under UNSCR 687*, Doc. S/23165, October 25, 1991, para. 10; Rod Barton, "Eliminating Strategic Weapons in Iraq," *Pacific Research* 6, no. 3 (August 1993): 11–13; "U.N. Prepares to Destroy Iraqi Chemical Weapons," *Washington Post*, September 13, 1992, A34; UN Security Council, *Letter Dated 25 January 1999 from the Executive Chairman of the Special Commission Established by the Secretary-General Pursuant to Paragraph 9 (b) (i) of Security Council Resolution 687 (1991) Addressed to the President of the Security Council*, Doc. S/1999/94, January 29, 1999, Appendix II, paras. 11, 16.

15. Manley, interview; former UNSCOM staff member, interview with author, New York City, September 2, 2005; Kelly, interview; Charles Duelfer (former UNSCOM deputy executive chairman), interview with author, Washington, DC, November 15, 2007; Huxsoll, interview; former senior UNSCOM official, interview with author, New York City, September 1, 2005; Barton, interview; former senior UNSCOM official, interview with author, August 30, 2005; Terence Taylor (former UNSCOM CBW commissioner and chief inspector), interview with author, Washington, DC, May 12, 2005; former UNSCOM staff member, interview with author, New York City, September 1, 2005; former UNSCOM CBW commissioner, interview with author, January 23, 2006; Richard Spertzel, PhD (former UNSCOM chief biological weapons inspector), interview with author, Washington, DC, July 1, 2005; foreign ministry official, interview with author, London, August 17, 2005.

16. Stephen Black (former UNSCOM historian), interview with author, Washington, DC, November 16, 2007.

17. Ekeus, interview. Agreeing, Pierce Corden, former UNSCOM deputy executive chairman, interview with author, Washington, DC, August 4, 2008; former senior UNSCOM official, interview with author, September 1, 2005.

18. Barton, interview; Taylor, interview.

19. Former senior UNSCOM official, interview with author, August 30, 2005. Similarly, Gallucci, interview; Corden, interview; former UNSCOM staff member, interview author, September 1, 2005.

20. Ekeus, interview.

21. Barton, interview. Agreeing, Spertzel, interview.

22. Former senior UNSCOM official, interview with author, August 30, 2005.

23. Quote from Ekeus, who characterized Jansen as being "very skeptical." Ekeus, interview. Also, Hamish Killip (former UNSCOM chief biological inspector), interview with author, Isle of Man, August 22, 2005; Manley, interview; Debra Krikorian, PhD (former UNSCOM biological weapons inspector), interview with author, Washington, DC, June 21, 2005; foreign ministry official, interview with author, August 17, 2005. See Karen M. Jansen, "Disarming Iraq—Lessons for the Chemical Weapons Convention," *Chemical Weapons Convention Bulletin*, no. 24 (June 1994): 6.

24. Peter Grier, "UN Inspectors in Iraq Get Chemical Surprise," *Christian Science Monitor*, June 23, 1992, 1; Karen M. Jansen, "Biological Weapons Proliferation," in *Multilateral Verification and the Post-Gulf Environment: Learning from the UNSCOM Experience*, ed. Steven Mataija and J. Marshall Beier, Centre for International and Strategic Studies (Toronto: York University, December 1992), 114–115.

25. Former UNSCOM chief inspector, interview with author, New York City, January 31, 2006; Taylor, interview; Krikorian, interview; Spertzel, interview; Raymond Zilinskas, PhD (former UNSCOM biological weapons inspector), interview with author, Washington, DC, October 4, 2005; Jeff Mohr, PhD (former UNSCOM chief biological weapons inspector), interview with author via telephone, June 27, 2005; Ake Sellstrom, PhD (former UNSCOM chief inspector), interview with author, Stockholm, August 24, 2005.

26. Huxsoll, interview; Krikorian, interview; Killip, interview; former senior UNSCOM official, interview with author, August 30, 2005.

27. Ekeus, interview. Also, Corden, interview; Gabriele Kraatz-Wadsack, DVM (former UNSCOM chief biological weapons inspector), interview with author, Berlin, August 15, 2005; former UNSCOM chief inspector, interview with author, August 18, 2005.

28. Letter from Kenneth Anderson, Human Rights Watch, and Andrew Whitley, Middle East Watch, to Rolf Ekeus, Chairman of UNSCOM (Human Rights Watch, New York, December 29, 1992). Also, "Document Says Iraq Has Biological Weapons, *New York Times*, December 30, 1992, A9; Shyam Bhatia, "Iraqi Scientist Tells 10-Year Secret: Saddam Hides Germ Tests from UN Inspectors," *The Observer* (London),

August 9, 1992 (in FBIS Doc. JPRS-TND-92-007-L, September 10, 1992), 6; Judith Miller, "Iraq: A Case of Genocide Accused," *New York Times Magazine*, March 1, 1993, 32.

29. Mark Skipworth and Jonathan Calvert, "Saddam Hid Missiles and Anthrax Bombs from UN," *Sunday Times* (London) February 19, 1995, 1; "Saddam Is Hiding Weapons from UN," *Gulf Daily News*, February 20, 1995, 7; Duelfer, *Hide and Seek*, 100–103.

30. Taylor, interview. Also, John Barry, "Unearthing the Truth: How a Team of Underdog Inspectors Finally Found Evidence of Iraq's Arsenal of Death," *Newsweek*, March 2, 1998, 40.

31. David Franz, DVM, PhD (former UNSCOM chief biological weapons inspector), interview with author, Washington, DC, June 29, 2005; UN Doc. S/25977, Appendix II, para. 8.

32. Franz, interview. Also, Mohr, interview; Robert Kadlec, MD (former UNSCOM biological weapons inspector), interview with author, Washington, DC, February 23, 2006.

33. Franz, interview. Also, Barton, *The Weapons Detective*, 118.

34. Franz, interview. Also, Spertzel, interview.

35. Franz, interview.

36. Franz, interview; UN Doc. S/25977, Appendix II, para. 8.

37. Spertzel, interview; Barton, *The Weapons Detective*, 118. On different views between teams, Huxsoll, interview; former UNSCOM CBW commissioner, interview with author, January 23, 2006.

38. Ekeus, interview.

39. UN Security Council, *Addendum to the Eighth Report of the Executive Chairman of the Special Commission, Established by the Secretary-General Pursuant to Paragraph 9 (b) (i) of Security Council Resolution 687 (1991)*, Doc. S/1994/1422/Add.1, December 15, 1994, Annex, para. 62.

40. Ekeus, interview. Similarly, Gallucci, interview; former UNSCOM CBW commissioner, interview with author, January 23, 2006; Corden, interview; Spertzel, interview. Also, Christopher Dickey and Colin Soloway, "The Secrets of Dr. Germ: U.N. Inspectors Have Begun Searching Iraqi Weapons Sites. But What Happens When They Investigate the Scientists? The 'Human Factor' Could Be a Trigger to War," *Newsweek*, December 9, 2002, 2.

41. Duelfer, interview; former senior UNSCOM official, interview with author, August 20, 2005; Barton, *The Weapons Detective*, 118–119. See also Trevan, *Saddam's Secrets*, 18; Barry, "Unearthing the Truth," 40.

42. UN Doc. S/22871/Rev.1, Annex A. Republic of Iraq, "Status of Iraq's Implementation of Its Obligations in Accordance with Paragraph (C) of SRC-687 (1991) and in Accordance with the Ongoing Monitoring Plan Annexed to SCR 715 (1991) for the Period of Sep. 1994 to Jan. 1995" (Baghdad, January 1995), 14–15; Pearson, *The UNSCOM Saga*, 136; Barry, "Unearthing the Truth," 40.

43. Gabriele Kraatz-Wadsack, "The Role of Scientists in Verification," in *Assessing the Threat of Weapons of Mass Destruction: The Role of Independent Scientists*, vol. 61, ed. J. L. Finney and I. Slaus, NATO Science for Peace and Security Series E: Human and Societal Dynamics (Amsterdam: IOS Press, 2010), 47.

44. Zilinskas, interview; former senior UNSCOM official, interview with author, September 1, 2005; former UNSCOM staff member, interview with author, September 2, 2005; Spertzel, interview.

45. Duelfer, *Hide and Seek*, 445.

46. Killip, interview with author, August 22, 2005; Krikorian, interview with author, June 21, 2005; Sellstrom, interview with author, August 24, 2005; Kraatz-Wadsack, interview; former UNSCOM staff member, interview with author, September 2, 2005; former UNSCOM chief inspector, interview with author, January 31, 2006; William Lebherz (former UNSCOM industrial biotechnology expert), interview with author, Washington, DC, February 13, 2006. Also, William J. Broad and Judith Miller, "The Deal on Iraq: Secret Arsenal: The Hunt for the Germs of War," *New York Times*, February 26, 1998, A1; Barton, *The Weapons Detective*, 120, 162–163.

47. Sellstrom, interview; former senior UNSCOM official, interview with author, August 30, 2005; Dickey and Soloway, "The Secrets of Dr. Germ;" Trevan, *Saddam's Secrets*, page x.

48. Spertzel, interview.

49. Ibid.; Krikorian, interview. On general recognition of the discrepancies in Iraq's stories, former UNSCOM senior official, interview with author, September 1, 2005. Also, John Barry and Gregory L. Vistica, "The Hunt for His Secret Weapons," *Newsweek*, December 1, 1997, 32.

50. Spertzel, interview; Zilinskas, interview.

51. Killip, interview; Kelly, interview.

52. The members of this brain trust are briefly introduced elsewhere. See Chapter 1 for Smidovich, Killip, Barton, and Ekeus, Chapter 2 for Kelly, and Chapter 4 for Kraatz-Wadsack.

53. Former UNSCOM staff member, interview with author, September 2, 2005.

54. Duelfer, *Hide and Seek*, footnote 13, pp. 495–496. Similarly, Krikorian, interview; Lebherz, interview.

55. Killip, interview.

56. Krikorian, interview; Lebherz, interview.

57. Pierson, *The UNSCOM Saga*, 136, 187.

58. Situation Report #11, To UNSCOM Executive Chairman, From CI UNSCOM 72, signed Volker Beck (Baghdad, April 18, 1994), 2–3; Situation Report #6, To UNSCOM Executive Chairman, From CI UNSCOM 72, signed Volker Beck (Baghdad, April 13, 1994), 1; Situation Report #5, To UNSCOM Executive Chairman, From CI UNSCOM 72, signed Volker Beck (Baghdad, April 12, 1994), 1; Situation Report #13, To UNSCOM Executive Chairman, From CI UNSCOM 72, signed Volker Beck (Baghdad, April 20, 1994), 1.

59. Mohr, interview. Also, Zilinskas, interview; Spertzel, interview.

60. "There Are No More Gaps Left: Expert, Iraq's Compliance with Resolutions on Biological Weapons," *Khaleej Times* (Bahrain), April 29, 1994, 5.

61. Spertzel, interview; Zilinskas, interview; Kelly, interview ; Situation Report #14, To UNSCOM Executive Chairman, From CI UNSCOM 72, signed Volker Beck (Baghdad, April 21, 1994), 2.

62. Ekeus, interview; Taylor, interview; Barton, interview; Spertzel, interview; Killip, interview.

63. Spertzel, interview.

64. Former UNSCOM inspector and chief of product development in an offensive biological weapons program, interview with author, Washington, DC, February 21, 2006.

65. Republic of Iraq, "List of Bacteriological Isolates Handed Over to the First Biological Lnspechon (sic) Team," in Annex 2, *A Full, Final and Comprehensive Report on {Biological Activity}*, May 1992, 13. Also, Dominic Kennedy, "Saddam's Germ War Plot Is Traced Back to One Oxford Cow," *London Times*, August 9, 2005, 19; Geoffrey Holland, *United States Exports of Biological Materials to Iraq: Compromising the Credibility of International Law* (Montreal: Center for Research on Globalization, July 7, 2005).

66. Former UNSCOM inspector and chief of product development in an offensive biological weapons program, interview with author, Washington, DC, February 21, 2006; Franz, interview; Kadlec, interview. Also, David R. Franz, Cheryl D. Parrott, and Ernest Takafuji, "The US Biological Warfare and Biological Defense Programs," in *Medical Aspects of Chemical and Biological Warfare*, ed. Frederick R. Sidell, Ernest T. Takafuji, and David R. Franz (Washington, DC: Office of the Surgeon General at Textbook of Military Medicine Publications, 1997), 425–436.

67. Former UNSCOM inspector and chief of product development in an offensive biological weapons program, interview with author, February 21, 2006. Similarly, Paul Lewis, "Telltale Clues Found by U.N. Inspectors in Iraq: No Documents, but Weapons-Knowledgeable Scientists," *New York Times*, September 29, 1991, A18.

68. UNSCOM, *Draft Inspection Report of UNSCOM 78/BW5* (New York, n.d.), 1–2, 11, 5–6.

69. UN Doc. S/1994/1422/Add.1, Annex, paras. 50–3.

70. UNSCOM, *UNSCOM 84/BW6: Draft Final Report*, A38-3 to A38-4, A38-6, A38-8.

71. Spertzel, interview; Mohr, interview.

72. *UNSCOM 84/BW 6: Draft Final Report; Site Report: Al Hakam*, June 20–July 12, 1994 (New York, n.d.), A19-1 to A-19-3; Spertzel, interview.

73. Mohr, interview.

74. Situation Report #3, To UNSCOM Executive Chairman, From CI UNSCOM 84/BW6, signed Jeff Mohr (Baghdad, June 27, 1994), 1; *UNSCOM 84/BW 6: Draft Final Report*, A16-2 to A-16-4, A-17.

75. *UNSCOM 84/BW 6: Draft Final Report*, A39-1; Killip, interview; Spertzel, interview; Kelly, interview; Kraatz-Wadsack, interview; Kadlec, interview.

76. Situation Report #4, To UNSCOM Executive Chairman, From CI UNSCOM 84/BW6, signed Jeff Mohr (Baghdad, June 28, 1994), 2, 10; Situation Report #5, To UNSCOM Executive Chairman, From CI UNSCOM 84/BW6, signed Jeff Mohr (Baghdad, June 29, 1994), 4–5; *UNSCOM 84/BW 6: Draft Final Report*, A39-5, A39-10. Also, Alan J. Mohr, "Biological Sampling and Analysis Procedures for the United Nations Special Commission (UNSCOM) in Iraq," *Politics and the Life Sciences* 14, no. 2 (August 1995): 243; Kadlec, interview.

77. Mohr, interview; Spertzel, interview; former UNSCOM chief inspector, interview with author, January 31, 2006.

78. *UNSCOM 84/BW 6: Draft Final Report*, A39-2, A39-11. Also, Mohr, interview; Spertzel, interview; Killip, interview; Kadlec, interview.

79. Spertzel, interview.

80. Caryle Murphy, "U.N. Inspectors in Iraq Prepare to Shift to Monitoring Role," *Washington Post*, July 14, 1994, A18; Terence Taylor, "The United Nations Special Commission on Iraq: A Period of Transition," Director's Series on Proliferation, no. 6 (Livermore, CA: Laurence Livermore National Laboratory, 1995).

81. Killip, interview. Also, Krikorian, interview.

82. Nabila Megalli, "Biological Experts Complete Survey, but Questions Remain," Associated Press, September 13, 1994.

83. Spertzel, interview; Kraatz-Wadsack, interview; UN Doc. S/1994/1422/Add.1, Annex, paras. 58–61.

84. Lebherz, interview.

85. Barton, interview; UN Security Council, *Report of the Secretary-General on the Status of the Implementation of the Special Commission's Plan for the Ongoing Monitoring and Verification of Iraq's Compliance with Relevant Parts of Section of Security Council Resolution 687 (1991)*, Doc. S/1995/864, October 11, 1995, Annex, para. 65.

86. Former senior UNSCOM official, interview with author, August 30, 2005.

87. Ekeus, interview.

88. Former senior UNSCOM official, interview with author, August 30, 2005; Spertzel, interview; Killip, interview; Krikorian, interview; Barton, *The Weapons Detective*, 136.

89. UN Security Council, *Report of the Secretary-General on the Status of the Implementation of the Special Commission's Plan for the Ongoing Monitoring and Verification of Iraq's Compliance with Relevant Parts of Section C of Security Council Resolution 687 (1991)*, Doc. S/1994/1138, October 7, 1994, para. 2, 10.

90. Thomas W. Lippman, "Baghdad Remains Far from Full Compliance with U.N. Resolutions," *Washington Post*, October 21, 1994, A28. Also, R. Jeffrey Smith, "Secretive Iraq Parries U.N. Arms Inspectors: Technology, Patience Pry Open Weapons Data," *Washington Post*, November 4, 1994, A1.

91. Spertzel, interview; former UNSCOM staff member, interview with author, September 2, 2005. Also, UN Security Council, *Second Report of the Executive Chairman of the Special Commission Following the Adoption of Security Council Resolution 1051 (1996)*, Doc. S/1996/848, October 11, 1996, Annex, para. 13.

92. Barton, *The Weapons Detective*, 125; Ekeus, interview.

93. Spertzel, interview; Barton, *The Weapons Detective*, 127; UN Doc. S/1994/1422/Add.1, Annex, para. 46.

94. Spertzel, interview; Barton, *The Weapons Detective*, 128–130.

95. Barton, interview. Also, Spertzel, interview; Killip, interview; Barton, *The Weapons Detective*, 127; UN Doc. S/1994/1422/Add.1, Annex, para. 47.

96. Killip, interview.

97. Spertzel, interview; Barry, "Unearthing the Truth," 40.

98. Barton, *The Weapons Detective*, 130–131.

99. Kelly, interview; Barton, interview; Spertzel, interview; Killip, interview. Also, Barton, *The Weapons Detective*, 131–132.

100. Spertzel, interview.

101. UN Doc. S/1994/1422/Add.1, Annex, para. 66.

102. Lebherz, interview.

103. Ibid.

104. Ibid.; Kelly, interview; Spertzel, interview; former UNSCOM inspector and chief of product development in an offensive biological weapons program, interview with author, February 21, 2006.

105. Lebherz, interview.

106. Spertzel, interview; Kraatz-Wadsack, interview.

107. UN Doc. S/1994/1422/Add.1, Annex, paras. 65–66.

108. Lebherz, interview; Kelly, interview.

109. UN Doc. S/1994/1422/Add.1, Annex, para. 20. Also, UN Doc. S/1996/848, Annex, para. 13.

110. Alan George, "Fears of Iraqi Biological Weapons Don't Abate," *Washington Times*, December 24, 1994, 9.

111. Kraatz-Wadsack, interview.

112. Spertzel, interview; Lebherz, interview.

113. Kelly, interview; Spertzel, interview; Kadlec, interview; former UNSCOM inspector and chief of product development in an offensive biological weapons program, interview with author, February 21, 2006.

114. Spertzel, interview; former UNSCOM inspector and chief of product development in an offensive biological weapons program, interview with author, February 21, 2006; Kadlec, interview; Franz, interview.

115. Kraatz-Wadsack, interview.

116. Ibid. Also, Kelly, interview; Kadlec, interview; Republic of Iraq, "Status of Iraq's Implementation Under Resolutions 687 and 715," 19.

Chapter 4

1. Richard Spertzel, PhD (former UNSCOM chief biological weapons inspector), interview with author, Washington, DC, July 1, 2005; David Kelly, PhD (former UNSCOM chief biological weapons inspector), interview with author, Washington, DC, December 17, 2002. Also, Rod Barton, *The Weapons Detective: The Inside Story of Australia's Top Weapons Inspector* (Melbourne: Black Inc. Agenda, 2006), 136–138; Tom Mangold and Jeff Goldberg, *Plague Wars* (New York: St. Martin's Press, 1999), 307.

2. Spertzel, interview. Also, Barton Gellman, "UN Arms Inspectors Relied on Israeli Leads," *International Herald Tribune*, September 30, 1998, 2.

3. Rod Barton (former UNSCOM biological weapons inspector), interview with author via telephone, May 20, 2005.

4. Barton, *The Weapons Detective*, 136–137. Also, Spertzel, interview with author, July 1, 2005.

5. Spertzel, interview; former senior UNSCOM official, interview with author, New York City, August 30, 2005; Barton, interview; Barton, *The Weapons Detective*, 138–139.

6. Former senior UNSCOM official, interview with author, August 30, 2005; Barton, interview.

7. Barton, *The Weapons Detective*, 145, 150–151. Also, Spertzel, interview.

8. Spertzel, interview; Terence Taylor (former UNSCOM CBW commissioner and chief inspector), interview with author, Washington, DC, May 12, 2005. Also, Barton, *The Weapons Detective*, 151, 154–157; William J. Broad and Judith Miller, "The Deal on Iraq: Secret Arsenal: The Hunt for the Germs of War," *New York Times*, February 26, 1998, A1.

9. Spertzel, interview; Barton, interview. Also, Barton, *The Weapons Detective*, 151–152, 154–155.

10. Spertzel, interview.

11. Ibid.; Charles Duelfer (former UNSCOM deputy executive chairman), interview with author, Washington, DC, November 15, 2007.

12. Former UNSCOM chief chemical weapons inspector, interview with author, New York City, January 31, 2006.

13. Spertzel, interview.

14. Ibid.; former UNSCOM inspector and chief of product development in an offensive biological weapons program, interview with author, Washington, DC, February 21, 2006; Robert Kadlec, MD, former UNSCOM inspector, interview with author, Washington, DC, February 23, 2006.

15. Gabriele Kraatz-Wadsack, DVM (former UNSCOM chief biological weapons inspector), interview with author, Berlin, August 15, 2005; Kadlec, interview; former UNSCOM biological weapons inspector, interview with author, Washington, DC, February 21, 2006.

16. Mangold and Goldberg, *Plague Wars*, 299.

17. Kraatz-Wadsack, interview; Spertzel, interview.

18. Hamish Killip (former UNSCOM chief biological weapons inspector), interview with author, Isle of Man, August 22, 2005; Kelly, interview; Spertzel, interview.

19. Kraatz-Wadsack, interview.

20. Ibid. Also, UNSCOM, "IBG 2 SitRep 12," from Gabriele Kraatz-Wadsack, CI IBG2, to Executive Chairman, UNSCOM (Baghdad, Baghdad Monitoring and Verification Center, March 15, 1995), 2; United Nations (UN) Security Council, *Report of the Secretary-General on the Status of the Implementation of the Special Commission's Plan for the Ongoing Monitoring and Verification of Iraq's Compliance with Relevant Parts of Section C of Security Council Resolution 687 (1991)*, Doc. S/1995/284, April 10, 1995, Annex, para. 65; Barton, *The Weapons Detective*, 151.

21. Kraatz-Wadsack, interview. Also, "IBG 2 SitRep 12," March 15, 1995, 1–3.

22. Jeff Mohr, PhD (former UNSCOM chief biological weapons inspector), interview with author via telephone, June 27, 2005. Also, Franz, interview; UNSCOM, *Final Report: UNSCOM 112/21, Executive Summary*, marked "UNSCOM Sensitive" (New York, UNSCOM, n.d.), 2, 10.

23. Spertzel, interview; Kraatz-Wadsack, interview. Also, UN Doc. S/1995/284, Annex, para. 75; Barton, *The Weapons Detective*, 140–141.

24. Spertzel, interview.

25. Ibid.; Kraatz-Wadsack, interview; Barton, *The Weapons Detective*, 140–142.

26. Spertzel, interview.

27. Ibid.; Kraatz-Wadsack, interview.

28. Barton, interview; Spertzel, interview; Barton, *The Weapons Detective*, 142–143.

29. Charles Duelfer, *Hide and Seek: The Search for Truth in Iraq* (New York: Public Affairs, 2009), 98–100.

30. Spertzel, interview; Barton, *The Weapons Detective*, 141.

31. Broad and Miller, "The Deal on Iraq: Secret Arsenal;" Barton, *The Weapons Detective*, 142–143.

32. Spertzel, interview; Barton, *The Weapons Detective*, 143; Broad and Miller, "The Deal on Iraq: Secret Arsenal."

33. Kelly, interview; Killip, interview; Spertzel, interview.

34. Kraatz-Wadsack, interview; Barton, interview; former senior UNSCOM official, interview with author, New York City, September 1, 2005; Debra Krikorian, PhD (former UNSCOM biological weapons inspector), interview with author, Washington, DC, June 21, 2005. Also, UN Security Council, *Report of the Secretary General on the Activities of the Special Commission Established by the Secretary-General Pursuant to Paragraph 9 (b)(i) of Resolution 687 (1991)*, Doc. S/1999/401, April 9, 1999, Annex, paras. 64, 66.

35. Barton, *The Weapons Detective*, 151.

36. Taylor, interview; Kraatz-Wadsack, interview; Spertzel, interview. Also, UN Doc. S/1999/401, Annex, para. 67.

37. Taylor, interview; Spertzel, interview; Barton, interview. Also, United Nations Special Commission, *Background Paper for the Biological Seminar* (seminar of international biological weapons experts, April 6–7, 1995), April 5, 1995, 4; Barton, *The Weapons Detective*, 145.

38. Spertzel, interview; Kelly, interview; Barton, *The Weapons Detective*, 138–139.

39. UN Security Council, *Report of the Secretary-General on the Status of the Implementation of the Special Commission's Plan for the Ongoing Monitoring and Verification of Iraq's Compliance with Relevant Parts of Section of Security Council Resolution 687 (1991)*, Doc. S/1995/864, October 11, 1995, Annex, para. 69.

40. Spertzel, interview. Also, Pierce Corden (former UNSCOM deputy executive chairman), interview with author, Washington, DC, August 4, 2008; Kelly, interview.

41. William Safire, "Iraq's Threat: Biological Warfare," *New York Times*, February 16, 1995, A27.

42. Evelyn Leopold, "Iraq Fails to Account for Bacteria 'Growth Media,'" Reuters (UN), February 27, 1995.

43. Robin Wright, "Iraq Concealing Biological Arms Effort, U.N. Says," *Los Angeles Times*, February 28, 1995, 1.

44. Taylor, interview. Also, former senior UNSCOM official, interview with author, August 30, 2005; Kraatz-Wadsack, interview.

45. Kraatz-Wadsack, interview; Taylor, interview.

46. Barton, interview; Kraatz-Wadsack, interview; Taylor, interview.

47. Quote from Taylor, interview. Also, Kraatz-Wadsack, interview.

48. UNSCOM, *Background Paper for the Biological Seminar*, 4.

49. Taylor, interview; Kraatz-Wadsack, interview; Barton, interview. Also, UN Doc. S/1995/284, Annex, para. 67.

50. Barton, interview; Taylor, interview.

51. Kraatz-Wadsack, interview; Taylor, interview.

52. Lee Michael Katz, "Iraq: Inspections Will Be 'Settled,' Will Open Up on Biological Arms, Ambassador Says," *USA Today*, March 7, 1995, 10.

53. Spertzel, interview; Kelly, interview. Also, UN Doc. S/1995/284, Annex, paras. 71–73; Stephen Black, "UNSCOM and the Iraqi Biological Weapons Program: Technical Success, Political Failure," in *Biological Warfare and Disarmament: New Problems, New Perspectives*, ed. Susan Wright (New York: Rowman & Littlefield, 2002), 293.

54. William Lebherz (former UNSCOM industrial biotechnology expert), interview with author, Washington, DC, February 13, 2006; former UNSCOM staff member, interview with author, New York City, September 2, 2005.

55. Barton, interview. Also, Christopher Dickey and Colin Soloway, "The Secrets of Dr. Germ: U.N. Inspectors Have Begun Searching Iraqi Weapons Sites. But What Happens When They Investigate the Scientists? The 'Human Factor' Could Be a Trigger to War," *Newsweek*, December 9, 2002, 2.

56. Ambassador Rolf Ekeus (former UNSCOM executive chairman), interview with author, Stockholm, August 24, 2005.

57. Barton, *The Weapons Detective*, 146–148. Also, UN Doc. S/1999/401, Annex, paras. 63–64.

58. Ekeus, interview; Spertzel, interview.

59. Ekeus, interview.

60. Ekeus, interview; Barton, interview; Spertzel, interview. Also, Barton, *The Weapons Detective*, 147–148; UNSCOM, *Background Paper for the Biological Seminar*, 4; UN Doc. S/1999/401, Annex, para. 64.

61. Barton, *The Weapons Detective*, 148.

62. Ekeus, interview.

63. Kraatz-Wadsack, interview; Spertzel, interview.

64. Spertzel, interview; Barton, interview; Kraatz-Wadsack, interview.

65. Kraatz-Wadsack, interview; Barton, interview; Spertzel, interview; Barton, *The Weapons Inspector*, 148.

66. Barton, interview; Kraatz-Wadsack, interview; Spertzel, interview. See also, Barton, *The Weapons Detective*, 150.

67. Ekeus, interview.

68. Lee Michael Katz and Judy Keen, "U.S. Fears Iraq Is Working on Biological Arms Again," *USA Today*, April 5, 1995, A1.

69. Former UNSCOM staff member, interview with author, September 2, 2005.

70. Kraatz-Wadsack, interview; former senior UNSCOM official, interview with author, August 30, 2005; Spertzel, interview; UNSCOM, *Background Paper for the Biological Seminar*, 1, 8–9.

71. Killip, interview.

72. Kraatz-Wadsack, interview.

73. Former senior UNSCOM official, interview with author, August 30, 2005; Kraatz-Wadsack, interview; Spertzel, interview.

74. UNSCOM, *Report Issued After Seminar of International Biological Weapons Experts* (New York: April 6–7, 1995), 3–4.

75. Ekeus, interview.

76. UN Doc. S/1999/401, Annex, para. 68.

77. Ibid., para. 60. Also, paras. 83–86.

78. Julia Preston, "Iraqi Accounting of Biological Arms Inadequate, U.N. Report Says," *Washington Post*, April 11, 1995, A14; Barbara Crossette, "Iraq Hides Biological Warfare Effort, Report Says," *New York Times*, April 12, 1995, A8; Ian Black, "Iraq Hides Stockpiles for Biological Arms; UN Envoy's Report Will Ask for Sanctions to Remain," *The Guardian*, April 10, 1995, 9; Barton, *The Weapons Detective*, 154.

79. William Safire, "Iraq's Ton of Germs," *New York Times*, April 13, 1995, A25.

80. Tom Aspell, "UN Monitoring of Plant in Iraq Shows Some Suspicious Activities," *NBC News*, April 4, 1995; Leon Barkho, "Iraq Shows Foreign Reporters Main

Biological Site," Reuters (Al Hakam, Iraq), April 22, 1995; "Iraqis Open Pesticide Factory Doors to Refute Germ War Claims," *Agence France Presse* (Baghdad), April 22, 1995; Robert Windrem, "The World's Deadliest Woman?" NBC News, September 23, 2004, http://www.msnbc.msn.com/id/3340765; Taylor, interview; Kraatz-Wadsack, interview.

81. Dilip Ganguly, "Iraqis Try to Build a Better Chicken at Former Weapons Plant," Associated Press, April 22, 1995.

82. Barkho, "Iraq Shows Foreign Reporters Main Biological Site."

83. Ganguly, "Iraqis Try to Build a Better Chicken at Former Weapons Plant."

84. Duelfer, interview; Spertzel, interview; Duelfer, *Hide and Seek*, 103–104. Also, UN Security Council, *Report of the Executive Chairman of the Special Commission Established by the Secretary-General Pursuant to Paragraph 9 (b) (i) of Security Council Resolution 687 (1991)*, Doc. S/1995/494, June 20, 1995, Annex, para. 5; Stephen Black, "The Death of UNSCOM: The CBW Colloquium," *ASA Newsletter*, no. 76 (January 2000).

85. Former senior UNSCOM official, interview with author, August 30, 2005; UN Doc. S/1995/494, Annex, paras. 6–7, 18.

86. Spertzel, interview; former senior UNSCOM official, interview with author, August 30, 2005; Kraatz-Wadsack, interview; Ake Sellstrom, PhD (former UNSCOM chief inspector), interview with author, Stockholm, August 24, 2005; UN Doc. S/1995/494, Annex, paras. 5–10.

87. "UN, Iraq at Odds on Weapons," *Boston Globe*, June 1, 1995, 21. Also, "Arms Issues Unresolved, U.N. Inspector Says," *Washington Post*, June 2, 1995, A27.

88. Spertzel, interview. Similarly, Kraatz-Wadsack, interview.

89. UN Doc. S/1995/494, Annex, para. 9.

90. Ibid., Annex, para. 17.

91. Khalil Matar, "Ekeus Sees No 'Total Guarantee' on Arms," interview with Rolf Ekeus (in New York, n.d.), *Al-Sharq Al-Awsat* (London), July 1, 1995 (translated by FBIS, Doc. FBIS-TAC-95-014-L, August 4, 1995, 72–74).

92. Ekeus, interview.

93. "Press Briefing by Rolf Ekeus, Executive Chairman of Commission Monitoring Iraqi Disarmament," Internal UN Document (New York, UN Secretariat, June 21, 1995), 3–4.

94. Ibid. Also, Matar, "Ekeus Sees No 'Total Guarantee' on Arms."

95. UN Doc. S/1995/864, Annex, para. 11.

96. Ibid., para. 71; Spertzel, interview with author, July 1, 2005; former senior UNSCOM official, interview with author; August 30, 2005; Kraatz-Wadsack, interview; Barton, *The Weapons Detective*, 156–157; Broad and Miller, "The Deal on Iraq: Secret Arsenal;" Milton Leitenberg, *Biological Weapons Arms Control*, PRAC Paper no. 16 (College Park, MD: Center for International and Security Studies at Maryland, May 1996), 25.

97. Ekeus, interview.

98. Spertzel, interview; Kraatz-Wadsack, interview; former senior UNSCOM official, interview with author, August 30, 2005. Also, Duelfer, *Hide and Seek*, 106; Barton, *The Weapons Detective*, 157.

99. Duelfer, interview.

100. Ekeus, interview; former senior UNSCOM official, interview with author, August 30, 2005.

101. Spertzel, interview; former senior UNSCOM official, interview with author, August 30, 2005. Also, Barton, *The Weapons Detective*, 158; UN Doc. S/1995/864, Annex, para. 71.

102. Republic of Iraq, Ministry of Defence, *Manual: Mobilization Use of Arms of Mass Destruction: Principles of Using Chemical and Biological Agents in Warfare*, vol. 2, part 1, first printing (Army General Staff, Training Department, Chemical Group Section, December 1987) (translated for the Armed Forces Medical Intelligence Center, Ft. Detrick, Maryland, Document AFMIC-HT-99-92). Also, Republic of Iraq, Ministry of Defence, *Manual: Meteorology*, vol. 10, section 1, first printing, *Behaviour of Chemical, Biological and Nuclear Agents in the Field* (Army General Staff, Training Department, Chemical Group Section, January 1988) (translated for the Armed Forces Medical Intelligence Center, Ft. Detrick, Maryland, Document AFMIC-HT-100-92).

103. UN Doc. S/1995/864, Annex, para. 11. Also, Black, "UNSCOM and the Iraqi Biological Weapons Program: Technical Success, Political Failure," 294.

104. R. Jeffrey Smith, "Iraq Had Program for Germ Warfare," *Washington Post*, July 6, 1995, A1; Stephen J. Hedges, Peter Cary, and Linda Fasulo, "Baghdad's Dirty Secrets," *U.S. News & World Report* 119, no. 10, September 11, 1995, 42.

105. Raghidah Dirgham, "Al-Sahhaf Says Iraq Destroyed Germ Program Because It Was Dangerous," *Al-Hayat* (London), July 7, 1995 (translated by FBIS, Doc. FBIS-TAC-95-014-L, August 4, 1995, 77–78).

106. Ambassador Madeleine K. Albright (U.S. Permanent Representative to the UN), Statement to the UN Security Council, Press Release (U.S. Department of State, July 5, 1995).

107. David A. Kay, "Denial and Deception Practices of WMD Proliferators: Iraq and Beyond," *Washington Quarterly* 17, no. 4 (Winter 1994): 96; Ibrahim al-Marashi, "How Iraq Conceals and Obtains Its Weapons of Mass Destruction," *Middle East Review of International Affairs* 7, no. 1 (March 2003): 53; Duelfer, *Hide and Seek*, 377. Also, p. 405.

Chapter 5

1. Richard Spertzel, PhD (former UNSCOM chief biological weapons inspector), interview with author, Washington, DC, July 1, 2005. See also United Nations (UN) Security Council, *Eighth Report of the Secretary-General on the Status of the Imple-*

mentation of the Special Commission's Plan for the Ongoing Monitoring and Verification of Iraq's Compliance with Relevant Parts of Section of Security Council Resolution 687 (1991), Doc. S/1995/864, October 11, 1995, Annex, para. 72–73.

2. Republic of Iraq, *Draft Full, Final and Complete Disclosure of Iraq's Past Biological Programme*, July 1995, 53–58.

3. Ibid., Section 5.6, 156–159.

4. Spertzel, interview. See also, UN Doc. S/1995/864, Annex, para. 72–73; Rod Barton, *The Weapons Detective: The Inside Story of Australia's Top Weapons Inspector* (Melbourne: Black Inc. Agenda, 2006), 159.

5. Rod Barton (former UNSCOM biological weapons inspector), telephone interview with author, May 20, 2005; Spertzel, interview; Barton, *The Weapons Detective*, 158–159.

6. Spertzel, interview.

7. "Notes of Nikita Smidovich on a Meeting Between Hussein Kamal and UNSCOM and IAEA," Note for the File, UNSCOM/IAEA Sensitive (Amman, Jordan, August 22, 1995), 2, available at: <http://www.unmovic.org>; William J. Broad and Judith Miller, "The Deal on Iraq: Secret Arsenal: The Hunt for the Germs of War," *New York Times*, February 26, 1998, A1; R. Jeffrey Smith, "Iraq Rushes to Preempt Defectors' Arms Disclosure," *Washington Post*, August 15, 1995, A13; UN Doc. S/1995/864, Annex, para. 12; "Iraq Threatens Halt in U.N. Cooperation," *Washington Times*, July 21, 1995, A23.

8. James Bruce, "Saddam Hopes BW Confession Is Enough to Convince USA," *Jane's Defence Weekly*, September 2, 1995, 27; UN Doc. S/1995/864, Annex, para. 13.

9. Spertzel, interview. Also, Bruce, "Saddam Hopes BW Confession Is Enough to Convince USA," 27; UN Doc. S/1995/864, Annex, para. 74; Charles Duelfer, *Hide and Seek: The Search for Truth in Iraq* (New York: Public Affairs, 2009), 106–107.

10. Leon Barkho, "Envoy Skeptical of Iraqi Report on Germ Weapons," *Washington Times*, August 7, 1995, A1; Bruce, "Saddam Hopes BW Confession Is Enough to Convince USA."

11. Republic of Iraq, *Full, Final and Complete Disclosure of Iraq's Past Biological Programme*, August 1995, section 1.2, p. 10. See also page 163 in Chapter VI and page 13 in section 1.2.

12. Nora Boustany, "Relatives, Top Aides of Saddam Defect to Jordan," *Washington Post*, August 11, 1995, A1; Broad and Miller, "The Deal on Iraq: Secret Arsenal;" Smith, "Iraq Rushes to Preempt Defectors' Arms Disclosure." Also, John Lancaster and David B. Ottaway, "Saddam Curbs Role of Kin in Iraq's Regime," *Washington Post*, October 22, 1995, A1; Central Intelligence Agency (CIA), "Regime Strategic Intent," in *Comprehensive Report of the Special Advisor to the DCI on Iraq's WMD* (Washington, DC, September 30, 2004): vol. 1, pp. 49–51.

13. Ibrahim al-Marashi, "How Iraq Conceals and Obtains Its Weapons of Mass Destruction," *Middle East Review of International Affairs* 7, no. 1 (March 2003): 57.

14. Quoted in Stephen J. Hedges, "Iraqi Arms Tests: Fears Strong, Proof Elusive," *The Gazette*, Montreal, January 31, 1999, A6.

15. Smith, "Iraq Rushes to Preempt Defectors' Arms Disclosure." Also, UN Security Council, *Fourth Report of the Executive Chairman of the Special Commission following the Adoption of Security Council Resolution 1051 (1996)*, Doc. S/1997/774, October 6, 1997, Annex, para. 107.

16. Daniel Williams, "U.S. Questions Top-Level Iraqis; Saddam Calls Defectors 'Judas,'" *Washington Post*, August 12, 1995, A15.

17. James Whittington, "Defections Good News and Bad News, Says Aziz," *Financial Times*, September 4, 1995, 3.

18. "Ekeus Sees No Lifting of Iraq Sanctions Soon," Reuters (Bonn) September 4, 1995. Also, Spertzel, interview; Smith, "Iraq Rushes to Preempt Defectors' Arms Disclosure"; UN Doc. S/1995/864, Annex, para. 9; Barbara Crossette, "Germ War Plan Underreporting, Iraq Tells U.N.," *New York Times*, August 23, 1995, A1; R. Jeffrey Smith, "Iraq Admits Working on Biological Weapons Systems," *Washington Post*, August 19, 1995, A17.

19. Williams, "U.S. Questions Top-Level Iraqis; Saddam Calls Defectors 'Judas;'" John Barry, "A Defector's Secrets," *Newsweek*, March 3, 2003, 2, 6.

20. Smith, "Iraq Rushes to Preempt Defectors' Arms Disclosure." Also, Crossette, "Germ War Plan Underreporting, Iraq Tells U.N."; Smith, "Iraq Admits Working on Biological Weapons Systems"; James Bruce, "Playing Hide and Seek with Saddam," *Jane's Defence Weekly*, January 3, 1996, 1; Catherine Toups, "Iraqis Fooled Weapons Monitors: Lack of Skepticism at IAEA Faulted," *Washington Times*, August 23, 1995, A1; Hedges, "Iraqi Arms Tests: Fears Strong, Proof Elusive."

21. John Barry, "Unearthing the Truth: How a team of Underdog Inspectors Finally Found Evidence of Iraq's Arsenal of Death," *Newsweek*, March 2, 1998, 40.

22. Barton Gellman, "Iraq's Arsenal Was Only on Paper; Since Gulf War Nonconventional Weapons Never Got Past the Planning Stage," *Washington Post*, January 7, 2004, A1.

23. Ambassador Rolf Ekeus (former UNSCOM executive chairman), interview with author, Stockholm, August 24, 2005. Also, Duelfer, *Hide and Seek*, 108.

24. UN Doc. S/1995/864, Annex, para. 14.

25. "U.N. Envoy Details Iraq's Admission of Germ Warfare," *Washington Times*, August 24, 1995, A1.

26. UN Doc. S/1995/864, Annex, para. 15; Duelfer, *Hide and Seek*, 108–109.

27. R. Jeffrey Smith, "U.N. Says Iraqis Prepared Germ Weapons in Gulf War," *Washington Post*, August 26, 1995, A1; "UN: What the New Iraqi Disclosures Reveal," Reuters (United Nations), August 26, 1995; "U.N. Envoy Details Iraq's Admission of Germ Warfare," *Washington Times*, August 24, 1995; Stephen J. Hedges, Peter Cary,

and Linda Fasulo, "Baghdad's Dirty Secrets," *U.S. News & World Report*, September 11, 1995, 41–42.

28. George Piro, interviewed by Scott Pelley, "Iraq War: Saddam's View," *60 Minutes*, CBS News Division, March 18, 2008.

29. Spertzel, interview; Smith, "Iraq Admits Working on Biological Weapons Systems"; "U.N. Envoy Details Iraq's Admission of Germ Warfare," *Washington Times*; Smith, "U.N. Says Iraqis Prepared Germ Weapons in Gulf War"; Barton, *The Weapons Detective*, 158–161.

30. Spertzel, interview.

31. Ibid.; Smith, "Iraq Admits Working on Biological Weapons Systems"; "U.N. Envoy Details Iraq's Admission of Germ Warfare"; Smith, "U.N. Says Iraqis Prepared Germ Weapons in Gulf War"; Barton, *The Weapons Detective*, 158–161.

32. Ekeus, interview.

33. Hedges, Cary, and Fasulo, "Baghdad's Dirty Secrets."

34. Duelfer, *Hide and Seek*, 108.

35. UN Doc. S/1995/864, Annex, Part III and IV.

36. Ekeus, interview.

37. Barton, interview; Spertzel, interview.

38. Crossette, "Germ War Plan Underreporting, Iraq Tells U.N." Also, former UNSCOM chief inspector, interview with author, London, August 18, 2005.

39. Spertzel, interview. Also, Smith, "U.N. Says Iraqis Prepared Germ Weapons in Gulf War"; "UN: What the New Iraqi Disclosures Reveal"; "U.N. Envoy Details Iraq's Admission of Germ Warfare"; Hedges, Cary, and Fasulo, "Baghdad's Dirty Secrets."

40. Hedges, Cary, and Fasulo, "Baghdad's Dirty Secrets."

41. Barton, *The Weapons Detective*, 160.

42. Ekeus, interview.

43. Ibid. Also, Spertzel, interview; Barton, *The Weapons Detective*, 161.

44. Ekeus, interview; Barton, interview; Spertzel, interview; "U.N. Envoy Details Iraq's Admission of Germ Warfare"; CIA, "Regime Strategic Intent," 55–56.

45. Rolf Ekeus, interviewed by Robert MacNeil and Jim Lehrer, *The MacNeil/Lehrer NewsHour*, PBS TV, August 28, 1995. Also, Duelfer, *Hide and Seek*, 106–107, 110.

46. Barton, interview; Spertzel, interview; Gabriele Kraatz-Wadsack, DVM (former UNSCOM chief biological weapons inspector), interview with author, Berlin, August 15, 2005; former UNSCOM chief chemical weapons inspector, interview with author, New York City, January 31, 2006; UN Doc. S/1995/864, Annex, para. 24.

47. Rasheed quoted in *ad-Dustour* (Jordan), as cited in "Iraqi Official Comments on Pending Ekeus Meeting with Defector," Reuters (Amman, Jordan), August 22, 1995. Also, Crossette, "Germ War Plan Underreporting, Iraq Tells U.N."

48. "U.N. Envoy Details Iraq's Admission of Germ Warfare."

49. Rolf Ekeus, *MacNeil/Lehrer NewsHour*, August 28, 1995. Also, Barton Gellman, "A Futile Game of Hide and Seek," *Washington Post*, October 11, 1998. A1; UN Security Council, *Report of the Secretary-General on the Activities of the Special Commission Established by the Secretary-General Pursuant to Paragraph 9 (b) (i) of Resolution 687 (1991)*, Doc. S/1997/301, April 11, 1997, para. 52; Duelfer, *Hide and Seek*, 109–110.

50. Al-Marashi, "How Iraq Conceals and Obtains Its Weapons of Mass Destruction," 14, 19; William J. Broad and Judith Miller, "The World; Germs, Atoms and Poison Gas: The Iraqi Shell Game," *New York Times*, December 20, 1998, section 4, p. 5. Also, UN Doc. S/1995/864, Annex, paras. 25, 27; Duelfer, *Hide and Seek*, 112.

51. Former UNSCOM chief chemical weapons inspector, interview with author, January 31, 2006.

52. UN Doc. S/1995/864, Annex, para. 26.

53. Spertzel, interview; Barton, interview.

54. "U.N. Says Iraqi Data Advances End to Oil Sanctions," Reuters (Amman, Jordan), August 23, 1995; "UN Gets More Iraq Information," Associated Press (Amman, Jordan), August 24, 1995; UN Doc. S/1995/864, Annex, para. 75.

55. Rolf Ekeus, *MacNeil/Lehrer NewsHour*, August 28, 1995.

56. Ekeus, interview.

57. Former senior UNSCOM official, interview with author, New York City, August 30, 2005. Also, "Smidovich Notes on Kamal Meeting," August 22, 1995, 1.

58. "Smidovich Notes on Kamal Meeting," August 22, 1995, 14. Also "Interview Transcript: Addendum to Transcript of Correspondent Brent Sadler's Exclusive Interview with Hussein Kamel," CNN, September 21, 1995, http://www.cnn.com/WORLD/9509/iraq_defector/kamel_transcript/index.html.

59. "Smidovich Notes on Kamal Meeting," quote from pages 7–8. Also, pages 11, 13; and "Interview Transcript with Hussein Kamel"; Al-Marashi, "How Iraq Conceals and Obtains Its Weapons of Mass Destruction," 56.

60. "Smidovich Notes on Kamal Meeting," 6, 9, 14. Also, "Interview Transcript with Hussein Kamel."

61. Former UNSCOM staff member, interview with author, New York City, September 1, 2005; Ekeus, interview with author, August 24, 2005. Also, Dean Fischer, "Inside Saddam's Brutal Regime," *Time*, September 18, 1995, http://www.time.com/time/magazine/article/0,9171,983427,00.html?promoid=cnn1.

62. John Lancaster, "Iraqi Opposition Tells of Wider Bloodshed After Defectors' Return," *Washington Post*, March 1, 1996, A24.

63. "U.N. Says Iraqi Data Advances End to Oil Sanctions;" "UN Gets More Iraq Information." Also, UN Doc. S/1995/864, Annex, para. 18.

64. Ron Manley, PhD (former UNSCOM chief chemical weapons inspector), interview with author, London, August 19, 2005.

65. Spertzel, interview. Also, UN Doc. S/1995/864, Annex, para. 75.

66. Barton, *The Weapons Detective*, 162.

67. Spertzel, interview; Kraatz-Wadsack, interview.

68. CIA, "Regime Strategic Intent," 54.

69. Spertzel, interview.

70. Kraatz-Wadsack, interview; Debra Krikorian, PhD (former UNSCOM biological weapons inspector), interview with author, Washington, DC, June 21, 2005.

71. Hamish Killip (former UNSCOM chief biological weapons inspector), interview with author, Isle of Man, August 22, 2005; Barton, interview; Spertzel, interview; Kraatz-Wadsack, interview; former senior UNSCOM official, interview with author, New York City, September 1, 2005. Also, UN Security Council, *Annex: Twenty-Second Quarterly Report on the Activities of the United Nations Monitoring, Verification and Inspection Commission in Accordance with Paragraph 12 of Security Council Resolution 1284 (1999)*, Doc. S/2005/545, August 30, 2005, 8, para. 11.

72. UN Special Commission, *Final Report: UNSCOM 139/BW33*, Chief Inspector Richard Spertzel (New York, n.d.), 6–7. Also, Barton, interview; Spertzel, interview; Killip, interview; Kraatz-Wadsack, interview; former senior UNSCOM official, interview with author, September 1, 2005.

73. Kraatz-Wadsack, interview; Killip, interview.

74. UN Doc. S/1995/864, Annex, para. 75, (j)(u)(v)(w), 78; Killip, interview; Tom Mangold and Jeff Goldberg, *Plague Wars* (New York: St. Martin's Press, 1999), 311.

75. Barton, *The Weapons Detective*, 170.

76. R. Jeffrey Smith, "Iraq's Drive for a Biological Arsenal," *Washington Post*, November 21, 1997, A1.

77. Spertzel, interview; Kraatz-Wadsack, interview; Barton, *The Weapons Detective*, 173.

78. UN Doc. S/1995/864, Annex, para. 28.

79. Robin Wright, "Iraqis Admit to Broad, Virulent Germ War Plan," *Los Angeles Times*, September 6, 1995, A1.

80. Spertzel, interview; David Kelly, PhD (former UNSCOM chief biological weapons inspector), interview with author, Washington, DC, December 17, 2002; Killip, interview; Manley, interview; Kraatz-Wadsack, interview; Krikorian, interview. Also, UN Doc. S/1995/864, Annex, para. 75 (a) to (t).

81. UN Doc. S/1995/864, Annex, para. 75 (y), (z). Also, Barton, *The Weapons Detective*, 169–170, 173.

82. UN Doc. S/1995/864, Annex, para. 79–80.

83. Thomas Wagner, "Iraq Condemns U.N. Weapons Inspector," Associated Press, Baghdad, October 12, 1995.

84. UN Security Council, *Second Report of the Executive Chairman of the Special Commission Following the Adoption of Security Council Resolution 1051 (1996)*, Doc.

S/1996/848, October 11, 1996, Annex, para. 84; Evelyn Leopold, "U.N. Council Maintains Sanctions Against Iraq," Reuters (United Nations), November 8, 1995.

85. UN Security Council, *Tenth Report of the Executive Chairman of the Special Commission Established by the Secretary-General Pursuant to Paragraph 9 (b) (i) of Security Council Resolution 687 (1991), and Paragraph 3 of Resolution 699 (1991) on the Activities of the Special Commission*, Doc. S/1995/1038, December 17, 1995, Annex, paras. 10, 61–65, 67.

86. "Officials Confirm Seizure of Gyroscopes," *Jordanian Times*, December 9, 1995, 1, 7 (translated in FBIS-TAC-95-007, December 27, 1995, 49).

87. Patrick Worsnip, "U.N. Official Sees New Tensions with Iraq," Reuters, Washington, DC, November 16, 1995.

88. Robert McMahon, "UN: Inspectors Will Press Iraqi Government On Interviews Of Experts," *Radio Free Europe/Radio Liberty*, broadcast on January 10, 2003.

89. Barry, "A Defector's Secrets."

90. "Chasing Saddam's Weapons", *Panorama*, BBC One, broadcast on February 9, 2003.

91. CIA, *Iraqi Weapons of Mass Destruction Programs* (Washington, DC, February 13, 1998), 4–5.

92. Philip Towle, *Enforced Disarmament: From the Napoleonic Campaigns to the Gulf* (Oxford: New Oxford University Press, 1997), 196.

93. Hedges, "Iraqi Arms Tests: Fears Strong, Proof Elusive." Also, Ken Alibek with Stephen Handelman, *Biohazard* (New York: Random House, 1999), 277–278.

94. "President Bush Outlines Iraqi Threat: Remarks by the President on Iraq," speech at Cincinnati Museum Center, Cincinnati, Ohio (Washington, DC, White House, Office of the Press Secretary, October 7, 2002).

95. "Prime Minister Statement on Iraq," briefing by Tony Blair at the House of Commons (London, Office of the Prime Minister, February 25, 2003).

96. Ekeus, interview; former senior UNSCOM official, interview with author, August 30, 2005; Charles Duelfer (former UNSCOM deputy executive chairman), interview with author, Washington, DC, November 15, 2007; Spertzel, interview. Also, Stephen Black, "UNSCOM and the Iraqi Biological Weapons Program: Technical Success, Political Failure," in *Biological Warfare and Disarmament: New Problems, New Perspectives*, ed. Susan Wright (New York: Rowman & Littlefield, 2002), 294; Gabriele Kraatz-Wadsack, "The Role of Scientists in Verification," in *Assessing the Threat of Weapons of Mass Destruction: The Role of Independent Scientists*, vol. 61, ed. J. L. Finney and I. Slaus, NATO Science for Peace and Security Series E: Human and Societal Dynamics (Amsterdam: IOS Press, 2010), 50.

97. Barry, "The Defector's Secrets."

98. *Letter from the Executive Chairman of the Special Commission Established by the Secretary-General Pursuant to Paragraph 9 (b) (i) of Security Council Resolution 687*

(1991) Addressed to the President of the Security Council (dated January 25, 1999), Doc. S/1999/94, January 29, 1999, Annex, para. 12.

99. Barton, interview.

100. Khidhir Hamza with Jeff Stein, *Saddam's Bombmaker: The Terrifying Inside Story of the Iraqi Nuclear and Biological Weapons Agenda* (New York: Scribner, 2000), 245.

101. Manley, interview.

102. Ekeus, interview.

103. Hamza with Stein, *Saddam's Bombmaker*, 245, 266–267. Also, Duelfer, *Hide and Seek*, 115.

104. Ekeus, interview; former UNSCOM chief chemical weapons inspector, interview with author, January 31, 2006; Barton, interview; former senior UNSCOM official, interview with author, August 30, 2005; Spertzel, interview.

105. Spertzel, interview. Similarly, former UNSCOM staff member, interview with author, New York City, September 2, 2005.

106. Barton, interview. Also on this point, former UNSCOM staff member, interview with author, September 2, 2005; former senior UNSCOM official, interview with author, August 30, 2005. Also, Daniel Williams, "Iraqi Defectors Killed on Return to Baghdad: Relatives Reportedly Shot Brothers," *Washington Post*, February 24, 1996, A1; John Barry and Gregory L. Vistica, "The Hunt for His Secret Weapons," *Newsweek*, December 1, 1997, 32.

107. Barry and Vistica, "The Hunt for His Secret Weapons."

108. Hedges, "Iraqi Arms Tests: Fears Strong, Proof Elusive." Also, Ruth Wedgwood, "Truth Sleuth in Iraq," *Washington Post*, June 19, 1996, A19.

109. Manley, interview; former UNSCOM chief inspector, interview with author, August 18, 2005.

110. CIA, *Iraqi Weapons of Mass Destruction Programs*, 4. Also, UN Doc. S/1997/301, para. 51.

111. Barton, interview. Also, former UNSCOM chief chemical weapons inspector, interview with author, January 31, 2006.

112. Spertzel, interview.

113. Ibid.; Barton, interview; Kraatz-Wadsack, interview; former senior UNSCOM official, interview with author, August 30, 2005.

114. Former senior UNSCOM official, interview with author, August 30, 2005.

115. Kraatz-Wadsack, interview.

116. Spertzel, interview; Barton, interview; Kraatz-Wadsack, interview.

117. UNSCOM Final Report: UNSCOM 139/BW 33, 31.

118. Kraatz-Wadsack, interview; Killip, interview; former senior UNSCOM official, interview with author, August 30, 2005. See also Barton, *The Weapons Detective*, 161.

119. Bruce Auster, Stephen J. Hedges, Linda Fasulo, "In Iraq, Hints of Biological Atrocities," *U.S. News & World Report*, January 26, 1998, 46.

120. Killip, interview; former UNSCOM chief chemical weapons inspector, interview with author, January 31, 2006; Kraatz-Wadsack, interview. Also, Alan George, "Iraq Used Animals to Test Germ Arsenal," *Washington Times*, September 27, 1995, A16.

121. Killip, interview. Also, Manley, interview; Krikorian, interview; Kraatz-Wadsack, interview.

122. Ekeus, interview.

123. Killip, interview; Manley, interview; Krikorian, interview; former UNSCOM chief inspector, interview with author, August 18, 2005.

124. Krikorian, interview.

125. Killip, interview; Krikorian, interview.

126. Barton, interview. Similarly, Spertzel, interview.

127. UN Doc. S/1999/94, Annex III, para. 7.

128. Killip, interview; Spertzel, interview; Kelly, interview; former UNSCOM chief chemical weapons inspector, interview with author, January 31, 2006.

129. Former UNSCOM chief inspector, interview with author, August 18, 2005; Ekeus, interview; Mamoun Fandy, "A Ruse by Saddam?" *Boston Globe*, August 26, 1995, 11.

130. Ekeus, interview. Also, Broad and Miller, "The Deal on Iraq: Secret Arsenal."

131. Ekeus, interview. Also, Spertzel, interview; foreign ministry official, interview with author, London, August 17, 2005. See Williams, "Iraqi Defectors Killed on Return to Baghdad."

132. Ekeus, interview. Also, former UNSCOM chief inspector, interview with author, August 18, 2005.

133. Former senior UNSCOM official, interview with author, August 30, 2005. Also, Duelfer, *Hide and Seek*, 115.

134. Ekeus, interview. Also, "Smidovich Notes on Kamal Meeting," August 22, 1995, p. 14.

135. Rolf Ekeus, "Defection and Detection," *New Perspective Quarterly* 20, no. 1 (Winter 2003): 58. Concurring, Barton, interview.

Chapter 6

1. Gabriele Kraatz-Wadsack, DVM (former UNSCOM chief biological weapons inspector), interview with author, Berlin, August 15, 2005; Debra Krikorian, PhD (former UNSCOM biological weapons inspector), interview with author, Washington, DC, June 21, 2005.

2. Krikorian, interview.

3. UNSCOM, *Draft Inspection Report: UNSCOM 145/BW35*, Chief Inspector David C. Kelly (New York, n.d.), 2, 24. Also, United Nations (UN) Security Council,

Report of the Secretary-General on the Activities of the Special Commission Established by the Secretary-General Pursuant to Paragraph 9 (b) (i) of Resolution 687 (1991), Doc. S/1996/258, April 11, 1996, para. 77; Kraatz-Wadsack, interview.

4. Kraatz-Wadsack, interview; David Kelly, PhD (former UNSCOM chief biological weapons inspector), interview with author, Washington, DC, December 17, 2002; Richard Spertzel, PhD (former UNSCOM chief biological weapons inspector), interview with author, Washington, DC, July 1, 2005; Krikorian, interview.

5. Terence Taylor (former CBW commissioner and UNSCOM chief inspector), interview with author, Washington, DC, May 12, 2005. Kraatz-Wadsack, interview.

6. Taylor, interview; Kraatz-Wadsack, interview.

7. Kraatz-Wadsack, interview; Kelly, interview; Spertzel, interview.

8. Taylor, interview; Krikorian, interview; Kraatz-Wadsack, interview. Also, UN Security Council, *Report of the Secretary-General on the Activities of the Special Commission Established by the Secretary-General Pursuant to Paragraph 9 (b) (i) of Resolution 687 (1991)*, Doc. S/1996/848, October 11, 1996, Annex, para. 15; Waiel Faleh, "Iraq Fells Plant for Germ Warfare," *Washington Times*, June 10, 1996, A13; Jon Leyne, "UN Destroys Iraqi Germ War Plant," *The Observer*, June 9, 1996, A1; Gabriele Kraatz-Wadsack, "The Role of Scientists in Verification," in *Assessing the Threat of Weapons of Mass Destruction: The Role of Independent Scientists*, vol. 61, ed. J. L. Finney and I. Slaus, NATO Science for Peace and Security Series E: Human and Societal Dynamics (Amsterdam: IOS Press, 2010), 51.

9. UN Security Council, *Report of the Secretary-General on the Activities of the Special Commission Established by the Secretary-General Pursuant to Paragraph 9 (b) (i) of Resolution 687 (1991)*, Doc. S/1995/864, October 11, 1995, paras. 64–67; Kraatz-Wadsack, "The Role of Scientists in Verification," 47–49.

10. Kraatz-Wadsack, interview; Krikorian, interview; UN Security Council, *Report of the Secretary-General on the Activities of the Special Commission Established by the Secretary-General Pursuant to Paragraph 9 (b) (i) of Resolution 687 (1991)*, Doc. S/1997/301, April 11, 1997, sect. 2 (B), para. 27.

11. On the perception that the biological monitors were not contributing significantly to UNSCOM's efforts to unravel Iraq's past and perhaps ongoing bioweapons activities, Stephen Black (former UNSCOM historian), interview with author, Washington, DC, November 16, 2007; Krikorian, interview; Kraatz-Wadsack, interview; former senior UNSCOM official, interview with author, August 30, 2005.

12. Krikorian, interview; Hamish Killip (former UNSCOM chief biological weapons inspector), interview with author, Isle of Man, August 22, 2005; Kraatz-Wadsack, interview. Also, Stephen Black, "UNSCOM and the Iraqi Biological Weapons Program: Technical Success, Political Failure," in *Biological Warfare and Disarmament: New Problems, New Perspectives*, ed. Susan Wright (New York: Rowman & Littlefield, 2002), 290–291.

13. Kraatz-Wadsack, "The Role of Scientists in Verification," 47–49.

14. Ibid.

15. Kelly, interview; Spertzel, interview; Kraatz-Wadsack, interview.

16. Krikorian, interview; Kraatz-Wadsack, interview; UN Security Council, *Report of the Secretary-General on the Activities of the Special Commission Established by the Secretary-General Pursuant to Paragraph 9 (b) (i) of Resolution 687 (1991)*, Doc. S/1999/401, April 9, 1999, para. 49.

17. Gordon K. Vachon, "Verifying the Biological Weapons Convention: The Role of Inspections and Visits" and Ali A. Mohammadi, "Verifying the Biological Weapons Convention: The Role of Visits and Inspections," in *Enhancing the Biological Weapons Convention*, ed. Oliver Thranert (Bonn: Dietz Nachfolger, 1996), 147–157; Jez Littlewood, *The Biological Weapons Convention: A Revolution Failed* (Aldershot, U.K.: Ashgate Publishing, 2005). The draft protocol can be found at <http://www.opbw.org>.

18. UNSCOM, *Draft Inspection Report: UNSCOM 145/BW35*, 1.

19. UNSCOM, *Report of UNSCOM 142/BW34: April 30–May 7, 1996*, Chief Inspector Hamish Killip (New York, n.d.), 1; UNSCOM, *Draft Inspection Report: UNSCOM 145/BW35*, 8–9.

20. William J. Broad and Judith Miller, "How Iraq's Biological Weapons Program Came to Light," *New York Times*, February 26, 1998, A1.

21. UNSCOM, *Report of UNSCOM 142/BW34*: paras. 13–14, 17, 20, 25, 42.

22. "Biological Terrorism," *Background Briefing*, ABC Radio National, August 29, 1999, http://www.abc.net.au/rn/talks/bbing/stories/s48674.htm.

23. Spertzel, interview with author, July 1, 2005.

24. UNSCOM, *Report of UNSCOM 142/BW34*: Annex D, Report from Subteam D.

25. Ibid., paras. 34, 36, 51–52.

26. UNSCOM, *Draft Inspection Report: UNSCOM 145/BW35*, 6–7.

27. Ibid., 12–13, L-8.

28. Ibid., K-5.

29. Ibid., 7, L-7.

30. Ibid., 13, K-9 to K-11.

31. Killip, interview.

32. UNSCOM, *Draft Inspection Report: UNSCOM 145/BW35*, 4–5, 7.

33. Spertzel, interview.

34. UNSCOM, *Draft Inspection Report: UNSCOM 145/BW35*, 4.

35. Cdr. James Burans, "Update on Sampling and Analysis of Samples Collected at Al Hakam and the Hoof and Mouth Vaccine Facility: 'Saddam, Are You Sure You Cleaned That Equipment?'" briefing slides (Washington, DC, Naval Medical Research Institute, n.d.); UNSCOM, *Draft Inspection Report: UNSCOM 145/BW35*, 4, 17–20, 24–25, 27. Also, Spertzel, interview.

36. Kraatz-Wadsack, interview.

37. UNSCOM, *Draft Inspection Report: UNSCOM 145/BW35*, 4.

38. National Monitoring Directorate, Republic of Iraq, *Full, Final and Complete Disclosure of Iraq's Past Biological Programme*, May 1996, Chapter VII, para. 7.1.1, page 187; UNSCOM, *Draft Inspection Report: UNSCOM 145/BW35*, K-9.

39. National Monitoring Directorate, Republic of Iraq, *Full, Final and Complete Disclosure of Iraq's Past Biological Programme*, para. 1.4.2.3, page 16; Chapter VII, para. 7.1.1, page 188–189.

40. UNSCOM, *Final Report: UNSCOM 139/BW33*, Chief Inspector Richard Spertzel, 30–31; Rod Barton (former UNSCOM biological weapons inspector), interview with author via telephone, May 20, 2005.

41. Robert Kadlec, MD (former UNSCOM biological weapons inspector), interview with author, Washington, DC, February 23, 2006. Also, Kelly, interview; Spertzel, interview; Killip, interview.

42. Murtada and Sinan were also senior military officers.

43. Spertzel, interview.

44. UN Doc. S/1997/301, Appendix I, Section I, para. 1.

45. Barbara Crossette, "Years After War, Iraq Is Probably Still Hiding Arms, U.N. Says," *New York Times*, June 13, 1996, A11. See also Barbara Crossette, "Iraq Isn't Doing So Well at Hide and Seek," *New York Times*, June 16, 1996, section 4, p. 3; Adnan Malik, "Iraq Gives U.N. Inspector Banned-Weapons Records," *Washington Post*, June 23, 1996, A27.

46. UN Doc. S/1996/848, para. 85, 88, 91.

47. UN Security Council, *Letter Dated 25 January 1999 from the Executive Chairman of the Special Commission Established by the Secretary-General Pursuant to Paragraph 9 (b) (i) of Security Council Resolution 687 (1991) Addressed to the President of the Security Council*, Doc. S/1999/94, January 29, 1999, Appendix III, para. 188.

48. Ibid., Annex, paras. 86–87.

49. Spertzel, interview; Killip, interview; Kelly, interview; former UNSCOM biological weapons inspector, interview with author, Washington, DC, February 4, 2005; former UNSCOM inspector and chief of product development in an offensive biological weapons program, interview with author, Washington, DC, February 21, 2006; Taylor, interview; Kraatz-Wadsack, interview.

50. Former UNSCOM inspector and chief of product development in an offensive biological weapons program, interview with author, February 21, 2006.

51. Spertzel, interview; Killip, interview. Also, UN Doc. S/1999/94, Appendix III, para. 40; UN Doc. S/1997/301, Appendix I, Section I, para. 3.

52. Former UNSCOM inspector and chief of product development in an offensive biological weapons program, interview with author, February 21, 2006; Kraatz-Wadsack, interview; former UNSCOM biological weapons inspector, interview with author, February 4, 2006; Kelly, interview; Spertzel, interview.

53. UNSCOM, *Final Report: UNSCOM 139/BW33*, 16. UN Security Council, *Report of the Secretary-General on the Activities of the Special Commission Established by the Secretary-General Pursuant to Paragraph 9 (b) (i) of Resolution 687 (1991)*, Doc. S/1996/259, April 11, 1996, paras. 72–4.

54. UNSCOM, *Final Report: UNSCOM 139/BW33*, 8.

55. Ibid., 10–11.

56. Ibid., 14.

57. Ibid., 12–13.

58. Ibid., 13–14.

59. As discussed in Chapters 3 and 4, analysis of the samples taken from the spray drier on the biopesticide line showed the particle size of ten microns or less, a size appropriate for dried biowarfare agents.

60. UNSCOM, *Final Report: UNSCOM 139/BW33*, 19.

61. Ibid., 11.

62. Ibid., 21–24. Also, Kraatz-Wadsack, "The Role of Scientists in Verification," 52.

63. UNSCOM, *Final Report: UNSCOM 139/BW33*, 24–25.

64. Ibid., 25. Also, "Report: Disarmament," Enclosure 1 attached to UN Doc. S/1999/94, Appendix III, para. 75.

65. UNSCOM, *Final Report: UNSCOM 139/BW33*, 25–28.

66. UN Doc. S/1996/259, paras. 75–76. Also, UN Doc. S/1996/848, para. 86.

67. Spertzel, interview.

68. Burans, "Update on Sampling and Analysis of Samples Collected at Al Hakam and the Hoof and Mouth Vaccine Facility," briefing slides; UNSCOM *Draft Inspection Report: UNSCOM 145/BW35*, 4, 17–20. Also, Kraatz-Wadsack, interview.

69. Burans, "Update on Sampling and Analysis of Samples Collected at Al Hakam and the Hoof and Mouth Vaccine Facility," briefing slides; UNSCOM, *Draft Inspection Report: UNSCOM 145/BW 35*, 21–23.

70. Spertzel, interview; Kadlec, interview; Kelly, interview; Kraatz-Wadsack, interview; Burans, "Update on Sampling and Analysis of Samples Collected at Al Hakam and the Hoof and Mouth Vaccine Facility," briefing slides; UN Doc. S/1999/94, Appendix III, para. 73.

71. Spertzel, interview; Kraatz-Wadsack, interview.

72. Spertzel, interview; Killip, interview; Kelly, interview; former UNSCOM biological weapons inspector, interview with author, Washington, DC, February 4, 2006; former UNSCOM inspector and chief of product development in an offensive biological weapons program, interview with author, Washington, DC, February 21, 2006; former UNSCOM biological weapons inspector, interview with author, Washington, DC, February 4, 2005; Taylor, interview; Kraatz-Wadsack, interview. Also, UN Security Council, "The Destruction, Removal or Rendering Harmless of Proscribed Items and Mate-

rials in Connection with Iraq's Biological Weapons Program Since 1991," in *Fifteenth Quarterly Report on the Activities of the United Nations Monitoring, Verification and Inspection Commission Submitted in Accordance with Paragraph 12 of Security Council Resolution 1284 (1999)*, Doc. S/2003/1135, November 26, 2003, Appendix I, para. 14, p. 11.

73. Spertzel, interview; former UNSCOM biological weapons inspector, interview with author, February 4, 2006.

74. UN Doc. S/1999/94, Appendix III, para. 74.

75. Kraatz-Wadsack, interview; Barton, interview.

76. William Lebherz (former UNSCOM industrial biotechnology expert), interview with author, Washington, DC, February 13, 2006; Spertzel, interview.

77. Spertzel, interview. Also, Robert Windrem, "The World's Deadliest Woman?" NBC News, September 23, 2004, http://www.msnbc.msn.com/id/3340765.

78. Spertzel, interview; Lebherz, interview; UN Doc. S/1997/301, Appendix I, Section I, para. 4.

79. Spertzel, interview. Also, UN Doc. S/1997/301, Appendix I, Section I, para. 6.

80. Kelly, interview; Kraatz-Wadsack, interview; Spertzel, interview; Barton, interview.

81. Kraatz-Wadsack, interview; Spertzel, interview.

82. Lebherz, interview. Kadlec, interview.

83. Kraatz-Wadsack, interview. Also, *U.S. Policy in Iraq: Next Steps, Hearing Before the Senate Committee on Governmental Affairs, Subcommittee on International Security, Proliferation, and Federal Services*, U.S. Senate (March 1, 2002) (testimony of Richard O. Spertzel).

84. Spertzel, interview. See also, *U.S. Policy in Iraq*, testimony of Richard O. Spertzel.

85. Kraatz-Wadsack, "The Role of Scientists in Verification," 53.

86. Spertzel, interview.

87. Killip, interview; UN Doc. S/1999/94, Appendix III, para. 47.

88. Ronald Manley, PhD (former UNSCOM chief chemical weapons inspector), interview.

89. Spertzel, interview.

90. UN Doc. S/1999/94, Appendix III, para. 40; UN Doc. S/1997/301, Appendix I, Section I, para. 2; UN Security Council, *Report of the Secretary-General on the Activities of the Special Commission Established by the Secretary-General Pursuant to Paragraph 9 (b) (i) of Resolution 687 (1991)*, Doc. S/1997/774, October 6, 1997, Annex, para. 77.

91. In addition to the other missions described, Killip headed the UNSCOM 187/BW50 team from May 16–20, 1997, and the UNSCOM 197/BW54 mission from August 20–26, 1997.

92. National Monitoring Directorate, Republic of Iraq, *Full, Final and Complete Disclosure of Iraq's Past Biological Programme*, para. 6.2, pages 165–170, 174.

93. Killip, interview; Kelly, interview; Kraatz-Wadsack, interview.

94. Killip, interview; Spertzel, interview. Also, National Monitoring Directorate, Republic of Iraq, *Full, Final and Complete Disclosure of Iraq's Past Biological Programme*, paras. 2.5, 6.6, 6.7, pages 41, 179–181, 183–184; UN Doc. S/1999/94, Appendix III, para. 32, 34; UN Doc. S/1997/774, Annex, para. 78–79.

95. UN Doc. S/1999/94, Appendix III, para. 202.

96. Spertzel, interview.

97. Ibid.; UN Doc. S/1997/774, Annex, para. 82.

98. Spertzel, interview.

99. John Barry, "Unearthing the Truth: How a Team of Underdog Inspectors Finally Found Evidence of Iraq's Arsenal of Death," *Newsweek*, March 2, 1998, 40.

100. UN Doc. S/1999/94, Appendix I, para. 27; Appendix III, para. 34.

101. Killip, interview. Also, Spertzel, interview; National Monitoring Directorate, Republic of Iraq, *Full, Final and Complete Disclosure of Iraq's Past Biological Programme*, para. 2.5, 6.6.1, 6.7, pp. 41, 180–183; Rod Barton, *The Weapons Detective: The Inside Story of Australia's Top Weapons Inspector* (Melbourne: Black Inc. Agenda, 2006), 82, 88–89, 171.

102. Spertzel, interview. UN Doc. S/1999/94, Appendix III, paras. 41–42, 47, 182, 202.

103. Killip, interview; Spertzel, interview; Kraatz-Wadsack, interview; Tom Mangold and Jeff Goldberg, *Plague Wars* (New York: St. Martin's Press, 1999), 310–311; UN Doc. S/1997/774, para. 81; UN Security Council, "Past Storage, Handling, and Deployment of Chemical and Biological Munitions by Iraq," in *Eighteenth Quarterly Report on the Activities of the United Nations Monitoring Verification and Inspection Commission Submitted in Accordance with Paragraph 12 of Security Council Resolution 1284 (1999)*, Doc. S/2004/693, August 27, 2004, Appendix I, para. 21, p. 11.

104. Spertzel, interview; Kraatz-Wadsack, interview; UN Doc. S/1999/94, Appendix III, para. 42, 47; UN Doc. S/1997/774, Annex, para. 81.

105. Killip, interview; Barton, interview.

106. Barton, interview; Kelly, interview; Killip, interview; Manley, interview; UN Doc. S/1999/94, Appendix III, paras. 47, 202.

107. Kelly, interview.

108. Spertzel, interview; UN Doc. S/1999/94, Appendix III, para. 47.

109. Killip, interview.

110. National Monitoring Directorate, Republic of Iraq, *Full, Final and Complete Disclosure of Iraq's Past Biological Programme*, Chapter VI, paras. 6.2.5, 6.2.8.4, 6.4.2, pp. 172, 174, 176; Chapter VII, para. 6.2.5, p. 172.

111. Kraatz-Wadsack, interview.

112. National Monitoring Directorate, Republic of Iraq, *Full, Final and Complete Disclosure of Iraq's Past Biological Programme*, Chapter VII, para. 6.2.5, 6.4.2.1, 6.2.2.4, pp. 167, 172, 177. Also, "Annual Confidential Report for 1990," marked "Top Secret" and "Personal," to the Minister of MIMI, from Ahmed Murtada Ahmed, Acting Director General (Iraq: Technical Research Centre, Al Hakam Division, January 15, 1991), 2, 6–9.

113. Kelly, interview.

114. National Monitoring Directorate, Republic of Iraq, *Full, Final and Complete Disclosure of Iraq's Past Biological Programme*, Chapter VI, para. 6.2.5, p. 172.

115. Spertzel, interview; Kelly, interview; Killip, interview. Also, National Monitoring Directorate, Republic of Iraq, *Full, Final and Complete Disclosure of Iraq's Past Biological Programme*, para. 6.2.4.4, p. 171; UN Doc. S/1999/94, para. 47.

116. National Monitoring Directorate, Republic of Iraq, *Full, Final and Complete Disclosure of Iraq's Past Biological Programme*, Chapter VI, para. 6.4.2.3, p. 178.

117. Kelly, interview; Spertzel, interview.

118. National Monitoring Directorate, Republic of Iraq, *Full, Final and Complete Disclosure of Iraq's Past Biological Programme*, Chapter VI, para. 6.2.5, p. 172, para. 6.4.2.1, p. 177.

119. UN Doc. S/1999/94, para. 34. Also, National Monitoring Directorate, Republic of Iraq, *Full, Final and Complete Disclosure of Iraq's Past Biological Programme*, Chapter VII, para. 6.2.5, p. 172.

120. Killip, interview; Barton, interview. Also, UN Doc. S/1999/94, para. 34, Appendix III, para. 47.

121. Spertzel, interview. UN Doc. S/1999/94, para. 34, Appendix II, para. 11.

122. Spertzel, interview. Also, Amb. Richard Butler, Presentation to the UN Security Council, June 3, 1998, http://www.fas.org/news/un/iraq/s/980603-unscom.htm, Section IV, Biological Weapons Related Issues; UN Doc. S/1997/774, Annex, para. 78–79, 81.

123. Kraatz-Wadsack, interview; Killip, interview.

124. UN Doc. S/1999/94, Appendix III, paras. 38, 47.

125. Spertzel, interview; Killip, interview; Kraatz-Wadsack, interview. Also, UN Doc. S/1999/94, Appendix III, paras. 34, 205; UN Security Council, *United Nations Monitoring, Verification and Inspection Commission, Summary of the Compendium of Iraq's Proscribed Weapons Programmes in the Chemical, Biological, and Missile Areas*, Doc. S/2006/420, June 21, 2006, para. 249, p. 64; Appendix I: "Past Storage, Handling, and Deployment of Chemical and Biological Munitions by Iraq," in UN Doc. S/2004/693, August 27, 2004, para. 20, p. 10.

126. Kraatz-Wadsack, interview; Spertzel, interview; former senior UNSCOM official, interview with author, August 30, 2005. Also, UN Doc. S/1999/94, Appendix III, paras. 35, 47, 205–206.

127. Spertzel, interview; Killip, interview; Kraatz-Wadsack, interview; former senior UNSCOM official, interview with author, August 30, 2005.

128. Former UNSCOM staff member, interview with author, New York City, September 2, 2005.

Chapter 7

1. Gabriele Kraatz-Wadsack, "The Role of Scientists in Verification," in *Assessing the Threat of Weapons of Mass Destruction: The Role of Independent Scientists*, vol. 61, ed. J. L. Finney and I. Slaus, NATO Science for Peace and Security Series E: Human and Societal Dynamics (Amsterdam: IOS Press, 2010), 53.

2. Terence Taylor (former UNSCOM CBW commissioner and chief inspector), interview with author, Washington, DC, May 12, 2005; Gabriele Kraatz-Wadsack, DVM (former UNSCOM chief biological weapons inspector), interview with author, Berlin, August 15, 2005.

3. Ibid.

4. Stephen Black (UNSCOM historian), interview with author, Washington, DC, November 16, 2007; Hamish Killip (former UNSCOM chief biological weapons inspector), interview with author, Isle of Man, August 22, 2005; Debra Krikorian, PhD (former UNSCOM inspector), interview with author, Washington, DC, June 21, 2005; Richard Spertzel, PhD (former UNSCOM chief biological weapons inspector), interview with author, Washington, DC, July 1, 2005; Kraatz-Wadsack, interview.

5. Taylor, interview.

6. Ibid. Also, Kraatz-Wadsack, interview; former senior UNSCOM official, interview with author, New York City, August 30, 2005.

7. Kraatz-Wadsack, interview. Also, Edith Lederer, "Team Uncovered Iraq Biological Weapon Plan, U.N. Says," Associated Press, April 24, 1997; United Nations (UN) Security Council, *Letter Dated 25 January 1999 from the Executive Chairman of the Special Commission Established by the Secretary-General Pursuant to Paragraph 9 (b) (i) of Security Council Resolution 687 (1991) Addressed to the President of the Security Council*, Doc. S/1999/94, January 29, 1999, Appendix III, para. 83; Central Intelligence Agency (CIA), *Iraqi Weapons of Mass Destruction Programs* (Washington, DC, February 13, 1998), 4–5.

8. Spertzel, interview.

9. Killip, interview; Kraatz-Wadsack, interview; Spertzel, interview.

10. David Franz, DVM, PhD (former UNSCOM chief biological weapons inspector), interview with author, Washington, DC, June 29, 2005; former UNSCOM inspector and chief of product development in an offensive biological weapons program, interview with author, Washington, DC, February 21, 2006; Spertzel, interview.

11. Kraatz-Wadsack, interview.; Also, UNSCOM, *UNSCOM 78/BW5, Draft Inspection Report* (New York, n.d.), 3.

12. Robert Kadlec, MD (former UNSCOM biological weapons inspector), interview with author, Washington, DC, February 23, 2006.

13. David Kelly, PhD (former UNSCOM chief biological weapons inspector), interview with author, Washington, DC, December 17, 2002.

14. Spertzel, interview.

15. William J. Broad and Judith Miller, "Government Report Says 3 Nations Hide Stocks of Smallpox," *New York Times*, June 13, 1999, A1. Also, Mike Wallace, "Smallpox: Years After Eradicating the Virus Among the General Population, Some Countries May Be Using the Smallpox Virus as a Biological Weapon," *60 Minutes*, CBS News, October 1, 2000; Kadlec, interview with author, February 23, 2006; Ken Alibek with Stephen Handleman, *Biohazard* (New York: Random House, 1992), 270–279.

16. Kelly, interview. Also, Kadlec, interview.

17. Kelly, interview; Spertzel, interview; Broad and Miller, "Government Report Says 3 Nations Hide Stocks of Smallpox."

18. Spertzel, interview; Kelly, interview; Kadlec, interview; CIA, "Biological Warfare" in *Comprehensive Report of the Special Advisor to the DCI on Iraq's WMD* (Washington, DC, September 30, 2004), vol. 3, pp. 25–28.

19. Kadlec, interview.

20. Ambassador Rolf Ekeus (former UNSCOM executive chairman), interview with author, Stockholm, August 24, 2005. Also, Article 2, paragraph 1, Charter of the United Nations, http://www.un.org/aboutun/charter/; Richard Butler, *The Greatest Threat: Iraq, Weapons of Mass Destruction, and the Crisis of Global Security* (New York: PublicAffairs, 2001); Charles Duelfer, *Hide and Seek: The Search for Truth in Iraq* (New York: Public Affairs, 2009), 164.

21. Stephen Black, "UNSCOM and the Iraqi Biological Weapons Program: Technical Success, Political Failure," in *Biological Warfare and Disarmament: New Problems, New Perspectives*, ed. Susan Wright (New York: Rowman & Littlefield, 2002), 305. Also, Duelfer, *Hide and Seek*, 129, 377–379; Philip Towle, *Enforced Disarmament: From the Napoleonic Campaigns to the Gulf* (Oxford: New Oxford University Press, 1997), 197–199.

22. Secretary of State Madeleine Albright, Remarks at Georgetown University, Washington, DC, March 26, 1997.

23. Ekeus, interview.

24. Black, "UNSCOM and the Iraqi Biological Weapons Program: Technical Success, Political Failure," 306.

25. Barbara Crossette, "Iraqis Still Defying Arms Ban, Departing U.N. Official Saying," *New York Times*, June 25, 1997, A1.

26. Barton Gellman, "A Futile Game of Hide and Seek: Ritter, UNSCOM Foiled by Saddam's Concealment Strategy," *Washington Post*, October 11, 1998, A1. Also, Spertzel, interview; Ekeus, interview.

27. Evelyn Leopold, "New UN Arms Chief Worried About Iraq's Germ Weapons," Reuters, July 1, 1997. Also, UN Security Council, *Report of the Secretary-General on the Activities of the Special Commission Established by the Secretary-General Pursuant to Paragraph 9 (b) (i) of Resolution 687 (1991)*, Doc. S/1997/774, October 6, 1997, para. 11.

28. Graham S. Pearson, *The UNSCOM Saga: Chemical and Biological Weapons Non-Proliferation* (New York: St. Martin's Press, 1999), 156–167.

29. Kraatz-Wadsack, interview. Also, Tom Mangold and Jeff Goldberg, *Plague Wars* (New York: St. Martin's Press, 1999), 297–299; Butler, *The Greatest Threat*, 163–164, 196; Duelfer, *Hide and Seek*, 152–153; UN Doc. S/1999/94, Annex D, para. 30; CIA, "Regime Strategic Intent," in *Comprehensive Report of the Special Advisor to the DCI on Iraq's WMD*, vol. 1, 60–61.

30. Spertzel, interview; former UNSCOM chief inspector, interview with author, New York City, January 31, 2006. Also, Butler, *The Greatest Threat*, 164–165.

31. UN Security Council, *Report of the Secretary-General on the Activities of the Special Commission Established by the Secretary-General Pursuant to Paragraph 9 (b) (i) of Resolution 687 (1991)*, Doc. S/1998/920, October 6, 1998, paras. 9, 11.

32. Spertzel, interview; Killip, interview.

33. Kraatz-Wadsack, interview; Spertzel, interview.

34. Kraatz-Wadsack, interview; Also, Gellman, "A Futile Game of Hide and Seek;" UN Doc. S/1999/94, Annex D, para. 27.

35. Kraatz-Wadsack, interview; Spertzel, interview. Also, UN Security Council, *Report of the Secretary-General on the Activities of the Special Commission Established by the Secretary-General Pursuant to Paragraph 9 (b) (i) of Resolution 687 (1991)*, Doc. S/1998/332, April 16, 1998, para. 67; R. Jeffrey Smith, "Did Russia Sell Iraq Germ Warfare Equipment? Document Seized by UN Inspectors Indicates Illicit Deal," *Washington Post*, February 12, 1998, A1; Alibek with Handelman, *Biohazard*, 275.

36. Spertzel, interview. Also, Kadlec, interview; Duelfer, *Hide and Seek*, 158.

37. Smith, "Did Russia Sell Iraq Germ Warfare Equipment?"; Knight-Ridder Financial, "Russia to Build Iraqi Energy Plants When Sanctions Lifted," *Journal of Commerce Newspaper*, June 7, 1995, B6. See also Duelfer, *Hide and Seek*, 105.

38. Former UNSCOM staff member, interview with author, New York City, September 2, 2005. Likewise, Kadlec, interview.

39. Spertzel, interview; Rod Barton (former UNSCOM biological weapons inspector), interview with author via telephone, May 20, 2005; Kraatz-Wadsack, interview; former UNSCOM staff member, interview with author, New York City, September 2, 2005.

40. International Covenant on Civil and Political Rights, Human Rights Committee, "Bosnia and Herzegovina Report" (UN, October 30, 1992); Ann Devroy, "Bosnia Croats, Muslims Agree to Confederate; Serb Stance Awaited," *Washington Post*, March 19, 1994, A17; John Pomfret, "NATO Jets Bomb Serb Airfield; Action Was Warning Against Repeated Cross-Border Attacks," *Washington Post*, November 22,

1994, A1; Elaine Sciolino, "Balkan Accord: The Overview; Accord Reached to End the War in Bosnia; Clinton Pledges U.S. Troops to Keep Peace," *New York Times*, November 22, 1995, A1; "Research Shows Estimates of Bosnian War Death Toll Were Inflated," Associated Press, June 21, 2007.

41. GlobalSecurity.org, "Rwanda Civil War," http://www.globalsecurity.org/military/world/war/rwanda.htm;UN,"Rwanda—UNAvMIRBackground,"http://www.un.org/Depts/dpko/dpko/co_mission/unamirFT.htm#HISTORICAL; Helen Vesperini, "No Consensus on Genocide Death Toll," April 6, 2004, http://iafrica.com/news/worldnews/314365.htm.

42. Spertzel, interview.

43. UN Doc. S/1997/774, para. 71–72, 75, 83, 78–79, 125. Also, Barbara Crossette, "New U.N. Monitor Reports Iraq Is Still Hiding Data on Weapons," *New York Times*, October 8, 1997, A7; Erik J. Leklem, "Iraqi BW Program May Be Key to Standoff with UN," *Arms Control Today* 27, no. 3 (October 7, 1997): 25.

44. UN Security Council, Resolution 1134 (1997), Doc. S/RES/1134, October 23, 1997; former UNSCOM staff member, interview with author, New York City, September 2, 2005; Barbara Crossette, "U.S. Fails to Get U.N. Backing to Widen Sanctions on Iraq," *New York Times*, October 23, 1997, A5; Rod Barton, *The Weapons Detective: The Inside Story of Australia's Top Weapons Inspector* (Melbourne: Black Inc. Agenda, 2006), 179–180; Duelfer, *Hide and Seek*, footnote 1, p. 485.

45. John M. Goshko, "Iraq Expels 6 American Inspectors; U.N. Orders Team to Leave Baghdad as Stakes Escalate in Standoff," *Washington Post*, November 14, 1997, A1; "Iraq: Road to the Current Crisis," *Washington Post*, February 15, 1998, A34; Duelfer, *Hide and Seek*, 139.

46. Kraatz-Wadsack, interview; Spertzel, interview.

47. UN Security Council, *Letter Dated 22 November 1998 from the Executive Chairman of the Special Commission Established by the Secretary-General Pursuant to Paragraph 9 (b) (i) of Security Council Resolution 687 (1991) Addressed to the President of the Security Council*, Doc. S/1998/922, November 24, 1997, Annex, paras. 20, 2. Also, "Russians Break Iraqi Deadlock," Reuters, November 21, 1997; "Iraq: Road to the Current Crisis," *Washington Post*, February 15, 1998, A34; Towle, *Enforced Disarmament*, 191–196.

48. Barbara Crossette and Tim Weiner, "U.N. Experts Face Daunting Task: Picking Up the Trail of Illicit Iraqi Arms," *New York Times*, November 21, 1997, A17.

49. "Saddam Set to Open Palaces for Arms Hunt," *Courier Mail*, November 28, 1997, 19; "Iraq: Road to the Current Crisis," *Washington Post*, February 15, 1998, A34.

50. John Barry and Gregory L. Vistica, "The Hunt for His Secret Weapons," *Newsweek*, December 1, 1997, 32.

51. "U.N. Aide Hopeful on Arms Talks with Iraq," *Washington Post*, December 15, 1997, A25; R. Jeffrey Smith, "Iraq Seeks to Rein in Inspectors," *Washington Post*, December 18, 1997, A1.

52. Former UNSCOM chief inspector, interview with author, New York City, January 31, 2006. Also, Marie Colvin and Uzi Mahnaimi, "Saddam Tested Anthrax on Human Guinea Pigs: Iraq Tested Anthrax on POWs," *Sunday Times* (London), January 18, 1998, 12.

53. Killip, interview.

54. Bruce Auster, Stephen J. Hedges, Linda Fasulo, "In Iraq, Hints of Biological Atrocities," *U.S. News & World Report*, January 26, 1998, 46; William J. Broad and Judith Miller, "The World; Germs, Atoms and Poison Gas: The Iraqi Shell Game," *New York Times*, December 20, 1998, section 4, p. 5.

55. Kraatz-Wadsack, interview. Also, Butler, *The Greatest Threat*, 120–125; Barbara Slavin, "Council Calls Iraqi Action 'Unacceptable,'" *USA Today*, January 15, 1998; Auster, Hedges, and Fasulo, "In Iraq, Hints of Biological Atrocities"; Stephen J. Hedges, "UN Seeks Proof of Iraqi Tests on Humans," *Chicago Tribune*, January 30, 1999, A6; Stephen J. Hedges, "Iraqi Arms Tests: Fears Strong, Proof Elusive," *The Gazette* (Montreal), January 31, 1999, A9; Mangold and Goldberg, *Plague Wars*, 299–300. Duelfer, *Hide and Seek*, 415–416; CIA, "Biological Warfare," 3.

56. James Bennet, "Clinton Describes Goals for a Strike on Iraqi Arsenals," *New York Times*, February 18, 1998, A1; John M. Goshko, "3 on Security Council Oppose 'Automatic Trigger' on Iraq," *Washington Post*, February 28, 1998, A20; Barton Gellman, Dana Priest, and Bradley Graham, "Diplomacy and Doubts on the Road to War," *Washington Post*, March 1, 1998, A1.

57. Julian Beltrame, "Annan Says He Trusts Saddam," *The Gazette* (Montreal), February 25, 1998, A1. Also, Duelfer, *Hide and Seek*, 141–142.

58. UN Security Council, Memorandum of Understanding Between the United Nations and Iraq, in *Letter Dated 25 February 1998 from the Secretary-General Addressed to the President of the Security Council*, Doc. S/1998/166, February 27, 1998.

59. UN Security Council, Annex, Procedures under Paragraph 4 (b) of the Memorandum of Understanding Between the United Nations and the Republic of Iraq of February 23, 1998, in *Letter Dated 9 March 1998 from the Secretary-General Addressed to the President of the Security Council*, Doc. S/1998/208, March 9, 1998, para. 11 (b).

60. Ekeus, interview.

61. Vijay Joshi, "U.N. Search of 8 Iraqi Palace Sites Turns Up Mostly Unfurnished Rooms," *Washington Times*, April 4, 1998, A6; "U.N. Teams Find Nothing at Iraqi Sites," *New York Times*, April 4, 1998, A4; UN Security Council, *Letter Dated 15 April 1998 from the Secretary-General Addressed to the President of the Security Council*, Doc. S/1998/326, April 15, 1998; Ekeus, interview; Duelfer, *Hide and Seek*, 145–151.

62. UN Doc. S/1998/332, para. 130. Also, para. 128; Barbara Crossette, "U.S. Report Sees No Iraqi Progress on Weapons Issue," *New York Times*, April 17, 1998, A1.

63. UN Doc. S/1998/332, para. 131. Also, para. 17.

64. UN Security Council, *Report of the Secretary-General on the Activities of the Special Commission Established by the Secretary-General Pursuant to Paragraph 9 (b) (i) of Resolution 687 (1991)*, Doc. S/1997/301, April 11, 1997, Appendix I, Section I, para. 7. Also, Tim Trevan, *Saddam's Secrets: The Hunt for Saddam's Hidden Weapons* (London: HarperCollins, 1999), 17; Spertzel, interview; Ekeus, interview.

65. UN Doc. S/1997/774, Annex II, para. 4. Also, paras. 2–3, 5 (a-k), 6; Leklem, "Iraqi BW Program May Be Key to Standoff with UN," 25.

66. Ake Sellstrom, PhD (former UNSCOM chief inspector), interview with author, Stockholm, August 24, 2005; Kraatz-Wadsack, interview; former senior UNSCOM official, interview with author, August 30, 2005.

67. Spertzel, interview. Also, UN Security Council, *Letter Dated 17 December 1997 From the Executive Chairman of the Special Commission Established by the Secretary-General Pursuant to Paragraph 9 (b)(i) of Security Council Resolution 687 (1991) Addressed to the President of the Security Council*, Doc. S/1997/987, December 17, 1997, para. 38.

68. Former UNSCOM chief chemical weapons inspector, January 31, 2006. Also, "Dispute Surrounds French Tests of Iraqi Warheads for Nerve Gas," *Washington Post*, October 8, 1998, A26; Jim Hoagland and Vernon Loeb, "Tests Show Nerve Gas in Iraqi Warheads," *Washington Post*, June 23, 1998, A1; Christopher S. Wren, "Lab Reports of Iraq Poison Bolster Case for Sanctions," *New York Times*, June 24, 1998, A7; Lee Michael Katz, "U.S. Vows to Keep Pressure on Iraq After Nerve Gas Report," *USA Today*, June 24, 1998, 11A; John M. Goshko, "Iraqi Nerve Gas Tests Confirmed," *Washington Post*, June 25, 1998, A30; Barbara Crossette, "New Tests Dispute U.S. Finding of Iraq Nerve Gas," *New York Times*, September 18, 1998, A8; Barbara Crossette, "France Detects Iraqi Nerve Gas, Experts Assert," *New York Times*, October 7, 1998, A1.

69. Former senior UNSCOM official, interview with author, August 30, 2005. Also, UN Security Council, *Letter Dated 19 February 1998 from the Executive Chairman of the Special Commission Established by the Secretary-General Pursuant to Paragraph 9 (b)(i) of Security Council Resolution 687 (1991)*, Doc. S/1998/176, February 27, 1998, Enclosures I and II.

70. Sellstrom, interview; Killip, interview; Kraatz-Wadsack, interview. Also, UN Security Council, *Letter Dated 8 April 1998 from the Executive Chairman of the Special Commission Established by the Secretary-General Pursuant to Paragraph 9(b)(i) of Security Council Resolution 687 (1991)*, Doc. S/1998/308, April 8, 1998, Annex: Report of the United Nations Special Commission's Team to the Technical Evaluation Meeting on the Proscribed Biological Warfare Programme, para. 2.

71. Sellstrom, interview; Killip, interview; Spertzel, interview.

72. Spertzel, interview; former UNSCOM chief biological weapons inspector, interview with author, Washington, DC, August 28, 2005.

73. Killip, interview.

74. UN Doc. S/1999/94, Appendix III, paras. 47, 50, 55–56.

75. Barton, interview; Spertzel, interview. Also, UN Doc. S/1999/94, Appendix III, para. 57–59; Mangold and Goldberg, *Plague Wars*, 312.

76. Sellstrom, interview.

77. Krikorian, interview. Also, Mangold and Goldberg, *Plague Wars*, 309.

78. Spertzel, interview; former UNSCOM chief biological weapons inspector, interview with author, August 28, 2005.

79. Kelly, interview.

80. Sellstrom, interview.

81. UN Doc. S/1998/308, Annex, paras. 4.1.1, 5.1, 5.2.

82. Ibid., para. 3.5. See also, para. 4.6.1.

83. Ibid., paras. 4.4.2, 4.6.4, 4.5.6, 4.7.3, 4.7.4, 4.8.2, 4.8.3. Also, Black, "UNSCOM and the Iraqi Biological Weapons Program: Technical Success, Political Failure," 297–298.

84. UN Doc. S/1998/308, Annex, para. 4.10.1.

85. Emphasis added. Ibid., paras. 5.3, 4.1.1.

86. Sellstrom, interview; Kraatz-Wadsack, interview.

87. Kraatz-Wadsack, interview; foreign ministry official, interview with author, London, August 17, 2005.

88. Ekeus, interview. Also, Barbara Crossette, "Experts Dispute Iraq's Claim It Ended Germ Warfare Effort," *New York Times*, April 10, 1998, A8; John M. Goshko, "Iraq Continued to Hide Arms Data, Experts Say," *Washington Post*, April 10, 1998, A20.

89. UN Doc. S/1998/332, para. 86. Also, paras. 64, 68–75.

90. Barbara Crossette, "Iraq Again Threatens to Halt Arms Inspections," *New York Times*, April 24, 1998, A3.

91. Amb. Richard Butler, Presentation to the UN Security Council (New York, UNSCOM, June 3, 1998), Section IV, Biological Weapons Related Issues.

92. Former UNSCOM staff member, interview with author, September 2, 2005.

93. Barton, *The Weapons Detective*, 181. Also, Butler, *The Greatest Threat*, 76–79.

94. UN Doc. S/1999/94, Appendix III, paras. 24–25.

95. Sellstrom, interview.

96. Spertzel, interview.

97. Sellstrom, interview. Also, Spertzel, interview.

98. Spertzel, interview. Also, UN Doc. S/1998/920, paras. 8, 34–35; UN Doc. S/1999/94, Appendix III, para. 25.

99. Barbara Crossette, "Russia Fails to Free Iraq from Intrusive Inspections," *New York Times*, July 30, 1998, A7.

100. Barton, *The Weapons Detective*, 182. Also, Butler, *The Greatest Threat*, 81–82; CIA, "Regime Strategic Intent," 61–62.

101. David Usborne, "Annan Seeks UN 'Rethink' on Iraq," *The Independent*, August 7, 1998, 13; Laura Silber, "Annan Suggests Surprise New Line on Iraq," *Financial Times*, August 8, 1998, 3.

102. "UN Officials at Odds Over Baghdad," Associated Press, August 7, 1998; Silber, "Annan Suggests Surprise New Line on Iraq."

103. Judith Miller, "American Inspector on Iraq Quits, Accusing U.N. and U.S. of Cave-In," *New York Times*, August 27, 1998, A1; Barton Gellman, "Inspector Quits UN Team; Says Council Bowing to Defiant Iraq," *Washington Post*, August 27, 1998, A1; Thomas W. Lippman, "Albright Defends Handling of Iraq," *Washington Post*, September 10, 1998, A2. Also, Barton Gellman, "Arms Inspectors 'Shake the Tree': UNSCOM Adds Covert Tactic," *Washington Post*, October 12, 1998, A1; UN Security Council, *Report of the Secretary-General on the Activities of the Special Commission Established by the Secretary-General Pursuant to Paragraph 9 (b) (i) of Resolution 687 (1991)*, Doc. S/1999/401, April 9, 1999, para. 5; UN Security Council, Resolution 1194 (1998), Doc. S/Res/1194, September 9, 1998, para. 3.

104. Barbara Crossette, "No Yielding to Inspectors by Baghdad," *New York Times*, October 3, 1998, A4. Also, Duelfer, *Hide and Seek*, 167, 117–135, and footnote 3, p. 492.

105. "Bitter Ritter Denies Spy Charge," *Courier Mail*, August 28, 1998, 12. Also, former UNSCOM chief biological weapons inspector, interview with author, August 28, 2005; Killip, interview; Mangold and Goldberg, *Plague Wars*, 316.

106. Duelfer, *Hide and Seek*, 155.

107. UN Doc. S/1998/920, paras. 67–72.

108. UN Doc. S/1999/94, Appendix III, para. 194.

109. UN Security Council Resolution 1194 (1998), Doc. S/RES/1194.

110. John M. Goshko, "Annan Says Iraq Will Never Be Fully Disarmed," *Washington Post*, October 17, 1998, A13. Also, UN Security Council, *Letter Dated 14 November 1998 from the Secretary-General Addressed to the President of the Security Council*, Doc. S/1998/1077, November 15, 1998.

111. Barbara Crossette, "Security Council Outlines New Strategy on Iraq Arms," *New York Times*, October 31, 1998, A7; UN Security Council, *Letter Dated 31 October 1998 from the Deputy Executive Chairman of the Special Commission Established by the Secretary-General Pursuant to Paragraph 9 (b)(i) of Security Council Resolution 687 (1991), Addressed to the President of the Security Council*, Doc. S/1998/1023, October 31, 1998.

112. John Lancaster, "Iraq to Oust American Inspectors," *Washington Post*, October 30, 1997, A1; John M. Goshko and Howard Schneider, "Iraq Halts All Work by U.N. Inspectors; Security Council Demands Reversal," *Washington Post*, November 1, 1998, A1; John M. Goshko and Thomas W. Lippman, "Iraq Blocks U.S. Arms Inspectors," *Washington Post*, November 3, 1997, A1. Also, UN Security Council, Resolution 1205 (1998), Doc. S/RES/1205, November 5, 1998; UN Doc. S/1999/401, paras. 3, 33.

113. This letter can be found at <http://www.meij.or.jp/text/Gulf%20War/1998111401 .htm>.

114. UN Security Council, *Letter Dated 20 November 1998 from the Executive Chairman of the Special Commission Established by the Secretary-General Pursuant to Paragraph 9 (b) (i) of Security Council Resolution 687 (1991) Addressed to the President of the Security Council*, Doc. S/1998/1106, November 20, 1998, Annex II.

115. Barton Gellman, "U.N. Team Downcast About Iraq Mission," *Washington Post*, November 22, 1998, A1.

116. John M. Goshko, "U.N. Panel on Iraq Supports Sanctions: Russian Bid to Ease Penalties Rejected," *Washington Post*, November 23, 1997, A1; Black, "UNSCOM and the Iraqi Biological Weapons Program: Technical Success, Political Failure," 298–302.

117. Spertzel, interview; Kelly, interview; Barton, interview; Kraatz-Wadsack, interview; UN Doc. S/1999/401, para. 34–36. Also, UN Security Council, *Letter Dated 15 December 1998 from the Executive Chairman of the Special Commission Established by the Secretary-General Pursuant to Paragraph 9 (b) (i) of Security Council Resolution 687 (1991) Addressed to the President of the Security Council*, Doc. S/1998/1172, December 15, 1998.

118. Kraatz-Wadsack, interview; Spertzel, interview. Also, UN Doc. S/1999/401, para. 34–36.

119. Barton, interview. Also, Spertzel, interview; Kraatz-Wadsack, interview. See also Barton, *The Weapons Detective*, 183–184.

120. UN Doc. S/1998/1172.

121. Taieb Mohjoub, "UN Quits as Iraq Blocks Access," *The Daily Telegraph* (Sydney), December 17, 1998, 32.

122. Colin Brown, "Attacks Legal and Justified, Says Blair," *The Independent*, December 17, 1998, 1; Francis X. Clines and Steven Lee Myers, "Attack on Iraq: The Overview; Impeachment Vote Delayed as Clinton Launches Iraq Air Strike, Citing Military Need to Move Swiftly," *New York Times*, December 17, 1998, A1; Timothy J. Burger and Kevin McCoy, "Clinton Foes Suspect a Stall," *New York Daily News*, December 17, 1998, 2; Bob Deans, "The Iraq Crisis: U.S. Begins Iraq Attacks; Impeachment Put on Hold; Destroying Saddam's Weaponry," *Atlanta Journal and Constitution*, December 17, 1998, A1.

123. Eugene Robinson, "U.S. Halts Attacks on Iraq After Four Days," *Washington Post*, December 20, 1998, A1; William M. Arkin, "Desert Fox Delivery; Precision Undermined Its Purpose," *Washington Post*, January 17, 1999, B1.

124. Ekeus, interview. Also, Tim Weiner, "U.S. Aides Say U.N. Team Helped to Install Spy Device in Iraq," *New York Times*, January 8, 1999, A1.

125. Philip Shenon, "C.I.A. Was with U.N. in Iraq for Years, Ex-Inspector Says," *New York Times*, February 23, 1999, A1; Amin Saikal, "The Coercive Disarmament of Iraq," in Wright, *Biological Warfare and Disarmament*, 265–283.

126. Thomas W. Lippman and Barton Gellman, "U.S. Says It Collected Iraq Intelligence via UNSCOM," *Washington Post*, January 8, 1999, A1; Barton Gellman, "U.S. Spied on Iraqi Military via U.N.: Arms Control Team Had No Knowledge of Eavesdropping," *Washington Post*, March 2, 1999, A1.

127. Philip Shenon, "Former U.N. Arms Inspector Is Criticized by State Dept.," *New York Times*, February 24, 1999, A6. Also, John M. Goshko, "U.N. Inspector Again Denies Spying Charge," *Washington Post*, January 9, 1999, A14; Tim Weiner, "U.S. Spied on Iraq Under U.N. Cover, Officials Now Say," *New York Times*, January 7, 1999, A1; John M. Goshko, "Chief U.N. Arms Inspector Sees Trouble in Spy Charge: Butler Says He Did Not Know of Espionage," *Washington Post*, March 4, 1999, A2.

128. Barton Gellman, "Annan Suspicious Of UNSCOM Role: Inspectors Possibly Tied to Eavesdropping," *Washington Post*, January 6, 1999, A1.

129. UN Doc. S/1999/94, Appendix III, paras. 7, 12.

130. Ibid., Appendix III, paras. 67–68, 78, 88.

131. Ibid., Appendix III, paras. 196–202.

132. Ibid., Appendix III, para. 173. Also, paras. 12, 43, 190–195, 199.

133. Barbara Crossette, "Iraq Still Tries to Hide Arms Programs, Report Says," *New York Times*, January 27, 1999, A8. Also, "U.N. Report: 'Confusion Reigns' on Details," *New York Times*, January 27, 1999, A9.

134. Hedges, "Iraqi Arms Tests: Fears Strong, Proof Elusive." Also, Duelfer, *Hide and Seek*, 137–161; 171–180.

135. Barton Gellman, "UNSCOM Losing Role in Iraqi Arms Drama: Bickering Security Council Seeks Alternatives," *Washington Post*, January 28, 1999, A19. Also, "UNSCOM Says Iraq Submitted New Data on Germs Warfare," Reuters, April 10, 1999.

136. UN Security Council, *Note by the President of the Security Council*, Doc. S/1999/100, January 30, 1999, para. 4.

137. Barbara Slavin, "U.N. Inspectors Lose Sight of Iraqi 'Duel-Use' Goods," *USA Today*, March 8, 1999, 10. Also, Judith Miller, "Besieged U.N. Commission Chief Will Not Seek Another Term," *New York Times*, February 5, 1999, A3.

138. UN Security Council, *Report of the First Panel Established Pursuant to the Note by the President of the Security Council on 30 January 1999 (S/1999/100) Concerning Disarmament and Current and Future Ongoing Monitoring and Verification Issues*, Doc. S/1999/356, March 30, 1999, Annex I, para. 24.

139. Ibid., paras. 41, 66. Also, para. 42.

140. Ibid., para. 67. Also, paras. 48–52. Black, "UNSCOM and the Iraqi Biological Weapons Program: Technical Success, Political Failure," 289. Also, Judith Miller, "U.N. Panel Urges New Inspections in Iraq," *New York Times*, March 28, 1999, A24.

141. Leon Barkho, "Iraq Rejects U.N. Monitoring Plan," *Washington Post*, April 15, 2000.

142. "U.N. Resolution on New Monitors in Iraq," *New York Times*, December 18, 1999, A8.

143. Lloyd Axworthy, "Iraq Impasse Over New Appointment Must End," *Toronto Star*, January 20, 2000, A30; Roula Khalaf, "Russia Rejects Annan Choice for Iraq Arms Inspectorate," *Financial Times*, January 18, 2000, 17.

144. Colum Lynch, "UNSCOM's Acting Director to Step Down," *Washington Post*, February 26, 2000, A17; Barbara Crossette, "Security Council Approves New Arms Inspection Agency for Iraq," *New York Times*, April 14, 2000, A12; David Kay, "With More at Stake, Less Will Be Verified," *Washington Post*, November 17, 2002, B1; James Drummond, "Iraq Set to Receive Arms Inspectors," *Financial Times*, November 18, 2002, 9; Helena Smith and Brian Whitaker, "Four Years On, UN Team Back in Iraq," *The Guardian*, November 26, 2002, A1.

145. Edith Lederer, "Butler Blames Death of UNSCOM on Russia, China and France," Associated Press, August 3, 1999. Also, Black, "UNSCOM and the Iraqi Biological Weapons Program: Technical Success, Political Failure," 286.

Chapter 8

1. The author is indebted to Dr. Joseph Barbera of George Washington University for raising the distinction between lessons learned and lessons experienced when explaining why emergency personnel repeatedly identify problems with communications, equipment, and training after disaster responses.

2. Tom Wolfe's book *The Right Stuff* (New York: Farrar, Straus & Giroux, 1979) and the subsequent movie made this phrase synonymous with finding the right person for a tough job.

3. Former UNSCOM chief inspector, PhD, interview with author, London, August 18, 2005. Seconding this view, foreign ministry official, interview with author, London, August 17, 2005, Ron Manley, PhD (former UNSCOM chief chemical weapons inspector), interview with author, London, August 19, 2005; Terence Taylor (former UNSCOM CBW commissioner and chief inspector), interview with author, Washington, DC, May 12, 2005; David Kelly, PhD (former UNSCOM chief biological weapons inspector), interview with author, Washington, DC, December 17, 2002; former UNSCOM staff member, interview with author, New York City, September 2, 2005; former senior UNSCOM official, interview with author, New York City, August 30, 2005.

4. Hamish Killip (former UNSCOM chief biological weapons inspector), interview with author, Isle of Man, August 22, 2005. Also, Rod Barton, PhD (former UNSCOM biological inspector), interview with author via telephone, May 20, 2005; Jeff Mohr, PhD (former UNSCOM chief biological weapons inspector), interview with author via telephone, June 27, 2005.

5. Killip, interview; William Lebherz (former UNSCOM industrial biotechnology expert), interview with author, Washington, DC, February 13, 2006; former senior

UNSCOM official, interview with author, August 30, 2005; Kelly, interview; Debra Krikorian, PhD (former UNSCOM biological weapons inspector), interview with author, Washington, DC, June 21, 2005; Richard Spertzel, PhD (former UNSCOM chief biological weapons inspector), interview with author, Washington, DC, July 1, 2005; Taylor, interview; former UNSCOM chief inspector, interview with author, August 18, 2005; former senior UNSCOM official, interview with author, August 30, 2005; former UNSCOM biological weapons inspector, interview with author, May 27, 2006; former UNSCOM CBW commissioner, interview with author via telephone, January 23, 2006.

6. Former UNSCOM chief inspector, interview with author, August 18, 2005.

7. Former UNSCOM inspector and chief of product development in an offensive biological weapons program, interview with author, Washington, DC, February 21, 2006. Also, Robert Kadlec, MD (former UNSCOM biological weapons inspector), interview with author, Washington, DC, February 23, 2006; Lebherz, interview.

8. Killip, interview; former UNSCOM chief inspector, interview with author, August 18, 2005; Lebherz, interview; Krikorian, interview.

9. Foreign ministry official, interview with author, August 17, 2005; Spertzel, interview.

10. Former UNSCOM inspector and chief of product development in an offensive biological weapons program, interview with author, February 21, 2006. Similarly, former senior UNSCOM official, interview with author, August 30, 2005.

11. Lebherz, interview.

12. David Franz, DVM, PhD (former UNSCOM chief biological weapons inspector), interview with author, Washington, DC, June 29, 2005. Likewise, Krikorian, interview.

13. Kelly, interview. Also, Gabriele Kraatz-Wadsack, "The Role of Scientists in Verification," in *Assessing the Threat of Weapons of Mass Destruction: The Role of Independent Scientists*, vol. 61, ed. J. L. Finney and I. Slaus, NATO Science for Peace and Security Series E: Human and Societal Dynamics (Amsterdam: IOS Press, 2010), 51–52.

14. Killip, interview; Stephen Black (UNSCOM historian), interview with author, Washington, DC, November 16, 2007.

15. David Huxsoll, DVM (former UNSCOM chief biological weapons inspector), interview with author, Washington, DC, June 21, 2005; Taylor, interview; Franz, interview.

16. Ambassador Robert Gallucci, PhD (former UNSCOM deputy executive chairman), interview with author, Washington, DC, March 13, 2006; Ake Sellstrom, PhD (former UNSCOM chief inspector), interview with author, Stockholm, August 24, 2005; Spertzel, interview; Kraatz-Wadsack, interview; foreign ministry official, interview with author, August 17, 2005.

17. For more, see U.S. Department of Health and Human Services, *Biosafety in Microbiological and Biomedical Laboratories*, 5th ed. (Washington, DC: U.S. Government

Printing Office, 2009); World Health Organization and U.S. biosafety procedures can be found, respectively, in *Laboratory Biosafety Manual*, 3rd ed. (Geneva: World Health Organization, 2006).

18. Huxsoll, interview; former UNSCOM biological weapons inspector, interview with author, Washington, DC, February 21, 2006; UNSCOM, *Report of UNSCOM 142/ BW34, April 30–May 7, 1996*, Chief Inspector Hamish Killip (New York, n.d.), paras. 13–14.

19. Sheldon H. Harris, *Factories of Death: Japanese Biological Warfare 1932–45 and the American Cover-Up* (New York: Routledge, 1994). On other programs, see Mark Wheelis, Lajos Rozsa, and Malcolm Dando, eds., *Deadly Cultures: Biological Weapons Since 1945* (Cambridge, MA: Harvard University Press, 2006).

20. Taylor, interview.

21. Kelly, interview; Krikorian, interview; Mohr, interview; Spertzel, interview; former UNSCOM inspector and chief of product development in an offensive biological weapons program, interview with author, February 21, 2006; former UNSCOM chief inspector, interview with author, New York City, January 31, 2006; former senior UNSCOM official, interview with author, August 30, 2005.

22. *Health Aspects of Chemical and Biological Weapons* (Geneva: World Health Organization, 1970), 93–94; Karle Lowe, "Analyzing Technical Constraints on Bio-Terrorism: Are They Still Important?" in *Terrorism with Chemical and Biological Weapons: Calibrating Risks and Responses*, ed. Brad Roberts (Arlington, VA: The Chemical and Biological Arms Control Institute, 1997); Office of Technology Assessment, *Technologies Underlying Weapons of Mass Destruction*, OTA-BP-ISC-115 (Washington, DC: U.S. Government Printing Office, December 1993), 94–96.

23. Rod Barton, "Profile of a Proliferator: Iraq's Biological Weapons Program," Briefing Series (Washington, DC: Center for Nonproliferation Studies, February 2, 2001); former UNSCOM staff member, interview with author, September 2, 2005.

24. Taylor, interview.

25. Manley, interview.

26. Kadlec, interview.

27. Kraatz-Wadsack, interview; Huxsoll, interview; Kelly, interview; Killip, interview; Lebherz, interview; former UNSCOM inspector and chief of product development in an offensive biological weapons program, interview with author, February 21, 2006; former senior UNSCOM official, interview with author, New York City, September 1, 2005.

28. Kadlec, interview. Puzzling over Amash's role, Spertzel, interview; Killip, interview; Kelly, interview; Kraatz-Wadsack, interview.

29. Barton, interview.

30. Kadlec, interview.

31. Taylor, interview.

32. Spertzel, interview; Huxsoll, interview.

33. Killip, interview; Mohr, interview; Krikorian, interview; Spertzel, interview.

34. Mohr, interview.

35. Ambassador Rolf Ekeus (former UNSCOM executive chairman), interview with author, Stockholm, August 24, 2005; Franz, interview; Mohr, interview; Spertzel, interview.

36. Christopher Dickey and Colin Soloway, "The Secrets of Dr. Germ: U.N. Inspectors Have Begun Searching Iraqi Weapons Sites," *Newsweek*, December 9, 2002, 2.

37. Kadlec, interview.

38. Barton, interview.

39. Killip, interview; Kelly, interview; Mohr, interview; Kraatz-Wadsack, interview; former UNSCOM biological weapons inspector, interview with author, Washington, DC, September 17, 2005.

40. Huxsoll, interview.

41. Former UNSCOM biological weapons inspector, interview with author, May 27, 2006.

42. Franz, interview. Similarly, Huxsoll, interview; Spertzel, interview; Killip, interview; Barton, interview; former UNSCOM inspector and chief of product development in an offensive biological weapons program, interview with author, February 21, 2006; former senior UNSCOM official, interview with author, September 1, 2005; former UNSCOM staff member, interview with author, September 2, 2005. Also, United Nations (UN) Security Council, *Twenty-Second Quarterly Report on the Activities of the United Nations Monitoring, Verification and Inspection Commission in Accordance with Paragraph 12 of Security Council Resolution 1284 (1999)*, Doc. S/2005/545, August 30, 2005, Annex, para. 39.

43. Mohr, interview.

44. Spertzel, interview; Kelly, interview; Mohr, interview; Manley, interview; former UNSCOM inspector and chief of product development in an offensive biological weapons program, interview with author, February 21, 2006; Office of Technology Assessment, *Technologies Underlying Weapons of Mass Destruction*, 91–93.

45. Former UNSCOM chief biological weapons inspector, interview with author, Washington, DC, August 28, 2005. Likewise, Spertzel, interview; Huxsoll, interview; Manley, interview; Killip, interview; former UNSCOM inspector and chief of product development in an offensive biological weapons program, interview with author, February 21, 2006.

46. Former UNSCOM biological weapons inspector, interview with author, May 27, 2006.

47. Killip, interview. Also on this point, Manley, interview.

48. Kelly, interview; Spertzel, interview; Mohr, interview; former UNSCOM inspector and chief of product development in an offensive biological weapons program,

interview with author, February 21, 2006; former UNSCOM biological weapons inspector, interview with author, May 27, 2006.

49. Manley, interview. For more on the Australia Group, go to <http://www .australiagroup.net>.

50. Former UNSCOM inspector and chief of product development in an offensive biological weapons program, interview with author, February 21, 2006.

51. Huxsoll, interview; Manley, interview; Franz, interview; Killip, interview; Kelly, interview; Barton, interview; Spertzel, interview; Mohr, interview; Kraatz-Wadsack, interview; former UNSCOM inspector and chief of product development in an offensive biological weapons program, interview with author, February 21, 2006; former senior UNSCOM official, interview with author, September 1, 2005; former senior UNSCOM official, interview with author, August 30, 2005; foreign ministry official, interview with author, August 17, 2005.

52. See "The Non-Inspection" segment in Chapter 3.

53. Lebherz, interview.

54. Mohr, interview; Taylor, interview; Krikorian, interview; Killip, interview; former UNSCOM biological weapons inspector, interview with author, May 27, 2006; former UNSCOM chief inspector, interview with author, August 18, 2005; foreign ministry official, interview with author, August 17, 2005.

55. Taylor, interview. Also, Kelly, interview; Kraatz-Wadsack, interview.

56. Former UNSCOM chief inspector, interview with author, August 18, 2005.

57. Killip, interview; Taylor, interview; Krikorian, interview; Kraatz-Wadsack, interview; former UNSCOM chief inspector, interview with author, August 18, 2005.

58. Kelly, interview; Franz, interview; Taylor, interview; Krikorian, interview; Killip, interview; former UNSCOM biological weapons inspector, interview with author, May 27, 2006; former UNSCOM chief inspector, interview with author, August 18, 2005.

59. Kraatz-Wadsack, interview. Likewise, Killip, interview; Krikorian, interview.

60. Taylor, interview; former UNSCOM inspector and chief of product development in an offensive biological weapons program, interview with author, February 21, 2006; Kelly, interview; Spertzel, interview.

61. Manley, interview. Also, Mohr, interview; Franz, interview; Killip, interview; Kelly, interview; Kraatz-Wadsack, interview; Barton, interview; foreign ministry official, interview with author, August 17, 2005; former UNSCOM inspector and chief of product development in an offensive biological weapons program, interview with author, February 21, 2006.

62. Taylor, interview.

63. Franz, interview; Kadlec, interview; Kraatz-Wadsack, interview; former UNSCOM chief inspector, interview with author, August 18, 2005; former UNSCOM CBW commissioner, interview with author, January 23, 2005.

64. Former UNSCOM chief biological weapons inspector, interview with author, August 28, 2005. Also, Gallucci, interview; former UNSCOM biological weapons inspector, interview with author, New York City, February 4, 2005; Lebherz, interview; Spertzel, interview; Kraatz-Wadsack, interview; former UNSCOM chief biological weapons inspector, interview with author, August 28, 2005; Richard Butler, *The Greatest Threat: Iraq, Weapons of Mass Destruction, and the Growing Crisis of Global Security* (New York: Public Affairs, 2000), 51, 81–82.

65. Manley, interview; Barton Gellman, "Iraq's Arsenal Was Only on Paper; Since Gulf War, Nonconventional Weapons Never Got Past the Planning Stage," *Washington Post*, January 7, 2004, A1.

66. Kadlec, interview.

67. Black, interview; former senior UNSCOM official, interview with author, August 30, 2005.

68. Spertzel, interview.

69. Huxsoll, interview. Calling the bad cop approach a recipe for failure, Mohr, interview with author, June 27, 2005; former senior UNSCOM official, interview with author, August 30, 2005.

70. Former UNSCOM chief biological weapons inspector, interview with author, August 28, 2005. Also recalling bad cop inspectors, Franz, interview; Krikorian, interview; Sellstrom, interview.

71. Huxsoll, interview. Seconding this approach, former UNSCOM chief inspector, interview with author, August 18, 2005.

72. Franz, interview.

73. Huxsoll, interview; Krikorian, interview.

74. Former senior UNSCOM official, interview with author, August 30, 2005. Similarly, Kraatz-Wadsack, interview; Spertzel, interview.

75. Mohr, interview; Taylor, interview; Kraatz-Wadsack, interview; former senior UNSCOM official, interview with author, August 30, 2005.

76. Taylor, interview. Agreeing, Killip, interview.

77. Dickey and Soloway, "The Secrets of Dr. Germ."

78. Former chief UNSCOM biological inspector, interview with author, August 28, 2005. Also, Killip, interview.

79. Killip, interview. Also, Taylor, interview; Kraatz-Wadsack, interview.

80. Killip, interview; Kraatz-Wadsack, interview; former senior UNSCOM official, interview with author, August 30, 2005; Taylor, interview; Spertzel, interview; former senior UNSCOM official, interview with author, August 30, 2005.

81. Spertzel, interview; Lebherz, interview; Kelly, interview; Killip, interview; Taylor, interview; Mohr, interview; Kraatz-Wadsack, interview.

82. Mohr, interview; former UNSCOM chief inspector, interview with author, August 18, 2005; former senior UNSCOM official, interview with author, August 30, 2005.

324   NOTES TO PAGES 183–186

83. Kelly, interview.

84. Kraatz-Wadsack, interview; Spertzel, interview; Killip, interview; Kelly, interview.

85. For example, *Increasing FDNY's Preparedness* (New York: McKinsey, 2002); *Improving NYPD Emergency Preparedness and Response* (New York: McKinsey, 2002).

86. Kadlec, interview. Also on compartmentalization, Gallucci, interview; Killip, interview; former UNSCOM chief inspector, interview with author, January 31, 2006; Barton Gellman, "A Futile Game of Hide and Seek; Ritter, UNSCOM Foiled by Saddam's Concealment Strategy," *Washington Post*, October 11, 1998, A1.

87. Mohr, interview; Taylor, interview; Huxsoll, interview; Kraatz-Wadsack, interview; former UNSCOM chief inspector, interview with author, January 31, 2006.

88. Taylor, interview; Kraatz-Wadsack, interview; former UNSCOM chief inspector, interview with author, January 31, 2006.

89. Taylor, interview; Krikorian, interview; Kadlec, interview; Raymond Zilinskas, PhD (former UNSCOM biological weapons inspector), interview with author, Washington, DC, October 4, 2005; former UNSCOM chief inspector, interview with author, January 31, 2006; Former UNSCOM chief inspector, interview with author, January 31, 2006.

90. Taylor, interview.

91. Manley, interview; former UNSCOM staff member, interview with author, September 1, 2005.

92. Spertzel, interview; Kadlec, interview.

93. Killip, interview.

94. Jeffrey T. Richelson, *The U.S. Intelligence Community* (Cambridge, MA: Ballinger, 1985); William E. Burrows, *Deep Black: Space Espionage and National Security* (New York: Random House, 1986).

95. Gallucci, interview; Killip, interview.

96. Ekeus, interview; Killip, interview; Sellstrom, interview; former senior UNSCOM official, interview with author, August 30, 2005.

97. Ekeus, interview; Gallucci, interview; former senior UNSCOM official, interview with author, September 1, 2005; "Disarming Iraq: The Work of the U.N. Special Commission," *The Interdependent* 18, no. 1 (January-February 1992), 1.

98. Ekeus, interview; Killip, interview; Doug Englund (former UNSCOM chief inspector), interview with author, Washington, DC, December 5, 2005; former senior UNSCOM official, interview with author, August 30, 2005; Pierce Corden (former UNSCOM deputy executive chairman), interview with author, Washington, DC, August 4, 2008; Gellman, "A Futile Game of Hide and Seek;" Tim Trevan, *Saddam's Secrets: The Hunt for Saddam's Hidden Weapons* (London: HarperCollins, 1999), 268–269, 287–288; Rod Barton, *The Weapons Detective: The Inside Story of Australia's Top Weapons Inspector* (Melbourne: Black Inc. Agenda, 2006), 126, 137–138.

99. Gallucci, interview. Also, Charles Duelfer, *Hide and Seek: The Search for Truth in Iraq* (New York: Public Affairs, 2009), 124–125; former UNSCOM staff member, interview with author, September 2, 2005.

100. "British Expert on Iraq's Secret Arms Program," *Sunday Times* (London), February 14, 1999, 12; Trevan, *Saddam's Secrets*, 58–59.

101. Gallucci, interview; Duelfer, *Hide and Seek*, 170.

102. Mohr, interview. Also, Krikorian, interview.

103. Ekeus, interview; former senior UNSCOM official, interview with author, August 30, 2005; former UNSCOM staff member, interview with author, September 2, 2005. For more, Jean E. Krasno and James S. Sutterlin, *The United Nations and Iraq: Defanging the Viper* (Westport, CT: Praeger, 2003), 85–90; Duelfer, *Hide and Seek*, 132.

104. Ekeus, interview; Corden, interview.

105. Kraatz-Wadsack, interview; Ekeus, interview; Kelly, interview; Killip, interview.

106. Killip, interview; Gallucci, interview; former UNSCOM chief inspector, interview with author, August 18, 2005; former senior UNSCOM official, interview with author, August 30, 2005. Also on GATEWAY, Barton, *The Weapons Detective*, 74–75; Krasno and Sutterlin, *Defanging the Viper*, 82; "Secrets, Spies, and Videotape," *Panorama*, BBC One, broadcast on March 22, 1999.

107. Manley, interview. Also, former UNSCOM staff member, interview with author, September 1, 2005; foreign ministry official, interview with author, August 17, 2005; former senior UNSCOM official, interview with author, August 30, 2005.

108. Krikorian, interview; Franz, interview; former UNSCOM chief inspector, interview with author, August 18, 2005. Also, Barton, *The Weapons Detective*, 77–8.

109. Killip, interview; former UNSCOM staff member, interview with author, September 2, 2005.

110. Killip, interview; former UNSCOM chief inspector, interview with author, August 18, 2005; former senior UNSCOM official, interview with author, August 30, 2005; former UNSCOM staff member, interview with author, September 2, 2005; former UNSCOM chief inspector, interview with author, August 18, 2005. See also, Barton, *The Weapons Detective*, 81.

111. Englund, interview; "Organizing for Dealing with Imagery and Inspection Reports," Memorandum from Douglas Englund to Chairman Rolf Ekeus (New York, UNSCOM, August 8, 1991).

112. Mohr, interview; Killip, interview; Gallucci, interview; Manley, interview; former senior UNSCOM official, interview with author, August 30, 2005; Taylor, interview; former UNSCOM biological weapons inspector, interview with author, February 4, 2005; former senior UNSCOM official, interview with author, September 1, 2005.

113. Taylor, interview.

114. Gallucci, interview; Taylor, interview.

115. Former UNSCOM chief biological weapons inspector, interview with author, August 28, 2005.

116. Gallucci, interview; Killip, interview; Taylor, interview.

117. Gallucci, interview.

118. Ibid. Also, Tim Weiner, "U.S. Used U.N. Team to Place Spy Device in Iraq, Aides Say," *New York Times*, January 8, 1999, A1; Barton, *The Weapons Detective*, 186.

119. Gallucci, interview; Killip, interview; former UNSCOM chief biological weapons inspector, interview with author, August 28, 2005; Duelfer, *Hide and Seek*, 117–135.

120. Killip, interview.

121. Inspectors who were briefed, including some who had prior direct involvement with intelligence analysis: Kelly, interview; Taylor, interview; Spertzel, interview; Krikorian, interview; Barton, interview; former UNSCOM biological weapons inspector, interview with author, September 17, 2005. Inspectors who had no intelligence briefing before deployment: Zilinskas, interview; Mohr, interview; Lebherz, interview; Franz, interview; former UNSCOM staff member, interview with author, September 2, 2005; former senior UNSCOM official, interview with author, August 30, 2005; former UNSCOM inspector and chief of product development in an offensive biological weapons program, interview with author, February 21, 2006. Killip manned the United Kingdom's chemical intelligence desk but was not specifically briefed on Iraq's bioweapons program. Killip, interview.

122. Killip, interview; Kelly, interview; Lebherz, interview.

123. Former senior UNSCOM official, interview with author, August 30, 2005; former UNSCOM staff member, interview with author, September 2, 2005; former UNSCOM biological weapons inspector, interview with author, February 21, 2006.

124. Kraatz-Wadsack, interview.

125. Taylor, interview.

126. See Table 1.2. Also, UN Doc. S/2005/545, Annex, para. 16.

127. Krikorian, interview.

128. Barton, interview; Spertzel, interview; Krikorian, interview; Kraatz-Wadsack, interview.

129. Englund, interview; Ekeus, interview; former senior UNSCOM official, interview with author, August 30, 2005; former senior UNSCOM official, interview with author, September 1, 2005.

130. Barton, interview; Krikorian, interview; Spertzel, interview.

131. Kraatz-Wadsack, interview. Similarly, Kelly, interview; Sellstrom, interview; Killip, interview; Barton, interview; Spertzel, interview; former senior UNSCOM official, interview with author, September 1, 2005.

132. Barton, interview.

133. Mohr, interview.

134. Kraatz-Wadsack, interview.

135. Englund, interview; Duelfer, *Hide and Seek*, 62, 312.

136. Kadlec, interview. Also, Manley, interview.

137. Franz, interview.

138. Englund, interview. Also, Gallucci, interview.

139. Kraatz-Wadsack, interview. Also, Duelfer, *Hide and Seek*, 253–254, 312. Arguing that using the mobile trailers to produce hydrogen was an implausible cover story, see *Iraqi Mobile Biological Warfare Agent Production Plants* (Washington, DC, Central Intelligence Agency/Defense Intelligence Agency, May 28, 2003). For an explanation of how the U.S. intelligence community botched the handling of the Curveball information, *Commission on the Intelligence Capabilities of the United States Regarding Weapons of Mass Destruction: Report to the President of the United States* (Washington, DC: U.S. Government Printing Office, March 31, 2005), 88–111. Also, Toby Harnden, "Iraqi Defector 'Curveball' Admits WMD Lies," *The Telegraph* (London), February 15, 2011, A1; Bob Drogin, *Curveball: Spies, Lies, and the Con Man Who Caused a War* (New York: Random House, 2007).

140. Ekeus, interview.

141. Former senior UNSCOM official, interview with author, August 30, 2005. Also, Duelfer, *Hide and Seek*, 125.

142. Sellstrom, interview; Charles Duelfer (former UNSCOM deputy executive chairman), interview with author, Washington, DC, November 15, 2007; former UNSCOM staff member, interview with author, September 2, 2005; former senior UNSCOM official, interview with author, August 30, 2005.

143. Barton, interview; former senior UNSCOM official, interview with author, September 1, 2005.

144. Franz, interview.

145. Ekeus, interview.

146. Former senior UNSCOM official, interview with author, September 1, 2005.

147. Sellstrom, interview. Similarly, Kraatz-Wadsack, interview.

148. Kelly, interview; Spertzel, interview; Killip, interview; Barton, interview; Taylor, interview; Krikorian, interview.

149. The Iraqis used the stainless fermenters at Al Hakam for bioweapons activities. Al Hakam's animal house and research buildings were built according to engineering drawings, which showed where imported ventilation equipment was to be installed to create high-level containment capacity for work with high-risk pathogens. Iraqi technicians modified the Al Daura fermenters to make *C. botulinum* in an anaerobic setting.

150. Barton, interview. Also, Killip, interview; Kelly, interview; Krikorian, interview; Kraatz-Wadsack, interview.

151. Killip, interview; Kelly, interview. For example, *Collateral Analysis and Verification of Biological and Toxin Research in Iraq* (Toronto: External Affairs and International Trade, October 1991).

152. Barton, interview; Spertzel, interview; Killip, interview; Taylor, interview; Kraatz-Wadsack, interview.

153. Krikorian, interview.

154. Black, interview; Spertzel, interview; former senior UNSCOM official, interview with author, August 30, 2005; Douglas J. MacEachin, "Routine and Challenge: Two Pillars of Verification," *The CBW Conventions Bulletin* 39 (March 1998), 3.

155. Kraatz-Wadsack, interview.

156. Former senior UNSCOM official, interview with author, August 30, 2005; Taylor, interview; Killip, interview; Kraatz-Wadsack, interview; former UNSCOM biological weapons inspector, interview with author, Washington, DC, February 4, 2005.

157. Black, interview.

158. Former senior UNSCOM official, interview with author, August 30, 2005; Black, interview; Ekeus, interview; Killip, interview; Kraatz-Wadsack, interview; Spertzel, interview.

159. Black, interview; former senior UNSCOM official, interview with author, August 30, 2005. On the Convention's monitoring challenges, Oliver Thranert, ed., *Enhancing the Biological Weapons Convention* (Bonn: Verlag J.H.W. Dietz Nachf., 1996); Malcolm Dando, *Biological Warfare in the 21st Century* (London: Brassey's, 1994); Amy E. Smithson, ed., *House of Cards: The Pivotal Importance of a Technically Sound BWC Monitoring Protocol,* Report no. 37 (Washington, DC: The Henry L. Stimson Center, May 2001). The Convention's provisions are at <http://www.opbw.org>.

160. Huxsoll, interview.

161. Kelly, interview.

162. Former senior UNSCOM official, interview with author, August 30, 2005; Killip, interview; Huxsoll, interview.

163. Killip, interview. Also, Ekeus, interview; Spertzel, interview; Barton, interview; Kraatz-Wadsack, interview; former UNSCOM CBW commissioner, interview with author, January 23, 2005; former senior UNSCOM official, interview with author, August 30, 2005.

164. Barton, interview.

165. Black, interview; Spertzel, interview; Killip, interview; Kraatz-Wadsack, interview.

166. Black, interview.

167. Kelly, interview; Killip, interview; Black, interview; Kraatz-Wadsack, interview; former senior UNSCOM official, interview with author, August 30, 2005. See also Chapter 2.

168. Duelfer, *Hide and Seek,* 252–253. For case studies, see Anne L. Clunan, Peter R. Lavoy, and Susan B. Martin, eds. *Terrorism, War, or Disease? Unraveling the Use of Biological Weapons* (Stanford, CA: Stanford Security Studies, June 2008).

169. Killip, interview; former senior UNSCOM official, interview with author, August 30, 2005; foreign ministry official, interview with author, August 17, 2005; Black, interview.

170. Kelly, interview.

171. Gallucci, interview. Similarly, Spertzel, interview; Black, interview; Killip, interview; Duelfer, *Hide and Seek*, 154, 254.

172. Kraatz-Wadsack, interview.

173. Lebherz, interview.

174. Kelly, interview.

175. Krikorian, interview. Likewise, Taylor, interview.

176. Mohr, interview; Huxsoll, interview; Kelly, interview; Kraatz-Wadsack, interview. Describing scientists as more skeptical and politicians as more amenable to hearing the evidence, Franz, interview.

177. United Nations Special Commission, *Report Issued After Seminar of International Biological Weapons Experts* (New York: April 6–7, 1995), 3–4.

178. Gallucci, interview. See David Albright and Mark Hibbs, "Iraq's Nuclear Hide-and-Seek," *Bulletin of the Atomic Scientists* 47, no. 7 (September 1991): 14–23; Rodger Claire, *Raid on the Sun: Inside Israel's Secret Campaign That Denied Saddam the Bomb* (New York: Broadway Publishing, 2004).

179. Former UNSCOM CBW commissioner, interview with author, January 23, 2006. Also, Mark M. Lowenthal, "The Politics of Verification: What's New, What's Not," in *Verification: The Key to Arms Control in the Late 1990s*, ed. John G. Tower, James Brown, and William K. Cheek (Washington, DC: Brassey's, 1992).

180. Mohr, interview; former UNSCOM chief inspector, interview with author, January 31, 2006; Killip, interview; former UNSCOM chief inspector, interview with author, August 18, 2005.

181. Kelly, interview.

182. Former UNSCOM chief biological weapons inspector, interview with author, August 28, 2005; Duelfer, *Hide and Seek*, 123.

183. Classic works on decision making include Hans J. Morgenthau, *Politics Among Nations: The Struggle for Power and Peace* (New York: Knopf, 1948); Graham Allison, *Essence of Decision: Explaining the Cuban Missile Crisis* (Boston: Little, Brown, 1971); Morton H. Halperin, *Bureaucratic Politics and Foreign Policy*, 2nd ed. (Washington, DC: Brookings Institution, 1974); and Irving L. Janis, *Groupthink: Psychological Studies of Policy Decisions and Fiascoes*, 2nd ed. (New York: Houghton Mifflin, 1982).

184. Duelfer, *Hide and Seek*, 96.

185. Manley, interview. Agreeing, former senior UNSCOM official, interview with author, September 1, 2005.

186. Ekeus, interview.

187. Former UNSCOM staff member, interview with author, September 2, 2005.

188. Ibid. Also, former senior UNSCOM official, interview with author, August 30, 2005.

189. Former UNSCOM chief inspector, interview with author, August 18, 2005. Concurring, Manley interview.

190. Former UNSCOM chief inspector, interview with author, January 31, 2006; former senior UNSCOM official, interview with author, August 30, 2005; former UNSCOM staff member, interview with author, September 1, 2005; former UNSCOM CBW commissioner, interview with author, January 23, 2006; former UNSCOM staff member, interview with author, September 2, 2005.

191. Kraatz-Wadsack, interview.

192. Spertzel, interview; former senior UNSCOM official, interview with author, August 30, 2005.

193. Englund, interview.

194. Kraatz-Wadsack, interview.

195. Killip, interview.

196. Franz, interview; former senior UNSCOM official, interview with author, September 1, 2005

197. Taylor, interview.

198. Franz, interview. With eerily similar comments, Gallucci, interview.

Chapter 9

1. United Nations (UN) Security Council, *Twenty-Seventh Quarterly Report on the Activities of the United Nations Monitoring, Verification, and Inspection Commission in Accordance with Paragraph 12 of Security Council Resolution 1284 (1999)*, Doc. S/2006/912, November 22, 2006, Annex, para. 16.

2. Dr. Joseph Barbera, a physician affiliated with George Washington University's Institute for Crisis, Disaster, and Risk Management, enlightened the author about the difference between lessons learned and lessons experienced because emergency personnel responding to disasters repeatedly experience the same problems.

3. David Huxsoll, DVM (former UNSCOM chief biological weapons inspector), interview with author, Washington, DC, June 21, 2005.

4. Office of Technology Assessment, *Nuclear Safeguards and the Atomic Energy Agency*, OTA-ISS-615 (Washington, DC: U.S. Government Printing Office, April 1995). For more on the IAEA's history and activities and on peaceful research reactors, go to <http://www.iaea.org>. See also the reactor database at <http://db.world-nuclear.org/reference/reactorsdb_index.php>. Information on the Organization for the Prohibition of Chemical Weapons is at <http://www.opcw.org>.

5. Debra Krikorian, PhD (former UNSCOM biological weapons inspector), interview with author, Washington, DC, June 21, 2005. Also, Ambassador Robert Gallucci,

PhD (former UNSCOM deputy executive chairman), interview with author, Washington, DC, March 13, 2006.

6. Former senior UNSCOM official, interview with author, New York City, August 30, 2005.

7. Terence Taylor (former UNSCOM CBW commissioner and chief inspector), interview with author, Washington, DC, May 12, 2005. Also, Rod Barton (former UNSCOM biological weapons inspector), interview with author via telephone, May 20, 2005; former UNSCOM chief inspector, interview with author, London, August 18, 2005. Expressing preferences for various inspection tools, Krikorian, interview; Stephen Black (UNSCOM historian), interview with author, Washington, DC, November 16, 2007; Charles Duelfer (former UNSCOM deputy executive chairman), interview with author, Washington, DC, November 15, 2007; David Franz, DVM, PhD (former UNSCOM chief biological weapons inspector), interview with author, Washington, DC, June 29, 2005, Richard Spertzel, PhD (former UNSCOM chief biological weapons inspector), interview with author, Washington, DC, July 1, 2005; Jeff Mohr, PhD (former UNSCOM chief biological weapons inspector), interview with author via telephone, June 27, 2005; William Lebherz (former UNSCOM industrial biotechnology expert), interview with author, Washington, DC, Washington, DC, February 13, 2006; Huxsoll, interview; Hamish Killip (former UNSCOM chief biological weapons inspector), interview with author, Isle of Man, August 22, 2005.

8. Former senior UNSCOM official, interview with author, August 30, 2005. Also, Barton, interview; former UNSCOM chief inspector, interview with author, August 18, 2005; former UNSCOM chief inspector, interview with author, New York City, January 31, 2006. Arguing that a combination of observation and sampling is the most powerful, Gabriele Kraatz-Wadsack, "The Role of Scientists in Verification," in *Assessing the Threat of Weapons of Mass Destruction: The Role of Independent Scientists*, vol. 61, ed. J. L. Finney and I. Slaus, NATO Science for Peace and Security Series E: Human and Societal Dynamics (Amsterdam: IOS Press, 2010), 52.

9. Killip, interview; Black, interview; Taylor, interview; Krikorian, interview.

10. Huxsoll, interview.

11. Taylor, interview; Killip, interview; Huxsoll, interview; David Kelly, PhD (former UNSCOM chief biological weapons inspector), interview with author, Washington, DC, December 17, 2002; Krikorian, interview; Gabriele Kraatz-Wadsack (former UNSCOM chief biological inspector), interview with author, Berlin, August 15, 2005.

12. Former senior UNSCOM official, interview with author, August 30, 2005. Similarly, Kraatz-Wadsack, interview.

13. Krikorian, interview.

14. Black, interview. Likewise, former senior UNSCOM official, interview with author, August 30, 2005.

15. Killip, interview.

16. Krikorian, interview.

17. Kraatz-Wadsack, interview; former UNSCOM inspector and chief of product development in an offensive biological weapons program, interview with author, Washington, DC, February 21, 2006.

18. Rod Barton, *The Weapons Detective: The Inside Story of Australia's Top Weapons Inspector* (Melbourne: Black Inc. Agenda, 2006), 86. Also, Kraatz-Wadsack, interview; Charles Duelfer, *Hide and Seek: The Search for Truth in Iraq* (New York: Public Affairs, 2009), 312.

19. Killip, interview; Black, interview.

20. Killip, interview.

21. Ibid.; Kelly, interview.

22. Kelly, interview. Also, Kraatz-Wadsack, interview; Spertzel, interview; Killip, interview.

23. Spertzel, interview.

24. Barton, interview; Franz, interview; Killip, interview; Krikorian, interview; Black, interview; Kraatz-Wadsack, interview.

25. Ronald Manley, PhD (former UNSCOM chief chemical weapons inspector), interview with author, London, August 19, 2005; Mohr, interview. Also, Isam al-Khafaji, "State Terror and the Degradation of Politics in Iraq," *Middle East Report*, no. 176 (May-June 1992): 15–21; Central Intelligence Agency (CIA), "Biological Warfare," in *Comprehensive Report of the Special Advisor to the DCI on Iraq's WMD* (Washington, DC, September 30, 2004), 12.

26. Former UNSCOM chief inspector, interview with author, January 31, 2006. Also, Manley, interview; Barton, interview; Duelfer, *Hide and Seek*, 94.

27. Spertzel, interview.

28. Taylor, interview; Killip, interview; Franz, interview; Barton, interview; Krikorian, interview; Spertzel, interview; former UNSCOM inspector and chief of product development in an offensive biological weapons program, interview with author, February 21, 2006. See also UN Security Council, *Letter Dated 25 January 1999 from the Executive Chairman of the Special Commission Established by the Secretary-General Pursuant to Paragraph 9 (b) (i) of Security Council Resolution 687 (1991) Addressed to the President of the Security Council*, Doc. S/1999/94, January 29, 1999, Annex D, para. 20.

29. Duelfer, interview.

30. Kraatz-Wadsack, interview; Spertzel, interview; former senior UNSCOM official, interview with author, August 30, 2005.

31. Killip, interview; former UNSCOM biological weapons inspector, interview with author, Washington, DC, February 4, 2005; Krikorian, interview; Taylor, interview; Gallucci, interview; Spertzel, interview; Kraatz-Wadsack, interview; Richard Butler, *The Greatest Threat: Iraq, Weapons of Mass Destruction, and the Growing Crisis of Global Security* (New York: Public Affairs, 2000), 51, 81–82.

32. Killip, interview. Also, Ambassador Rolf Ekeus (former UNSCOM executive chairman), interview with author, Stockholm, August 24, 2005.

33. Black, interview; former senior UNSCOM official, interview with author, August 30, 2005; Killip, interview.

34. The Iraqis' antics are described in Chapter 1. Mohr, interview with author, June 27, 2005; Spertzel, interview; former UNSCOM chief inspector, interview with author, January 31, 2006; Killip, interview.

35. Killip, interview; Spertzel, interview; former senior UNSCOM official, interview with author, August 30, 2005; former UNSCOM chief inspector, interview with author, August 18, 2005; Ake Sellstrom, PhD (former UNSCOM chief inspector), interview with author, Stockholm, August 24, 2005; Franz, interview; Krikorian, interview.

36. Spertzel, interview; Killip, interview; Huxsoll, interview; Kraatz-Wadsack, interview; former senior UNSCOM official, interview with author, August 30, 2005.

37. Killip, interview. Also, Kraatz-Wadsack, interview; Huxsoll, interview; former senior UNSCOM official, interview with author, August 30, 2005.

38. Spertzel, interview; Killip, interview; Krikorian, interview; Lebherz, interview; Kraatz-Wadsack, interview; former senior UNSCOM official, interview with author, August 30, 2005.

39. Killip, interview; Spertzel, interview; Kelly, interview; Kraatz-Wadsack, interview.

40. Spertzel, interview; Huxsoll, interview; former senior UNSCOM official, interview with author, August 30, 2005.

41. Franz, interview; Barton, interview; Krikorian, interview; Spertzel, interview; former UNSCOM inspector and chief of product development in an offensive biological weapons program, interview with author, February 21, 2006.

42. Former senior UNSCOM official, interview with author, August 30, 2005.

43. Former UNSCOM chief biological weapons inspector, interview with author, August 28, 2005. Also, senior UNSCOM official, interview with author, August 30, 2005.

44. Killip, interview; Kraatz-Wadsack, interview.

45. Manley, interview; Mohr, interview; Killip, interview; Krikorian, interview; Spertzel, interview; Kraatz-Wadsack, interview. On the science of detecting deception, Committee on Military and Intelligence Methodology for Emergent Neurophysiological and Cognitive/Neural Research in the Next Two Decades, National Research Council, *Emerging Cognitive Neuroscience and Related Technologies* (Washington, DC: National Academies Press, 2008), 32–41; Paul Ekman and Maureen O'Sullivan, "From Flawed Self-assessment to Blatant Whoppers: The Utility of Voluntary and Involuntary Behavior in Detecting Deception," *Behavioral Sciences and the Law* 24, no. 5 (September 2006): 673–86.

46. Krikorian, interview. Agreeing, Killip, interview.

47. Former senior UNSCOM official, interview with author, August 30, 2005.

48. Taylor, interview.

49. Spertzel, interview; Kelly, interview; Black, interview; Kraatz-Wadsack, interview; Killip, interview; Mohr, interview; former senior UNSCOM official, interview with author, August 30, 2005.

50. Killip, interview; Kraatz-Wadsack, interview; Spertzel, interview; Mohr, interview; Kelly, interview; Franz, interview; former senior UNSCOM official, interview with author, August 30, 2005.

51. Killip, interview. Similarly, Huxsoll, interview; Manley, interview; Krikorian, interview; Kraatz-Wadsack, interview.

52. Black, interview.

53. Former senior UNSCOM inspector, interview with author, August 30, 2005.

54. Taylor, interview.

55. Franz, interview; former UNSCOM inspector and chief of product development in an offensive biological weapons program, interview with author, February 21, 2006; foreign ministry official, interview with author, London, August 17, 2005.

56. Killip, interview. Also, Kelly, interview; Kraatz-Wadsack, interview; Black, interview; Krikorian, interview; Franz, interview; Taylor, interview.

57. Barton, interview. Also, Spertzel, interview; Kelly, interview; Killip, interview; Black, interview; Taylor, interview; Kraatz-Wadsack, interview; former UNSCOM chief inspector, interview with author, January 31, 2006; Duelfer, *Hide and Seek*, 341.

58. Ekeus, interview; Killip, interview; Kraatz-Wadsack, interview; former senior UNSCOM official, interview with author, August 30, 2005; Kelly, interview; Barton, interview; Spertzel, interview; Taylor, interview; former senior UNSCOM official, interview with author, August 30, 2005; foreign ministry official, interview with author, August 17, 2005.

59. Ekeus, interview. Also on this point, Robert Kadlec, MD (former UNSCOM inspector), interview with author, Washington, DC, February 23, 2006; former UNSCOM chief inspector, interview with author, January 31, 2006; former UNSCOM staff member, interview with author, September 2, 2005; Kraatz-Wadsack, interview.

60. Killip, interview.

61. Kraatz-Wadsack, "The Role of Scientists in Verification," 47–49. Also, Killip, interview; former senior UNSCOM official, interview with author, August 30, 2005. For the ongoing monitoring and verification provisions, see UN Security Council, Resolution 715 (1991), Doc. S/RES/715, October 11, 1991.

62. Quote on the Haidar farm documents, former senior UNSCOM official, interview with author, August 30, 2005.

63. Kraatz-Wadsack, interview; Krikorian, interview; Spertzel, interview; UN Doc. S/1999/94, Annex D, para. 25.

64. Kraatz-Wadsack, interview; Spertzel, interview; Barton, interview; former senior UNSCOM official, interview with author, August 30, 2005.

65. Pierce Corden (former UNSCOM deputy executive chairman), interview with author, Washington, DC, August 4, 2008. See David Albright and Mark Hibbs, "Iraq's Bomb: Blueprints and Artifacts," *Bulletin of the Atomic Scientists* 48, no. 1 (January-February 1992): 31–40; Paul Lewis, "44 U.N. Inspectors Freed by Iraq with Secret Nuclear Documents," *New York Times*, September 28, 1991, section 1, p. 1; R. Jeffrey Smith and Michael Z. Wise, "Report Shows Extensive Iraqi Nuclear Effort; Records Seized by U.N. Team Indicate Testing of Missile Capable of Carrying A-Bomb" *Washington Post*, October 5, 1991, A1.

66. Lebherz, interview; Krikorian, interview; Kraatz-Wadsack, interview; Killip, interview; former senior UNSCOM official, interview with author, August 30, 2005.

67. Kraatz-Wadsack, interview; Spertzel, interview.

68. Taylor, interview; Kraatz-Wadsack, interview.

69. Killip, interview; Duelfer, interview.

70. George Pierce, PhD (Professor, Georgia State University), interview with author, November 27, 2007.

71. Kelly, interview; Ekeus, interview; Barton, interview; Spertzel, interview; Killip, interview; Kraatz-Wadsack, interview; former UNSCOM chief inspector, interview with author, January 31, 2006; foreign ministry official, interview with author, August 17, 2005.

72. Former senior UNSCOM official, interview with author, August 30, 2005; Duelfer, *Hide and Seek*, 340.

73. Mohr, interview. Also, Ekeus, interview.

74. Former senior UNSCOM official, interview with author, August 30, 2005.

75. Wilfred H. Nelson, *Modern Techniques for Rapid Microbiology Analyses* (Hoboken, NJ: John Wiley & Sons, 1991); Jiang Gu, ed., *In Situ Polymerase Chain Reaction and Related Technology* (Westborough, MA: Eaton, 1995).

76. Huxsoll, interview.

77. Former senior UNSCOM official, interview with author, August 30, 2005; Kraatz-Wadsack, "The Role of Scientists in Verification," 52.

78. Killip, interview. Similarly, Black, interview; Mohr, interview; Spertzel, interview; Kraatz-Wadsack, interview; Barton, interview.

79. Mohr, interview; Lebherz, interview; Killip, interview; Franz, interview; Kelly, interview; Huxsoll, interview.

80. Kadlec, interview; Kelly interview.

81. Huxsoll, interview; Mohr, interview; Killip, interview; Kelly, interview; Spertzel, interview.

82. Alan J. Mohr, "Biological Sampling and Analysis Procedures for the United Nations Special Commission (UNSCOM) in Iraq," *Politics and the Life Sciences* 14, no. 2 (August 1995): 241–242.

83. Kelly, interview; Kraatz-Wadsack, interview; Spertzel, interview; Kadlec, interview; Mohr, interview; former UNSCOM staff member, interview with author, New York City, September 1, 2005.

84. Barton, interview; Franz, interview; Mohr, interview; Spertzel, interview; former senior UNSCOM official, interview with author, August 30, 2005.

85. Mohr, interview. Also, Huxsoll, interview.

86. Killip, interview. Likewise, Huxsoll, interview; Kelly, interview; Mohr, interview; Kraatz-Wadsack, interview; former senior UNSCOM official, interview with author, August 30, 2005.

87. Mohr, interview; Kelly, interview; Spertzel, interview; former UNSCOM staff member interview with author, September 1, 2005.

88. Paul Keim, "Microbial Forensics: A Scientific Assessment" (Washington, DC: American Academy of Microbiology, 2003); Craig A. Cummings and David A. Relman, "Microbial Forensics—'Cross-Examining Pathogens,'" *Science* 296, no. 5575 (June 14, 2002): 1976–1977; Bruce Budowle et al., "Toward a System of Microbial Forensics: From Sample Collection to Interpretation of Evidence," *Applied Environmental Microbiology* 71, no. 5 (May 2005): 2209–2213; Bruce Budowle et al., "Building Microbial Forensics as a Response to Bioterrorism," *Science* 301, no. 5641 (September 26, 2003): 1852–1853; , Bruce Budowle, Stephen E. Schutzer, Roger G. Breeze, Paul G. Keim, and Stephen A. Morse, eds., *Microbial Forensics,* 2nd ed. (San Diego: Elsevier Academic Press, 2011). See also Gregory D. Koblentz and Jonathan B. Tucker, "Tracing an Attack: The Promise and Pitfalls of Microbial Forensics," *Survival* 52, no. 1 (February 2010): 159–186.

89. These specialized areas of science combine to allow the establishment of a molecular trail of evidence related to bioweapons manufacture or the dispersal of biowarfare agents. Developments at the forefront of these fields of science can be followed in journals such as *Bioinformatics, Metabolomics, Briefings in Functional Genomics and Proteomics, Genomics,* and *International Journal of Mass Spectrometry.*

90. Mohr, interview.

91. Franz, interview; Mohr, interview; Spertzel, interview.

92. Mohr, interview. Also, former UNSCOM inspector and chief of product development in an offensive biological weapons program, interview with author, February 21, 2006; Kelly, interview.

93. Former UNSCOM biological weapons inspector, interview with author, February 21, 2006. Similarly, Mohr, interview. Also, Government of the United Kingdom, "UN Special Commission BW Inspections in Iraq: Lessons for the Ad Hoc Experts' Group on Verification," BWC/CONF-III/VEREX-WP5 (White Paper presented during Third Review Conference of the Parties to the BWC, Geneva, UN, March 30–April 10, 1992), 2.

94. Kelly, interview; Kraatz-Wadsack, interview; Spertzel, interview; former UNSCOM inspector and chief of product development in an offensive biological weapons program, interview with author, February 21, 2006.

95. Killip, interview.

96. Barton, interview. Agreeing, Mohr, interview.

97. Kelly, interview; Lebherz, interview; Killip, interview; Kraatz-Wadsack, interview.

98. See Chapter 8 on the utility of hot washes. Killip, interview; Barton, interview; Mohr, interview.

99. Franz, interview.

100. Mohr, interview. Agreeing, former UNSCOM staff member, interview with author, New York City, September 2, 2005; former senior UNSCOM official, interview with author, September 1, 2005.

101. Killip, interview. Also, Kelly, interview. For example, *Collateral Analysis and Verification of Biological and Toxin Research in Iraq* (Toronto: External Affairs and International Trade, October 1991).

102. United Nations, *Special Conference of the States Parties to the Convention on the Prohibition of the Development, Production, and Stockpiling of Bacteriological (Biological) and Toxin Weapons and on Their Destruction: Final Report*, Doc. BWC/SPCONF/1, Geneva, September 19–30, 1994.

103. Jez Littlewood, *The Biological Weapons Convention: A Revolution Failed* (Aldershot, U.K.: Ashgate, 2005); Marie Chevrier, "The Biological Weapons Convention: The Protocol That Almost Was," in *Verification Yearbook 2001*, ed. Trevor Findlay and Oliver Meier (London: Verification, Inspection, and Training Centre, 2001), 79–97. On the U.S. rejection of the draft protocol, Donald Mahley, *Statement by the United States to the Ad Hoc Group of Biological Weapons Convention States Parties* (statement made in Geneva, July 25, 2001); John R. Bolton, undersecretary for arms control and international security, *The U.S. Position on the Biological Weapons Convention: Combating the BW Threat* (remarks at the Tokyo American Center, Tokyo, August 26, 2006). For the proposals of U.S. pharmaceutical scientists, see Amy E. Smithson, ed., *House of Cards: The Pivotal Importance of a Technically Sound BWC Monitoring Protocol*, Report no. 37 (Washington, DC: The Henry L. Stimson Center, May 2001): 49–84, 93; *Resuscitating the Bioweapons Ban* (Washington, DC: Center for Strategic and International Studies, November 2004).

104. "Text: Albright Addresses UNSCOM Inspectors," Remarks in Manama, Bahrain, *Global Security Newswire*, November 17, 1997. Also, John R. Bolton, undersecretary for arms control and international security, *Remarks to the Fifth Biological Weapons Convention RevCon Meeting in Geneva* (remarks made in Geneva, UN, November 19, 2001), 5. See also Kathleen C. Bailey, *The UN Inspections in Iraq: Lessons for On-Site Verification* (Boulder, CO: Westview Press, 1995), 37–53.

105. See the essays of former UNSCOM inspectors in *Politics and the Life Sciences* 14, no. 2 (August 1995), including Raymond A. Zilinskas, "UNSCOM and the UNSCOM Experience in Iraq" and "Detecting and Deterring Biological Weapons in Iraq: The Role of Aerial Surveillance," pp. 230–235 and 255–258, respectively; David L. Huxsoll, "On-Site Inspection Measures and Interviews," pp. 238–239; David R. Franz, "Inventory Control of Dual-Use Equipment," pp. 244–247; Allen A. St-Onge, "United

Nations Biological Warfare Inspectors in Iraq: Implications for Biological Arms Control—One Canadian's Perspective," pp. 259–261. Also, Raymond A. Zilinskas, "Iraq's Biological Weapons: The Past as Future?" *Journal of American Medical Association* 278, no. 5 (August 6, 1997): 418–424.

106. Mohr, interview. Also, former UNSCOM biological weapons inspector, interview with author, May 27, 2006; Spertzel, interview; former UNSCOM chief biological weapons inspector, interview with author, August 28, 2005; Mohr, "Biological Sampling and Analysis Procedures for UNSCOM in Iraq," 243.

107. See Fred Charles Ikle, "After Detection—What?" *Foreign Affairs* 39, no 2 (January 1961): 208–220. Also on this debate, Kosta Tsipis, David W. Hafemeister, and Penny Janeway, eds., *Arms Control Verification: The Technologies That Make It Possible* (Washington: Pergamon-Brassey's, 1986); John G. Tower, James Brown and William K. Cheek, eds., *Verification: The Key to Arms Control in the 1990s* (Washington: Brassey's, 1992); Brad Roberts, "Revisiting Fred Ikle's 1961 Question: After Detection—What?" *Nonproliferation Review* 8, no. 1 (Spring 2001): 10–24.

108. *U.S. Policy in Iraq: Next Steps, Hearing Before the Senate Committee on Governmental Affairs, Subcommittee on International Security, Proliferation, and Federal Services,* U.S. Senate (March 1, 2002) (testimony of Richard O. Spertzel). Also, Robert P. Kadlec, "First, Do No Harm," *Arms Control Today* 31, no. 4 (May 2001): 16–17; Karen M. Jansen, "Disarming Iraq—Lessons for the Chemical Weapons Convention," *Chemical Weapons Convention Bulletin*, no. 24 (June 1994): 6.

109. Huxsoll, interview; Sellstrom, interview.

110. Ekeus, interview. Also, Duelfer, *Hide and Seek*, 170.

111. CIA, *Comprehensive Report of the Special Advisor to the DCI on Iraq's WMD*, vol. 1; vol. II, nuclear key findings, 7–8, 73–74, 83–112; vol. III, Iraq's chemical warfare program key findings, 29–60, 97–106, 113–125; biological warfare key findings, annexes A–D.

112. Kraatz-Wadsack, interview. Also, Government of the United Kingdom, "United Nations Special Commission BW Inspections in Iraq: Lessons for the Ad Hoc Experts' Group on Verification," 8–9, 10, 16.

113. Kelly, interview; Taylor, interview; Kraatz-Wadsack, interview; Lebherz, interview; former UNSCOM biological weapons inspector, interview with author, May 27, 2006; former UNSCOM CBW commissioner, interview with author via telephone, January 23, 2005; former senior UNSCOM official, interview with author, August 30, 2005.

114. Killip, interview. Also, Taylor, interview; foreign ministry official, interview with author, August 17, 2005; Kraatz-Wadsack, interview; former senior UNSCOM official, interview with author, August 30, 2005; Stephen Black, "UNSCOM and the Iraqi Biological Weapons Program: Technical Success, Political Failure," in *Biological Warfare and Disarmament: New Problems, New Perspectives*, ed. Susan Wright (New York: Rowman & Littlefield, 2002), 303.

115. Stephen Black, "The UN Special Commission and CBW Verification," *Chemical Weapons Convention Bulletin*, no. 32 (June 1996): 8.

116. Former senior UNSCOM official, interview with author, August 30, 2005. Also, Mohr, interview; former senior UNSCOM official, interview with author, September 1, 2005.

117. UN Security Council, *Twenty-Second Quarterly Report on the Activities of the United Nations Monitoring, Verification and Inspection Commission in accordance with Paragraph 12 of Security Council Resolution 1284 (1999)*, Doc. S/2005/545, August 30, 2005, Annex, para. 45. Also, Black, "UNSCOM and the Iraqi Biological Weapons Program," 303.

118. Killip, interview; Kelly, interview; Kraatz-Wadsack, interview; Mohr, interview; former senior UNSCOM official, interview with author, August 30, 2005. Also, Christian Seelos, "Lessons from Iraq on Bioweapons," *Nature* 398 (March 19, 1999): 187–188; Kraatz-Wadsack, "The Role of Scientists in Verification," 52.

119. Former UNSCOM biological weapons inspector, interview with author, May 27, 2006. Similarly, Killip, interview; Kraatz-Wadsack, interview; Kelly, interview.

120. Kadlec, interview. Also, Kadlec, "First, Do No Harm," 16. Likewise, Trevor Findlay, "A Standing United Nations Verification Body: Necessary and Feasible," *Compliance Chronicles* no. 1 (Ottawa: Canadian Centre for Treaty Compliance, December 2005); Terence Taylor, "Building on the Experience: Lessons from UNSCOM and UNMOVIC," *Disarmament Diplomacy* 75 (January/February 2004), http://www.acronym.org.uk/dd/dd75/75tt.htm.

121. Kadlec, interview. Also, Taylor, interview; Krikorian, interview; Killip, interview; former UNSCOM biological weapons inspector, interview with author, May 27, 2006; former UNSCOM chief inspector, interview with author, August 18, 2005.

Chapter 10

1. International Atomic Energy Agency (IAEA), General Conference, *Strengthening the Effectiveness and Improving the Efficiency of the Safeguards System*, Doc. GC (40)/17, August 23, 1996; IAEA, *Model Protocol Additional to the Agreement(s) Between State(s) and the International Atomic Energy Agency for the Application of Safeguards*, Doc. INFCIRC/540, September 1997; Joseph P. Harahan, *On-Site Inspections Under the INF Treaty* (Washington, DC: U.S. Department of Defense, 1993); Frank Barnaby, ed., *A Handbook of Verification Procedures* (London: Macmillan, 1990); Ola Dahlman, Svein Mykkeltveit, Hein Haak, *Nuclear Test Ban: Converting Political Visions to Reality* (New York: Springer, 2009); Elmer Engstrom, *Comprehensive Test Ban Negotiations, 1954 to 1981: Including the History of the Limited Test Ban Treaty, Threshold Test Ban Treaty, Peaceful Nuclear Explosions Treaty* (Cambridge, MA: Institute for Defense and Disarmament Studies, 1989).

2. Jez Littlewood, *The Biological Weapons Convention: A Revolution Failed* (Aldershot, U.K.: Ashgate, 2005); Mike Allen and Steve Mufson, "U.S. Scuttles Germ War

Conference; Move to Halt Talks Stuns European Allies," *Washington Post*, December 8, 2001, A1; Graham S. Pearson, "The US Rejection of the Protocol at the Eleventh Hour Damages International Security Against Biological Weapons," *CBW Conventions Bulletin*, no. 53 (September 2001): 6–9.

3. At the 56th session of the United Nations (UN) General Assembly, Canadian Foreign Minister John Manley (45th plenary meeting, November 10, 2001); German Minister of Foreign Affairs Joschka Fischer (48th plenary meeting, November 12, 2001); Polish Minister of Foreign Affairs Wlodzimierz Cimoszewicz (49th plenary meeting, November 12, 2001); New Zealand Minister of Foreign Affairs and Trade Phil Goff (49th plenary meeting, November 12, 2001); Dutch Minister of Foreign Affairs Jozias Van Aartsen (50th plenary meeting, November 13, 2001); Japanese Member of Parliament and former Prime Minister Kiichi Miyazawa (47th plenary meeting, November 11, 2001); U.S. President George W. Bush (46th plenary, November 10, 2001); Hungarian Minister of Foreign Affairs Janos Martonyi (51st plenary meeting, November 13, 2001). Their statements can be found at <http://www.un.org>.

4. Adrienne Mayor, *Greek Fire, Poison Arrows & Scorpion Bombs: Biological and Chemical Warfare in the Ancient World* (Woodstock, NY: Overlook Press, 2003), 41–205; Mark Wheelis, "Biological Warfare Before 1914," in *Biological and Toxin Weapons: Research, Development and Use from the Middle Ages to 1945*, ed. Erhard Geissler and John Ellis van Courtland Moon (Oxford: Oxford University Press, 1999), 10–34; Edward M. Eitzen and Ernest T. Takafuji, "Historical Overview of Biological Warfare," in *Medical Aspects of Chemical and Biological Warfare*, ed. Frederick R. Sidell, Ernest T. Takafuji, and David R. Franz (Washington, DC: Office of the Surgeon General at Textbook of Military Medicine Publications, 1997), 416–417.

5. John Ellis van Courtland Moon, "The US Biological Weapons Program," in *Deadly Cultures: Biological Weapons Since 1945*, ed. Mark Wheelis, Lajos Rozsa, and Malcolm Dando (Cambridge, MA: Harvard University Press, 2004), 11; Erhard Geissler, John Ellis van Courtland Moon, and Graham Pearson, "Lessons from the History of Biological and Toxin Warfare," in Geissler and van Courtland Moon, *Biological and Toxin Weapons*, 259–260; Edward M. Eitzen, "Use of Biological Weapons," in Sidell, Takafuji, and Franz, *Medical Aspects of Chemical and Biological Warfare*, 442–445.

6. Mark Wheelis, "Biological Sabotage in World War I," in Geissler and van Courtland Moon, *Biological and Toxin Weapons*, 35–62.

7. Erhard Geissler, "Biological Warfare Activities in Germany, 1923–45," in Geissler and van Courtland Moon, *Biological and Toxin Weapons*, 91–126; Jeffrey K. Smart, "History of Chemical and Biological Warfare: An American Perspective," in Sidell, Takafuji, and Franz, *Medical Aspects of Chemical and Biological Warfare*, 32; Jeanne Guillemin, *Biological Weapons: From the Invention of State-Sponsored Programs to Contemporary Bioterrorism* (New York: Columbia University Press, 2005), 26, 41, 136.

8. Olivier Lepick, "French Activities Related to Biological Warfare, 1919–45," in Geissler and van Courtland Moon, *Biological and Toxin Weapons*, 70–90; Olivier Lepick, "The French Biological Weapons Program," in Wheelis, Rozsa, and Dando, *Deadly Cultures*, 108–131.

9. Gradon B. Carter and Graham S. Pearson, "British Biological Warfare and Biological Defence, 1925–45," in Geissler and van Courtland Moon, *Biological and Toxin Weapons*, 168–189; Guillemin, *Biological Weapons*, 40–56.

10. Brian Balmer, "The UK Biological Weapons Program," in Wheelis, Rozsa, and Dando, *Deadly Cultures*, 47–83.

11. David E. Hoffman, *The Dead Hand: The Untold Story of the Cold War Arms Race and Its Dangerous Legacy* (New York: Doubleday, 2009), 330–342, 345–357, 431–437; Richard Preston, "Annals of Biowarfare: The Bioweaponeers," *New Yorker* 74, no. 3 (March 9, 1998): 52–65. David C. Kelly, "The Trilateral Agreement: Lessons for Biological Weapons Verification," in *Verification Yearbook 2002*, ed. Trevor Findlay and Oliver Meier (London: Verification, Inspection, and Training Centre,, 2002), 93–109; Tom Mangold and Jeff Goldberg, *Plague Wars* (New York: St. Martin's Press, 1999), 83–84; 130–131, 198–199.

12. Donald Avery, "Canadian Biological and Toxin Warfare Research, Development and Planning, 1925–45," in Geissler and van Courtland Moon, *Biological and Toxin Weapons*, 190–214.

13. Sheldon Harris, *Factories of Death: Japanese Biological Warfare, 1932–45 and the American Cover-Up* (London: Routledge, 2002); Peter Williams and David Wallace, *Unit 731: Japan's Secret Biological Warfare in World War II* (New York: Free Press, 1989); Eitzen and Takafuji, "Historical Overview of Biological Warfare," 417–418; Smart, "History of Chemical and Biological Warfare: An American Perspective," 32–33.

14. Smart, "History of Chemical and Biological Warfare: An American Perspective," 42–44, 52, 60–61; David R. Franz, Cheryl D. Parrott, and Ernest T. Takafuji, "The U.S. Biological Warfare and Biological Defense Programs," in Sidell, Takafuji, and Franz, *Medical Aspects of Chemical and Biological Warfare*, 427–429; John Ellis van Courtland Moon, "The US Biological Weapons Program," in Wheelis, Rozsa, and Dando, *Deadly Cultures*, 19, 25–26; Guillemin, *Biological Weapons*, 75–80, 86–90, 96–111; John Ellis van Courtland Moon, "US Biological Warfare Planning and Preparedness: The Dilemmas of Policy," in Geissler and van Courtland Moon, *Biological and Toxin Weapons*, 213–254.

15. Smart, "History of Chemical and Biological Warfare: An American Perspective," 50, 52, 60; Franz, Parrott, and Takafuji, "The U.S. Biological Warfare and Biological Defense Programs," 428–429; van Courtland Moon, "The US Biological Weapons Program," 24–28.

16. Smart, "History of Chemical and Biological Warfare: An American Perspective," 50–52, 60; van Courtland Moon, "The US Biological Weapons Program," 22–23,

37; Simon M. Whitby, "Anticrop Biological Weapons Programs," in Wheelis, Rozsa, and Dando, *Deadly Cultures*, 214–218.

17. Piers Millett, "Antianimal Biological Weapons Programs," in Wheelis, Rozsa, and Dando, *Deadly Cultures*, 224–228; U.S. Department of Homeland Security, *Fact Sheet: Plum Island Animal Disease Research Center Transition* (Washington, DC, June 6, 2003).

18. Smart, "History of Chemical and Biological Warfare: An American Perspective," 50–52, 59–60; Whitby, "Anticrop Biological Weapons Programs," 217–218; Millett, "Antianimal Biological Weapons Programs," 228.

19. Guillemin, *Biological Weapons*, 113–130. Quote on pages 125–126. Also, Smart, "History of Chemical and Biological Warfare: An American Perspective," 64; Franz, Parrott, and Takafuji, "The U.S. Biological Warfare and Biological Defense Programs," 431–435.

20. Valentin Bojtzov and Erhard Geissler, "Military Biology in the USSR, 1930–45," in Geissler and van Courtland Moon, *Biological and Toxin Weapons*, 153–167; Jonathan B. Tucker and Ray Zilinskas, eds., *The 1971 Smallpox Epidemic in Aralsk Kazakhstan and the Soviet Biological Warfare Program*, Occ. Paper no. 9 (Monterey, CA: Center for Nonproliferation Studies, 2002), 5–6.

21. For more information on the Convention, go to <http://www.opbw.org>.

22. For insider accounts, Ivan Domaradski and Wendy Orent, *Biowarrior: Inside the Soviet/Russian Biological War Machine* (Amherst, NY: Prometheus, 2003); Ken Alibek with Stephen Handelman, *Biohazard: The Chilling True Story of the Largest Covert Biological Weapons Program in the World* (New York: Random House, 1999). On the trilateral inspections, Kelly, "The Trilateral Agreement," 93–109; Hoffman, *The Dead Hand*, 345–357, 431–437. On collaborative research programs with former Soviet weaponeers, Amy E. Smithson, *Toxic Archipelago: Preventing Proliferation from the Former Soviet Chemical and Biological Weapons Complexes*, Report no. 32 (Washington, DC: Henry L. Stimson Center, December 1999).

23. Anthony Rimmington, "From Military to Industrial Complex? The Conversion of Biological Weapons Facilities in the Russian Federation," *Contemporary Security Policy* 17 (April 1996): 81–112; John Hart, "The Soviet Biological Weapons Program," in Wheelis, Rozsa, and Dando, *Deadly Cultures*, 140–141; Mangold and Goldberg, *Plague Wars*, 62–213; Guillemin, *Biological Weapons*, 141–147; "Section F: Declaration of Past Activities in Offensive/Defensive Biological Research and Development Programs," UN doc. DDA/4-92/BWIII/ADD.2, Moscow, Russian Federation, 1992, 85.

24. Hoffman, *The Dead Hand*, 460–466, 479; Gulbarshyn Bozheyeva, Yerlan Kunakbayev, and Dastan Yeleukenov, *Former Soviet Biological Weapons Facilities in Kazakhstan: Past, Present, and Future*, Occasional paper no. 1 (Monterey, CA: Center for Nonproliferation Studies, June 1999), 4–5, 8–12; Alibek with Handelman, *Biohazard*, 82–93, 96–99, 105–106.

25. Tucker and Zilinskas, eds., *The 1971 Smallpox Epidemic*, 12–7; Hoffman, *The Dead Hand*, 467–469; Bozheyeva, Kunakbayev, and Yeleukenov, *Former Soviet Biological Weapons Facilities in Kazakhstan*, 4–5.

26. Whitby, "Anticrop Biological Weapons Programs," 223–224; Millett, "Antianimal Biological Weapons Programs," 229–231.

27. Bozheyeva, Kunakbayev, and Yeleukenov, *Former Soviet Biological Weapons Facilities in Kazakhstan*, 12; Alibek with Handelman, *Biohazard*, 301–302.

28. Alibek with Handelman, *Biohazard*, 113–118, 126–127, 175, 202; Hart, "The Soviet Biological Weapons Program," 141, 144. "Interview with Ken Alibek," *Journal of Homeland Security* (September 28, 2000), http://www.homelandsecurity.org/journal/Search.aspx?s=Ken+Alibek.

29. "Interview with Sergei Popov," *Journal of Homeland Security* (November 1, 2000, updated November 19, 2002), http://www.homelandsecurity.org/journal/Default.aspx?oid=3&ocat=4. See also Alibek with Handelman, *Biohazard*, 66–67, 78, 87–89, 97, 105, 153–167, 261–262, 281; Hoffman, *The Dead Hand*, 130–134, 296–299, 325, 335, 347–248, 352, 425–426.

30. "Interview with Ken Alibek"; Alibek with Handelman, *Biohazard*, x–xi, 20–21, 78, 111–114, 140–141, 166, 272, 281. Whitby, "Anticrop Biological Weapons Programs," 223–224; Millett, "Antianimal Biological Weapons Programs," 229–231.

31. "Section F: Declaration of Past Activities in Offensive/Defensive Biological Research and Development Programs," 85. Quote translated from Russian. For more on voluntary data declarations, see Erhard Geissler, ed., *Strengthening the Biological Weapons Convention by Confidence-Building Measures*, SIPRI Chemical & Biological Warfare Studies no. 10 (Oxford: Oxford University Press, 1990).

32. "Interview with Ken Alibek." Also, "Interview with Sergei Popov." On opposition to Yeltsin's efforts to shut down the program, see Hoffman, *The Dead Hand*, 424–438. See as well, Decree of the President of the Russian Federation on Providing Fulfillment of International Obligations in the Field of Biological Weapons, Decree no. 390 (Moscow: April 11, 1992); R. Jeffrey Smith, "Yeltsin Blames '79 Anthrax on Germ Warfare Efforts," *Washington Post*, June 16, 1992, A1. On concerns about a continuing program, see Hart, "The Soviet Biological Weapons Program," 154–156.

33. Chandre Gould and Alastair Hay, "The South African Biological Weapons Program," in Wheelis, Rozsa, and Dando, *Deadly Cultures*, 191–212; Mangold and Goldberg, *Plague Wars*, 214–282; Nuclear Threat Initiative, "South Africa: Biological Overview," http://www.nti.org/e_research/profiles/index.html.

34. Joshua Sinai, "Libya's Pursuit of WMD," *Nonproliferation Review* 4, no. 3 (Spring-Summer 1997): 92–99; Sharon Squassoni, *Disarming Libya: Weapons of Mass Destruction* (Washington, DC: Library of Congress, Congressional Research Service, September 22, 2006), 1–3; Patrick E. Tyler and James Risen, "Secret Diplomacy Won Libyan Pledge on Arms," *New York Times*, December 21, 2003, A1.

35. Mangold and Goldberg, *Plague Wars*, 322–334; Nuclear Threat Initiative, "North Korea Profile: Biological Weapons Overview," http://www.nti.org/e_research/profiles/index.html; Russian Federation, Foreign Intelligence Service Report, *A New Challenge After the Cold War: Proliferation of Mass Destruction Weapons*, JPRS-TND-93-007 (Arlington, VA: Joint Publications Research Service, March 5, 1993); Alibek with Handelman, *Biohazard*, 273.

36. Avner Cohen, "Israel and Chemical/Biological Weapons: History, Deterrence, and Arms Control," *Nonproliferation Review* 8, no. 3 (Fall-Winter 2001): 27–53; M. Zuhair Diab, "Syria's Chemical and Biological Weapons: Assessing Capabilities and Motivations," *Nonproliferation Review* 5, no. 1 (Fall 1997): 104–111; Nuclear Threat Initiative, "Syria Profile: Biological Overview" and "Iran Profile: Biological Overview," http://www.nti.org/e_research/profiles/index.html. For U.S. charges that China has sustained some offensive bioweapons activities and abetted the proliferation of such weapons, see *Hearing on China's Proliferation Practices and the North Korean Nuclear Crisis, Before the United States–China Economic and Security Review Commission*, 108th Cong., 1st sess. (July 24, 2003) (statement of Paula A. DeSutter, Assistant Secretary of State for Verification and Compliance), 7–31; *Hearing on China's Proliferation to North Korea and Iran, and Its Role in Addressing the Nuclear and Missile Situation in Both Nations, Before the United States–China Economic and Security Review Commission*, 109th Cong., 2nd sess. (September 14, 2006) (statement of Paula A. DeSutter, Assistant Secretary of State for Verification and Compliance), 5–12. The U.S.S.R. had indications that China was weaponizing viral agents and had a possible biowarfare facility in the vicinity of Lop Nur. Alibek with Handelman, *Biohazard*, 273.

37. Amy E. Smithson, with Leslie-Anne Levy, *Ataxia: The Chemical and Biological Terrorism Threat and the US Response*, report no. 35 (Washington, DC: Stimson Center, October 2000), 71–91, 106; Milton Leitenberg, "Aum Shinrikyo's Efforts to Produce Biological Weapons: A Case Study in the Serial Propagation of Misinformation," *Terrorism and Political Violence* 11, no. 4 (1999): 149–158.

38. *Global Proliferation of Weapons of Mass Destruction, Hearings Before the Permanent Subcommittee on Investigations of the Senate Committee on Governmental Affairs*, 104th Cong., 1st sess. (1996), 273–276.

39. Thomas J. Torok et al., "A Large Community Outbreak of Salmonellosis Caused by Intentional Contamination of Restaurant Salad Bars," in *Biological Weapons: Limiting the Threat*, ed. Joshua Lederberg (Cambridge: MIT Press, 1999), 167–184; W. Seth Carus, "The Rajneeshees (1984)," in *Toxic Terror: Assessing the Terrorist Use of Chemical and Biological Weapons*, ed. Jonathon B. Tucker (Cambridge: MIT Press, 2000), 115–137; Mark Wheelis and Masaaki Sugishima, "Terrorist Use of Biological Weapons," in Wheelis, Rozsa, and Dando, *Deadly Cultures*, 286–293.

40. William J. Broad, "A Nation Challenged: The Spores; Contradicting Some U.S. Officials, 3 Scientists Call Anthrax Powder High-Grade," *New York Times*, October 25,

2001, B6; William J. Broad and David Johnson, "Anthrax Sent Through Mail Gained Potency by the Letter," *New York Times*, May 7, 2002, A1; Gary Matsumoto, "Anthrax Powder: State of the Art?" *Science* 302, no. 5650 (November 28, 2003): 1492–1497; "Investigation of Bioterrorism Related Anthrax," *Journal of the American Medical Association* 286, no. 21 (5 December 2001): 2662–2663; National Research Council, *Review of the Scientific Approaches Used During the FBI's Investigation of the 2001 Anthrax Letters* (Washington, DC: National Academies Press, 2011); Philipp Sarasin and Giselle Weiss, *Anthrax: Bioterror as Fact and Fantasy* (Cambridge, MA: Harvard University Press, 2006); Marilyn Thompson, *The Killer Strain, Anthrax, and a Government Exposed* (New York: HarperCollins, 2003).

41. Dan Eggen, "Letter with Ricin Vial Sent to White House," *Washington Post*, February 4, 2004, A7; Federal Bureau of Investigation, "Ricin Letter," press release, Washington, DC, February 23, 2004; *Hearings on Bioterrorism, Before the Senate Judiciary Subcommittee on Technology, Terrorism and Government Information*, U.S. Senate (November 6, 2001) (testimony of J. T. Caruso, deputy assistant director, Counterterrorism Division, FBI).

42. Databases on terrorist activities are available at <http://www.mipt.org> and <http://www.nti.org/db/cbw/index.htm>. Briefly, Jonathan B. Tucker and Amy Sands, "An Unlikely Threat," *Bulletin of the Atomic Scientists* 44, no. 4 (July-August 1999): 46–52.

43. Bruce Hoffman, *Inside Terrorism* (New York: Columbia University Press, 1998); Brian Jenkins, ed., *Countering the New Terrorism* (Santa Monica, CA: RAND, 1999); The Advisory Panel to Assess Domestic Response Capabilities for Terrorism Involving Weapons of Mass Destruction, *First Annual Report to the President and Congress of the Advisory Panel to Assess Domestic Response Capabilities for Terrorism Involving Weapons of Mass Destruction: I. Assessing the Threat* (Washington, DC: RAND, December 15, 1999); Robert K. Mullen, "Mass Destruction and Terrorism," *Journal of International Affairs* 32, no. 1 (Spring-Summer 1978): 63–89; Roberta Wohlstetter, "Terror on a Grand Scale," *Survival* 18, no. 3 (1978): 98–104.

44. Commission on the Prevention of Weapons of Mass Destruction Proliferation and Terrorism, *World at Risk: The Report of the Commission on the Prevention of Weapons of Mass Destruction Proliferation and Terrorism* (New York: Vintage Books, 2008), xi; National Intelligence Council, *Mapping the Global Future*, NIC-2004-13 (Washington, DC: U.S. Government Printing Office, December 2004), 100; National Intelligence Council, *Global Trends 2025: A Transformed World*, NIC-2008-003 (Washington, DC: U.S. Government Printing Office, November 2008), 70; *The Biological Weapons Threat and Nonproliferation Options: A Survey of Senior U.S. Decision Makers and Policy Shapers* (Washington, DC: Center for Strategic and International Studies, November 2006), 10, 15–19.

45. Martin Shubik, "Terrorism, Technology, and Socioeconomics of Death," *Comparative Strategy* 16, no. 4 (October 1997): 399, 406, 408.

46. For a synopsis of the appeal of biological weapons, see the Introduction.

47. Terence Taylor, "Safeguarding Advances in the Life Sciences: The International Council for the Life Sciences Is Committed to Becoming the Authoritative Source for Identifying and Managing Biological Risks," *EMBO Reports* 7, no. SI (2006): S61.

48. Institute of Medicine, *Emerging Infections: Microbial Threats to Health in the United States*, (Washington, DC: National Academies Press, January 1992); Institute of Medicine, *Emerging Infectious Diseases from the Global to the Local Perspective: Workshop Summary*, (Washington, DC: National Academies Press, April 2001); Laurie Garrett, *The Coming Plague* (New York: Farrar, Straus & Giroux, 1994); Felissa R. Lashley and Jerry D. Durham, eds., *Emerging Infectious Diseases: Trends and Issues*, 2nd ed. (New York: Springer, 2007). Current developments can be followed in journals such as *Emerging Infectious Diseases* and at the World Health Organization's Global Health Atlas at <http://www.who.org>.

49. United Nations, *Final Document of the Fifth Review Conference of the States Parties to the Convention on the Prohibition of the Development, Production, and Stockpiling of Bacteriological (Biological) and Toxin Weapons and on Their Destruction*, Doc. BWC/CONF.V/17, Geneva, November 11–22, 2002, 18(a); United Nations, *Final Document of the Sixth Review Conference of the States Parties to the Convention on the Prohibition of the Development, Production, and Stockpiling of Bacteriological (Biological) and Toxin Weapons and on Their Destruction*, Doc. BWC/CONF.VI/16, Geneva, November 20–December 8, 2006, Part III, para. 7 (a). Documents from these meetings are available at <http://www.opbw.org> and at <http://www.unog.ch>.

50. For more on biosafety, see U.S. Department of Health and Human Services, *Biosafety in Microbiological and Biomedical Laboratories*, 5th ed. (Washington, DC: U.S. Government Printing Office, 2009).

51. U.S. Department of State, "New Ways to Strengthen the International Regime Against Biological Weapons," Fact Sheet (Washington, DC: Department of State, October 19, 2001); John R. Bolton, *Remarks to the Fifth Biological Weapons Convention Review Conference Meeting*, Geneva, November 19, 2001; Jonathan B. Tucker, "The BWC Process: A Preliminary Assessment," *Nonproliferation Review* 11, no. 1 (March 2004): 32–33.

52. For example, National Institutes of Health, *Biosafety in Microbiological and Biomedical Laboratories*; Amy E. Smithson, ed., *Beijing on Biohazards: Chinese Experts on Bioweapons Nonproliferation Issues* (Washington, DC: Center for Nonproliferation Studies, August 2007); *Laboratory Biosafety Manual*, 3rd ed. (Geneva: World Health Organization, 2004). For more on WHO's biosafety training and resources, see <http://www.who.int/csr/bioriskreduction/biosafety/en/>.

53. Tucker and Zilinskas, *The 1971 Smallpox Epidemic*, 10; *Symposium on Opportunities and Challenges in the Emerging Field of Synthetic Biology: Synthesis Report* (Paris: Organization for Economic Cooperation and Development, The Royal Society, 2010), 35.

54. Council for Responsible Genetics, "Mistakes Happen: Accidents and Security Breaches at Biocontainment Facilities" (Cambridge, MA: Council for Responsible Genetics, July 5, 2007). U.S. cases of laboratory acquired infections are reported in *Morbidity and Mortality Weekly Report*.

55. On the 2007 outbreaks, see <http://www.defra.gov.uk/FootandMouth/2007/index.htm>. On the 2001 outbreak, see *Origin of the UK Foot and Mouth Disease Epidemic in 2001* (London: Department of Environment, Food and Rural Affairs, June 2002).

56. C. H. Collins and D. A. Kennedy, *Laboratory-Acquired Infections: History, Incidences, Causes, and Preventions* (London: Hodder Arnold, 1999); Marilyn P. Ogren, "An Accident Waiting to Happen," *Scientist* 17, no. 2 (January 27, 2003): 30–33; Council for Responsible Genetics, "Mistakes Happen: Accidents and Security Breaches at Biocontainment Facilities."

57. Jennifer Gaudioso, Susan Caskey, Tamera Zemlo, "Understanding Current Laboratory Biosafety and Biosecurity Practices Around the World," presentation at the 50th Annual Biosafety Conference, Nashville, TN, October 2007.

58. National Intelligence Council, *Global Trends 2025: A Transformed World*, 47–48.

59. Malcolm Dando, *Biological Warfare in the 21st Century: Biotechnology and the Proliferation of Biological Weapons* (New York: Macmillan, 1994), 210. See also Robert Carlson, "The Pace and Proliferation of Biological Technologies," *Biosecurity, Bioterrorism: Biodefense Strategy, Practice, and Science* 1, no. 3 (2003): 203–214.

60. Jan van Aken and Darrell Hammond, "Genetic Engineering and Biological Weapons: New Technologies, Desires and Threats from Biological Research," *EMBO Reports* 4, no. S1 (2003): S57–S60. Also on the Soviet bioweapons program, see Mangold and Goldberg, *Plague Wars*, 93–94; Alibek with Handelman, *Biohazard*, 40–42, 153–167, 234, 259–260; Hart, "The Soviet Biological Weapons Program," 132–156.

61. Ronald Jackson et al., "Expression of Mouse Interleukin-4 by a Recombinant Ectromelia Virus Suppresses Cytolytic Lymphocyte Responses and Overcomes Genetic Resistance to Mousepox," *Journal of Virology* 75, no. 3 (February 2001): 1205–1210; Rachel Nowak, "Disaster in the Making: An Engineered Mouse Virus Leaves Us One Step Away from the Ultimate Bioweapon," *New Scientist* 169, no. 2273 (January 13, 2001): 4–5. With another controversial experiment, Ariella M. Rosengard et al., "Variola Virus Immune Evasion Design: Expression of a Highly Efficient Inhibitor of Human Complement," *Proceedings of the National Academy of Sciences* 99, no. 13 (June 25, 2002): 8808–8813.

62. J. Cello, A. V. Paul, E. Wimmer, "Chemical Synthesis of Poliovirus cDNA: Generation of Infectious Virus in the Absence of Natural Template," *Science* 297, no. 5583 (2002); Terence M. Tumpey et al., "Characterization of the Reconstructed 1918 Spanish Influenza Pandemic Virus," *Science* 310, no. 5745 (October 7, 2005): 77–80; Jeffrey K. Tautenberger et al., "Characterization of the 1918 Influenza Virus Polymerase Genes," *Nature* 437 (October 6, 2005): 889–893.

63. Daniel G. Gibson et al., "Creation of a Bacterial Cell Controlled by a Chemically Synthesized Genome," *Science* 328, 5987 (July 2, 2010): 52–56; S. Enterlain et al., "Rescue of Recombinant Marburg Virus from cDNA Is Dependent on Nucleocapsid Protein VP30," *Journal of Virology* 80, no. 2 (2006): 1038–1043; Michelle M. Becker et al., "Synthetic Recombinant Bat SARS-like Coronavirus Is Infectious in Cultured Cells and in Mice," *Proceedings of the National Academy of Sciences* 105, no. 50 (November 26, 2008): 19944–19949; Daniel G. Gibson et al., "Complete Chemical Synthesis, Assembly, and Cloning of a *Mycoplasma genitalium* Genome," *Science* 319, no. 5867 (February 29, 2008): 1215–1220.

64. Robert F. Massung et al., "Potential Virulence Determinants in Terminal Regions of Variola Smallpox Virus Genome," *Nature* 366 (December 30, 1993): 748–751.

65. J. Tian, et al., "Accurate Multiplex Gene Synthesis from Programmable DNA Microchips," *Nature* 432, no. 7020 (December 23–30, 2004): 1050–1054; *Symposium on Opportunities and Challenges in the Emerging Field of Synthetic Biology: Synthesis Report*, 35.

66. Committee on Advances in Technology and the Prevention of Their Application to Next Generation Biowarfare Threats, *Globalization, Biosecurity, and the Future of the Life Sciences* (Washington, DC: National Academies Press, 2006), 139–212, 214; National Research Council, *Biotechnology Research in an Age of Terrorism* (Washington, DC: National Academies Press, 2004).

67. Matthew Meselson, "Averting the Hostile Exploitation of Biotechnology," *The CBW Conventions Bulletin*, no. 48 (June 2000): 16. Similarly, British Medical Association Board of Science and BMA Science & Education Department, *The Use of Drugs as Weapons: The Concerns and Responsibilities of Healthcare Professionals* (London: British Medical Association, May 2007), 1. On the implications of the revolution in the life sciences for the bioweapons threat, see Malcolm Dando, *Biological Warfare in the 21st Century*; British Medical Association, *Biotechnology, Weapons and Humanity II* (London: Harwood Academic, 2004); David G. Victor and C. Ford Runge, "Farming the Genetic Frontier," *Foreign Affairs* 81, no. 3 (May-June 2002): 107–121; Jonathan B. Tucker and Craig Hooper, "Protein Engineering: Security Implications," *EMBO Reports* 7, no. SI (2006): S14–S17; Mark Wheelis, "Biotechnology and Biochemical Weapons," *Nonproliferation Review* 9, no. 1 (2002): 48–53; Stephen M. Block, "Biological Threats Enabled by Molecular Biology," in *The New Terror: Facing the Threat of Biological and Chemical Weapons*, ed. Sidney D. Drell, Abraham D. Sofaer, and George D. Wilson (Stanford, CA: Hoover Institution Press, 1999), 39–75; Richard Danzig, *Catastrophic Bioterrorism: What Is to Be Done?* (Blue Ridge Summit, PA: Bernan Press, 2003); Jonathan B. Tucker and Raymond A. Zilinskas, "The Promise and Perils of Synthetic Biology," *The New Atlantis*, no. 12 (Spring 2006): 25–45; Margaret Kosal, *Nanotechnology for Chemical and Biological Defense* (New York: Springer, 2009), 89–98.

68. Paul Berg, "Meetings That Changed the World: Asilomar 1975: DNA Modification Secured," *Nature* 445 (September 18, 2008): 290–291; Michael Rogers, *Biohazard* (New York: Alfred A. Knopf, 1977). See *NIH Guidelines for Research Involving Recombinant DNA Molecules* (Washington, DC: National Institutes of Health, April 2002).

69. Jeanne Whalen, "In Attics and in Closets, 'Biohackers' Discover Their Inner Frankenstein: Using Mail-Order DNA and Iguana Heaters, Hobbyists Brew New Life Forms; Is It Risky?" *Wall Street Journal*, May 12, 2009, 1; Chris Ayres, "Why Frankenstein's Monster Might Come to Life in a Garage; United States," *The Times* (London), December 27, 2008, 55. Also, go to <http://bio.org>.

70. Act on the Regulation of Genetic Engineering, as revised December 16, 1993, Section 3 (4)(5)(6), Section 39. For an overview of the United Kingdom's oversight system, see John Steinbruner, Elisa D. Harris, Nancy Gallagher, and Stacy Okutani, *Controlling Dangerous Pathogens: A Prototype Protective Oversight System* (College Park, MD: Center for International and Security Studies, March 2007), 15–18.

71. Quote from Jan van Aiken, "When Risk Outweighs Benefit," *EMBO Reports* 7, no. SI (2006): S13. On the malfunction of U.S. institutional biosafety committees, see Filippa Corneliussen, "Adequate Regulation, a Stopgap Measure, or Part of a Package?" *EMBO Reports* 7, no. SI (2006): S52–S53.

72. National Research Council, *Biotechnology Research in an Age of Terrorism*, 5–6. Also, U.S. National Science Advisory Board on Biosecurity, *Proposed Framework for the Oversight of Duel Use Life Sciences Research: Strategies for Minimizing the Potential Misuse of Information* (Washington, DC: National Institutes of Health, June 2007). See as well The Royal Society and Wellcome Trust, "Do No Harm: Reducing the Potential for the Misuse of Life Science Research" (report of a Royal Society-Wellcome Trust meeting at The Royal Society, London, October 7, 2004).

73. Jessica Eve Stern, "Larry Wayne Harris (1998)," in Tucker, *Toxic Terror*, 227–246; Smithson with Levy, *Ataxia*, 40–42.

74. The 1996 Antiterrorism and Effective Death Penalty Act, Pub. L. No. 104–132 (April 24, 1996); 2001 USA Patriot Act, Pub. L. No. 107–156 (October 26, 2001); The 2002 Public Health and Bioterrorism Preparedness Act, Pub. L. No. 107–188 (June 12, 2002); Reynolds M. Salerno and Jennifer Gaudioso, *Laboratory Biosecurity Handbook* (New York: CRC, 2007).

75. Marilyn W. Thompson, Carrie Johnson, Rob Stein, "FBI to Show How Genetics Led to Anthrax Researcher," *Washington Post*, August 6, 2008, A3; Scott Shane and Eric Lichtblau, "F.B.I Presents Anthrax Case, Saying Scientist Acted Alone," *New York Times*, August 7, 2008, A1; Carrie Johnson, Del Quentin Wilber, Dan Eggen, "Government to Assert Researcher Acted Alone; Detail Evidence, Suspicions Linger," *Washington Post*, August 7, 2008, A1; Joby Warrick, "Documents List Essential Clues; Taken

Together Data Called Compelling," *Washington Post*, August 7, 2008, A17. Also, go to <http://www.fbi.gov/anthrax/amerithraxlinks.htm>.

76. Scott Shane, "Portrait Emerges of Anthrax Suspect's Troubled Life," *New York Times*, January 4, 2009, A1; Amy Gold Stein, Nelson Hernandez, Anne Hull, "Tales of Addiction, Anxiety, Ranting; Scientist, Counselor Recount Recent Turmoil in Anthrax Suspect's Life," *Washington Post*, August 6, 2008, A1.

77. Scott Shane, "Army Suspends Germ Research at Maryland Lab," *New York Times*, February 10, 2009, A16; David Dishneau, "Md. Lab Research Halted for Records," Associated Press, February 9, 2009; Nelson Hernandez, "Most Research Suspended at Ft. Detrick," *Washington Post*, February 10, 2009, B2; Nelson Hernandez, "Inventory Uncovers 9,200 More Pathogens," *Washington Post*, June 18, 2009, B8; Martin Matishak, "Thousands of Uncounted Disease Samples Found at Army Biodefense Lab," *Global Security Newswire*, June 18, 2009.

78. U.S. National Science Advisory Board on Biosecurity, *Enhancing Personnel Reliability Among Individuals with Access to Select Agents* (Washington, DC: National Institutes of Health, May 2009). Also, 42 Code of Federal Regulations, Part 73, "Possession, Use, and Transfer of Select Agents and Toxins; Interim Final Rule," *Federal Register* 240, no. 67 (December 13, 2002): 76889–76890.

79. Julie E. Fischer, *Stewardship or Censorship? Balancing Biosecurity, the Public Health and the Benefits of Scientific Openness* (Washington, DC: Henry L. Stimson Center, February 2006), 19–39; *Globalization, Biosecurity, and the Future of the Life Sciences*, 54; Marc L. Ostfeld, "Pathogen Security: The Illusion of Security in Foreign Policy and Biodefense," *International Journal of Risk Assessment and Management* 12, nos. 2, 3, 4 (2009): 208–211; Jonathan B. Tucker, *Biosecurity: Limiting Terrorist Access to Deadly Pathogens*, report no. 52 (Washington, DC: U.S. Institute of Peace, November 2003).

80. Jonathan B. Tucker, "Strategies to Prevent Bioterrorism: Biosecurity Policies in the United States and Germany," *Disarmament Diplomacy*, no. 84 (Spring 2007): 36–47.

81. *Globalization, Biosecurity, and the Future of the Life Sciences*, 95–129; Kathleen M. Vogel, "Biodefense: Considering the Sociotechnical Dimension," in *Biosecurity Interventions: Global Health and Security in Question*, ed. Andrew Lakoff and Stephen J. Collier (New York: Columbia University Press, 2008): 227–249; Kendall Hoyt and Stephen G. Brooks, "A Double-Edged Sword: Globalization and Biosecurity," *International Security* 28, no. 3 (Winter 2003-2004): 123–148; Rita Grossman-Vermaas, Brian D. Findlay, and Elizabeth Turpen, *Old Plagues, New Threats: The Biotech Revolution and Its Impact on US National Security* (Washington, DC: Henry L. Stimson Center, March 2008); Rita Grossman-Vermaas, Brian D. Findlay, and Elizabeth Turpen, *Regulating Access to and Control of Pathogens: Implications for the Pharmaceutical Industry*, report no. 58 (Washington, DC: Henry L. Stimson Center, February 2007);

Brian D. Finlay, "Minding Our Business: The Role of the Private Sector in Managing the WMD Supply Chain," *WMD Insights* (February 2009), http://www.wmdinsights.com/I30/I30_G1_MindingBusiness.htm.

82. *Globalization, Biosecurity, and the Future of the Life Sciences*, 84–97,112–119.

83. Go to <http://www.niaid.nih.gov/factsheets/facilityconstruct_06.htm>. Also, *Preliminary Observations on the Oversight of the Proliferation of BSL-3 and BSL-4 in the United States*, GAO-08-108T (Washington, DC: U.S. Government Accountability Office, October 4, 2007), 9–10; World Health Organization, "Biosafety and Biosecurity in Health Laboratories" (report of the regional workshop, Pune, India, July 8–11, 2008), 8.

84. *Biorisk Management: Laboratory Biosecurity Guidance*, Doc. WHO/CDS/EPR/2006.6 (Geneva: World Health Organization, 2006). For more on WHO's biosecurity training and resources, go to <http://www.who.int/csr/bioriskreduction/biosafety/en/>.

85. United Nations, *Report of the 2007 Meeting of States Parties*, Doc. BWC/MSP/2007/5, Geneva, December 10–14, 2007, paras. 21–6. For national laws, regulations, decrees, and guidelines, go to <http://www.un.org/sc/1540/>.

86. World Health Organization, *SARS: How a Global Epidemic Was Stopped* (Manila: WHO Regional Office for the Western Pacific, 2006). To track the progress of H5N1 influenza virus, go to <http://www.who.int/csr/disease/avian_influenza/en/>. On Ebola outbreaks from 1997 forward, go to <http://www.cdc.gov/ncidod/dvrd/spb/mnpages/dispages/ebola/ebolatable.htm>.

87. The responsible sales conduct codes of two groups of gene synthesis companies, the International Association of Synthetic Biology and the International Gene Synthesis Consortium, announced in November 2009, can be found at <http://www.ia-sb.eu/tasks/sites/synthetic-biology/assets/File/pdf/iasb_code_of_conduct_final.pdf> and <http://www.genesynthesisconsortium.org/Harmonized_Screening_Protocol.html>. See also Hubert Bernauer et al., "Technical Solutions for Biosecurity in Synthetic Biology," report on the Workshop, Industry Association of Synthetic Biology, Munich, April 3, 2008, http://www.synbiosafe.eu/uploads///pdf/iasb_report_biosecurity_syntheticbiology.pdf. As well, see Michelle S. Garfinkel, Drew Endy, Gerald L. Epstein, and Robert M. Friedman, *Synthetic Genomics: Options for Governance* (Rockville, MD: J. Craig Venter Institute, October 2007); Ali Nouri and Christopher F. Chyba, "Proliferation-Resistant Biotechnology: A Novel Approach to Improve Biosecurity," *Nature Biotechnology* 27, no. 3 (2009): 234–236; U.S. National Science Advisory Board on Biosecurity, *Addressing Biosecurity Concerns Related to the Synthesis of Select Agents* (Washington, DC: National Institutes of Health, December 2006), 11.

88. E. Check Hayden, "Experiments of Concern to Be Vetted On-Line," *Nature* 457 (February 5, 2009): 643. The screening portal can be accessed at <http://gsppi.berkeley.edu/EoC/uc-berkeley-synthetic-biology-security-program/experiments-of-concern>.

89. Gabriele Kraatz-Wadsack, "The Role of Scientists in Verification," in *Assessing the Threat of Weapons of Mass Destruction: The Role of Independent Scientists*, ed. J. L. Finney and I. Slaus, vol. 61, NATO Science for Peace and Security Series E: Human and Societal Dynamics (Amsterdam: IOS Press), 46. On requirements for a bioweapons program, see Office of Technology Assessment, *Technologies Underlying Weapons of Mass Destruction*, OTA-BP-ISC-115 (Washington, DC: U.S. Government Printing Office, December 1993), 71–117; Smithson with Levy, *Ataxia*, 37–56.

90. *Commission on the Intelligence Capabilities of the United States Regarding Weapons of Mass Destruction: Report to the President of the United States* (Washington, DC: U.S. Government Printing Office, March 31, 2005), quotes from pages 1, 82. Also, 88–111. Charles Duelfer, *Hide and Seek: The Search for Truth in Iraq* (New York: Public Affairs, 2009), 456, 470; Bob Drogin, *Curveball: Spies, Lies, and the Con Man Who Caused a War* (New York: Random House, 2007).

91. Central Intelligence Agency (CIA), *Comprehensive Report of the Special Advisor to the DCI on Iraq's WMD*, (Washington, DC, September 30, 2004), vol. 1, vol. III, Iraq's chemical warfare program key findings, 29–60, 97–106, 113–125; biological warfare key findings, annexes A-D.

92. John D. Negroponte and Edward M. Wittenstein, "Urgency, Opportunity, and Frustration: Implementing the Terrorism Reform and Prevention Act of 2004," *Yale Law & Policy Review* 28, no. 2 (June 2010): 379–461. Observing that Congress can "add resources and organizations," but that "[i]ncreased quality . . . cannot be legislated," Duelfer, *Hide and Seek*, 476.

93. David Hoffman, "Wastes of War: A Puzzle of Epidemic Proportions," *Washington Post*, December 16, 1998, A1; Victor Israelyan, "Fighting Anthrax: A Cold Warrior's Confession," *Washington Quarterly* 25, no. 2 (Spring 2002): 17–29; Mangold and Goldberg, *Plague Wars*, 66–82; Alibek with Handelman, *Biohazard*, 70–86; M. Meselson, J. Guillemin, M. Hugh-Jones, I. Popova, et al., "The Sverdlovsk Anthrax Outbreak of 1979," *Science* 266, no. 5188 (November 18, 1994): 1202–1208; Jeanne Guillemin, *Anthrax: The Investigation of a Deadly Outbreak* (Berkeley, CA: University of California Press, 1999).

94. On Ishii, see Harris, *Factories of Death*; Williams and Wallace, *Unit 731*. On the Nazi doctor who experimented on prisoners at Auschwitz, see Gerald Astor, *The Last Nazi: The Life and Times of Dr. Joseph Mengele* (New York: Donald I. Fine, 1985.)

95. The World Health Organization coordinates and aids implementation of the International Health Regulations. For more, go to <http://www.searo.who.int/en/Section10/Section2362.htm>.

96. "Annan Calls for Strategy to Prevent Biological Weapons Falling into Terrorists' Hands," *UN News Centre*, November 20, 2006.

97. For related proposals, see "Annan Calls for Strategy to Prevent Biological Weapons Falling into Terrorists' Hands;" David P. Fidler and Lawrence O. Gostin,

Biosecurity in the Global Age: Biological Weapons, Public Health, and the Rule of Law (Stanford, CA: Stanford University Press, 2007); Ronald M. Atlas, "National Security and the Biological Research Community," *Science* 298, no. 5594 (October 2002): 753–754; Fischer, *Stewardship or Censorship*, 90–91.

98. Mary Beth Sheridan, "Obama Secures 47-Nation Pact at Nuclear Summit," *Washington Post*, April 14, 2010, A1; Office of the Press Secretary, "Work Plan of the Washington Security Summit" (Washington, DC, White House, April 13, 2010), or go to <http://www.nti.org/e_research/in_focus_nuclear_summit.html>.

99. The biosafety guidelines of the World Health Organization might be agreed to be the "floor" or first-phase standard, with states allotted time to implement these measures fully, then tougher biosafety standards and phased compliance deadlines could be enacted.

100. Tucker, *Limiting Terrorist Access to Deadly Pathogens*, 35–36; Jonathan B. Tucker, "Preventing the Misuse of Pathogens: The Need for Global Biosecurity," *Arms Control Today* 33, no. 5 (June 2003): 3–10. On the need to identify and protect biological materials of greatest risk, see Reynolds M. Salerno and Lauren T. Hickok, "Strengthening Bioterrorism Prevention: Global Biological Materials Banagement," *Biosecurity and Bioterrorism* 5, no. 2 (June 2007): 107–116.

101. For more detail on full-scope screening programs, see U.S. Department of Energy, "Document 50.2: Personnel Assurance Program" and "Document 50.3 : Personnel Security Assurance Program," in *Environment Safety and Health Manual* (Washington, DC, April 1, 2001); "Nuclear Personnel Reliability Program," GAO/NSI-AD-92-193R (Washington, DC: U.S. Government Accountability Office, May 1992).

102. Lisa M. Astuto-Gribble, Jennifer M. Gaudioso, Susan A. Caskey, and Tamara R. Zemlo, "A Survey of Bioscience Research and Biosafety and Biosecurity Practices in Asia, Eastern Europe, Latin America, and the Middle East," *Applied Biosafety* 14, no. 4 (April 2009): 181–196.

103. Nancy L. Jones, "A Code of Ethics for the Life Sciences," *Science and Engineering Ethics* 13, no. 1 (March 2007): 25–43; Margaret A. Somerville and Ronald M. Atlas, "Ethics: A Weapon to Counter Bioterrorism," *Science* 307, no. 5717 (March 25, 2005): 1881–1882; James Revill and Malcolm R. Dando, "A Hippocratic Oath for Life Scientists," *EMBO Reports* 7, no. SI (2006): S55–S60. For model education programs, see the Federation of American Scientists at <http://www.fas.org/biosecurity/education/dualuse/index.html>, the Center for Arms Control and Non-proliferation at <http://www.politicsandthelifesciences.org/Biosecurity_course_folder/base.html>, and the University of Bradford/Exeter Project on Life Sciences, Biosecurity, and Dual-Use Research at <http://projects.exeter.ac.uk/codesofconduct/BiosecuritySeminar/Education/index.htm>.

104. The main burden for oversight of biosafety, biosecurity, and genetic engineering research would reside with the scientists serving as principal investigators, facility

management, and an Institutional Biosafety Committee, which might request a national or international review of an unusually serious breach of standards or for proposed experiments. Scientists from the U.S. pharmaceutical industry first proposed a triple-tiered structure in Amy E. Smithson, ed., *Compliance Through Science: U.S. Pharmaceutical Industry Experts on a Strengthened Bioweapons Nonproliferation Regime*, Report no. 48 (Washington, DC: Stimson Center, September 2002), 61–65. Also suggesting global research standards and a strong role for scientific advisory panels: "Royal Society Submission to the Foreign and Commonwealth Office: Green Paper on Strengthening the Biological and Toxin Weapons Convention," policy doc. 25/02 (London: Royal Society, September 2002). Proposing an international structure, John D. Steinbruner and Elisa D. Harris, "Controlling Dangerous Pathogens," *Issues in Science and Technology* (Spring 2003): 47–54; Steinbruner, Harris, Gallagher, Okutani, *Controlling Dangerous Pathogens*, 37–44.

105. Elizabeth Turpen, "Achieving Nonproliferation Goals: Moving from Denial to Technology Governance," Policy Analysis Brief (Muscatine, IA: Stanley Foundation, June 2009).

106. For more on the International Organization on Standardization, which certifies safe and efficient practices in a variety of domains, go to www.iso.org/homt.htm.

107. Giving the Obama Administration's verdict on a verification protocol for the convention, Under Secretary of State Ellen Tauscher said it "would not achieve meaningful verification or greater security" or "keep pace with the rapidly changing nature of the biological weapons threat." "Under Secretary of State Ellen Tauscher: Address to States Parties of the BWC" (Geneva, Permanent Mission of the United States of America, December 9, 2009). See also the remarks of Stephen Rademaker, U.S. assistant secretary of state for arms control, "U.S. Welcomes Biological Work Plan," press release (Washington, DC, U.S. Department of State, November 15, 2002.) For more on verification skeptics, see Henrietta Wilson, *The Biological Weapons Convention Protocol: Politics, Science and Industry*, Report no. 2 (London: Verification, Inspection, and Training Centre, December 2001), 13–14.

108. As noted in Chapter 9, numerous UNSCOM inspectors endorse this argument. See also Robert P. Kadlec, "First, Do No Harm," *Arms Control Today* 31, no. 4 (May 2001): 16; Yang Ruifu, "Biological Inspections in Iraq: Lessons for BWC Compliance and Verification," in Smithson, *Beijing on Biohazards*, 91–105.

109. Amy E. Smithson, ed., *House of Cards: The Pivotal Importance of a Technically Sound BWC Monitoring Protocol*, Report no. 37 (Washington, DC: Stimson Center, May 2001): 39–77. U.S. biotechnology and pharmaceutical industry scientists expound their counsel on these matters in Amy E. Smithson, ed., *Resuscitating the Bioweapons Ban: U.S. Industry Experts' Plans for Treaty Monitoring* (Washington, DC: Center for Strategic and International Studies, November 2004).

110. On faulty intelligence, *Commission of the Intelligence Capabilities of the United States Regarding Weapons of Mass Destruction: Report to the President of the*

United States. Giving the case for the 2003 invasion of Iraq, President George W. Bush, "President Discusses Beginning of Operation Iraqi Freedom," Presidential Radio Address (Washington, DC, White House, March 22, 2003); CIA/Defense Intelligence Agency, *Iraqi Mobile Biological Warfare Agent Production Plants* (Washington, DC, May 28, 2003) and "Transcript of Powell's U.N. Presentation," (New York, U.S. Department of State, February 6, 2003); "Iraq's Weapons of Mass Destruction: The Assessment of the British Government" (London, September 24, 2002), 17–18; Duelfer, *Hide and Seek*, 4.

111. Arms control critics have downplayed the importance of declarations, but as Chapter 4 describes, inconsistencies in Iraq's declarations helped tip UNSCOM chief bioweapons inspector Richard Spertzel to Iraq's bioweapons program. Also, see Bio-Weapons Prevention Project, *BioWeapons Report 2004* (Geneva: BioWeapons Prevention Project, 2004), 25–33; Marie Chevrier, "Doubts About Confidence: The Potential Limits of Confidence-Building Measures for the Biological Weapons Convention," in *Biological Weapons Proliferation: Reasons for Concern, Courses of Action*, report no. 24, ed. Amy E. Smithson (Washington: Stimson Center, January 1998); "New Unit Created to Help World Effort Against Biological Weapon Threat," press release DC/3079 (New York, UN Department of Public Information, August 20, 2007). This unit's webpage is at <http://www.unog/ch>.

112. Many years could pass during the process of negotiation and ratification of a verification protocol, so policymakers may want to establish a temporary mechanism to investigate charges of cheating on the Convention. Rather than a standing inspectorate, an on-call roster of inspectors could be mobilized, as needed. See Jez Littlewood, "Investigating Allegations of CBW Use: Reviving the UN Secretary-General's Mechanism," *Compliance Chronicles* no. 3 (December 2006): 1–36; Jonathan B. Tucker, "Multilateral Approaches to the Investigation and Attribution of Biological Weapons Use," in *Terrorism, War, or Disease? Unraveling the Use of Biological Weapons*, ed. Anne L. Clunan, Peter R. Lavoy, and Susan B. Martin (Stanford, CA: Stanford University Press, 2008), 269–292.

113. For example, the International Organization for Standardization and the World Health Organization would be the natural choices to oversee implementation of biosafety and biosecurity standards, whereas oversight of genetic engineering standards might be affiliated with an existing scientific body, such as the International Union of Biochemistry and Molecular Biology. If a verification protocol for the Convention were created, a biological inspector corps could be appended to the Technical Secretariat of the Organization for the Prohibition of Chemical Weapons, which conducts inspections for the chemical weapons ban, allowing both groups of inspectors to use the same administrative infrastructure. Additional resources to enable existing organizations to perform their new duties fully would be required, and a modest amount of new international infrastructure may also be needed to uphold some summit directives.

INDEX

Abu Ghraib prison, 156

Aflatoxin: disclosures about production of, 111, 115, 133, 157, 160; weaponization of, 100, 105, 124, 139, 140–145; Western view of, 107, 174

Ahmed, Ali Shehab, 132

Airfield 37, 190

Akashi, Yasushi, 12

Al Adile Medical Warehouse, 79–80, 84, 184–185, 195

al-Akidy, Shakir, 147–148, 216

Al Ameriyah (Al Ameriyah Serum and Vaccine Institute): biosafety conditions at, 177; documents clarifying biological weapons role of, 126; growth media discovered at, 80; Iraq's initial declaration about, 15; not bombed during 1991 Gulf War, 20; UNSCOM BW2's inspection of, 53, 54

Al Azziziyah: bombs stored at, 99, 113; munitions destroyed at, 140–141, 142, 143

Albright, Madeleine, 93, 150–151, 224

Al Daura (Al Daura Foot and Mouth Disease Vaccine Production Department): baseline inspections at, 64, 67, 68; biological agents produced at, 98, 135; destruction of biological weapons capability of, 120, 121, 122; documents found at, 125; early biological inspection of, 38, 53–54, 55, 61; Iraq's initial declaration about, 15; and Kamal's defection, 102, 103, 105; not bombed during 1991 Gulf War, 20;

observations at, 194, 198–199; viral agent research at, 149

Al-Diyat, Mohammed Emad, 107, 133

Al Fallujah, IAEA/UNSCOM inspection of, 26, 27

Al Faw Construction Establishment, 81, 153–154

Al Fudhaliyah (Al Fudhaliyah Agricultural and Water Research Center): information from Kamal about, 102, 111; Iraq's initial declaration about, 15–16; production of aflatoxin at, 18, 100, 107, 115; sampling at, 126–127; UNSCOM BW2's inspection of, 52

Al Hakam (Al Hukm): anthrax at, 66, 72, 91–92, 131–132, 134–136; *Bacillus thuringiensis* at, 61, 66, 72, 78, 132, 197, 226; baseline biological inspections at, 64, 66, 67, 68; biosafety precautions at, 87, 178; botulinum toxin at, 72, 91–92, 131, 134, 135; biological weapons activities suspected at, 28, 38, 61; cameras for monitoring at, 73–74; chickens at, 125, 195; confirmation of dual purpose of, 78, 80–81, 86–88, 201–202; declarations about, 15, 95; destruction of, 120–122; determining link between military and, 43, 70, 71; disclosure of dual purpose of, 46, 91–93, 196–197; evidence at, 130, 148; growth media at, 72–73, 78–79, 80; incongruities noted at, 198, 199; information about, in UNSCOM report to Security

Council, 88, 89; not bombed during 1991 Gulf War, 20, 21; opportunities missed by inspectors at, 194, 195; propaganda television report from, 89–90; UNSCOM BW2's inspection of, 49–52, 54–55

Al Hammadiyat, 116

Al Hazen Institute, 39, 40, 70, 216

Al-Hindawi, Nassir: as director of Al Hakam, 50, 67; questioned by inspectors, 105, 136; role in biological weapons program, 102, 103, 176

Ali, Hazem, 53, 105, 149, 150

Alibek, Ken, 236

Al Jaboori, Moona, 147

Al Kanat Hotel, 79

Al Kindi (Al Kindi Veterinary Vaccine Production Plant): anthrax production at, 123; baseline biological inspections of, 66, 67–68; biological inspections of, 52–53, 54, 61, 64; bombed during 1991 Gulf War, 20; fermenters from, moved to other sites, 43, 51; growth media discovered at, 80; Iraq's initial declaration about, 15; viral agent production suspected at, 149

Al Latifayah (Al Latifayah Explosives and Ammunition Plant), 20

Al Muthanna (Al Muthanna State Establishment for Pesticide Production): biological laboratory testing at, 116; bombed during 1991 Gulf War, 18; biological weapons tests at, 139; documents clarifying biological weapons role of, 126; first inspection at, 23–26; information from Kamal about, 102, 103, 111, 112; as Iraq's main chemical weapons production facility, 19, 88; markings on R-400s at, 25, 26, 141–142, 143, 195, 222; possible biological capabilities at, 89; role in Iraqi biological weapons program, 19, 25, 89, 95, 99, 102–103, 110–111, 116, 125–126, 130, 142; statements to first biological inspection team about, 43; weaponization of biological agents at, 95, 99, 130–131

Al Nibai, 103, 139–140

Al Qaysi, Riyad, 86, 91

Al Razi Institute, 80, 149

Al Sa'adi, Amir: contributed to Iraqi declarations, 138, 145; documentation allegedly sent to, 42; headed Iraqi delegation to technical evaluation meetings, 159–160, 162; information from Kamal about, 103;

interviewed by inspectors, 104; on military contribution to biological weapons program, 128; ordered revised disclosure of aflatoxin production, 133; said Iraq had furnished all documents, 124; on wheat smut field trial, 133

al-Sahhaf, Muhammad Sa'id, 93

Al-Sammarra'i, Wafiq, 60

Al Taji (Al Taji Single-Cell Protein Plant), 15, 18, 88, 105, 125, 131, 158

Al Tarmiya, 22

Al Tuwaitha, 22, 66, 137, 147, 148, 155

Al Za'ag, Ali, 126

Al-Zubaidy, Tariq, 99

Amash, Huda, 175

Amin, Hossam: admitted Iraqi military biological research, 36–38, 44; delayed destruction of Al Hakam, 121; directed Ekeus to Haidar farm, 100; interviewed about links between biological facilities and military, 70, 71; presented "farmer" at Salman Pak, 68; queried about Iraq's growth media imports, 76, 82, 84, 85

Amorim, Celso, 168

Anfeng, Guo, 159

Annan, Kofi: on disarmament of Iraq, 164; nominated Ekeus to lead UNMOVIC, 168; reached agreement on access for inspectors, 156–157; role in demise of UNSCOM, 166, 169; suggested "comprehensive review," 163, 164

Anthrax: at Al Daura, 135; at Al Hakam, 66, 72, 91–92, 131–132, 134–136; at Al Kindi, 123; alleged burial of bombs filled with, 60; attempted Iraqi purchase of strains of, 85–86; biosafety mistakes with, 240, 247; bioterrorist attacks with, in U.S., 237–238, 243; Coalition troops vaccinated for, 17; countries conducting biowarfare research on, 230, 231, 232, 233, 234, 235, 236; endemic in Iraq, 42; and Kamal, 102, 106; munitions filled with, 140–145; pre–1991 Gulf War intelligence on Iraq's production of, 16, 17; research at Salman Pak, 37; simulated, 61. *See also Bacillus anthracis*

Arnett, Peter, 20

Aum Shinrikyo cult, 237

Australia, 17, 187

Aziz, Tariq: blamed Kamal, 97, 98–100; body language during interviews, 211; interactions with Butler, 152, 161, 162; on Iraq's biological research program as defensive, 56; lobbied UNSCOM about destruction of biological weapons capability, 121; meeting with Ekeus to break biological logjam, 90–91, 96; in questioning about growth media quantity, 86–87; reached agreement on access for inspectors, 156–157; requested lifting of sanctions, 161, 162; and technical evaluation meetings, 158, 162

Bacillus anthracis, 134, 135, 142, 143. See also *anthrax*
Bacillus subtilis, 41, 132, 177
Bacillus thuringiensis: at Al Hakam, 61, 66, 72, 78, 132, 197, 226; at Salman Pak, 41
Bangladesh, 245
Barton, Rod: background of, 21, 24; on cascading inspections, 221; conducted interviews during inspection focused on growth media (BW70), 165; on Haidar farm documents, 115, 117; helped break the code on Iraq's biological import records, 77; on information obtained from Kamal, 114; and inspections of Al Hakam, 80, 88, 197; as inspector on interview mission (BW15), 70; on interviews as inspection tool, 205; investigated Iraq's growth media imports, 76, 77, 82; involved in biological inspections, 63; as member of first UNSCOM inspection, 23–24, 25–26, 141; on need to follow up on intelligence, 191; on observation technique, 207; on opportunities missed by inspectors, 194; on possible origin of Iraqi biological weapons program, 17; questioned Iraqis about July 1995 admission, 92; on Taha as head of biological weapons program, 176; on value of intelligence to UNSCOM biological inspections, 193
Beck, Volker, 64, 65
Bender, Patrice, 64, 65
Bhutan, 245
Bilal, Mohammed Mahmoud, 117, 125–126, 128, 135, 136
Biological agents: information from Kamal about, 102–103; Iraqi claims of disposal of, 26, 92, 107, 134–136, 197–198; munitions filled with, 140–145; suspected testing on humans, 156; viral, 149–150; Western view of choice of, 174. *See also* Anthrax; Botulinum toxin; Weaponization of biological agents
Biological and Toxin Weapons Convention (1975): lack of verification under, 5–6, 229; monitoring compliance with, 14, 223; provisions of, 170–171, 204, 229, 250; research permitted under, 37, 196; signed by Iraq, 2; U.S.S.R. and, 234, 236
Biological facilities: Al-Hakam confirmed as bioweapons facility, 78, 80–81, 86–88; Butler's warning about, 168; data produced by inspections of, 6; destruction of, 119–122; difficulty of inspecting, 202, 204; "dual use" defined, 2; equipment at, 62, 65–69, 83–86; intelligence on, 16, 18–19, 59, 60; Iraq's initial declarations about, 15–16; lack of biosafety precautions at, 57, 60, 61, 87; lessons about utility of inspecting, 223–227; list of, provided by Iraq, 15–16; mission (BW15) to determine links between military and, 70–72; monitoring, 122–124; 1991 Gulf War bombing of, 18–21; rated by UNSCOM for monitoring, 68–69; role in Iraq's bioweapons program, 18–19; sampling at, 126–127; searching for documents of, 124–126; UNSCOM questionnaire to obtain information about, 36. *See also specific facilities*
Biological inspections. *See* UNSCOM biological inspections
Biological risks: advances in life science techniques and technologies, 241–243; biosafety mistakes, 240–241; biosecurity lapses, 243–245; bioterrorism, 237–238; biowarfare research activities, 229–237, 238–239; overview of, 239, 245–247; recommendations for curbing, 247–252; state-level bioweapons programs, 229–241
Biological weapons: ambiguous Iraqi accounts of testing and disposing of, 137–145; delivery systems for, 16, 106; Iraq's claim to have destroyed, 58, 103, 107; markings on munitions identifying, 25, 26, 141–142, 143, 195, 222; medical precautions for troops possibly encountering, 17; myth of Iraqi possession of, 30–31; Western view of agents for, 174–175. *See also* Biological weapons program; Biowarfare research
Biological weapons program: advocates of UNSCOM investigating, 64; chain of

command for, 103, 176; defensive vs. offensive, 37–38, 44–45, 55–56; destroying infrastructure of, 119–122; doubt over existence of, 60–61; Haidar farm documents on, 100–102, 114–117; information about, from inspections following Kamal's defection, 105–107; information about, from Kamal's debriefing, 102–103, 108–114; Iraq's concealment and deception strategy on, 28–31; Iraq's initial declarations to UNSCOM about, 13–16; military declared not involved with, 127–128, 175; partial-truth tactic for disclosing, 62, 196–197; pre–Gulf War intelligence on, 16–21; revised declarations on, 94, 95, 96, 98, 102, 108, 127; searching for documents of, 124–126; UNSCOM report to Security Council presenting evidence of, 88–89; Western view of management of, 175–176. *See also* Biowarfare research

Biosafety procedures: at Al Ameriyah, 177; at Al Hakam, 87, 178; assessing according to Western standards, 176–178; defined, 239; Iraq's lack of, 57, 60, 61, 177–178, 240; risk of human error in, 240–241

Biosecurity: as biorisk management tool, 249–250; defined, 239; risk of lapses in, 243–245

Bioterrorism, 237–238

Biowarfare research: difficulty of detecting program for, 4–6, 246–247; history of countries conducting, 229–237, 238–239. *See also* Biological weapons; Biological weapons program

Black, Stephen: on challenge facing inspectors, 151; on creation of verification tools, 32; on Iraq's cover stories, 197; on observation technique, 206, 208; on uncovering biological weapons program, 59, 225–226

Blair, Tony, 109, 166

Blix, Hans, 169

Bolton, John, 224

Botulinum toxin: at Al Taji, 18, 105; countries conducting biowarfare research on, 230, 231, 233, 234, 235; munitions filled with, 16, 99, 109, 130, 140–145; pre–1991 Gulf War intelligence on Iraq's production of, 16, 18; produced at Al Daura, 98, 105, 115; produced at Al Hakam, 72, 91–92, 131, 134, 135; at Salman Pak, 37, 95;

vaccination of U.S. troops against, 17. *See also Clostridium botulinum*

Brazil, 245

Britain. *See* United Kingdom

Bush, George H. W., 5–6

Bush, George W., 5–6, 109, 239

Butler, Richard: appointed Kraatz-Wadsack head of UNSCOM's biological desk, 164; arbitrated access for inspectors, 156; biological weapons as concern of, 151; and demise of UNSCOM, 166, 169; interactions with Aziz, 152, 161, 162; pulled biological inspectors from Iraq, 155; released "Final Compendium Report," 166–167; reported to Security Council on biological inspections, 154–155, 157, 161; resignation of, 168; technical evaluation meetings initiated by, 158–162; wrote letters to Russian UN ambassador, 153

Camel pox, 149

Canada: biowarfare research by, 231–232; intelligence shared between UNSCOM and, 187; proposed tri-panel approach to Iraq situation, 166, 167–168

Canal Hotel, 79

Cascading inspections, 220–223

Central Intelligence Agency. *See* CIA (Central Intelligence Agency)

Chemap AG, 77

Chemical Engineering Design Center, 148

Chemical weapons: Al Muthanna as main facility for producing, 19, 88; biological weapons as offshoot of, 175; Haidar farm documents on, 115; Iraq's declarations about, 14–15, 57–58; and nerve agent VX, 158; pre–Gulf war intelligence on, 21; recommendation to destroy Iraq's chemical arsenal, 200–201; UNSCOM inspections focused on, 23–26, 58, 59, 184–185; used in Iran-Iraq war, 23, 27, 30, 152

Chemical Weapons Convention (1993), 5, 32, 204

China, 169, 237, 240

Cholera, 15, 37, 53, 72, 232, 234

Churchill, Winston, 230

CIA (Central Intelligence Agency), 16–17, 187

Clinton, Bill, 166

Clostridium botulinum, 42, 53, 105, 134, 137, 141, 219. *See also* Botulinum toxin

Clostridium perfringens, 37, 41, 100, 132, 142, 174
Conventional Forces in Europe Treaty (1990), 32
Corden, Pierce, 61, 62
Cuba, 245
Cultural differences: in management of biological weapons program, 175–176; need for training about, 180–181, regarding lies, 181. *See also* Western frame of mind
"Curveball," 192
Dando, Malcolm, 241
Dedouchkine, Vladimir, 167
Diplomats. *See* Political issues
Disarmament of Iraq: Annan on, 164; Bolton on, 224; by destroying biological weapons program infrastructure, 119–122; by destroying chemical weapons, 59; by destroying the supergun, 59; Ekeus on, i, 225; Final Compendium Report's statement on, 167; and lifting sanctions, 150–151; by monitoring dual-use biological facilities, 122–124; report to Security Council on progress on (Oct. 1998), 163–164; sampling activities to confirm, 126–127; by searching for documents, 124–126; Security Council panel on, 168; as UNSCOM's responsibility, 119
Duelfer, Charles: on Aziz-Ekeus discussions, 90; on expectations of UNSCOM, 13; on expertise of Spertzel, 62–63; as inspector on interview mission (BW15), 70; on Iraqi cover stories, 82, 209; on political forces impeding UNSCOM's work, 163; on Resolution 707, 27; on UNSCOM vs. Security Council, 200; on work methods of biological inspectors, 64
Dunn, Peter, 23, 25

Ebola virus, 240
Egypt, 245
Ekeus, Rolf: actions and comments regarding intelligence, 59, 60, 186, 187, 190, 192, 193; authorized no-notice inspections of nondeclared sites, 32, 221; background of, 12–13; communicated with Security Council, 68, 69, 83, 88–89, 91, 102, 112; considered political consequences of actions, 150, 200–201; did not institute training program for inspectors, 179; dispatched biological inspection teams, 35, 58, 68, 83–84, 129; ended chase of Iraqi

convoy from Al Fallujah, 26; evolution of thoughts about Iraqi biological research program, 14, 35, 56, 61–62, 73; frustrated by Iraqi deception and obstructionism, 57–58, 69, 83, 151, 214; Haidar farm documents "discovered" by, 100–102; on inspections' success in disarming Iraq, 225; and investigation of Al Hakam's capabilities, 86–87, 88, 93; Iraqi statements about, 29, 107; Kamal debriefed by, 97–98, 102–103, 108–114, 118; met with Aziz, 90–91, 96, 98–100; named executive chairman of UNSCOM, 12–13; nominated to lead UNMOVIC, 168; personnel decisions by, 21–22, 63; pursued information on Iraq's growth media imports, 76; secured access for inspectors, 157, 220
England. *See* United Kingdom
Englund, Doug, 192, 202
Experts, outside technical, 157–161, 174

Fluka AG, 77, 82, 86
Food testing laboratory, Baghdad University, 152–153
France: biowarfare research by, 230; debriefed inspectors, 187; and demise of UNSCOM, 155, 168, 169; ready to lift sanctions, 89
Franz, David: on difficulty of uncovering biological noncompliance, 202; as head of inspection teams (BW3, BW5), 61, 66; on intelligence analysts vs. inspectors, 191; interviewing technique of, 182; on sampling, 222; on technical expertise of inspectors, 172; on value of intelligence to biological inspections, 193

Gallucci, Robert: on founding of UNSCOM, 10–13; on initial Iraqi declarations, 14; on Iraqi concealment practices' effect on inspectors, 31; on pre–1991 Gulf War intelligence about Iraq's weapons capabilities, 21; on proof of weapons programs, 198, 199–200; requested sharing U.S. intelligence with UNSCOM, 186; on Resolution 687, 10, 11; on Rolf Ekeus, 23; on "Scott Ritter factor" in intelligence, 189; in talks to establish UNSCOM, 12, 13
GATEWAY debriefing program, 187t
Genetic engineering: as an advanced life sciences discipline, 241–243; in Iraqi

bioweapons program, 126; in Soviet bioweapons program, 235–236

Geneva Protocol (1925), 170, 229

Germany: attempted disarmament after World War I, ix, xii, 32; biological research oversight in, 242; intelligence cooperation with UNSCOM, 69; UNSCOM inspectors visit to, 95–96; World War I– and World War II–era biowarfare activities, 230

Germ warfare. *See* Biological weapons; Biological weapons program; Biowarfare research

Ghazi, Faisal, 126

Glanders, 230, 232, 234, 236

Gorbachev, Mikhail, 22

Growth media: clarifying Iraqi information on, 136–137; companies selling, 77; destruction of, 122, 137; discovery of huge quantities of, 79–80; Final Compendium Report's statement on production of, 167; intelligence about importation of, 76–77; Iraqi cover story for hospital diagnostic use of, 79–80, 81, 82–83, 85, 86–87; last inspections focusing on, 164–165; other Iraqi tales about, 82, 83–85, 86–87, 133

Gulf War (1991): intelligence on Iraq's biological weapons capabilities prior to, 16–21, 190, 223, 246; suspected biological weapons facilities bombed during, 18–21, 39

Gulf War (2003), 246

Haidar farm documents: biological weapons field test information from, 138–139; discovery of, 100–102; on smallpox, 150; value of, 114–117

Hammond, Owen, 122

Hamza, Khidhir, 113, 114

Harris, Larry Wayne, 243

Hasen, Sinan Abdul, 43, 117, 140

Hemorrhagic fever, 235, 240

Hitler, Adolph, 230

Hot washes, 183–184

Hussein, Saddam: access to presidential facilities of, 155, 156–157; called Kamal a traitor, 97; and concealment of biological weapons program, 28; conflicting policy objectives of, 197–198; gave UNSCOM deadline for finishing inspections, 96; interactions with Iraqi researchers, 136, 149; international response to nerve agent use by, 16; and myth of Iraqi possession of WMDs, 30–31; pre–1991 Gulf War comments on Iraq's biological weapons capabilities, 16, 17; program to test food and clothing of, 153; speculated he could outlast support for UNSCOM, 146. *See also* Iraq

Huxsoll, David: background of, 36; as biological inspector at Salman Pak, 36, 37, 38, 41, 42, 46; on difficulty of biological inspections, 204; interviewing technique of, 182; on Iraqi biosafety conditions, 177; on Iraq's admission of military biological research program, 36, 38, 196; as leader of inspection team (BW2), 49–55; observation technique as used by, 206; on sampling, 218, 219

IAEA (International Atomic Energy Agency): inspection at Al Fallujah, with UNSCOM, 26–27; inspections worldwide, 204; other joint inspections, with UNSCOM, 22, 31–32, 47, 55; pre–1991 Gulf War inspections of Iraq, 10, 27; relationship with UNSCOM, 10

Ibn-Sina Center, 40

India, 245

Infant Formula Plant (Project 600), 20

Inspections. *See* IAEA (International Atomic Energy Agency) inspections; UNSCOM biological inspections; UNSCOM inspections

Inspection techniques: cascading inspections, 220–223; document reviews, 214–218; interviews, 205, 208–214; mass balance of materials method, 33; sampling, 218–220; on-site observation, 205–208; UNSCOM innovation of, 31–34

Inspectors. *See* UNSCOM inspectors

Intelligence: about importation of growth media, 69, 76–77; assertions that UNSCOM shared with U.S., 163, 166, 187; biological, from various countries, 69; clarified by inspections, 80–83; collaborating governments' of a two-way street, 188; lack of, about biological weapons program, 59, 60; pre–1991 Gulf War, on Iraq's biological weapons capabilities, 16–17, 18–19, 21, 190, 246; role of, in UNSCOM biological inspections, 185–192; shared by Ritter with Israel, 163; UNSCOM requests cooperation from governments, 186–189; value to UNSCOM biological inspections, 192–194

Intermediate-Range Nuclear Forces Treaty (1987), 32

International Health Regulations, 248

Interpreters, 173

Interviews: lessons about, as inspection technique, 208–214; need for training in how to conduct, 179; opinions on value of, 205, 208; protocol for formal, 211; quandary of Iraqis in, 181, 209;

Iran: chemical weapons used against, 23, 27, 30, 152; growth media orders as result of war with, 82; Iraqi biological weapons program as deterrent to, 37–38, 103, 127–128; Iraqi claim of buried remains of soldiers from, 67–68; military threat from, 73, 106, 127–128; plan to contaminate crops and water of, 112; suspected biowarfare research by, 237

Iraq: biological declarations of, xi, 13–16, 83, 88, 94–96, 108, 127–128, 138–139, 154, 157; blamed Kamal for hiding weapons program, 97, 98, 99, 100; concealment and deception strategy with UNSCOM inspections, 27–31, 60; detained inspection team that obtained evidence of nuclear weapons program, 31–32, 55; errors of, in UNSCOM biological inspections, 195–198; gave UNSCOM ultimatum for finishing its work, 96, 98; initial weapons declarations of, to UNSCOM, 13–16; limits of admission strategy of, 214; myth of possession of WMDs by, 30–31; noncooperation with UNSCOM biological inspections, 28–29, 37–38, 40–45, 155–157, 162–163

Iraqi leaders: destroyed prohibited weapons after Al Fallujah incident, 26; ordered biological weapons and bulk agent destroyed, 196

Iraq's biological weapons. See Biological weapons

Iraq's biological weapons program. See Biological weapons program

Iraq's chemical weapons. See Chemical weapons

Iraq Survey Group, 7, 225, 246

Ishii, Shiro, 247

Ismael, Majid, 128

Israel: article on impact of anthrax on, 106; attacked Iraq nuclear plant, 2; inspector

allegedly sharing intelligence with, 163; intelligence from, 16, 69, 76; Iraq's biological weapons program as deterrent to, 37–38, 128; suspected biowarfare research by, 237

Ivins, Bruce, 243

Jansen, Karen, 60

Japan, 232, 237

Kadlec, Robert: on failure of intelligence to detect Al Hakam, 20; on loyalty to Hussein as criteria to work in Iraq's WMD programs, 176; on management of Iraq's biological weapons program, 175; on need to learn lessons of UNSCOM's biological inspections, 226–227; on pressures facing Iraqi weaponeers, 181; on UNSCOM's handling of intelligence, 184; on U.S. intelligence analysts stonewalling inspectors, 191

Kamal, Hussein: approved biological program at Salman Pak, 45; blamed for hiding weapons program, 97, 98, 99, 100; biological weapons program as pet project of, 128, 175; debriefing of, 102–103, 108–114; defection of, 97, 117–118; Haidar farm of, 100–102; made decision not to reveal Al Hakam's military purpose, 28; possible impairment of due to brain tumor surgery, 114; pushed for better biological delivery system, 106; returned to Iraq, 103, 120; Taha believed to report to, 70

Kay, David, 22, 26, 27, 31–32, 47, 55

Kelly, David C.: advocated investigating Iraq's covert biological weapons program, 64; background of, 36; on inspections to Al Hakam, 72, 73, 80; as inspector on baseline inspection (BW8), 68; as inspector on interview mission (BW15), 70, 71; on inspectors sharing observations, 183; interview skill of, 208–209; led biological document search mission (BW35), 125–127; led first biological inspection (BW1), 36–38, 41, 42, 43, 44–45, 46, 47–48; led inspection (BW28) following Kamal's defection, 104, 105; led inspection (BW43) searching for physical evidence, 129–130; member of second biological inspection (BW2), 49, 51, 52, 53, 54; on missiles unaccounted for in Iraq,

200; on reason for disclosures about Al Hakam, 196–197; role in UNSCOM's biological inspections, 63, 76; on scheduling inspections, 222; on scientific vs. political views of proof, 198; on statements by Iraqis, 160, 199; on suspected smallpox production by Iraq, 149, 150; on technical expertise of UNSCOM inspectors, 172

Killip, Hamish: as advocate for investigating Iraq's covert biological weapons program, 64, 225; background of, 24; on biological TEM, 159; on biosafety precautions in Iraq, 177–178; comments on first biological inspection, 38, 46, 47; increased involvement in biological inspections, 63; on inspection after Kamal's defection, 105; on inspectors' intelligence connections, 189; on Iraqi lies in interviews, 209, 210, 213; led biological document search mission (BW34), 124–125; led inspections focused on field tests and disposal of munitions, 139, 140–141; as member of biological inspection missions (BW8, BW15, BW22), 68, 70, 80; as member of first UNSCOM inspection, 24, 25, 26, 32, 33; observation skills of, 130, 207; and techniques used by inspectors, 33, 64, 183, 219, 223

Kraatz-Wadsack, Gabriele: at Al Adile warehouse, 79, 184–185; Al Hakam inspected by, 78–79, 87–88, 120, 195; on Ali-Hussein connection, 149; background of, 78; believed Iraq was hiding documents, 124–125; explained UNSCOM findings to international experts, 88, 159; on intelligence and inspectors, 189–190, 191, 192; on interaction between inspectors and diplomats, 202; investigated growth media at Iraqi sites, 79–80, 137, 165, 184–185; led 1997 inspection teams, 151–152, 153; led inspection to Abu Ghraib prison, 156; led monitoring of dual-use biological facilities, 122–124; observations by, 198–199; role in UNSCOM's biological inspections, 63, 78, 124, 164; on training inspectors, 179

Krikorian, Debra: believed Iraqi gave some truthful accounts about agent production, 120; on delay in UNSCOM's biological inspections, 204; on inspectors missing opportunities, 195; on interview technique, 212; on objectivity of

scientists, 199; on observation technique, 206, 207

Lavrov, Sergei, 153

Lebherz, William (Bill): assessing Al Hakam's earliest operational date, 86; on lack of training for inspectors, 178; as a member of BW13, 72–73; on need for inspectors with production expertise, 172

Lessons experienced: advance training of inspectors, 178–183; cascading inspections, 220–223; data sharing during inspections, 183–185; document searches and reviews, 214–218; errors made by biological inspectors and Iraqis, 184–185; explanation of term, 170, 203; interviews, 208–214; on-site observation, 205–208; operational details of inspections, 183–185; required expertise of inspectors, 171–174; role of intelligence in biological inspections, 185–192; sampling, 218–220; scientific vs. political views of proof, 198–202; utility of dual-use biological facilities inspections, 223–227; value of intelligence to biological inspections, 192–194; Western frame of reference, 159, 174–178

Libya, 237

Lies: exposing, in interviews, 212–213; Iraqi cultural view of, 181, 211; as part of cover stories, 36–38, 41–43, 45, 83–85, 87–88, 126, 138, 209–210; physical signs of, in interviews, 211–212

Maarouf, Taha Muhieddine, 107

Manley, Ron, 15, 17, 180, 187, 200–201

Mass balance of materials method, 33

Melkonian, Alice, 153

Meselson, Matthew, 242

Mexico, 245

Military Industrialization Commission: and Al Hakam, 81; Al Sa'adi at, 128; documents about, 101, 126; Iraqi statements on involvement in biological weapons program, 95, 128; Kamal as head of, 45, 97, 175

Ministry of Agriculture, 60

Ministry of Defense: declared not involved in biological weapons program, 95, 96, 127; documents about, 101, 125; links between Al Hakam and, 51, 67

Ministry of Health: growth media allegedly purchased for, 81–83, 84, 85, 87, 90; vaccinated Iraqi citizens, 37

Missiles: for delivering biological weapons, 16, 106; destroyed by Iraqis, 26; Haidar farm documents on, 115; SCUD, 30, 58, 99; unaccounted for in Iraq, 200

Mitrokin, Igor, 33

Mohr, Jeff: complaints about ineffective inspection leaders, 65; on conditions for doing inspections, 220; on lack of biosafety precautions in Iraq, 177; led inspection (BW6) to Al Hakam and Al Daura, 67; on sampling, 219, 220, 222; on Taha as head of biological weapons program, 175

Monitoring: authorized by Resolution 715, 57; biological facilities rated by UNSCOM for, 68–69; by cameras at Al Hakam, 73–74; of dual-use biological facilities, 122–124; Ekeus's communication to Security Council about starting, 68, 69

Mosul sugar factory, 20, 58

Murtada, Ahmed: claimed to have ended ricin production, 133; ordered Iraqis to tell truth in interviews with inspectors, 104; role in biological weapons program, 36–37, 42–43, 103; statements to inspectors about biological weapons work, 44–45, 136; tales about growth media, 165

N bomb, 230, 231

Nepal, 245

Nerve agent VX, 158

Niro Atomizer Inc., 77

Nixon, Richard M., 234

North Korea, 150, 237

Nuclear Nonproliferation Treaty, 5, 228

Nuclear weapons: documents containing evidence of, 115, 216; inspections focused on, 10, 59, 204; Iraqi sites inspected for, 22–23, 31, 55; obstruction of inspection team finding evidence of, 31–32, 55; pre-1991 Gulf war intelligence on, 21; Security Council's standard of proof for, 199–200

Obama, Barack, 6, 248

Observations, on-site, 183, 205–208

Olsa S.P.A., 77

Operation Desert Fox, 166

Oxoid, Ltd., 76, 77, 82, 86

Pasechnik, Vladimir, 180, 231

Paul-Henriot, Annick, 60, 63, 64, 65

Peptone, 82, 136, 137, 167

Peres de Cuellar, Javier, 12

Pickering, Thomas, 12

Plague: biosecurity lapse with, 243; countries conducting biowarfare research on, 230, 232, 234, 235, 236; possible Iraqi production of, 66, 174; vaccination of British troops against, 17. See also Yersinia pestis

Political issues: diplomats accompanying UNSCOM inspectors, 156–157; geographic balance of inspection teams, 174; loyalty of people in Iraqi biological weapons program, 175; political support for or against lifting sanctions, 89, 150–151, 154; political support for UNSCOM, 163, 198; scientific vs. political views of proof, 198–202

Project 85, 76

Project 324, 63, 76, 81

Project 600, 20

Project 900, 81

Rajneesh cult, 237

Rasheed, Amer: assessed inspectors' acceptance of Iraqi cover stories, 210; on biological agents in warheads, 144–145; informed of need for full declaration by Iraq, 58; led delegation to New York, 61; in meetings about Al Hakam's capabilities, 86, 88, 91, 92; meeting with Ekeus and Aziz after Kamal's defection, 98–100; position in biological weapons program, 103; queried about Iraq's growth media imports, 76; on value of Haidar farm documents, 101

Razzack Jasem, Abdul, 84–85

Reagan, Ronald, 5

Ricin: bioterrorist attack in U.S. with, 238; Iraqi production of, 133, 148, 195; Iraqi research on, 100, 104, 112, 126; monitoring residue of, 124

Ritter, Scott, 163, 189

Russia: admitting Soviet bioweapons program, 236; biological intelligence from, 69; biosafety mistakes in, 240, 247; biotechnology industry in, 245; biowarfare research by, 150, 180, 231, 234–236; concerns about continuing bioweapons program, 236; and demise of UNSCOM, 167, 169; helped Iraqi bioweapons program, 17, 108, 153–154; on missiles unaccounted for in Iraq, 200; proposed resolution on

UNSCOM inspections, 162, 164; ready to lift sanctions, 89, 150, 161; U.S.-U.K. inspection of Soviet bioweapons facilities, 22, 36, 61

Salman Pak: admissions and declarations about, 16, 36–37, 38, 95, 196; bombed during 1991 Gulf War, 18, 21, 39, 45; equipment and supplies bought for, 81–82, 85; initial biological inspection of, 38–46, 48, 195; Iraqi claim of animal carcasses buried at, 130; Iraqi mandated concealment of biological weapons activities at, 28; pre–1991 Gulf War intelligence on, 15, 16; subsequent biological inspections of (BW6, BW15, BW16), 67–68, 70–72, 73
Salmonella typhimurium, 237
Samarra Drug Industries, 52, 54, 125–126, 165
Sampling: at Iraqi biological facilities, 44, 52, 68, 73, 126–127, 129–130, 141, 143; lessons about, as inspection technique, 218–220; need for plan for, 222–223
Sanctions: confirmation of Iraqi efforts to evade, 108; Iraqi noncooperation threatened if no lifting of, 96, 161, 162–163; lifting of, dependent on closing biological portfolio, 80, 86; political support for or against lifting, 89, 150–151, 154
Santesson, Johan, 57, 62
Sarin, 237
SARS, 240
Scientists: interviews of Iraqi, 41--44, 66, 69–72, 80–82, 84, 126, 133, 147–148, 194–195, 223; proof as viewed by diplomats vs., 198–202; publications by Iraqi, 42; viral agent research by Iraqi, 149–150
SCUD missiles, 16, 30, 58, 99, 105, 111, 138–145, 162
Seaman, Diane, 153
Security Council. *See* United Nations (UN) Security Council
Sellstrom, Ake, 158, 159, 161–162, 193–194
Shubik, Martin, 238
Singapore, 245
Smallpox: British attempts to transmit, 229; Iraqi activities related to, 149–150; Soviet biowarfare research on, 235, 236
Smidovich, Nikita: background of, 21–22; co-developed questionnaire prior to UNSCOM's first biological inspection, 36; explained UNSCOM findings to international experts, 88, 159; helped break the code on Iraq's biological import records, 77; led inspection focused on biological agents in warheads, 144; questioned Iraqis about July 1995 admission, 92; role of, at UNSCOM, 21–22, 63
South Africa, 236–237
South Korea, 245
Special Security Organization (SSO), 97, 101, 152–153
Spertzel, Richard: analyzed all biological data at UNSCOM (spring of 1994), 63–64, 185; background of, 62–63; on camel pox research, 149; explained UNSCOM findings to international experts, 88, 159; on Haidar farm documents, 115; helped break the code on Iraq's biological import records, 77; on inability of inspections to shut down bioweapons program, 224–225; on inspections clarifying purpose of Al Hakam, 80, 81, 83, 87, 88, 92; intelligence data analyzed by, 63–64; on interview mission (BW15) clarifying Salman Pak links, 70, 71; on interview technique, 181, 208; Iraqi delay tactics with, 136; on Kamal, 97, 114; led 1996 inspection missions, 131, 138, 139; led inspection (BW27) following Kamal's defection, 104, 105; led inspections clarifying Iraqi declarations and reports, 95, 123, 154; led interview mission (BW56), 153; left UNSCOM, 164; pursued information on Iraq's growth media imports, 76, 77; questioned Iraqis about July 1995 admission, 92
State Organization for Technical Industries, 95
Synthetic biology, 241
Syria, 237

Taha, Rihab: admissions and denials about offensive biowarfare activities, 37, 41, 43, 45, 62, 67, 71, 80, 87–88, 90–92, 95–96, 98–99; answered questions about Al Hakam's capabilities, 87, 88; assembled biological Haidar farm documents, 115; background of, 71, 126; compelled scientists to conceal biological weapons development, 28, 209; emotional displays by, 71, 88, 176; gave presentation about consumption of growth media, 87; gave presentation about Salman Pak, 62;

given award by Saddam for developing bioweapons, 136; interacted with first biological inspection team, 36–37, 39–40, 41–42, 43, 44, 45, 215; interactions with inspectors at Al Hakam, 67, 78, 80, 81, 83; on lies in cover stories, 209; propaganda television appearance at Al Hakam, 89–90; reticence to discuss scientific matters, 198; role in biological weapons program, 62, 103, 116–117, 136, 176; tales from, about growth media, 165

Taiwan, 245

Taylor, Terence (Terry): headed inspection focused on military use of dual-use biological items (BW23), 84–85, 86; on intelligence briefings for inspectors, 187, 190; interview approach of, 182; on interviews as inspection tool, 205, 212, 213–214; led BW31's destruction of Iraq's biological weapons capability, 121; led inspection interviewing Iraqi scientists (BW48), 147–149; on need for inspectors to share information, 184; on spectrum of biological risks, 239; on training UNSCOM biological inspectors, 178–179; on UNSCOM as scientific and political, 202; on Western frame of mind of inspectors, 174, 175, 180

Technical evaluation meetings (TEMs), 158–162

Technical Scientific Materials Import Division (TSMID): growth media purchased by, 76, 81–82, 84, 136–137; interviews with employees of, 70–1; investigating activities of, 85–86; investigating records of, 77–78

Thamer, Abdul Rahman, 8, 67, 125, 126, 130, 165

Training, for UNSCOM biological inspectors, 178–183

Trichothecene, 133

U-2 aircraft, 186–187, 214

United Kingdom: biosafety mistake in, 240; past biowarfare activities of, 229, 230–231; intelligence shared between UNSCOM and, 186, 187; medical precautions for troops of, 17; pre–1991 Gulf War intelligence from, 17

United Nations (UN) Security Council: attitudes on, regarding demise of UNSCOM, 167–168; Butler's reports to,
154–155, 161; declining support by, for UNSCOM, 150–151, 154–155, 161–164; Ekeus's reports about Iraq's biological weapons program to, 48, 57, 68, 69, 73, 83, 89, 91, 102, 109, 112, 129; level of noncompliance proof required by, 200, 201–202; Resolution 687, 9, 10–11, 48–49, 186–187; Resolution 707, 27, 48–49; Resolution 715, 57, 58, 62; Resolution 1284, 168; stripped Iraq of right of civilian nuclear activity, 55; tri-panel approach of, to Iraq situation, 166, 167–168; UNSCOM joke about proof required by, 199–200

United States: anthrax bioterrorist attacks in, 237–238, 243; biosafety mistake in, 240; biosecurity lapses in, 243–244; medical precautions for troops of, 17; pre–1991 Gulf War intelligence on Iraq's biological weapons capabilities, 16–17, 18–19; reports of manipulation of UNSCOM for, 163, 166, 187; sharing of intelligence with UNSCOM, 186–187, 188–189; World War II–era biowarfare research by, 232–234

UNMOVIC, 168–169

UNSCOM: accused of intelligence activities for U.S. government, 163, 166; decline in Security Council support for, 150–151, 154–155, 161–164; demise of, 166–169; departures from standard UN culture, 4, 12–13, 171, 185–186, 190; establishment of, 9, 10, 11, 12–13; given ultimatum by Iraq for finishing its work, 96; Iraq's initial weapons declarations to, 13–16; level of noncompliance proof United Nations (UN) Security Council expected from, 200, 201–202; mandate of, 9; operating method of, 171, 182–183, 187–188; opinions within, about destruction of Iraq's biological weapons capability, 120–121; outside technical experts' view supporting, 157–161; political support for, 163, 198; released "Final Compendium Report," 166–167; report to Security Council on disarmament progress (Oct. 1998), 163–164; report to Security Council presenting evidence of Iraqi biological weapons program, 88–89; Saddam's speculation he could outlast, 146; sharing data across inspection portfolios, 184–185

UNSCOM biological inspections: achievements of, 250–251; baseline, 62, 64–69; to clarify Iraqi information about testing and disposal of biological weapons, 137–145; destroying Iraq's biological weapons capability (BW31), 120–122; errors made by Iraq in, 195–198; first (BW1), 36–49, 199; focused on biological agent production and weaponization, 131–145; focused on growth media, 79–80, 136–137, 164–165; hiatus in (1992–1993), 58–62, 194, 204; intelligence and, 80–83, 185–194; interviewing Iraqi scientists (BW48), 147–149, 194–195; Iraq's noncooperation with, 60, 155–157; lessons about utility of, of dual-use biological facilities, 223–227; monitoring dual-use biological facilities, 122–124; objectives of, 203; vs. pressure to lift sanctions, 90–1, 150–151, 154; recommended improvements in operational details of, 183–185; Resolution 715's impact on, 62; sampling activities of, 44, 52, 68, 73, 126–127, 129–130, 134–135, 141, 143; searching for documents (BW34 and BW35), 124–127; searching for hard evidence (BW43), 129–130; second (BW2), 49–55; staff added with biological expertise for, 62–65; value of Haidar farm documents to, 114–117; value of Kamal's debriefing to, 104–114. See also Inspection techniques; UNSCOM inspections; specific locations

UNSCOM inspections: chemical inspections, 23–26, 58, 59, 184–185; historical guidance for, 32; Iraqi concealment and deception strategy with, 27–31, 60; Iraqi efforts to hinder, 26–27; joint, with IAEA, 22, 47; lack of biological expertise for, 59–60; personnel for, 12–13, 21–22; priority given to chemical, nuclear, and missile inspections, 59; role of Iraqi biological weapons facilities discovered by, 18–19. See also Inspection techniques; UNSCOM biological inspections

UNSCOM inspectors: accused of being American spies, 163; diplomats accompanying, 156–157; doubting existence of Iraqi biological weapons program, 60–61; expertise and experience of, 59–60, 62–65, 171–174, 206; held hostage over nuclear program documents, 31–32,

55; intelligence briefings for, 189–190; Iraqi denial of access for, 155–156, 157; Iraqi "minders" for, 29; opportunities missed by, 194–195; rights granted by Iraq to, 23; training of, 178–183; Western frame of reference of, 174–178

U.S.S.R.. See Russia

Ustinov, Nikolai, 240

Vaccinations: of Coalition troops, 17; of Iraqi citizens and soldiers, 37, 43, 150

Viral agents, 149–150, 235, 236

Weaponization of biological agents: freeze dried vs. wet slurry form of agents, 175, 178; Haidar farm documents confirming Iraq's, 116–117; inspections to clarify information about Iraq's, 137–145; investigation of Iraqi munitions and markings indicating, 140–145; Iraq's admission of, 98–99; Iraq's ambiguous disclosures about, 92–93, 95–96, 104–105, 130–134; and Kamal, 102, 103, 106; past, by the United Kingdom, 231; past, by the United States, 233–234; by the Soviet Union, 235–236; UNSCOM suspicions of Iraq's, 66, 92, 95, 109

Weapons of mass destruction, 30–31, 228–229. See also Biological weapons; Chemical weapons; Nuclear weapons

Webster, William, 16

Western armies, 17, 106

Western frame of mind: about biosafety precautions, 61, 64–65, 176–178; about choice of biological weapons, 174–175; about management of biological weapons program, 175–176; about offensive biological weapons programs, 180; training needed to overcome, 180–181

Wheat smut, 99, 102, 133–134

World Health Organization, 87, 150, 235, 240, 245

World War I, 230

Yeltsin, Boris, 236

Yersinia pestis, 72, 243. See also Plague

Zilinskas, Raymond, 62

Zubaidy device, 96, 132, 159